ENGLISH PLACE-NAME SOCIETY. VOLUME LXXXI
FOR 2003–2004

GENERAL EDITOR

RICHARD COATES

THE PLACE-NAMES OF LEICESTERSHIRE

PART III

THE SURVEY OF ENGLISH PLACE-NAMES
UNDERTAKEN WITH THE APPROVAL AND SUPPORT OF
THE BRITISH ACADEMY
AND
THE ARTS AND HUMANITIES RESEARCH BOARD

THE PLACE-NAMES OF LEICESTERSHIRE

BY

BARRIE COX

PART THREE

EAST GOSCOTE HUNDRED

NOTTINGHAM
ENGLISH PLACE-NAME SOCIETY
2004

Published by the English Place-Name Society,
School of English Studies, University of Nottingham,
Nottingham NG7 2RD.

Registered Charity No. 257891

ISBN 0 904889 68 8

Typeset by Paul Cavill & Printed in Great Britain
by Woolnough Bookbinding, Irthlingborough, Northants.

CONTENTS

PREFACE

This third volume of *The Place-Names of Leicestershire* follows the format which I adopted for my two previous volumes, in that each as far as possible is self-contained and, I trust, user-friendly.

Again I extend my grateful thanks to the staffs of the Record Office for Leicestershire, Leicester and Rutland at Wigston Magna and of the Lincolnshire Archives Office, Lincoln, for their splendid assistance in locating and presenting such manuscripts and early maps as I requested to view in researching the East Goscote Hundred.

I am indebted to Dr Anne Tarver for her work on the parish map of the Hundred. I am fortunate indeed always to be able to call upon her cartographic expertise.

Finally (and once again) my best thanks are due to Dr Paul Cavill of the English Place-Name Society for his meticulous application and patience in preparing for publication the camera-ready copy of each completed volume of my survey of Leicestershire's place-names. May the contents of this present volume be worthy of the elegance of their presentation.

Barrie Cox — June 2004

INTRODUCTION TO THE PLACE-NAMES OF EAST GOSCOTE HUNDRED

The territory of East Goscote Hundred comprises the western end of the Leicestershire Wolds, the Soar Valley east of the river, the lower Wreake Valley, rich in meadowland, and in its south-eastern region, a large tranche of High Leicestershire, land over 400 ft above sea level, in places rising to 600 ft. In the north-west of its area, Boulder Clay dominates with Keuper Marl, but with sand and gravel patches lining the river Soar. Further south-east is the alluvium of the lower Wreake Valley, also with sand and gravel patches and with Boulder Clay overlying Lower Lias and Keuper Marl. Furthest south-east are the soils of the Middle and Upper Lias, with sand and gravel spreads, again with some Boulder Clay.

The major Roman roads of East Goscote Hundred are the Fosse Way, which runs south-west from the county boundary near Wymeswold through Thurmaston to Leicester, and Margary 58a which crosses the Wolds from Ermine Street. This forms the northern parish boundaries of Grimston and Hoby with Rotherby parishes and, crossing the Fosse Way, continues at least to Barrow upon Soar where Roman cremation burials are known.

An ancient route which forded the river Wreake at Melton Mowbray and passed close to the Iron Age hill-fort at Burrough on the Hill continued southwards through Tilton and Skeffington. The Anglo-Saxons knew this as the *Ferdgate* 'the army road, the military road' (with Old English *ferd* 'an army, a troop' and Old Norse *gata* 'a road'). This was no doubt a prehistoric trackway, later used by the Romans and by the English-speaking peoples after them. Another very early route in this region is the Ridgeway (also known as Ridgemere Lane) which runs south-east through the heart of East Goscote Hundred from the site of its hundred-moot overlooking Syston as far as Cold Newton and thence in all probability to Tugby and East Norton. From this, a branch led south-westwards through Hungarton and Keyham parishes via Humberstone to Leicester. Another early track ran south-east from Queniborough via South Croxton and

Lowesby, presumably to join the *Ferdgate* on its way to Tilton. It is to be assumed that these trackways were in use from earliest times, through the periods of the Roman occupation, the Anglo-Saxon settlements, the Scandinavian incursions and so into the Middle Ages. Such routes may in part be traced by the survival of minor names and field-names with Old English *strǣt* 'a Roman road, a paved road' (*v.* The Elements in East Goscote Hundred's Place-Names *s.v.*) but, of course, not all earlier names containing this element necessarily indicate a road that had its origins in the Roman period or before.

The principal evidence for the survival of Romano-British inhabitants in the territory of East Goscote Hundred is to be found in the adjoining parishes of Wymeswold, Burton on the Wolds, Walton on the Wolds and Seagrave in its north-west. Walton is Old English *wala-tūn* 'the farmstead of the Britons or British serfs'. In Wymeswold, *Cumberdale* and in Seagrave, *Cumberlea* each record the *Cumbre* 'the Britons'. In Burton on the Wolds, *Tralleswellehul* may remember the former presence of such serfs, if indeed the name derives from *þrǣll* 'a thrall, a serf'. In contiguous Walton on the Wolds and Seagrave are *Severn Acre* and *Seuene Wong*, field-names containing the pre-English stream-name Severn (cf. River Severn, Gl **1** 10 and Saffron Brook, Lei **1** 226) of doubtful etymology.

Of great interest in Wymeswold, the most northerly of East Goscote Hundred parishes, is the survival of names which may record Romano-British religious sites. Wymeswold's north-eastern parish boundary is shared with Willoughby on the Wolds (in Notts.) whose territory contains the Romano-British settlement of *Vernemeto*(*n*), the name meaning 'great sacred grove'. A major pagan Anglo-Saxon inhumation cemetery was located beside the Fosse Way here, its siting perhaps determined by the ancient sanctity of the place (*v.* I. A. Richmond, *Roman Britain* (London, 1955), 145, for other British sites with names in *nemeton* 'sacred grove'). In the Romano-British period, such a major holy place probably gave rise to a series of surrounding temple enclosures. Early minor names in the east of Wymeswold parish include *Horrou* and *Harrowefeld*, possibly from Old English *hærg* 'a heathen temple' (cf. Harrow, Mx 51) and *Alfletford'* (1292) and *Alfletethorn* (13th cent.), both perhaps with Old English *alh* 'a heathen temple' and thus meaning 'the ford of the temple stream' and 'the thorn (patch) at the temple stream' respectively (cf. *Alhfleot* 815 (9) BCS 353 (S 178) in Kent).

Such a sacred area on the Wolds would long have been a natural meeting place for the inhabitants of the region. North of the present village site of Wymeswold was the location of the curious *Gosefot* or *Gosfote* recorded from the early 13th century and surviving as late as *Goose Foot Close* in its Enclosure Award (*v.* Wymeswold field-names (a) *s.n.*). The tentative interpretation of this name offered in the text of Wymeswold's field-names is 'the foot of the hill where geese are pastured', a suggestion based on John Dodgson's explanation of *Oxefotemor* (Ch **3** 96, n.1) as 'marshland at the foot of a hill where oxen graze'. But could *Gosfote* rather be the original Goscote, the former moot-site of the early undivided Goscote Wapentake? The continuity of such a place of congregation from the time of the Iron Age Corieltauvi, through the Romano-British period into Anglo-Saxon England and later may be reasonably argued. However, the surviving evidence can only provoke the question. Certainly the construction of *Gosefot* and *Oxefote* is otherwise unique in the known canon of English place-names and one must wonder whether both were originally names with *cot* 'a shelter, a hut, a cottage' rather than with *fōt* 'a foot (of something)'.

The earliest Anglo-Saxon presence in East Goscote Hundred is evidenced by the pagan cemetery at Thurmaston beside the Roman Fosse Way and by the pagan inhumation cemetery at Twyford which relates to the ancient routeway called the *Ferdgate* mentioned above. Isolated pagan Anglo-Saxon inhumations are known at Baggrave, Hungarton and Queniborough, and in the Scandinavian-named Beeby, Ingarsby, Lowesby and Tugby. Only Barrow upon Soar, Keyham and Twyford can be argued strongly to be of the earliest stratum of the place-names of the Anglo-Saxons (with maybe the lost *Luffnum* in Humberstone parish, perhaps to be compared with Luffenham in neighbouring Rutland, *v.* Ru 256), but Old English settlement names are dominant in the north-west and in the south-east of the Hundred.

Place-names which are thought to represent the earliest evidence for Scandinavian settlement in East Goscote Hundred are those compounded with a Scandinavian personal name as the first element and Old English *tūn* 'a village, an estate'. These are presumed to be original Anglo-Saxon settlements appropriated by the men of that Viking army which disbanded in 877. Here, they are South Croxton, Grimston, Thrussington and Thurmaston. All occupy prime sites. South Croxton lies on Queniborough Brook, neighbouring the former royal Anglo-Saxon vill of Queniborough, 'the queen's manor'. Grimston is located on a sheltered, south-facing slope beside the Roman road Margary 58a across the Wolds, while Thrussington and Thurmaston are adjacent to the Roman Fosse Way, to the rivers

Wreake and Soar, and within a few miles of the Scandinavian borough of Leicester.

Place-names with *bȳ* 'a farmstead, a village', which in some cases probably mark the division of earlier large Anglo-Saxon estates, are numerous and dominate east of the Fosse Way and the centre of the Hundred. They are Asfordby, Ashby Folville, Barkby, Barsby, Beeby, Brooksby, the lost *Canby* (in Sileby), the lost *Colby* (in Thurmaston), Frisby on the Wreake, Gaddesby, Hoby, Old Ingarsby, Lowesby, Quenby, Rearsby, Rotherby, Saxelby, Shoby, Sileby, Tugby and Welby. In the lower Wreake Valley, Asfordby, Brooksby, Frisby, Hoby, Rearsby, Rotherby and Welby are closely related to the river itself. To these may be added Kirby Bellars, probably a former Anglo-Saxon vill with its own church, appropriated and renamed by Scandinavians. Saxelby and Shoby lie to the north of the river Wreake on streams flowing south-west into it. Ashby Folville, Barkby, Barsby, Beeby, Gaddesby, Ingarsby, Lowesby and Quenby are located to the south of the Wreake on streams flowing north-west to join it. Only Sileby, beside a stream running directly into the river Soar north of Leicester, and Tugby in the far south-east of the Hundred on a tributary of Eye Brook, are unrelated to the Wreake Valley. Wreake, of course, is a Scandinavian name *Vreþk*, from the adjective *vreiðr* 'winding, twisting', entirely appropriate to the nature of the river's channel. Of these 21 place-names with *bȳ*, 16 (plus one possible, i.e. 76% or 81%) have a Scandinavian personal name as first element. Recorded lost Anglo-Saxon settlements or estates in the territories of townships now with Scandinavian names in *bȳ* are *Alwolton* (Hoby), *Dodyngton* (Rearsby), *Hogston* (Sileby) and *Weston* (Beeby).

Of the 56 major township names in current use in the Hundred, 29 (i.e. 52%) are Old English, 17 (plus 2 possible, i.e. 30% or 34%) are Scandinavian, 8 (plus 2 possible, i.e. 14% or 18%) are hybrid Old English/Scandinavian. These eight include the four early townships, listed above, which evidence the disbanding of a Viking army in 877.

The influence of the Normans was minimal on the toponomy of East Goscote Hundred. The Old English township name *Merdegrave* had its first element *mearð* 'a marten, a weasel' (> *merde*) replaced by Old French *bel* 'beautiful' because *merde* was associated with Old French *merde* 'excrement, filth', hence the remodelled Belgrave, while in what was eventually to become the extra-parochial liberty of Launde (Old French *lande* 'a forest glade') was founded c.1120 a priory for Augustinian Canons which perpetuated the Norman name of a minor topographical feature.

Unlike in Framland Hundred, however, religious houses did not establish a large number of granges in East Goscote Hundred. Garendon Abbey had a grange at Burton on the Wolds and another at Welby as early as the late twelfth century, while Croxton Abbey held a grange at Skeffington, recorded from the later fifteenth century. A grange at Cold Newton in the possession of the leper Hospital of St Lazarus in Burton Lazars is recorded from 1539, while a grange at Cossington, presumably once belonging to the Knights Templars of Rothley, appears in a Rothley Temple deed of 1551. The late medieval *Colley Grange* (1537) in Thorpe Satchville cannot be assigned to a religious house.

The earliest medieval hunting park in East Goscote Hundred is that of the manor of Barrow, recorded as *parco* (*meo*) *de Barow* in the mid-twelfth century. This was a secular hunting park, part of an estate held at the date of Domesday Book by Earl Hugh of Chester. An unassigned *the parke* (1559) is recorded at Gaddesby, again presumably secular, while Launde Priory's park is only recorded from 1375. *Oldpark* (1517), which appears in records for Belgrave, refers to an early park associated with the nearby Abbey of St Mary de Pratis, Leicester (*v.* Abbey Park, Lei **1** 223).

Finally a note concerning medieval saltways in the Hundred. The line of the modern A607 road was used as an important route skirting the south bank of the river Wreake. From Burton Lazars in Framland Hundred, it passed by way of Kirby Bellars (*Saltgate* p.1250 (1404)), through Rotherby (*the Streetway* 1601), Rearsby (cf. *Salters Cloase* 1648), Barkby (*Saltergate* 1467×84) and so by Thurmaston (*Saltergate* 1320×40) to Leicester. Branches from this route crossed the river Wreake at Asfordby (cf. *Sawtrum* 1580 and *Grenestrete* 1439) and Hoby (*Salteforde* 1322 and cf. *Salterewonges* 1322). These river crossings were presumably related to saltway(s) en route north-west to Wymeswold (in which *Saltstrete* 1412) and beyond. The minor Roman road from the north-east mentioned above via Keyham (cf. *the Salters Cloase* 1788) and Humberstone (cf. *Saltersford Bridge* 1835) on its way to Leicester was also used as a saltway.

NOTES ON ARRANGEMENT

1. The East Goscote Hundred name is discussed first. After this, the place-names are treated within the civil parishes. Within each civil parish, the townships are dealt with in alphabetical order. For each township, the township name is followed by names of primary historical or etymological interest, also arranged in alphabetical order. At the end of these sections, all the remaining names related to the township appearing on the 1956–7 O.S. 6" maps, on the 1951–66 O.S. 2½" maps and on the 1967–8 O.S. 1" maps (and any names recorded only locally) are listed with such early forms and etymological comment as can be provided. These names, however, are sometimes of obvious origin or are ones about whose history it is unwise to speculate. The forms of all names in the above sections are presented in the order: spelling, date, source. The final section for each township lists field-names, divided into modern (i.e. post-1750) and earlier. The pre-1750 field-names are printed in italic.

2. Place-names believed to be no longer current are marked '(lost)', e.g. 'WILLOUGHES (lost)'. This does not necessarily mean that the site to which the name was once applied is unknown. We are dealing primarily with names and it is the names which are lost. Such names are printed in italic in the index. Place-names marked '(local)' are believed to be current locally.

3. In explaining the various toponyms, summary reference is always made, by printing the elements in bold type, to the analysis of elements at the end of this volume and to more extended treatment of these in *English Place-Name Elements* (EPNS 25 and 26), in the *Addenda and Corrigenda* to these volumes in JEPNS 1 and in *The Vocabulary of English Place-Names* (CENS), in progress: e.g. '*Peiselondes* 1322 (*v.* **pise**, **land**)'.

4. Manuscript sources of the early spellings of the names are indicated by printing the abbreviations of the sources in italic. The abbreviations for published sources are printed in roman type.

5. Where two dates are given for a spelling, e.g.'1156 (1318)' or '1328 (e.15)' or '14 (1449)', the first date is the date at which the document purports to have been composed, the second the date of the

copy that has come down to us. Sources whose dates cannot be fixed to a particular year are dated by century, e.g.'12', '13', '14' etc. (often more specifically 'e.13', 'm.13', 'l.13' etc., early, mid and late thirteenth century respectively); by regnal date, e.g.'Edw 1', 'Hy 2', 'John' etc.; or by a range of years, e.g.'1209 × 35', such a date meaning that the form belongs to a particular year within those limits but cannot be more precisely fixed.

6. The sign '(p)' after a source indicates that the particular spelling given appears in that source as a person's surname, not primarily as a reference to a place; thus '*Hathelakeston* 1223 ClR (p)' refers to one *Hacon de Hathelakeston*, bearing *Hathelakeston* as his surname.

7. When a letter or letter (sometimes words or phrases) in an early place-name form are enclosed in parentheses, it means that spellings with and without the enclosed letter(s) occur: e.g. '*Asseford(e)by*' means that the forms *Assefordeby* and *Assefordby* are found. When only one part of a place-name spelling is given as a variant, preceded or followed by a tilde or tildes, it means that the particular spelling only differs in respect of the cited part from the preceding or following spelling, e.g. '*Holm Meadow, ~ Middow*', '*Croake hades, Croke ~*', '*Far ~ ~, Near Hirst Croft*'.

8. When an entry reads, e.g. 'BARKBY GRANGE, 1877 White', the name appears in its modern spelling in the source quoted.

9. Cross references to other names are sometimes given with *supra* or *infra*, the former referring to a name already dealt with, the latter to a name dealt with later in the text.

10. When a place-name is compared with an example from another county, that county is indicated: e.g.'Berkeley Harness, Gl **2** 206' which refers to Berkeley Harness in Gloucestershire and to a specific volume and page in the EPNS survey *The Place-Names of Gloucestershire.*

11. In order to save space in presenting early spellings of a name, *et passim* and *et freq* are sometimes used to indicate that the preceding form occurs from time to time or frequently from the date of the last quoted source to that of the following one.

12. Putative forms of the place-name elements which appear asterisked in the analysis at the end of this volume are not asterisked in the text, although the discussion will often make it clear which are on independent record and which are inferred.

ABBREVIATIONS AND BIBLIOGRAPHY

Abbreviations printed in roman type refer to printed sources and those in italic to manuscript sources.

a.	*ante.*
AAS	Reports and Papers of the Associated Architectural Societies.
Abbr	*Placitorum Abbrevatio* (RC), 1811.
abl.sg.	ablative singular.
AC	*Ancient Charters* (PRS 10), 1883.
acc.sg.	accusative singular.
AD	*Catalogue of Ancient Deeds* (PRO), in progress.
adj.	adjective.
AFr	Anglo-French.
AllS	Archives in the Muniments Room of All Souls' College, Oxford.
AN	Anglo-Norman.
Angl	Anglian dialect of Old English.
Anglo-Scand	Anglo-Scandinavian.
ASC	*The Anglo-Saxon Chronicle*, ed. B. Thorpe (RS), 1861.
Ass	Assize Rolls in various publications.
ASWills	*Anglo-Saxon Wills*, ed. D. Whitelock, Cambridge 1930.
Ave	Avenue (in street-names).
Banco	*Index of Placita de Banco 1327–8* (PRO Lists and Indexes 32), 1909 and De Banco Rolls in Farnham.
BCS	*Cartularium Saxonicum*, ed. W. de G. Birch, 3 vols., 1885-93.
Beau	Cartulary of Beauchief Abbey, National Library of Wales, Aberystwyth.
BdHu	*The Place-Names of Bedfordshire and Huntingdonshire* (EPNS 3), 1926.
BelCartB	Large Cartulary of Belvoir Priory (Add. MS 105), Duke of Rutland's Muniments Room, Belvoir Castle, Leics.
Berkeley	*Catalogue of the Charters at Berkeley Castle*, ed. I. H. Jeayes, 1892.
BHosp	Barrow Hospital Trustees MSS, The Record Office for Leicestershire, Leicester and Rutland, Wigston Magna.
Billson	C. J. Billson, *Mediaeval Leicester*, Leicester 1920.
Bk	Buckinghamshire; *The Place-Names of Buckinghamshire* (EPNS 2), 1925.
BM	*Index to the Charters and Rolls in the Department of Manuscripts, British Museum*, 1900–12.
BodlCh	*Calendar of Charters and Rolls preserved in the Bodleian Library*, ed. W. H. Turner and H. O. Coxe, 1878.

BPR	*The Register of Edward the Black Prince* (PRO), 4 vols., 1930–33.
Brk	Berkshire; *The Place-Names of Berkshire* (EPNS 49–51), 1973–76.
Burton	W. Burton, *The Description of Leicestershire*, 1622.
BurtonCart	*The Burton Cartulary* in Salt, vol. 5.
c.	*circa.*
Ca	Cambridgeshire; *The Place-Names of Cambridgeshire and the Isle of Ely* (EPNS 19), 1943.
Camd	Publications of the Camden Society.
CartAnt	*The Cartae Antiquae Rolls* 1–20 (PRS NS 17, 33), 1939, 1960.
CCart	Cossington Cartulary (2/77/80) in the Middleton MSS, University of Nottingham Archives, Nottingham.
CCR	Croxton Kerrial Court Rolls, Duke of Rutland's Muniments Room, Belvoir Castle, Leics.
CENS	Publications of the Centre for English Name Studies, University of Nottingham, Nottingham.
cent.	century.
Census	Censuses in various publications.
cf.	compare.
Ch	*Calendar of Charter Rolls* (PRO), 6 vols., 1903–27.
Ch	Cheshire; *The Place-Names of Cheshire* (EPNS 44–47), 1970–72, (EPNS 48, 54), 1981, (EPNS 74), 1997.
ChAccts	Chamberlains' Accounts in RBL.
ChancP	*Calendars of Proceedings in Chancery in the reign of Queen Elizabeth*, 3 vols., London 1827–32; *Index of Chancery Proceedings* (Series ii) (PRO Lists and Indexes, nos. 7, 24, 30).
ChancR	Chancellor's Rolls (as footnotes to *Pipe Rolls* (PRS), in progress).
Charyte	Charyte's Novum Rentale of Leicester Abbey, incorporating Geryn's Rental (Bodleian Laud Misc 625), Bodleian Library, Oxford.
ChPr	*Chronicon Petroburgense* (Camd 47), 1849.
ChR	*Rotuli Chartarum* (RC), London 1837.
Cl	*Calendar of Close Rolls* (PRO), in progress.
Cl(s)	Close(s) (in field-names).
Clay	Clayton MSS, The Record Office for Leicestershire, Leicester and Rutland, Wigston Magna.
ClR	*Rotuli Litterarum Clausarum* (RC), 1833–44.
Comp	Compotus Rolls, Duke of Rutland's Muniments Room, Belvoir Castle, Leics.; The Record Office for Leicestershire, Leicester and Rutland, Wigston Magna; in Middleton MSS, University of Nottingham Archives, Nottingham.
comp.	comparative.
Conant	Conant MSS, The Record Office for Leicestershire, Leicester and Rutland, Wigston Magna.
ContGerm	Continental Germanic.
CoPleas	Common Pleas in various publications.

Cor	Coroners' Rolls in various publications.
Coram	Coram Rege Rolls in various publications.
CRCart	Roll Cartulary of Croxton Abbey (II. 29. iii), Duke of Rutland's Muniments Room, Belvoir Castle, Leics.
Cresc	Crescent (in street-names).
Crox	The Large Cartulary of Croxton Abbey (Add. MS 70), Duke of Rutland's Muniments Room, Belvoir Castle, Leics.
CroxR	Croxton Abbey Register (Add. MS 71), Duke of Rutland's Muniments Room, Belvoir Castle, Leics.
Ct	Court Rolls in the Ferrers MSS, the Hazlerigg MSS, the Rothley Temple Deeds and the Winstanley MSS, The Record Office for Leicestershire, Leicester and Rutland, Wigston Magna; in the Middleton MSS, University of Nottingham Archives, Nottingham.
Ct	Court Rolls in various publications.
Cu	Cumberland; *The Place-Names of Cumberland* (EPNS 20–22), 1950–52.
Cur	*Curia Regis Rolls* (PRO), in progress.
Curtis	J. Curtis, *A Topographical History of the County of Leicester*, 1831.
CustRo	*The Custumary of the Manor and Soke of Rothley in the County of Leicester*, ed. G. T. Clark, *Archaeologia*, vol. 47, 1882.
D	Devon; *The Place-Names of Devon* (EPNS 8–9), 1931–32.
d.	died.
Dan	Danish.
Dane	F. M. Stenton, *Documents illustrative of the Social and Economic History of the Danelaw*, 1920.
dat.sg.	dative singular.
DB	Domesday Book; *Domesday Book: Leicestershire*, ed. P. Morgan, 1979.
Db	Derbyshire; *The Place-Names of Derbyshire* (EPNS 27–29), 1959.
Deed	Miscellaneous deeds in The Record Office for Leicestershire, Leicester and Rutland, Wigston Magna; in Lincolnshire Archives Office, Lincoln; in private collections.
def.art.	definite article.
DEPN	E. Ekwall, *The Concise Oxford Dictionary of English Place-Names*, 4th edn, 1960.
Deposition	Exchequer Special Depositions in PRO.
Derby	*Descriptive Catalogue of Derbyshire Charters*, ed. I. H. Jeayes, 1906.
DgP	*Danmarks Gamle Personnavne*, ed. G. Knudsen, M. Kristensen and R. Hornby, Copenhagen 1936–64.
DI	*The Domesday of Inclosures 1517–1518*, ed. I. S. Leadam, 2 vols., London 1897, reprinted New York 1971.
dial.	dialect(al).
Dixie	Dixie or Market Bosworth Grammar School MSS, The Record Office for Leicestershire, Leicester and Rutland, Wigston Magna.

DKR	*Reports of the Deputy Keeper of the Public Records* (PRO).
DLPN	K. Cameron (with J. Insley), *A Dictionary of Lincolnshire Place-Names*, EPNS Popular Series, vol. 1, 1998.
Dugd	W. Dugdale, *Monasticon Anglicanum*, 6 vols. in 8, 1817–30.
e.	early.
ECP	*Early Chancery Proceedings* (PRO Lists and Indexes 1–10).
ed.	edited by.
EDD	J. Wright, *The English Dialect Dictionary*, 6 vols., 1898–1905.
edn	edition.
Edw 1, Edw 2	Regnal date, t. Edward I, t. Edward II etc.
EETS	Publications of the Early English Text Society.
Ekwall Studies[2]	E. Ekwall, *Studies on English Place-Names,* Stockholm 1936.
el.	place-name element.
Elements	A. H. Smith, *English Place-Name Elements* (EPNS 25–26), 1956.
ELiW	*Early Lincoln Wills*, ed. A. Gibbons, 1888.
Eliz 1	Regnal date, t. Elizabeth I.
eModE	early Modern English.
EnclA	Unpublished Enclosure Awards, The Record Office for Leicestershire, Leicester and Rutland, Wigston Magna.
EpCB	*An Episcopal Court Book for the Diocese of Lincoln, 1514–20* (LRS 61), 1967.
EPNS	Publications of the English Place-Name Society.
esp.	especially.
et freq	*et frequenter* (and frequently (thereafter)).
et passim	and occasionally (thereafter).
ExchKR	Exchequer King's Remembrancer Memoranda Rolls in PRO.
Ex-Rel	*The State of the Ex-Religious and Former Chantry Priests in the Diocese of Lincoln 1547–74* (LRS 53), 1959.
FA	*Feudal Aids* (PRO), 6 vols., 1899–1920.
Farnham	G. F. Farnham, *Leicestershire Medieval Village Notes*, 6 vols., 1929–33.
Fd(s)	Field(s) (in field-names).
Fees	*The Book of Fees* (PRO), 3 vols., 1921–31.
FF	Feet of Fines in various publications.
Ferrers	Ferrers MSS, The Record Office for Leicestershire, Leicester and Rutland, Wigston Magna.
Feilitzen	O. von Feilitzen, *The Pre-Conquest Personal Names of Domesday Book*, Uppsala 1937.
fem.	feminine.
Field	J. Field, *A History of English Field-Names*, 1993.
Fine	*Calendar of Fine Rolls* (PRO), in progress.
FineR	*Excerpta e rotulis finium* (RC), 2 vols., 1835–36.
Fisher	Fisher MSS, The Record Office for Leicestershire, Leicester and Rutland, Wigston Magna.
Flo	*Florence of Worcester's Chronicle* in MHB.
Fm	Farm.
f.ns.	field-name(s).

For	*Select Pleas of the Forest* (Seld 13), 1901.
For	Forest Proceedings in PRO.
France	*Calendar of Documents preserved in France* (RS), 1899.
freq	frequently.
GarCart	Cartulary of Garendon Abbey (BL Lansdown 415), British Library, London.
GarCh	Garendon Abbey Charters, The Record Office for Leicestershire, Leicester and Rutland, Wigston Magna.
GauntReg	*John of Gaunt's Register* (Camd), 2 vols., 1911, 1937.
gen.	genitive.
gen.pl.	genitive plural.
gen.sg.	genitive singular.
Gilb	*Gilbertine Charters* (LRS 18), 1922.
GildR	Merchant Gild Rolls in RBL and RFL.
Gl	Gloucestershire; *The Place-Names of Gloucestershire* (EPNS 38–41), 1964–65.
Ha	Hampshire; R. Coates, *The Place-Names of Hampshire,* 1989.
Harl	Harley MSS, British Library, London.
Hastings	*The Manuscripts of the late Reginald Rawdon Hastings of the Manor House, Ashby de la Zouch*, vol. 1 (HMC), 1928.
Hazlerigg	Hazlerigg MSS, The Record Office for Leicestershire, Leicester and Rutland, Wigston Magna.
HighwayB	Keyham Highway Book, The Record Office for Leicestershire, Leicester and Rutland, Wigston Magna.
Hilton	R. H. Hilton, *The Economic Development of Some Leicestershire Estates in the Fourteenth and Fifteenth Centuries*, 1947.
HMC	Historical Manuscripts Commission.
HMCVar	Historical Manuscripts Commission Reports on Manuscripts in Various Collections, 1901–23.
Ho.	House.
HP	Hall Papers in RBL.
Hrt	Hertfordshire; *The Place-Names of Hertfordshire* (EPNS 15), 1938.
Hy 1, Hy 2	Regnal date, t. Henry I, t. Henry II etc.
ib, *ib*	*ibidem.*
Inqaqd	*Inquisitiones ad quod Damnum* (RC), 1803.
Ipm	*Calendar of Inquisitions post mortem* (PRO), in progress.
IpmR	*Inquisitiones post mortem* (RC), 4 vols., 1802–28.
ISLR	F. A. Greenhill, *The Incised Slabs of Leicestershire and Rutland*, 1958.
Jackson	K. Jackson, *Language and History in Early Britain*, 1953.
JEPNS	Journal of the English Place-Name Society.
John	Regnal date, t. John.
K	Kent.
KB	Cartulary of Kirby Bellars Priory, Rockingham Castle Library, Rockingham, Northants.
Kelly	*Kelly's Directory of the Counties of Leicester and Rutland*, 1925.
KPN	J. K. Wallenberg, *Kentish Place-Names*, Uppsala 1931.

L	Lincolnshire; *The Place-Names of Lincolnshire* (EPNS 58, 64–66, 71, 73, 77), 1985-2001, in progress.
l.	late.
La	Lancashire; E. Ekwall, *The Place-Names of Lancashire*, 1922.
LAS	Transactions of the Leicestershire Archaeological Society, later Leicestershire Archaeological and Historical Society.
Lat	Latin.
Laz	Cartulary of Burton Lazars (BL Cotton Nero C XII), British Library, London.
LCDeeds	Leicester Corporation Deeds, The Record Office for Leicestershire, Leicester and Rutland, Wigston Magna.
LCh	Leicestershire Charters, The Record Office for Leicestershire, Leicester and Rutland, Wigston Magna.
Lei	Leicestershire; *The Place-Names of Leicestershire* (EPNS 75, 78), 1998–2002, in progress.
LeicSurv	*The Leicestershire Survey*, ed. C. F. Slade, 1956.
LeicW	*Leicester Wills*, ed. H. Hartopp, 2 vols., 1902–20.
LEpis	*Lincoln Episcopal Records* (LRS 2), 1912.
Lib	*Calendar of Liberate Rolls* (PRO), in progress.
LibCl	Liber Cleri in *The State of the Church*, vol. 1 (LRS 23), 1926.
Lind	E. H. Lind, *Norsk-Isländska Personbinamn från Medeltiden*, Uppsala 1920–21.
LML	*Leicestershire Marriage Licences 1570–1729*, ed. H. Hartopp, 1910.
LN	*Liber Niger Scaccarii*, 1774.
Löfvenberg	M. T. Löfvenberg, *Studies on Middle English Local Surnames*, Lund 1942.
LP	*Letters and Papers Foreign and Domestic, Henry VIII* (PRO), 1864–1933.
LRoll	'The Lincoln Roll' – a Noseley Cartulary in the Hazlerigg MSS, The Record Office for Leicestershire, Leicester and Rutland, Wigston Magna.
LRS	Publications of the Lincolnshire Record Society.
LTD	Liber de terris Dominicalibus of Leicester Abbey (BL Cotton Galba B III), British Library, London.
LWills	*Lincoln Wills* (LRS 5, 10, 24), 1914–30.
m.	mid.
MagBrit	D. Lysons and S. Lysons, *Magna Britannia being a Concise Topographical Account of the several Counties of Great Britain*, 1816.
Map	Various printed maps.
Map	Unpublished maps in local and private collections.
Margary	I. D. Margary, *Roman Roads in Britain*, vol. 1, 1955.
masc.	masculine.
Mdw	Meadow (in field-names).
ME	Middle English.
MemR	*Memoranda Rolls* (PRS NS 11, 21, 31).
Merton	Maps and deeds in the archives of Merton College, Oxford.

MHB *Monumenta Historica Britannica*, ed. H. Petrie, 1848.
MHG Middle High German.
MHW The Matriculus of Hugh de Wells in *Rotuli Hugonis de Welles*, (LRS 3), 1912.
MiD Middleton MSS, University of Nottingham Archives, Nottingham.
MinAccts *Ministers' Accounts: List of the Lands of Dissolved Religious Houses* (PRO Lists and Indexes, Supplementary Series III, vols. 1–4).
Misc *Calendar of Inquisitions Miscellaneous* (PRO), in progress.
MiscAccts Miscellaneous accounts in local and private collections.
MLat Medieval Latin.
ModE Modern English.
Moule T. Moule, *The English Counties Delineated*, 1830.
Moulton *Paleography, Genealogy and Topography: Selections from the Collection of H. R. Moulton*, 1930.
MS(S) Manuscript(s).
Mx *The Place-Names of Middlesex* (EPNS 18), 1942.
Names *Names*, Journal of the American Name Society.
n.d. not dated.
neut. neuter.
Nichols J. Nichols, *The History and Antiquities of the County of Leicester*, 4 vols. in 8, 1795–1811.
nom.pl. nominative plural.
nom.sg. nominative singular.
Norw Norwegian.
NS New series in a run of publications.
Nt Nottinghamshire; *The Place-Names of Nottinghamshire* (EPNS 17), 1940.
Nth Northamptonshire; *The Place-Names of Northamptonshire* (EPNS 10), 1933.
num. numeral.
O First edition O.S. 1" maps.
OblR *Rotuli de Oblatis* (RC), 1835.
obl.sg. oblique singular.
OBret Old Breton.
ODan Old Danish.
OE Old English.
OEBede *The Old English Version of Bede's Ecclesiastical History* (EETS 95–96, 110–11), 1890–98.
OED *A New English Dictionary*, ed. J. A. H. Murray *et al.*, 1884–1928; re-issued with a supplement in 1933 as *The Oxford English Dictionary*.
OEScand Old East Scandinavian.
OFr Old French.
OGer Old German.
OIcel Old Icelandic.
ON Old Norse.

ONFr	Old Northern French.
Ord	Ordericus Vitalis, *Ecclesiasticae Historiae*, vols. 2–3, Paris 1840–45.
O.S.	The Ordnance Survey.
OSut	*The Rolls and Registers of Bishop Oliver Sutton* (LRS 39, 43, 52, 60), 1948–65.
OSwed	Old Swedish.
OWScand	Old West Scandinavian.
P	*Pipe Rolls* (PRS), in progress.
p.	*post.*
(p)	place-name used as a personal name.
Pap	*Calendar of Entries in the Papal Registers* (PRO), in progress.
Pat	*Calendar of Patent Rolls* (PRO), in progress.
Pat	Patent Rolls in the Public Record Office.
Peake	Peake MSS (Neville of Holt), The Record Office for Leicestershire, Leicester and Rutland, Wigston Magna.
perh.	perhaps.
pers.n(s).	personal name(s).
P.H.	Public House.
Plan	Unpublished plans in The Record Office for Leicestershire, Leicester and Rutland, Wigston Magna.
p.n.	place-name.
Pochin	Pochin MSS, The Record Office for Leicestershire, Leicester and Rutland, Wigston Magna.
poss.	possible, possibly.
Potter	S. P. Potter, *A History of Wymeswold*, 1915.
ppl.adj.	participial adjective.
PR	Parish registers in various publications.
PRep	*The Register of Bishop Philip Repingdon* (LRS 57–58), 1963.
prep.	preposition.
pres.part.	present participle.
presum.	presumably.
PRO	Records preserved in or published by the Public Record Office.
prob.	probable, probably.
PRS	Publications of the Pipe Roll Society.
PrW	Primitive Welsh.
Queen's	Rentals and surveys of the lands of the Bishop of Lincoln, Queen's College, Oxford, MS 366.
QuR	*Quorndon Records,* ed. G. F. Farnham, 1912 and 1913.
q.v.	*quod vide.*
R.	River.
RB	Romano-British.
RBE	*Red Book of the Exchequer* (RS 99), 1896.
RBL	*Records of the Borough of Leicester*, vols. 1–3, ed. M. Bateson 1899–1905; vol. 4, ed. H. Stocks 1923; vols. 5–6, ed. G. A. Chinnery 1965–67.
RC	Publications of the Record Commission.
Rd	Road (in street-names).

Reaney	P. H. Reaney, *A Dictionary of English Surnames*, revised by R. M. Wilson, 3rd edn with appendix by D. Hey, 1995.
Reeve	Documents in the Reeve Collection, Lincolnshire Archives Office, Lincoln.
Reg	*Regesta Regum Anglo-Normannorum*, 1913–68.
RegAnt	*Registrum Antiquissimum of the Cathedral Church of Lincoln* (LRS 27–29, 51), 1931–58.
Rental	Various unpublished rentals in local and private collections.
Req	Court of Requests Rolls in Farnham.
RFinib	*Rotuli de Finibus* in *Rotuli de Oblatis et Finibus in Turri Londinensi* (RC), 1835.
RFL	*Register of the Freemen of Leicester*, ed. H. Hartopp, 2 vols., 1927–33.
RGrav	*Rotuli Ricardi Gravesend Episcopi Lincolniensis* (LRS 20), 1925.
RGros	*Rotuli Roberti Grosseteste Episcopi Lincolniensis* (LRS 11), 1914.
RH	*Rotuli Hundredorum* (RC), 1812–18.
RHug	*Rotuli Hugonis de Welles Episcopi Lincolniensis* (LRS 3, 6), 1912–13.
Ric 1, Ric 2	Regnal dates, t. Richard I, t. Richard II etc.
RN	E. Ekwall, *English River-Names*, 1928.
RotNorm	*Rotuli Normanniae in Turri Londinensi* (RC), 1835.
RTAL	*Rotulus Taxationis Archidiaconatus Leicestrie* (LRS 3), 1912.
RTemple	Rothley Temple Deeds, The Record Office for Leicestershire, Leicester and Rutland, Wigston Magna.
Ru	Rutland; *The Place-Names of Rutland* (EPNS 67–69), 1994.
Rut	Duke of Rutland's MSS, Muniments Room, Belvoir Castle, Leics.
S	P. H. Sawyer, *Anglo-Saxon Charters*, 1968.
s.a.	*sub anno.*
Sale	Particulars of sales in local and private collections.
Salt	Publications of the William Salt Society.
Sandred	K. I. Sandred, *English Place-Names in -stead*, Uppsala 1963.
Saxton	C. Saxton, *Atlas of England and Wales*, 1576.
sb.	substantive.
Scand	Scandinavian.
Searle	W. G. Searle, *Onomasticon Anglo-Saxonicum*, 1897.
Selby	*The Selby Abbey Cartulary* (YAA, vols. 10, 13), 1891–93.
Seld	Publications of the Selden Society.
ShR	Shangton Records, The Record Office for Leicestershire, Leicester and Rutland, Wigston Magna.
Sloane	Sloane MSS, The British Library, London.
s.n(n).	*sub nomine, sub nominibus.*
SP	State Papers Domestic in PRO.
Speed	J. Speed, *The Theatre of the Empire of Great Britain*, 1610.
SPNLY	G. Fellows Jensen, *Scandinavian Personal Names in Lincolnshire and Yorkshire*, Copenhagen 1968.

SR	Subsidy Rolls in various publications.
Sr	Surrey; *The Place-Names of Surrey* (EPNS 11), 1934.
SSNEM	G. Fellows Jensen, *Scandinavian Settlement Names in the East Midlands*, Copenhagen 1978.
St	Street (in street-names).
Stephen	Regnal date, t. Stephen.
surn(s).	surname(s).
Surv	Surveys in various publications.
Surv	Surveys in local and private collections.
s.v.	*sub voce.*
Swed	Swedish.
Sx	Sussex; *The Place-Names of Sussex* (EPNS 6–7), 1929–30.
t.	*tempore.*
TA	Tithe Awards in The Record Office for Leicestershire, Leicester and Rutland, Wigston Magna.
Tax	*Taxatio Ecclesiastica* (RC), 1802.
TB	Tryon of Bulwick MSS, Northamptonshire Record Office, Northampton.
Templar	*Records of the Templars in England in the Twelfth Century*, ed. B. A. Lees, 1935.
Terrier	Terriers in various publications.
Terrier	Terriers in local and private collections.
Thoroton	*The Antiquities of Nottinghamshire*, ed. R. Thoroton, 1677.
TRE	*tempore Regis Edwardi*, the DB term for 'on the day that King Edward the Confesssor was alive and dead'.
TutP	*Cartulary of Tutbury Priory* (HMC, vol. JP 2), 1962.
v.	*vide.*
Val	*The Valuation of Norwich*, ed. W. E. Lunt, 1926.
Valuation	Valuations in local and private collections.
vbl.sb.	verbal substantive.
VE	*Valor Ecclesiasticus* (RC), 1810–34.
VEPN	*The Vocabulary of English Place-Names* (CENS), in progress.
Visit	*Visitations of Religious Houses in the Diocese of Lincoln* (LRS 14, 21, 33, 35, 37), 1918–47.
W	Wiltshire; *The Place-Names of Wiltshire* (EPNS 16), 1939, reprinted 1970.
Wa	Warwickshire; *The Place-Names of Warwickshire* (EPNS 13), 1936, reprinted 1970.
Whit	Whitfield Documents, Lincolnshire Archives Office, Lincoln.
White	*History, Gazetteer and Directory of Leicestershire and Rutland*, ed. W. White, 1846, 1863, 1877.
Will	Wills in various publications.
Will	Unpublished wills in local and private collections.
Win	Winstanley MSS, The Record Office for Leicestershire, Leicester and Rutland, Wigston Magna.
wk.obl.	weak oblique.
Wo	Worcestershire; *The Place-Names of Worcestershire* (EPNS 4), 1927.

WoCart	John de Wodeford's Cartulary (BL Claudius A XIII), British Library, London.
Works	*Public Works in Medieval Law* (Seld 40), 1915.
Wyg	Wyggeston Hospital MSS, The Record Office for Leicestershire, Leicester and Rutland, Wigston Magna.
XenLid	E. Hellquist, 'Fornsvenska tillnamn', *Xenia Lideniana: Festskrift Tillägnad Professor Evald Lidén*, Stockholm 1912.
YAA	Publications of the Yorkshire Archaeological Association: Record Series.
YE	Yorkshire East Riding; *The Place-Names of the East Riding of Yorkshire and York* (EPNS 14), 1937.
YN	Yorkshire North Riding; *The Place-Names of the North Riding of Yorkshire* (EPNS 5), 1928.
YW	Yorkshire West Riding; *The Place-Names of the West Riding of Yorkshire* (EPNS 30-37), 1961-63.
ZEN	E. Björkman, *Zur englischen Namenkunde*, Halle 1912.
*	a postulated form.
1"	O.S. 1" maps, editions of 1967–68.
2½"	O.S. 2½" maps, editions of 1951–66.
6"	O.S. 6" maps, editions of 1956–67.
(x2), (x3)	Two instances of a particular name; three instances etc.

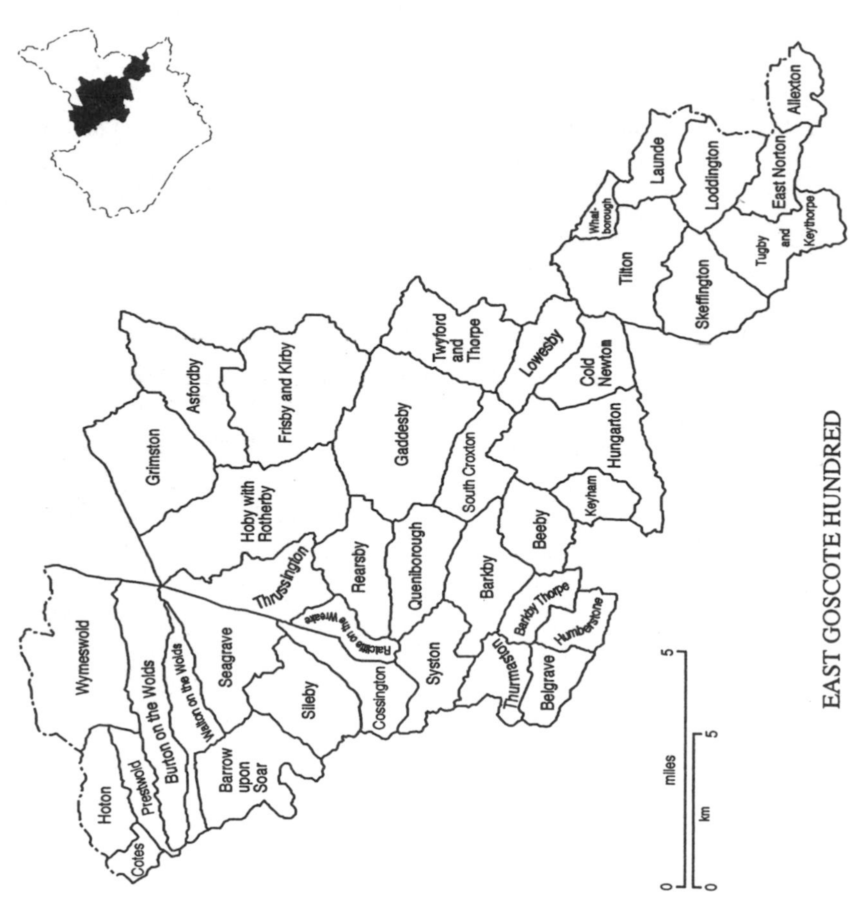
EAST GOSCOTE HUNDRED
Allexton
Launde
Loddington
East Norton
Whatborough
Tilton
Skeffington
Tugby and Keythorpe
Twyford and Thorpe
Lowesby
Cold Newton
Asfordby
Frisby and Kirby
Gaddesby
Hungarton
Grimston
South Croxton
Keyham
Hoby with Rotherby
Queniborough
Beeby
Rearsby
Barkby
Thrussington
Ratcliffe on the Wreake
Barkby Thorpe
Humberstone
Wymeswold
Seagrave
Syston
Thurmaston
Belgrave
Walton on the Wolds
Burton on the Wolds
Sileby
Cossington
Prestwold
Hoton
Barrow upon Soar
Cotes
miles
km
0
5
0
5

East Goscote Hundred

The East Goscote Hundred was once part of an extensive original Goscote Wapentake which was eventually divided into East and West Goscote Hundreds, the boundary between them formed by the river Soar. The division of the early wapentake/hundred into two is said by Nichols (Vol. 3, Pt. 1, 1) to have occurred in 1346. He cites a taxation (his Rot.Aux.20 Edw III) for this. However, as late as an entry dated 1553 in the *Calendar of Patent Rolls*, the Goscote Hundred is still presented as a unit and the earliest evidence for its division into two parts that the editor has noted is in *State Papers Domestic* for 1571 which records the *hundred of East Goscott.*

GOSCOTE HUNDRED

Gosencote 1086 DB

Gosecot 1086 DB (x 5), 1203 P, 1229 Cl *et passim* to 1242, 1255 Cl, *Gosecote* 1086 DB (x 8), c.1130 LeicSurv, 1166 P *et freq* to 1276 RH, c.1291 Tax *et passim* to 1360, 1363 BPR, *Gosecota* 1168 ChancR, *Gosekote* 1242, 1252 Fees

Goscot 1276 RH, c.1291 Tax, *Goscote* 1316 FA, 1327 Pat *et passim* to 1363 BPR, 1369 *Fisher et freq* to 1509 LP, *Goscotte* 1454 *Comp*, *Goscort* 1457 *MiD*, *Gosgate* (sic) 1553 Pat

East Goscott 1571 *SP*, *Eastgoscott*(*e*) 1604 SR, 1607 LAS, *East Goscoate* 1610 Speed

The division is styled

wapentaco, *-tacum*, *-tagio* 1086 DB *et freq* to 1230 P, 1242 ChR *et passim* to 1509 LP

hundred, *-o*, *-um* 1230 P, 1233 Ch, 1242 Cl *et freq*

v. **vápnatak, hundred**.

The area of the original Goscote Wapentake was roughly twice that of Framland and twice that of Gartree. It extended from the Rutland border in the east to the Derbyshire and Nottinghamshire boundaries in the north-west. The heavy soils of western Leicestershire were exploited later than those of the east of the county and the size of the original wapentake doubtlessly reflects, as does that of the original Guthlaxton Wapentake, its more sparsely spread population.

The East Goscote Hundred moot assembled on an impressive promontory lying in Barkby parish, overlooking Syston to its north-west and Queniborough to its north. The site is a mile and a half from the Roman Fosse Way and beside an early ridgeway (now called Ridgemere Lane) running south-east towards Allexton at the county boundary. The earliest evidence for a moot-site here is *Mothowes* 1467 × 84 *LTD*, with OE *mōt* 'an assembly'. The implications of the plural form of the generic are uncertain. It may have been an original singular OE *hōh*, modified as a plural of ON *haugr* 'a mound, a hill', or even have been the plural of *haugr* from the name's formation, suggesting the erstwhile presence of ancient burial mounds which marked the assembly site on the headland. If so, such tumuli are no longer visible on the ground, perhaps having been long ploughed out. The moot-site appears as *Mute Bush* on a Barkby map of 1609, and on another of 1635 as *Moote Bush* (OE *mōt-busc* 'the bush or thicket at which the assembly meets'). In 1798, Nichols noted, 'In this lordship is a place called *Mowdebush-hill* on which stands a stone with *Mowdebush-hill* inserted thereon'; and again, 'The Hundred Court is called at a large stone at a place at the top of Syston field'. The East Goscote Hundred *Mute Bush* is located reasonably near the centre of the original Goscote Wapentake area and, as for the other Leicestershire hundred moot-sites, positioned conveniently near a Roman road leading to the Borough of Leicester (*v.* Barrie Cox, 'Leicestershire moot-sites: the place-name evidence', *Transactions of the Leicestershire Archaeological and Historical Society*, vol. 47 (1971–72), 14–21). However, whether this was the moot-site of the original undivided Goscote Wapentake is uncertain. In Wymeswold parish further to the north-west, at a headland to the west of the Fosse Way and more central to the extent of the undivided Goscote Wapentake, is a location which by the early thirteenth century is initially recorded as an unusual *Gosefot*. This may have been an earlier *Gosecot* at which the men of the wapentake assembled and which gave it its name (*v.* Introduction xiii and Wymeswold f.ns. (a)). Whether the unique survival *Gosecoteho* (*wap'*) 1168 P (with OE *hōh* 'a promontory') preserves the name of the later East Goscote Hundred moot-site or that of the postulated site in

Wymeswold must remain unresolved.

The other Leicestershire hundreds of Framland, Gartree, Guthlaxton and Sparkenhoe are all named from topographical features. Not so Goscote. It is uncertain, however, whether the name Goscote specifies a habitation site, a 'Gōsa's cottage' (with the OE masc. pers.n. *Gōsa* (*Gōsan* gen.sg.) and *cot*), or whether it simply represents an OE *gōsacot* 'a shelter for geese' (with OE *gōs* (*gōsa* gen.pl.)). The former interpretation may seem the likelier, since a shelter for geese must have been an ephemeral thing and so perhaps an unlikely landmark for a moot-site. However, the surviving form *Gosencote* 1086 DB, upon which a pers.n. interpretation of the name may be postulated, is unique and because it has to be set beside thirteen forms in *Gosecot*(*e*) in the same earliest source, it is uncertain what weight may be given to it. It may be thought that a 'goose-cote' was a common medieval phenomenon and for that reason the latter explanation of the name of the hundred is likelier. However, it should be noted that only one very late possible instance (*Goose coat* 1842 *TA*, YW **6** 9) is otherwise recorded in the entire published corpus of the English Place-Name Survey.

Allexton

ALLEXTON

Adelachestone 1086 DB (x3), *Adelakeston(e)* 1168 P, 1211 ChancR (p), 1214, 1215 P, *Adelacston'* c.1130 P

Aðelacheston' 1167 P, *Athelakeston'* 1222 ClR (p), 1225 FineR (p) *et freq* to 1269 For, 1275 RGrav, *Athelakestun'* 1241 Cl, *Adthelakestone* 1226 RHug, *Hathelakeston'* 1220 Pat (p), 1220 Cur (p) *et passim* to 1239 Lib (p), 1239 Cl (p), *Hathelakestun'* 1225, 1226 ClR (p)

Aðelochestona 1167 ChancP, *Athelokeston'* 1254 Val, 1346 Pap *et passim* to 1362 Ipm, 1388 Misc, *Atelokeston* 1228 Pat (p), 1301 Coram (p), *Hathelokeston* 1236 Fees, 1338 Pat

Athelaxton 1252 Derby, 1267 Cur (p), 1385 Banco, *Atheloxton'* 1276 Pat, 1327 SR *et passim* to 1373 Ipm, 1375 Ass, *Athelocston* 1313 Cl, 1313 Ipm

Adelokeston' 1254 Val, 1328 (e.15) *BelCartB*, *Adelokiston* 1376 Cl, *Adelokston* c.1291 Tax, 1375 Ipm, 1376 Cl

Adlakeston(e) 1211 P (p), 1226 RHug, 1277 Abbr, *Adlokiston'* 13 *BHosp* (p)

Adloxton' 1333 *Peake*, 1358 Pat *et freq* to 1451 Cl, 1486 Ipm, *Adlaxton'* 1405 PRep, *Adlaxston* 1501 Cl

Aselakeston(e) 1212 RBE (p), 1220 MHW, 1259 RGrav, *Aslaketon* 1209 × 35 RHug

Alakestona l.12 BM, *Halakestona* l.12 Dane, *Al(l)okeston'* 1361 Pat, 14 (1449) *WoCart* (p), *Alhokeston* 1378 Pat

Alexton Hy 2 *AllS*, 1318 Pat, 1509 *Deed*, 1576 Saxton, 1610 Speed, *Al(l)oxton* 1327 SR (p), 1331 *MiD* (p) *et passim* to 1428 FA, 1453 Cl, *Al(l)oxton* 1327 SR (p), 1331 *MiD* (p) *et passim* to 1428 FA, 1453 Cl, *Al(l)axton* 1518 Visit, 1535 VE *et passim* to 1576 LibCl, 1578 LEpis, *Allaxson* 1552, 1553 Moulton

'Æðellāc's farmstead, village', *v.* **tūn**. The OE pers.n. *Æðellāc* is otherwise unrecorded. Ekwall DEPN offers, rather, the OE pers.n. *Ēadlāc* which occurs once only (*v.* Searle 182), but the shortening of

Ēad- > *Æd-* > *Ad-* is not evidenced in DB material (*v.* Feilitzen 60). Note that some early spellings may have been influenced by the ON pers.n. *Áslákr* (ODan *Aslak*) and by the ME pers.n. *Havelok* (an Anglicized form of the Irish *Abloc*), that of the hero of the popular medieval romance 'The Lay of Havelock the Dane' which is set in neighbouring Lincs., particularly in Lincoln itself. The form *Allaxson* shows typical 16th cent. (and later) Leics. loss of *t* in the group *-ston.*

ALLEXTON HALL, 1925 Kelly, *the Hall* 1806 Map, 1824 O *et passim* to 1925 Kelly; earlier halls at Allexton are recorded as *Needham Halle* 1427 (1798) Nichols (the *Nedham* family is cited 1427 (1798) ib, while *Anne Nedham* was baptized here in 1599 PR), *Nether halle* 1428 Inqaqd (*v.* **neoðera**) and *ye Mannor house* 1635, 1638 *Terrier*, *The Manor House* 1749 *Deed* (*v.* **maner**), *v.* **hall**. ALLEXTON LODGE. ALLEXTON WOOD, c.1800, 1806 Map, 1824 O, *Alexton Wood* 1651 (18), 1671 (1768) *Deed*, 1781 *Terrier*, 1847 *TA*, *Alaxton* ~ 1657 (18) *Deed*; it is *the Wood* 1625 (1730), 1708 *Terrier*, 1797 *Surv*, *v.* **wudu**. BERNERS' ARMS (P.H.) (lost), *Berners' Arms* 1846 White; *Lord Berners* is lord of the manor 1846 ib. DOCKEY FM, cf. *Dockey Close* 1797 *Surv*, 1847 *TA*, *v.* **docce**, **-ig**[3], cf. *Dockey Wonge*, Lei **2** 48. FLOODGATES, *v.* **flod-gate.** HALLATON RD. HIGH FM (LODGE FM 2½"). THE RECTORY, 1925 Kelly, *v.* **rectory**; earlier is *The Parsonage House* 1635, 1638 *Terrier et passim* to 1781 *ib*, *v.* **personage**. ST PETER'S CHURCH, *Church (St Peter)* 1846, 1863, 1877 White, 1925 Kelly; it is earlier recorded as *ecclesie de Aslakeston* 1220 MHW, ~ *de Adloxton* 1358 *Pat*, ~ *de Allokeston* 1361 *ib, The Church* 1635, 1638 *Terrier et passim* to 1721 *ib.* Note also *The Church Yard(e)* 1635, 1697 *ib et passim* to 1745 *ib*, *the Churchyeard* 1674 *ib*, *v.* **chirche-ȝeard**. SHEEP WASH, cf. *Wash Pit* 1793 (1878) *Whit,* 1847 *TA*, *Wash Pitt Close* 1822 (1878) *ib*, *v.* **scēp-wæsce, wæsce, pytt**. STOCKERSTON RD, Stockerston lying 2 miles to the south-east. WILSON ARMS (P.H.) (lost), *The Wilsons Arms Inn* 1847 *TA*, *Wilson's Arms* 1863, 1877 White, *Wilson Arms* 1925 Kelly; *the Hon. H. Tyrwhitt Wilson* is lord of the manor 1863 White.

FIELD-NAMES

Forms in (a) dated 1770 are *Deed*; 1781 are *Terrier*; 1793 (1878), 1822 (1878) and 1869 are *Whit*; 1797 are *Surv*; 1847 are *TA*. Forms throughout dated 1598 are Req; 1625 (1730), 1635, 1638, 1674, 1697, 1708, 1708 (18), 1721, 1724 and 1745 are *Terrier*; 1651 (18), 1657 (18), 1658, 1664, 1671 (1768), 1675 (1768), 1675 (18), 1682, 1693 (1768) and 1749 are *Deed*; 17 are *Clay*.

(a) Three Acres 1797, 1847, Four ~ 1781, 1797 (1721, 1724, 1745, cf. *Four Acre Close* 1721), Five ~ 1797, 1847, Six ~ 1797, 1847, Seven Acres 1797, 1847, Seven Acre Mdw 1797, 1847, Eight Acres 1797, 1847, Johnsons Eight Acre 1847 (with the surn. *Johnson*), Twelve ~ 1797, 1847, Thirteen Acres 1797 (*v.* **æcer**); the Apron piece 1781 (1721, 1745, ~ ~ *peice* 1724, (*a little spong called*) *the Apron* 1625 (1730), 1708, 1708 (18) (*v.* **spang, spong**), *v.* **napperone, pece**; with reference to a narrow strip of land fronting another); Barn Cl 1797, 1847; Bridget's Cl 1781 (*Bridgetts Close* 1625 (1730), 1671 (1768), 1674, 1693 (1768), *Bridgets* ~ 1635, 1638 *et passim* to 1745, *Bridgets Close Meadow* 1635, 1638, 1708; with the surn. *Bridget*, cf. Bridget's Covert, Lei **2** 50); the Brook 1781, 1797 (1638, 1708 *et passim* to 1745, *the Brooke that runs by the towne side* 1625 (1730), *v.* **brōc**; also called *the little Ee* 1721, *the Little Eye* 1724, *the Ee* 1781, *v.* **ēa**; now Eye Brook, it was styled 'Little' to distinguish it from the river Eye; note also *ye Brookside* 1708, *v.* **sīde**); Burton's Cl 1781, 1869, Burton ~ 1847 (*Burtons Close* 1625 (1730), 1635 *et passim* to 1745; with the surn. *Burton*); Castor's Cl 1781, Castons ~ 1797, Custons ~ 1847 (*Casters Close* 1625 (1730), *Castors* ~ 1635, 1638 *et passim* to 1745; with the surn. *Castor* of a family prob. originally from Castor, 19 miles to the east in Northants.); Catlins Mdw 1847 (with the surn. *Catlin*, from the pers.n. *Catelin*, an OFr form of Catharine); Corner Mdw 1797, the Corner(s) 1797, 1847 (*v.* **corner** and the Wood Corner *infra*); Corporation Cl 1847, Corporation Land 1847, Corporation Mdw 1847 (presum. once the property of Leicester Corporation although no authority has been traced for this assumption); Crabtree Cl 1770, 1822 (1878) ((*the*) *Crabtree Close* 1658, 1664, 1682, cf. *Crabtree feild* 1598 (*v.* **feld**), *v.* **crabtre**); Far Cl 1797; Far Mdw 1847; Fence Cl 1797 (*The Upper* ~ ~, *The Nether or Lower Fence Close* 1749, *v.* **fence**); Firn Mdw 1847, the Fern Mdw 1869 (*v.* **fearn**); First Mdw 1847; Gilfords Cl 1847, Guilford's ~ 1869, Gilfords Mdw 1847, Guilford's ~ 1869 (with the surn. *Gilford/Guilford*, *v.* Reaney *s.nn*); Glebe Cl 1847, Glebe Land 1797, 1847 (*v.* **glebe**); Great Cl 1797, 1847, 1869 (x4) (*the Great close* 1598, *v.* **grēat, clos(e)**); Green Gate, ~ ~ Mdw 1797, Great ~ ~, Little Green Gate 1847, Nether Green Gate 1797, 1847 (*Greengate* 1721, 1724, 1745, *v.* **grēne**[1], **gata**); Grimes's Cl 1797 (with the surn. *Grimes*); (The) Hall Cl 1797, 1847, Hall Close Mdw 1797, 1847, Hall Fd 1797, ~ ~ Mdw 1797, 1847 (cf. *Hall Meadow* 1749, *v.* Allexton Hall *supra*); Hawkins Mdw 1797, 1847 (with the surn. *Hawkins*); Hill Cl 1797; the Hole Fd 1770,1822 (1878) (*Holefeild* 1635, 1638 *et passim* to 1682, *Holefield*, ~ *Meadow* 1749, *Hole Field Close* 17, *Hole Field Meadow Close* 17, *v.* **hol**[1], **feld**; one of the early great fields of the township); Home Cl 1847 (*v.* **home**); Homestead 1797 (*The Homestead* 1625 (1730), *v.* **hām-stede**); Humphry's Cl 1797, Humphreys Cl 1847, Humphry's Mdw 1797 (with the surn. *Humphr(e)y*); Knights Cl 1770, 1822 (1878) (1658, 1664, 1682; with the surn. *Knight*, *v.* Tubford(s) Cl *infra*); Little Mdw 1797, 1847; Long Cl 1797, 1847; Middle Cl 1797 (*the Middle close* 1598, *v.* **middel, clos(e)**); (The) Middle Ground 1822 (1878), 1847, 1869 (*v.* **grund**); Mill Cl 1797, 1847, Mill Holm(e) 1797, 1847 (*ye Mill Holme* 1635, *ye Miln Holmes* 1638, *v.* **myln, holmr**); Near Cl 1797; Near Mdw 1797; Nether Cl 1822 (1878), 1847, 1869, Nether Close Mdw 1822 (1878), 1869; the Nether Fd 1781 ((*the*) *Nether Field* 1625 (1730), 1635, 1638 *et passim* to 1708, *the Neitherfield* 1671 (1768), 1675 (1768), 1721, *the nether feilde* 1697, *the Neither feild* 1724, *the Neather field* 1745, *v.* **neoðera, feld**; one of the early great fields, cf. *Nether Field Close* 1651 (18), 17, *Netherfield Meadow* 1651 (18), *Nether Field Meadow Close* 17); The Paddock 1847 (*v.* **paddock**); Pinfold

1847 (*v.* **pynd-fald**); Plowed Cl 1797, Plow'd ~ 1847; Pochins First Cl, ~ Second ~ 1847 (with the surn. *Pochin*); (The) Poor Mdw 1797, 1847 (*v.* **pouer(e)**; land endowed to provide funds for assistance to the poor of the parish); Rookery 1797, The Rookery Fm 1847 (*v.* **rookery**); Scotts Cl 1847, Scott's ~ 1869 (with the surn. *Scott*); Spinney Mdw 1847 (*v.* **spinney**); Stocking(s) 1781, 1847 (*Stockings* 1625 (1730), 1635 *et passim* to 1745, *Stockins* 1697, cf. *Stockings Close* 1635, 1708, 1708 (18), *the Upper Stockings* 1635, 1638 *et passim* to 1745, *the upper stockins* 1721, *v.* **stocking**); Stonefield Cl 1770, 1822 (1878) (*Stonefeild Close* 1658, 1664, 1682, *Stone Field* ~ 17, cf. *Stone Close* 1635, 1638), Stonefield Mdw 1770, 1822 (1878) (*Stonefeild me(a)dow* 1658, 1664, 1682, cf. *Stone Field Meadow Close* 17) (*v.* **stān**); Swansons Cl 1797, 1847 (with the surn. *Swanson*); Sweet Hedge 1781 (1635, 1638, 1708, 1721, 1724, *Sweet Hedges* 1745, *v.* **swēte**; with **edisc** or **etisc**); Tippet's Wood 1781, Tippetts ~ 1797, 1847 (*Tippets Wood* 1635, 1638 *et passim* to 1745, *tippits* ~ 1697, cf. *Tippet(t)s Wood Close* 1675 (1768), 1675 (18); with the surn. *Tippett*, *v.* Reaney *s.n.*); Tomkins Mdw 1847 (with the surn. *Tomkin(s)*); Top Cl 1847; Tubford(s) Cl otherwise Knights Cl 1770, 1822 (1878) (*Tubfords Close* 1635, 1638, 1664, *Tubford* ~ 1658, 1664, 1682, cf. *Tubsford grounds* 1598 (*v.* **grund**); *Tubford* is poss. a surn. here, as from a p.n. such as *tubba ford* 965 (c.1200) BCS 1169 (S 734), Brk **2** 426; otherwise itself a p.n. 'Tubba's ford', with the OE pers.n. *Tubba* (a poss. short form of *Tūnbeorht*), *v.* **ford**); Wades Cl 1797, 1847 (with the surn. *Wade*); the Water Mill 1797 (*v.* **water-mylne**); West Fd 1797 (*Westfield* 1635, 1638, 1651 (18), *the Westfeild* 1671 (1768), *v.* **feld**); Wood Cl 1847 (1693 (1768)), the Wood Corner 1781 (1721, 1724, 1745, *v.* **corner**; a close so called), Wood Nooks 1797 (*v.* **nōk**) (*v.* Allexton Wood *supra*).

(b) *Banky(e) Close* 1635, 1651 (18), 1671 (1768), *Bankie* ~ 1638, *Bancky* ~ 1675 (1768), *Bankey* ~ 1675 (18), 1693 (1781) (*v.* **banke**, **-ig**[3]); *Bell peice (a peice of ground belonging to the bells)* 1708, *Bell piece* 1708 (18) (*v.* **belle**, **pece**; land endowed for the maintenance of the bells of the parish church); *Belton peice* 1708, ~ *piece* 1708 (18) (*v.* **pece**; Belton in Rutland adjoins to the north); *Brounes close* 1598 (*v.* **clos(e)**; with the surn. *Broune/Brown*); *Church Meadow* 1635, 1638, 1671 (1768) (*v.* St Peter's Church *supra*); *Crabs Close* 1635, *Crabbs* ~ 1638 (either with the surn. *Crabb* or with ME **crabbe** 'the wild apple', cf. Crabtree Cl in f.ns. (a)); *Cranwells Two Closes* 1675 (18), *Cramwells* ~ ~ 1675 (1768), 1693 (1768) (with the surn. *Cranwell*, poss. of a family originally from Cranwell, 35 miles to the north-east in Lincs.); *Glovers Close* 1635, 1638 *et passim* to 1675 (18), 1693 (1768) (with the surn. *Glover*); (*the*) *Hay Close* 1625 (1730), 1635, 1638 *et passim* to 1708 (18), *Hey* ~ 1651 (18) (*v.* **hēg**); (*the*) *Headless Cross* 1635, 1708, 1708 (18) (*v.* **hēafodlēas**, **cros**); *the Highway* 1708, 1708 (18) (*v.* **hēah-weg**); (*the*) *Horse Close* 1651 (18), 1657 (18), 1671 (1768) (*v.* **hors**); *the Kilne close* 1598 (*v.* **cyln**, **clos(e)**); *the Little close* 1598, 1749 (*v.* **lȳtel**, **clos(e)**); *May Bankes Close* 1749 (*v.* **banke**; *May* presum. refers to the blossoms of the hawthorn or to the hawthorn itself rather than being a careless spelling of *many*, but note *Banky(e) Close*, *supra*); *the New piece* 1675 (1768), 1675 (18), 1698 (1768) (*v.* **pece**); *Nortons leas* 1598 (*v.* **leys**; with the surn. *Norton*); *the Orchard* 1749; (*the*) *Overfield* 1625 (1730), 1635, 1638 *et passim* to 1745 (*v.* **uferra**, **feld**; one of the early great fields); *Putts Close* 1635, 1638 *et passim* to 1675 (18), 1693 (1768) (with the surn. *Putt* (from OE *pytt* 'a pit, a hollow'), *v.* Reaney *s.n.*); *Roberts his Close* 1625 (1730); *the towne side* 1625 (1730) (*v.* **tūn**, **sīde**); *Upperfield formerly part of Overfield* 1651 (18), 1657 (18), *Upper Field Close*

17; *atte Welle* 1327 SR (p) (*v.* **atte, wella**); *West Hedge* 1708 (18) (with **hecg** or **edisc**, *v.* Sweet Hedge *supra*).

Asfordby

1. ASFORDBY

Esseberie 1086 DB
Osferdebie 1086 DB
Osfordebi 1102 × 06 Reg bis, *Osfordeby* c.1291 Tax
Asfordebi 1184, 1185 P (p) *et passim* to 1195 ib (p), 13 (1404) *Laz*, *Asfordebia* c.1130 LeicSurv, *Asfordeby* 1225 Cur, 1232 RHug *et freq* to 1409 Pat, 1428 FA *et passim* to 1547 Pat, 1552 *MiD*, *Asfortheby* 1295 ChPr (p)
Asseford(e)by 1316 FA, 1367 Pat, *Assford(e)by* 1375 (p), 1377 *LCDeeds* (p), 1505 *Peake*
Aisfordeby 1156 (1318) Ch, Hy 2 Dugd, *Eisfordby* 1218 RegAnt
Esfordebi 1190 × 1204 BM, e.13 (1404) *Laz* (p), l.13 *CRCart*, *Esfordeby* 1205 Dugd, 1218 RegAnt *et passim* to 1253 × 58 RHug, 1263 GildR (p)
Essefordebi 1204 RegAnt, 1204 ChR, *Esseford(e)by* 1204, 1218 RegAnt *et passim* to 1254 Val, 1329 Ch, *Essfordeby* 1205 ChR, 1217 BodCh, *Esfordby* 1218 RegAnt, 1234 RHug
Assh(e)ford(e)by 1291 OSut, 1294 Ass (p), *Ashford(e)by*, 1294 OSut, 1335 LAS *et passim* to 1412 Nichols, 1537 MinAccts
Eschefordeby m.13 (1404), *Aschefordeby* 1349 *Queen's*, *Aschfordby* 1505 *RTemple* (p)
Asfordby 1232 RHug, 1288 OSut (p) *et passim* to 1499 Banco, 1505 *Peake et freq*, *Asforby(e)* 1528 LWills,1552 Pat, 1625 LML, *Asforbie* 1581 LEpis
Assorby(e) 1529 AAS, 1537 *RTemple*, *Asorby(e)* 1576 Saxton, 1610 Speed *Hasford(e)by* 1528 *LWills*, *Hasforby* 1528 ib, *Hassorby* 1529 AAS

This is a difficult name because of the disparities evidenced in the 11th and 12th cent. forms. The two DB spellings attributed by historians to Asfordby, i.e. *Esseberie* and *Osferdebie*, are greatly at variance. *Esseberie* has as its first el. OE **æsc** 'ash-tree', perhaps influenced by the cognate ON **eski** with the same meaning. An OE collective **esce** 'a group of ash-trees' may also have existed. The form of the generic of this unique spelling is one in a number of East Goscote Hundred p.ns. whose final el. is actually Scand *-bȳ* 'farmstead, village', but whose Norman scribe mismanaged as *-berie*: these are Asfordby, Barkby, Gaddesby, Ingarsby, Quenby and Shoby. It has been suggested that such *-berie* generics may in some instances represent earlier OE *-byrig* (the dat.sg. of *burh* 'a fortified site') later replaced by *-bȳ*. However, all Leics. p.ns. with *burh* whose etymologies are unequivocal have their generics in the nom.sg. *burh*. For this county, *-byrig* > *-berie* may be safely dismissed. If the form *Esseberie* does not represent Ashby Folville, four miles to the south, then the spelling may be explained by the scribe's attributing to it the four syllables of *Osferdebie*/*Asfordebi*. Even so, and perhaps significantly, he fixed on the ash-tree as shaping the name of the site.

The forms *Osferdebie*, *Osfordebi* and *Asfordebi*, on the other hand, appear to contain as first el. the ON pers.n. *Ásfrøðr* (reflex *Asford*, *v.* Feilitzen 165), but perhaps showing early confusion with ODan *Āsfrith* and maybe OE *Ōsferð*, *Ōsfrið*. However, the weight of the forms following these earliest instances suggests that we may have, rather, an early OE p.n. **Æscford* 'ford at the ash-trees' to which Scand *-bȳ* was later appended. This concurs with the DB form *Esseberie* as a name relating to the local tree-cover. Four miles to the south lies Ashby Folville, another major p.n. indicating the regional presence of ash-trees. Also, Asfordby is on the river Wreake at an important crossing point, used in the medieval period by salt-merchants and no doubt on a time-honoured route. Six miles to the east, also on the river, is Wyfordby (*v.* Lei **2** 142), an OE ford-name **Wīgford* to which Scand *-bȳ* was later appended, while to the west, Blackfordby in West Goscote Hundred offers a parallel construction with *-bȳ* added to an OE ford-name **Blæcford*. Across R. Wreake from Asfordby in Kirby Bellars was *Asfordewong'*/*Assefordewong'* (surviving forms from 1347 onwards). This may be interpreted as either 'the field at Ashford' or 'Asford's field' (*v.* **vangr**), although one may question whether the river as a natural estate boundary negates the notion of a postulated *Ásfrøðr* owning and farming land to its south in another estate unit.

The unresolved problems of the p.n. Asfordby are: (i) whether it is to be interpreted as 'the farmstead, village at Ashford' (*v.* **æsc**, **eski, ford**, **bȳ**) or 'Asford's farmstead, village' (*v.* **bȳ** and cf. Asserby, DLPN 5); (ii) whether the later forms which describe a settlement at an 'ash-ford' are rationalizations of a misunderstood and forgotten Scand pers.n.; (iii) whether the lost *Asfordewong'*/*Assefordewong'* south of R. Wreake in Kirby Bellars contains acceptable evidence for the original name of the ford.

ALL SAINTS' CHURCH, *the Church* 1708 (18) *Terrier*, *Church (All Saints)* 1846, 1863 White, 1925 Kelly; it is earlier recorded as *ecclesie de Esseforde by* 1220 MHW, ~ *de Asfordby* 1409 *Pat*. Note also (*the*) *Church Yard* 1708 (18), 1824 *Terrier*. ALMA LODGE (lost), *Alma Lodge* 1863 White, *v.* **loge**; named from the battle of the Alma (1854) in the Crimean War. ASFORDBY HALL (2½") (lost), *Asfordby Hall* 1863, 1877 White, 1925 Kelly, *the Hall* 1846 White, *v.* **hall**; built in 1840, the hall was demolished in 1965. ASFORDBY HILL, 1925 Kelly. ASFORDBY HO. (lost), *Asfordby house* 1877 White. ASFORDBY OLD HALL is *Asfordby Hall* 1831 Curtis, *v.* **hall**. BLUE BELL INN, *Blue Bell* 1846, 1863, 1877 White, *The Bell* 1925 Kelly. BRADGATE LANE, *v.* **brād**, **gata**. BROOK LANE, cf. *Broke* 1349 *Queen's*, *the brooke* 1601 *Terrier*, *v.* **brōc**. CROWN (P.H.) (lost), *Crown* 1846, 1863, 1877 White, 1925 Kelly. GLEBE RD, *v.* **glebe**. THE GROVE, 1925 Kelly. THE HOME FM (1"), *v.* **home**. THE HORSE SHOES (P.H.), *Horse Shoes* 1863, 1877 White, 1925 Kelly. LADY LODGE (lost), *Lady Lodge* 1877 White, *v.* **loge**. LORD WILTON'S GORSE, *v.* **gorst**; a fox-covert of gorse-bushes. Egerton Lodge in neighbouring Melton Mowbray was the hunting-lodge of the Earl of Wilton. MANOR FM. MELTON RD is *Melton Gate* 1605, 1674, 1679, 1690, 1697, 1777 *Terrier*, *v.* **gata**; the road to Melton Mowbray which lies 2½ miles to the east. MILL HO., MILL LANE, cf. *le Milnecroft* 1634 Ipm (*v.* **croft**), *the Mill Holm* 1708 (18), c.1777 *Terrier*, *the Mill Holme and Mill* 1824 *ib*, *v.* **myln**, **holmr**. NEWFOUNDLAND LODGE (lost), *Newfoundland Lodge* 1877 White, *v.* **loge**; poss commemorating the establishment of self-government for the province in 1855, otherwise a name indicating remoteness from the township. PASTURE FM (PASTURE HO. 2½"), *Pasture house* 1877 White, cf. *the Pasture* 1824 *Terrier*, *v.* **pasture**. PUMP LANE, *v.* **pumpe**. THE RECTORY, 1877 White, 1925 Kelly, *v.* **rectory**; earlier is *the Parsonadge* 1601 *Terrier*, *the Pars(s)onage house* 1605, 1674, 1824 *ib*, *v.* **personage**. SANDLEN'S LODGE, *Sandlands* 1674 *Terrier*, 1835 O, *v.* **sand**, **land**, **loge**. SAXELBYE ROAD FM. THE SHIELING. THE VALLEY, 1925 Kelly, *v.* **valeie**.

Note also: BROOK CRESC, COMPTON RD, DALGLIESH WAY, JUBILEE AVE, KLONDYKE WAY (this street-name may preserve an earlier name alluding to the discovery of gold in the Klondyke in Canada in 1896), LOUGHBOROUGH RD, MAIN ST, NEW ST, REGENCY RD, SAXELBY RD, STANTON RD, WOODHOUSE RD.

FIELD-NAMES

Forms throughout are *Terrier*, except those few otherwise specified.

(a) Alestow 1777 (1708, *alistoe al's welbie horne* 1601, 1602, *Allesto(w)* 1674, 1679, *Alestowe* 1690, *Alesto* 1697, *Alestou* 1708 (18), *v.* **stōw**; the first el. is an OE pers.n. such as *Ælle* (as in Allesley, Wa 152) or a reduced *Aðelheard* (as in Allestree, Db 423) or similarly *Ælfnōð* (as in Alstoe, Ru 4); *v.* Stow(e) Cl *infra* and *welbie horne* in f.ns. (b)); Barn Cl 1824; the Bastards 1777 (1690, 1708, 1708 (18), *v.* **bastard**; used of fields of abnormal shape or poor yield); Bawlands 1777 (1690, 1700, e.18, *longe* ~, *shorte bawlandes* 1601, 1602, *long* ~, *short baulands* 1674, *long* ~, *short Bawlands* 1679, 1697, 1700, *long* ~, *Bawlands* 1708, 1708 (18), *bawlands hades* 1605 (*v.* **hēafod**), *bawlandes stye* 1602, 1605 (*v.* **stīg**), *v.* **bord-land**; cf. Bawdland Hole in Barsby f.ns. (a)); (the) Bishop Mdw 1777, 1824, Bishops ~ 1852 *TA* (*the Bishops meadow* 1634 Ipm, *Bishop-Meadow* 1708 (18); poss. with reference to the Bishop of Lincoln who, according to 1349 *Queen's*, held land in Asfordby; but note *Gilbert Bishops lands* 1605 in f.ns (b) *infra*); Blackmole 1777 (*blakemould(e)* 1601, 1602, 1605, 1674, *Blackmold* 1679, 1700, 1708 (18), *Bla(c)kemold* 1690, 1697, e.18, *Black Mould* 1708, 1708 (18), *v.* **blæc, molde**); (the) Bridge Cl 1824; Brockholes 1777 (1601, 1602, 1674 *et passim* to 1708 (18), *brockeholes* 1605, *Brockhole(s) hades* 1605, 1708, 1708 (18) (*v.* **hēafod**), *Brockhole hades end* 1690 (*v.* **ende**), *Cross Brockholes* 1690, 1700, e.18, 1708, 1708 (18) (*v.* **cross**), *v.* **brocc-hol**); the Car 1777 (1690, 1708, *the Carre* 1601, 1602, 1605, *the Carr* 1679, 1700, *v.* **kjarr**); Church Cl 1824 (*v.* All Saints' Church *supra*); Constable Hades 1777 (e.18, 1708 (18), *the cunstables hades* 1605, *Constables hades* 1697, 1700, *v.* **conestable, hēafod**); Croaks 1777, 1824 (1708 (18), *the Hither and Far Crokes* 1634 Ipm), Croak Hades 1777 (1674, 1700, 1708 (18), *crokes hades* 1601, 1602, *Croaks hads* 1679, *Croake hades* 1690, *Croke* ~ 1697, *Crook* ~ 1708, *v.* **hēafod**) (*v.* **krókr**); Debdale 1777 (1708, 1708 (18), *v.* **dēop, dalr**); Dimsdale 1777 (1697, 1708, 1708 (18), e.18, *Diminggedale* l.12 *GarCart* bis, *dimingsdale* 1601, 1602, 1605, *Diminsdale* 1674, 1679, *diminsdaile, diminsdayle* 1690, *Dymsdale* 1700, *long(e)* ~, *short*(e) *dimingsdale* 1601, 1602, 1605, *long* ~, *short(t) diminsdale* 1674, 1679, cf. *Dumenyngedalewange* 1297 Banco (*v.* **vangr**), 'the valley which darkens quickly', *v.* **dimming, dalr** and Dimsdale in Frisby on the Wreake f.ns. (a)); Dunspool 1777 (e.18, *Dunspoole* 1601, 1602, 1605, 1697, 1708 (18), *dunspole* 1605, *dunchpoole* 1674 bis, 1679 bis, *Duns pooll* 1700, 'muck pool, dung pool', *v.* **dyncge, pōl**[1]); East Fd 1777 (1697, 1700, 1708, 1708 (18), e.18, *East Fielde* 1601, 1602, (*The*) *East Feild* 1674, 1679 1690, *v.* **ēast, feld**; one of the early great fields of the township); Eastings 1777 (1605, 1674 *et passim* to 1708 (18), *Yestyng* 1580 Nichols (with prosthetic *y*), *eastinges* 1601, 1602, *Estings* 1700), Far ~ ~, 1st Easting Mdw 1824 (*Eastings meadow(e)* 1601, 1602, 1605, 1690, 1708, 1708 (18), *easting(e) meadow* 1605, 1697, 1708 (18), *eastin* ~ 1674, *esting middow* 1679), Easting Meadow Leas 1824 (cf. *Eastinge leas* 1601, *Easting*(s) *leas* 1605, *Easting Leay(e)s* 1674, 1679, *Esting Lees* 1700, *v.* **leys**) (*v.* **ēast, eng**); Fourheadlands 1777 (1700, 1708 (18), e.18, *four(e)hadland(e)s* 1601, 1602, 1605, *forehedlandes* 1674, *forehadlands* 1679, *four*(*e*) *he(a)dlands* 1674, 1697, *v.* **fēower, hēafod-land**); Five Acres 1777 (1697, 1708, 1708 (18), *fiue acres* 1601, 1602, 1605, 1690, ~ *a(c)kers* 1674, 1679, *Five*

Acres Headland 1697, 1700 (*v.* **hēafod-land**), *v.* **fīf, æcer**); ye Gravell 1777, Gravel Hill Cl 1824 (*v.* **gravel**); Great Pasture 1824 (*v.* **pasture**); Gregory's Fm 1824 (*Gregory's Farme* 1708 (18) (*v.* **ferme**), cf. (*William*) *Gregories hadland* 1601, 1602, 1605, 1679, *gregorie*(*s*) *he*(*a*)*dland* 1674 (*v.* **hēafod-land**), *Gregory's headley* 1708 (18) (*v.* **headley**), *Gregory's Land* 1708 (18) (*v.* **land**), *John Gregorie lea* 1674 (*v.* **ley**)); *ye Ham in Holme* 1777 (*v.* **hamm** and Holm(e) *infra*); Hart-Livers 1777 (*hart*(*e*)*cliffs* 1601, 1602, *hartlifts* 1674, *Hartclifts* 1679, 1697, 1700, *Hartliues* 1690, *Hartlives* 1708, 1708 (18), *Hart Cliffs* 1708 (18) (*v.* **clif**; prob. with **heard, harðr** rather than with **heort**); Hobeck ford 1777 (1697, 1700, 1708 (18), *v.* **ford**), Hobeck hill 1777 (1601, 1602, 1674, *hoback* ~ 1679) (*Hobeck* 1601, 1602, 1700, 1708 (18), e.18, ~ *hades* 1601, 1602, 1697, 1700, 1708 (18), *hoback hades* 1674, 1679 (*v.* **hēafod**), *Hobeck yate* 1674 (*v.* **gata**), *v.* **hol**[2], **bekkr**); Holm(e) 1777 (*le Holme* 1580 Nichols, *home* 1605, *the Holme* 1690, *Holm* 1697, 1700, 1708, 1708 (18), *ye Holm against ye Car* 1708 (*v.* the Car *supra*)), Holm Gate 1777 (e.18, *hoome*(*s*) *yate* 1601, 1602, *ho*(*o*)*mes gate* 1601, 1602, 1679, *home yate* 1605, 1679, *holme yate* 1674, ~ *gate* 1674, *holms gate* 1697, 1700, *Holm's* ~ 1708 (18), *v.* **gata**), Holm leas 1777 (1697, 1700, *holm lees* e.18, ~ *Leys* 1708 (18), *v.* **leys**) (*Holm Close* e.18, *holmes dike* 1412 (c.1430) *KB* (*v.* **dík**), *ho*(*o*)*me headge* 1601, 1605, *holme hedg* 1674, *home hedge* 1679 (*v.* **hecg**), *Hoome Innam al's Shobye Innam* 1601, *Home Innam* (*al's Shobie Innam*) 1605, 1679 (*v.* **innām** and *Shobye Innam, infra*), *Hoome meadowe* 1601, *Holm Meadow* 1674, ~ *Middow* 1679 (*v.* **mǣd** (**mǣdwe** obl.sg.)) (*v.* **holmr**); Hoods leas 1777 (*v.* **leys**; with the surn. *Hood*); Horndale 1777, Bottom ~, Middle ~, Top Horndale 1824 (*Hornedale* 1601, 1602, 1700, *Horndale* 1674, 1679 *et passim* to 1708 (18), *Horndaile, Horndayle* 1690, *v.* **horn, dalr**); Horse Cl 1824; Incroft Gate 1777 (*v.* **gata**) (*Incrofte* 1580 Nichols, 1605, *Incroft* 1690, 1697, 1700, 1708, 1708 (18), e.18), Incroft Mdw 1824 (1674, *Incroft meadowe* 1601, 1602, ~ *Middow* 1679, *v.* **mǣd** (**mǣdwe** obl.sg.)) (*v.* **in, croft**); Little Beck 1777 (1679, 1697, 1708 (18), e.18, *littleback* 1674, 1679, *little becke* 1690, *Litlebeck* 1708, *v.* **bekkr**); Little Mdw 1824; Longlands 1777 (1605, 1674 *et passim* to 1708 (18), *longelandes* 1601, 1602, *long land hades* 1605 (*v.* **hēafod**), *v.* **lang**[1], **land**); Long Marrows 1777 (1601, 1602 *et passim* to 1708 (18); earlier forms are needed, but poss. is **mareis** 'a marsh', otherwise (**ge**)**mǣre** 'a boundary'; *mares beck*(*e*) 1601, 1602, 1605, 1674, ~ *back* 1679, 1708, *marsebacke* 1690 may belong here and if so, either 'marsh stream' or 'boundary stream', *v.* **bekkr**); Lorput Gate 1777 (*larpit gate* 1601, 1602, 1605, *lorpit*(*t*) ~ 1674, 1679, *Lorpodgate* 1697, 1700, ~ *end* 1708 (18) (*v.* **ende**), *larpit gate hole* 1601, 1602, 1605, *lorpitt gate* ~ 1674, 1679, *Lorpodgate* ~ 1697, 1708 (18) (*v.* **hol**[1]), *Larpit Innam* 1601, 1602, 1605, *Lorpitt Inam* 1679 (*v.* **innām**), *v.* **lort(e), pytt, gata**); Marshside 1777 (1679, 1697 *et passim* to 1708 (18), *March side* 1690 (*v.* **sīde**), *le Merssh* 1384 (c. 1430) *KB*, (*the*) *marsh* 1605, e.18, *Marshe* 1605, *March* 1674, 1690, 1700, 1708, 1708 (18), *Marsh heage* 1601, 1602, 1605 (*v.* **hecg**), *Marsh meadow*(*e*) 1601, 1674, ~ *Middow* 1679 (*v.* **mǣd** (**mǣdwe** obl.sg.)), *March Nook* 1697, 1700, 1708 (18), *Marsh* ~ e.18 (*v.* **nōk**), *v.* **mersc**); Middle Fd 1777 (1697, 1700, 1708 (18), e.18, *Midle fielde* 1601, (*the*) *Middle Feild*(*e*) 1605, 1679, 1690, *the Middell feild* 1674, *v.* **middel, feld**; one of the early great fields); Middle Hill Cl 1824; Middle Road Cl 1824; Mildthorne 1777 (*ne*(*i*)*ther* ~, *ouer Milethorne* 1601, 1602, 1605, 1674, 1679 (*v.* **neoðera, uferra**), *Ne*(*a*)*ther* ~ ~, *Upper Mild Thorn*(*e*) 1690, 1697, 1700, 1708 (18), e.18, *v.* **mīl, þorn**; evidently a mile marker from the township); More side 1777 (1690, 1700, 1708, 1708 (18), *Moor*(*e*) *Side* 1697, 1708

(18) (*v.* **sīde**), *the Moor(e)* 1605, 1708 (18), *the moare* 1679, *mores gate* 1601, 1602 *et passim* to 1708 (18), *moores gate* 1605 (*v.* **gata**), *mores head* 1601, 1602, 1674, *the moores head* 1605, *the morehead* 1679, *the Moore head* 1697, 1708 (18), *More Head* 1700, e.18 (*v.* **hēafod**), (*the*) *more heage* 1601, 1602, 1605, *the moore heage* 1605, *the more hedge* 1674, *the mores headg* 1679 (*v.* **hecg**), *smale more(s) al's brawater* 1601, 1602, *small moore* 1605, *smallmore al's breuwaters* 1674, *Small moare al's Breuwaters* 1679 (*v.* **smæl** and *brawater* in f.ns. (b)), *v.* **mōr**[1]); New Cl 1777 ((*the*) *New Close* 1708, 1708 (18), e.18, *the new closse* 1690, *New Closs* 1700, *v.* **clos(e)**); Old Mdw 1824 ((*the*) *olde meadow(e)* 1601, 1602, 1605, *ye oulde meddow* 1674, (*the*) *ould middow* 1679, *the Old Meadow* 1690, 1697, 1700, e.18, *Old Meadow Side* 1708, 1708 (18) (*v.* **sīde**), *v.* **ald, mǣd (mǣdwe** obl.sg.)); Old ~ ~, New Pasture Mdw 1824; Plough Cl 1824 (*v.* **plōg**); Red Banks 1824 (1700, 1708, 1708 (18), e.18, *Redbankes* 1697, *v.* **banke**; with **hrēod** or **rēad**); Robinrig 1777 (1605, 1679, 1697, *Robynrig* 1601, 1602, *robbinrig* 1674, *Robinrigg* 1700, 1708 (18), e.18, *Robyn rig hades* 1605 (*v.* **hēafod**), *v.* **hryggr**; a diminutive of *Rob* (Robert), *Robin* is also found as a surn. in ME and may be so used here); Saddleback 1777 (1690, 1697, 1700, e.18, *Sadleback* 1708, 1708 (18), *Saddle Back Baulk* 1708 (18) (*v.* **balca**), *v.* **sadol, bæc**; describing a ridge resembling a saddle in shape); Sholby Hedge 1777 (1690, 1697, 1708, 1708 (18), *shobie headge* 1601, 1602, 1605, *Shobye headge* 1605, *shobe hedg* 1674, *Shob(e)y hedge* 1679, e.18, *Sholdby* ~ 1700 (*v.* **hecg**; a boundary hedge), cf. *Sewolbygate* 1387 (c.1430) *KB*, *shobie gate* 1601, 1602, 1605, *shobe(y)* ~ 1674, 1679, *Sholby(e)* ~ 1679, 1690, 1708, 1708 (18), *Sholdby* ~ 1697, 1700, *Shoby* ~ e.18 (*v.* **gata**), *Shobye Innam* 1601, *Shobie* ~ 1605 (*v.* **innām**), *under Sholby* 1708, 1708 (18); Shoby adjoins to the north-west); Spellows Mdw 1824, Long Spellows Cl 1824 (*long speller(e)s* 1601, 1602, *long spellors* 1674, 1679, *Long Spellow* 1697, 1700, 1708 (18), e.18, *v.* **spell, hlāw**; a moot-site to the east of the township); Stonyfurlong 1777 (1674, 1679 *et passim* to 1708 (18), *stooney furlong* 1601, 1602, *stonie* ~ 1605, *Stoney* ~ 1690, *v.* **stānig, furlang**); Stow(e) Cl 1777, 1824 (1708 (18), e.18, *a little close or tofte called the stoo* 1601 (*v.* **toft**), (*the*) *sto(o) close* 1601, 1602, 1605, 1674, 1679, (*the*) *stoe close* 1605, 1679, *Stow Closs* 1697, 1700 (*v.* **clos(e)**), (*the*) *stoo(e)* 1601, 1602, 1605, *Stow* 1708 (18), cf. *stooe dale* 1601, 1602, *stoodale* 1605, *Stodale* 1674, 1679, 1708, *Stowdayle* 1690, *Stowdale* 1697, 1708 (18), e.18 (*v.* **dalr**), *Stow hill* 1700, *Stoo Innam* 1601, *Sto Inam* 1679 (*v.* **innām**), (*the*) *sto(o) way* 1601, 1602, 1674, 1679 (*v.* **weg**), *sto hie way* 1679 (*v.* **hēah-weg**), *the stoo yate* 1601, 1602, *stogate* 1674, *stoeyate* 1679, *Stow gate* 1700, 1708 (18), e.18 (*v.* **gata**), *v.* **stōw**; it is uncertain whether *the stoo* is to be identified with Alestow *supra*); Sysonby Gate Cl 1824 (*Sysonby Gate* 1708 (18) (*v.* **gata**), cf. *Sisonbie headge* 1601, *Sisonbye hedg* 1674, 1679, *Sisonby hedg(e)* 1679, *v.* **hecg**; a boundary hedge, Sysonby adjoining to the north-east); Townend 1777, Townsend Cl 1824, ~ ~ Mdw 1824 (*the townes end* 1601, 1602, (*the*) *Townsend* 1674, 1679, 1708 (18), e.18, *Townes end* 1697, 1700, *v.* **tūn**, **ende**); Wakoe 1777 (1679, 1697, 1700, e.18, *Wakooe* 1601, 1602, *Wako* 1605, *wackoe* 1674, *Wacku* 1690, *Wacklow* 1708, *Wakoe half acre* 1708 (18) (*v.* **half-aker**), *v.* **wacu, hōh**; poss. a look-out place); Waltons headland 1777 (*Waltons hadland* 1679, *v.* **hēafod-land**; with the surn. *Walton* of a family prob. originally from Walton on the Wolds, 7 miles to the west); Warblong 1777 (1700, 1708 (18), e.18, *warble wong(e)* 1601, 1602, 1679, *worble wong* 1674, *v.* **vangr**; earlier forms are needed for *warble*, but the unique *Weruel* l.12 *GarCart* may belong, and if so,

v. **hwerfel**, cf. *Werueldike* in Queniborough f.ns. (b)); West Fd 1777 (1679, 1700, 1708, e.18, *Weast(e) fielde* 1601, 1602, *the weaste feilde* 1605, *the West feild(e)* 1674, 1679, 1690, *v.* **west, feld**; one of the early great fields of the township); Wiggo 1777 (1690, 1708, 1708 (18); earlier forms are needed, but prob. as the generic is OE **hōh** 'a spur of land', with the OE pers.n. *Wicga* or less likely, the OE sb. **wigga** 'a beetle' (surviving in *earwig*)).

(b) *Abbottesmede* 1349 *Queen's* (*v.* **abbat, mǣd**; with reference to the Abbot of Garendon Abbey); *at ye Allems* 1708, *at the Alloms* 1708 (18) (*v.* **almr**); *the arbour hades* 1605 (*v.* **erber, hēafod**); *arlestub hades* 1605 (*v.* **alor (alres** gen.sg.), **stubb, hēafod**); *Henry Austins yards end* 1679 (*v.* **geard, ende**; note also *Robert Austen* 1524 SR, *Henry Austin* 1628 ib, *John Austin* 1666 ib); *Gilbert Bishops lands* 1605, ~ ~ *(grasse) hadland* 1605 (*v.* **land, græs, hēafod-land**); *bloepoole* 1601, 1602, *Blowpool(e)* 1674, 1679 *et passim* to e.18 (*v.* **blár, pōl**[1]); *William Blunts hadlands* 1605 (*v.* **hēafod-land**); *Bondehirne* 1389 (c.1430) *KB* (*v.* **hyrne**; either with **bond** 'held by tenure of bond service' or **bóndi** 'a peasant landowner' or its derived ON pers.n. *Bóndi* or their ME surn. reflex *Bonde*); *brawater* 1601, 1602, *Breuwaters* 1674, 1679 (*v.* **breiðr, wæter** and *smale more(s)* in More side *supra*); *Calf holme* 1690, *Calf(e) Home* 1708, 1708 (18) (*v.* **calf, holmr**); *Cheuerall Balk* 1700, *Cheverall Baulk* 1708 (18) (*v.* **balca**; with the surn. *Cheverall*, *v.* Reaney *s.n.*); *(the) Chicken wong(e)* 1601, 1602 *et passim* to 1708, *(the) Chickinwong(e)* 1674, 1679, *Chicken wong end* 1697 (*v.* **ende**) (*v.* **cīcen, vangr**); *le Church Hooke* 1580 Nichols (*v.* **hōc** and All Saints' Church *supra*); *Crosse hades* 1601, 1602, 1679, *crosshads* 1674 (*v.* **cross, hēafod**); *Cust wong(e)* 1601, 1602 *et passim* to 1708 (18), *Cust wong had(e)s* 1674,1679 (*v.* **hēafod**) (*v.* **vangr**; with the surn. *Cust* (from the short form of the fem. pers.n. *Custance*, the anglicized version of OFr *Constance*); *darbie style* 1601, 1602, *darby stile* 1605, 1674, 1679 (prob. with **stīg** 'a narrow road' rather than with **stigel** 'a stile' (since the former often gives spellings in *stile* in later Leics. f.ns.) and with the surn. *Darby* (from the p.n. Derby)); *debdayle* 1690 (*v.* **dēop, dalr**); *Demarke* (sic) 1580 Nichols, *Denmark(e)* 1605, 1679 *et passim* to e.18, *Denmack* 1708 (18), *denmarke ditch(e)* 1601, 1602, 1605 (*v.* **dīc**), *denmark dike* 1679 (*v.* **dík**), *denmarke hedge* 1674 (*v.* **hecg**), *Denmark(e) meadow(e)* 1601, 1602, 1674 (*v.* **mǣd (mǣdwe** obl.sg.)) (poss. an early example of a transferred name signifying a location remote from the township (cf. Denmark Fm, Ca 225)); *dukenpites* 1601, *duckenpittes hades* 1602, *dickenpit(t) had(e)s* 1605, *dickinpitt hades* 1674, 1679 (*v.* **hēafod**) (*v.* **dūce (dūcena** gen.pl.), **pytt**); *edgecroft* 1601, 1602, 1605, 1697, *edgcroft* 1674 (*v.* **ecg, croft**; note *Edgcroft* in Lei **2** 57, the interpretation of which must now be revised); *the Ellmes* 1690 (*v.* **elm** and cf. *at ye Allems*, *supra*); *Five Land Furlong* 1690, 1708, 1708 (18) (*v.* **land, furlang**; a furlong with five units of arable); *Five Leys* 1708 (18), ~ ~ *hedge* 1708 (18) (*v.* **hecg**) (*v.* **leys**; five units of grassland); *(the) hie ~, hye flate al's ouer flate* 1601, 1602, 1605, 1674, *high flate* 1697, *the High Flatt* 1708 (18) (*v.* **hēah**[1]), *(the) ouer flate* 1679, 1700, ~ ~ *hades* 1605, 1679 (*v.* **hēafod**) (*v.* **uferra**), *Neither flate* 1674, 1679 (*v.* **neoðera**) (*v.* **flat**); *(the) flax(e) furlong* 1601, 1602, 1605 *et passim* to 1708 (18) (*v.* **fleax, furlang**); *flaxen furlong(e) al's nether flate* 1601, 1602, 1605, *flaxen furlong al's ye neither flate* 1674 (*v.* **flaxen** and *Neither flate*, *supra*; the adj. *flaxen* was used here to distinguish this flax-growing furlong in Middle Fd from that (above) in East Fd); *Flaxlands* 1690, 1697, 1708, 1708 (18), e.18 (*v.* **fleax, land**); *over the foot pad* 1690, *over the Foot path* 1708 (18) (*v.* **pad**; a furlong so called); *the fordings* 1679 (*v.* **ford, eng**); *Fowlers Farme* 1708

(18) (*v.* **ferme**; with the surn. *Fowler*); *Anthonye Frankes land* 1605 (*v.* **land**); *Fulfords ~*, *Fulforths hadland* 1679 (*v.* **hēafod-land**; *Tho. Fulforth* is cited 1679); *the long ~*, *the short furlong* 1601, 1605, 1674, 1679 (*v.* **furlang**; in West Fd); *the Furne Hades* 1708, 1708 (18) (*v.* **fearn**, **hēafod**); *the further furthinge* 1601, 1602 (*v.* **furðra**, **fēorðung**); *Gambles land* 1708 (18), *George Gambles hadland* 1605 (*v.* **hēafod-land**), *William Gambles land* 1605 (*v.* **land**), *the homestall of William Gamble* 1605 (*v.* **hām-stall**); *Gelstropt(s) h(e)adland* 1674, 1679 (*v.* **hēafod-land**); the surn. *Gelstropt* is presum. from a metathesized *Gerlthorp*, an early form of Garthorpe in Lincs., *v.* DLPN 49); *the Glebe Meadow* 1708 (18) (*v.* **glebe**); *gossy close* 1697 (*v.* **gorstig**); *the Grass headland* 1708 (18) (*v.* **græs**, **hēafod-land**); *the great balke in diminsdayle* 1690, *the Great Ba(u)lk* (*in Dimsdale*) 1708, 1708(18) (*v.* **balca** and Dimsdale in f.ns. (a)); *ye Great hadland* 1708 (18) (*v.* **hēafod-land**); (*into*) *greene* 1605, (*uppon*) *Greene* 1605 (*v.* **grēne**[2]); *Green(e) willow sick* 1601, 1602 *et passim* to 1700 (*v.* **grēne**[1], **wilig**, **sík**); *grymson meare* 1601, 1602 (*v.* **(ge)mære**; the boundary of Grimston which adjoins to the north-west); *Hampton gate* 1601, 1690, 1700, 1708, 1708 (18) (*v.* **gata**; the road due south to Northampton); *haulfe acre* 1602 (*v.* **half-aker**); *the heage towardes Saxelbie* 1601 (*v.* **hecg**; Saxelby adjoins to the north); *heanes close* 1601, 1602, *heines ~* 1605 (*v.* **clos(e)**; *Richard Heine* is cited 1605); *Richard Hensons lands* 1605 (*v.* **land**); *the hie hades al's bawlands* 1601, 1605, (*the*) *hie hades* 1605, 1679, *High had(d)es* 1697, 1708 (18), e.18 (*v.* **hēah**[1], **hēafod** and Bawlands in f.ns. (a)); *the hie way* 1601, 1602, 1674, 1679, *the Highway* 1708 (18), *the queenes hye way* 1601, 1602 (with reference to Elizabeth I), *the kings high waye* 1605 (with reference to James I), *the hie way side* 1601, 1602 (*v.* **sīde**) (*v.* **hēah-weg**); *Mr Hills great piece* 1700, 1708 (18) (*v.* **pece**); *Hinckl(e)y dale* 1601, 1602 *et passim* to 1700, *~ dayle* 1690, *hincklye dale* 1605, *Hinkle ~* 1697, 1708, 1708 (18), *Hinkly ~* 1708 (18), *Hincklydale Hill* 1700 (with the surn. *Hinckley* of a family originally from the township of this name 24 miles to the south-west; with **dalr** or **deill**); *the homestall* 1605 (*v.* **hām-stall**; belonging to *the Parsonage house*, *v.* The Rectory); *John Humberstons land* 1605, *~ ~ hadland* 1605 (*v.* **land**, **hēafod-land**; the *Humberston* family presum. was originally from Humberstone, 9 miles to the south-west); *Innoms* 1690, *Innome* 1697 (*v.* **innām**); (*William*) *Kellams H(e)adland* 1690, 1708, 1708 (18) (*v.* **hēafod-land**; with the surn. *Kellam* of a family originally from Kelham, 24 miles to the north in Notts., cf. *Will' Kelom* 1327 SR of Leics.); *the kings land* 1605, *~ ~ hadland* 1605 (*v.* **land**, **hēafod-land**; with reference to James I); *Leadenwell* 1601, 1602 *et passim* to 1708 (18), *~ close* 1605, 1674, 1679, 1708 (18), *~ Closs* 1697 (*v.* **wella**; with the OE pers.n. *Lēoda* (*Lēodan* gen.sg.), cf. Leadenham in Lincs., *v.* DLPN 79); *Lees hedge Balk* 1700 (*v.* **hecg**, **balca**; prob. with **leys** rather than with the surn. *Lee* in the possessive case); *lilland(e)s* 1601, 1602, 1605, 1674, 1679 (*v.* **līn**, **land**, with assimilation of *-nl-* to *-ll-*; cf. The Lillands, YW **3** 39); *ye litle Balk in Thurnborow* 1708, *the little Baulk* 1708 (18) (*v.* **balca** and *thurnebarrow hill*, *infra*); *William Loues hadland al's Jack Milners hadland* 1605 (*v.* **hēafod-land**); *manyedikes* 1601, 1602, *manie dikes* 1605, *Manydikes* 1674, 1679 *et passim* to 1708 (18) (*v.* **manig**, **dík**); *the meere* 1605, *the mear(e)* 1605, 1674, 1697 (*v.* **(ge)mære**); *Melton gap(p)* 1601, 1602, 1674, 1679 (*v.* **gap**; presum. referring to the gap in the parish boundary hedge through which the road to Melton Mowbray ran); *Melton gate al's sto gate* 1674, *~ ~ al's sto(w) way* 1679, 1697, *Melton Gate Side* (*v.* **sīde**), *v.* Melton Rd *supra*, Alestow and Stow(e) Cl in f.ns. (a)); *Jack Millers h(e)adland* 1601, 1602, 1697, 1708 (18), e.18, *Jack Milner(s) ~* 1605, 1674, 1700 (*v.* **hēafod-**

land and *William Loues hadland, supra*); *John Mor(r)ice his hadland* 1601, 1602, 1605, ~ ~ *his land* 1605 (*v.* **hēafod-land, land**), *John Morrice his side grasse* 1605 (*v.* **sīde, græs**), *John Morrice his wiues land* 1601, 1602, 1605, ~ ~ ~ ~ *hadland* 1605 (*v.* **wīf**), *Morris grasse hadland* 1679 (in the possession of *Jo. Morris* 1679), *Morris Closse* 1690, *Morises Close* 1708, *Morris's* ~ 1708 (18)); *Neckacres* 1708, 1708 (18) (*v.* **hnecca, æcer**); *Nuttal(l)s hadland* 1679 (*v.* **hēafod-land**), ~ *land* 1679 (*v.* **land**) (with the surn. *Nuttall* of a family originally from Nuthall, 18 miles to the north-west in Notts.); *oodykes* 1601, 1602, *odikes* 1605, 1679, *oadikes* 1674, *Old dikes* 1690, 1697, 1700 *et passim* to e.18 (*v.* **ald, dīk**); *Osgar Well* 1601, 1602, 1679, 1697, e.18, *Osgarrwell* 1674 (*v.* **wella**; with the OE pers.n. *Ōsgār*); *Parsey half Acre* 1674, 1708 (18) (*v.* **half-aker**; the first word is poss. ME **berse** 'a hedge made with stakes', cf. *Parsie cowdale*, Lei **2** 112); *the parsonadge ditch* 1601 (*v.* **dīc**), *the parsonadge dreane or scoure* 1602 (*v.* **drain, scoure**), *the parsonadge yard* 1601, 1602 (*v.* **geard**) (*v.* The Rectory *supra*); *the parsons ston(e)* 1601, 1674, ~ *persons* ~ 1602, *the ston(n)e* 1601, 1602, 1605, 1679 (*v.* **persone, stān**; a boundary marker); *Pye howse* 1528 LWills (*v.* **hūs**; with the surn. *Pye*, *v.* Reaney *s.n.*); *Quagmire* 1708 (18) (*v.* **quagmire**); *the queenes hadland* 1601, 1602 (*v.* **hēafod-land**), *the queenes man(n)or land* 1601, 1602 (*v.* **maner, land**) (with reference to Elizabeth I); *Riggat(e)s* 1679, 1697, 1700, 1708 (18), e.18, *Riggate furlong* 1601, 1602, 1697, *Riggit* ~ 1674, *Riggats* ~ 1679 (*v.* **furlang**), *Riggate leas* 1601, 1602, ~ *Leayes* 1674 (*v.* **leys**) (*v.* **ryge, gata**); *Saint Nicholas Meadow* 1580 Nichols, *Saint Pulchres Meadow* 1580 ib (*v.* **mǣd** (**mǣdwe** obl.sg.); both poss. with reference to chapel endowments in the parish church); *Sandpit leas* 1601, 1602, 1605, *sand(e) pit(t) leas* 1605, *San(d)pitt leayes* 1674, 1679 (*v.* **sand-pytt, leys**); *Sawtrum Stones* 1580 Nichols (*v.* **saltere, hamm, stān**; formally, the first word is identical to the p.n. Saltram (D 255), but a surn. based on this p.n. is unlikely here at this date; a salters' way ran east to west, south of R. Wreake via Burton Lazars and Kirby Bellars, and a branch appears to have crossed the river by the ford at Asfordby on its way north-west via Wymeswold; the nature of the stones is uncertain); *Saxelbie meare* 1601, 1602, *Saxelbye* ~ 1605 (*v.* **(ge)mǣre**), *Saxilby Hill* e.18 (Saxelby adjoins to the north); *Scole furlong(e)* 1601, 1602, 1605, 1674, 1679, *Scholes Furlong* 1697, 1700, 1708 (18) (*v.* **skáli, furlang** and neighbouring Shoby Scholes); *Seghoome* 1601, 1602, *Seghome* 1674, 1679, 1697, *Segholm* 1700, *Segum(m)* 1708 (18) (*v.* **secg**[1], **holmr**); *Segwonge* 1605 (*v.* **secg**[1], **vangr**); *sholbreade* 1605 (*v.* **scofl-brǣdu**); *Sliperhook(e)* 1601, 1674, 1679 (*v.* **slipor, hōc**); *Smiths close* 1674, 1679, *Smiths headland* 1674 (*v.* **hēafod-land**) (with the surn. *Smith*); *Spongs Nook* 1697 (*v.* **spang, spong, nōk**); *Stannion furlong(e)* 1601, 1602, 1605, 1674, *stanion* ~ 1679 (*v.* **furlang**; with the surn. *Stan(n)ion* of a family originally from Stanion, 24 miles to the south-east in Northants.); *Stean hill* 1697, 1700, 1708 (18) (*v.* **steinn**); *the stone bryge* 1528 LWills, (*the*) *stone bridge* 1601, 1602, 1679 (*v.* **stān, brycg**); *Sylverwoods Land* 1708 (18) (the property of *John Silverwood* 1708 (18)); *thislie landes* 1601, *thistlye lands* 1605, *thisleylands* 1674, *thistlelands* 1679 (*v.* **thist(e)ly, land**); *Thorn(e)y Balk(e)* 1690, 1697, 1700, 1708, e.18, *Thorney Baulk* 1708 (18) (*v.* **þornig, balca**); (*the*) *Three Roods* 1690, 1697, 1708, 1708 (18) (*v.* **rōd**[3]); *thurnebarrow hill* 1601, *thornborow hill* 1674, 1679, *Thunborrow* 1690, *Thurnborow* 1697, 1700, 1708, 1708 (18), *Thornborow* e.18, *Thunborrow* ~, *Thurnborow Hades* 1690, 1708, 1708 (18) (*v.* **hēafod**) (*v.* **berg**; the specific varies between **þyrne** and **þorn**); *Twelue foote* (*being a hadland stoned on the east side*) 1602 (*v.* **twelf, fōt**, (**hēafod-land, stoned**)); *the Waterfurrow(e)s* 1690, 1708, 1708 (18) (*v.* **wæter, furh**; prob. 'furrows where water tends to lie'; Field 50 argues that these were deeper furrows so ploughed in order to carry off surface water, but such furrows appear to be called alternatively *Wet furrowes* in Coston (Lei **2** 155–6) and *Watriforowis* in Eaton (Lei **2** 121)); *the water gapp* 1690, *Water Gap* 1708, 1708 (18) (*v.* **wæter, gap**); *Weans Gate* 1708 (18) (*v.* **wægn, gata**); *welbie gate* 1601, ~ *yate* 1602, 1679 (*v.* **gata**), *welbie headge* 1601, *welbey hedg* 1674, *welbye hedge* 1679 (*v.* **hecg**; a boundary hedge), *welbie horne* 1601, 1602 (*v.* **horn** and Alestow in f.ns. (a)) (Welby adjoins to the north-east); (*at*) *wells* 1601, 1602, 1605, 1674, 1679, *Wells Ford* 1700 (*v.* **ford**) (*v.* **wella**); *Woolsdale* 1601, 1602, 1679, ~ *hole* 1674, 1697, 1700, e.18, *Wolsdale hole* 1708 (18) (*v.* **hol**[1]) (the first el. is poss. a pers.n., an anglicized ON *Úlfr*; otherwise **wald**, with **dalr** or **deill**; note that the latter compound recurs in Lei **2** 53, 132 and 165); *wrongeland(e)s* 1601, 1602, 1605, (*the*) *Wranglands* 1674, 1679 *et passim* to 1708 (18) (*v.* **wrang, vrangr, land**).

2. WELBY

Welby is a member of Framland Hundred.

Alebi 1086 DB (x3), 1162 × 70 *Rut* (p), l.12 *GarCart* (freq) *et passim* to c.1220 Berkeley, a.1250 *GarCh* (p), *Alebie* 1086 DB, *Alebia* c.1130 LeicSurv, *Aleby* a.1211 *Rut* (p), e.13 *GarCart et freq* to 1295, 1299 Ipm *et passim* to 1347, 1351 BPR
Halebi l.12 *GarCart*, *Haleby* Hy 3 RBE, c.1310 (1449) *WoCart* (p)
Oleby 1225 Cur, 1243 Fees, m.13 *Deed* (p) *et freq* to 1459, 1467 Banco *et passim* to 1524 Ipm, 1552 AAS, *Olebye* 1537 LeicW, *Olabye* 1576 Saxton, *Olebe alias Welbe* 1573 Fine
Ouleby 1276 RH, *Owelby* 1507 Ipm
Welby 1371 *Rut* (p), 1398 ISLR bis, 1518 Visit, 1610 Speed *et freq*, *Welyby* 1425 Cl, *Welbye* 1535 VE, 1607 LeicW
Wolby alias dicta Welby 1541 Nichols

'Āli's farmstead, village', *v.* **bȳ**, cf. Ailby, DLPN 1. For the ODan pers.n. *Āli*, *v.* SPNLY 9.

ASH PLANTATION. FISHPONDS SPINNEY, cf. *Spinney Close* 1838 *TA*, *v.* **spinney**. GRANGE COTTAGE, *v.* Welby Grange *Infra*. OAK PLANTATION. OLD HALL (2½"), *Old Hall* 1877 White, 1925 Kelly, cf. *atte Halle* 1377 SR (p) (*v.* **atte**), *v.* **hall**. POTTER HILL, ~ ~ FM, *Potters Hill* 1631 Ipm, 1806 Map, *Potter Hill* 1824 O, 1828 *Plan*, 1838 *TA*, 1846 White, *v.* **pottere**; hill-top sites were common for medieval pottery kilns. ST BARTHOLOMEW'S CHURCH. STANTON PLANTATION. STONESBY HOUSE

FM. THORNEY PLANTATION, cf. *Thorney Close* 1838 *TA*, *v.* **þornig**. WELBY GRANGE, *grangie de Alebi* l.12 *GarCart*, *Halebi Grangia* l.12 *ib*, *Grang' de Oleby* 13 *ib*, *v.* **grange**; the grange was an outlier of Garendon Abbey. WELBY HOUSE FM (WELBY HO., 2½"). WELBY LANE. WELBY LODGE, 1836 O, *v.* **loge**. WELBY OSIER BEDS, cf. *Osier Holt* 1838 *TA*, *v.* **oyser**, **holt**. YAXLEY HO.

FIELD-NAMES

Undated forms in (a) are 1838 *TA*. Forms throughout dated l.12 are *GarCart*, 1439 are *Ct* and 1631 are Ipm.

(a) Far ~ ~, First ~ ~, Four Acres, Five ~, Seven ~, Nine ~, Fifteen ~, Eighteen Acres (*v.* **æcer**); First ~ ~, Second ~ ~, Third Ashey Cl (*v.* **æsc**, **-ig**[3]); Bottom ~ ~, Top Austins Cl (with the surn. *Austin*, cf. *Henry Austin* 1679 *Terrier* of Asfordby); Backside (*v.* **bak-side**); Bottom ~ ~, Middle ~ ~, Top ~ ~, Barn Cl (*Barne close* 1631, *v.* **bern**); Bastards (*v.* **bastard**; used of fields of abnormal shape or poor yield); Bottom Cl (*v.* **bottom**); Burdricks Yard (*v.* **geard**; with the surn. *Burdrick*); Calf Cl (*v.* **calf**); Far ~, Near ~, Copy (*v.* **copis**; the spelling *copy* is due to the popular reconstruction of a 'singular' form); Far ~ ~, First Cow Pasture; Dog Kennel Cl (*v.* **kenel**; with reference to kennels for hounds); Doubledays Cl (cf. *Will' Dubilday* 14 AD of Leics.); Low ~ ~, Top ~ ~, Far Cl; Far Mdw; Fish Pond Cl (cf. Fishponds Spinney *supra*); Gorsey Cl (cf. *Gosseclose* 1631, *v.* **gorstig**, **gorst**); Gravel Pit Cl (*v.* **gravel**, **pytt**); Bottom ~ ~, Top Great Cl; Gunder Pits (*Further* ~, *Hither Gunderpittes* 1631, *v.* **gandra**, **pytt**); Far ~ ~, First Halls Cl, Far ~ ~, First Halls Wolds (*v.* **wald**) (with either the surn. *Hall* in the possessive case or **hall**, cf. Old Hall *supra*); Hill Cl; Hogs Fd (cf. *Hogges close* 1631, *v.* **hogg**); Holow Drain Cl (*v.* **holh**, **drain**); Home Cl (freq) (*v.* **home**); Jacksons Yard (*v.* **geard**; with the surn. *Jackson*); Langleys (*v.* **lang**[1], **leys**); Far ~ ~, First Lewyns Cl; (with the surn. *Lewin* (a reflex of the OE pers.n. *Lēofwine*)); Little Mdw; Top ~ ~, Long Cl; Low Long Mdw (*longemad* 1439, *v.* **lang**[1], **mǣd**); Bottom ~ ~, Middle ~ ~, Top Marriotts Cl (with the surn. *Marriott*); Middle Cl; Far ~ ~, Mill Hill (cf. *Mellefeld* 1439, *Milfeild* 1631, *v.* **myln**, **feld**; one of the early great fields of the township); Near Mdw; Nursery (*v.* **nursery**); Pig Yard or Orchard; Pingle (*v.* **pingel**); Far ~, First Plough Cl (*v.* **plōg**); Far ~ ~ ~, Turnpike Potter Hill (*v.* **turnepike** and Potter Hill *supra*); Bottom ~ ~, Top ~ ~, Peas Fd (*v.* **pise**); Princes Cl (with the surn. *Prince*); Rough Cl (*v.* **rūh**[1]); Top Seed, First Seedy Cl (*v.* **sǣd**, **-ig**[3]; in modern f.ns., often used of areas of sown grass); Top Cl; Town Cl (*v.* **tūn**); Tup Cl (*v.* **tup**); Wash Dike Cl (*v.* **wash-dyke**; a close containing a sheep-dip); Far ~, First Wolds (cf. *Nether* ~, *Upper Oldes* 1631, *v.* **wald**).

(b) *Aspedic* l.12 (*v.* **dīc**, **dík**; the first el. is either **æspe** 'an aspen-tree' or else **hæpse** 'a hasp, a hinge' (with metathesis) used topographically of 'something which bends (sharply)'); *Bakers* 1439 (naming a tenement, this is presum. the surn. *Baker* in the possessive case); *Bradeslandes* l.12 (prob. 'broad selions', *v.* **brād**, **land**); *Brocholes* l.12 (*v.* **brocc-hol**); *Clerkyscroft* 1439 (*v.* **croft**; with the surn. *Clerk*);

unum tenementum voc' Cobbys 1439 (with MLat *tenementum* 'a tenement'), *Cobbyscroft* 1439 (*v.* **croft**) (both with the surn. *Cobb(e)*); *Forthermorefeld* 1439 (*v.* **furðra, mōr**[1], **feld**; one of the early great fields); *Gagyscroft* 1439 (*v.* **croft**; with the surn. *Gage*); *Garrets close* 1631 (with the surn. *Garret(t)*); *Grenedale* l.12 (*v.* **grēne**[1], **dalr**); *Grenestrete* 1439 (*v.* **grēne**[1], **strǣt**); *hassokbregge* 1439 (*v.* **hassuc, brycg**; either a bridge growing with coarse grass or located near an area of such growth); *helagre* l.12 (*v.* **æcer**; the first el. is prob. **hyll**, since **hell** 'hell' as a term of contempt for land is unlikely at this date); *Hyndecroft* 1439 (*v.* **croft**; prob. with the surn. *Hind(e)*, as Welby's 15th cent. croft-names are thus compounded); *ladyacre* 1439 (*v.* **lavedi, æcer**; land endowed for the upkeep of a chapel dedicated to Our Lady, the Blessed Virgin Mary); *ladyredyng* 1439 (*v.* **lavedi, ryding**); *laylondes* 1439, *Leyland* 1631 (*v.* **lǣge, land**); *Longcroft* 13 Nichols (*v.* **lang**[1], **croft**); *lytyllachemere* 1439 (*v.* **lȳtel, lache, mere**[1]); *Monkkewode* 1439 (*v.* **munuc, wudu**; Garendon Abbey held land here, *v.* Welby Grange *supra*); *le more* 1439 (*v.* **mōr**[1]); *Myngeys* 1439 (naming a tenement; hence the surn. *Mingey* in the possessive case, *v.* Reaney *s.n.*); *Nelmys* 1439 (an acre of land so called; the surn. *Nelm(e)s* in the possessive case); *New close* 1631; *Newlond* 1439 (*v.* **nīwe, land**); *Osebec* l.12 (*v.* **bekkr**; more forms are needed to be certain of the first el., but poss. are **ōsle** 'an ouzel, a blackbird' (cf. Izle Beck, Lei **2** 91 and *Owsell Welles*, Lei **2** 13) and **oyser** 'an osier', cf. Welby Osier Beds *supra*); *Pakyscroft* 1439 (*v.* **croft**; with the surn. *Pack(e)* in the possessive case, cf. *Rog' Pake* 1195 P of Leics. and the Packe family, lords of the manor of Hoton *infra*); *Peryfeld* 1439 (*v.* **pirige, feld**); *Smalbregge* 1439 (*v.* **smæl, brycg**); *Spenyfeld* 1439 (*v.* **spinney, feld**; one of the early great fields); *Stykeryscroft* 1439 (*v.* **croft**; with the surn. *Sticker* (a derivative of OE *stician* 'to stick, to kill', a nickname for a butcher)); *Thorne close* 1631 (*v.* **þorn**); *Twelfeacres* 1439 (*v.* **twelf, æcer**); *Walbrygge* 1439 (*v.* **brycg**; either the bridge was associated with a ditch or some kind of embankment (*v.* **walu**), or was provided with a parapet on each side (*v.* **wall**)); *Wallyscroft* 1439 (*v.* **croft**; presum. with the surn. *Wall* in the possessive case, in the style of Welby's other 15th cent. croft-names, but the sb. **wall** is also poss., cf. the local *atte Wall'* 1439 (p) bis, *v.* **atte, wall**); *le Walwode* 1439 (*v.* **wudu**; with either **wall** or **walu** in its sense 'ditch' or 'embankment'; in each case, some sort of containing demarcation for the wood is implied); *Wlfewel* l.12 (*v.* **wella**; with the OE pers.n. *Wulf(a)*); *Woodefeld* 1439 (*v.* **wudu, feld**; one of the early great fields of the township).

Barkby

BARKBY

Barchebi 1086 DB
Barcheberie 1086 DB
Barkebia c.1130 LeicSurv, *Barkebi* 1200 FF, 1227 GildR (p), c.1270 AD, 1292 GildR (p), *Barkeby* 1156 (1318) Ch, 1209 × 35 RHug, 1237 Cur *et freq* to 1423, 1427 *Rut et passim* to 1537, 1539 MinAccts
Barkesby 1242 Fees
Barkby 1251, 1252 Cur *et passim* to 1510 CoPleas, 1514 Ipm *et freq*
Berkeby 1442 Fine, 1473 *MiD*, 1553 Pat, *Mikeberkby* 1494 Banco

'Bark's farmstead, village', *v.* **bȳ**. The Scand pers.n. *Bark* is a reflex of either *Bǫrkr* (*Barkar* gen.) or *Barki*. The DB spelling *Barcheberie* is erratic and does not suppose an earlier OE p.n. with a generic in *-byrig* (dat.sg. of *burh* 'a fortified place'), *v.* Asfordby.

Both DB forms have AN orthographic *ch* for the voiceless stop *k* before *e*. The late form *Mikeberkby* is prefixed by Scand **mikill** 'great' to distinguish the village from its neighbouring daughter settlement Barkby Thorpe.

BARKBY BROOK, *le Brok'* 1467 × 84 *LTD*, *v.* **brōc**. BARKBY GRANGE, 1877 White, *v.* **grange**. BARKBY HOLT, ~ ~ FM, BARKBY HOLT LANE, *Barkby Holt* 1806 Map, 1870 *Sale*, *v.* **holt**. BARKBY LODGE, 1925 Kelly, *v.* **loge**. BARKBY THORPE LANE is *Saltergate* 1467 × 84 *LTD* bis, 1477 (e.16) *Charyte*, 1609 *Merton*, *Saltregate* 1477 (e.16) *Charyte*, *Saltersway* 1635 *Merton* (*v.* **weg**), *v.* **saltere**, **gata**. BEEBY RD is *Bebygate* 1467 × 84 *LTD*, *v.* **gata**; the road to Beeby, 2 miles to the south-east. BROOKFIELD HO., *Brookfield house* 1925 Kelly. BROOKLANDS FM. THE DAIRY FM. EBURY, 1925 Kelly. THE HALL is *Barkby Hall* 1798 Nichols, 1806 Map *et passim* to 1925 Kelly, *v.* **hall.** MAIN ST. THE MALT SHOVEL INN, *Malt Shovel* 1846, 1863, 1877 White, ~ ~ *Inn* 1925 Kelly. MANOR HO., *Manor house* 1635 *Merton*, 1877 White, 1925 Kelly, *v.* **maner**. MERTON FM, referring to Merton College, Oxford, a landowner locally. MILL HO., *Mill* *house* 1925 Kelly. NEW YORK, 1835 O, 1846 White, *New York Lodge* 1863 ib, *v.* **loge**; a 'remoteness' name, the farmstead being situated at the north-eastern extremity of the parish. QUENIBOROUGH RD is *Quenyburgate* 1467 × 84 *LTD*, *v.* **gata**; Queniborough adjoins to the north. RIDGEMERE LANE, *Ridg Mere* 1609 *Merton*, (*The*) *Ridgemere* 1968 *Surv*, cf. *The Ridgeway* c.1785, 1788 *ib*, 1835 O (*v.* **weg**), *v.* **hrycg**, **(ge)mǣre**; an ancient trackway running south-east through the length of East Goscote Hundred and forming the boundary between Barkby and Queniborough parishes. ST MARY'S CHURCH, *Church (St Mary)* 1846, 1863, 1877 White, 1925 Kelly; it is earlier recorded as *ecclesia* ~ ~, *ecclesie de Barkeby* 1220 MHW, 1248 RGros, 1253 × 58 RTAL, 1304 *Pat*. Note also *the Churchyard*(*e*) 1625, 1709 *Terrier*, *v.* **chirche-ȝeard**. SYSTON GRANGE, 1863 White, *v.* **grange**; adjacent to Syston parish boundary. THE VICARAGE, 1877 White, 1925 Kelly, *the Vicaridge house* 1625 *Terrier*, ~ *Vicarage* ~ 1700 *ib*, *v.* **vikerage**; cf. *the Parsonage house* 1635 *Merton*, *v.* **personage**. WHITE COTTAGE, 1968 *Surv*. WOODGATE, 1609 *Merton*, c.1635 *Terrier*, 1648, 1779 *Pochin*, 1925 Kelly, *le Wodegate* 1467 × 84 *LTD* bis, *Woodgate Way* 1635 *Merton* (*v.* **weg**), *v.* **wudu**, **gata**.

FIELD-NAMES

Undated forms in (a) are 1968 *Surv*; those dated 1779, 1826 and 1896 are *Pochin*; 1821 are *Terrier*; 1883 and 1886 are *Merton*. Forms throughout dated 1467 × 84 are *LTD*; 1477 (e.16) are *Charyte*; 1609 and 1635 are *Merton*; 1630, 1633, 1640, 1648 and 1688 are *Pochin*; c.1635, 1650, 1672 and 1709 are *Terrier*.

(a) The 4 Acres 1886, 5 Acre(s) (*Fiuea(c)kres* 1467 × 84, *v.* **fīf**), 8 Acres 1826, Hill's ~ ~, 13 Acre (with the surn. *Hill*), 14 Acres, Hill's 15 Acre, 16 Acres, 18 ~, 20 Acre, 26 Acres (*v.* **æcer**); Bailey's Nook 1826 (*v.* **nōk**) (cf. *Balies Clo(a)se* 1609, *v.* **clos(e)**; with the surn. *Bailey*); Barn Cl 1826, 1886, 1968, Top ~ ~ 1826; Barn Fd; Barn Mdw 1826; Beeby Cl 1826 (Beeby adjoins to the south-east); Belton's Top Fd (with the surn. *Belton*; townships with the name Belton lie in neighbouring Rutland and Lincs., from one of which this family originally came); Bennets Mdw 1968, Little Bennets Mdw 1896, Bennets Pen 1896 (*v.* **penn**[2]) (with the surn. *Bennet*); Berridges 1968, Far ~, Near Berridges 1886 (with the surn. *Berridge* in the possessive case); Bigg Cl 1886, Near Big Cl 1886, Big Cl 1968, Big Mdw 1968 (*v.* **big**); Bottom Cl 1826, Bottom Mdw 1826 (*Bottoms* 1609, 1635, ~ *Cloas* 1609 (*v.* **clos(e)**), *Bottomes hedge* 1609 (*v.* **hecg**), *v.* **botm**); Bramley's (the surn. *Bramley* in the possessive case); Brickkilen Cl (sic) 1826 (*v.* **brike-kiln**); Bridge Fd; Brook Cl 1886, Brook Fd 1968, Brookfurlongs 1779 (*Brooke fur'* 1609, *v.* **furlang** and Barkby

Brook *supra*); Burnett Hills 1779 (*Burnethill* 1467 × 84, *Burnet Hills* c.1635, *Bernet Hill medow* 1609, *v.* **hyll**; with the surn. *Burnet*, from OFr *burnete/brunette*, a diminutive of *brun* 'brown', used of complexion, cf. *Burnetcroft* in neighbouring Thurmaston f.ns. (b) and *v.* Reaney *s.n.*); Byagate South 1779 (*Byhou* 1467 × 84, *Byhougate* 1467 × 84, *Byegate* 1650, 1672 (*v.* **gata**), *Byagate Feilde* 1635, *Bigate field alias Clayfield* c.1635, *Bigate feild* 1650, 1672, (*in campo de Bihou*, *campis de Byhou* 1467 × 84, with MLat *campus* 'a field'), *Biofe(e)lde*, *Biofeild* 1609 (*v.* **feld**; one of the early great fields of the township)), By-Meer Cl 1826 (*Bio Mear* 1609, *Byameere Feild* 1688, *v.* **(ge)mǣre**) (*v.* **bī**, **haugr**); Carnall's Little Fd (with the surn. *Carnall*, *v.* Reaney *s.n.*); Cemetery Fd (adjacent to a local burial ground); Chestnut Fd (a field containing the sweet chestnut tree (*Castanea sativa*), the wood of which was used for fencing, gate-posts, hurdles etc.); Church Headland 1779, 1826, 1968 (*Church hadland*, *~ ~ fur'* 1609 (*v.* **furlang**), *Church hadland feeld* 1609, *~ ~ Field* 1635, *the Church headland feilde* 1648, *Church hadland Meere* 1609 (*v.* **(ge)mǣre**), *v.* **hēafod-land** and St Mary's Church *supra*); Clayton's Cl 1826 (with the surn. *Clayton*); Cleay Cliff 1779 (cf. *Cleclif furlong* c.1635 (*v.* **furlang**), *v.* **clǣg**, **clif**); Clover Cl 1886 (*v.* **clāfre**; a crop used for fodder); College Leys 1883 (*v.* **leys**; with reference to Merton College, Oxford, a landowner locally); The Corner Fd (*v.* **corner**); Little Cottage Cl 1886, Cottage Cl 1968, Cottage Mdw 1968 (*v.* **cotage**); Cow Cl 1826, 1968; Cowpen 1779 (*ye cowpen* c.1635, *v.* **cowpenn**); Cow Pool 1826, 1968 (*v.* **pōl**[1]); The Craft 1883, 1968 (*v.* **croft**); Cricket Fd (for the game of cricket); Croxton Cl, Croxton Fd, Crowson Road Cl 1886, Croxton ~ ~ 1968 (South Croxton adjoins to the east); The Dale Furlong 1779 (*Dale fur'* 1609, (*the*) *Dale furlong*(*e*) 1635, c.1635 (*v.* **furlang**), (*le*) *Dales* 1467 × 84, 1477 (e.16), *þe Dalys*, *Dayls* 1467 × 84, (*in campo de ~*, *campis de Dales* 1467 × 84; with MLat *campus* 'a field'), *the dale feild* 1648 (one of the early great fields of the township)), Dale Cl 1826, First ~ ~, Second ~ ~, Third Dale Cl 1883, 1886, Near Dale Cl (the early plural forms point to **deill** rather than to **dalr** as the source of this group of f.ns.); Far Mdw 1883; The Flats 1883 (*v.* **flat**); Flaxland Leys 1779 (*v.* **leys**) (*Flaxlandes* 1467 × 84, c.1635, *Flaxlandys* 1467 × 84, *Flaxelands* 1635, *v.* **fleax**, **land**); Fiddle Cl 1826 (descriptive of shape, *v.* Field 137–8); Front Fd; Gadfly Lane (a lane infested by gadfly (horsefly or botfly) which bite or annoy livestock); Garners Cl (with the surn. *Garner*); Glass House (may allude to the manufacture of glass rather than to greenhouses, *v.* Field 225); Glebe (*v.* **glebe**); Goose Cl (*v.* **gōs**); Half Moon Spinney (with reference to shape); Hall Warren 1779 (*v.* **wareine** and The Hall *supra*); Hamps 1968, Far ~ ~, Near Hemps Cl 1883 (both *Hamp* and *Hemp* are current surns., here presum. in the possessive case; but **hænep** is poss.); Harbards Cl 1779 (with the surn. *Harberd*, *v.* Reaney *s.n.*); Hill Cl 1826; Holt Fd 1968, Holt Furlong or Smallborough 1826, Short Holt Furlong 1826 (*v.* **furlang**, Barkby Holt *supra* and Long Smallborough *infra*); Home Fd (*v.* **home**); Horse Cl; Horse Pasture (*v.* **pasture**); House Cl; Hovel Cl 1886, ~ ~ or John Willie Sharpless's 1968 (*v.* **hovel**); Hone Hill 1886 (a hill from which sharpening-stones or hones were obtained, *v.* **hān**); Honey Hole Cl 1826 (many such names allude to sticky soil, *v.* Field 42); Hungerfield (sic) 1779 (*Hungar hill feeld* 1609 (*v.* **feld**), *Hungirhul(l)* 1467 × 84, *Hungar Hill* 1635, *Hunger hill furlong* c.1635 (*v.* **furlang**), *v.* **hungor**, **hyll**); Illston's Cl (with the surn. *Illston* of a family originally from Illston on the Hill, 8 miles to the south-east); New Intake 1826, Intek 1968 (*v.* **inntak**); Lady Acre 1826, 1968 (*Ladiaker*, *Ladyaker* 1467 × 84, *Ladiacer* 1609, *Farr Ladi Acar* 1609, *Ladi acar fur'* 1609, *Ladyacre little ~*, *Ladyacre long* *furlong* 1635, *Our Lady furlong* c.1635 (*v.* **furlang**), *Ladyacar sicke* 1635, *Lady acre sicke* c.1635 (*v.* **sík**)), Overlady acre 1779 (*v.* **uferra**) (cf. *Upperlady-Acar-Furlonge* 1635, *v.* **upper, furlang**) (*v.* **lavedi, æcer**; land endowed for the upkeep of a chapel dedicated to Our Lady, the Blessed Virgin Mary); The Lanty Fd (if this records an old name, then 'the long enclosure' may be thought of, *v.* **lang**[1], **tēag**); Lewins Cl 1826, 1968 (with the surn. *Lewin*, a reflex of the OE pers.n. *Lēofwine*); Little Hill; Little Mdw 1883, 1968 (*Littelmedowe, Littilmedow* 1467 × 84, *Lit(t)ell Medow* 1609, *Litle Mead* 1635, *the Little Medowe* c.1635), Little Meadow furlong 1779 (*v.* **furlang**) (*v.* **lȳtel, mǣd** (**mǣdwe** obl.sg.)); Long Cl 1883; Long Crofts 1779 (*Longcroft* 1467 × 84, *v.* **lang**[1], **croft**); Long Mdw (*Longe Meadow* 1609); Lower Fd 1821; Lower furlong upon Cleay Cliff 1779 (*v.* **furlang** and Cleay Cliff *supra*); the Malt Sic, Malt Syke 1779 (*v.* **mealt, sík**); Marl furlong 1779 (*v.* **furlang**), Marl Hole 1968 (*v.* **hol**[1]) (*v.* **marle**); Marl Pit Cl 1883 (*le Marlepit* 1467 × 84, *Marlepit furlong* c.1635 (*v.* **furlang**), *v.* **marle-pytt**); First Meer Cl 1883, Far ~ ~, Meer Cl 1886 (*v.* **(ge)mǣre**); Middle Cl 1886; Middle furlong adjoining Byagate South 1779 (*v.* **furlang** and Byagate South *supra*); Middle Pasture 1826 (*v.* **pasture**); Mill Cl 1886, 1968; Top ~ ~, Mill Hill 1968, Mill Hill Cl 1826 (*Mill Hill* 1635, *Milhill furlong* c.1635 (*v.* **furlang**), *v.* **myln**); Moota Bush 1779 *EnclA*, Moody Bush 1798 Nichols, 1968 (*Mute Bush* 1609, *Moote* ~ 1635, cf. *the thre Moote-bush furlongs* 1635 (*v.* **furlang**)), Mowdebush hill 1798 Nichols, 1846, 1863 White, Mootee Bush Hill 1877 ib (cf. *Mothowes* 1467 × 84 in f.ns. (b)) (*v.* **mōt, busc**; on the promontory which was the meeting place of East Goscote Hundred; it is uncertain whether the unique form *Mothowes* implies early burial mounds (if so, now ploughed out) which originally signalled the moot-site prior to the 'bush', for which landmark there is no early evidence); the Moor 1779, Bottom ~, Middle~, Top ~, Far Moor 1826 (*le Mor* 1467 × 84 (freq), *The Moore* 1635, *Barkby Common Moore* 1609 (*v.* **commun**), *Morfurlong* 14 AD (*v.* **furlang**)), Moor Cl 1826, Moor Mdw 1826 (*v.* **mōr**[1]); Near Mdw 1883; Needhams Cl (with the surn. *Needham*, cf. *Anne Nedham* 1599 of Allexton); the Northings 1779, 1883, the Northerns, Big Northings 1968 (*Northenges* 1467 × 84, *Northinges* 1467 × 84, 1477 (e.16), (*pratum de Northynges* 1467 × 84, with MLat *pratum* 'a meadow, meadowland'), *Nordens* c.1635, *Northing meadow* c.1635, *Northen-Mead* 1635 (*v.* **mǣd** (**mǣdwe** obl.sg.)), *Northinges Gutter* 1609 (*v.* **goter**), *Northen bottoms* c.1635 (*v.* **botm**), *v.* **norð, eng**); Odens Little Fd (with the surn. *Oden*, a reflex of the ON pers.n. *Auðunn*); Far ~ ~, Near ~ ~, Old Cl 1886; Old Mdw 1826, 1968; Old Ploughed Fd; Old Syke 1826 (*Old sicke* c.1635, *the oute sicke* 1635, *v.* **sík**; with **ald** or **wald**, *v.* *le Woldsyke* in f.ns. (b)); Orton's Little Fd, Orton's Orchard (with the surn. *Orton*); the Ould Mear furlong 1779 (*v.* **(ge)mǣre, furlang**; with **ald** or **wald**); the Over Pasture 1779 (*v.* **uferra, pasture**); The Paddock (*v.* **paddock**); The Park (*v.* **park**); Pasture Cl 1825 (*v.* **pasture**); Bottom ~ ~, Top Pear Tree 1826, Pear Tree Cl 1826 (*v.* **pertre**); Pen Cl 1826 (*v.* **penn**[2]); George Pick's Orchard; The Pingle (*v.* **pingel**); Pit Cl (*le Pitt, le Pyt* 1467 × 84, *v.* **pytt**); Ploughed Cl 1826; Plumb Tree Syke 1826 (*Plumtre* 1467 × 84, *Pluntre* 1477 (e.16), *Plumtresyke, Plumtreissyke* 1467 × 84, *Plomtre sick(e), Plumtre sick, Plumtree sicke* c.1635, *Plumtree sick furlonge* 1609 (*v.* **furlang**), cf. *Plumtregate* 1477 (e.16) (*v.* **gata**), *v.* **plūm-trēow, sík**); Pond Fd; Pump Fd (*v.* **pumpe**); Rabbits Hill (*v.* **rabet**); Railway Fd (abuts the former Midland Counties Railway); Reads Cl 1883 (with the surn. *Read*); (The) Redlands, Road Redlands 1883, Syston Road Redlands 1968 (Syston adjoins to the north-west) (*Redelandes, Redlandys* 1467 × 84, *Redd Lands*,

Redlands 1635, *Re(a)dlandes* c.1635, *Redlandes fur'* 1609 (*v.* **furlang**), *v.* **rēad, land**); Richardson's Little Fd, Richo's ~ ~ (in the second form, the surn. *Richardson* is familiarly abbreviated); The Rose Gardens; Rough Cl (*v.* **rūh**[1]); Ruddle Cl 1826 (either with the surn. *Ruddle* (a diminutive *Rudd-el* of ME *rudde* 'red') or with **ruddle** 'red dye' used for marking sheep when tupping); Sandhill Furlong 1779 (1609, c.1635 (*v.* **furlang**), *Sondhull* 1467 × 84 bis, *Sandhull* 1477 (e.16), *Sand hill* 1609, 1635, (*campis de Sondhull* 1467 × 84, with MLat *campus* 'a field'), *Sandell feild* c.1635 (*v.* **feld**; one of the early great fields), *Sandhill Balke* c.1635 (*v.* **balca**), *Sandhill Balke fur(long)* 1609, c.1635 (*v.* **furlang**), *Sandhill hades* c.1635, *Sandell* ~ 1648 (*v.* **hēafod**), *v.* **sand, hyll**); Sarson's Nook Bottom (*v.* **botm**), ~ ~ Top 1826, 1968 (*v.* **nōk**; with the surn. *Sarson*, from OFr *Sarrazin* 'a Saracen', used as a by-name for a swarthy person, cf. *Oliverus Sarazin* 12 Dane of Leics.); Searchlight (the location of a Second World War searchlight battery); Seed Fd (*v.* **sǣd**; used often in f.ns. for areas of sown grass); John Willie Sharpless's (*v.* Hovel Cl *supra*); (The) Shed Fd (*v.* **shed**); Short Mdw (*v.* **sc(e)ort**); Simison Leys 1779 (*v.* **leys**; with the surn. *Simison*, *v.* Reaney *s.n.*); Slade Cl 1826, Slades ~ 1826, 1968 (*v.* **slæd**); Slang, The Slangs (*v.* **slang**); Long Smallborough 1826, Little Smallborough or Short Holt Furlong 1826 (*v.* Holt Furlong *supra*), Small Berry, ~ ~ Plantation 1968 (*Smereberwe* 1467 × 84 bis, *Smaleburrows* 1609, *Longesmereberwe* 1467 × 84 (*v.* **lang**[1]), cf. *Smereberwesyke* 1467 × 84, *Smaleburrow Sicke* 1609, *Smalborow sicke*, *Smalle Burrow Sicke* c.1635 (*v.* **sīk**), *v.* **smeoru, smjǫr, berg**); Smith Mdw (with either the surn. *Smith* or **smið**); Southerdole 1762 Nichols (*Sutherdole* 1477 (e.16), *Southirdol(is)* 1467 × 84, *v.* **suðer, dāl**); South furlong in the Malt Sic 1779 (*v.* **furlang** and the Malt Sic *supra*); Spickacre Fd 1779, Spit Acre (sic) 1886, Spickacre 1968 (*Spikakar*, *Spikaker* 1467 × 84, *Spickacar* 1635, *Spickacre feild* c.1635, 1640, 1648 (*v.* **feld**), *Spickacre Hades* c.1635 (*v.* **hēafod**), *v.* **spic**[2], **æcer**); Spinney Cl 1826, Spinney 1968 (*Spinney Close* 1635, *v.* **spinney**); Springfield (*v.* **spring**[1]); Steels Cl 1883, 1968, Steels Big ~, Steels Far ~ 1883, 1968, Steels Hovel Cl 1883 (*v.* **hovel**) (with the surn. *Steel*); The Stoughton's (the surn. *Stoughton* in the possessive case, of a family originally from the village of Stoughton, 6 miles to the south); The Styway Fds 1779, Styway 1826, 1968, ~ Mead 1826 (*v.* **mǣd**) (*v.* **sty-way**); Sugar Hill 1826, 1968, Little ~ ~ 1826 (either a complimentary name for a location with 'sweet' pasture or reference to a hill of conical (i.e. sugar-loaf) shape, *v.* Field 41); Sutton's Cl (with the surn. *Sutton*); Syston Cl 1883, 1968 (cf. *Siston old close* c.1635; Syston adjoins to the north-west); Ten Foot Pool (*Tent pool fur'* (sic) 1609 (*v.* **furlang**), *v.* **pōl**[1]; poss. originally with **tentour**, otherwise unexplained); Thistle Hill (*Thistle Hill hades* c.1635 (*v.* **hēafod**), *v.* **þistel**); Far ~, Great ~, Middle Thornhill 1826 (cf. *le Thyrnhou* 14 AD, *Thirnhou*, *Thyrnehow* 1467 × 84, *v.* **þyrne, þyrnir, haugr**; replaced by **þorn** and **hyll**); Top Pasture 1826 (*v.* **pasture**); Townside (*v.* **tūn, sīde**); Turnpike Cl 1826 (*v.* **turnepike**); Upper Fd 1821 (*the Upper feild called Bigate feild* 1650, 1672, *v.* Byagate South *supra*); Wheatholm 1826 (*Wheteholm*, *Whytholme* 1467 × 84, *Wheathome*, *Wheete home* 1609, *Wheate holme* 1633, *Great Wheatholme* c.1635, *Wheatholme little furlong* 1635 (*v.* **furlang**), *v.* **hwǣte, hveiti, holmr**); White's Cl (with the surn. *White*); Wilderness (*v.* **wildernesse**); Windmill Fd (cf. *Windmill Hill* 1635, *v.* **wind-mylne**); the Would Cls 1779 Nichols, Wolts Cls 1779 *Pochin*, 1780 *Map* (cf. *the ould woult close* c.1635 (*v.* **ald**), *v.* **wald**).

(b) *Abouethebrok'* 1467 × 84 (*v.* **aboven, þe, brōc**; a furlong so called); *Arlons Bush* c.1635, *Arlong Bush balk* c.1635 (*v.* **balca**), *Arlon bush furlong* c.1635 (*v.*

furlang), *Arland Bush meare* c.1635 (*v.* **(ge)mǣre**) (*v.* **busc**; in Leics. f.ns., *bush* is typically compounded with a surn. indicating ownership, here perh. with *Arling* (a reflex of the OFr pers.n. *Arluin*), *v.* Reaney *s.n.*, but the forms are too disparate for certainty; alternatively **á** (**ár** gen.sg.) 'a river, a stream', with **land**, may be thought of, cf. *Arlandsyke* in Skeffington f.ns. (b)); *Atteblakeforth* 1467 × 84 bis (*v.* **atte**, **blæc**, **ford**; cf. Blackfordby in West Goscote Hundred); *Banlond'* 1467 × 84, *Banlandes* 1609, *Ouerbanlondes* 1467 × 84 (*v.* **uferra**) (*v.* **bēan**, **land**); *Barkby Common Pasture* 1609 (*v.* **commun**, **pasture**); *Barkby Leyes* 1635 (*v.* **leys**); *Barliholme* 1467 × 84 (*v.* **bærlic**, **holmr**); *Barnesbygate*, *Barnysbygate* 1467 × 84 (*v.* **gata**; the road to Barsby which lies 4 miles to the north-east); *Blackmiers furlong* 1609 (*v.* **blæc**, **mýrr**, **furlang**); *Blakemilde*, *Blakemylde* 1467 × 84 (*v.* **blæc**, **mylde**); *Brantclyf* 1467 × 84, *le Branteclif* 1477 (e.16) (*v.* **brant**, **clif**); *le Breche* 1467 × 84, *Breach hades* c.1635 (*v.* **hēafod**); *Upper Breach fur'* 1609 (*v.* **furlang**) (*v.* **brēc**); *Bridoles fur' alias Long Clift* 1609, *Bridehill furlong* c.1635 (earlier forms are needed to explain the first word; *v.* **furlang** and *Longclif*, *infra*); *Brodale* 1477 (e.16) (*v.* **brād**, **dalr**); *le Brodessherd* 1467 × 84, *Brodscherd* 1477 (e.16) (*v.* **brād**, **sceard**); *le Brokfurlong* 1467 × 84, *Brook furlong* 1609 (*v.* **brōc**, **furlang**); *Burnardeshul* 1477 (e.16) (*v.* **hyll**; with the surn. *Burnard*, a compound of OFr *brun* and *hard*, originally a by-name for a person with brownish, dark hair or complexion, cf. Burnt arse Leys in nearby Hungarton f.ns. (a)); *the butt lane* c.1635 (with either **but** or **butte**); *Calfdale* 1467 × 84 (*v.* **calf**, **dalr**); *Carters Close* 1609; with either the surn. *Carter* or **cartere**); *Church Meare* c.1635 (*v.* **(ge)mǣre**), *the Church peece* 1635 (*v.* **pece**), *Church Way* 1635 (*v.* **weg**) (*v.* St Mary's Church *supra*); *Clay field* c.1635 (*v.* Byagate South *supra*), *Lower Clay furlong* c.1635 (*v.* **furlang**) (*v.* **clǣg**); *the Upper ~ ~, Cow Pasture* 1635 (*v.* **pasture**); *Crabtree* 1635, *~ feelde* 1609 (*v.* **feld**), *~ fur'* 1609 (*v.* **furlang**) (*v.* **crabtre**); *Crochou* 1467 × 84, *Crokhougate* 1467 × 84 (*v.* **gata**) (*v.* **haugr**; prob. with **crocc** and referring to a hill where pots were made, cf. *Crokehou* in Hoby f.ns. (b)); *le Crokefeld* 1477 (e.16) (*v.* **krókr**, **feld**; one of the early great fields of the township); *Crokesgate* 1477 (e.16), *Krokesgate* 1467 × 84 (*v.* **krókr**, **gata**); *Croston gapp* c.1635 (*v.* **gap**; South Croxton adjoins to the east); *Croswell* 1467 × 84 (*v.* **cros**, **wella**; presum. a sacred spring marked by a standing cross); *Depforou* 1467 × 84 (*v.* **dēop**, **furh** (in its sense 'a trench or drain')); *Dicfurlongfeld'*, *Dikefurlongfelde* 1467 × 84 (*v.* **feld**, one of the early great fields), *le Nethirdykefurlong'* 1467 × 84 (*v.* **neoðera**), *Ouirdikefurlong'*, *Ouirdykfurlong* 1467 × 84 (*v.* **uferra**) (*v.* **dík**, **furlang**); *le Dykeshende* 1477 (e.16) (*v.* **dík**, **ende**); *Elrinstubbes*, *Elrinstubbis* 1467 × 84 (*v.* **ellern**, **stubb**); *Elthornhurst* 1467 × 84 bis (*v.* **þorn**, **hyrst**; the first el. is poss. the OE pers.n. *Ella*); *Est medue* 1477 (e.16), *the East Med(d)ow* 1609, *Estmedewende* 1467 × 84 (*v.* **ende**) (*v.* **ēast**, **mǣd** (**mǣdwe** obl.sg.)); *Flaxleys* c.1635 (*v.* **fleax**, **leys** and cf. Flaxland Leys in f.ns. (a)); *Frot(t)hewellessyke* 1467 × 84, *Frowell sick*, *~ ~ furlonge* c.1635, *Froowell sick furlonge* 1635 (*v.* **furlang**) (*v.* **frothe**, **wella**, **sík**); *Gallow Hill* c.1635 (prob. with **calu** rather than with **galga**, *v.* *Caleberg* in neighbouring Barkby Thorpe f.ns. (b)); *tofto Will' Ganger* 1477 (e.16) (with MLat *tofta* 'a house-place, a curtilage'); *Bottom Gibsons Close* 1609 (*v.* **bottom**, **clos(e)**; with the surn. *Gibson*); *Goose grene* c.1635 (*v.* **gōs**, **grēne**[2]); *le Gorebrode* 1467 × 84 (*v.* **gorebrode**); *le Gores* 1467 × 84, *the Long Gores* 1609 (*v.* **gāra**); *pratum de Goscote* 1477 (e.16) (with MLat *pratum* 'a meadow, meadowland', *v.* Goscote Hundred); *le Hardemedewe* 1467 × 84, *Hardmedwe* 1477 (e.16) (*v.* **heard**, **mǣd** (**mǣdwe** obl.sg.); literally descriptive of hard soil, *v.* Field 37); *Harewelmere* 1467 × 84 (*v.* **(ge)mǣre**), *Harewelslade* 1467 × 84 (*v.* **slæd**), 'boundary stream', *v.* **hār**[2], **wella**); *Hell Hadland* 1609 (*v.* **hēafod-land**; the first word could be **hell** used as a term of contempt or else be the surn. *Hell* (*v.* Reaney *s.n.*), but may alternatively relate to the following f.n.); *Heluhou* 1467 × 84 (*v.* **haugr**; poss. with **hjallr** 'a shed'); *Highmeare* c.1635 (*v.* **hēah**[1], **(ge)mǣre**); *Hobb Baulk* 1635 (*v.* **balca**; either with the surn. *Hobb* (from the pet-form of Robert, rhymed on *Rob*) or with **hobb(e)** 'a hummock'); *Holewell slade*, *Holwelslade* 1609 (*v.* **hol**[2], **wella**, **slæd**); *Holland meare* c.1635 (with **(ge)mǣre** or **mere**[1]), *Holands slade* c.1635 (*v.* **slæd**) (*v.* **hol**[2], **land**); *Homans lane* c.1635 (*v.* **lane**; with the surn. *Homan*, *v.* Reaney *s.n.*); *horn* 1635 (*v.* **horn**); *le Houeforlong* 1477 (e.16) (*v.* **haugr, furlang**); *Howesgate*, *Howegate* 1467 × 84, *Howsegate* 1477 (e.16), *Hoose Gate* 1609 (*v.* **hōh, haugr, gata**; cf. *Mothowes*, *infra*); *Johnsons Close* 1635, *Johnsons holme* c.1635 (*v.* **holmr**), *Johnsons Pen(n)* 1609, 1635 (*v.* **penn**[2]) (all with the surn. *Johnson*); *Kettellbarrow woonge fur'* 1609 (*v.* **berg, vangr, furlang**; the first el. is prob. the ON pers.n. *Ketill* (an original by-name 'cauldron, cauldron-shaped helmet') or, less likely, its surn. reflex *Kettle*); *the Kinges highe way* 1609 (*v.* **hēah-weg**; with reference to James I); *Kyrkegate* 1477 (e.16) (*v.* **kirkja, gata**; the road to St Mary's Church *supra*); *Langedale* 1477 (e.16) (*v.* **lang**[1], **dalr**); *Langley wonge* 1609 (*v.* **lang**[1], **lēah, vangr**); *Lapidem Josep'* 1467 × 84 ('Joseph's stone'; with MLat *lapis* (*lapidem* acc.sg.) 'a stone'; presum. a boundary marker; *Joseph* may be either a pers.n. or a surn. here); *Leyrstedes*, *Leyrstedis*, *Leyrstedys* 1467 × 84 (*v.* **leirr, stede**); *Little Short furlong* c.1635 (*v.* **furlang**); *Lombe place* 1588 Ipm (*v.* **place**; with the surn. *Lomb*, *v.* Reaney *s.n.*); *Longclif*, *Longclyf* 1467 × 84, *Longe Clift* 1609 (*v.* **lang**[1], **clif**); *Long Crocroft* c.1635 (a scribal duplication of *cro-* may be present here (*v.* Long Crofts in f.ns. (a)), but note *le Crokefeld* and *Crochou*, *supra*, *v.* **lang**[1], **croft**); *le Longewold* 1467 × 84 (*v.* **lang**[1], **wald**); *Martch Dale* 1609 (*v.* **mersc, dalr**); *Longmeyrewong'* 1467 × 84 (*v.* **lang**[1]), *Schortmerewong* 1467 × 84 (*v.* **sc(e)ort**) (*v.* **vangr**; with **(ge)mǣre** or **mere**[1]); *Merstalwong'* 1467 × 84 (*v.* **mere-stall, vangr**); *Middelclyf* 1467 × 84 (*v.* **middel, clif**); *Mill Balke* 1609, c.1635, ~ *Bawke* c.1635 (*v.* **balca**), *the Mill brook* c.1635 (*v.* **brōc**), *Mill Home* 1635 (*v.* **holmr**) (*v.* **myln**); *Millstone way*, *Milston Waye* c.1635 (*v.* **milne-stone, weg**; a road strengthened with worn millstones, cf. Millstone Lane, Lei **1** 50 and *milnestonlane*, Lei **2** 236); *Mothowes* 1467 × 84, *Nether* ~, *Over Motus* 1640, 1648 (*v.* **uferra**) (*v.* **mōt, hōh, haugr** and Moody Bush in f.ns. (a)); *the Neather feild* 1633 (*v.* **neoðera, feld**); *the Neets Penn* 1609, *Ould Neetes Penn* 1609 (with **ald** or **wald**) (*v.* **nēat, penn**[2]); *New Close* 1635, c.1635 (*v. the wong*, *infra*); *Newdikes* 1467 × 84, *New Dickes* 1609, *Neudikgate* 1467 × 84 (*v.* **gata**) (*v.* **nīwe, dík**); *Osmoundesdikys* 1467 × 84 (*v.* **dík**; the first el. may be a pers.n., either OE *Ōsmund* or ON *Ásmundr* (ODan *Asmund*), or the surn. reflex *Osmond/Osmund* to which they gave rise); *the Oulte* 1635 (*v.* **wald**); *Oustontoftis* 1467 × 84 (*v.* **toft**; with the surn. *Ouston* of a family originally from Owston, 9 miles to the east); *Peper Cloase* 1609 (*v.* **clos(e)**; with the surn. *Pepper*); *Poole balk* c.1635 (*v.* **pōl**[1], **balca**); *le Portwey(e)* 1467 × 84 (*v.* **port-weg**; the road to Leicester, 4 miles to the south-west); *le Preestes Clos* 1467 × 84 (*v.* **prēost, clos(e)**); *Mr Putchings new close* 1609, *Mr Putchens (new) close* 1635 (the modern local form of the surn. is *Pochin*, *v.* the list of consulted MSS *supra*); *le Pynfold* 1477 (e.16), *le Pynfeld* 1539 MinAccts, *the Pinfold* 1541 Nichols, *Pinfould* c.1635, *Old Pinfold Leyes* 1635 (*v.* **leys**), *Pinfold Leys furlong* c.1635 (*v.* **furlang**) (*v.* **pynd-fald**); *Queniburhull*, *Quenyburhull*, *Quenyngborwhull* 1467 × 84, *Quiniborow Hill* 1609,

Quinaburrow ~ 1635, *Queniborrow* ~ 1640 (*v.* **hyll**), *Queniborrow furlong* 1648 (*v.* **furlang**) (Queniborough adjoins to the north); *Rauenshyd* 1477 (e.16) (*v.* **hēafod**), *Rauenesedesti* 1467 × 84, *Rauenesty* 1467 × 84 (*v.* **stig**) (either with a pers.n., OE *Hræfn* or ON *Hrafn*, or with their surn. reflex *Raven*); *Redemere* n.d. Nichols (*v.* **hrēod, mere**[1] and the following f.n. which may refer to the same feature); (*in*) *Redemoram* 1477 (e.16) (*v.* **hrēod, mōr**[1]); *le Rekyart* 1477 (e.16) (*v.* **reke-yard**; this compound sb. is otherwise unrecorded before 1712 OED); *the Rie field or Sandell field* c.1635 (*v.* **ryge** and Sandhill *supra*); *Rischebusk'* 1467 × 84 (*v.* **risc, buskr**); *Rowell Sick(e)* c.1635, 1648 (*v.* **sík**; with the surn. *Rowell* of a family prob. originally from Rothwell, 20 miles to the south-east in Northants.; *v.* Nth 118 for the relevant early p.n. form which gave rise to the surn.); *Rush Balk*, ~ *Baulke* c.1635 (*v.* **risc, balca**); *Ryleyes Closse* 1609 (*v.* **clos(e)**; with the surn *Riley* in the possessive case); *Sand feylde alias Crabtree* 1635 (*v.* **feld** and *Crabtree*, *supra*), *Sandfurlong* c.1635 (*v.* **furlang**) (*v.* **sand**); *Sheaffeld Close* c.1635 (with the surn. *Sheffield*); *Sison Meere* 1609, ~ *meare* c.1635 (*v.* **(ge)mǣre**), *Siston old sicke* c.1635 (*v.* **sík**), *Sison Woult*, ~ ~ *Close* 1609 (*v.* **wald**) (Syston adjoins to the north-west); *Souterdole* 1467 × 84, *Sowterdolys* 1467 × 84 bis, *Souter Doles* 1609, *Sowters Doale* 1635, *Sowter dole medow* c.1635 (*v.* **dāl**; poss. with **sūtere** 'a shoemaker' or its surn. reflex *Souter/ Sowter*, *v.* Reaney *s.n.* Soutar, but note Southerdole in f.ns. (a) where this may rather belong); *the Southwong* 1648 (*v.* **vangr**); *Spensar Spindle* 1635 (*v.* **spinele**; with the surn. *Spenser*); *Starkeswong'* 1467 × 84 (*v.* **vangr**; poss. with the surn. *Stark* (*v.* Reaney *s.n.*), but a shortened form of a poss. Anglo-Scand pers.n. *Starkulfr* (cf. ContGerm *Starculf*) may be thought of, *v.* SPNLY 263); *the North* ~, *the South Stints* 1640 (*v.* **stint**); *le Stret'* 1467 × 84 bis, *le Stretes* 1467 × 84 (*v.* **strǣt**; with reference to a Roman road or roads); *le Thirne* 1467 × 84 (*v.* **þyrne**); *Thorpe Lease* 1635, *Thorp Leys* 1688 (*v.* **leys**), *Thorpe Mere* 1609 (*v.* **(ge)mǣre**) (Barkby Thorpe adjoins to the south); *þe thre rudes* 1301 Banco (*v.* **þe, þrēo, rōd**[3]); *le Thwerewong* 14 AD (*v.* **þverr, vangr**); *Thurmestongate* 1467 × 84 bis (*v.* **gata**), *Thromerson Hadland* 1609 (*v.* **hēafod-land**), *Thurmaston Moor(e)* 1635, c.1635 (*v.* **mōr**[1]) (Thurmaston adjoins to the south-west); *Thurnclyf* 1467 × 84 (*v.* **þyrne, clif**); *Nether* ~, *Upper Thurne fur'* 1609 (*v.* **þyrne, furlang**); *Thurnwell furlong* 1635 (*v.* **þyrne, wella, furlang**); *the Vicarage Barn* 1709, *the Vicarage Lane* 1709 (*v.* **vikerage**); *le Vicarslane* 1477 (e.16) (*v.* **vikere, lane**; presum. identical with the previously listed lane); *le Waterforowes* 1467 × 84, *Waterthorow fur'* 1609 (*v.* **furlang**) (*v.* **wæter, furh** and *the Waterfurrow(e)s* in Asfordby f.ns. (b)); *the Watring places* 1609 (*v.* **wateryng**); *the wayn balk* c.1635 (*v.* **wægn, balca**); *West brook* c.1635, *West Brookes fur'* 1609 (*v.* **furlang**) (*v.* **brōc**); *Westgate* 1477 (e.16) (*v.* **west, vestr, gata**); *Westhorpbirimedow(e)*, *Westthorpebirimedow* 1467 × 84 (*v.* **west, vestr, þorp, bȳre, mǣd** (**mǣdwe** obl.sg.) and the West Rope end in adjoining South Croxton f.ns. (a)); *Whythows* 1467 × 84 bis, *Whitehouse furlong* c.1635 (*v.* **furlang**), *Wite-house Lese* 1635 (*v.* **leys**) (*v.* **hwīt, hvítr, haugr**); *le Witeston'* 1467 × 84 (*v.* **hwīt, stān**); *le Witewong'* 1467 × 84, *Whitewonge* 1650, 1672 (*v.* **hwīt, hvítr, vangr**); *le Longewold* 1467 × 84 (*v.* **lang**[1]), *le Schortewolde* 1467 × 84 (*v.* **sc(e)ort**), *le Woldclos* 1467 × 84 (*v.* **clos(e)**), *le Woldgate* 1467 × 84, *Wouldie gate* 1650, 1672 (*v.* **gata**; cf. *Ouldwaie* c.1635, *v.* **weg**), *le Woldsyke* 1467 × 84, *le woult sick* c.1635 (*v.* **sík**) (*v.* **wald**); *the Wong Close* 1630, *the wong or new close* 1635 (*v.* **vangr**).

Barkby Thorpe

1. BARKBY THORPE

Thorp c.1130 LeicSurv, 1200 Fine, 1237 Cur *et passim* to 1347 *MiD*, 1380 *Win*, (- *iuxta Bark(e)by* 1306, 1313 Banco *et passim* to 1327 SR, 1346 *Deed*)
Torp(e) 1199 Cur, 1220 ib (p), 1236 Fees
Thorpe 1287 Banco, 1318 Pat, 1338, 1408 AD, 1535 VE, 1553 Pat, (- *iuxta Barkeby* 1287 Banco, c.1290 Dugd, 1295 Ipm)
Thorp' Berkeby 1473 *MiD*, *Thorp(e) Bark(e)by* 1481, 1489 *ib*, 1494 Banco, 1502 Ipm, 1529 MinAccts
Barkeby Thorpe 1536 Dugd, *Barkby(e) Thorpe* 1604 SR, 1610 Speed *et freq*

'The outlying farmstead', *v.* **þorp**. This was in origin a secondary settlement dependent on Barkby.

ABBOT'S SPINNEY, cf. *Abbotts Clos(s)e* 1650, 1672 *Terrier*, *Abbots close* 1798 Nichols, *v.* **abbat**; the manor was once held by the Abbey of St Mary de Pratis, Leicester. BARKBY THORPE SPINNEY is *Thorpe Spinny* 1835 O, *v.* **spinney**. HILL TOP FM. KING ST. MANOR FM. QUEEN ST. SPINNEY HO., adjacent to Barkby Thorpe Spinney.

FIELD-NAMES

Forms dated 1346 are *Deed*; 1467 × 84 are *LTD*; 1477 (e.16) are *Charyte*; 1630, c.1635, 1650, 1655, 1660 and 1672 are *Terrier*; 1631, 1655, 1682, 1688, 1693, 1694, 1701, 1706, 1717 and 1718 are *Pochin*.

(b) *Brownes wonge* 1650, 1672 (*v.* **vangr**; with the surn. *Browne*); *Bull leyes* 1650, 1672 (*v.* **bula**, **leys**); *Caleberge* 1477 (e.16), *Calbaro*, *Calobaro*, *Calberowgh*, *Caluberwe* 1467 × 84, *Caleborge in campo de Thorp* e.16 Nichols, *Galloborrow* 1650, 1672, *Gallowborow* 1655, *Galloburrough* 1660, *Galloborrow(e) baulk(e)* 1650, 1672 (*v.* **balca**), *Gallaborow feilde* 1630, *Galloborrowe field* c.1635, *Galloborrowe feild(e)* 1650, 1672 (*v.* **feld**; one of the early great fields of the township), *Gallaborow hades* 1630 (*v.* **hēafod**) (*v.* **calu**, **berg** and *Gallow Hill* in Barkby f.ns. (b)); *campis de Thorp* 1467 × 84 (with MLat *campus* 'a field'); *nether* ~, *upper Cawkells* 1650, 1672 (*v.* **calc**, **hyll**); *the Colledge land* 1655, 1682, 1717 (*v.* **land**; with reference to Merton College, Oxford, landowners locally); (*the*) *Combes* 1650, 1672 (*v.* **cumb**); *Crook*(*e*) *sick*(*e*) *hadland* 1650, 1672 (*v.* **krókr**, **sík**, **hēafod-land**); *Dewell furlong* 1650, 1672 (*v.* **furlang**), *Dewell leyes* 1650, 1672 (*v.* **leys**), *Dewell streame* 1650, 1672 (*v.* **strēam**), *the Dowell Close* 1693, 1706 (*v.* **dēaw**, **wella**); *a close called Farme Yard* 1717 (*v.* **farmyard**; the earliest citation in OED is for 1748); *the Great*(*e*) *Close* 1694, 1701, 1748; *atte Grene* 1312 QuR (p) (*v.* **atte**, **grēne**[2]); *Hall Dales* 1650, 1672 (*v.* **hall**, **deill** and *the Whyne plowlands*, *infra*); *Horse Leyes* 1650, 1672 (*v.* **hors**, **leys**); *Lampert greene* 1650, 1672 (*v.* **grēne**[2]; with the surn. *Lampert*, a reflex of the OFr pers.n. *Lambert*); *Leic' way* 1630 (*v.* **weg**; the road to Leicester); *the Longe Close* 1693, 1706; *le Longedoles* 1346, *Long*(*e*) *Doles* 1630, 1650, 1672 (*v.* **lang**[1], **dāl**); *the Middle Close* 1693, 1706; *the Middle feild*(*e*) 1630, 1650, 1672 (*v.* **feld**; one of the early great fields); *the Middle furlonge* 1650, 1672 (*v.* **furlang**; i.e. of *Galloborrowe feild*); *the neather close* 1631 (*v.* **neoðera**); *Nyne Ridges* 1630 (*v.* **nigon**, **hrycg**; cf. the Nine Ridges, Db 463); *the orchard garden* 1655 (*v.* **gardin**); *the Pingle* 1693, 1706 (*v.* **pingel**); (*the*) *Poole Sicke* 1650, 1672, ~ ~ *furlong*(*e*) 1630, 1650, 1672 (*v.* **furlang**), *atte pol sik ende* 1346 (*v.* **atte**, **ende**) (*v.* **pōl**[1], **sík**); *over Posterne Hill* 1650, 1672 (*v.* **ofer**[3]; *Posterne* may be a surn. here (*v.* Reaney *s.n.* Postan), from OFr *posterne* 'a postern-gate', unless the name refers to the postern-gate of a former hall of the township); *Power place* 1386 Banco (*v.* **place**; with the surn. *Power*, *v.* Reaney *s.n.* Poor); *Sandhill pitt*(*e*)*s* 1650, 1672 (*v.* **pytt** and Sandhill Furlong in Barkby f.ns. (a)); *Soure Butts* 1650, 1672 (*v.* **sūr**, **butte**); *Stocweldole* 1477 (e.16) (*v.* **stocc**, **wella**, **dāl**; referring to a stream with a footbridge consisting of a tree-trunk); *Stonhill sicke* 1650, 1672 (*v.* **stān**, **hyll**, **sík**); *Thorp croft* 1477 (e.16) (*v.* **croft**); *Thorpe meadow* 1630, *the meadow* 1650, 1672, (*in prat' de Thorp* 1346 (with MLat *pratum* 'a meadow, meadowland')); (*the*) *Three Acre*(*s*) *Close* 1694, 1701, 1718 (*v.* **æcer**); *Tincroft alias Thurmaston close* 1631 (*v.* **croft**; the first el. of *Tincroft* is poss. a surn. such as *Ting* or *Tinn*, both of which are current; Thurmaston adjoins to the north-west); *Waynes bridge* 1650, 1672, *Waines* ~ 1650 (*v.* **wægn**); *over Westerling*(*e*)*s* 1650, 1672 (*v.* **uferra**, **lyng**; with either **vestr** or **wester**); *the Whyne plowlands al*(*ia*)*s Hall Dales* 1650, 1672 (*v.* **whinny**, **plōg(a)-land** and *Hall Dales*, *supra*); *the Wonge Closes* 1630 (*v.* **vangr**); *le Wynnidole* 1346 (*v.* **whinny**, **dāl**).

2. HAMILTON

Hamelton' c.1130 LeicSurv, 1199 Cur, 1200 Fine *et passim* to 1306 Banco, 1316 FA *et freq* to 1371 Banco, 1395 Cl *et passim* to 1449 *MiD* bis, 1492 Banco

Hameleton 1199 Cur (p)

Hameldon 1220 MHW, 1324 GildR (p), 1353 Ipm, 1494 Banco, *Hameld'* 1236 Fees

Hamilton' l.13 *RTemple* (p), 1294 *MiD et passim* to 1408 AD

Hamulton' 1406 AD, 1434, 1435 *MiD et passim* to 1481 *ib*, 1539 MinAccts
Homulton' 1489 *MiD* bis
Hambleton 1609 *Terrier*, 1835 O

Possibly 'Hamela's farmstead, village'. The preponderance of spellings point to **tūn** 'farmstead, village' as the generic rather than to **dūn** 'a hill' (cf. Hambleton, YW **4** 28 and La 155) and the medial *e* of the unique form *Hameleton* 1199 Cur (p) hints at a pers.n. in the possessive case as the specific. The OE pers.n. *Hamela* is unrecorded outside p.ns., but it has a recorded Scand parallel *Hamall* (cf. ON *hamall* 'maimed'). The specific may alternatively be OE **hamol**, **hamel** 'maimed, mutilated' used as a noun denoting 'a cut-off, flat-topped hill' or the like (cf. MHG *hamel* 'a steep, abrupt cliff'), hence 'farmstead, village near the flat-topped or steep hill'. Less likely, the p.n. may simply represent the common OE topographical name **hamol-dūn* 'cut-off, flat-topped hill' (cf. Hambleton, Ru 179), although spellings with **dūn** as the generic are sparse and even the cited 1324 GildR (p) form may rather represent Hambleton in Rutland.

Examination of local topography is inconclusive for the name's interpretation. The village site lies on slightly shelving ground in a wide valley bottom beside a ford across a major brook which runs westwards into the river Soar. To its north-east, beyond the brook, rises an impressive east–west ridge with a flat, seemingly sliced-off top, declining shallowly east to west. To the south of the village, another major east–west ridge rises quite steeply, again to a flat top. However, there is nothing to suggest that the village migrated from either ridge top to its present location and that the p.n. once denoted an earlier hill-top settlement.

Hamilton is now a deserted medieval village of which extensive earthworks remain, including manor house and probable chapel sites. As a community, the township ceased to exist in the 15th cent., presumably through enclosure for sheep pasture by the Abbey of St Mary de Pratis, Leicester.

HAMILTON GROUNDS, 1877 White, *v.* **grund**.

FIELD-NAMES

Forms throughout are *Pochin* except where otherwise specified.

(a) Four Acre Piece 1760, 1764, 1794 (*Four Acre peece* 1723, *v.* **æcer, pece**); the Hovell Cl 1794 (*v.* **hovel**); the Middle Mdw 1760, 1764, 1794 (1723); the Mill Fd 1760, 1764, 1794 (1723, *the Milne field* 1635, *v.* **myln, feld**; one of the early great fields of the township); the Mill Field Mdw 1760, 1764, 1794 (1723); the Over Mdw 1760, 1764, 1794 (1723, *v.* **uferra**); the Pen Cl 1760, 1764, 1794 (*the Penn Close* 1723, *v.* **penn**[2]); the Ram(m) Yard 1760, 1764, 1794 (1723, cf. *Rams close* 1635, *v.* **ramm**); the Thorney Cl 1760, 1764, 1794 (*Thorny close* 1635, *v.* **þornig**); the Township 1760, 1764, 1794 (1723, *the Towneshipp* 1635, *v.* **tounshipe**; a close so called, with reference to the site of the deserted medieval village, as for the site of *Willoughes*, *v.* Ragdale f.ns. (a) *s.n.* (The) Township).

(b) *capellam de Hameldon* 1220 MHW (with MLat *capella* 'a chapel'; Hamilton was a chapelry of Barkby); *Hambleton Closes* 1635; *Hambleton hedge* 1609 *Terrier* (*v.* **hecg**; on the boundary of the former township); *Long Dolus* 1406 AD (*v.* **lang**[1], **dāl**; poss. identical with *le Longedoles* in Barkby Thorpe f.ns. (b)); *the new mead* 1635 (*v.* **mǣd**).

Barrow upon Soar

BARROW UPON SOAR

Barhov 1086 DB, *Barhou* 1086 ib, *Baru* 1158 France, *Barew* 1209 × 35
Barua l.12 *GarCart*, 12 *GarCh* (p), *Baruha* John Berkeley, *Baruwe* 1227 Cur, 1274 Cl *et passim* to 1316 FA, 1338 Hosp (p), *Barue* 1261 Cur, 1273 Ipm, 1277 Hastings, 13 *MiD*
Barwa e.Hy 2 BM, Hy 2 Dane, 1192 × 1227 Hastings, *Barwe* 1198 GildR, 1212 *GarCart et freq* to 1375 *Ferrers*, 1385 Banco *et passim* to 1415 *LCDeeds* (p), 1424 Cl
Barewa Hy 2 Dugd, 1228, 1253 × 58 RHug, *Barewe* 1182, 1184 P, 1228 RHug *et passim* to 1240 FF, 1250 *RTemple et freq* to 1396 Banco, 1403 *RTemple*
Baroua 1214 × 26 BM, 1340 Ch, *Barowe* 1209 × 35 RHug, 1284 Ass *et passim* to 1361 *Ferrers* (p), 1367 *LCDeeds* (p) *et freq* to 1500 *Wyg*, 1507 *Ferrers*, 1517 *Dixie et passim* to 1549, 1552 Pat, *Barouwe* 1325, 1326, 1340 Ipm
Barugh 1336 Ct, 1395 Cl *et passim* to 1404 FF, 1420 Pat, *Barogh* 1376 ib, 1391 Banco *et passim* to 1447 *Ferrers*, 1532 FF, *Barough* 1422 AD, 1424 Coram *et passim* to 1445 *LCDeeds*, 1449 *RTemple*, *Barroughe* 1557 FF
Barow 1449 *MiD*, 1454 *RTemple et passim* to 1518 Visit, 1522 Will, *Barrow(e)* 1413 *RTemple*, 1452 *LCDeeds et passim* to 1556 ISLR, 1576 Saxton *et freq*

Affixes are added as:
~ *super Sore* 1294 Ass, 1302 IpmR, 1307 *Ferrers et freq* to 1450 *RTemple*, 1452 *LCDeeds*, ~ *sup. Soore* 1550 ISLR, ~ *sup' Zoare* 1604 SR, ~ *super Soram* 1395, 1454 *RTemple*, 1543 *Wyg*
~ *upon Sore* 1457 *Win*, ~ *vpon sowre* 1546 AAS, 1549 Pat, ~ *vpon Zoram* 1610 Speed

'(At) the grove', *v.* **b(e)aru** (**b(e)arwe** dat.sg.). The dominant form of the p.n. is the OE dat.sg. *b(e)arwe*. Most likely, it was originally preceded by the OE prep. *æt* 'at', the expression for 'homestead' o 'village' being understood (cf. *Æt Bearwe* c.890 (10) OEBede, Barrov upon Humber, L **2** 15). Barrow stands on the river Soar, hence affixe with MLat *super* 'on, upon'; and *v.* **uppan**.

BARLEY HILL HO., *Barlyhyll* 1391 *Deed*, *Barl(e)yhille* 1454 *RTemple* bis *Barlyhul* 1477 (e.16) *Charyte*, *Barlihill*, *Barlihull* 1467 × 84 *LTD*, *Barlie hille* 1651 *Terrier*, *Barley Hill* 1967 × 71 *Surv*, *v.* **bærlic**, **hyll**. BARROW BARN, cf. *Barrow Barn farm* 1925 Kelly, *v.* **bern**. BARROWCLIFFE, *Barrowcliff* 1925 Kelly, *v.* **clif**. BARROW HILL, 1967 × 71 *Surv*. BARROW LOCK, cf. *Lock Meadow* 1967 × 71 *Surv*, *v.* **lock**. BARROW LODGE. BARROW MILL, *le Mylne* 1560 Ct, *Barrow Mylne* 1557 QuR, *Barrow Mill* 1835 O, 1863, 1877 White; it is *Water Mill* 1846 ib, *v.* **myln**. BEVERIDGE ST, named from Bishop Beveridge, Bishop of St Asaph, born here in 1636. BILLHEDGE COTTAGES, 1967 × 71 *Surv*, *Billhedge* 1967 × 71 *ib*. BREADCROFT LANE, *Bradecrofte* 1544 Surv, *v.* **brād**, **croft**. BRIDGE ST, *Bridge street* 1846, 1863, 1877 White; cf. *Barewebrigg* 1347 Hastings, *Baroghbrygge* 1444 ib, *Barrobrigge* c.1474 ib, *Barrowbrig* 1481 MinAccts, *Barbridges* 1651 *Terrier*, *atte Brig* 1332 SR (p), *atte brygende* 1467 × 84 *LTD* (p) (*v.* **atte**, **ende**), (*ad Ponte'* 1327 SR (p), *pontem de Barewe* 1276 RH (with MLat *pons* (*pontem* acc.sg.) 'a bridge')), *v.* **brycg**, **bryggja**. BUCKNALL HILL, 1846, 1863 White; prob. with the surn. *Bucknall*, *v.* Reaney *s.n.* CATSICK HILL, CATSICK LANE, *v.* **sík**; the first el. is poss. a surn., cf. *Walter Cat* 1315, 1320 QuR, *Roger le Cat* 1318 ib; otherwise *v.* **cat(t)**. CHIPPINGDALE HO., *Chippingdale house* 1925 Kelly. CHURCH ST, *Church street* 1846, 1863, 1877 White, *v.* Holy Trinity Church *infra*. CLIFF COTTAGE, 1846 White, *Cliffe* ~ 1863, 1877 ib, CLIFF HILL, 1925 Kelly, CLIFF HO., *Cliff House* 1846 White, *Cliffe* ~ 1863, 1877 ib, 1925 Kelly, CLIFF TERRACE, *v.* **clif**. CREAM LODGE, 1846 White, 1925 Kelly, *v.* **loge**; cf. Cream Lodge, Kirby Bellars. ELM FM. FISHPOOL BROOK, *le Fisshpole(s)*, *Fysshpole* c.1474 Hastings, *Fisshpoles* 1481 MinAccts, *Fishpo(o)le* 1564 Ct, *le Fisshepooles*, *Fishpoole(s)* 1615 Ipm, *Fish Pools* 1967 × 71 *Surv*, *v.* **fisc-pōl**. FOXHILL FM, *Foxhill farm* 1925 Kelly, *Foxhyll* 1391 *Deed*, *Foxhull'* 1477 (e.16) *Charyte*, *Foxhul* 1467 × 84 *LTD*, *Foxehill* 1651 *Terrier*, *v.* **fox**, **hyll**. GLENWORTH FM. GRANGE COTTAGE, 1925 Kelly, *v.* **grange**; note also *Grange poultry farm* 1925 ib. GROVE LANE, *le Grove* 1316 QuR, *The Grove* 1967 × 71 *Surv*, cf. *atte Grove* 1326 Hastings (p), 1364 Banco (p), *at groue* 1381 (15) *Deed* (p), *att(e) Groue* 1395 *RTemple* (p), 1398 (15) *Deed* (p) (*v.* **atte**), (*ad Gravam* 1274 Cl (p), *ad graua'* 1327 SR (p), with MLat *grava* (*gravam* acc.sg.) 'a grove'), *v.* **grāf**. HAYHILL

LANE, *Hay* 1347 Hastings bis, *Hay Hill* 1967 × 71 *Surv*, *v.* **(ge)hæg**. HIGHFIELD FM, *Highfield farm* 1925 Kelly. HOLY TRINITY CHURCH, *the Church* 1708 (18) *Terrier*, *Church (Holy Trinity)* 1846, 1863, 1877 White, 1925 Kelly; it is earlier recorded as *ecclesie de Barowe* 1220 MHW, ~ *de Barwa'* 1235 RGros, ~ *de Barwe* 1248 ib, 1335, 1337 *Pat*, *ecclesia de Barewe* 1253 × 58 RTAL, *in ecclesia parochiali* 1549 *Pat*. Note also *the Church Yard* 1639, 1690, 1708 (18), 1822 *Terrier*, *v.* **chirche-ʒeard**; it is uncertain whether *capella de Barowe* 1381 *Pat* (with MLat *capella* 'a chapel') refers to the chapel at Quorndon which was part of the Manor of Barrow. THE LEYS, 1877 White, *v.* **leys**. MAYCROFT, 1925 Kelly. MEADOW VIEW FM, *Meadow View Farm* 1967 × 71 *Surv*. MELTON RD is *Mellton Gate* 1651 *Terrier*, 1797 *Plan* (*v.* **gata**), *Melton Way* 1797 *ib*; the road to Melton Mowbray which lies 11 miles to the east. MILL LANE, 1846, 1863 White, 1925 Kelly, *v.* Barrow Mill *supra*. NETHERFIELD, *Netherfeld* c.1474 Hastings, *Nether Feld* 1568 Ct, *the nether field* 1708 (18) *Terrier*, *v.* **neoðera**, **feld**; one of the early great fields of the township. NEWTON VILLAS. THE NOOK, *Nooke* 1560 Ct, NOOK LANE, 1877 White, *v.* **nōk**. NORTHFIELD, *ye North Feld* 1568 Ct, (*ye*) *North field* 1697, 1700 *Terrier*, 1925 Kelly, *v.* **norð**, **feld**; one of the early great fields. NORTH ST, *the North street* 1630, 1690 *Terrier*, 1846, 1863, 1877 White. OLD MEN'S HOSPITAL, *Men's Hospital* 1846, 1863, 1877 White, *Barrow Hospital(l)* 1730, 1751, 1772 ChAccts, *the Hospital of Barrow upon Soar* 1793, 1814 ib, OLD WOMEN'S HOSPITAL, *Women's Hospital* 1846, 1863, 1877 White, *v.* **hospital**. PAUDY FM, *Pawdy farm* 1925 Kelly, PAUDY LANE, *Pawdy Lane* 1835 O, PAUDY LODGE, 1877 White, *v.* **loge**, PAUDY RISE FM, *Pawdy rise* 1925 Kell, *v.* **rise**; all named from Paudy Lane which runs from Barrow upon Soar north-east by way of Seagrave parish to the Fosse Way and was a continuation south-westwards of the Roman road Margary 58a across the Wolds from Ermine Street. Perh. the lane was styled **paued(e)**, **paved** 'paved' with reference to the original Roman road surface, but such a phonological development seems unlikely. Earlier forms are needed. RECTORY FM, *Rectory farm* 1925 Kelly, *v.* **rectory**. THE ROOKERY, 1925 Kelly, *v.* **rookery**. RYECROFT FM, *Ryecroft farm* 1925 Kelly, *Ryecroft* 1391 *Deed*, 1477 (e.16) *Charyte*, 1544 Surv, *Ricrofte* 1454 *RTemple* bis, *Rycrofte* 1454 *ib*, 1651 *Terrier*, *Riecrofte* c.1474 Hastings, *Ryecrofte* 1481 MinAccts, 1544 Surv, *Riecroft* 1467 × 84 *LTD*, (*le*) *Rycroft* 1544 Surv, 1568 Ct, cf. *Riecroftwey* 1467 × 84 *LTD* (*v.* **weg**), *v.* **ryge**, **croft**. SILEBY RD, *Sileby road* 1877 White, 1925 Kelly; Sileby lies 3 miles to the south-east. SOUTH FIELDS, 1925 Kelly, *Southfelde* 1544 Surv, *ye Sowth Feld* 1568 Ct, *the South Feild* 1651 *Terrier*, *South field* 1700 *ib*, *Southend* *field* 1797 *Plan* (*v*. **ende**), *v*. **sūð**, **feld**; one of the early great fields of the township. SOUTH ST, *South street* 1846, 1863, 1877 White. STRANCLIFFE, 1651 *Terrier*, 1877 White, 1967 × 71 *Surv*, *Stranclyfe* 1454 *RTemple*, *Strangclyf* 1467 × 84 *LTD*, *Strankcliffe* 1544 Surv, STRANCLIFFE HO., *Strancliffe house* 1925 Kelly, STRANCLIFFE LANE, *v*. **strang**, **clif**. THORNTREE COTTAGE, 1863 White. TITHE FM, *The Tithe Farm* 1835 O, *Tythe farm* 1925 Kelly, 1967 × 71 *Surv*, *v*. **tēoða**. THE VICARAGE, 1925 Kelly; it is *the Vicaridge house* 1697, 1703 *Terrier*, ~ *Vicarage* ~ 1708 (18) *ib*, *v*. **vikerage**. WALTON LANE, leading to Walton on the Wolds, 2 miles to the north-east. WARNER ST. WEST END, *v*. **ende**. WHITE LEES, 1877 White, *v*. **hwīt**, **leys**; prob. here is ModEdial. *white* used of dry, open pasture, cf. White Leys, Lei **2** 38. THE WILLOWS, cf. *the Willowes Baulk* 1708 (18) *Terrier*, *v*. **wilig**, **balca**.

INNS AND TAVERNS

BISHOP BLAIZE (lost), *Bishop Blaize* 1846, 1863, 1877 White, 1925 Kelly. BLACKSMITHS' ARMS (lost), *Blacksmiths' Arms* 1846, 1863, 1877 White. FOX (lost), *Fox* 1846, 1863 White, *Fox Inn* 1877 ib. HAMMER AND PINCERS, 1925 Kelly. KING'S HEAD (lost), *King's Head* 1846 White. NAVIGATION INN, 1846, 1863, 1877 White, 1925 Kelly. RAILWAY INN (lost), *Railway Inn* 1863, 1877 White, 1925 Kelly; named from *the Midland Railway* 1863 White. RAM (lost), *Ram* 1846, 1863 White. ROYAL OAK (lost), *Royal Oak* 1846, 1863, 1877 White. THREE CROWNS INN, *Three Crowns* 1846, 1863, 1877 White, 1925 Kelly.

FIELD-NAMES

Undated forms in (a) are 1967 × 71 *Surv*; 1797 are *Plan*. Forms throughout dated 1139 × 47, 1242, Hy 3, 1298, 1313, 1326, 1343, 1347, 1350, 1388, 1426, 1444, 1456, c.1474, 1508 and 1530 are Hastings; a.1279, 1312, 1314, 1315, 1316, 1318, 1320, 1324, 1344, 1432, 1557, 1585 and 1588 are QuR; 1327 and 1332 are SR; 1391 are *Deed*; 1454 are *RTemple*; 1477 (e.16) are *Charyte*; 1467 × 84 are *LTD*; 1481 are MinAccts; 1544 are Surv; 1560, 1564, 1568 and 1587 are Ct; 1615, 1626 and 1639 are Ipm; 1651, 1690, 1697, 1700 and 1708 (18) are *Terrier*.

(a) Barn Cl; The Big Fd; Bottom Fd; Bridge Mdw (*Bridge Meadowe* 1700); Brook Fd (*le Broke* c.1474, 1477 (e.16), 1481, *The Broke* 1651, *Brokefelde* 1467 × 84, 1544 bis, *Brokefeld* 1544, *The Broke Feild* 1521 Will (*v*. **feld**; one of the early great fields of the township), cf. *Brokefurlong(e)* 1454, *Brocfurlong* 1477 (e.16), *Brokeforlong* 1467 × 84, *the Brooke Furlounge* 1651 (*v.* **furlang**); note also *the Easte Brooke Feilde or the Cuningrie Feilde* 1651 (*v. the Cuningrie Feilde* in f.ns. (b)), *v.* **brōc**); The Bryans (prob. the surn. *Bryan* in the possessive case, *v.* Reaney *s.n.*); Bungalow Fd; Bottom ~ ~, Top Campion Brook 1967 × 71, Campion brook Common 1797 (*v.* **commun**) (*Campion brooke* 1615, *v.* **brōc**, cf. *Gilbert' Campion* 1320); Conigreen Brook Common 1797 (*v.* **coni**, **grēne**[2], **coningre**, **brōc**, **commun**); The Cricket Fd (x2) (for the game of cricket); Big Daddy (cf. *Daddyplowe* 1391 (*v.* **plōg**); the property of *Joh'e Daddy* 1391; *plowe* may here be an incomplete *ploweland* 'a ploughland' (in the Danelaw about 120 acres and equivalent to a DB carucate or the area capable of being tilled by one plough-team of eight oxen in the year), or be used with the same meaning, or may simply refer to an unspecified area of arable land); Eastlands (*v.* **land**); Ellis Cl (with the surn. *Ellis*); Fewkes (the surn. *Fewkes* in the possessive case); The Five Acres (*v.* **æcer**); Flatsick (*v.* **flatr**, **sík**); Footpath Cl; Middle ~ ~, Top Fox Hill (*v.* Foxhill Fm *supra*); Front Cl; The Furrows (*v.* **furh**); The Gandes (sic) (poss. the surn. *Gander* in the possessive case, *v.* Reaney *s.n.* Gander and cf. The Bryans *supra*); The Gardens; Gas House Mdw; Haggs 1797 (*v.* **hǫgg**); Hale Cl (may belong with Hayles following); First ~, Top Hayles or Hay Hill (*v.* Hayhill Lane *supra*); Haysick, ~ furlong 1797 (*v.* **furlang**) (*Haysick* 1708 (18), *v.* **(ge)hæg**, **sík**); Hazel Croft 1967 × 71, South hazle Croft 1797 (*Heselcroft* 1477 (e.16), *v.* **hæsel**, **hesli**, **croft**; The Headings (*v.* **heading**); Bottom ~ ~, Middle ~ ~, Top Hey Hole (*v.* **hēg**, **hol**[1]); Holm Cls 1797 (*the Holme Close* 1630 Nichols, *v.* **holmr**); Home Fd (*v.* **home**); Homestead (*v.* **hām-stede**); Horse Cl; Hungerfield 1797 (*v.* **hungor**); Labour Gate (*v.* **gata**; the first el. may be **lǣfer** 'a rush, a reed, a reed-bed'); Lamb Croft (*lambecroft* 1391 bis, 1454 bis, 1477 (e.16), 1467 × 84, *lamcrofthe* 1454 bis, *Lamcroft(e)* 1454 bis, 1544 bis, *le Lamcrofte* 1544, *Lambe Croft* 1568, *Lambcrofte* 1651, *Lamb craft* 1700, *Lamcroft(e)felde* 1544, *Lambcrofte Feilde* 1651 (*v.* **feld**; one of the early great fields), *v.* **lamb**, **croft**); The Leasures (*v.* **lǣs** (**lǣswe** gen.sg., dat.sg.)); Lime Kiln Cl (*v.* **lim-kilne**) (cf. *Kilneclose* 1560, *v.* **cyln**, **clos(e)**); Long Cl; Far ~ ~, First Long Hedge; Lords Orchard (with the surn. *Lord*); The Magazine (presum. a close which once contained a storehouse for explosives); Joe Marshall Fd; First ~ ~, Top ~ ~, Melton Gate (*v.* Melton Rd *supra*); Far ~ ~, First Middle Cl; Mill Mdw (*le Milnemedowe* 1326, *Milnmedow* c.1474, *Milne Medowe* 1481, *v.* **myln**, **mǣd** (**mǣdwe** obl.sg.) and Barrow Mill *supra*); Nether field Leas 1797 (*v.* **leys**); New Brighton Row; Northend (*v.* **ende**); Oak Tree Mdw; Occupation Lane (a common name, often dating from the Enclosures and meaning 'a private road for the use of the occupiers of the land', *v.* OED *s.v.* occupation, 7; it signified a green lane, an access road through what were originally great fields); Old Eleven Acres (*v.* **æcer**); Old Man's Fd; The Paddock (*v.* **paddock**); The Parks (*le Parke* c.1474, 1481, *Barrow Parke* 1508, (*parco* (*meo*) *de Barow* 1139 × 47, *parco de Barwe* 1340 Dugd (with MLat *parcus* 'a park, an enclosure')), *v.* **park**); Parting Peace (sic) (*v.* **parting**, **pece**); Parsons Cl (*v.* **persone**); Pauday Fd 1797, Pawdy Fds 1925 Kelly, Pawdy furlong 1797 (*v.* **furlang**), Behind Pawdy 1797 (*v.* Paudy Lane *supra*); Far ~ ~, First Petty Lands (*Pitelandys* 1467 × 84, *Pittilandes* 1651, *v.* **pety**, **land**); The Pingles (*v.* **pingel**); The Pleasures (prob. with **lǣs** (**lǣswe** gen.sg., dat.sg.), cf. The Leasures *supra*); Pond Fd; Quarry Cl; Red Hill (*v.* **rēad**; referring to the colour of the soil); Redlands (1651, *Redelandes* 1454, *Redelond'* 1477 (e.16), *Redelandys* 1467 × 84, *v.* **rēad**, **land**); Roadside Fd; Rough Cl (*v.* **rūh**[1]); Round Cl (*v.* **round**); Big ~ ~, Little Sand Pit (*v.* **sand-pytt**); Second Fd (cf. Third Fd *infra*); Shepherds Hill Fd (cf. *Sheperdowe* 1530, *v.* **scēp-hirde, haugr**); Bottom Six Hills (*v.* **bottom**) (*le Sikes* c.1474, *les Sykes* 1481, *v.* **sík**); Sledge Cl (poss. a reflex of *the slade* 1467 × 84, *v.* **slæd** and cf. Sledge Spinney, Lei **2** 85; otherwise **secg**[1] with intrusive *l*); South Holme 1797 (*Southolm* 1298, 1432 bis, *Suthholm* 1314, 1316, *Sutholm* 1315, *Sowthholme* 1391, *Southolme* 1391, c.1474, *le Sowtheholme* 1560, *Southeholme* 1564, *Sowth Holme* 1568, *South Holme* 1615 (*v.* **sūð, holmr**); Stack Yard Fd (*v.* **stak-ȝeard**); Third Fd (cf. Second Fd *supra*); Thompsons Shallows (perh. land beside a shallow reach of the river Soar, but more likely is **salh** 'a sallow' in the pl.); The Thoroughfare (a close beside a (main) road); Top Cl; Top Fd; Top Eight Acres, Top Two Acre (*v.* **æcer**); Great ~ ~, Little Town Cl (*v.* **tūn**); Two Waters (*v.* **wæter**; a close containing two streams); Understile (*v.* **under, stīg**); Vera's Fd; Warren hedge Furlong 1797 (*v.* **wareine, hecg, furlang**); Weir Mdw (*v.* **wer**); Far ~ ~, First Wollax Wong (*v.* **vangr**; earlier forms are needed for *Wollax*, but 'wold oaks' may be thought of, *v.* **wald, āc**; note that Walton on the Wolds adjoins); Big ~, Little Worm (prob. with **vangr**, but otherwise with **wamb, womb** used topographically of a hollow, cf. Hall Worm in Wymeswold f.ns. (a)).

(b) *lez Acres* 1474, 1481, *les Akers* 1568, 1585, *ye Akers* 1568, *The Akers* 1615, *The Acres* 1630 Nichols, 1651, ~ ~ *in the South Feild* 1651 (*v.* **æcer** and South Fields *supra*); *Akyrlondes* 1314 bis, *Akyrlandes* 1432, *le Akerlands* 1544 (*v.* **æcer, land**); *Ansons Baulk* 1708 (18) (*v.* **balca**; with the surn. *Anson*); *atte As(s)he* 1327 (p), 1332 (p) (*v.* **atte, æsc**); *Bancrofte* 1454 bis, 1651, *Bancrofthe* 1454, *Bancroft* 1477 (e.16), *Bancrofte Feilde* 1651 (*v.* **feld** and *the Middle Feilde*, *infra*), *Bancrofte hades* c.1474, *Bankecrofthades* 1481, *Bancroft Hades* 1639 (*v.* **hēafod**) (*v.* **bēan, croft**); *Banlandys* 1467 × 84, *Benelondeslade* 1477 (e.16) (*v.* **slæd**) (*v.* **bēan, land**); *Barlehillfelde* 1544 (*v.* **feld** and Barley Hill Ho. *supra*); *Barneȝarte* 1477 (e.16) (*v.* **bern, garðr**); *Barroholme* c.1474 bis, *Bar(r)owholme* 1481 bis, *Baroholme* 1477 (e.16), *Bar(r)ow Holme* 1560 bis, 1564, 1568, 1615, *(le) Holme* 1430 Banco, 1456, c.1474, *le Holm* 1477 (e.16), *ye Holme* 1700 (*v.* **holmr**); *Ben(e)hilstye* c.1474, 1481, *Benelsti(e)* 1564, 1615 (*v.* **bēan, hyll, stīg**); *Betwixte the ditches* 1651 (*v.* **betwixt, dīc**; a furlong so called); *the hille called Beyonde the Sicke* 1651 (*v.* **sík**); *Bondman medow* c.1474, *Bondeman Medowe* 1481 (*v.* **bond-man, mǣd (mǣdwe** obl.sg.)); *(le) Breche* c.1474, 1477 (e.16), 1481 (*v.* **brēc**); *Brokenlond* c.1474, *Brokenlande* 1481, *Brokine Lands* 1564, *Brokenlands* 1564, 1615 (*v.* **brocen, land**); *Broweshouse* 1615 (*v.* **hūs**; prob. with the surn. *Brower* in the possessive case rather than a **brew-hous**, *v.* Reaney *s.n.*); *Bydwell'* 1391, *Bidewell* 1477 (e.16), *Bydewellhyl* Hy 3, *Bydewellehyl* a.1291, *Bidewellhill* 1343, *Bydewelhyle* 1454, *Bidewellhull* 1477 (e.16) (*v.* **hyll**) (*v.* **byden, wella**); *Caldewellesyke* 1344, *Cawdewellesike* c.1474, *Caudewellsike* 1481, *Cawdwell sicke* 1651 (*v.* **sík**), *Caldewellewong* 1477 (e.16) (*v.* **vangr**) (*v.* **cald, wella**); *le Cawsey* 1560 (*v.* **caucie**); *bosco qui vocatur la Chaleng'* 1236 Cur, ~ ~ ~ *le Chaleng'* 1239 ib (with MLat *boscus* 'a wood') (*v.* **calenge**; used of 'land in dispute'); *The Chickines*, *Chickins* 1651 (*v.* **cīcen**; perh. an early form of the modern f.n. Hen and Chickens which may allude to the birdsfoot trefoil (*Lotus corniculatus*), *v.* Field 71; otherwise, land on which chickens were regularly kept may be thought of, cf. *(the) Chicken wonge* in Asfordby f.ns. (b)); *ye Cliff Meadowes* 1700 (*v.* **clif**); *Cokpoole* c.1474, *Cokkespole* 1481, *Coxpoole* 1560 bis, 1564, 1615 bis, *Coxe Poole* 1564, *Cokkuspol medowe* 1326 (*v.* **mǣd (mǣdwe** obl.sg.)) (*v.* **cocc**[2], **pōl**[1]); *Copthorn* 1467 × 84 (*v.* **copped**[2], **þorn**); *Corduwanleyes* 1326, *Cordeweyn leisse* c.1474,

Cordwynelies 1481 (*v.* **lǣs**; ME *corduan/cordewan* (OFr *cordoan* 'Spanish leather made originally at Cordoba', and used for shoes) seems to be an occupational surn. here (*v.* Reaney *s.n.* Corden), and used as a metonymic for *Cordner* (AFr *cordewaner* 'a cordwainer, a shoemaker')); *le Croft* 1388 (*v.* **croft**); *Cuningrie Feilde* 1651 (*v.* **feld**), *the Cuningrie leaies* 1651 (*v.* **leys**) (*v.* **coningre**); *Dedewong* 1477 (e.16) (*v.* **dēad**, **vangr**; poss. alluding to the discovery of human bones); *le Dernforthe* 1298, 1314 (*v.* **derne**, **ford**); *Douuecrofteshende* 1477 (e.16) (*v.* **croft**, **ende**; either with **dowe** or with the surn. *Dow(e)*, cf. *Dowwongus* in Humberstone f.ns. (b)); *Drift Nooke* 1690 LAS (*v.* **drift**, **nōk**); *Durrands Howse* 1530 (*v.* **hūs**; with the surn. *Durrand*); *Eastwell*, ~ *landes* 1651 (*v.* **ēast**, **wella**, **land**); *estowlandes* 1391 bis, *Esthouland'* 1477 (e.16), *Esthoulandes* 1467 × 84 bis (*v.* **ēast**, **haugr**, **land**); *les Flagges* 1326, *Flagmere* c.1474, *Flaggymere* 1481, *Flaggie Meare* 1651 (*v.* **mere**[1]) (*v.* **flagge**, **-ig**[3]); *Flitwong* 1477 (e.16) (*v.* **(ge)flit**, **vangr**); *Follerscrofte*, *Foulescrofte* c.1474 (*v.* **croft**; either with the occupational term OE **fullere** (OFr *fouleor*, *foleur*) or its surn. reflex *Fuller*); *(the) Fordewaie* 1651 bis, *the Furdway* 1708 (18) (*v.* **ford**, **weg**); *Fotwong* 1477 (e.16) (*v.* **fōt**, **fótr**, **vangr**); *Fullewellegate* 1324 (*v.* **gata**), *Fulwell Lane* 1568 (*v.* **lane**) (*v.* **fūl**, **wella**); *Gildal Dale* 1347 bis (*v.* **gild**, **deill**, **dalr**); *Gilesnoke* 1481 (*v.* **nōk**; with the surn. *Giles*, *v.* Reaney *s.n.*); *le Gore* 1477 (e.16) (*v.* **gāra**); *atte Grene* 1332 SR (p), 1365 Banco (p) (*v.* **atte**, **grēne**[2]); *Greneclyffe* 1391 (*v.* **grēne**[1], **clif**); *Grimmeswelle* 1298, 1316 (*v.* **wella**; prob. with the pers.n. *Grim*, either from OE *Grīm* or, less likely here, ON *Grímr* (ODan *Grim*)); *Hall Orchard* 1560 (*v.* **hall**, **orceard**); *Haregharedyke* 1477 (e.16) (*v.* **hār**[2], **æcer**, **dík**); *Hartclif* 1467 × 84 (*v.* **clif**), *Hartlandis* a.1279 (*v.* **land**) (prob. with **heard**, **harðr** in the sense 'hard to till' rather than with **heort**); *Harvie Close* 1564, *Harveys* ~ 1615, *Harvy* ~ 1615, 1626 (*v.* **clos(e)**; with the surn. *Harvey/Harvie*); *Hauekerescroft* 1298, 1316 (*v.* **croft**), *Hauekeremedowe* 1298, 1314, *Hauekerlsmedowe* 1315, *Haukeresmedowe* 1316 (*v.* **mǣd (mǣdwe** obl.sg.)) (poss. with the sb. **hafocere** 'a falconer, a hawker' rather than with its occupational surn. reflex, esp. when compounded with *medowe*, although the f.n. with *croft* may rather point to the latter); *Hawlandis*, *Hawlandys* 1467 × 84 (*v.* **haga**[1], **land**); *Hegh Strete* 1391 Banco (*v.* **hēah**[1], **strǣt**; this may refer to the continuation of the Roman road Margary 58a from the Fosse Way through Barrow upon Soar); *(le) Hogge* c.1474, 1481 (*v.* **hǫgg** 'a felling of trees; a part of a wood marked off for cutting'; at this period, described as a meadow); *Holborne* 1626, *le Overholborne*, *Overholborn* 1615 (*v.* **ofer**[3]) (*v.* **hol**[2], **burna**); *le Hold* 1275 Coram, *Holdhull* 1467 × 84 (*v.* **hyll**) (*v.* **hald**[1] 'shelter, refuge; a stronghold'); *Hollandys* 1391, *Holandes* 1477 (e.16) (*v.* **hol**[2], **land**); *Holme dyche* 1568 (*v.* **dīc**) (*v.* *Barroholme*, *supra*); *The Homestall* 1708 (18) (*v.* **hām-stall**; belonging to *the Vicarage House*); *Hothornhull*, *Huthornhil* 1477 (e.16), *Othornhull* 1467 × 84 (*v.* **hagu-þorn**, **hyll**); *Hunwell'* 1391, *Honwellhyll* 1467 × 84 (*v.* **hyll**) (*v.* **wella**; the first el. is either the OE pers.n. *Hūna* or **hūne** 'hoarhound'); *la Launde* 1312, 13, *Barolawnde* 1477 (e.16), *Bar(r)owlaunde* 1481 (*v.* **launde**); *Lentoncrofte* c.1474 (*v.* **croft**; in the tenure of *Thomas Lenton* c.1474), *Lenton Thing* 1585 (*v.* **thing**; property of the *Lenton* family, originally from the Notts. village of this name, 13 miles to the north); *Litileberwe* Hy 3, *Litleber'* a.1279, *Lytul baro* 1467 × 84, *Little Barrowe* 1651, *Lytelbaro slade* 1467 × 84, *little Barrowe slade* 1651 (*v.* **slæd**) (*v.* **lȳtel**, **lítill**, **berg**); *Litleclyff* c.1474, *Litelcliff alias Southcliff* 1481 (*v.* **lȳtel**, **clif** and *Southcliff*, *infra*); *Liteldoles* c.1474 (*v.* **lȳtel**, **dāl**); *Littelhagh* 1253 Lib, *Littelhawe* 13 AD bis, 1325 Banco (*v.* **lȳtel**, **haga**[1]); *Lokholm(e)* c.1474 bis, 1481 bis, *Lokholmeplassh* c.1474, 1481 (*v.* **plæsc**) (*v.* **loc, loca, holmr**); *Lokyngton thynge* c.1474 bis, 1481 bis (*v.* **thing**; property of the *Lockington* family, originally from the village of this name, 9 miles to the north-west); *Lymputes* 1396 Cor bis, *the Limepittes* 1651, *the Common Lyme Pitt(e)s* 1564, 1615 (*v.* **commun**), *Lymepitholes* c.1474, 1544, *Lymepittholes* 1481, 1564, *Lyme Pytt Holles* 1568, *Lyme Pitt Holes* 1615, *the Lymepitt hooles* 1651 (*v.* **hol**[1]) (*v.* **lyme-pytt**); *Merelond* c.1474, *Merelande* 1481 (*v.* **land**; either with **(ge)mǣre** or with **mere**[1] in its sense 'wetland'); *the Middle Feilde under the Towne called Bancrofte Feilde* 1651 (*v. Bancrofte*, *supra*); *Monkesbroke* c.1474, 1481 (*v.* **brōc**), *Monkesdam* 1588 (*v.* **damme**) (*v.* **munuc**; the manor was once the property of the Abbey of St Mary de Pratis, Leicester); *the mylne brynke* 16 *Rental*, *Millnebrincke* 1615 bis (*v.* **brink**), *Mil(l)ne close* 1564, 1615 (*v.* **clos(e)**), *le Milnescrofte* c.1474 (*v.* **croft**), *Mulnehul* 1477 (e.16), *le Milhill* 1587, *Myll Hill* 1626 (*v.* **hyll**) (*v.* **myln**; the 'mill hill' indicates a windmill here in addition to the waterside Barrow Mill *supra*); *Northwillodole* 1481 (*v.* **norð, wilig, dāl**); *le Norty* Hy 3 (*v.* **norð, tēag**); *Oldhull* 1467 × 84 bis, *Under Ouldhill* 1651 (*v.* **wald, hyll**; the first el. appears to represent an early instance of *wald* > *old*, which occurs more commonly in Leics. from the mid 16th cent.); *Oneclif* 1247 Ass (*v.* **ān, clif**); *le Orchard* c.1474 (*v.* **orceard**); *le Oxlesuwe in le Holme* 1456, *Oxlesew* c.1474, *Oxleysue* 1481, *Ox Leasue* 1568, 1585, *(le) Oxleasowe* 1615 bis (*v.* **oxa, lǣs (lǣswe** gen.sg., dat.sg.) and *Barroholme*, *supra*); *Philypwode*, *Phylypwode* 1477 (e.16), *Philipwode* 1481 (*v.* **wudu**; prob. with the surn. *Philip* rather than with the pers.n. from which it developed); *(le) Pole* c.1474, 1481 (*v.* **pōl**[1]); *Portegate* 1347 (*v.* **port**[2], **gata**; the market town to which this road led was presum. Mountsorrel, 2 miles to the south); *Rederodes* 1477 (e.16) (*v.* **rēad, rōd**[3]); *Ryecrofte medowe* 1381, 1391, *Ryecraft Meadowe* 1700 (*v.* **mǣd (mǣdwe** obl.sg.) and Ryecroft Fm *supra*); *Sanderyerdes* c.1474, *Saunderyerdes* 1481 (*v.* **geard**; with the surn. *Sander/Saunder* (from the pers.n. *Sander*, a pet form of Alexander)); *(the) Sandie Furlonge* 1651 (*v.* **sandig, furlang**); *Scortewellebrok* 1477 (e.16) (*v.* **sc(e)ort, wella, brōc**); *Seyntemariesedlond* 1477 (e.16), *St Maries headland* 1651 (*v.* **hēafod-land**; the manor was once held by the Abbey of St Mary de Pratis, Leicester); *the Slade Baulk* 1708 (18) (*v.* **slæd, balca**); *Small Acres* 1651 (*v.* **smæl, æcer**); *lez Smithleies* c.1474, *lez Smythleis* 1481 (*v.* **smið, lǣs**); *Smithisbuttes* 1477 (e.16) (*v.* **butte**; prob. with **smið** rather than with its surn. reflex *Smith*); *Southcliff* 1481, *Southclyffeild* 1560 (*v.* **feld**; one of the early great fields of the township) (*v.* **sūð, clif**); *South Willoes* c.1474, *South Willowes* 1481 (*v.* **sūð, wilig**); *Spencers Nooke or Drift Nooke* 1690 LAS (*v.* **nōk**; with the surn. *Spencer*, *v. Drift Nooke*, *supra*); *Stanford* 1477 (e.16), *Stanefordegate* 1467 × 84 (*v.* **gata**), *Stanford waie* 1651, ~ *way* 1708 (18) (*v.* **weg**) (*v.* **stān, ford** and *Stonyforth*, *infra*); *Stodwellewong* 1477 (e.16) (*v.* **stōd, wella, vangr**); *Stonyforth* c.1474, *Stonyford* 1481 (*v.* **stānig, ford**; presum. an alternative style for *Stanford*, *supra*); *Stonylandys* 1347 (*v.* **stānig, land**); *Strangcliffelde*, *Strangclyffeld* 1544 (*v.* **feld** and Strancliffe *supra*; one of the great fields of the township); *the Streetewaie* 1651 (*v.* **street-waie**; no doubt referring to the continuation of the Roman road Margary 58a from the Fosse Way into Barrow upon Soar); *Suthwude* 1242, *Suthwode* 1282 Banco, *le Southwode* c.1474, *Sowthewode* 1477 (e.16) (*v.* **sūð, wudu**); *Summer(e)stenement* 1426, 1432 (*v.* **tenement**; with the surn. *Summer*, prob. from OFr *somier* 'a sumpter', *v.* Reaney *s.n.*); *Titfordemere* 1467 × 84 (*v.* **tit, ford, mere**[1], cf. *Tythow*, Lei **2** 131); *attetounsende* 1467 × 84 (p) (*v.* **atte**), *the Townes ende* 1651 (*v.* **tūn, ende**); *Vtterhull* 1477 (e.16), *Outer hille* 1651 (*v.* **ūterra, hyll**); *Walkemylnenoke* c.1474, 1481 (*v.* **walke-milne, nōk**; this may be *ye Walkmill Nook* of adjoining Walton on the Wolds f.ns. (b)); *Walton Cunyngre* 1544, ~ *Coningrie* 1651 (*v.* **coningre**), *Walton had*(*e*)*s* 1651 (*v.* **hēafod**), *Walton mere* 1467 × 84 (*v.* **(ge)mǣre**) (Walton on the Wolds adjoins to the north-east); *atte Watere* 1269 Cur (p) (*v.* **atte, wæter**; presum. with reference to the river Soar); *le Waterfal* 1467 × 84 (*v.* **wæter-(ge)fall**); *the Waterthorrowes* 1651 (*v.* **wæter, furh** and *the Waterfurrow*(*e*)*s* in Asfordby f.ns. (b)); (*le*) *Weddermedow*(*e*) 1544 bis (*v.* **weðer, mǣd (mǣdwe** obl.sg.)); *Wellespringe*, ~ *Forlainge* 1651 (*v.* **furlang**) (*v.* **wella, spring**[1]); *Wyghtwere* 1313, (*le*) *Wyggewere* 1314, 1324, 1432, *Wygwere* 1560 bis, *Wigwere* 1564 bis, *Wigwore* 1568, *Wigwear* 1615 (*v.* **wiht, wer**; a weir or fishing-enclosure at a bend in the river Soar); *Wylinghaw*, *Wylynghaw* 1477 (e.16) (*v.* **haga**[1]; with **wiligen** or **wilign**); *le Wyluwe*(*s*) *doles* 1314, *le Weludoles*, *le Wyludoles* 1432 (*v.* **wilig, dāl**).

Beeby

BEEBY

Bebi 1086 DB, c.1125 Ord, 1199 GildR (p), 1316 Pap (p), 1327 SR, *Bebia* c.1130 LeicSurv
Beby 1209 × 19, 1220 RHug *et passim* to 1300 *LCDeeds* (p), 1302 *RTemple* (p) *et freq* to 1553 Pat, 1576 LibCl
Bebe 1518 Visit, 1527 LWills, 1536 ISLR, *Beybe* 1527 LWills
Beebie 1603 LibCl, 1610 Speed, *Beeby* 1620 LeicW *et freq*

'The village where bees are kept', *v.* **bēo, bȳ**. The forms clearly indicate that it is the OE word *bēo* rather than its ON cognate *bý* 'a bee' which constitutes the first element of the place-name as it has survived. The DB valuation of Beeby is high, equivalent to that of the important manor of Queniborough. It is probable that Beeby was an English settlement taken over and partly renamed by Scandinavians. Note also *hundredum de Bebia* c.1130 LeicSurv, which suggests that shortly after DB it had become an administrative centre of some kind and was thus a vill of significance.

ALL SAINTS' CHURCH, *the Church* 1708 (18) *Terrier*, *Church (All Saints)* 1846, 1863, 1877 White, 1925 Kelly; it is earlier recorded as *ecclesiam ~ ~*, *ecclesie de Beby* a.1219 RHug, 1220 MHW. Note also *the Church yard* 1605, 1674, 1708 (18) *Terrier*, 1839 *TA*, *v.* **chirche-ȝeard**. BARKBY RD, Barkby adjoins to the north. BEEBY HO., *Beeby house* 1835 O, 1925 Kelly. BEEBY SPRING, *v.* **spring**[1]. BEEBY SPRING GRANGE, *The Grange* 1863 White, 1925 Kelly, *v.* **grange**. BREWERY COTTAGES. CROXTON RD, South Croxton adjoins to the north-east. HOME FM, *v.* **home**. HUNGARTON LANE is *hungarton gate* 1601 *Terrier*, *hungerton ~* 1605 *ib*, *v.* **gata**; Hungarton adjoins to the east. KEYHAM LANE is *keame gate* 1601, 1605 *Terrier*, *v.* **gata**; Keyham adjoins to the south-east. LITTLE BEEBY is the name given to a mid 17th cent. timber-framed farmhouse, one of a number of scattered dwellings that remain of the shrunken medieval village. THE LODGE (lost), *The Lodge* 1863 White, *v.* **loge**. MAIN ST. MANOR FM, *Manor farm* 1925 Kelly, MANOR HO., *Manor*

House 1846, 1863, 1877 White, 1925 Kelly, *v.* **maner**. THE RECTORY, 1877 White, 1925 Kelly, *v.* **rectory**; cf. *the Parsonage Howse* 1605 *Terrier*, ~ ~ *house* 1674, e.18, 1708 (18) *ib*, 1839 *TA*, *v.* **personage**. SCRAPTOFT LANE, Scraptoft adjoins to the south-west. SPRING GRANGE, *v.* **spring**[1], **grange**. STEPPING STONES FORD (2½"), *v.* **stepping-stone**. WHITE HOUSE FM.

FIELD-NAMES

Undated forms in (a) are 1839 *TA*. Forms throughout dated 1601, 1605, 1674 and 1708 (18) are *Terrier*.

(a) The Acre (cf. *the acre hades* 1601, 1605, *v.* **hēafod**), The Three Acres, Three Acre Mdw, (The) Four Acres, Top Five ~, (The) Eight ~ (x2), The Fourteen Acres (*v.* **æcer**); Banks (*v.* **banke**); Lower ~ ~, Upper ~ ~, New ~ ~, Old ~ ~, Barn Cl, Top end ~ ~ ~, Behind the Barn; Bottom ~ ~, Top Baileys Cl (with the surn. *Bailey*); Bartons Cl, Bartons Mdw (with the surn. *Barton*); Best Cl (*v.* **best**; a complimentary name for very fertile land); Boarden Bridge Mdw (*v.* **borden**); Bottom Mdw (*v.* Bottom Meadow Watering *infra*); Little ~, Bridewell (a poss. instance of a 'brides' spring', a name prob. denoting a fertility spring, *v.* **brȳd, wella**, cf. Bridewell (W 150) and Bridwell (D 537); but earlier forms are needed); Bridle Gate Cl (*v.* **brigdels, gata**); Brook Mdw, ~ ~ Bottom (*v.* **botm**); Bottom ~ ~, Burn Thorn, Burn Thorn Mdw, Big Burn Thorn Hill (*v.* **þorn**; these fields lie beside a small watercourse, so it is poss. that **burna** 'a stream' is present here; otherwise reference may be to a place cleared by burning (as OE **bryne** or ON **bruni**); perh. cf. *Burnelandez* Lei **2** 38, *byrnelandys* Lei **2** 27, *le Burnhassokis* Lei **2** 235); Bush Cl (*v.* **busc**); Calf Cl (*v.* **calf**); Middle ~, Top Clayton, Top Clayton's Cl, Claytons Platt (*v.* **plat**) (with the surn. *Clayton*); Clover Cl (*v.* **clāfre**; used as a fodder crop); Nether ~ ~, Upper Coopers Cl (with the surn. *Cooper*); Corn Cl (*v.* **corn**[1]); Cow Cl, ~ ~ Mdw; Digby's Bit (*v.* **bit**; with the surn. *Digby* of a family originally from Digby, 35 miles to the north-east in Lincs.); Dumble (*v.* **dumbel**; here, a deep shady dell); Far Cl; Far Leys (*v.* **leys**); Far Mdw; First Cl; Foot Road Cl (*v.* **foot-road**); Franks Acre (*v.* **æcer**; prob. with the surn. *Frank*, often from OFr, ME *franc* 'free', i.e. not a serf, *v.* Reaney *s.n.*); Garth (*v.* **garðr**); Great ~ ~, Little ~ ~, George Cl (with the surn. *George*); Gorse Cl (*v.* **gorst**); Gravel Pit Cl (*v.* **gravel, pytt** and *foxe grauel* in f.ns. (b)); Great Cl; Great Mdw; Hall Cl (*the hall(e) closse* 1601, 1605, *the hall close* 1605, *v.* **clos(e)**), Hall Yards (*v.* **geard**) (*v.* **hall**); Bottom ~ ~, Highway Cl (*v.* **hēah-weg**); Far ~ ~, Near Hirst Croft (*v.* **hyrst, croft**); Bottom ~, Middle ~, Top Holdel, Far ~, First Holdel, Foot Road Holdel (*v.* **foot-road**) (*hodal(l)* 1601, 1605, *hodall feild* 1601, 1605 (*v.* **feld**; one of the great fields of the township) (*v.* **hol**[2], **deill**); Holland Dale (*v.* Holland Dale in adjoining Hungarton f.ns. (a)); Great Holt, Lower ~ ~, Upper Clayton Holt (with the surn. *Clayton*), Holt Cl (cf. *the olt close of Bryan Winbye* 1601), Holt Mdw (adjoining Barkby Holt *q.v.*); Home Cl, ~ ~ Bottom (*v.* **botm**) (*v.* **home**); The Homestead, Little ~, Homestead (*v.* **hām-stede**); Hooks, ~ Bottom (*v.* **botm**) (*v.* **hōc**); Horse Cl; House Cl; Far ~ ~, Judds Cl (with the surn.

Judd); Keyham Cl, Big ~ ~, Nether Keyham Gate (*v.* **gata**) (Keyham adjoins to the south-east); Lane end Cl (*v.* **lane-ende**); Leesons Home Cl (*v.* **home**), Leesons Platts (*v.* **plat**) (with the surn. *Leeson*); Little Mdw; Long Leys (*v.* **leys**); Long Mdw; (The) Middle Cl; Middle Leys (*v.* **leys**); Near Cl; New Planting (*v.* **planting**); Pages Cl (with the surn. *Page*); Pingle (*v.* **pingel**); Plantation Pond (*v.* **plantation**); Plough Cl (*v.* **plōg**); Bottom ~ ~, Lower ~ ~, Upper ~ ~, Ploughed Cl, New Ploughed Cl; Ploughed Fd; Ram Cl (*v.* **ramm**); Road, ~ Cl, Road Piece (*v.* **pece**) (enclosures adjoining a road); Rough Cl (*v.* **rūh**[1]); Scots Cl, Scotts Mdw (with the surn. *Scott*); Screatons Cl (with the surn. *Screaton* of a family originally from Screveton, 22 miles to the north-east in Notts. (forms in *Screton* from the early 14th cent., *v.* Nt 229)); Smithill (*v.* **hyll**; either with the surn. *Smith* or with **smið**); Western ~ ~, South Brook, ~ ~ Mdw, ~ ~ Spinney (*Sowbroke* 1601, 1605, *Sowbrooke* 1601, *v.* **sūð**, **brōc**); The Spinney Cl, Spinney Mdw (*v.* **spinney**); Spring Cl (*v.* **spring**[1]); Stack Yard (*v.* **stak-ȝeard**); Stensons Cl, Stensons Mdw (with the surn. *Stenson*); Sugar Cl, Bottom ~ ~, Top ~ ~, Sugar Hill (complimentary names for 'sweet' land); Upper ~ ~, Tags Hill (*v.* **tagga**); Town(s) End (*v.* **tūn**, **ende**); Bottom Meadow Watering, Plantation Watering (*v.* **plantation**) (*v.* **wateryng**); Websters Mdw (with the surn. *Webster*); The Far West Mdw (cf. *the west medowe* 1601, 1605, *v.* **mǣd** (**mǣdwe** obl.sg.)); Workhouse Orchard (*v.* **workhouse**; an orchard beside, or belonging to, a Poor Law institution).

(b) *the acres* 1601, 1605 (*v.* **æcer**); *beby fylde* Hy 7 *Terrier* (*v.* **feld**); *Betwe(e)ne the gates* 1601, 1605 (*v.* **betwēonan**, **gata**; a furlong so called); *Bruntes* 1601, 1605 (*v.* **brend**); *Brymble feild* 1601, 1605 (*v.* **brēmel**, **feld**; one of the early great fields); *Byall feild* 1601 (*v.* **feld**; earlier forms are needed for *Byall*, but prob. **bī** with **halh** in origin; one of the early great fields, called *Hambleton feild* in 1605, that is, the field adjoining Hamilton); *the Church hadlande* 1605 (*v.* **hēafod-land** and All Saints' Church *supra*); *the common pasture* 1605 (*v.* **commun**, **pasture**); *the Earl of Shaftesbury's ground* 1708 (18) (*v.* **grund**); *Foxe grauel(l)* 1601, 1605 (*v.* **fox**, **gravel**; presum. a gravel bank where foxes dug their lairs); *fussull* 1601, *Fussle* 1605 (*v.* **fyrs**, **hyll**); *the Glebe Closes* 1708 (18) (*v.* **glebe**); *Thomas Goddards close* 1601; *in the grayne* 1601, 1605 (a furlong so called), *graynwell* 1601, 1605 (*v.* **wella**) (*v.* **grein**); *the hall layes* 1605 (*v.* **hall**, **leys**); *Hambleton feild* 1605 (*v. Byall feild*, *supra*); *the Homestall* 1605 (*v.* **hām-stall**; belonging to *the Parsonage Howse*, *v.* The Rectory *supra*); *hoobarrow* 1601, 1605 (*v.* **hōh**, **berg**); *the ingate* 1601, 1605 (*v.* **in**, **gata**); *Ingle sicke* 1605 (*v.* **sík**; prob. with the surn. *Ingle*, the reflex of a Scand pers.n. such as ON *Ingulfr* (ODan *Ingulf*) or ON *Ingjaldr* (ODan *Ingeld*), *v.* Reaney *s.n.*); *lankeley* 1601, *lankley* 1605 (*v.* **lang**[1], **lēah**); (*in*) *litle dale* 1601, *lytle dale* 1605 (*v.* **lȳtel**, **lítill**, **dalr**); *the lytle feild* 1601, 1605 (*v.* **lȳtel**, **feld**); *marlpitt* 1601, *Marlepitte* 1605 (*v.* **marle-pytt**); *martley* 1601, *Markley* 1605 (*v.* **mearð**, **lēah**, cf. Martley, Wo 62; the local area must have been a good habitat for the marten or weasel, since Belgrave (whose pre-Norman name was also compounded with *mearð*) is only 4 miles to the west); *the meere* 1605 (*v.* **(ge)mǣre**); *the mylne* 1601 (*v.* **myln**); *the Parsonage closes* 1674 (*v.* **personage**); *parson crafte hades* 1601, ~ *croft* ~ 1605 (*v.* **persone**, **croft**, **hēafod**); *port sicke* 1601, 1605 (*v.* **sík**; the first word is problematical, poss. **port**[2], perh. with reference to an outlying possession of the townspeople of Leicester, or to a market site of some sort; or else it is the surn. *Port* (*v.* Reaney *s.n.*), since f.ns. in *sík* are freq. compounded with a surn.); *raddells* 1601, *Raddels* 1605 (*v.* **rēad**, **deill**); *rowdal* 1601, *roudalles* 1605 (*v.* **rūh**[1], **deill**); *royley* *close* 1605 (*v.* **clos(e)**; in the tenure of *Richard Royley* 1605); *the sheephosse* 1601, *the shipe hosse* 1605 (*v.* **scēp-hūs**); *stony landes* 1605 (*v.* **stānig, land**); *thorow hilles* 1601, 1605 (*v.* **furh, hyll**); *the towne hadland* 1601 (*v.* **tūn, hēafod-land**); *wattes sicke* 1601, 1605 (*v.* **sík**; with the surn. *Watt*(*s*)); *Weston feild* 1601, 1605 (*v.* **feld**; one of the great fields of the township, lying to its south-east; evidently with the name of a lost settlement *Weston* (*v.* **west, tūn**), presum 'west' in relation to Hungarton); *wheteland gate* 1601, 1605 (*v.* **hwǣte, land, gata**).

Belgrave

BELGRAVE

Belgrave is now part of the Borough of Leicester.

Merdegrave 1086 DB (x2), *Merdegraue* 1086 ib
Merthegrava (*quæ nunc alio nomine Belegrava dicitur*) s.a. 1081 (c.1130) Ord
Mardegraue c.1130 LeicSurv
Belegraua, -grava s.a. 1081 (c.1130) Ord, 1191, 1192 P *et freq* to 1201, 1202 ib *et passim* to 1267 *LCDeeds* (p), l.13 *RTemple*, *Belegraue, -grave* 1185 P (p), a.1186 Dane, 1186 P (p) *et passim* to 1200, 1201 ib *et freq* to 1333 *MiD*, 1352 *LCDeeds* (p) *et passim* to 1368 *ib* (p), 1442 *RTemple*
Bellagrave 1199 Cur (p), 1252 GildR (p), *Bellagraua, -grava* 1205 ChancR (p), 1211 P (p), 1265 GildR (p), *Bella Grava* 1234 Ch (p), *Bellegraue, -grave* 1205 P (p), c.1240 AD, 1308 Pap (p), 1311 GildR (p)
Belgraue, -grave 1205 P, 1227 RHug *et passim* to 1343 *RTemple*, 1344 *MiD et freq*

Originally 'the small wood or grove frequented by marten, weasel', *v.* **mearð, grāf**. Such AN forms as *Merdegrave* became associated with OFr *merde* 'excrement, filth' so that, presumably in the early 12th century, the name of the manor was deliberately altered to *Belegrave* with OFr *bel* 'beautiful' as the new specific, *v.* **bel**[2]. The early form *Marthegrevegate* a.1183 (l.14) *Beau* 'the road to *Merdegrave*' (*v.* **gata**), a minor name recorded for Wymeswold parish, refers to the Fosse Way.

ABBEY LANE, 1657 *Map*, *v.* **abbaye, lane**; leading to the Abbey of St Mary de Pratis, *v.* Lei **1** 90. BELGRAVE HALL, completed 1713; an earlier hall is recorded as *þe halle* 1477 (e.16) *Charyte*, *le Hall* 1621 Ipm, *Belgrave Hall* 1657 *Surv*, *v.* **hall**. BELGRAVE LOCK, *v.* **lock**. BELGRAVE MILL (lost), *molendinum de Belgraue* 1477 (e.16) *Charyte* (with MLat *molendinum* 'a mill'), *Belegrave mylne* 1621 Ipm, *the mylne* 1621 *Deed*,

Belgrave Mill c.1660 HP, 1863 White, cf. *Belgrave Mill house* 1845 *TA*, *v.* **myln**. BERRIDGE LANE, cf. *Berridge his land* 1657 *Map* (held by *Henry Berridge* 1657 *Surv*), *v.* **land**. BRICKLAYERS' ARMS (P.H.) (lost), *The Bricklayers Arms Public House* 1845 *TA*. BULL'S HEAD (P.H.) (lost), *The Bulls Head Public House* 1845 *TA*, *Bulls Head* 1846, 1877 White. CHAMPION INN (P.H.) (lost), *The Champion Public House* 1845 *TA*, *Champion Inn* 1877 White. CHECKETTS CLOSE, 1845 *TA*, cf. *Checkitts Paddock* 1845 *ib* (*v.* **paddock**), CHECKETTS RD; with the surn. *Checkett*. CLOWES ARMS (P.H.) (lost), *Clowes Arms* 1877 White. DEVON FM. EDENHURST. GIPSY LANE, *v.* **gipsy**; a former venue for itinerants. THE GRANGE (lost), *The Grange* 1877 White, *v.* **grange**. LORD LYON (P.H.) (lost), *Lord Lyon* 1877 White. MELTON BROOK. METHODIST CHAPEL, 1845 *TA*. NELSON (P.H.) (lost), *The Nelson Public House* 1845 *TA*, *Nelson* 1863 White. NEW BRIDGE. NEW INN (P.H.) (lost), *The New Inn Public House* 1845 *TA*, *New Inn* 1877 White. NEW LODGE FM. OLD BRIDGE, cf. *pontem de Belgrave* 1357 Works (with MLat *pons* (*pontem* acc.sg.) 'a bridge'), *Belgrave Bridge* 1709, 1730, 1751, 1772 ChAccts. RED HOUSE FM (lost), *The Red house farm* 1845 *TA*. RUSHEY FIELDS (RUSHEY FM 2½"), cf. *Rushey Meadow* 1743 *Deed*, 1784 *Surv*, *Rushy ~* 1845 *TA*, *v.* **riscig**. ST PETER'S CHURCH, *Church (St Peter)* 1846, 1863, 1877 White, 1925 Kelly; it is earlier recorded as *ecclesiam ~ ~, ecclesie de Belegraue* 1220 MHW, 1227 *Pat*, 1238 RGros *et passim* to 1338 *Pat*, *ecclesie de Belgrave* 1344, 1358 *ib et passim* to 1404 *ib*, *St Peters Church* 1657 *Map*. Note also *The Church Yard* c.1700, 1708 (18) *Terrier*. TALBOT INN (P.H.) (lost), (*The*) *Talbot Inn* 1845 *TA*, 1846, 1877 White. TOLL GATE HO. (lost), *Toll Gate house* 1845 *TA*, *v.* **toll-gate**. THE VICARAGE, 1877 White, *the Vicarage house* 1845 *TA*, *v.* **vikerage**; cf. *the Parsonage house* 1625 *Terrier*, 1650 Surv, *v.* **personage**. VICARAGE LANE.

No early forms have been noted for the following Belgrave street-names: ACORN ST, AGAR ST, ANCHOR ST, ANTLIFFE ST, ARBOUR RD, ARDATH RD, ARGYLE ST, ASCOT RD, BARKBY RD, BARDOLPH ST, BATH ST, BELGRAVE AVE, BELPER ST, BERKLEY ST, BRANDON ST, BRUN ST, BURFIELD ST, CANON ST, CATHERINE ST, CLARKE ST, CORPORATION ST, COSSINGTON ST, CRANBOURNE ST, DEAN RD, DONCASTER RD, DORSET ST, DOWN ST, DRUMMOND RD, ELLIS AVE, EPSOM RD, FINSBURY RD, FLAX RD, FLETCHER ST, GIPSY RD, GLEN ST, GLENCOE AVE, GLENDON ST, GLENEAGLES AVE, GLENMORE RD, GRESHAM ST, HALKIN ST, HARDY'S AVE, HARRINGTON ST, HARRISON RD, HIGHBURY RD, HOBSON RD, HOLDEN ST, JERMYN ST, KERRYSDALE AVE, LANCASHIRE ST, LEIRE

ST, LEXHAM ST, LINFORD ST, LOCKERBIE AVE, LOUGHBOROUGH RD, MARFITT ST, MARTIN ST, MELROSE ST, MELTON AVE, MELTON RD, MOIRA ST, NEWINGTON ST, OAKLAND AVE, OLIVER RD, ORTON RD, PAULINE AVE, PAYNE ST, PENRITH RD, PORTMAN ST, PORTSMOUTH RD, PUNSHON ST, PURLEY RD, QUENIBOROUGH RD, READING ST, REDCAR RD, RENDELL RD, ROBERT HALL ST, ROSE ST, ROSENEATH AVE, ROSEWAY, ROTHERBY AVE, ROYAL RD, ST BERNARD ST, SALTCOATS AVE, SANDRINGHAM AVE, SCARBOROUGH RD, SHAFTESBURY AVE, SHETLAND RD, SHIRLEY ST, SPURGEON RD, STAFFORD ST, STRATHMORE AVE, SURREY ST, SUTTON AVE, THURCASTON RD, TIVERTON AVE, ULVERSCROFT RD, VANN ST, VICTORIA RD, VIOLET ST, WATSON RD, WAVERTREE AVE, WESLEY ST, WEYMOUTH ST, WINDSOR AVE, WOODBINE ST, WOODBRIDGE RD, WYVERN AVE, YORKSHIRE RD.

It is uncertain whether the following street-names are directly related to the cited f.ns. or are the result of local government's road-name creation via archive material: FLAX RD (cf. *Flax Leys* 1845), ORTON RD (cf *Ortons Cl*, *Ortons Mdws*, *Ortons Willows* 1845). For these, *v*. f.ns. (a) *infra*.

FIELD-NAMES

Forms in (a) dated 1751, 1772, 1793 and 1835 are ChAccts; 1758, 1763, 1769, 1776, 1781 and 1814 are *Deed*; 1784 are *Surv*; 1845 are *TA*. Forms throughout dated 1327 and 1332 are SR; 1399, 1609, 1621, 1624 and 1628 are Ipm; 1446 and 1447 are Banco; 1477 (e.16) are *Charyte*; 1467 × 84 are *LTD*; 1625, 1658 and 1708 (18) are *Terrier*; 1635, 1675, 1687, 1688, 1689, 1696, l.17, 1709, 1710, 1724, 1731 and 1743 are *Deed*; 1650 are Surv; 1657 are *Map*; 1662 are Nichols; 1730 are ChAccts.

(a) Abbey Lane Cl 1769, 1784 (*v*. Abbey Lane *supra*); Abbey Mdw 1835 O (adjoining the Abbey of St Mary de Pratis, Leicester); Adcocks First ~, Adcocks Second Cl, Adcocks Great Cl, Adcocks Mdw 1845 (with the surn. *Adcock*); Back Water 1845 (*v*. **backwater**; land beside a backwater of the river Soar); Bannel 1784, The Bannells 1845 (*Bannells* 1657), Bannells Cl or Foxholes 1776 (*v*. Foxholes *infra*), Bannell Mdw 1845 (*v*. **bēan**, **hyll**); Barn Cls 1784, The Barn Cl, Second ~ ~, Third Barn Cl 1845; (The) Barn Mdw 1845; The Barn Orchard 1845; Belgrave Meer 1863 White (*v*. **(ge)mǣre**); Belgrave Pasture 1845 (*v*. **pasture**); Belholme 1814 (*Bellholme* 1657, 1709, *v*. **belle**, **holmr**); Bentleys Orchard 1845 (with the surn. *Bentley*); Berridges Cl 1784, 1845 (*v*. Berridge Lane *supra*); the Bishops Yard 1784 (*v*. **geard** and Walled Paddock *infra*; with reference to the Bishop of Lincoln who possessed much land around Belgrave Gate); Bottles Orchard 1845 (with the surn.

Bottle); Bottom Fd 1845; Bottom Mdw 1845; 3 Bowers 1784, First ~, Second ~, Third Bowers 1845 (cf. *Bow(w)ood Field* 1657, 1688, 1696 (*v*. **feld**; poss. one of the early great fields of the township), *Bow(w)ood Leys* 1688, 1696 (*v*. **leys**), *v*. **boga, wudu**); Bradley Mdw 1845, Bradleys Cl 1845 (with the surn. *Bradley*); Bratlands 1784 (*Bretlands* 1657), Bretlands Cl or Leys now New Barklands and Far Barklands 1776 (*v*. **leys**) (*Bratland Close* 1635, *the Brackland close* 1650) (*v*. **breiðr**, **land**; with attraction to **bræc**[1] and late metathesis); Bridge Cl 1776, Belgrave Bridge Cl 1793 ChAccts, 1801 HB, 1814, 1835 ((*le*) *Bridge close* 1621, 1657, *v*. Old Bridge *supra* and Cow Cl *infra*); Bridge Leys 1769, 1784, 1845, ~ ~ Mdw 1845 (*Bridg Layes* 1657, *v*. **leys**); Brook Mdw 1845 (*v*. Melton Brook *supra*); Bull Piece 1784, 1845 (*the Bull Piece* 1710, *v*. **bula, pece**); Callis's Fd 1845 (with the surn. *Callis*, *v*. Reaney *s.n.*); Camp Cl 1764 *EnclA*, 1769, 1784, 1845 (*v*. **camp**; this seems to be a survival of *camp* in its early sense 'open land', a borrowing by the Anglo-Saxons of Lat *campus*, which for the RB inhabitants of the area would have described stretches of uncultivated open country in the northern vicinity of the Roman town of *Ratae Corieltavorum* (Leicester); the later use of the word as a term for a military encampment is unlikely in this f.n., since no record of such an earthwork in Belgrave occurs and the location's proximity to a major Roman walled town effectively negates the former existence of such a fortified site; the early presence of English speakers here who would have adopted the Latin word is confirmed by the large pagan Anglo-Saxon cremation cemetery at adjacent Thurmaston); Carters Hill Cl 1784, 1845, Carters Mdw 1784, 1845 (with the surn. *Carter*, cf. *Carters house* 1609, 1628); Cartwright's Mead 1784 (*v*. **mǣd**; with the surn. *Cartwright*); Chadwick Cl 1845 (with the surn. *Chadwick*); Church Mdw 1845 (*v*. St Peter's Church *supra*); Clay Lands 1784 (*Clelands* 1625, *Cley-lands* 1657, *Cleyland field* 1650, *v*. **clǣg, land** and *Johnsons Plot* in f.ns. (b)); The Clover Cl 1845 (*v*. **clāfre**; used as a fodder crop); Coney Cl 1769 (cf. *Conebalk* 1467 × 84 (*v*. **balca**), *v*. **coni** and Home Cl *infra*); Coopers Cl 1845 (with the surn. *Cooper*); Cow Cl or Bridge Cl 1776, (the) Cow Cl 1784, 1845 (*v*. Bridge Cl *supra*); Cow Gate 1776, 1784, 1845 (*Cowgate* 1467 × 84, cf. *Cougatewonge* 1399 (*v*. **vangr**); prob. 'the cow road' with **cū, gata** rather than the later **cowgate** 'pasture for a single cow'); Cranes Nest 1784, 1845 (*v*. **cran, nest**); (The) Cunnery 1784, 1845 (*the Cunnyngre* 1467 × 84, *the Cunnery* 1625, *the Connery* 1650, cf. *Connery leas* 1650 (*v*. **leys**), *v*. **coningre**); Davies Two Cls 1784 (the property of *Mr Davie* 1784); Davis Cl 1784, 1814, Davis's ~ 1845, Davis's Mdw 1845 (prob. containing the surn. *Davie* of the previous name; otherwise *Davis*); The Dead Hole 1845 (*v*. **dēad, hol**[1]; often in f.ns., *dead* is used with reference to the site of a violent death or to the discovery of human bones, but on occasion may allude to infertile land); East Mdw 1784, 1845 (1635, 1657, 1675, 1.17, 1743, *le estmedowe* 1467 × 84, *the East Medow* 1625, ~ ~ *Meadow* 1658, *the east Medow dich* 1625 (*v*. **dīc**), *East medow Leas* 1625 (*v*. **leys**), *the East Medow slade* 1625 (*v*. **slæd**)), East Meadow Bushes 1845 (1657, 1675, *East Medow bushes* 1625, *v*. **busc**) (*v*. **ēast, mǣd (mǣdwe** obl.sg.)); The Elms 1845 (*v*. **elm**; a pasture so called); Elms and Wytches 1784 (*v*. **elm, wice**; land where wych-elms grew); Flax Leys 1769, 1784, 1845 (*the flax leaes* 1625, *Flax Layes* 1657, *v*. **fleax, leys**); Folley hill 1877 White (*v*. **folie**); Forty Rood 1784, ~ Roods 1845 (cf. *The 40 rood piece* 1635 (*v*. **pece**), *Forty Rood Meadow* 1657, *the Forty Rood Close* 1687, *v*. **rōd**[3]); Foxholes 1776 (*v*. **fox-hol**); The Garden Cl 1845 (*v*. **gardin**); Glebe Cl 1784, 1845 (*v*. **glebe**); Goodes Mdw 1845 (with the surn. *Goode*); The Gorsey Mdw 1845 (*v*. **gorstig**);

(The) Great Cl 1784, 1845; Grundy's Cl 1776 (with the surn. *Grundy*, *v.* Reaney *s.n.*); Haffords Orchard (sic) 1845, Halfords Cls 1784 (with the surn. *Halford*); Hagars Cl 1784 (with the surn. *Hager*, *v.* Reaney *s.n.*); Hall Mdw 1784, 1845 (1635, 1650, 1657, 1662, *the hall medow* 1625, *Great Hall Meadow* 1731, *v.* Belgrave Hall *supra*); The Hays 1763, 1767, 1845, Crab Hays 1845 (*v.* **crabbe**), Glovers Hays 1784 (held by *Mr Glover* 1784), Great Hays 1758 (*Great Hayes* 1657, cf. *Little Hayes* 1657), Hawley Hays 1784, Hauling ~ 1845 (with the surn. *Hawley*), Wards Hays 1845 (with the surn. *Ward*) (*v.* **(ge)hæg**); Headland Cls 1784 (cf. *the Church Hadland* 1625, *Church Headland* 1657, *Churchhadlandfield* 1662, *Church Headland Field* 1689, *Hadland field* 1650, *Headland Field Closes* 1709 (*v.* **feld**), *v.* **hēafod-land**); (The) Hill Cl 1784, 1845 (*Hill Close* 1657, *v.* **hyll**); Hills Two Cls 1784, First ~ ~, Second Hills Cl 1845 (either with the surn. *Hill* in the possessive case or **hyll**); Holme Cl 1814 (cf. *The Holmes* 1743, *v.* **holmr**); Home Cl formerly Coney Cl 1769, Home Cl 1784 (*v.* **home** and Coney Cl *supra*); Homesteads 1718 (*v.* **hām-stede**); Hopkins Mdw 1845 (with the surn. *Hopkin*(*s*)); Hopp Yard 1781, Hopyard 1784, The Hop Yard 1845 (*v.* **hop-yard**); Horse Cl 1845; (The) Hospital Cl 1845 (*v.* **hospital**; referring to the Hospital of St John, Leicester (*v.* Lei **1** 93–4 and 88) whose *Spittle house* 1741 *Plan* lay beside Belgrave Gate); House Cls 1784, ~ Cl 1845; Hovel Mdw 1784, 1845 (*v.* **hovel**); Iliffe's Penn 1784 (*v.* **penn**[2]; the property of *Mr Iliffe* 1784); Intake 1845 (*v.* **inntak**); The Island 1845 (*v.* **island**; a piece of ground completely enclosed by others); Kempe's Yard 1776 (*v.* **geard**; with the surn. *Kempe*); Kimpton Hill Leys 1751 ChAccts, Knipton Hill Leys 1772, 1793, 1814, 1835 ib, ~ ~ Leas 1801 HB (*Kimpton Hill Leys* 1730 ChAccts (*v.* **leys**), *Kympton Hill* 1589 Charter, 1591 MiscAccts, *Kymton* ~ 1595 Rental, *Kimpton* ~ 1689 ChAccts; with the surn. *Kimpton*, *v.* Reaney *s.n.*, the later spellings having been attracted to the Leics. village-name Knipton, *v.* Lei **2** 14); Kings Mdw 1845 (cf. *Kings Croft Close* 1688 (*v.* **croft**), *Kings Croft Nooke* 1687 (*v.* **nōk**); with the surn. *King*); Kinnes Mdw 1784 (cf. *Katharine Kinnes* d. 1680 and *Charles Kinnes* d. 1723; from parish church monuments); Kinseys Mdw 1845 (with the surn. *Kinsey*); Two Lings 1784, The Great ~, The Little Lings 1845, Lewins Lings 1784, First ~ ~, Second Lewins Lings 1845 (with the surn. *Lewin*) (*The Lings* 1657, 1743, cf. *Lyngbreche* 1467 × 84 (*v.* **brēc**), *v.* **lyng**); Little Cl 1845 (1624); (the) Little Mdw 1784, 1845 (1621, 1650, 1657, *the little Medow* 1625); the Little Mere 1845 (*v.* **(ge)mǣre**); the Little Wong 1845 (*v.* **vangr**); The Lodge Barn 1835 O (*v.* **loge**); (the) Long Cl 1769, 1784, 1845 (1657, 1675, cf. *Long close bridge* 1621); Long Mdw 1784, 1845; Lowdhams Cl 1784 (in the possession of *Mr Lowdham* in 1784, whose family came originally from Lowdham, 25 miles to the north in Notts.); The Meadows 1845; High Mears 1784, The Bottom ~ ~, The Top High Mere 1845, Adcocks ~ ~, Scamptons High Mere 1845 (with the surns. *Adcock* and *Scampton* (of a family originally from Scampton, some 40 miles to the north-east along the Fosse Way in Lincs.)) (*Hye mere* 1467 × 84, *High Mear alias Above Meadow* 1743, *v.* **hēah**[1], **(ge)mǣre** and *Above Meadow* in f.ns. (b)); Middle Cl 1845; Mill Dam 1845 (*v.* **damme**), Mill Hill or Camp Cl 1769 (*the Milne hill* 1625, *Mill Hill* 1657, cf. *Mill hill field* 1650, *v.* Camp Cl *supra*), Mill Holme 1784 (*Mill Home* 1657, *v.* **holmr**), Mill Mdw 1784, 1769, 1845 (*v.* **myln**; both a watermill and a windmill are indicated); (The) Millers Holme 1845 (*v.* **mylnere, holmr**; prob. a later style for Mill Holme *supra*); Moor furlong 1784, First ~ ~, Second ~ ~, Third moor furlong 1845 (*Morfurlong'* 1467 × 84, *Moor*(*e*) *furlong* 1650, 1657, l.17, *Moor furlond* (sic) 1743, *v.* **furlang**), Moore Mdw 1784, (The)

Moor Mdw 1814, 1845 (*Moremedow* 1467 × 84, *Moor(e) Meadow* 1657, *v.* **mǣd (mǣdwe** obl.sg.)) (*v.* **mōr**[1]); Mow Macre Hill 1835 O, 1877 White, Momeacre Hill Cl 1845 (*Momeacre Hill* 1657, *Momacre* ~ 1687, 1688 (*v.* **malm, æcer**); Needhams Cl 1784, Nedhams ~ 1845 (with the surn. *Needham*); The New Fd 1845; Oldershaws Cls 1784, Great ~, Little Oldershaw 1845 (with the surn. *Oldershaw*, *v.* Reaney *s.n.*); Old Womans Cl 1845 (land assigned for a widow's or a dowager's benefit, *v.* Field 167); The Orchard 1845; Ortons Cl 1769, 1784, 1845, Ortons Mdw 1845, Ortons Willows 1784, 1845 (*v.* **wilig**), Ortons Yard 1784 (*v.* **geard**) (with the surn. *Orton*); (The) Paddock 1784, 1845 (*v.* **paddock**); Peaches Cl 1845 (cf. *John Peach* 1767); Peakes Cl 1845 (with the surn. *Peak(e)*); Pinfold Cl 1758, 1784, 1845 (*le Pynfould close* 1621, *v.* **pynd-fald**); The Pingle 1814, 1845 (*v.* **pingel**); Reed Bed 1845 (*v.* **hrēod, bedd**); Red Hill Cl 1784 (*Red Hill* 1688, *Redhill Close* 1731, cf. *Red Hill Foot* 1657 (*v.* **fōt**), *v.* **rēad, hyll**); Scampton leases 1784 (*v.* **lǣs (lǣswe** gen.sg., dat.sg.); for the surn. Scampton, *v.* Scamptons High Mere *supra*); Shepherds nook 1845 (*v.* **nōk**; either with the surn. *Shepherd* or with **scēp-hirde**); Shipleys Cl 1784, Shipleys Mdw 1784 (with the surn. *Shipley*); Side Cl 1845 (*v.* **sīde**); Simpkins Cl 1845 (with the surn. *Simpkin(s)*); Sopers Cl 1784 (this f.n. may contain the surn. *Soper* or the late reflex of its source **sāpere** 'a soap maker', *v.* the following f.n.); The Soap House Cl 1845 (this may be a phonetic development of the previous f.n. or may refer literally to the local manufacture of soap; *v.* Field 87 for other f.ns. with Soaphouse and discussion of parochial soap-making); Staples Cl 1784, 1845 (with the surn. *Staple(s)*); Stubble Cl 1784, 1845 (land on which stubble after harvesting was allowed to remain for an abnormally long time); Swains Mdw 1784, Swains East ~ 1845 (with the surn. *Swain*); Three Cornered Cl 1845 (*v.* **three-cornered**); Thurmaston Hill 1784, 1845 (1625, l.17, 1743, *montem de Thurmaston* 1467 × 84 (with MLat *mons* (*montem* acc.sg.) 'a hill')), Thurmaston Hill Cl 1845, Thurmaston Hill Fd 1845 (Thurmaston adjoins to the north-east); Tillage Land 1784, Top Tillage 1845, the Little Tillage Cl 1845 (*v.* **tillage**; referring to land enclosed for arable use); Top Cl 1845; Top Mdw 1845; Top Orchard 1845; Townside Cls 1784 (cf. *the Townside field* 1650, *Townside Fields* 1657, *v.* **tūn, sīde**); Two Acre Mdw 1845 (*v.* **æcer**); Walkers Two Mdws 1784 (with the surn. *Walker*); Wards Cl 1776, 1845 (with the surn. *Ward*); Warners Cl 1784, Bottom ~ ~, Top Warners Cl 1845, Warners Long Cl 1845, Warners Pen(n) 1784, 1845 (*v.* **penn**[2]) (with the surn. *Warner*, cf. *Miss Warner* 1784, who owned the pen); Waterman's Mdw 1845 (cf. *Thomas Waterman* d. 1763, *Elizabeth Waterman* d. 1775; from monuments in the parish church); Watkins Mdw 1845, Watkins 4 Acre Mdw 1845 (with the surn. *Watkins*); Wells 2 Closes 1784 (in the tenure of *John Wells* 1784), Wells Cl 1845, Bottom ~ ~, Top Wells's Cl 1845, Wells Mdw 1845; White's Mdw 1784 (in the tenure of *Mr White* 1784), Whites Cl 1845; Willow Mdw 1845 (*v.* **wilig**).

(b) *Abbey hedge* 1621 (*v.* **abbaye, hecg**; the boundary hedge of St Mary de Pratis Abbey, Leicester); *Abbotispool subtus Barschawe* 1390 Pat (*v.* **abbat**, **pōl**[1] and *Barshaw Field*, *infra*); *Above Meadow* 1657, *High Mear alias Above Meadow* 1743 (*v.* **aboven**; with reference to land above East Mdw, *v.* East Mdw and High Mears *supra*); *Barschawe* 1390 Pat, *Barshaw Field* 1657, *v.* **bār**, **scaga** and *Abbotispool*, *supra*); *Belegraue Ling* 1278 AD, *le Belegrauelyng* 1297 Cor (*v.* **lyng**); *Billington Closes* 1709 (with the surn. *Billington*, *v.* Reaney *s.n.*); *Blackland Leas* 1625 (*v.* **blæc, land, leys**); *Blakewonge* 1399, *Blakwong'* 1467 × 84 (*v.* **vangr**; either with the surn. *Black*/*Blake* or with **blæc**, alluding to the soil); *le Breche* 1467 × 84, *Breach*

1625, *the Hye breche* 1467 × 84, *High Breache* 1657 (*v.* **hēah**[1]), *the Long breche* 1467 × 84, *Long Breache* 1657, *Long Breach or Keene's Close* 1709 (*v.* **lang**[1] and *Keene's Close, infra*), *Breachfield* 1650 (*v.* **brēc**); *Bridg Fields* 1657 (*v.* **brycg**); *Burblad(e)syk* 1477 (e.16), 1467 × 84, *Burbladsyk'*, *Burblau(d)syke* 1467 × 84, *v.* **bur-blade** and VEPN *s.v.*); *Burstall moor* 1628 (*v.* **mōr**[1]; Birstall lies beyond R. Soar to the north-west); *Caterrode furlong'* 1467 × 84 (*v.* **furlang**; prob. with **rōd**[3], otherwise **rod**[1]; it is unfortunate that only this single form survives and is that of a monastic (though local) copyist, since the first el. which appears here as *cater* may be that in a series of difficult names such as Caterham (Sr 311), Catherington (Ha 49), Catterton (Cu 182), Catterall (La 162) and Chadderton (La 50) and may be a surviving British hill-name *Cater* (PrW *cateir*, *cadeir* 'chair' used in a transferred sense 'hill'), *v.* Elements *s.v.* ***cadeir**, DEPN *s.n.* Chadderton and Jackson 555); *le Closfurlong* 1477 (e.16) (*v.* **clos(e)**, **furlang**); *the coale pitt way* 1657 (*v.* **col-pytt**; referring to a place where charcoal was made); *Coweswade* 1357 Works (*v.* **cū**, **(ge)wæd**); *the Crabtree* 1625 *v.* **crabtre**); *Crosses Plots* 1657 (*v.* **plot**; held by *Eduard Crosse* 1657); *Dalsyk* 1477 (e.16) (*v.* **dalr**, **sík**); *the Dew wong* 1467 × 84 (*v.* **dēaw**, **vangr**); *(le) Dovecoate close* 1621, 1635 (*v.* **dove-cot(e)**); *Foulkes Plots* 1657 (*v.* **plot**; held by *Richard Foulkes* 1657); *Goseholme* 1446, 1447 (*v.* **gōs**, **holmr**); *atte Grene* 1260 Cl (p) (*v.* **atte**), *on the grene* 1327 (p), 1332 (p) (*v.* **grēne**[2]); *Harcott Hill* 1657, *Harcourt Hill* 1635, 1688, 1724 ('boundary cottage', *v.* **hār**[2], **cot**; on the parish boundary); *Heyrigg* 1399 (*v.* **hēg**, **hryggr**); *le Holly Crosse* 1556 Pat (*v.* **hālig**, **cros**); *The Homestall* 1708 (18) (*v.* **hām-stall**; i.e. of *the Parsonage House*); *de Hull* 1345 GildR (p) (*v.* **hyll**); *Humberstone Bridge Closes* 1709, *Humberstone Fields alias Bridg Fields* 1657, *Humberston Meare* 1625 (*v.* **(ge)mǣre**) (Humberstone adjoins to the south-east); *Johnsons Plot or Cley-lands* 1657 (*v.* **plot** and Clay Lands *supra*; with the surn. *Johnson*); *Keenes Close(s)* 1709, 1731 (with the surn. *Keene*); *Kent croft* 1467 × 84 (*v.* **croft**; with the surn. *Kent*); *le kylne yard* 1621 (*v.* **cyln**, **geard**); *Kyrkehull* 1399 (*v.* **kirkja**, **hyll**), *Kyrkland furlong'* 1467 × 84 (*v.* **kirkja**, **land**, **furlang** and St Peter's Church *supra*); *le Lammas close* 1621 (*v.* **lammas**; land used for grazing after the first day of August when the hay had been cut, *v.* Field 118); *Lane Fields* 1657 (*v.* **lane**); *Leicester way* 1625, *Lincolne way* 1625 (both referring to the Roman road, the Fosse Way, on its route to Lincoln in the north-east and to Leicester in the south-west); *Longelands* 1625, *Longland* 1650 (*v.* **lang**[1], **land**); *Lymstall* 1467 × 84 (*v.* **līm**, **stall**); *Mansdale* 1625, 1657, *Mandalls* 1657 (*v.* **(ge)mǣnnes**, **deill**); *Marks Yard* 1710 (*v.* **geard**; with the surn. *Mark(s)*); *the Marlepitt*, *Marlpitts* 1625 (*v.* **marle-pytt**); *the Middle furlonge* 1625 (*v.* **furlang**); *Moore Close* 1635, *Moores Plot* 1657 (*v.* **plot**) (*Will'm Moore* held the plot in 1657, but the close may belong with the group subsumed with Moor furlong in f.ns. (a) *supra*); *New Pasture*, *~ ~ Foot* 1657 (*v.* **fōt**) (*v.* **pasture**); *Oldpark* 1517 DI (*v.* **ald**, **park**); *the Parsonage Medow* 1625 (*v.* The Vicarage *supra*); *Perkin Arbor Layes* 1657, *Parkin Arbor Leys* 1675 (*v.* **erber**, **leys**; with the surn. *Perkin/Parkin*); *The Poores Plot* 1657, *The Poors Plot(t)* 1662, 1710 (*v.* **pouer(e)**, **plot**; land dedicated to poor relief or charity); *Pudyng Row* 1467 × 84 (*v.* **pudding**, **vrá**); *Roger hedge* 1625 (*v.* **hecg**; a property boundary, with the surn. *Roger*, *v.* Reaney *s.n.*); *Long ~ ~*, *Schort schepis wong'* 1467 × 84 (*v.* **lang**[1], **sc(e)ort**, **scēp**, **vangr**); *le Seven acres* 1621 (*v.* **æcer**); *Suthforth* 1467 × 84 (*v.* **sūð**, **ford**); *Syde furlong* 1467 × 84 (*v.* **sīde**, **furlang**); *Taylerwong* 1467 × 84 (*v.* **vangr**; presum. with the surn. *Tayler/Taylor* rather than its source AFr *taillour*, OFr *tailleur* 'a tailor'); *Thorp on le Toftis* 1278

AD (*v.* **þorp, toft**; with an early use of *toft* as 'a hillock', otherwise first recorded in this sense in Langland's *Piers Plowman* A 14 (c.1370); a lost farmstead, described in 1278 as a tillage), *Thorp felde* 1467 × 84, *Thorp(e) Field* 1657, 1709, 1743 (*v.* **feld**; one of the early great fields of the township); *the Felde aboue the towne* 1467 × 84 (*v.* **feld, aboven, tūn**; one of the early great fields); *the Felde be nethe the Town* 1467 × 84 (*v.* **feld, benethe, tūn**; one of the early great fields); *the Town Close* 1710 (*v.* **tūn**); *Townesend Close* 1675, 1743 (*v.* **tūn, ende**); *the Upper Leas* 1625 (*v.* **leys**); *Wadlowhadlond'* 1467 × 84 (*v.* **hēafod-land**; *Wadlow* could be 'Wada's hill or mound', *v.* **hlāw** and cf. Wadlow (BdHu 138), or 'woad hill' with **wād** 'woad'; note that *Wadlow* also exists as a surn., *v.* Reaney *s.n.*, but is unlikely to figure here at this date); *Walled Paddock alias the Bishops Yard* 1743 (*v.* **paddock** and the Bishops Yard *supra*); *Welshes Yard* 1687 (*v.* **geard**; with the surn. *Welsh(e)*); *Whitlands* 1625 (*v.* **hwīt, land**; in eModE, *white* 'infertile' is contrasted with *black* 'fertile'); *in the Wro* 1327 (p), *in le Wro* 1332 (p) (*v.* **vrá**).

Burton on the Wolds

BURTON ON THE WOLDS

Bvrtone 1086 DB (x3), Hy 2 Dugd, *Burtona* l.12 *GarCart* (freq), John BM, 13 *GarCart*, *Burtonie* l.12 *ib*, *Burton(')* l.12 *ib*, l.12 *BHosp*, 12 *GarCart*, e.13 *BHosp*, 1212 *GarCart et freq*, *Burthon'* 1314 *ib*
Burtun l.12 *GarCart* (freq), *Burtuna* l.12 *ib* (freq), *Burtune* l.12 *ib*
Bortone 1086 DB

Affixes are variously:
~ *iuxta Prestwo(u)ld* 1295 Banco, 1719 LML
~ *super Waldas* 1301 MinAccts, Edw 1 BM, 1336 *GarCart*, ~ *super Wald(e)* 1488 *MiD*, 1541 Nichols, ~ *super Wolds* 1623 LML
~ *sur le Would* 1372 Nichols, ~ *de Wolds* 1534 VE
~ *othe Wold* 1413 Pat, ~ *upon Wold* 1486 × 1515 ECP
~ *sup' Olds* 1604 SR, ~ *on the Owles* 1604 LML

'The farmstead, village near a fortification' or 'the fortified farmstead, village' (later '~ on the high open ground or wold country'), *v.* **burh-tūn, wald**. Note the affixes with MLat *super* and AFr *sur*, both meaning 'on, upon'; and *v.* **uppan**.

BROOK FM, BROOKFIELD, both beside Walton Brook, the parish boundary with Walton on the Wolds to the south. BURTON BANDALLS, BANDALLS FM, BURTON BANDALLS FM, *Bandale* l.13 BM, *Burton Bandal(l)s* 1739 LeicW, 1836 O, 1871 *Plan*, 1925 Kelly, *v.* **bēan**; prob. with **dalr**, otherwise with **deill**. BURTON HALL, 1831 Curtis, 1863, 1877 White, 1925 Kelly, *the Hall House* 1701 *Terrier*, *The Hall* 1846 White, *v.* **hall**. BURTON WOLDS, 1836 O, 1925 Kelly, *Burton Woldes* 1537 MinAccts, *v.* **wald**. CHALKPIT FM (lost), *Chalkpit Farm* 1836 O, *v.* **calc, pytt**. THE CLIFF, *the Clife* 1701 *Terrier*, *v.* **clif**. CLIFF HO., *Cliff house* 1925 Kelly. THE CLUMP, *v.* **clump**; a small plantation of trees. EGGLESTON FM. EGYPT LODGE FM, a 'remoteness' name, the site being at the eastern extremity of the parish. FISHPOND PLANTATION. FOUR

ACRE WOOD. FOXCOVERT HO., *v.* **cover(t)**. GLOVER'S FM (lost), *Glovers Farm* 1931 *Sale*; with the surn. *Glover*. GREYHOUND INN, *Greyhound* 1846, 1863 White, 1925 Kelly. HARROW FM, *Harrow Farm* 1944 *Sale*, *v.* Arrow Fd in Wymeswold f.ns. (a). HORSE LEYS FM, *Horse Leys farm* 1925 Kelly, cf. *the Greate Horse Leas*, ~ ~ ~ *Leyes* 1701 *Terrier*, *the Little Horse Leas* 1701 *ib*, *v.* **hors**, **leys**. MANOR FM, *Manor farm* 1925 Kelly, *v.* **maner**. MANOR LODGE FM is *Low Farm* 1836 O, *v.* **la(g)h**. NEW FM, *New farm* 1925 Kelly. OLD BARN. PARK FM (THE OLD PARK FM 1"). PLASTER PIT BARN, *the Plaster Pitt* 1694 *Reeve*, *Plaister Pitts* 1700 *Deed*, *Plaster Pitt* 1701 *Terrier*, cf. *Plaster Pitt Lane* 1701 *ib*, *v.* **plaster**, **pytt**; a site of the extraction of gypsum, *v.* Field 227. RANCLIFF WOOD, *v.* **hræfn**, **clif**; the wood lies on a steep hillside. RED HILL BARN, *Redd Hill* 1701 *Terrier*, *v.* **rēad**, **hyll**. SIX HILLS RD, leading to Six Hills (*q.v.*) on the Fosse Way. SOWTER'S LANE, with the surn. *Sowter*, *v.* Reaney *s.n.* SPINNEY FM. TOP FM is *Angraves Lodge* 1836 O, *v.* **loge**; with the surn. *Angrave*. TOWN END PLANTATION, cf. (*the*) *Town*(*e*) *end close* 1701 *Terrier*, 1811 *Will*, *v.* **tūn**, **ende**. TWENTY ACRE, *Twenty Acres* 1700 *Deed*, 1701 *Terrier*, *v.* **æcer**; it is *Mundy's Gorse* 1836 O, *v.* **gorst**; with the surn. *Mundy*, a reflex of the ON pers.n. *Mundi*, a short form of names in *-mundr*, *v.* SPNLY 198. UPPER MILL (lost), *Upper Mill* 1877 White.

The following dwellings are listed in 1701 *Terrier*, together with some of their tenants: *Bridges old house*, *Burbages Cottage* (*Joseph Burbage*), *the Cottage House*, *Earl of Huntingdons house*, *Greasleys Cottage*, *Hentons Farme house*, *Loes Cottage* (*John Loe*), *Matlockes Cottage* (*John Mattlocke*), *Melbornes Cottage* (*William Melborne*), *Palmers Cottage* (1) (*Edward Palmer*), *Palmers Cottage* (2) (*Thomas Palmer*), *Peabodys Cottage*, *Raggs Cottage* (*Elizabeth Ragg*), *Shallcross Cottage* (*Samuel Shallcross*), *Smiths house and homestead* (*v.* **hām-stede**), *Toones house* (*William Toone*), *the Upper House*, *Whites Cottage* (*Sarah White*), *v.* **cotage**. It is worthy of note that a quarter of the surns. which appear here may be based on Derbyshire township names (i.e. Burbage, Gresley, Matlock and Melbourne) and could represent lead-mining families which migrated to Burton on the Wolds to work the local gypsum.

FIELD-NAMES

Undated forms in (a) are 1871 *Plan*; those dated 1766 are *Will*; 1759 are *EnclA*; 1807, 1826 and 1828 are *Deed*; 1836 are O. Forms throughout dated l.12, 1212 and 13 are *GarCart*; Hy 2, l.Hy 2 and John are Berkeley; 1543, c.1625 and 1701 are *Terrier*; 1666, 1700 and 1744 are *Deed*; 1687, 1694 and 1702 are *Reeve*.

(a) Barn Cl (*Barne close* 1701, *v.* **bern** and *Robert the Millers close* in f.ns. (b)); Bingham Cl, Bingham Mdw, Little Bingham (with the surn. *Bingham* of a family originally from the village of this name, 14 miles to the north-east in Notts.); Brook Cls 1799 Nichols ((*the*) *Brooke close* 1700, 1701, *v.* **brōc**); Burton Cl 1871; Burton Pasture 1836 (*v.* **pasture**); Burton Woulds Cl 1759 (*v.* Burton Wolds *supra*); Deepdales 1836 (*the deep dale alias delph dales* 1701, *Debtdale close* (sic) 1701, *v.* **dēop, dalr** and *delph dales* in f.ns. (b)); Hardys Cl (*Hardy close* 1701; with the surn. *Hardy*); Hill Top; Holm Cls 1797 (*v.* **holmr**); Homestead (*the Homestead* 1701, *v.* **hām-stede**); House Cl; Little Cl; Middle Cl; Mill Hill (*the Mill Hill Close*(*s*) 1701, *v.* **myln**; a windmill site); Parsons Plat (*v.* **plat**) (cf. *Parsons alias Bucknalls close* 1701, 1702; prob. with **persone** rather than with the surn. *Parsons*, although note that Burton on the Wolds has no parish church, *v. Bucknalls close* in f.ns. (b)); East ~ ~, West Plaister Cl (cf. *the Nether ~ ~, Over Plaister Pitts* 1700 (*v.* **uferra**), *the Little ~ ~ ~, the Neather ~ ~ ~, the Upper ~ ~ ~, Plaster Pitt close* 1701, *the Plaster Pitt Leas* 1701 (*v.* **leys**), *v.* Plaster Pit Barn *supra*); the Plowed Cl 1766, 1807, 1826, 1828 (1744; land under arable cultivation); Pool Cl (*v.* **pōl**[1]); Spring Cl (*v.* **spring**[1]).

(b) *Arrow leas Close* c.1625 (*v.* **leys** and Harrow Fm *supra*); *the Barley close, ~ ~ ~ alias Rayles close* 1701 (*v.* **bærlic** and *Rayles close, infra*); (*the*) *Little Barne Close* 1701 (*v.* **bern**); (*William*) *Beltons Close* 1701 (the *Belton* family prob. originally came from Belton, 9 miles to the west); *Blacclif* 1212, *Blacclifueshende* 1212 (*v.* **ende**), *the Black Leaves* (sic) 1701 (*v.* **blæc, clif**); *the Bramleyes close* 1701 (with the local surn. *Bramley*); *the Brooke Platt, ~ ~ ~ close* 1701 (*v.* **brōc, plat**); *ouer the brok* 1327 SR (p) (*v.* **ofer**[3], **brōc**); *Bucknalls* 1700, *~ close* 1701, 1702 (with the surn. *Bucknall*, *v.* Parsons Plat in f.ns. (a)); *Burton felde* 1543, *~ feilde* c.1625 (*v.* **feld**; the only great field recorded for the township); *Burton Grange* 1589, 1609 Nichols, (*grangia ~ ~, grangie de Burton'* l.12, 13, with MLat *grangia* 'a grange') (*v.* **grange**; an outlier of Garendon Abbey); *the Bushey close* 1701 (*v.* **busshi**); *the Church Leys* 1700, *~ ~ Leas* 1701 (*v.* **leys**; Burton on the Wolds has no parish church and thus these pastures presum. provided income for a neighbouring church, prob. that of Wymeswold; perh. cf. Parsons Plat in f.ns. (a)); *the Nether Cliffe alias Little Cliffe* 1700 (*v.* **clif**); *the Cole Pitt close* 1701 (*v.* **col-pytt**; a place where charcoal was made); *the Cow Close* 1700, 1701, 1702; *the Cow Grange Plot*(*t*) 1687 (*v.* **cū, grange, plot**); *Crackhole* c.1625 (*v.* **craca**; ostensibly with **hol**[1], but an earlier **hōh** appears poss., cf. Cracoe, YW **6** 88); *Cumedwe hauedes* 1212 (*v.* **cū, mǣd (mǣdwe** obl.sg.), **hēafod**); *Davis Long Close* 1701, *Davis yard* 1701 (*v.* **geard**) (with the surn. *Davis*); *delph dales* 1701 (*v.* **(ge)delf** and Deepdales in f.ns. (a)); *the Dovecoats yard* 1700, *the Dove coate Yard* 1701 (*v.* **dove-cot(e), geard**); *Drakestan* 1212 (*v.* **draca, stān**; presum. recording an item of early folklore); *the Eight Acres* 1701 (*v.* **æcer**); *Elrenestub* 1212 (*v.* **ellern, stubb**); *the Farr Sicke* c.1625 (*v.* **feor, sík**); *Fewekes*

Close, *the Fewex close* 1701 (with the surn. *Fewkes*, *v.* Reaney *s.n.* Folk); *Fintesdale* 1212 (the first el. is the ON pers.n. *Finnr* (ODan *Fin*), with final AN inorganic *t* after *n*, *v.* Feilitzen 95–6; with **dalr** or **deill**); *the Fisele Close* 1701 bis (*v.* **þistel**); *Fisher Nooke Close* 1666, 1701 (*v.* **nōk**; with the surn. *Fisher*); *the Flatt nookes* 1701 (*v.* **flat, nōk**); *the Flax leyes* 1701 (*v.* **fleax, leys**); *Fowlers Close* 1701 (with the surn. *Fowler*); *the Gardeners Platt* 1701 (*v.* **plat**; prob. with the surn. *Gardener* rather than with its occupational source ONFr *gardinier* 'a gardener'); *the Gate Close adjoining Burton Lane* 1701 (*v.* **gata**); *the Gosse close* 1701, *the Goss(e)y close* 1701 (*v.* **gorst, gorstig**); *Grange closes* 1701, *the Grange Leas*, *~ ~ Leyes* 1701 (*v.* **leys**), *Grange Leyes Plott* 1687 (*v.* **plot**) (*v. Burton Grange*, *supra*); *the greate ground* 1701 (*v.* **grēat, grund**); *the Hall Crofts* 1700, 1702 (*v.* **croft** and Burton Hall *supra*); *Hawcraft Leas* 1701, *Hawcroft Leyes* 1702 (*v.* **leys**; prob. with forms of the previous f.n., but if not, *v.* **haga**[1], **croft**); *the Hemp Yard* 1700, 1701 (*v.* **hemp-yard**); *the Home Close(s)* 1701, 1702, *the Home Nooke* 1701 (*v.* **nōk**) (at this date poss. with **holmr** rather than with **home**); *the Honey Suckles close* 1701 (*v.* **hunisuccle**; here either a name for flowers of clover, esp. the common red clover, or of the woodbine (*Lonicera periclymenum*), *v.* Field 98 and the Honeysuckle in neighbouring Wymeswold f.ns. (a)); *Horseley(e)s Close* 1701, 1702, *the Greate Horse leas Sick close* 1701 (*v.* **sík**) (*v.* Horse Leys Fm *supra*); *Hubbards close* 1701 (with the surn. *Hubbard*); *Hulfstaredale* 1212, *the Great Husterdale* 1700, 1701, *the Greate Hurste dale* 1701, *the Little Husterdale* 1701, *the Greate and Little Husterdales* 1701 (*v.* **hulfestre, dalr**); *Ironmungers Barne Closes* 1701 (cf. *William Iremonger* 1630 Nichols); *Johnsons Yard* 1700 (*v.* **geard**; with the surn. *Johnson*); (*the*) *Kiln*(*e*) *Close* 1701 (*v.* **cyln**); *the Lady Day closes*, *the little Lady Day close* 1701 (land whose rent fell due on 25 March, Lady Day); *Lamcotte hill* c.1625 (*v.* **lamb**, **cot**); *the Lane Close* 1701 (*v.* **lane**); *the Ling Close* 1701 (*v.* **lyng**); *the Longleyes close* 1701 (*v.* **lang**[1], **leys**); *the Upper Lords Leas* 1701 (*v.* **leys**; *Lord* may be a surn., but more likely alludes to the Earl of Huntingdon whose house is recorded in 1701, *v. supra*); *the Mald ~*, *the Mauld Close* 1701 (*v.* **marled(e)**); *Merehull'* 1212 (*v.* **(ge)mǣre, hyll**); *Munetilandes* 1212, *Muntilandes* l.13 Nichols (*v.* **land**; the first el. appears to be **minte** 'wild mint', poss. with the adj. suffix **-ig**[3], cf. Minety, W 61-2); *the Old Grange* 1701 (a close so called, *v.* Burton Grange *supra*); *Old Hollands yard* 1701 (*v.* **geard**; with the surn. *Holland*); *Palmers close* 1701 (cf. *Edward Palmer* and *Thomas Palmer* 1701 and *v. the Towne end close*, *infra*); *the Pingle* 1701 (*v.* **pingel**); *the Platts* 1701 (*v.* **plat**); *the Plowed Platt* 1701 (*v.* **plat**; under arable cultivation); *Rayles Close*, *the Reale Close* 1701 (*v.* **raile, reille**; land enclosed by a rail fence, *v. the Barley Close*, *supra*); *the Redd Hill close* 1701 (*v.* Red Hill Barn *supra*); *Robert the Millers close alias Barne Close*, *Robin the Millers close ~ ~ ~* 1701 (*v.* **mylnere** and Barn Cl in f.ns. (a)); *Scoueldale* 1212 (*v.* **scofl, deill**); *the Scrubby close*, *~ ~ ~ alias Parsons Close* 1701 (*v.* **scrubby** and Parsons Plat in f.ns. (a)); *Segehishou* Hy 2, *Segishou* l.Hy 2, *Seggeshou* John, 1212 (this represents either an original OE **Seccgeshōh*, containing the pers.n. of the same Anglo-Saxon landowner as in **Seccgeswald* (now Six Hills *q.v.*), with the OE generic **hōh** refashioned as ON **haugr**, or it forms an intermediate step in a sequence **Seccgeswald* > *Seggeshou* > *Seggs Hill* > *Sex Hill* > *Six Hill* > *Six Hills*, in which *haugr* replaced *wald* rather than *hōh*, and *hill* eventually replaced *haugr*); *the Seggs Hill house close* 1701 (adjoining Six Hills *q.v.*); *the Sheep leyes* 1701, *the Sheep Leys alias Twenty acres* 1701, *the Upper Shipp leas* 1701 (*v.* **scēp, leys** and Twenty Acre *supra*); *the Shurbbs alias*

Srubbs (sic) 1701, *the neather Srubbs close* (sic) 1701 (*v.* **neoðera**) (*v.* **scrubb**); *the Sixteen acres* 1701 (*v.* **æcer**); *Standart* 1212 (*v.* **standard**); (*the*) *Stone Bridge Close* 1694, 1701; *Stone Pitt Close* 1694 (*v.* **stān-pytt**); *Strawberrys close* 1701 (*v.* **streberie**; land on which strawberries were grown); *the Street close* 1701 (*v.* **strǣt**; poss. with reference to the Roman Fosse Way, otherwise to the village main street); *Swans Upper Close* 1701 (with the surn. *Swan*); *the Towne end close alias Palmers close* 1701 (*v.* **tūn**, **ende** and *Palmers close*, *supra*); *Tralleswellehul* 1212 (*v.* **wella**, **hyll**; the first el. is prob. **þrǽll** with AN orthographic *t* for *th*, but **troll** 'a troll, a supernatural being' cannot be discounted here, to be compared with *Drakestan*, *supra*); *the Turnopp close*, *Levetts Turnopp close* 1701 (*v.* **turnepe**; cf. *Thomas Levett* 1701); *Tuttebrugge* 1212 (*v.* **brycg**; with the OE pers.n. *Tutta*); *the Twenty Leas*, ~ ~ ~ *Close* 1701 (*v.* **leys**; when compounded with a numeral, *leys* represents grassland units of tenure corresponding to *lands* (i.e. selions or strips) similarly used of arable); *the Watering Platt* 1701, *the Old Watering Platt*, ~ ~ ~ ~ *Close* 1701 (*v.* **wateryng**, **plat**); *the well close* 1701 (*v.* **wella**); *Wheat*(*e*)*s close* 1701 (with the surn. *Wheat*(*e*), *v.* Reaney *s.n.*); *Wimeswould Lane Close* 1701 (*v.* **lane**; Wymeswold adjoins to the north-east); *the Woulds close* 1701, *Little Woulds meadow* 1701 (*v.* **wald**).

Cossington

COSSINGTON

Cosintone 1086 DB, *Cosinton'* c.1130 LeicSurv, 1242 Fees *et passim* to 1316 FA, 1335 *MiD*, *Cosintun* 1236 Fees, c.1237 GildR (p), 13 *MiD*, *Cosynton'* 1319, 1328 Banco *et passim* to 1389 *RTemple*, 1391 *Wyg*

Cosenton' l.13 *RTemple*

Cosington' 1220 MHW, 1254 Val *et passim* to 1314 *GarCart*, 1316 *RTemple et freq* to 1528 *ib*, 1538 *MiD et passim* to 1549 LAS, Eliz 1 *Surv*, *Cosingtona* c.1280 *RTemple*, *Cosingthon'* 1294 *MiD*, *Cosyngton'* 1290 *RTemple*, l.13 *MiD* (freq) *et freq* to 1539 *RTemple*, 1546 *Rental et passim* to 1560 ISLR, 1566 *Ct*, *Cosynkton* 1481 *RTemple*, *Coshington* 1522 *MiD*, *Cosingetone* 1572 *ib*

Cossyngton 1330 FA, *Cossynton* 1525 AD, *Cossington* 1540 Ipm *et passim*

Cousington 1304 Pat

Cusintona 1175 P, 1196 × 1216 Berkeley, *Cusintun* 1199 × 1216 ib (p), *Cusinton'* 1176, 1183 P *et passim* to 1299 Banco (p), 13 *MiD*, *Cusynton* 1269 Cur

Cusenton 1253 × 58 RHug

Cusington' 1221, 1222 Fine *et passim* to 1331 Banco, 1343 *RTemple*, *Cusyngton'* 1352 *Peake*, 1357, 1384 Pat, 1504 *RTemple*

Cussington 1251 Cur, 1254 Ass, 1604 SR, 1613, 1625, 1628 LML, *Cussyngton'* 1389 *RTemple*, *Cussinton* 1576 Saxton, 1610 Speed

'The village or estate associated with or called after a man named Cos(s)a or Cus(s)a', *v.* **-ingtūn**. The specific of this p.n. is an OE pers.n. While *Cus(s)a* is recorded (*v.* Searle 147), *Cos(s)a* survives only in p.ns., as in Corshaw (W 95) and Cosham (Ha 59). Spellings of Cossington with *-ss-* are as a whole rather late, which suggests either *Cosa* or *Cusa* as the form of the pers.n.

In Leics., p.ns. of this type appear to belong to the eighth cent., and may indicate a developing manorial structure. They are present in particular in a group in the west of the county, an area which was exploited comparatively late, *v.* Barrie Cox, 'Aspects of place-name evidence for early medieval settlement in England', *Viator* 11 (1980), 35–50 at 44–5.

ALL SAINTS' CHURCH, *the Church* 1708, 1708 (18) *Terrier*, *Church (All Saints)* 1846, 1863, 1877 White, 1925 Kelly; it is earlier recorded as *ecclesie de Cosington* 1220 MHW, *ecclesiam de Cusinton* 1238 RGros, *ecclesie de Cosyngton* 1357, 1361, 1362, 1378 *Pat*, ~ *de Cusyngton* 1357 *ib*, ~ *de Cosynton* 1378 *ib*, *Omnium Sanctorum Cosyngton* 1392 *ib*, and in the groups *ecclesiarum de ... Walton Cosyngton et Raveneston* 1337 *ib*, ~ ~ *Walton on le Wold et Cosyngton* 1464, 1467, 1475 *ib*. Note also *the Church Yard*(*e*) 1564 *RTemple*, 1697, 17, 1704, 1708, 1708 (18), 1762 *Terrier*, *v.* **chirche-ȝeard**. BLACKBERRY LANE, 1835 O, *v.* **lane**; with reference to the blackberry (*Rubus fructicosus*). BLACKSMITH'S SHOP (lost), *Blacksmiths shop* 1842 *TA*, *v.* **blacksmith**, **sc(e)oppa**. CARPENTER'S SHOP (lost), *Carpenters shop* 1842 *TA*, *v.* **carpenter**, **sc(e)oppa**. CARTHEGENA (2½"), *Carthagena* 1806 Map, 1835 O, *Carthegena* 1863 White, 1925 Kelly, *Carthagenia House* 1846 White; named from the port of Cartagena, founded as a Spanish city in 1533 in north-west Colombia on the Caribbean Sea. Cartagena was freq. attacked by British privateers, including Sir Francis Drake. In Cossington, Carthegena is a 'remoteness' name, the site of the dwelling being located in the extreme north-east of the parish. CHINE HO., *Chine house* 1925 Kelly; either with the surn. *Chine* (*v.* Reaney *s.n.*) or with its source, OE **cinu** 'a fissure, a cleft', but if the latter is the case, no early forms are recorded in f.ns. COLLEGE FM is *Cossington Lodge* 1835 O, *College farm* 1925 Kelly, *v.* **loge**; adjoining Ratcliffe Roman Catholic College. COSSINGTON GORSE, 1806 Map, 1835 O, 1842 *TA*, *v.* **gorst**. COSSINGTON GRANGE, *le Grange* 1551 *RTemple*, *the Grange* 1559 *ib*, 1925 Kelly, *v.* **grange**. COSSINGTON OLD MILL (COSSINGTON MILL 2½"), *Cosyngton' milne* 1450, 1479 *RTemple*, (*molendini aquatici de Cosyngton* 1477 *ib*, with MLat *molendinum* 'a mill' and MLat *aquaticum* 'worked by water'), *Cossington Mill* 1842 *TA*, 1925 Kelly; it is *the Mill* 1591, 1666 *Surv*, *the Water Corn Mill* 1842 *TA*, *the Water Mill* 1846, 1863 White. Note also *le milnedame* 1477 *RTemple* (*v.* **damme**), *the milne doore* 1635 *Surv* (*v.* **duru**), *le milne gate* 1331 *RTemple* (*v.* **gata**), *v.* **myln**. FLAGSTAFF BUTTS, *v.* **but**. GLEBE FM, *Glebe Farm* 1846 White, *v.* **glebe**. THE GROVE, 1877 White, 1925 Kelly. THE HALL, 1635 *Surv*, 1877 White, *the Hall House* c.1634 LAS, *v.* **hall**. HUMBLE FM, *Homble Farm* 1846 White, *Humble* ~ 1863 ib, *Hamble* ~ 1925 Kelly; the site is that of *Humble Barn* 1835 O. HUMBLE LANE, 1835 O; this is *Lambogate* 1467

× 84 *LTD*, *Lamble Gate* 1585 LAS, *v.* **gata** and Lambles in f.ns. (a). LOCK HO., *Lock House* 1842 *TA*, *v.* **lock**; beside the Grand Union Canal. MARSHDALE FM, *v.* Marsh Dale in f.ns. (a). PADGE HALL, *Podge Hall* 1835 O; a stream-side location and thus poss. in origin 'the frog-infested water-meadow, nook of land', *v.* **padde, halh** and to be compared with the common Frog Hall. RATCLIFFE ROMAN CATHOLIC COLLEGE, 1925 Kelly, *Ratcliffe College* 1846, 1863, 1877 White. THE RECTORY, 1877 White, 1925 Kelly, *v.* **rectory**; cf. *the Parsonage House* 1697, 17, 1704, 1708, 1708 (18), 1762, *v.* **personage**. ROYAL OAK (P.H.), *Royal Oak* 1842 *TA*, 1877 White, 1925 Kelly. RYEFIELD LODGE (lost), *Ryefield Lodge* 1846, 1863 White, *v.* **loge** and Great Rye Fd in f.ns. (a). WHEELWRIGHT'S SHOP (lost), *Wheelwrights shop* 1842 *TA*, *v.* **whelewryght, sc(e)oppa**. WHITE LODGE is *Cossington Lodge* 1835 O, 1846, 1863 White, *The Lodge* 1925 Kelly, *v.* **loge**.

FIELD-NAMES

Undated forms in (a) are 1842 *TA*; those dated 1762 are *Terrier* and 1803 are *Map*. Forms throughout dated c.1280, c.1285, 1287, 1270 × 90, p.1290, l.13[1], 13[1], 1325, 1331, 1332, 1389, 1450, 1477 and 1479 are *RTemple*; l.13[2], 13[2] and 1349 are *MiD*; 13 (15) are *CCart*; 14 are HMCVar; 14 (1467 × 84) and 1467 × 84 are *LTD*; 1529, 1554, 1563, 1577, 1585, 1598, 1608, 1610, 1634, c.1634, 1647, 1649, 1673, 1677, 1699, 1700, 1719, 1726 and 1743 are LAS; 1546 are *Rental*; c.1575 are *Plan*; 1591, Eliz 1, 1635, 1666, 1668, 1676, 1678 and e.18 are *Surv*; 1601, 17, 1704, 1708 and 1708 (18) are *Terrier*.

(a) First ~ ~ ~, Second three Acre Cl, Four ~, Eight acres, Ten Acre Fd, the Ten acre flat (*v.* **flat**) (*v.* **æcer**); Ash Cls 1803, Ash Close High 1803, Barn ~ ~, Upper Ash Cl 1842 (*the Ash Close* 1703, *v.* **æsc**); Ashbys far ~, Ashbys near Wolds (*v.* **wald**; with the surn. *Ashby*); Astills Lane (*v.* **lane**; cf. *John Astill* and *Edward Astill* 1842); Barn Cl 1803, 1842, Far ~ ~, First ~ ~, Bottom ~ ~, Top ~ ~, Upper ~ ~ 1842 (*Barn Close* 1719, *v.* **bern**); The Bastard (*v.* **bastard**; a field of irregular shape); Best Mdw (*v.* **best**; a complimentary name for very fertile land); Second Bottom Cl, Bottom Mdw (*v.* **bottom**); Brook Cl (*v.* **brōc**); Bull piece 1842 *TA*, 1846, 1863, 1877 White, 1925 Kelly (*the bullpyece* 1554, *bull peece* 1649, *Bull peice* 1666, 1668, *the Bull piece* 1666, *v.* **bula, pece**); Upper ~ ~, Bushy Cl 1803 (*v.* **busshi**); Butchers Cl (with the surn. *Butcher*); Cherry Orchard; Church Yard Cl (*v.* All Saints' Church *supra*); Clarke's Cl 1803, Clarkes ~, West Clarkes ~ 1842 (with the surn. *Clarke*); Corn Cl (*v.* **corn**[1]); Cross Cl (*the Crosse close* 1666, (*the*) *Cross Close* 1666, e.18, *v.* **cross**); Dakins Cl (in the tenure of *Jonathan Dakin* 1842); Doctors Cl ((*the*) *Doctors Close* 1577, 1677, 1697, 17, 1704, e.18, 1708, 1708 (18), *Doctors Cloase*

17, *the Doctor Close* 1762, *v.* **doctour**); Far Cl; Ferrimans Cl(s) 1791 LAS, 1803, Bottom ~ ~, Top Ferrymans Cl 1842 (in the tenure of *Thomas Ferriman* of Sileby 1743); First Cl; Great Fowks ~, Little Fowkes Cl (with the surn. *Fowkes*, *v.* Reaney *s.n.*); The Gaultry, The North Gaultry, Gaultry Cl (*Galtree* 1649, *Gaultrey* 1666, *Gaultre* ~, *Gaultrey leas* 1635, *Gaultrey ley(e)s* 1666, 1668 (*v.* **leys**), *Gaultrey Meadow* 1676, *v.* **galg-trēow**); the Glebe 1755 LAS (*the gleab land* 1666, *the gleabland plotts* 1666 (*v.* **plot**), *the gleab meadow*, *Gleeb Meadow* 1666, *the gleab platt* 1704 (*v.* **plat**), *the Great Gleeb Close* 1704, 1708, ~ ~ *Glebe* ~ 1708 (18), 1762, *v.* **glebe**); John Goude's Farm 1803; Hall Homestead (*v.* **hām-stede** and The Hall *supra*); Halls far ~, Halls near Cl (in the tenure of *William Hall* 1842); Hill Cl; Home Cl, ~ ~ Spinney (*ye Home Cloase* 17, *the Home Close(s)* 1647, 1666, *v.* **home**, **clos(e)**); Home Mdw (*the Holme meddow* 1668, *the Holme* 1635, 1704, *the Home* 1708, 1708 (18), 1762, *v.* **holmr**); Homestead (*homstid* 17, *the Homestead* 1666, *v.* **hām-stede**); House Cl; House Spinney; Hovel Cl (*v.* **hovel**); Hulses Cl (in the tenure of *Francis Hulse* 1842, cf. *Henry Hulses land* 1666 (*v.* **land**), *Wm. Hulses homestead* e.18 (*v.* **hām-stede**)); Junction 1835 O, Junction Mdw 1842 (at the junction of *Leicester Canal* 1835 O and the river Wreake); Barn ~, Little ~, Long ~, Road ~, Top Lambles (*Lambowe* 1287, *Lawmbull* 1467 × 84, *(the) Lamble* 1601, 1610, 1666, 1676, 1708, *Forlawmbull* 1467 × 84 (*v.* **feor**), *Lamble or the Round Hill plott*, *Laumble or the round hill plot* 1666 (*v. the Round Hill plott* in f.ns. (b)), cf. *lamble gos(s)e* 1563 (*v.* **gorst**), *Lamble hill* 1635, *the Lawmble plott* 1668 (*v.* **plot**), *Lambulsyke* 1467 × 84, *Lamblesick(e)* 1601, 1610, 1635, 1649 (*v.* **sík**)), Lambleys 1842 (*Lawmbulleys* 1467 × 84, *Lamble leas* 1635, *La(u)mble ley(e)s* 1666 (*v.* **lǣs**) (*v.* **lām**, **boga** and note the form *Lambogate* 1467 × 84 for Humble Lane *supra*; **boga** here is in its sense 'a curving hill or hill-side, a circular hill, something curved', hence *Lamble or the Round Hill plott*; **boga** is early confused with **hyll** in *Lawmbull* etc., while in the 19th cent. *Lamble* > *Humble*); Lower ~ ~, Upper Lentile Cl (with the surn. *Lentell/Lentle*, *v.* Reaney *s.nn.*); Little Mdw; Far ~ ~, Near ~ ~, Third Lower Cl; Lyel Mdw (with the surn. *Lile/Lyle*, *v.* Reaney *s.nn.*); Bottom ~ ~, First ~ ~, Middle Marsh Dale (*Marchedales* 1601, *Marshdales* 1610, 1635, *Great* ~, *Short Marshdales* 1635, *v.* **mersc**, **deill**); the Meadow, Bottom ~ ~, Top Meadow Cl; Mickle Mdw (1661, 1666, 1677, *Mykul Mydow* 1467 × 84, *Mickle medowe* 1601, *Micle* ~, *Mycle meadowe* 1635), Mickle Meadow Lane (*v.* **micel**, **mikill**, **mǣd** (**mǣdwe** obl.sg.)); North ~ ~, South ~ ~, Middle Cl; Mill Cl (*the miln(e) close* 1635, *Mill Closse* 1676, *(the) milne close end* 1598 (*v.* **ende**), *v.* **myln**, **clos(e)**), Mill Close Bit (*v.* **bit**), Mill Holme and Park (*v.* **park**) (*Mill Holme* c.1634, *v.* **holmr**); Great ~ ~, Little Mill Leys (*Milne Layes* 1601, *(the) miln(e) leas* 1635, *(the) Mill leyes* 1662, 1666, *Mill Leys* 1666, 1668, e.18, *v.* **leys**) (*v.* Cossington Old Mill *supra*); Little ~ ~, Needhams Cl (in the tenure of *William Needham* 1842); The Newks (*v.* **nōk**); North East Cl; North West Cl; Nursery Cl (*v.* **nursery**); Ox Holm 1754 LAS (*v.* **oxa**, **holmr**); Platt Cl, Platt Mdw, The Platts, Poors Platts (*the Poores plot* 1666, *the Poor(e)s Plott*, *(the) Poors Plott* e.18, 1708 (18), 1782, *v.* **pouer(e)**, **plot**; land dedicated to poor-law relief or charity), Sand Hole Platt (*v.* **sand-hol**) (all 1842 forms are with **plat**); Pound (*v.* **pund**); Bottom ~ ~, Top Railway Cl, Middle Railway Leys (*v.* **leys**) (beside the lines of *The Midland Counties Railway* 1842); Ranglands 1755 LAS, Bottom ~, Middle Ranglands, First Top ~, Middle Top Ranglands (*Wranglandis*, *Wronglondis* 1467 × 84, *Wranglands* 1598, 1601, 1635, *v.* **wrang**, **vrangr**, **land**); Rasdales Mdw, Rasdales piece (*v.* **pece**) (*Rasdale* appears to be a surn., perh. a form of *Rastall*, *v.* Reaney *s.n.*); Ratcliffe Cross 1835 O (*v.* **cross**; a cross-roads towards Ratcliffe on the Wreake), Top Ratcliffe Cl (cf. *Ratcliffe End Close* 1699, *v.* **ende**) (Ratcliffe on the Wreake adjoins to the east); Bottom ~ ~, Top Rushey Cl (*Rushey Close* 1719), Grass ~ ~, Ploughed Rushy platt (*v.* **plat**) (*v.* **riscig**); Great Rye Fd (*the grete Ryfelde* 1467 × 84, (*the*) *Great Riefeild* 1601, 1666, *Great Ryefeild* 1635, ~ *Rye Field* 1647, 1666, *v.* **grēat**), Little Rye Fd (*the Lytul Ryfelde* 1467 × 84, *Little Riefeild*, (*the*) *Little Ryefeild* 1635, *Little Rye Field* 1666, *the Lesser Riefeild* 1601, *v.* **lӯtel**; both Great and Little Rye Fd were open-fields of the township), South Rye Fd (cf. *Ryefield Close* 1647, e.18, *Riefield* ~ 1649) (*v.* **ryge**, **feld**); the Sand Cl, Sand Mdw (*v.* **sand**); Sand Pit Cl (*v.* **sand-pytt** and cf. Sand Hole Platt *supra*); Seggs (*þe Seygys* 1467 × 84, (*the*) *Seggs* 1666, cf. *Seggs lane* e.18 (*v.* **lane**)), Seggs Mdw (cf. *Seggs Close* 1647, 1677, e.18), Seggs Willow Holt (*v.* **wilig**, **holt**) (*v.* **secg**[1]; *cg* > *gg* is due to Scand influence); Sheep Dole, ~ ~ Mdw, North East Sheep Doles (*sheepe dooles* 1601, *Sheepdoles* 1635, 1666, 1668, *Shepe doles* 1666, (*the*) *Sheepe Doles* 1666, 1676, *Shepe dolles ende* 1563, *Shepdoules ende* 1598 (*v.* **ende**), *v.* **scēp**, **dāl**); Smithy Cl (e.18, *v.* **smiððe**); Snail Horn Hill (presum. a fanciful allusion to shape); Soar Bridge 1793 LAS (*pontem trans Soram* 1331 *Pat*, 'the bridge across the river Soar' at Cossington Mill (with MLat *pons* (*pontem* acc.sg.) 'a bridge' and MLat *trans* 'across, over')); Sough Garden (*v.* **gardin**) (*the Soue* 1467 × 84 bis, cf. *Sough close* 1647, *Suf* ~ 1666, (*the*) *Suff* ~ 1704, e.18, 1708, 1708 (18), 1762, *v.* **sōg**); South East Cl; South West Cl; Great ~ ~, Little Southernwood Cl (held by *Thomas Southernwood* 1843); Sunhill, Hill Sun Hill (sic), Willow ~ ~ (*v.* **wilig**) (*Sunne hill* 1601, *Sunhill* 1601, 1635, *little sonhill* 1610, *little Sunhill* 1635, cf. *Sun hill plot* 1668 (*v.* **plot**), *Sunhill Close* 1743, *v.* **sunne**, **hyll**; alluding to ground which catches the best of the sun); Swines Bridge Mdw (*Swines Bridge* 1666, cf. *the Swines bridge close* 1678; prob. with **swin**[2] 'a creek, a channel' rather than with **swīn**[1] 'a swine, a pig', cf. Swine bridge in Loddington f.ns. (a)); Syston Mill Home Cl (*v.* **holmr**; on the Cossington side of the river Wreake; Syston adjoins to the south-east); Thackracks (1676, 1677, 1697, e.18, *Thackbracks*, *Thackwacks* 1666, *the Thatchwracks* 1704, 1762, *the Thatch Racks* 1708, 1708 (18), *the Thatchwraks* 1762, cf. *Thackaras bushes* (sic) 1635 (*v.* **busc**) (*v.* **þæc**, **þak**; the final el. is poss. a Scandinavianized form of OE **rǣc**, *v.* *Longe Ratche*, *infra*; otherwise **bræc**[1]); Top Bowling Leys (*the bowling leyes* 1649, *Bowling Leas* 1719, *v.* **bowling**, **leys**); Far ~ ~, Near ~ ~, First ~ ~, Second ~ ~, Third ~ ~, Top Cl (*v.* **top**); Far ~ ~, Near Toplis Cl (with the surn. *Toplis*); Far ~ ~, First ~ ~, Second ~ ~, Townsend Cl (*Townsend* 1635, ~ *Close* 1649, 1673, e.18, *v.* **tūn**, **ende**); (The) Turnwater 1835 O, 1842, Turn Water Mdw 1759 Nichols, 1842 (cf. *Thurnwater Close* 1666, *Turn Water Close* 1762, *Thurn Water Close and Nook* 1704, 1708, *Thurnwater Nook*(*e*), *Turnwater Nook* 1666 (*v.* **nōk**), *v.* **trun**, **turn**, **wæter**; at a great bend in the river Wreake); Upper Cl; Watts Cl 1842, Watts's Croft 1803 (*v.* **croft**) (with the surn. *Watts*); West Mdw; The Wharf in Gaultry Cl (*v.* **hwearf** and The Gaultry *supra*); Wheatleys Cl (with the surn. *Wheatley*); Bottom ~ ~, Top ~ ~, Far ~ ~, Middle Whites Cl (*Whites Close* 1708; with the surn. *White*); North ~, South Willimot (with the surn. *Willimott*, *v.* Reaney *s.n.*); Willow Holt (*v.* **holt**) (cf. *Willows closse*, (*the*) *Willowes Close* 1666, *Willows* ~ e.18, *v.* **wilig**, **clos(e)**); The Wolds, Bottom ~, Top Wolds, Far Bottom ~, Far Top Wolds, First Top ~, Middle Top Wolds, Halls near ~, Halls far Wolds (with the surn. *Hall*), Spinney Wolds (*v.* **spinney**) (*Wold* l.13, *the Woulds* 1601, 17, *the Ouldes* 1635, *the Oldes* 1666, *the Olds* 1666, 1668, 1704, *the Oulds* 1666, 1668,

1697, 1704, 1708, 1708 (18), 1762, cf. *the closse of tholdes* 1554, *the close of the Wouldes* 1585, *Woulds Cloase* 17, *the Oulds close* 1668 (*v.* **clos(e)**), *the closse of tholdes ende* 1554 (*v.* **clos(e), ende**), *v.* **wald**); Bottom ~, Top Woolridge (with the surn. *Woolridge*, a reflex of the OE pers.n. *Wulfrīc*); Wreake Cl, Little Wreake, Bottom ~ ~, Middle ~ ~, Top ~ ~, Little Wreake Cl, Wreake Hill (beside the river Wreake).

(b) *le apiltrestub* c.1285 (*v.* **æppel-trēow, stubb**); *Apple Holme* 1635 (*v.* **æppel, holmr**); *Apple Yard* 1704, 1708, 1708 (18) (*v.* **æppel, geard** and *Doctors Orch(y)ard, infra*); *the As(s)hes* 1601, 1635, 1677, *Ashfield* 1634, *Ashe hilles* 1601 (*v.* **hyll**), *Ashmeere* 1635 (*v.* **(ge)mǣre**), *(the) Ash Plot(t)* 1668, 1676, 17 (*v.* **plot**) (*v.* **æsc**); *Matthew Babingtons plott* 1666 (*v.* **plot**), *Babingtons Woulds* 1700 (*v.* **wald**); *Banlandis* c.1285, *le Banelondes* 13, *Ballands* 1601 (*v.* **bēan, land**); *Barley Feild* 1610 (*v.* **bærlic, feld**); *the Barne Plott* 1678 (*v.* **bern, plot**); *Beaste gate* 1591 (*v.* **beste, gata**); *Beebyes farme* 1666 (*v.* **ferme**; with the surn. *Beeby* of a family originally from the village of Beeby, 5 miles to the south-east); *Belles close* 1608 (either with the surn. *Bell* in the possessive case, or land endowed for the provision and maintenance of church bells or for the payment of bell-ringers, *v.* **belle**); *Belmans yard* 1546 (*v.* **geard**; with the surn. *Belman*, *v.* Reaney *s.n.*); *Bennetts lane Close* e.18 (*v.* **lane**; with the surn. *Bennett*); *Bessons close* c.1634 (with the surn. *Besson*); *Betwynedeke* 1389 (prob. a furlong 'between the drainage ditches', *v.* **betwēonan, dík**); *Birdlip*, *~ thornes* 1635 (*v.* **þorn**) ('a steep place frequented by birds', *v.* **bridd, hlēp**, cf. Birdlip, Gl **1** 156); *Bonacres* 17 (*v.* **æcer**, with either **bān** or **bōn**; perh. cf. *Bony dolys*, *infra* and *v.* VEPN *s.v.* **bón**); *Bony dolys* 1467 × 84 (*v.* **dāl**; the first el. may be an early use of the adj. **bony** (earliest OED citation dated a.1535) in the sense 'abounding in bones' and alluding to a disturbed burial site; cf. *le Bonydole* in Thorpe Satchville f.ns. (a) *s.n.* Bundells); *Borow* 1331 bis (prob. from **berg** rather than **burh**; cf. *The Hill, infra*); *Mr Bouthes Close ende* 1598 (*v.* **clos(e), ende**; with the surn. *Booth(e)*); *Bradegate* c.1285, l.13² bis, *Bradgate* 1389 (*v.* **brād, gata**); *Bradewong* p.1290, 1325, 1332, *Brodewong* 1325 (*v.* **brād, vangr**); *le Breche* 1287, 1325, 1332, *þe breche* 1325, *the Breche* 1467 × 84, *(the) Breach* 1601, 1635, *breach furlong* 1635 (*v.* **furlang**) (*v.* **brēc**); *Bremehou* l.13¹, 1325, *Bremoue* 13², 13 (15), *Bremehow* 1325, 1331, 1332, *Bremoe* 1601, *Breamoe* 1649, *Longebremhow* l.13², *Longe bremhou* 13², *Longbremow* 1467 × 84, *long breemoe* 1635 (*v.* **lang¹**), *short breemoe* 1635, *Houerbremhou* c.1285 (*v.* **uferra**), *neþerbremhou* 13², *Netherbremhow*, *Nethir bremhow* l.13² (*v.* **neoðera**) (*v.* **brēme, haugr**); *Brewings homestead* e.18 (*v.* **hām-stede**; with the surn. *Brewin(g)*); *(le) Briggefurlong* 1287, l.13², 1325, 1331, 1332, *Breggefurlong* l.13¹, *Bryggefurlong'* 1467 × 84 (*v.* **furlang**), cf. *the bridge end* 1635 (*v.* **ende**) (*v.* **brycg**; prob. with reference to Soar Bridge *supra*); *brodedol'* 1325, *le Brodedoles* 1332 (*v.* **brād, dāl**); *Broad(e) Sick* 1661, 1666, 1668, *Broadsike* 1666 (*v.* **brād, sík**); *le Brog* (sic) c.1285, *the Brooke* 1635, 1649, *Cussington Brooke* 17, *le brock dick* 1331 bis (*v.* **dík**), *Brokefelde* 1467 × 84, *Brook(e)feild* 1635, 1666, *Brook(e) Field* 1649, 1666 (*v.* **feld**; one of the early great fields of the township) (*v.* **brōc**); *Brounshow* l.13², *Brounsou* 1325, *Brounsow* 1332 (*v.* **haugr**; the first el. may be the surn. *Broun/Brown*, but likelier is one of its pers.n. sources such as ON *Brúnn* (ODan *Brun*), OE *Brūn* or a by-name from OE *brūn* 'brown', *v.* Reaney *s.n.* Brown); *Burbladehyl* c.1280, c.1285 bis, 14, *Burbladhill'* l.13² bis, *Burbladhil* 1325, 1332, *Burbladil* 1331, *Burblade hill*, *~ hyll* 1467 × 84 (*v.* **bur-blade, hyll**); *Butt Close* e.18 (*v.* **butte**); *Calkhill'*, *Calkhull'* l.13², *Calcehull* 13²,

13 (15), *Calchil* 1325, 1331, 1332, *Kauke hill* 1601 (*v*. **calc, hyll**); *Caunts Close* 1699, 1700, *Caunts plot* 1668 (*v*. **plot**) (with the surn. *Caunt*); *Tho. Chamberleins headland* 1601 (*v*. **hēafod-land**), *Chamberlains Homestead* 1719 (*v*. **hām-stede**); *Charphyll* 1467 × 84, *Sharp(e) hill* 1601, 1635 (*v*. **scearp, hyll**); *Cheescake nook* 1649 (*v*. **cheesecake, nōk**); *the Medow close that Choyes holds* 1668, *Choises Meadow* 1676 (with the surn. *Joyce*); *le Cleyclif* c.1280, *Clayclif* 1270 × 90, *Cleclif, Cleiclif* l.13[2], 1331, *Nethercleiclif* 1331 (*v*. **neoðera**) (*v*. **clǣg, clif**); *Cleyclos* 1349 (*v*. **clǣg, clos(e)**); *Cleypytt'* 1467 × 84 (*v*. **cley-pytt**); (*le*) *Clif* l.13[2], 13[2], 1325, 1332, *þe Clif* 1331, *Clyfe* 1467 × 84, *Vnderclyf* 1467 × 84 (*v*. **under**), *Clyffelde* 1467 × 84, *Cliff feild alias Syson miln feild* 1635 (*v*. **feld**; one of the early great fields, this adjoining Syston Mill (*q.v.*)) (*v*. **clif**); *Coates headland* 1601 (*v*. **cot, hēafod-land**); *Cockislandis* 13[2], 13 (15), *Kokeslandes* p.1290, *Koklandys* 1467 × 84 (*v*. **land**; either with **cocc**[2] or with the OE pers.n. *Cocc* or its surn. reflex *Cock*); *the Common* 1635, *the Com(m)on Hedge* 1635, 1679 (*v*. **hecg**; a boundary hedge), *Common way* 1662 (*v*. **weg**) (*v*. **commun**); *Conniegrey close* c.1634, *Conygrey close*, *Cunnery clos(s)e* 1666, *Connery* ~, *Cunnery head* 1635, *Coningrey head* 1649 (*v*. **hēafod**) (*v*. **coningre**); *Constable peice* 1668 (*v*. **conestable, pece**); *Cosyngton Woldys* 1467 × 84 (*v*. **wald**); *Cottage Close* 1726 (*v*. **cotage**); *Cow Close or Bowling Leas* 1719 (*v*. Top Bowling Leys *supra*); *the Cowpasture*, *the pasture* 1635 (*v*. **pasture**); *Crokenest* c.1285, 1325, 1332, *Crokenes* 1601, *Crokenest furlong* 1635 (*v*. **furlang**), *Croknest thornes* 1635 (*v*. **þorn**) (*v*. **kráka, nest**); *Crosforlong* l.13[2], *Crosfurlong* 1331, *Crosse furlong'* 1467 × 84 (*v*. **cross, furlang**); *Croslandes* p.1290, *Croslandys*, *Crosselandis* l.13[2] (*v*. **cross, land**); *Croseleys* 1467 × 84, *Crosse Leyes* 1601, ~ *leas* 1635 (*v*. **cross, lǣs**); *iuxta crucem* 1467 × 84 ('(furlong) beside the cross'; with MLat *crux* (*crucem* acc.sg.) 'a cross'); *Crowe holme garden* 1635 (*v*. **crāwe, holmr, gardin**); *Dickforlong* 1325, *Dickfurlong* 1325, 1331, 1332 (*v*. **dík, furlang**); *Doctors Orch(y)ard or Apple Yard* 1704, 1708, 1708 (18) (*v*. **orceard** and *Apple Yard*, *supra*), *Doctors stints* 1635 (*v*. **stint**) (*v*. **doctour** and Doctors Cl *supra*); *dorendale gate* l.13[2] (*v*. **gata**), *Ouerdorindale* p.1290 (*v*. **ofer**[3]) (*v*. **dora, dalr**); *Long Drabs* 17 (*v*. **drabbe**, cf. The Drabble, Lei **2** 263); (*the*) *Eight Hades*, *ye 8 hades* 1666 (*v*. **hēafod**); *the elboes*, *the elbowes* 1635 (*v*. **elbowe**; alluding to land with sharp turns in its boundaries, esp. adjacent to a stream; here presum. the name of a group of selions); *John Fishers homestead* 1666 (*v*. **hām-stede**); *Flaxlands* 17 (*v*. **fleax, land**); *the foure leas* 1666 (*v*. **fēower, leys**; when compounded with a numeral, *leys* represents grassland units of tenure corresponding to *lands* (i.e. selions or strips) similarly used of arable); *brodefoxholl'* l.13[2] (*v*. **brād**), *Clefoxholl'* l.13[2], *Cleyfoshol'* 1467 × 84, *Cleafoxholes* 1635, *Cley foxholes* 1649 (*v*. **clǣg**), *littelfoxol'* 1325, *littel foxoles* 1333 (*v*. **lȳtel**), *Ryefoxoles* 1332, *Rie foxeho(o)les* 1601, *Rye foxhill* (sic) 1610 (*v*. **ryge**), *Schortfoshol'* 1467 × 84 (*v*. **sc(e)ort**) (*v*. **fox-hol**); *Houerfuldolys* c.1280, 14 (*v*. **uferra**), *Netherefouldoles* l.13[1] (*v*. **neoðera**) (*v*. **fūl, dāl**); *le Gatys* l.13[2], *le Gates* 1332 (*v*. **gata**); *Gibsons Close* 1649 (with the surn. *Gibson*); *Gilby Rowe* 1649 (*v*. **vrá** and *le Wro*, *infra*; the surn. *Gilby* is that of a family originally from Gilby, 20 miles north-west of Lincoln); *John Goffs plot* 1668 (*v*. **plot**), *Goffs Meadow* 1676 (with the surn. *Goffe*; *v*. *Gouges house and homestead*, *infra*); *Goldhou* 1325, *Goldhow* 1331, 1332 (*v*. **haugr**; either with **gold**, which may refer to the discovery of gold treasure in an early burial, but more likely used in the sense 'golden-hued' with reference to flowers, or less likely **golde** 'a (marsh) marigold'); *le Gore* l.13[2] (*v*. **gāra**); *Gorebrode* c.1575 (*v*. **gorebrode**); *Gouges house and homestead* 1666 (*v*. **hām-**

stede; with the surn. *Gouge* which here may be an earlier spelling for *Goffe* (*v. Goffes Meadow*, *supra* and Reaney *s.nn.*)); *Grahalega* 1199 Cur (*v.* **grǣg**[2], **lēah**; at this date *grǣg* poss. refers to the wolf rather than to the badger); *Graves his close* 1678; *Greneham Wonge* 1601 (*v.* **vangr**), *Greenum baulke* 1649 (*v.* **balca**) (with the surn. *Greenham*); *grenehou*, *Grenhou* 1325, *le Grenehow* 1332 (*v.* **grēne**[1], **haugr**); *Grenishou* c.1285, *Greynsow* 1467 × 84 (*v.* **grein, haugr**); *greenknowles* 1649 (*v.* **grēne**[1], **cnoll**); *Green shawe* 1635 (*v.* **grēne**[1], **sceaga**); *Little* ~ ~, *Greene Stye* 17 (*v.* **grēne**[1], **stīg**); *the hades* 1610 (*v.* **hēafod**); *the Hall close* 1666, ~ ~ ~ *yate* 1635 (*v.* **geat**), *the nether Hall peece* 1635 (*v.* **pece**), *Over* ~ ~ (*v.* **uferra**), *Nether Hall wong* 1635 (*v.* **vangr**) (*v.* The Hall *supra*); *le Hengende* 1270 × 90, *hangeinge* 1610, *Hangin hill* 1635 (*v.* **hangende, hengjandi**; the OE pres.part., meaning 'hanging', in the earliest form influenced by its ON cognate, is here used as a sb. meaning 'a steep slope, a steep hillside'); *Hennelandys* l.13[2] bis, *Henelandes* 1331, *Heynlandys* 1467 × 84 (*v.* **henn, land**); *Henton Close* 1666 (with the surn. *Henton*); *Herstenhow* l.13[2] bis, 1331 ('boundary-stone hill', *v.* **hār**[2], **stān**, **haugr**, with the influence of Scand **steinn**); *Hestecrofte*, *Hestecraft* 1325, *Hestcroft* 1332 (*v.* **croft**; prob. with ON **hestr** 'a horse, a stallion'); *Heyscroft'* 1467 × 84, *Heascroft* 1635, *Hescroftes Leyes* 1601, *Heascroft leas* 1635 (*v.* **leys**) (*v.* **hǣs**, **croft**; but in consideration of the late date of the earliest form, the surn. *Heyes* is also poss. as the first el., *v.* Reaney *s.n.* Hease); *the Highway plott* 1678 (*v.* **hēah-weg, plot**); *the Hill* 1635; *the Hogg Yard* 1702, *ye Hog yarde* 1708, *the Hog Yards* 1708 (18) (*v.* **geard**), *the Hogpoole* 1635 (*v.* **pōl**[1]) (*v.* **hogg**); *Holgate* l.13[2], 1467 × 84, *Olgate* 1467 × 84 (*v.* **hol**[2], **gata**); *Hollowe furlonge* 1601 (*v.* **holh, furlang**); *Hollowe furre*, *Hollow furroe* 1635 (*v.* **holh, furh**); *Holme close* c.1634 (*v.* **holmr**); *Holtons close* 1673 (with the surn. *Holton* of a family originally from one of three Lincs. villages of this name: Holton cum Beckering, Holton le Clay, Holton le Moor); *the Home plott* 1668 (*v.* **home, plot**); *the Homestall* 1704, 1708, 1708 (18) (*v.* **hām-stall**; i.e. of *the Parsonage House*, *v.* The Rectory *supra*); *Honys close* c.1634, *honeyes closse* 1649 (*v.* **clos(e)**; with the surn. *Honey*, from OE *hunig* 'honey' used as a term of endearment, as 'sweetheart'); *horse croft* 1649 (*v.* **hors, croft**, cf. *Hestecrofte*, *supra*); *Horshades* p.1290, *Horshadehyl* c.1285 bis, *Horshadehul* l.13[1], *Horsadhill'*, *Horsadyl* l.13[2], *Horsadil* 1325 bis, 1332 bis, *Horsecle*, *Horsicle* 1601 (*v.* **hyll**), *Horseydylboske*, *Horseydelbuske* 1467 × 84 (*v.* **buskr**), *Horseydylgate* 1467 × 84 (*v.* **gata**), *Horsicle meare*, ~ *meere* 1635 (*v.* **(ge)mǣre**), *Horsickel(l) way* 1666 (*v.* **weg**) (*v.* **hors, hēafod**); *Horsnoll* 1467 × 84 (*v.* **hors, cnoll**); *Hous his hadland* 1635, *Wid. Hous hadland* 1635 (i.e. *Widow* ~ ~) (*v.* **hēafod-land**; with the surn. *House*, *v.* Reaney *s.n.*); *Howgate* 1601 bis (*v.* **haugr, gata**); *Hundehoge* 1124 ASC E, *Hundehaug* c.1285, *Hundaue* 1325, *Hundauc* 1332, *Hundauk* 1467 × 84, *Hundie hoole* 1601 (*v.* **hol**[1]) (*v.* **haugr**; the first el. is either the ON pers.n. *Hundi* or the sb. **hund**, *v.* Barrie Cox, 'Leicestershire moot-sites: the place-name evidence', *Transactions of the Leicestershire Archaeological and Historical Society* 47 (1971–72), 14–21 at 14–15); *Hungerhil* 1325, 1332 bis, 14, *Hungurhyll* 1467 × 84, *Hungerhill* 1467 × 84, 1601, 1635, 1649, *Hungarhill* 1635 (*v.* **hungor, hyll**); *Hyboro* 1467 × 84 bis, *Hyborowe* 1601 (*v.* **hēah**[1], **berg**); *Hyclyf* 1467 × 84 (*v.* **hēah**[1], **clif**); *Hyridolis* c.1285, *heridol'* 1325, *le Hiridoles* 1331, *le Hyridoles* 1332 (*v.* **dāl**; poss. with OE **higre** 'a magpie, a jay', and if so, the 1325 form may have been influenced by the ON cognate **hegri** 'a heron'; otherwise with ME **hyrid** 'let out in return for payment'); *the Island* 1708 (18), 1762 (*v.* **island**; part of *the Parsonage House* environs, it was a piece of ground completely enclosed by others); *Widdowe Kirbyes hadland* 1635 (*v*. **hēafod-land**), *Wid. Kirbyes hadlea* 1635 (*v*. **headley**); *Kylne Yard* c.1634 (*v*. **cyln, geard**); *Lane Close* e.18 (*v*. **lane**); *Langbothyl* 1287, *Langebythul* l.13[2], *langebothil* 1325, *langbothul* 1332, *langbotilsyke* c.1285 (*v*. **sík**) (*v*. **lang**[1], **hyll**; the second el. is poss. **bōð**, with the l.13 cent. form containing its variant **búð**; otherwise **bot**); *Leapoole* 1601, 1649, *Leapole* 1601, *Leypoole* 1649, *Leypulleyes* 1467 × 84, *the leapoole leas, the Leypoole leyes* 1635, *Leypoole leys* 1666 (*v*. **lǣs**) (*v*. **laie**; **pull** of the 15th cent. form was replaced by **pōl**[1]); *the Ley(e)s Close* 1666, *the Leas* ~ 1719 (*v*. **leys**); *Leylandys* 1467 × 84 (*v*. **lǣge, land**); *Leyvyngys* 1467 × 84, *the leavings peece* 1635 (*v*. **pece**) (*v*. **lẹvenges** 'remainder, residue'; here of uncertain application); *Luin bridg way* 1635 (the road to Lewin Bridge in Ratcliffe on the Wreake); *Mr Lumners bush* 1635 (*v*. **busc**), *Mr Lumners close* 1635, *Mr Lumners (grass) hadland* 1635 (*v*. **hēafod-land**); *Marlepitt'* 1467 × 84, *Marlepit(t)* 1635, 1649 (*v*. **marle-pytt**); *Tobias Marshalls meadow* 1666, *Marshalls pingle* 1649 (*v*. **pingel**); *Malmberthorn* 1325, 1331, 1332 bis, 14, *Mamethorn* (sic) 1467 × 84 (*v*. **malm, berg, þorn**); *Widdow Masons land* 1666 (*v*. **land**); *Merstalles* 1331, 1467 × 84, *be nethe the Merstals* 1467 × 84 (*v*. **benethe**), *Gosmastal', Gosmastalis, Gosmastalys* 1467 × 84, *Garmastalles* 1601, *Garmestalls* 1635 bis (*v*. **gōs**), *Narow Merstallus* 1467 × 84 (*v*. **nearu**), *Nether Merstals* 1467 × 84 (*v*. **neoðera**) (*v*. **mere-stall** and Ch **3** 158–9 *s.n. le Merstal'*); *the middle meere* 1635 (*v*. **mere**[1]); *Milne furlonge* 1601 (*v*. **myln, furlang**); *Mirehilles* 1331, *Myrhillis* 1467 × 84 (*v*. **mýrr, hyll**); *Mydulfelde* 1467 × 84, *Midle feild* 1601, *(the) Middle feild* 1635, 1666, ~ *Field* 1649, 1666 (*v*. **middel, feld**; one of the early great fields of the township); *Mydulfurlong'* 1467 × 84 (*v*. **middel, furlang**; i.e. of Great Rye Fd); *Netharde yarde* 1554 (*v*. **neetherd, geard**); *Nether Close or Seggs Close* 1677 (*v*. Seggs *supra*); *Nether douedale* l.13[2] (*v*. **neoðera, dalr**; poss. with a pers.n., either OE *Dūfe* or ON *Dúfa*, but a bird-name OE **dūfe**/ON **dúfa** may be present, cf. *Dovedale* in Hoby f.ns. (b)); *Nethurfurlong'* 1467 × 84 (of Little Rye Fd), *Nethurfurlong'* 1467 × 84, *the nether furlong(e)* 1601, 1635 (of Great Rye Fd) (*v*. **neoðera, furlang**); *the North feild* 1601 (also called *Brokefeld, q.v.*); *Northings* 17 (*v*. **norð, eng**); *Nyne leyes* 1649 (*v*. **nigon, leys**; grassland units of tenure corresponding to *lands* (i.e. selions or strips) similarly used of arable); *Osseps close* 1662, 1666 (with a surn., presum. *Allsep/Allsop*); *Oswoldacr'* l.13[2] (*v*. **æcer**; either with a pers.n., OE *Ōswald* or ON *Ásvaldr*, or their ME surn. reflex *Oswald*, *v*. Reaney *s.n.*); *Oswins Bridge* 1666, *William Oswins house*, ~ ~ *land*, *John Oswins Home Plott* e.18 (*v*. **home, plot**); *Old Close* 1668 (with either **ald** or **wald**); *the old Inclosure* 1666, 1762 (*v*. **ald, inclosure**); *the parsonage homestead* 1666, *the Homestead* 1762 (*v*. **personage, hām-stede**); *the Parsons sevynstynt'* 1467 × 84, *the Seven Styntes* 1601 (*v*. **persone, seofon, stint**); *Pears his plott* 1678 (*v*. **plot**); *Pease Field* 1610, *Peasehill* 17 (*v*. **pise**); *Pencroft* 1666 (*v*. **penn**[2], **croft**); *Tho. Peppers close* 1601, *Peppers or Holtons Close* 1673 (*v*. *Holtons close, supra*); *Peselondys* c.1285 bis, *Peselandes* 1270 × 90, *le peselandes* l.13[1], *Peyslandis, Peyselandys* l.13[2], *Peyslondis* 13[1], *peiseland'* 1325 bis, *Peyselandes* 1331, 1332 bis, *Peaseland(e)s* 1601, 1635, *Peyseland(ys) grene* l.13[2], *Peyslondegren, Peyslondgrene* 1467 × 84 (*v*. **grēne**[2]) (*v*. **pise, land**); *the Pingle* c.1634 (*v*. **pingel**); *the Pitt Close or Ratcliffe End Close* 1699 (*v*. **pytt, ende**; Ratcliffe on the Wreake adjoins to the east); *the Pump Court* 1708, 1708 (18), 1762 (*v*. **pumpe, court**; part of *the Homestall* of *the Parsonage House*); *Quallerie*, ~ *leyes* 1601 (*v*. **leys**) (either with **quarrere** 'a quarry', with dissimilation of *rr* > *ll*, or **quarrelle** 'a quarry', with metathesis); *Radclifgate*

1467 × 84 (*v.* **gata**; the road to Ratcliffe on the Wreake); *Longe Ratche* 1601, *long ratch*, ~ ~ *furlong* 1635 (*v.* **furlang**) (*v.* **rǣc** and Thackracks *supra*); *Ratcliff(e) Broad* 1601, 1635, *Ratcliffe broard* 1610 (*v.* **brǣdu**), *Ratcliff leas* 1635 (*v.* **leys**), *Ratcliff meere* 1635, *Ratcliffe meare* 1666 (*v.* **(ge)mǣre**) (lands bordering Ratcliffe on the Wreake); *the Reed(e)s* 1635 (*v.* **hrēod**); *Rencheston* l.13[1], 14, *Rengiston* c.1285, *Rengeston* l.13[2], 1325, 1331, 1332, *Rynston* 14 (1467 × 84) (*v.* **tūn**; perh. with an unrecorded OE pers.n. *Hrencge*, which may be compared with the postulated *Hrencga* of Rangeworthy (*Rengeswurda* 1167, *Renchewrth* 1261), Gl **3** 11; the lost farmstead was in the region of the later great Middle Fd); *le rid* 13[2], *le Ryd* 1331 (*v.* **ryde**); *Rie meare* 1601 (*v.* **ryge, (ge)mǣre**); *Round hill plott, the Round Hill plot* 1666 (*v.* **round, plot** and Lambles *supra*); *rundell* 1601, *the Rundells*, ~ *furlong* 1635 (*v.* **furlang**) (*v.* **rynel**); *Rychemere* 1467 × 84 (*v.* **ric**; with **mere**[1] or **(ge)mǣre**); *Ryele* 1331, *Ryhill, Ryhyll* 1467 × 84, *Rie hill* 1601, *Ryehill* 1635 (*v.* **ryge, hyll**); *Ryhades* 1467 × 84 (*v.* **ryge, hēafod**); *Schardewelforlong, Schardewellfurlong* 1325, *Schardewelfurlong* 1332, *Schardewil furlong* 14 (*v.* **sceard**, **wella**, **furlang**); *Schepecotes* 1331, *le Schepecote furlong* 13[2], ~ *furlang* 13 (15) (*v.* **furlang**), *Sheepcote close* 1647, 1666, *the Sheepcoat close* 1666 (*v.* **scēp-cot**); *Schortfurholm* c.1280, c.1285 (*v.* **sc(e)ort, furh, holmr**); *Seagrave End Plott* 1699, 1700 (*v.* **ende, plot**; Cossington shares a short length of its parish boundary in the extreme north-east with Seagrave); *Seynt Mary hadland'*, ~ ~ *hadlond'* 1467 × 84 (*v.* **hēafod-land**; with reference to land of the Abbey of St Mary de Pratis, Leicester); *Sharpes nooke* 1635, 1649, 1666, *Sharps Nook* 1666, 1668 (*v.* **nōk**; with the surn. *Sharp*); *Sheepgate* 1591 (*v.* **shepe-gate**); *Shrubb feild* 17 (*v.* **scrubb, feld**); *Silbyholme* 1467 × 84 (*v.* **holmr**), *Sileby Inclosure* 1762 (*v.* **inclosure**) (Sileby adjoins to the north); *Sison Mille feild* 1601, *Sison miln feild* 1635, *Sison* ~ ~, *Siston Mill field* 1666 (also known as *Cliff feild*, one of the great fields of Cossington township, lying towards Syston Mill (*q.v.*), *v.* **feld**), *Sison mille hill* 1601, *Syson miln hill* 1635, *Siston Mill hill* 1649, *Syson miln way* 1635 (*v.* **weg**) (*v.* **myln**); *(ye) Six Leas* 1666, 1673 (*v.* **leys**; a close made up of six former units of pasture land); *(the) South close* 1666; *Southfeild* c.1634, 17, ~ *hades* 17 (*v.* **hēafod**) (*v.* **sūð, feld**); *Sowtholme* 1467 × 84 bis, *Sowth Holme* c.1575, Eliz 1, *South holm* 1610, *Southom(e)* 1635, *Schortsowtholme* 1467 × 84, *Short Southam* 1601, *Short Southome* 1635, *short south holme* 1649 (*v.* **sc(e)ort**), *Great Southam* 1601, *Long Southome* 1635, *South thum banke* (sic) 1563 (*v.* **banke**) (*v.* **sūð, holmr**); *Robt. Spencers plot* 1668 (*v.* **plot**), *Spencers Meadow* 1676; *Stacfurlang'* 13[2], 13 (15), *Stacforlong* l.13[2], 1325, *Stackforlong* l.13[2] bis, *Stacfurlong* p.1290, 13[2], 13 (15), 1325, 1331, 1332, *Stakfurlong* 1467 × 84, *Stackfurlonge* 1601, *Stacke ferlong* 1610, *Stackfurlong* 1635, 1649 (*v.* **staca, furlang**); *Stanilandes* l.13[1], 1332, *Steynilondis* c.1285, *Stanilandis* l.13[2], 13[2], 1325, *Stonylands* 17 (*v.* **stānig, land**; the c.1285 form influenced by ON **steinn**); *Mr Stavelys Home meadow* 1676 (*v.* **home**); *Stevens leas* 1635, ~ *leyes* 1649 (*v.* **leys**; with the surn. *Stevens*); *above the stone* 1601, *the Stone* 1635 (*v.* **stān**; naming a furlong and a boundary marker); *Stongate* 1467 × 84, *Stonegate* 1601, ~ *way* 1635 (*v.* **weg**) (*v.* **stān, gata**); *Stonie hill* 1601, *Stonhill* 1610, 1635, 1649, *Stone hill* 1666, *Stonhill furlong* 1635 (*v.* **furlang**) (*v.* **stānig, stān, hyll**); *Stonhou* 1325, *Stonehow* 1325, 1332, *Stonow* 1467 × 84 (*v.* **stān, haugr**; prob. the earlier name for *Stone hill, supra*); *the Sonne shoote* 1649 (*v.* **sunne, scēot**[3] and Sunhill *supra*); *Swine poole* 1598 (*v.* **pōl**[1]; with either **swin**[2] or **swīn**[1]; *v.* Swines Bridge Mdw *supra*); *le syke* l.13[2] (*v.* **sík**); *Syson meadowe* 1635 (Syston adjoins to the south); *Thakecroft* 1467 × 84 (*v.* **þak, croft**); *Thickebusk* l.13[2],

1332, *Thikebusk* 1325 (*v.* **þicce**², **buskr**); *Thokeslandys* l.13², *Thokeslandes* 1331, *Thoklandis* 1467 × 84 bis (*v.* **land**; with a Scand pers.n., either a by-name *Tōk* (perh. meaning 'fool'), which is deduced from Danish p.ns. (*v.* SPNLY 288), or *Tóki* accorded a ME *-es* gen.sg.); *Long* ~, *Short thorne* 1601 (*v.* **þorn**); *Thorntons Meadow* 1676 (with the surn. *Thornton*); *Togdoles* 1467 × 84, *Togge dooles* 1601, (*the*) *Dogdoles* (sic) 1635, 1649 (*v.* **dāl**; perh. with the OE pers.n. *Tocga*); (*the*) *Town Close* 1708, e.18, *the Townes Holme* 1601 (*v.* **holmr**), *the towne land* 1601, *ye Towne Side* 1666 (*v.* **sīde**), *the Town Street* 1704, 1708, 1708 (18), 1762 (*v.* **strǣt**) (*v.* **tūn**); (*the*) *Townsend leas* 1635 (*v.* **leys**), *Townsend Plot* 1673 (*v.* **plot**) (*v.* **tūn, ende**); *the upper furlonge* 1601 (*v.* **furlang**; i.e. of Little Rye Fd); *Wadefurlong* 1331 bis (*v.* **(ge)wæd, furlang**); *Wadetorn* 1325, *Wadethorn* 1325, 1332, 14, *Wadethornforlong* l.13² (*v.* **furlang**), *Wadethornrissches* l.13² (*v.* **risc**) (*v.* **(ge)wæd, þorn**); *Warteborow* l.13² (*v.* **weard, varða, berg**); *Waterresschus* 1467 × 84, *Waterish Wong* 1635, 1666, *Waterisse Wonge* 1649 (*v.* **vangr**), *Waterish Wong hedge* 1649 (*v.* **hecg**) (*v.* **wæter, risc**); *Waterforowes*, *þe Watriforoues* 1325, *le Watryforowes* 1332 bis, *Waterthorowes* 1635 (*v.* **wæter, wæterig, furh** and *the Waterfurrow*(*e*)*s* in Asfordby f.ns. (b)); *ye Water syde* c.1575 (*v.* **wæter, sīde**); *Wellbucke Feild* 17 (*v.* **wella, bekkr, feld**); *Welslade* 1635, *Wellslade* 1649 (*v.* **wella, slæd**); *Weteborow* l.13² bis (*v.* **hwǣte, berg**); *Mr Whalleyes great peace* (sic), *Mr Whalley great peeice* 1601 (*v.* **grēat, pece**); *Richard Wilkins hadland* 1635 (*v.* **hēafod-land**); *Wiloforlong'*, *Wylefurlong'*, *Wyloforlong'*, *Wylwefurlong'* 1467 × 84, *Willow*(*e*) *furlong*(*e*) 1601, 1635 (*v.* **wilig, furlang**); *Mr Willoughbies hadland* c.1575 (*v.* **hēafod-land**); *le Woldacr'*, *Woldacre* l.13², *Woldakr* 13² bis (*v.* **wald, æcer**); *le Woldgatehend* l.13² (*v.* **wald, gata, ende**); *Wlfethwong* l.13², *Wolfetewong* 13¹, 14 (*v.* **vangr**; either with the OE pers.n. *Wulfgēat* or with its surn. reflex *Wolfit/Woolfit*); *le Wro* c.1285, 1331, 1349, 14 (*v.* **vrá** and *Gilby Rowe*, *supra*); *Wydeboro* 1467 × 84 bis (*v.* **wīd, berg**); *Wymanstead* 1649 (perh. 'the woman's homestead', *v.* **wīfmann, stede**, cf. Winestead YE 29-30; the OE pers.n. *Wīgmund* is also formally poss. as the first el., although pers.ns. are rare in compound with *stede*); *yarmshalle* 1610 (the generic is poss. **hall** in its later sense 'a farmhouse', with the surn. *Yarm* (*v.* Reaney *s.n.*), but **halh** is also poss. and if so, earlier forms are needed to ascertain the first el.); *yokefurlong* 1635 (*v.* **geoc**¹, **furlang**; the furlong may have resembled a yoke in shape, but the precise implications of its name are uncertain).

Cotes

COTES

Chotes Wm 1 Nichols, Stephen ib
les cotes n.d. AD
Cotes l.12 *GarCart*, l.12, c.1200 Dane *et passim* to 13 *MiD*, 1306 *GarCart et freq*, (~ *super Soram* 1271 Abbr), (~ *Poutrel* 1343 Ipm, 1344 Cl), *Cothes* l.Hy 2 Dane, Hy 3 Ipm, *Cotis* 1220 MHW, c.1237 GildR (p) *et passim* to 1277 *GarCart*, 1325 Ipm, *Cotys* 1326 ib
Kotes l.12 Nichols, e.13 BM, 1341 GildR (p)
Cootes 1396 HMCVar, 1416 Nichols, *Cootys* 1541 MinAccts
Coates 1558 Will, 1598 LML, *Coats* 1619, 1623 ib

'The cottages', *v.* **cot**; here an early instance of the ME nom.pl. **cotes**. The two earliest forms have AN orthographic *ch* for *c* before the back vowel *o*. *Robertus Putrel de Cotes* held the manor in the late 12th century (Dane) and the Poutrell family is recorded in possession until at least *Rogerus Poutrell* 1396 HMC. The settlement lies beside the river Soar, hence ~ *super Soram* 1271 Abbr (with MLat *super* 'on, upon').

CHURCH (site of . . .), cf. *capellam Cotis* 1220 MHW (with MLat *capella* 'a chapel'). COTES BRIDGE, 1798 Nichols, cf. *pontium inter Loughteburg et Cotes* 1332 ib (with MLat *pons* (*pontium* gen.pl.) 'a bridge'). FISHPOND SPINNEY. HALL FM, *v.* Old Hall *infra*. MANOR FM (lost), *Manor farm* 1877 White, *v.* **maner**. MOAT HILL, *Motts* 1735 *Map*; evidently a former moot-site, *v.* **mōt**. MOAT HILL SPINNEY is *Moat Spinney* 1806 Map, *Moat-hill Spinny* 1836 O, *v.* **spinney**. OLD HALL. PARKS FM, *Parks* 1877 White, cf. *Cotes park house* 1719 Nichols, *v.* **park**.

FIELD-NAMES

Undated forms in (a) are 1871 *Plan*. Throughout, forms dated 1735 are *Map*.

(a) Seven Acres, Eight ~, Sixteen ~, Bottom ~ ~, Top Twenty Acres (*v.* **æcer**); Far ~, Middle ~, Near Brandbury (*Brandbury Close* 1735, *v.* **berg**, with **brand** or **brant**; the close was on a steep hillside); Bridle Gate Cl (*v.* **brigdels, gata**); Brook Cl (cf. *Brook Meadow* 1735, *v.* **brōc**; beside King's Brook); Bullock Yard (*v.* **bulluc, geard**); Cow Cl (1735); Far Cl; Far ~ ~, Near Furmety Mdw (*v.* **furmente**); Far ~ ~, Near ~ ~, Great Cl; Hall Garden, Hall Orchard (*v.* Old Hall *supra*); Hill Cl; South ~, Homestead (*v.* **hām-stede**); Lower ~ ~, Upper Long Croft (*v.* **croft**); Lower Mdw; Meadow Leys (*v.* **leys**); East ~ ~, West Moat Cl, Moat Orchard (*v.* Moat Hill *supra*); Far ~ ~, First ~ ~, Near Nether Cl (*Neather Close* 1735, *v.* **neoðera**); Over Mdw (*v.* **uferra**); Home Park (*v.* **home**), Long Park, Seed Park (*v.* **sǣd**; used in f.ns. of areas of sown grass), Park Mdw (*Old Park* 1735; originally parkland of the Old Hall, *v.* Old Hall and Parks Fm *supra*); Small Mdw; Spring Cl (*v.* **spring**[1]); Tree Cl; Windmill Fd (1735, *v.* **wind-mylne**); Workhouse Cl (1735, *v.* **workhouse**).

(b) *Corn Close* 1735 (*v.* **corn**[1]); *Cotesfeld* 1556 × 58 ECP (*v.* **feld**; a great field of the township, but whether the only one is uncertain since no others are recorded); (*the*) *Hall Close* 1539 Ipm, 1735 (*v.* **clos(e)**), *Hall Meadow* 1735 (*v.* **hall** and Old Hall *supra*); *le Louuefurlong* 13 *MiD* (*v.* **la(g)h, furlang**); *Plashe* 1735 (*v.* **plæsc**); *Townend Close* 1735 (*v.* **tūn, ende**); *Wheathead Close* 1735 (presum. with the surn. *Whitehead*, but if not, *v.* **hwǣte, hēafod**).

South Croxton

SOUTH CROXTON

Crochestone 1086 DB, *Crocheston'* c.1130 LeicSurv, *Crokeston*(*e*) 1201 Abbr, 1203 Ass, 1297 AD
Croxton(') 1199, 1203 Fine, 1205 FF *et passim* to 1265 Misc, 1270 *MiD*, Hy 3 *Crox* (freq) *et freq*, *Croxtona* a.1250 (1404) *Laz*, *Croxtun* 1236 Fees, *Chroxton'* 13 *MiD* bis, *Crouxton'* 1343 *ib* bis
Croxston 1202 FF, 1220 MHW, 1316 FA, 1343 *MiD* (freq), *Crocston* c.1300 AD
Crowston 1529 × 32 ECP, *Crouston* 1576 LibCl, *Croston* 1580 LEpis, 1610 Speed, 1688 LML
Croson 1568 Ct, c.1570 *Rental et passim* to 1679, 1690 *Terrier*, *Crowson* 1607, 1629 LML

The affix is added as:
Sut- 1199 Fine, 1205, 1212 FF
Sud- 1201 Abbr, 1203 Ass *et passim* to 1224 RHug, 13 *MiD*
Suth- 1202 FF, 1203 Fine, 1264 RGrav *et freq* to Edw 1 *CroxR*, 1324 *MiD*, *Suð-* 1204 Nichols, *Suht-* 13 *MiD*
Sou(*t*)- Hy 3 *Crox*, 13 *MiD*, 1302 *Rut*, 1343 *MiD* (freq)
South ~ Hy 3 *Crox*, 1294 *MiD*, Edw 1 *CroxR et passim* to 1343, 1346 *MiD et freq*, *Sowth* ~ 1529 MinAccts, c.1570 *Rental*, 1604 SR

'Krōk's farmstead, village', *v.* **tūn**. The ODan pers.n. *Krōk* (ON *Krókr*) is an original by-name 'crook-backed' (cf. OIcel *krókr* 'a hook') or poss. 'crooked-dealer', *v.* SPNLY 181. Note the typical 16th century (and later) Leics. loss of *t* in the group *-ston*, a loss still evidenced in the modern local pronunciation of Croxton. For further discussion of this recurring p.n., *v.* L **2** 98–100 *s.n.* The suffix **sūð** 'south' distinguishes South Croxton from Croxton Kerrial (Lei **2** 102) in Framland Hundred.

BELL DIP FM (~ ~ LODGE 2½") is *Barsby Lodge* 1835 O, *v.* **loge** and Bell Pits in f.ns. (a). BLACKSMITH'S SHOP (lost), *Blacksmiths Shop* 1844 *TA*, *v.* **blacksmith, sc(e)oppa**. BRANCLIFF FM (~ COTTAGE 2½") is *Brancliffe* *cottage* 1877 White, *Browncliffe lodge* 1925 Kelly, *v.* **cotage, loge** and Brancliff Furlong in f.ns. (a). FOX COTTAGES. GOLDEN FLEECE (P.H.), (*The*) *Golden Fleece* 1844 *TA*, 1846, 1877 White, 1925 Kelly, *Fleece* 1863 White. THE GRANGE, 1863, 1877 White, 1925 Kelly, *v.* **grange**. KINGS LANE, with the surn. *King*, cf. Kings Cl in f.ns (a). MAIDA HO., *Maida house* 1877 White, commemorating the British victory over the French at Maida in Calabria, 4 July 1806. MALT SHOVEL (P.H.) (lost), *the Malt Shovel* 1863 *Sale*. MASONS' ARMS (P.H.) (lost), *Masons' Arms* 1846 White. NEW COVERT, *v.* **cover(t)**. NORTH MANOR HO., *North Manor* (*house*) 1877 White, 1925 Kelly, *v.* **maner**. THE RECTORY, 1877 White, 1925 Kelly, *v.* **rectory**; cf. *the Parsonage House* 1583, 1625, 1708, 1708 (18) *Terrier*, *v.* **personage**. RIDGEMERE LANE, *v.* Barkby *s.n.* ST JOHN THE BAPTIST'S CHURCH, *the Church* 1583, 1708 *Terrier*, *Church (St John)* 1846, 1863, 1877 White, 1925 Kelly, *v.* **cirice**; it is earlier recorded as *ecclesie de Croxton* 1220 MHW, 1310 *Pat*, ~ *de Southcroxton* 1400, 1410 *ib.* Note also *ye Churchyard* 1690, 1697 *Terrier*. SOUTH CROXTON GRANGE is *High Thurning Lodge* 1835 O, *South Croxton lodge* 1877 White, *v.* **loge**; for the earlier name, *v.* **þyrning**. SOUTH MANOR HO. is *Manor house* 1877 White, 1925 Kelly, *v.* **maner**.

FIELD-NAMES

In (a), forms dated 1757 are *Map*, 1798 are *EnclA*, 1844 are *TA*, 1863 and 1877 are *Sale*, 1969 are *Surv*. Forms throughout dated 13 are *MiD*, 1477 (e.16) are *Charyte*, 1467 × 84 are *LTD*, 1583, 1601, 1625, 1674, 1679, 1690, 1697, 1700, e.18, 1708 and 1708 (18) are *Terrier*.

(a) Eight ~, Ten ~, Fourteen Acre 1969 (*v.* **æcer**); The Allotments 1969 (*v.* **allotment**); Baggrave Brook 1798 (1583, *v.* **brōc**; Baggrave adjoins to the south-east); Barley Leys 1798, 1969 (*v.* **bærlic, leys**); Beeby Gate Cl 1757, 1844 (*v.* **gata**; Beeby lies 2 miles to the south-west); Bellpits 1798, Bell Dip (sic) 1969 (*Bell pitt*(*e*)*s* 1601, 1625, 1700, 1708 (18)), Bellpits Furlong 1798 (*Bell Pitts Furlong* 1708, 1708 (18), *v.* **furlang**) (*v.* **belle, pytt**; located in the great *Upper Feild* of the township and too far from the parish church to be the site for the local casting of church bells; *belle* here must refer to the rounded hill spur on which Bell Dip Fm stands, while the pits are presum. the result of mineral extraction; the late form *Bell Dip* may be either the result of the association of sheep-dip with bell-wether or else simply metathesis and voicing of *pit* > *dip*); Big Cl 1969; Big Mdw 1969; Bottom Cl 1863; Brancliff Furlong 1798 (*v.* **furlang**) (*Brancliff* 1583, 1674, 1679 *et passim* to 1708 (18), *Brantliffe* 1625, *Brantlife* 1700, cf. *Brancliff Nook* 1708, 1708 (18) (*v.* **nōk**), *v.* **brant, clif** and Brancliff Furlong in neighbouring Queniborough f.ns.(a)); Brick Kiln Cl, ~

~ Furlong 1798 (*v.* **furlang**) (*v.* **brike-kiln**); Brook Furlong 1757, 1844 (*the Brooke furlong* 1583, *v.* **brōc**, **furlang**); Bull Heads 1798 (*v.* **hēafod**; either with the surn. *Bull* or **bula**); Chace Headland Furlong 1798 (*v.* **hēafod-land**, **furlang**; with the surn. *Chace*, prob. metonymic for *chaser*, from OFr *chaceur* 'a hunter'); Church Headland Furlong 1798 (*churche hadland* 1583, 1601, *the Church hadeland* 1625, *Croxton Church H(e)adland* 1708, 1708 (18), *Church H(e)adland Furlong* 1708, 1708 (18), *v.* **cirice**, **hēafod-land**, **furlang** and St John the Baptist's Church *supra*); Clapperdale Furlong 1798 (*v.* **furlang**), Clapperdale Leys 1798 (*v.* **leys**) (*v.* **clapere**, **dalr**); Court Cl 1798 (1708, 1708 (18), *Cote Close* 1583, *v.* **cot**, **clos(e)**); Nether ~ ~, Upper Cow Cl 1757, Cow Cl 1969; Great ~, Little Cowdam 1757, 1844 (*v.* **cū**, **damme**; an artificially-created watering-place for cattle); Cow Pasture 1757, 1844 (*v.* **pasture**); Cross Furlong 1798 (*v.* **cross**, **furlang**); Cross Leys 1757, 1844 (*v.* **cross**, **leys**); Croxton Brook 1798; Deadmans Grave 1757, 1798 (1708, 1708 (18), *Deadmans Grave furlong* 1700 (*v.* **furlang**)), Little Deadmans 1969 (*v.* **dede-man**, **græf**; on the parish boundary with Beeby and thus poss. an Anglo-Saxon pagan cemetery site); Farthing's (sic) 1757, Farthings 1844 (*v.* **fēorðung** 'a fourth part'; regularly used to indicate land divided into four parts, or more specifically, land which had an area of a quarter of a virgate; alternatively, some such names may allude to the rental of a farthing); Flaxlands Furlong 1798 (*v.* **furlang**), Flax Lands 1969 (*Flaxlandes* 1467 × 84, *Flaxlands* 1583, 1708, 1708 (18), *v.* **fleax**, **land**); Bottom ~ ~, Fox Covert 1870 (*v.* **cover(t)**); Fox's Mdw 1969 (with the surn. *Fox*); Franks 1969 (with the surn. *Frank(s)* in the possessive case); Garden Cl 1969 (*v.* **gardin**); Gravel Pit Cl 1757, 1844, Gravel Pit 1969 (*v.* **gravel**, **pytt**); Hall Leys 1798 (*v.* **leys**), Nether ~, Upper Hallsick, Hallsick Cl, Hallsick Mdw, Hallsick Spinney 1757 (*v.* **spinney**) (*v.* **hall**, **sík**); Great ~, Little Harle 1757, 1844, Harle Cl, Harle Furlong 1798 (*v.* **furlang**) (*Long Harle* 1583, *Harle hades* 1708, 1708 (18) (*v.* **hēafod**), *Harley sicke*, *Harle Sycke* 1583 (*v.* **sík**), *v.* **lēah**; either with **hār**[2] 'grey' or 'boundary' or **hær** 'a heap of stones, stony ground', cf. Swed *har* 'stony ground'); Heeld Acre Furlong 1798 (*Heldakir* 1467 × 84, *Heldakyr* 1477 (e.16), 1467 × 84, *Heldiker* 1477 (e.16), *Heldacre* 1583, *heeldaker* 1601, *Heild Acres* 1674, 1679, 1708 (18), *heeldacers* 1700, *Hield Acres* 1708, *Heild acar furlong* 1625, *Heildacres* ~ 1690, 1697 (*v.* **furlang**), *Heldakerholme* 1467 × 84 bis (*v.* **holmr**), *Heldacre sicke* 1583, *hilde acre sicke*1625 (*v.* **sík**), *v.* **helde**, **æcer**); Herring Cl 1798, Herrings ~ 1969 (poss. with the surn. *Herring*; but note the Herring Shoot in Walton on the Wolds f.ns.(a)); High Ash 1798 (*v.* **æsc**); High Brinks Cl 1798 (*High Brinkes* 1583, *hybrinks* 1700, *High Brinks* 1708, 1708 (18), *v.* **hēah**[1], **brink**); Nether ~, Upper Highleys, Little Highleys 1757 (*v.* **hēah**[1], **leys**); Holes 1757, The Holes 1844 (*v.* **hol**[1]); (The) Holt Cl 1757, 1844 (adjoins Barkby Holt, *q.v.*); Home Cl 1863, Home Fd 1969 (*v.* **home**); Hooks Furlong 1798 (*the Hookes* 1583, (*the*) *Hook(s) Furlong* 1700, 1708, 1708 (18), *v.* **hōc**, **furlang**); Hop Yard 1798 (*v.* **hop-yard**); Hospital 1969 (a late example, but poss. land once endowed for a charitable institution, *v.* **hospital**); Hovel Cl 1969 (*v.* **hovel**); Hut Cl 1969 (*v.* **hut**); Jack Cl 1757, 1844, Far ~ ~, Middle ~ ~, Near Jack Leys 1757, Jack Leys 1844 (*v.* **leys**) (either with the surn. *Jack* (*v.* Reaney *s.n.*) or with dial. *jack* 'unused', often with pejorative overtones, *v.* Field 106); Kilby Cl 1969 (with the surn. *Kilby* of a family originally from the village of this name, 10 miles to the south-west); Kings Cl 1798 (with the surn. *King*); Knights Cl 1757 (with the surn. *Knight*); Leicester Sick, Little ~ ~ 1757, 1844 (*Leicester Sick* 1674, *v.* **sík**; beside *Leicester Gate* 1679, 1690, 1697, *v.* **gata**, the road to Leicester); Little Cl 1798; Little

Fd 1969; Little Mdw 1969; Long Mdw 1757, 1844, 1969; Longborough Sick Furlong 1798 (*v.* **sík**, **furlang**) (*Longborowe* 1583, *Longborrow* 1674, 1679, 1690, *Long Burrow* 1697, 1708, 1708 (18), *v.* **lang**[1], **berg**); Long Holme Furlong 1798 (*v.* **furlang**) (*Long Holm* 1708, *Long holms* 1708 (18), *v.* **holmr**); Lustygate 1969 (*lustye gate* 1601, 1625, *Lusty* ~ 1674, 1679 *et passim* to 1708 (18), *Lusty gate Furlong* 1708, 1708 (18) (*v.* **furlang**), *Lusty gate side* 1700 (*v.* **sīde**), *v.* **gata**; poss. with a reduced **lūs-þorn** (cf. Lostiford, Sr 255) and attraction to *Leicester Gate*; that both *Lusty Gate* and *Leicester Gate* are present in the same terriers with reference to the same great field would seem to preclude the former's being a development of the latter or vice versa; an alternative explanation for *Lusty* is **lūs** 'a louse', often used to describe something small and insignificant, compounded with **tēag** 'a small enclosure'); Match Dike 1798, Matchdyke 1969 (*v.* **mersc**, **dík**); Mearend Cl 1757 (*v.* **(ge)mǣre**, **ende**; on the parish boundary); Middle Cl 1757, 1844; Middle Mdw 1757, 1844; Mill Furlong 1798 (*v.* **furlang**), Mill Hill 1798, 1969 (cf. *the olde myll hill* 1601, *thould Mill hill* 1625, *the Old Mill Hill* 1679, 1690, 1697), Mill Sick Furlong 1798 (*v.* **furlang**) (cf. *Millsick hades* 1700, *v.* **sík**, **hēafod**) (*v.* **myln**); Millery Leys 1757, 1844 (*v.* **leys**; perh. with *milliary* 'a Roman milestone', note Streethill *infra*; but a base **mylnere** 'a miller' seems likelier); Milkers Bridge 1798 (*v.* **mylker**); The Moat 1969 (*v.* **mote**; the field contains a medieval moated site); Moor Cl 1757, Bottom ~ ~, Top ~ ~ 1844, Moor End Cl 1844 (*v.* **ende**), Moors Bastard 1798 (*v.* **bastard**) (*v.* **mōr**[1]); Mountain 1969 (alluding to hilly land); Muckil Hill 1798 (*Mikilhill*, *Mikulhull*, *Mikylhill* 1467 × 84, *Mokelhill* 1583, *Mucklehill* 1601, *Muckall hill* 1625, *Muckill Hill* 1674, 1679, 1708, *Muckilhil(l)* 1690, 1700, *Muckhil(l) Hill* 1690, 1708, 1708 (18), *Schortmykylhyl* 1467 × 84 (*v.* **sc(e)ort**)), Muckil Hole Furlong (sic) 1798 (*v.* **furlang**) (*Muck(h)ill Hole* 1708, 1708 (18), *v.* **hol**[1]) (*v.* **micel**, **mikill**, **hyll**); Mussels Furlong 1798 (*v.* **furlang**) (*Muswel* 1467 × 84, *Muzzils* 1708, 1708 (18), *Longemuswell* 1467 × 84 (*v.* **lang**[1]), *v.* **mūs**, **wella**); Nether Barn 1757, ~ ~ Cl 1757, 1844, ~ ~ Paddock 1844 (*v.* **paddock**); (the) Nether End 1798, 1844, Nether End Road 1798 (*ye neither end* 1697, *the nether* ~ 1708, 1708 (18), *Nether End Fields* 1732 *Deed*, *v.* **neoðera**, **ende**; with reference to the lower region of the parish, cf. Upper End *infra*); Nether Mdw 1757, 1844; New Cl 1969; Old Ploughed Fd 1969; Old Yard 1757, 1844 (*v.* **ald**, **geard**); Little Parlour 1757 (*v.* **parlur**); Nether ~ ~, Upper Pen Cl 1757, 1844 (*v.* **penn**[2]); Plummers Cl 1969 (cf. *Plummers lane* 1477 (e.16), *v.* **lane**; with the surn. *Plummer*, cf. *Osbertus le plummer* 1225 RFL); Little Poverty 1969 (a f.n. indicating infertile land and financial loss, *v.* Field 108); Rabe's Cupboard 1969 (a complimentary name for productive land; *Rabe* represents either a pet name for Robert or is the surn. *Rabb* (for *Robb*)); Road Cl 1757, 1844 (in 1757, a road passed *through* the close); Road Fd 1969; Rough Cl 1969 (*v.* **rūh**[1]); Saddle Backs 1798 (*v.* **sadol**, **bæc**; with reference to the shape of a hill ridge); Sand Road 1969; Sarsons Barn Cl 1757, 1844, Above Sarsons Barn 1757, Sarsons Homestead 1757, 1844 (*v.* **hām-stede**) (cf. *William Sarson* 1844); Big ~ ~, Little Seed Fd 1969 (*v.* **sǣd**; used in f.ns. of areas of sown grass); Skip-a-dale 1969 (*Scipperdale*, *Scypperdale* 1583, *Skipperdale* 1601, 1625 *et passim* to 1708 (18), *Sciperdale furlong* 1700 (*v.* **furlang**), *Scipperdale Sicke* 1583 (*v.* **sík**); the surviving forms are late, so either a Scandinavianized form of **scypen** with **dalr**, or the surn. *Skipper* (*v.* Reaney *s.n.*) with **deill**); Snipe Wong 1798 (*Snypwong* 1467 × 84 bis, *Snipe Wong(e)* 1583, 1601 *et passim* to 1708 (18), *Snype wonge* 1625, *Snepe Wong* 1708 (18), *Longsnypwong'* 1467 × 84 (*v.* **lang**[1]), *v.* **vangr**; either with the Scand pers.n. *Snípr* or with its surn. reflex *Snipe*); Sowbrook Cl 1757, 1798, Sowbrook Furlong 1798 (*v.* **furlang**), Sowbrook Mdw 1798 (*Sowthbroke* 1467 × 84, *Sowebrok* 1601, *Sowbrooke* 1625, *Sowebrook(e)* 1674, 1679 *et passim* to 1700, *Sowth brooke* 1697, *South Brook* 1708, 1708 (18), *v.* **sūð, brōc**; otherwise known as Queniborough Brook); Spindle Banks, ~ ~ Cl, ~ ~ Mdw 1757 (*v.* **spinele, banke**); Spinney 1757, ~ Cl 1757, 1844, 1969, Spinney Mdw 1969 (*v.* **spinney**); Sprig Thorne 1798 (*v.* **sprigge** (OED *s.v.* sprig sb.², 1), **þorn**); Spring Fd 1757, 1844 (1708, 1708 (18), *v.* **spring**¹); Streethill, ~ Meer 1798 (*v.* **(ge)mǣre**), ~ Side Furlong 1798 (*v.* **sīde, furlang**), Strettle Bridge Cl 1798 (cf. *Strithill hedge* 1583, *Streethill hedge* 1708, 1708 (18) (with **hecg** or **edisc**), *v.* **strǣt, hyll**; recording a Roman road, *v.* Streethill Fm in adjoining Lowesby); Taft Leys 1757 (*v.* **toft, leys**); Tenter Leys Cl 1798 (*v.* **tentour, leys**); Great, Little Thorney, Thorney Spinney 1757 (*v.* **spinney**) (*v.* **þornig**); Three Corner Cl 1757 (*v.* **three-corner**), *Three cornered* ~ 1844 (*v.* **three-cornered**); Allotment ~ (*v.* **allotment**), Big ~, Four ~ (*v.* **fēower**), Middle Thurns 1969, Thurn Cl 1844, Thurn Side Furlong 1798 (*v.* **sīde, furlang**) (cf. *three thurne* 1625 (cf. *Threthornis* in f.ns. (b)), *the Thurnegreene* 1625, *Thurn Greene* 1700 (*v.* **grēne**²), *Thurne sicke* 1625 (*v.* **sík**), *v.* **þyrne**); Far ~ ~, Near Townsend Cl 1757 (*v.* **tūn, ende**); Upper End 1844 (*ye Upper End* (*of South Croxton*) 1697, 1708, 1708 (18), *v.* **upper, ende**); Walley Cl, Walley Furlong 1798 (*v.* **furlang**) (poss. with the surn. *Walley*, *v.* Reaney *s.n.*); West Ford 1969 (*v.* **ford**); Far ~ ~, Near ~ ~, Top West Leys 1757, 1844 (*v.* **leys**); the West Rope end (sic) 1798 (*v.* **ende**) (*Westrope* 1583, *v.* **west, vestr, þorp**; a former farmstead, prob. to be identified with the *Westhorp-* listed in adjoining Barkby f.ns. (b)); West Wong Cl, West Wong Furlong 1798 (*v.* **furlang**) ((*the*) *West Wonges* 1583, 1674, 1679, 1690, *West Wonge* 1697, *v.* **west, vestr, vangr**); Whetstone Cl 1757 (prob. with the surn. *Whetstone* of a family originally from the village of this name, 12 miles to the south-west); The Wilderness 1969 (*v.* **wildernesse**; used of barren or uncultivated land); First ~, Second Willows 1969 (*v.* **wilig**); Far Windmill Furlong 1798 (*the Wynde Mill* 1625, *the Wind Mill* 1674, 1679, 1690, 1697, cf. *ye old Wind Mill* 1679, *Wine Mill Close* 1700, *Wind Mill* ~ 1708, 1708 (18), *Wind Mill Hades* 1708, 1708 (18) (*v.* **hēafod**), *Wyndmill hill* 1601, *v.* **wind-mylne**); The Wong 1798, Wong Fd 1969 (*v.* **vangr**); Worm Row 1969 (*Wormroe* 1583, *v.* **wyrm, vrá**) .

(b) *Abb(e)y Closes* 1674, 1679, 1697, *Abby Cloases* 1690, *Abbye sicke* 1625, *Abby Sick* 1674, 1679, 1690, 1697, *Abbey Sick* 1708 (*v.* **sík**) (*v.* **abbaie**; the Abbey of St Mary de Pratis, Leicester, held land here); *Abedylsyke* 1467 × 84 (*v.* **abbod, hyll, sík**; alluding to the Abbot of St Mary de Pratis); *Mr Allens Close* 1679, 1697; *Armeston Hookes* 1605 Ipm (*v.* **hōk**), *Armeston Wonge* 1605 ib (*v.* **vangr**), *Armson sicke* 1583 (*v.* **sík**) (with the surn. *Armston* of a family originally from the Northants. village of this name, 30 miles to the south-east); *Arnoldiswong* 1467 × 84 (*v.* **vangr**; either with the surn. *Arnold* or with its pers.n. source OGer *Arnald/Arnold*); *Arpingate* 1700, ~ *Side* 1708, 1708 (18) (*v.* **sīde**) (*v.* **gata**; with the surn. *Arpin*, *v.* Reaney *s.n.*); *Ashby(e) hedge* 1601, 1674 (*v.* **hecg**; the boundary hedge of Ashby Folville which adjoins to the north-east); *de Aula* 1467 × 84 (p) (with MLat *aula* 'a hall'); *Baggrave Gate* 1583 (*v.* **gata**; Baggrave adjoins to the south-east); *Bagodeswong* 1467 × 84 bis (*v.* **vangr**; either with the surn. *Bagot* or with its pers.n. source *Bagot* (a diminutive of OGer *Bago*), *v.* Reaney *s.n.*); *Banethorn'* 1467 × 84 (*v.* **þorn**; the first el. is problematical but appears to be either OE *bana* 'a killer' in the sense 'that which kills' (ME **bane** 'poison'), perh. alluding to poisonous berries or OE *bēan* 'a bean', giving a compound **bēan-þorn** which may be an alternative name for gorse; gorse, as a member of the *Leguminosae* family, produces small seed pods similar to those of the broad bean and the pea; note Bean Thorn Furlong in Grimston f.ns. (a) and Great Beanthorn in Shoby f.ns. (a) which represent the modern reflex of the compound); *Banlond'* 1467 × 84, *Ballance* 1583, 1708, 1708 (18), *Bandlands* 1679, 1690, 1697, *Long Ballance*, ~ ~ *Sycke* 1583 (*v.* **lang**[1], **sík**), *Bandland hole* 1700 (*v.* **hol**[1]), *Shortbanelond*, *Shortbanlond'* 1467 × 84, *Shortballondholme* 1301 Banco (*v.* **sc(e)ort**, **holmr**), *v.* **bēan**, **land**); *Barsby waye* 1601 (*v.* **weg**; Barsby adjoins to the north-east); *Bernardhul* 13 (*v.* **hyll**; either with the surn. *Bernard* or its pers.n. source OFr *Bernart*); *Blackmyles* 1583 (*v.* **blæc**, **mylde**); *Bossycke* 1583 (*v.* **bōs**, **sík**); *Braken* 1467 × 84 (*v.* **braken**); *brantclos* 1601 (*v.* **clos(e)**; prob. with **brand** 'a place cleared by burning, a place where burning has occurred' rather than with **brant** 'steep', cf. *le brend wong* and perh. *Burne Wong*, *infra*); *the breach* 1583 (*v.* **brēc**); *Brec(c)lond* 1467 × 84 (*v.* **bræc**[1], **land**); *le brend wong* 13, *Brendewong'* 1467 × 84 bis (*v.* **brend**, **vangr**); *Brodhome* 1583 (*v.* **brād**, **holmr**); *Brodsike* 1467 × 84 (*v.* **brād**, **sík**); *Bromcliffe*, ~ *Sicke*, *Bromclyffe Sycke* 1583 (*v.* **brōm**, **clif**); *Richard Burchnalls Close* 1674; *Burne Wong* 1583, *Burn woome* (sic) 1601, *burnewonge* 1625 (*v.* **vangr**; the first el. is either **burna** 'a stream' or one of the cognates OE **bryne**/ON **bruni** '(a place cleared by) burning'); *Calles leays* 1583 (*v.* **leys**; poss. with the surn. *Callis*, *v.* Reaney *s.n.*, but note *Colisakyr*, *infra*); *in campo occidentali* 1467 × 84 (with MLat *campus* 'a field' and *occidentalis* 'western'; one of the early great fields); *in campo orientali* 1467 × 84 (with MLat *orientalis* 'eastern'; another of the early great fields); *the Lord Carringtons ground* 1700 (*v.* **grund**); *Church hadley* 1700 (*v.* **headley** and St John the Baptist's Church *supra*); *cobb hadland* 1601, *Cobh(e)adland* 1708, 1708 (18) (*v.* **cobb(e)**, **hēafod-land** and Cob Headland Furlong in Barsby f.ns. (b)); *Colisakyr* 1467 × 84 (*v.* **æcer**; either with a pers.n., ON *Kollr* (an original by-name 'the bald-headed one') or ON *Kolr* (ODan *Kol*) (either an original by-name 'dark-skinned' or a short form of names in *Kol-*), or a surn. reflex *Coll*, *v.* Reaney *s.n.*); *the common pasture* 1625 (*v.* **commun**, **pasture**); *Cotewong* 1477 (e.16) (*v.* **cot**, **vangr**); *Cotte Croft* 1473 *CCR* (*v.* **cot**, **croft**); *Croft leyes* 1583 (*v.* **croft**, **leys**); *Long Croft(s)* 1674, 1679, 1690, 1697, 1708, 1708 (18), *Long Crafts* 1700, *longe crafte layes* 1601, *Croft leyes* 1583 (*v.* **leys**) (*v.* **lang**[1], **croft**); *Crokisthorn* 1467 × 84 (*v.* **þorn**; presum. with the ODan pers.n. *Krōk* (ON *Krókr*) as in the name of the township); *Croson hooks* 1674, 1679, 1690, *Croxton* ~ 1697 (*v.* **hōc**); *Debdale* 1583, 1601 *et passim* to 1700, 1708, ~ *Sycke* 1583 (*v.* **sík**), *Debdale Top Hade* 1708 (18) (*v.* **topp**, **hēafod**) (*v.* **dēop**, **dalr**); *Eassicke* 1625 (*v.* **ēast**, **sík**); *East Field* 1674 (*v.* *Upper Feild*, *infra*); *Edemerth* 1583 (earlier forms are needed, but poss. is **erð**, with the surn. *Adem*, *v.* Reaney *s.n.*); *ye Eight Lands* 1690, 1697 (*v.* **land**; a unit consisting of eight selions of a former great field); *Endegatis* 1467 × 84 bis (*v.* **ende**, **gata**); *le Espinee* 1238 Nichols, 1289 Coram, 1290 Abbr (*v.* **spinney**; here OFr *espinei* survives); *Estgate* 1467 × 84 (*v.* **ēast**, **gata**); *Estrenegate* 1467 × 84, *Easternegate* 1625 (either 'the road lying towards the east' (in this sense, OED 1593) or 'the road having an eastward direction' (in this sense, OED a.1719), *v.* **estren**, **gata**); *Falhul(l)* 1467 × 84 (*v.* **(ge)fall**, **hyll**); *Flithulleswong* 1467 × 84 (*v.* **(ge)flit**, **hyll**, **vangr**); *Foldhull* 1467 × 84 (*v.* **fald**, **hyll**); *Forsland Sick* 1679, 1690, 1697 (*v.* **forst**, **land**, **sík**); *Foshill Sycke* 1583 (*v.* **sík**; poss. a later form of *Foxwellesyke* following, otherwise *v.* **fox**, **hyll**); *Foxwell'* 1477 (e.16), 1467 × 84 bis, *Foxuell* 1467 × 84, *Foxwelles* 1477 (e.16),

Foxuelles 1467 × 84, *Foxwellesyke* 1477 (e.16), *Foxuellesike* 1467 × 84) (*v.* **fox, wella**); *Fromcliffe*, ~ *sicke*, *Fromclyffe Sycke* 1583, *Front Cliff Sick* 1708, 1708 (18) (*v.* **front, clif, sík**); *gadsbye gate* 1601, *gadsbye waye* 1601 (*v.* **gata, weg**; the road to Gaddesby which lies 2 miles to the north); *Gatelandes* 1601 (*v.* **gata, land**); *Glebe bastard Ley* 1674 (*v.* **bastard, ley**; with reference to a selion of arable not completely swarded over, *v.* Field 96), *the Glebe Seaven Landes* 1674 (*v.* **seofon**), *the Glebe two land(e)s* 1674, 1679, 1690 (*v.* **land**) (*v.* **glebe**); *Gosewelsyke* 1467 × 84 bis (*v.* **gōs, wella, sík**); *the Greene* 1605 Ipm (*v.* **grēne**[2]); *Grundisbutts*, *Grundibuttes* 1477 (e.16), *Grundesbuttes*, *Grundibuttis* 1467 × 84 (*v.* **grund, butte**); *a sick called Hallams* 1583 (*v.* **sík**; with the surn. *Hallam* in the possessive case); *Herbertlane* 1467 × 84 (*v.* **lane**; with the surn. *Herbert*, a reflex of the OFr pers.n. *Herbert*); *Hi(e)gate*, *Hyegate* 1583, *(the) Highgate* 1583, 1625, 1708, 1708 (18), *highe gate* 1601, *hygate*, ~ *hades* 1700 (*v.* **hēafod**) (*v.* **hēah**[1], **gata**), *the highe waye* 1601, *the High Way* 1679, 1697 (*v.* **hēah-weg**); *Hodes* 1708, 1708 (18) (*v.* **hōd**; the word had two meanings in OE: 'a hood', used topographically of 'a hood-shaped hill', and 'a shelter', the latter likelier here); *Holegate* 1467 × 84 (*v.* **hol**[2], **gata**); *the Home Close of William Stevenson* 1708, 1708 (18) (*v.* **home**); *the Homestall* 1708, 1708 (18) (that of *the Parsonage House*), *the Homestall of Mr Smith* 1708, 1708 (18) (*v.* **hām-stall**); *the homestead* 1625 (*v.* **hām-stede**; that of *the Parsonage House*); *the hook furlong* 1700 (*v.* **hōc, furlang**); *Hordpit* 1467 × 84 bis (*v.* **hord, pytt**; presum. the site of the discovery of buried treasure); *Kalengewong'* 1467 × 84 (*v.* **calenge, vangr**); *Langley Hoockes* 1583 (*v.* **lang**[1], **lēah, hōc**); *(the) Long furlong(e)* 1674, 1679 *et passim* to 1708 (18) (*v.* **furlang**; i.e. of the Nether Fd); *Longe hauerhul* 13 (*v.* **lang**[1], **hæfera, hafri, hyll**); *Longehouedis* 1467 × 84 bis (*v.* **lang**[1], **hēafod**); *Longemere* 1467 × 84 bis (*v.* **lang**[1]; with **(ge)mǣre** or **mere**[1]); *Margyt(t)s laye* 1601 (*v.* **ley**; with the surn. *Margetts*, *v.* Reaney *s.n.*; a reflex of the pers.n. Margaret); *Medwegate* 1467 × 84 bis, *Middow gate* 1700, *Meadow* ~ 1708, 1708 (18) (*v.* **mǣd (mǣdwe** obl.sg.), **gata**); *Meer ba(u)lk* 1690, *Meere balk* 1697 (*v.* **balca**; with **(ge)mǣre** or **mere**[1]); *(The) Middle Feild* 1583, (~) ~ *Field* 1625, 1690, 1697, 1708 (18), *The Myddle Feelde* 1601, *Midle Field* 1674, 1679, 1708 (*v.* **middel, feld**; one of the great fields of the township); *Milnested* 1477 (e.16) (*v.* **myln, stede**); *Mill Close* 1708, 1708 (18); *Mill Sick* 1708, 1708 (18) (*v.* **sík**); *the Moore balke* 1674 (*v.* **balca**), *Moardale*, *Moredall*, *Mordale* 1583, *Moredale* 1601, *Moor(e)dale* 1625, 1674, 1679, 1690, 1697 (*v.* **dalr**) (*v.* **mōr**[1], **mór**); *Newbolde* 1625, ~ *hedge* 1601, 1674 (*v.* **hecg**; a boundary hedge), *Newbold Closes* 1679, *Newbald* ~ 1690, 1697 (Newbold Folville adjoins to the north-east); *the Neyther Feild* 1583, *the Nether Feelde* 1601, *(the) Nether Field* 1625, 1679, 1708, 1708 (18), ~ ~ *or West Field* 1674, *(ye) Neather field* 1690, 1697 (*v.* **neoðera, feld**; one of the great fields); *Osgoteacre* 1324 Banco, *Osegodacres*, *Osgodacres* 1467 × 84 (*v.* **æcer**; with the late OE pers.n. *Ōsgod/Ōsgot* (from ON *Ásgautr* (ODan *Asgot*))); *the Over feelde* 1601, ~ *field* 1625 (*v.* **uferra** and *Upper Feild*, *infra*); *Peysul* 1467 × 84, *Pease Hill*, ~ ~ *Stye* 1583 (*v.* **pise, hyll, stīg**); *Qwerinhou*, *Qwernishou* 1467 × 84 (*v.* **cweorn, haugr**); *Qweyldale* 1467 × 84 (*v.* **cwelle, dalr**); *Rauensakir'* 1467 × 84 bis, *Ransacar* 1625 (*v.* **æcer**), *Raunsdale* 1605 (*v.* **deill**) (either with the ON pers.n. *Hrafn* (or less likely OE *Hræfn*), or their surn. reflex *Raven*); *Redegres*, *Radgresse* 1467 × 84 (*v.* **hrēod, græs**); *Saltfengate* 1467 × 84 (*v.* **salt**[2], **fenn, gata** and Sauving in adjoining Barsby f.ns. (a)); *Schormere* 1467 × 84 bis (*v.* **scor(a), (ge)mǣre**); *Schortecrofte*, *Sortecroft* 1477 (e.16) (*v.* **sc(e)ort, croft**); *Schortlond* 1467 × 84 bis (*v.* **sc(e)ort, land**); *Schortpeislond'* 1467 × 84 (*v.* **sc(e)ort,**

pise, land); *Scuitelsty* 1467 × 84 (*v.* **scyt(t)el, stig**); *Sendebusk* 1467 × 84 (*v.* **sende, buskr**); *Senlond* 1467 × 84 bis (*v.* **sænna, senna, land**); *Sheapheards borde* 1601, *Shepherd*(*s*) *Board* 1679, 1690, *Shepheard board* 1697, *Shepard bo*(*a*)*rd Furlong* 1700, 1708, 1708 (18) (*v.* **furlang**) (*v.* **scēp-hirde, bord**, evidently alluding to good grazing for sheep; a derivation from OFr *bord* 'a cottage' seems unlikely); *Shrubland* 1601, *Shrublandes furlong* 1625 (*v.* **furlang**), *Shrobland sicke*, ~ *sycke* 1583, *Shrubland Sick* 1674, 1697 *et passim* to 1708 (18) (*v.* **sík**) (*v.* **scrubb, land**); *Siwordlong* 1467 × 84 (*v.* **lang**[2]; the first el. is either the ME surn. *Siward* (ModE *Seward*) or a precursor, prob. the ON pers.n. *Sigvarðr* (ODan *Sigwarth*) or, less likely, OE *Sigeweard*); *Sproweslond'* 1467 × 84 bis (*v.* **land**; prob. with the OE pers.n. *Sprow* (cf. Sproston, Ch **2** 254)); *Stackhill bridge hooke* 1583 (*v.* **staca, hyll, brycg, hōc**); *Stanbryg* 1467 × 84, *Stan brig*(*g*) 1708, 1708 (18) (*v.* **stān, brycg, bryggja**); *Stanilond'* 1467 × 84, *Stonyelands* 1583, *Stony Lands* 1674, 1700, 1708, 1708 (18) (*v.* **stānig, land**); *the Stone* 1679, 1690 (*v.* **stān**; prob. a boundary marker); *Stubbes* 1674, *Stubbs* 1679, 1690, 1697, 1700, 1708, *Stubs* 1708, 1708 (18), *Stubbs Sicke* 1583 (*v.* **sík**) (*v.* **stubb**); *Schortstobullys* 1467 × 84 (*v.* **sc(e)ort**), *Stuble furlong* 1583 (*v.* **furlang**), *Stuble sicke* 1583 (*v.* **sík**) (*v.* **stubbil**); *Suthenmerche* 1467 × 84 (*v.* **sūðan, mersc**); *Suthwranglond'* 1467 × 84 bis (*v.* **sūð, wrang, vrangr, land**); *Swetebuske* 1477 (e.16), *Swetbusk'* 1467 × 84 (*v.* **buskr**; with **swēte** or **sviða**); *Theuisdene* 1467 × 84, *Thieve Denne* 1708, *Theive Denn* 1708 (18) (*v.* **þēof, denu**; cf. *þeofa denn* 816 (11) BCS 356 (S 179) and Thievesdale, Nt 109); *the Thorn* 1708, 1708 (18) (*v.* **þorn**); *Thornehill* 1583, *Thorn hill* 1708, 1708 (18) (*v.* **þorn, hyll**); *Threthornis* 1467 × 84 bis, *three thorn*(*e*) 1601, 1625, 1674 (*v.* **þrēo, þorn**); *Twelfrodisbrod*(*e*) 1477 (e.16), 1467 × 84, *Twelfrodesbrode* 1467 × 84 (*v.* **twelf, rōd**[3], **brǣdu**); *Twyforde Crosse* 1601, 1625, *Twyford Cross* 1674, 1679, 1690, *Twiford* ~ 1697 (*v.* **cros**), *Lower Twyford* 1708, 1708 (18) (Twyford lies 2 miles to the east); *Upper Feild* 1583, ~ *Field* 1674, 1679 *et passim* to 1708 (18), *Uperfeild* 1700 (*v.* **upper, feld**; one of the great fields of the township, also called *The Over Feelde* 1601 and *East Field* 1674); *ad vadum de Baggraue* 1467 × 84 (with MLat *vadum* 'a ford'; Baggrave adjoins to the south-east); *Wayngatewong'* Hy 3 *Crox* (*v.* **wægn, gata, vangr**); *West Field* 1674 (an alternative name for the Nether Fd); *Wetelond'* 1467 × 84 (*v.* **hwǣte, land**); *Whorlo* 1583 bis, *Wharlowe* 1601, *Wharloe* 1708, 1708 (18) (*v.* **hlāw**; poss with **hwerfel**, cf. Whorl Hill, YN 177); *Wheatdal*(*l*)*e*, *Whetedal*(*l*)*e* 1583 (*v.* **hwǣte, dalr**); *Whethill* 1708, 1708 (18) (*v.* **hwǣte, hyll**); *Yenbrook field* 1583 (*v.* **ēan, brōc, feld**).

Frisby and Kirby

1. FRISBY ON THE WREAKE

Frisebie 1086 DB, *Frisebia* c.1130 LeicSurv, e.13 (1404) *Laz*, *Frisebi* Hy 1 Dugd, 1190 P, 1200 Cur, m.13 (1404) *Laz* bis, *Friseby* Hy 1 Dugd, 1202 Fine, 1213 Cur *et freq* to 1349 *LCDeeds*, 1359 BPR *et passim* to 1444 AD, 1472 Hastings, *Frisseby* 1357 Pap, 1419 FF, 1419 Cl, *Fryseby* 1271 Ipm, Hy 3 *Crox*, c.1291 Tax *et freq* to 1392 Cl, 1406 Pat *et passim* to 1460 Banco, *Frysseby* 1351 (1449), 1361 (1449), 1363 (1449) *WoCart*, 1428 FA

Freseby Hy 2 Dugd, 1244 Cl *et passim* to 1351 *Wyg* (p), 1367 Misc bis, *Fresby* 1409, 1412 Pat

Frisby 1404 *Laz*, 1413 Pat, 1438 *Peake et passim* to 1535 VE, 1576 Saxton *et freq*, *Frysby* 1412, 1421 Banco *et passim* to 1535 VE, 1541 MinAccts

Affixes are variously added as:

~ *Hernis* 1242 Fees

~ *super Wrethek*(*e*) 1329 Pat, 1329 IpmR *et passim* to 1349 *LCDeeds* 1498 Pat, ~ *super Wreke* 1483 *AllS*, 1510 LP, 1541 MinAccts, ~ *super le Wreake* 1580 LEpis, ~ *on Wreke* 1510 CoPleas, ~ *on the Wreake* 1628 LML

~ *in Kyrkeby* 1365 FA, l.14 AD

'The farmstead, village of the Frisians', *v.* **Frīsa**, **Frēsa**, **bӯ**, cf. Frisby (by Galby) in Gartree Hundred. Frisby lies on the river Wreake, adjacent to Kirby Bellars. The early affix ~ *Hernis* is from OE **(ge)hērness** 'a district obedient to a single jurisdiction, a jurisdiction', cf. Berkeley Harness, Gl **2** 206. Note also affixes with MLat *super* 'on, upon'.

ASHFIELD, 1925 Kelly. BELL INN, 1877 White, *Bell* 1846 ib, 1925 Kelly, *Blue Bell* 1863 White. BLACK HORSE (P.H.) (lost), *Black Horse* 1846, 1863, 1877 White, 1925 Kelly. BRIGGS'S HOSPITAL (lost), *Briggs's*

Hospital 1846, 1863, 1877 White, *v.* **hospital**; founded by Judith Briggs in 1718 for six poor old maids or widows. CHEAP END, *v.* **cēap**, **ende**; presum. with reference to the market at Melton Mowbray which lies 4 miles to the east. CHURCH OF ST THOMAS OF CANTERBURY, *Church (St Thomas à Becket)* 1846, 1863, 1877 White, 1925 Kelly; it is earlier recorded as *ecclesie de Friseby* 1220 MHW, *ecclesiam de Fresby* 1309 *Pat*, *~ de Freseby* 1310 *ib*. Note also *the Church yard* 1761 *EnclA*. FRISBY GRANGE is *The Grange* 1877 White, *v.* **grange**. FRISBY HAGS, 1800 Nichols, 1846, 1863, 1877 White, cf. *the Hag Way* 1800 Nichols, *v.* **hǫgg**. FRISBY LODGE, 1835 O, *v.* **loge**. GREAT LANE, ~ ~ HILL, *the Great Lane* 1761 *EnclA*. HALL ORCHARD, *the Orchard* 17 *Rental*, *(the) Hall Orchard* 1708 (18) *Terrier*, 1761 *EnclA*, 1969 *Surv*, *v.* **hall**, **orceard**. THE KNOLL, 1925 Kelly, *v.* **cnoll**. THE LAURELS. PENNYHAVEN. STUMP CROSS, *(The) Stump Cross* 1761 *EnclA*, 1800 Nichols, 1846, 1863, 1877 White, 1925 Kelly, *v.* **stump**, **cros**; a headless wayside cross. THE VICARAGE, 1877 White, 1925 Kelly; cf. *the Vicaridge howse* 1625 *Terrier*, *~ ~ house* 1690 *ib*, *the Vicarage House* 1708, 1708 (18) *ib*, *v.* **vikerage**. WASHSTONES BRIDGE, *(the) Wash Stones* 1761 *EnclA*, 1969 *Surv*, *v.* **wæsce**, **stān**; at R.Wreake. WATER LANE, cf. *Water Lane End* 1761 *EnclA*, *v.* **wæter**, **lane-ende**. YORK FM is *New York farm* 1846, 1863 White; a 'remoteness' name.

FIELD-NAMES

Undated forms in (a) are 1969 *Surv*, while those dated 1761 are *EnclA*. Forms throughout dated 1555 are Pat; 1601, 1625, 1674, 1679, 1690, l.17, 1700, 1708 and 1708 (18) are *Terrier*; 1680 are *Reeve*.

(a) Two ~, Six ~, Nine Acre, Eighteen Acres (*v.* **æcer**); Asfordby foot road 1761 (the common Leics. compound **foot-road** is not cited in OED; Asfordby adjoins to the north-east); Big ~, Bandlands (*v.* **bēan**, **land**); Barbers Cl 1761, Barbers Corner 1969 (*v.* **corner**) (with the surn. *Barber*); Bennet(t) Leys 1761 (*v.* **leys**), Bennets Stile 1761 (*v.* **stigel**) (with the surn. *Bennet*); Biddles (the surn. *Biddle* in the possessive case); Big Fd; Mary Blacks Cl 1761; Boat House (a field thus called, beside the river); the Bog (*v.* **bog**); First ~, Second Born (sic) (*v.* **brún**[2]); Branstons (the surn. *Branston* in the possessive case, of a family prob. originally from the village of this name 10 miles to the north-east); Bottom ~, Top Car, Car Paddock (*v.* **paddock**) (*le Carre* 1555 Pat, 1578 Ipm, *v.* **kjarr**); Middle ~, Road Chesters (prob. with **ceaster** in the sense 'a Roman site' rather than with the surn. *Chester(s)* in the possessive case; the fields so named occupy a broad, flat-topped promontory overlooking a road south and appear to be sited ideally for a small RB township, although there are no obvious earthworks evident viewed from the ground; the road southwards defines the west and south of the site by an unusual right-angled turn); Bottom ~, Top Claypits (*v.* **cley-pytt**); the Common Pasture 1761 (*v.* **commun, pasture**); Corner Cl (*v.* **corner**); Cottage Cl (*v.* **cotage**); Cowdam Hades 1761 (*v.* **cū, damme, hēafod**; with reference to an artificially-created watering-place for cattle); Bottom ~, Cowpens (*v.* **cowpenn**); The Croft 1761 (*v.* **croft**); The Cuckoos (alluding to the cuckoo bird, but the association is unclear); Top ~, Dam (*v.* **damme**; on a stream); (Mary Blacks) Dimisdale Cl 1761, Bottom ~, Top ~, Dimsdale (*Diminsdale* 1625, 1700, 1708, 1708 (18), *Diminsdaile* 1674, *Dimmingdale* 1679, *Dimin*(*i*)*sdayle* 1690, l.17, 'the valley which darkens quickly', *v.* **dimming, dalr**; Dimsdale is the name of a small valley opening out to the north, whose west shoulder with earlier woodland cuts off light from the setting sun, causing a rapidly darkening hollow; this site clears up the long-standing problem of the interpretation of this common p.n., *v.* YW **6** 108 *s.n.* Dimingdale and L **2** 218 *s.n. Dimigdale*); Dockhams (*v.* **docce, hamm**); Dovecoat Cl 1761 (*v.* **dove-cot(e)**); Fishpond piece 1761 (*v.* **pece**), Bottom ~, Top Fishponds 1969; Folds (either the surn. *Fold*(*s*) in the possessive case (*v.* Reaney *s.n.*) or **fald** 'a small enclosure for animals'); Big ~, Top Foxstoles (sic) (*v.* **fox-hol**); Frannum Cl 1761 (*Frannam* 1601, 1625, *Franham* 1708, 1708 (18), *Frannum furlong* 1679 (*v.* **furlang**), *Franam Head* l.17, 1700, *Frannem head* 1690 (*v.* **hēafod**), *Frannam hill* 1674 (*v.* **fearn, hamm**); Frisby Station 1854 O (on the *Syston and Peterborough Branch Railway* 1854 ib); Front Fd; Gadsby foot road 1761 (*v.* **foot-road**), Gadsby Road 1761 (Gaddesby lies 3 miles to the south); Top Glebe (*v.* **glebe**); Gooses Neck (descriptive of a looping side channel of the river Wreake beside which the field is situated); Goss No. 2 (cf. *Goss ground* 1708, 1708 (18), *v.* **gorst, grund**); Gravel Holes (*v.* **gravel, hol**[1]); the Hall Cl 1761, the Hall Farm Yard 1761 (*v.* **farmyard**) (cf. *atte Halle* 1362 (1449) *WoCart* (p), 1377 SR (p) (*v.* **atte**), *v.* **hall**); Hoby Road, Hoby Bridle Road 1761 (*v.* **brigdels**) (Hoby adjoins to the west); the Hill Cl 1761; Bottom ~, Middle ~, Top Hillside; Hollings Croft 1761 (*v.* **croft**; with the surn. *Holling*(*s*)); (the) Home Cl 1761, 1969, Home Fd 1969 (*v.* **home**); Hornbuckles (the surn. *Hornbuckle* in the possessive case, *v.* Reaney *s.n.*); Horse Cl; Hose Cl (earlier forms are needed, but poss. with **hōh** (**hōs** nom.pl.) or **haugr**); the House Cl 1761 (cf. *the mansion house* 17, *v.* **mansion-house**); the Howbeck Cl, Howbeck Dyke 1761 (*v.* **dík**) (*Howbeck* 1625, *Hobeck*(*e*) 1674, 1679 *et passim* to 1708 (18), *v.* **hol**[2], **holr, bekkr**); Hubbard Cl 1761, Hubbard Way 1761 (*Hubbard Way* 1679, *Hubbert way* 1690 (*v.* **weg**), *the high way called Hubbert*(*e*)*s gate* 1625, *Hubbard gate* 1674, *Hubbart* ~ l.17, *Hubbert* ~ l.17, 1700, *Hubberd* ~ 1708, 1708 (18) (*v.* **gata**); cf. *James Hubbert* 1625); The Jessons (cf. *John Jesson* 1761); Johnsons Garden 1761; (a furlong called) Kerby Debdale 1761 (*Debdale* 1601, 1625, 1708, 1708 (18), *Debdaile* 1674, 1690, *Debdayle* l.17, *Depdale* 1679, *Dibdale* 1700, *Debdale hill* 1625, *v.* **dēop, dalr**; with reference in 1761 to neighbouring Kirby Bellars); King Hill Gate 1761 (*v.* **gata**; it is uncertain whether *King* is a surn. here or whether the whole refers to *the kinges high way called the Streete* 1625, *v.* **strǣt**); Kirby foot road 1761 (*v.* **foot-road**; with reference to adjoining Kirby Bellars); Ladies Cl 1761, Ladys ~ 1969 (*v.* **lavedi**; alluding to a female proprietor or to a dowager or to the lady of the manor); the Lammas Cl 1761 (*v.* **lammas**); Lawn Way 1761 (*v.* **launde**); Leicester Road 1761 (Leicester lies 10 miles to the south-west); the Little Lane 1761 (*v.* **lane**); Little Mdw 1761; Locks, ~ Mdw, Bottom Lock (*v.* **lock**; beside a canalized reach of R. Wreake); Long Hedge 1761 (*v.* **hecg**); Mantons (the surn. *Manton* in the possessive case, of a family prob. originally from Manton, 12 miles to the south-east in Rutland); Melton Gate 1761 (1625, 1674 *et passim* to 1708 (18), *v.* **gata**; the road to Melton Mowbray which lies 4 miles to the east); the Mill, ~ ~ Cl, ~ ~ Holm (*v.* **holmr**), ~ ~ Leys (*v.* **leys**) all 1761, Mill Mdw 1969 (cf. *atte milne* 1327 SR (p), *at Milne* 1332 ib (p) (*v.* **atte**), *v.* **myln**); (the) Nether Cl 1761; Newcombs (the surn. *Newcomb* in the possessive case); Little Normans (with the surn. *Norman* in the possessive case; cf. The Normans in Ragdale f.ns. (a)); Old Cricket Fd (for the game of cricket); Osier Beds 1968 (*v.* **bedd**), the Osier Holt 1761 (*v.* **holt**) (*v.* **oyser**); (the) Paddock, Pony Paddock (*v.* **pony**) (*v.* **paddock**); Palings Croft 1761 (*v.* **croft**; cf. *Robt. Paling* 1791 *TB* of nearby Ashby Folville); Pearsons (the surn. *Pearson* in the possessive case); Pocklington (the surn. *Pocklington* (*v.* Reaney *s.n.*), indicating ownership or tenure of the land unit); Pump Cl, ~ Fd (*v.* **pumpe**); Rabbit Warren (*v.* **rabet**, **wareine**); Rotherby Road 1761, Rotherby foot road 1761 (*v.* **foot-road**) (Rotherby adjoins to the south-west); the Scower 1761 (*v.* **scoure**); Shortlands (*v.* **sc(e)ort**, **land**); The Slip, Slips (*v.* **slipe**); the Spinney, ~ ~ Cl 1761 (*v.* **spinney**); Stackyard Cl (*v.* **stak-ȝeard**); Stokes's Yard 1761 (*v.* **geard**; with the surn. *Stokes*); Stoughton Church Land 1761 (land endowed for the upkeep of the parish church in Stoughton, 10 miles to the south-west); Streetway 1761, Bottom ~, Middle ~, Top Straightways 1969 (*v.* **street-waie**; with reference to a minor Roman road, also recorded in *the kinges high way called the Streete* 1625, *v.* **strǣt**); the Taslands, Tasland Cls 1761 (*v.* **tǣsel**, **land**); Ting Hills (*Tynge Hill* 1680; earlier it is *Thingou* c.1200 Dane, *v.* **þing**, **haugr**, a moot-site on the parish boundary with Rotherby which adjoins to the south-west; for additional forms, *v.* Rotherby f.ns. (a) *s.n.* Tinghill); Tuckham 1761 (*v.* **hamm**; poss. with a Scandinavianized **þæc** as first el.); (the) Upper Mdw 1761; Voyces (the surn. *Voyce* in the possessive case); the Wails Cl 1761, Top ~, Wales 1969 (perh. with the surn. *Wailes*/*Wales* (*v.* Reaney *s.nn.*), although the site on the parish boundary in the west may indicate an early humorous 'remoteness' name referring to the Principality; cf. The Wales in Ragdale f.ns. (a)); Wards Cl 1761 (with the surn. *Ward*); the Water Furrows 1761 (*v.* **wæter**, **furh** and *the Waterfurrow*(*e*)*s* in Asfordby f.ns. (b)); Wet Mdw (*v.* **wēt**); Whites Fd (with the surn. *White*); Windmills (cf. (*the*) *Wind-Mill hill* 1680, *v.* **wind-mylne**).

(b) *broding*(*e*) 1601, 1625, *Brodin* 1674, *Broading* 1679, 1690 *et passim* to 1708 (18) (*v.* **brād**, **eng**); *Catlyf* 1601, 1625 (*v.* **cat(t)**, **clif**); *the common balke* 1601, *ye Comon Balk* 1708, *the Common Baulk* 1708 (18) (*v.* **commun**, **balca**); *the cowes pasture* 1625, *the Cowpasture* 1680 (*v.* **cū**, **pasture**); *le Estfeilde* 1555, *the East feilde* 1601, 1625, 1674, 1680, ~ ~ *Field* 1700, 1708, 1708 (18) (*v.* **ēast**, **feld**; one of the great fields of the township); *le Estmede* 1555, *the east medow* 1625, *the medow* 1601, *the Meadow* 1679, 1.17, 1700, 1708, ~ ~ *side* 1674, 1679 (*v.* **sīde**) (*v.* **ēast**, **mǣd** (**mǣdwe** obl.sg.)); *Frisebyhoue* 1275 GildR (*v.* **haugr**); *Gadsbie Meare* 1625, *gadsby meere* 1674 (*v.* **(ge)mǣre**; Gaddesby adjoins to the south); *James Goodmans grasse headland* 1625 (*v.* **græs**, **hēafod-land**); *the ground of Richard Sharpe* 1625 (*v.* **grund**); *lez Hades* 1555, *les Hades* 1578 Ipm (*v.* **hēafod**); *the high way* 1625 (*v.* **hēah-weg**); *le holme* 1555 (*v.* **holmr**); *the Homestall* 1625 (i.e. of *the Vicaridge howse*), *the homestall of John Milner* 1625 (*v.* **hām-stall**); *the homestead* 17 (*v.* **hām-stede**); *Iron furlong* 1601 (*v.* **hyrne**, **furlang**); *litle beck* 1601, *Little Beck* 1680 (*v.* **lȳtel**, **lítill**, **bekkr**); *Marlepitt hades* 1625 (*v.* **marle-pytt**, **hēafod**); *the Meadow furlong* 1680 (*v.* **furlang**); *Middelfeilde* 1555, *the Middle fielde* 1601, 1625, *the Middel*(*l*) *feild* 1674, 1690, *the Midle field* 1679, 1700, 1708, *the Middle Feild* 1680, 1.17, ~ ~ *Field* 1708, 1708 (18) (*v.* **middel**, **feld**; one of the early great fields); *John*

Miller's Orchard 1708 (18); *the ne(a)ther meadow* 1674, 1690 (*v*. **neoðera**); *the Orcharde of Mr Bartholomew Brookesbie* 1625 (*v*. **orceard**; the *Brooksby* family was originally from the village of this name, 2 miles to the south-west); *Pinder balke* 1679 (*v*. **pinder**, **balca**); *James Quickes grasse headland* 1625 (*v*. **græs**, **hēafod-land**); *Mr Sharpe his Wonge* 1601 (*v*. **vangr**), *Richard Sharpes headland* 1625 (*v*. **hēafod-land**); *the Short furlong* 1680 (*v*. **furlang**); *Toftessike* c.1200 Dane (*v*. **toft**, **sík**); *the Vicars hades* 1625, *Vicker* ~ 1674, *viccar* ~ 1690, l.17, (*the*) *Vicar Hades* 1700, 1708, 1708 (18) (*v*. **vikere**, **hēafod**; in both the East Fd and Middle Fd); *atte Well* 1327 SR (p) (*v*. **atte**, **wella**); *le Westfeilde* 1555, *the West fielde* 1601, 1625, ~ ~ *feild* 1674, 1680, 1690, l.17, ~ ~ *Field* 1679, 1700, 1708, 1708 (18) (*v*. **west**, **feld**; one of the great fields); *le Westmede* 1555, *the West medowe* 1625 (*v*. **west**, **mǣd** (**mǣdwe** obl.sg.)); *Witters wonge* 1625 (*v*. **vangr**; the first el. is presum. a surn., prob. *Whitter* (cf. *Henry le Wytter'* 1221 of Warwks.), recording the medieval trade of 'whitener, whitewasher'; or less likely the surn. *Wither*, a reflex of the ON pers.n. *Viðarr* (ODan *Withar*), *v*. Reaney *s.nn*.).

2. KIRBY BELLARS

Kirby Bellars is a member of Framland Hundred.

Cherchebi 1086 DB

Chirchebi 1086 DB, *Chirchebia* c.1130 LeicSurv

Kirchebia 1163 RegAnt, *Kyrchebia* 1163 ib, *Kercheby* m.13 (1404) *Laz*

Kirkebi 1166, Hy 2 Dane, 1198 Cur *et passim* to c.1235 AD, m.13 (1404) *Laz*, *Kirkebia* e.13 (1404) *ib* bis, *Kyrkebi* 1169 AD, e.13 Berkeley, 1237 AD, *Kierkebi* 1204 P, *Kirkeby* Hy 2 Dugd, 1200, 1203 Fine, e.13 *Peake et passim* to 1226 TutP, 1228 Ch *et freq* to 1486 Cl, 1494 Will *et passim* to 1535 VE, 1551 *Deed*, *Kirkebya* p.1250 (1404) *Laz*, *Kyrkeby* 1214 Cur, 1226 TutP, 1227 Fees *et freq* to 1537 MinAccts, 1542 Fine *et passim* to 1556 ib, 1574 Ipm

Kerkebi Hy 2 Dane, *Kerkeby* m.13 (1404) *Laz*, 1290 Ipm (p) *et passim* to 1377 ELiW, 1428 FA

Kirkby 1436, 1467 Pat *et passim* to 1518 Visit, 1526 Fine *et freq* to 1576 Saxton, 1584 Ipm, *Kyrkeby* 1429 Fine, 1446 AD *et passim* to 1548, 1553 Pat

Kerkby 1538 × 44 ECP, 1610 Speed

Kirby 1539 *Deed*, 1604 SR, 1614 Ipm *et freq*, *Kyrby* 1428 FA, 1502 *MiscAccts et passim* to 1573, 1588 Fine

Kerbie 1630 LML

Affixes are variously added as:

~ *iuxta Maltunam* 1166 Dane, ~ *Meltonam* Hy 2 ib, ~ *Meltun* Hy 2 ib, ~ *iuxta Malton* 1275 RH, ~ *iuxta Melton* 1293 Banco, 1319 BM

~ *super Werc* Hy 2 Dane, ~ *super Wreþech* 1224 × 30 Fees, ~ *super Wrethek* e.Hy 3 Hastings, ~ *super Wreic* 1243 Fees (and with various spellings for R. Wreake freq to 1542 Fine), ~ *super aquam de Wreyk* 1301 IpmR

~ *Beler* 1332 SR, 1372 Ipm, 1383 *Rut*, ~ *Bel(l)ers* 1375 Misc, 1377, 1380 ELiW (and with various spellings of the feudal surn. suffix from 1404 Coram freq)

~ *super Wrethek alias Vellers* (sic) 1510 LP, ~ *super Wretheke alias Beler* 1539 AAS

'The village with a church', *v.* **kirkju-bý(r)**. The *ch* spellings in some early forms are AN for *k* rather than representing OE *cirice* 'a church'.

Hamo Beler held the manor in 1166 Dane and it remained in the Beler family as late as *Alicia Beler* 1327 SR and *Radulfus Beler* 1361 Ipm. In 1242 Fees, parts of Kirby are variously described as ~ *de Auvill'*, ~ *de Fouker*, ~ *Prioris*, ~ *de Sancto Amante* and ~ *de Wasteneys*. *Juliana de Ayvill* held land in Kirby in the reign of John, while *Robertus de Hevill'* possessed a knight's fee here in 1236 Fees. *Fouker*, a name surviving in the Kirby f.n. *Foucherdyke* 1407 Hilton, is poss. the ME surn. reflex of the ODan pers.n. *Folkar* (*Fulcarius* 12 Dane is recorded in Leics.). Alternatively, it may represent the OFr pers.n. *Foucher* < OGer *Fulchar*, *v.* Reaney *s.n.* Fulcher. The suffix ~ *Prioris* refers to that part of Kirby in the possession of the Prior of Kirby Bellars Priory, a house of Augustinian Canons (MLat *prior* (*prioris* gen.sg.) 'a prior'). *Amaury de Sancto Amando* is recorded as receiving a grant of land in Kirby in 1228 Ch, while *John de Wasteneys* owned *Wasteneyscroft* here in 1302 Ipm. Earlier, a *Willelmus de Wasteneys* held land in Osgathorpe (1236 Fees). Presumably he also possessed a fee in Kirby. Note affixes with MLat *iuxta* 'next to', *super* 'on, upon' and *aqua* (*aquam* acc.sg.) 'water, a river'.

ASHBY PASTURES is *Flindells* 1835 O, *Flendell Lodge* 1846, 1863 White, *v.* **loge** and Flindell's Cl in f.ns. (a); adjoining Ashby Folville. ASH TREE FM is *The New Close Lodge* 1835 O, *v.* **loge**. BRAN HILLS, *Bran Hill* 1679 *Terrier*, 1969 *Surv*; prob. with **brand** 'a place cleared by burning', cf. Bran, Ch **4** 178. BROCKLEYS FM (BROCKLEYS 2½"). CHALK POOL HILL, *Chalk Pool* 1969 *Surv*, *v.* **calc**, **pōl**[1] and cf. *Calkland* in f.ns. (b). CREAM GORSE, 1835 O, *v.* **gorst**. CREAM LODGE, 1806 Map, 1835 O,

1846, 1863, 1877 White, *v.* **loge** and cf. Cream Lodge in Barrow upon Soar. THE ELMS. ELMS COTTAGES. FLYING CHILDERS (P.H.), *Flying Childers* 1846, 1863, 1877 White, 1925 Kelly. GADDESBY LANE, leading to Gaddesby, 3 miles to the south-west. HAWTHORNE HO. HIGHFIELDS FM. HILLCREST FM. THE HOLLIES. IVY COTTAGE is *Chandlers Lodge* 1835 O, 1846, 1863 White; occupied by *Wm. Chandler, farmer* 1846 ib, *v.* **loge**. KIRBY BELLARS PRIORY (lost), *priorie de Kirk(e)by* 1467 *Pat*, ~ *de Kyrkebye Bellers* 1551 *ib*, *Kirkeby Bellers monasterii* 1550 *ib* (with MLat *monasterium* 'a monastery'), *v.* **priorie**; founded in 1320 as a chantry by Roger Beler, but converted to a priory for Augustinian Canons by his widow in 1359. KIRBY COTTAGE, 1835 O, 1877 White, 1925 Kelly, *v.* **cotage**. KIRBY GATE, ~ ~ FM, *Kirby Gate* 1925 Kelly, *v.* **gata**. KIRBY HALL, 1863 White, *The Hall* 1877 ib, *v.* **hall**. KIRBY HALL FM. KIRBY LODGE FM, cf. *Kirby Lodges* 1835 O, *v.* **loge**. KIRBY OLD MILL (lost), *Kirby Old Mill* 1824 *Terrier*. KIRBY PARK, 1846, 1863, 1877 White, 1970 *Surv*, *The Park* 1925 Kelly; it is *The Park House* 1835 O, *v.* **park**. LOSEBY HO. MAIN ST. PEACOCK FM. PICK'S LODGE, cf. *Arthur Pick, farmer and landowner* 1925 Kelly, *v.* **loge**. POPLARS FM. PRINGLE, 1970 *Surv*, *v.* **pingel**. RED LODGE. ST PETER'S CHURCH, *Kirby Church* 1690, 1708, 1708 (18), e.18 *Terrier*, *the Church* 1708 (18) *ib*, *Church (St Peter)* 1846, 1863, 1877 White, 1925 Kelly; it is earlier recorded as *ecclesie de Kyrkeby* 1220 MHW, ~ *de Kirkeby* 1316, 1319 *Pat*, *ecclesie Sancti Petri de Kyrkeby sup' Wrethek* 1366 (c.1430) *KB*, *ecclesiam de Kirkebebellers* 1555 *Pat*, *ecclesia de Kirkebie Bellers* 1561 *ib*. SANHAM HO., *Sanham House* 1863, 1877 White, *v.* *Senholm(e)* in f.ns. (b). STATION LANE, leading to *Kirby Station* 1854 O, on the *Syston and Peterborough Branch Railway* 1854 ib. WHITE LODGE. WINDYRIDGE FM. YEW TREE FM.

FIELD-NAMES

Undated forms in (a) are 1970 *Surv*. Forms throughout dated a.1250 (1404), m.13 (1404), p.1250 (1404) and l.13 (1404) are *Laz*; 1340 (c.1430), 1342 (c.1430), 1343 (c.1430), 1354 (c.1430), 1357 (c.1430), 1365 (c.1430), 1377 (c.1430), Edw 3 (c.1430) and 1400 (c.1430) are *KB*; 1395 × 1407, 1399 × 1407 and 1407 are Hilton; 14 (1467 × 84) are *LTD*; 1477 (e.16) are *Charyte*; 1486 are Cl; 1548 and 1556 are Pat; 1708 are *Reeve*.

(a) 4 ~, 4½ ~, 5 Acre, Barn 5 Acre, 7 Acres, Barn 7 Acre, 10 ~, 11 Acre, 12 Acres, Top 12 Acre, 16 ~, 17 ~, 19 ~, 20 Acre, Far ~, Near 20 ~, 22 ~, 40 Acre (*v.* **æcer**); Barn Cl; The Best Fd (*v.* **best**; a complimentary name for very fertile land); Big Fd; Bottom Fd; Brandy Mdw (*v.* **brand** and Bran Hills *supra*); Bridle Road Fd (*v.* **brigdels**); The Brummels (*Bromhull* Edw 3 Nichols, *le Netherbromehill* 1548 (*v.* **neoðera**), *le Over bromehill* 1548 (*v.* **uferra**) (*v.* **brōm, hyll**); Brutnall's Fd (cf. *Mrs. H. Brutnall* who is cited 1970); Burton Mdws (with reference to neighbouring Burton Lazars); Calf Cl, Calf Fd, Calf Holme (*v.* **holmr**) (*v.* **calf**); Chandler's Land (cf. *Wm. Chandler, farmer* 1846 White); Church Fd (*v.* St Peter's Church *supra*); Cluer's Cl (with the surn. *Cluer*, *v.* Reaney *s.n.*); Coal Place Fd (*v.* **col**[1]); the Conduits Fd (cf. *the Conduit Closes* 1708, *v.* **cundite**); the Cover (*v.* **cover(t)**); Crow Park (*v.* **park**; a humorous name for land frequented by crows); Dalby Road Fd (Great Dalby adjoins to the south-east); the Dovecote Fd (*v.* **dove-cote**); Debdale (*Depedale* 14 (1467 × 84), 1365 (c.1430), 1407, 1477 (e.16), *Depdale* 1395 × 1407, *the Deb Dayles* 1708, cf. *Depedalesyke* 1407 (*v.* **sík**), *Depedalewong* 1486 (*v.* **vangr**), *v.* **dēop, dalr** and Kerby Debdale in Frisby on the Wreake f.ns.(a)); Far Acre (*v.* **æcer**); Flindell's Cl (*flinttedele* m.13 (1404), *Flintedele* p.1250 (1404), *Scorteflintedel'*, *Scortflintedeyle* m.13 (1404) (*v.* **sc(e)ort**), *flintedole* p.1250 (1404) (*v.* **dāl**), *v.* **flint, deill** and Ashby Pastures *supra*); the Frisby Fd, the Frisby Mdw (Frisby on the Wreake adjoins to the west); the Galls (*v.* **galla**); the Haddocks (sic) (prob. with **hassuc**); Hampton Gates (*v.* **gata**; beside the old road south to Northampton); Hemsleys (the surn. *Hemsley* in the possessive case); Bottom ~, Top Hillybanks (*v.* **hyllig, banke**); Hinckley's Cl (with the surn. *Hinckley* of a family originally from the township of this name, 24 miles to the south-west); Home Cl, Bottom ~ ~, Home Fd, The Home Fd (*v.* **home**); Horse Cl; the Hossups (*Horshou* 1319 Inqaqd, *Horshow* 14 (1467 × 84), 1395 × 1407, *Attehorshow* 1477 (e.16) (*v.* **atte**), *v.* **hors, haugr**); House Cl; the Lea (*v.* **ley**); Little Hills (*litlehil* p.1250 (1404), *Litlehull* 1395 × 1407, *v.* **lȳtel, hyll**); the Long Cl; Long Mdw; Middle Fd (*Medelfelde*, *Middelfelde*, *Middilfelde*, *Middulfelde*, *Myddelfelde* 14 (1467 × 84), *Midelfeld*, *Midulfeld*, *Mydelfeld*, *Mydulfeld* 1477 (e.16), *le Myddlefelde* 1548, 1556 (*in campo medio* 1357 (c.1430); with MLat *campus* 'a field' and *medius* 'middle'), *v.* **middel, feld**; one of the great fields of the township); The Moat (*v.* **mote**; the site of the early hall); Moat Cl (a small enclosure in the far south of the parish, poss. a moot-site, since there is no evidence of the earthworks of a moat, *v.* **mōt**); Oak Tree Cl; Paddock (*v.* **paddock**); Parr Cross (*v.* **cros**; either with the surn. *Parr* or its pers.n. source, OFr *Perre/Pierre*); the Pikeshaft Cl 1761 *EnclA* (*Pekesers* m.13 (1404), *Pekyshers* m.13 (1404), p.1250 (1404) bis, *Pekeshers*, *Pekishers* p.1250 (1404), *Pikeshers*, *Pikishers* 14 (1467 × 84), *Pykeshers* 14 (1467 × 84), 1477 (e.16), *Pykisers* 1357 (c.1430), *Pikeshearfe or Pikesheaves* 1708, *v.* **ears** 'a rounded hill'; the first el. is the ME surn. *Peke*, *v.* Reaney *s.n.* Peak); Pinfold (*v.* **pynd-fald**); Platts (either the surn. *Platt* in the possessive case or **plat**); Plumtree Mdws (either with **plūm-trēow** or with the surn. *Plumtree* of a family originally from the village of this name 12 miles to the north-west in Notts.); the Reservoir Fd; Road Fd; Romeo's Fd (a very small enclosure; perh. named from a horse); Seagrass Mdw (*v.* **sǣd, græs**; referring to sown grass); Seven Sisters (unexplained; poss. a close containing a row of seven planted trees); Simpkin's Cl (with the surn. *Simpkin*); the Slip (*v.* **slipe**); Skellet's Cl (with the surn. *Skellett*); the Summer Fd (*v.* **sumor**; land used only in summer); Three Cornered Fd (*v.* **three-cornered**); T Mdw (with reference to shape); Townend Fd (*v.* **tūn, ende**);

Uplands (self-explanatory); Watley's Close 10 Acres, 2nd Watley's Cl (with the surn. *Watley*); Watts Cl (with the surn. *Watts*); Weathers Acres (*Wethirisakir* m.13 (1404), *Wetherisacre* 1357 (c.1430), *Longwetherisacre* 14 (1467 × 84), 1477 (e.16), *Longwetheracre* 1395 × 1407 (*v.* **lang**[1]), *Schortwethisaker'* 14 (1467 × 84) (*v.* **sc(e)ort**), *v.* **æcer**; either with an early form of the surn. *Weather* (*v.* Reaney *s.n.*) or with its source, OE **weðer** 'a wether, a castrated ram'; the ON pers.n. *Viðarr* (ODan *Withar*) appears to be precluded because of the recurring *e* in the first syllable); White Gate Cl (*v.* **geat**); Windmill Fd (*v.* **wind-mylne**); 1st Wood Cl also Well Fd (*v.* **wudu, wella**); Wool Fds (perh. with **wald**; but here rather may belong *Wlfhull* 1357 (c.1430), *Wolfhull'* 14 (1467 × 84) bis, *Wolfhull syke* 1407 (*v.* **sík**), *v.* **hyll**; if so, the first el. could be **wulf** 'a wolf' or a by-name derived from it, but more likely is a surn. *Wolf* or the ON pers.n. *Úlfr* which in part gave rise to it, *v.* Reaney *s.n.* Wolf).

(b) *Achterode* p.1250 (1404), *Aghtrode* 1407, *Haghtrodesterte* 1395 × 1407 (*v.* **steort**) (*v.* **æhta, rōd**[3]); *Adeynetlond* 1407 (*v.* **land**; either with the surn. *Adnet*, reflex of the OFr pers.n. *Adenet* (a diminutive of Adam), or less likely, with the pers.n. itself); *Aldeclif(f)* p.1250 (1404), 1395 × 1407, 1477 (e.16), *Aldeclyf* 1467 × 84 bis (*v.* **clif**; the first el. formally could be the OE pers.n. *Alda*, but pers.ns. compounded with *clif* are rare; more likely is **ald** 'old', which may denote 'formerly used' or 'long used'); *Ancherode, Anchrerode* 1467 × 84, *Anchire rode* 1477 (e.16) (*v.* **rōd**[3]; either with the surn. *Anker*, a reflex of the OFr pers.n. *Anchier*, or with the pers.n. itself; ME **ancre** 'a hermit' is also formally poss. but unlikely in compound with a word for a land unit); *Asfordewong'* 1357 (c.1430), 1467 × 84, *Assefordewong'* 1467 × 84, *Asfordwong* 1467 × 84, 1477 (e.16) (either 'the field by the ford at the ash-trees (or at Ashford)' or 'Asford's field', *v.* **æsc, ford, vangr**; it is uncertain whether the ford leading to Asfordby, which lies across R. Wreake, gave its name to Asfordby or whether this township gave a folk-etymology of its name to the ford, *v.* the discussion of the p.n. Asfordby *supra*); *Assebygate, Essebigate* m.13 (1404), *Asshbygate* 1477 (e.16), *Ayhschebygate, Ayschebygate* 1467 × 84 (*v.* **gata**; the road to Ashby Folville which adjoins to the south); *Ayleshou* 14 (1467 × 84) (*v.* **haugr**; the first el. is a pers.n., prob. ON *Egill*, but could be OE *Ægel* (cf. Aylestone (Guthlaxton Hundred) which could also contain either pers.n.)); *le balke* m.13 (1404) (*v.* **balca**); *Banecroft diche* m.13 (1404), *Bancroftdike* 1357, *Bancroft(e)dyke* 14 (1467 × 84) bis, 1395 × 1407, 1477 (e.16) (*v.* **bēan, croft, dīc, dík**); *Banelond* 14 (1467 × 84), *fattebanlond'* a.1250 (1404), *Fatbanlond'* 14 (1467 × 84), *Fatbanland(e)* 1395 × 1407, 1436 AD, 1477 (e.16) (*v.* **fætt**), *longebanlond'* a.1250 (1404), *langebanlond* m.13 (1404), *Longbanlond* 1395 × 1407 (*v.* **lang**[1]), *hardebanland* m.13 (1404), *hardebanlond'* p.1250 (1404) bis, *hardebanlont* p.1250 (1404) (*v.* **heard**), *Humblibanland, Humblybanland* 14 (1467 × 84) (*v.* **humol, humul**), *Shortbanlond* 1407 (*v.* **sc(e)ort**), *banlandhole* m.13 (1404) (*v.* **hol**[1]) (*v.* **bēan, land**); *le Barneclose* 1548 (*v.* **bern, clos(e)**); *Bathpol'* p.1250 (1404), 14 (1467 × 84), *Bathepol, Batepoel* 14 (1467 × 84), *Batepole* 1395 × 1407, 1477 (e.16) (*v.* **bæð, pōl**[1]); *Belleholme* 14 (1467 × 84) (*v.* **belle, holmr**); *Belloue* a.1250 (1404), *Belhou* m.13 (1404), *Belhowe* 1382 AD, *Bellehow* 14 (1467 × 84), 1477 (e.16), *Bellowe by Saltgate* 1395 × 1407 (*v.* *Saltgate*, *infra*) (*v.* **haugr**; the first el. is prob. **belle**, but a pers.n. ON *Beli* or OE *Bella* may also be thought of); *Bernardes Crosse* 1319 Inqaqd, 1319 Pat (*v.* **cros**; either with the pers.n. OFr *Bernart* or with its surn. reflex *Bernard*); *Bernewonge* l.13 (1404), *Berneswong'* 14 (1467 × 84), 1477 (e.16) bis, *Berniswong* 14 (1467 × 84), *v.* **vangr**; prob. with **bern** 'a barn', but the possessive case in the later forms may indicate a pers.n. such as ON *Bjǫrn* or OE *Beorn*); *betwene the gat(t)es* 1357 (c.1430), 1365 (c.1430) (a furlong so called, *v.* **betwēonan, gata**); *Bille pasture* 1486 (*v.* **pasture**; either with **bile** 'a beak' in its sense 'a narrow promontory' or **bill** 'a sword' in its transferred topographical sense 'a ridge'); *Blakemilde* a.1250 (1404), 14 (1467 × 84), *Blakmyld* 1395 × 1407, 1407 (*v.* **blæc, mylde**); *Bosseferthyng* 1395 × 1407 (*v.* **fēorðung**), *Bosseland* 1407 (*v.* **land**) (perh. with the OE pers.n. *Bōsa* or with the ME surn. *Bosse* (*v.* Reaney *s.n.* Boss for a range of its origins, esp. the OFr pers.n. *Bos*), but note also *Bossehowhyll'* in Wymeswold f.ns. (b)); *Brantcroftdyke* 14 (1467 × 84), *Brancroftdyke* 1477 (e.16) (*v.* **brant, croft, dík**); *Brecchou* c.1200 Dane, *Braicho* 1203 FF, 1203 Fine, *Breikehou* a.1250 (1404), *Breychou* p.1250 (1404), *Breychhow*, *Breychowe* 14 (1467 × 84), *Breychow* 14 (1467 × 84), 1477 (e.16), *Braychow(e)* 1407 bis, *longe Breychou* p.1250 (1404) (*v.* **lang**[1]), *scortebreychou* p.1250 (1404), *Schortbreyc(h)hou* 14 (1467 × 84) (*v.* **sc(e)ort**), *Brechougrene* m.13 (1404) (*v.* **grēne**[2]) (*v.* **brēc, haugr**); *Brecland(e)* 1467 × 84 (*v.* **bræc**[1], **land**); *le Brodedole* 14 (1467 × 84) (*v.* **brād, dāl**); *le Brok* 1407, *the Brooke Closes* 1708 (*v.* **brōc**); *Brotherne* 1407 (*v.* **brū, þyrne**); *Buckpool* n.d. Nichols (*v.* **bucca, pōl**[1]); *the Bullins* 1708 (*v.* **bula, eng**); *Calkland* 14 (1467 × 84), *calklond* 14 (1467 × 84), 1407 (*v.* **calc, land**); *Calvercroft* 1302 Ipm (*v.* **calf (calfra** gen.pl.), **croft**); *Catteshou* 14 (1467 × 84), 1477 (e.16), *Cattishou* 14 (1467 × 84) (*v.* **cat(t), haugr**); *Cawland* 1477 (e.16) (*v.* **cāl, cawel, land**); *Caytestou'* m.13 (1404), *Kaytistowe* 14 (1467 × 84), *Caystowellwong* 1395 × 1407 (*v.* **wella, vangr**) (*v.* **stōw**, poss. in its later sense 'a place where animals are herded and restrained from straying'; with the ON pers.n. *Kátr*, an original by-name from the adj. *kátr* 'glad'); *Chalhoum* m.13 (1404) (*v.* **holmr**; prob. with **cāl, kál**); *Closdyke* 1395 × 1407 (*v.* **clos(e), dík**); *Colhille* a.1250 (1404), *Colehull* 14 (1467 × 84) (*v.* **cāl, hyll**); *le Covent Close* 1548, 1556 (*v.* **convent, clos(e)**; with reference to Kirby Bellars Priory); *le Crokedole* 1548, 1556 (*v.* **krókr, dāl**); *(le) Croshou* p.1250 (1404), 14 (1467 × 84) (*v.* **haugr**; prob. with **cross** rather than with **cros**); *Dokeplace* 1391 Ipm (*v.* **place**; with the surn. *Doke*, *v.* Reaney *s.n.*); *Duffehous Yerde close* 1486 (*v.* **dove-hous, geard, clos(e)**); *elrenestub* m.13 (1404), *Elrenstubbe* 1365 (c.1430) (*v.* **ellern, stubb**); *Enedewell* 14 (1467 × 84), *Enedwell(e)* 14 (1467 × 84), 1477 (e.16), *Endewell* 1486 (*v.* **ened, wella**); *Endlies* 14 (1467 × 84), *Endlyes* 1477 (e.16) (*v.* **ende, lǣs**); *Estfeld(e)* 14 (1467 × 84, 1477 (e.16), *le Estefeld(e)* 1548, 1556, (*in campo orient'* 1357 (c.1430), with MLat *campus* 'a field' and *orientalis* 'eastern'), *v.* **ēast, feld**; one of the early great fields of the township); *le Esthorp* Edw 3 (c.1430), 1387 AD, *Estthorp* 1395 × 1407, *Estthorpleys* p.1250 (1404) (*v.* **lǣs**) (*v.* **ēast, þorp**); *Estynge* 14 (1467 × 84) (*v.* **ēast, eng**); *the Eye Meadow* 1708 (with reference to the river Eye or to the stream (**ēa**) which separates Kirby from Eye Kettleby); *le Farre Close* 1548, 1556 (*v.* **feor, clos(e)**); *le Feehous* 1420 Ipm (*v.* **fé-hús**); *le fen* m.13 (1404), *atte fen* 14 (1467 × 84) (*v.* **atte**), *Fensyke* 1395 × 1407 (*v.* **sík**) (*v.* **fenn**); *Firreswong* 1395 × 1407 (*v.* **fyrs, vangr**); *Flintedene* 14 (1467 × 84), *Flyntdene* 14 (1467 × 84), 1477 (e.16), *Flyntedene* 1477 (e.16) (*v.* **flint, denu**); *Foucherdyke* 1407 bis (*v.* **dík**; with the ME surn. *Foucher*, here either a reflex of the OFr pers.n. *Foucher* or the ODan pers.n. *Folkar*, *v.* Reaney *s.n.* Fulcher); *Frydaywong* 1395 × 1407 (*v.* **vangr**; with the surn. *Friday*, cf. *Radulphus Fridai* c.1167 AC of Leics.); *Frysebegate* 14 (1467 × 84) (*v.* **gata**), *Frisebymere* 1357 (c.1430), 14 (1467 × 84), *Frisebemere* 14 (1467 × 84), *Frysebymere* 1477 (e.16) (*v.* **(ge)mǣre**) (Frisby on the Wreake adjoins to the west); *Geruiswong* 14 (1467 × 84) (*v.* **vangr**; with the ME surn. *Gerveys*, a reflex of the OFr pers.n. *Gervais*, *v.* Reaney *s.n.* Jarvis); *Godelis* m.13 (1404), *Godeleyhes* 14 (1467 × 84), 1477 (e.16) (*v.* **gōd**[2], **lǣs**); *Goldsburgh* 1395 × 1407 (*v.* **burh**; poss. the late survival of the earlier Anglo-Saxon name for the settlement site of Kirby, with its first el. a pers.n. in the possessive case, such as OE *Godel* (with metathesis, cf. Goldsborough, YW 15) or OE *Golde* (later accorded a ME *-es* gen.sg., cf. Goldsborough, YN 137)); *le Gore* 1395 × 1407, 1548 (*v.* **gāra**); *le grene* m.13 (1404) (*v.* **grēne**[2]); *Grenesti* a.1250 (1404), *Grenesty(e)* 1357 (c.1430), 14 (1467 × 84), *Grenestywong* 1395 × 1407 (*v.* **vangr**) (*v.* **grēne**[1], **stīg**); *Grop(e)cuntlane* 1377 (c.1430), 1400 (c.1430) (*v.* **co(u)nte**, **lane**, with the first el. from OE *grāpian* 'to grope'; referring no doubt to a dark alley, the site of sexual exchanges); *Haliwell(e)* m.13 (1404), p.1250 (1404) (*v.* **hālig**, **wella**; a sacred spring or well); *Halls alias Fowlers meadow* 1708 (with the surns. *Hall* and *Fowler*); *Hamperland* 1407 (*v.* **land**; with the surn. *Hamper*, the reflex of OFr *hanapier* 'a maker or seller of goblets'); *Ham(p)tongate* 14 (1467 × 84), 1477 (e.16), *Hamptongatewong* 1395 × 1407 (*v.* **vangr**) (*v.* **gata**; the road south to Northampton); *hauerberghe* a.1250 (1404), *hauerberewe* m.13 (1404), *Harebergh* 14 (1467 × 84) bis, 1477 (e.16), *Longeharbergh'* 14 (1467 × 84), *Longhareberowe* 1395 × 1407 (*v.* **lang**[1]), *Harberwesyke* 14 (1467 × 84), *Herbersyke* 1395 × 1407 bis, 1407 (*v.* **sík**) (*v.* **hæfera, hafri, berg**); *Hayleshou* 14 (1467 × 84), *Haylyshou* 1477 (e.16), *Shorthailssoue* 1395 × 1407 (*v.* **sc(e)ort**) (*v.* **haugr**; with a pers.n., poss. ON *Hagall* or *Egill*, less likely OE *Hægel* or *Ægel*); *Herdewell* 1395 × 1407 (*v.* **heord**, **heorde, wella**); *Herdwych* m.13 (1404), *Herdewyc* p.1250 (1404), *Herd(e)wyke* 14 (1467 × 84), *Herdwyk* 1407, 1477 (e.16), *Hardwyk* 1407, *Herdwyghole* 1407, *Herdwykhole* 1407 bis (*v.* **hol**[1]) (*v.* **heorde-wīc**); *Holebek* 1407, *Holebeckhil* p.1250 (1404), *Hollebekhull* 1357 (c.1430), 14 (1467 × 84), 1407, 1477 (e.16) (*v.* **hyll**), *Holbeklond'*, *Holbuklond* 14 (1467 × 84) (*v.* **land**), *Holebeckhelongke* m.13 (1404), *Holbeklong'* 1340 (c.1430), 14 (1467 × 84) (*v.* **lang**[2]), *Holbeknetherȝente* 1395 × 1407 (*v.* **neoðera, ende**), *Holbeksyke* 1407 bis (*v.* **sík**), *Holebeckewade* p.1250 (1404), *Holbekwade* 1395 × 1407 (*v.* **(ge)wæd**) (*v.* **hol**[2], **bekkr**); *Holmeshades* 1357 (c.1430), *le Holmishauedis* 14 (1467 × 84) (*v.* **holmr, hēafod**); *Horswey* 14 (1467 × 84) (*v.* **hors, weg**); *How(e)manholm* 14 (1467 × 84), 1477 (e.16) (*v.* **holmr**; with the surn. *Howman*, a reflex of the late OE pers.n. *Hygemann*, *v.* Reaney *s.n.* Human); *atte Hulles in to þe gate, the hullis in þe gate, the hylles in ythe gate* 14 (1467 × 84), *Attehulles in to the gate, Attehulles in þe gate* 1477 (e.16) (*v.* **atte, hyll, þe, gata**; a furlong thus called); *Hyndesdale* m.13 (1404), 14 (1467 × 84), 1477 (e.16), *Hindisdale* 14 (1467 × 84), *longehindesdale, longehindisdale* p.1250 (1404), *Longhyndesdale, Long hyndisdale* 14 (1467 × 84), *Longehyndesdale* 1477 (e.16) (*v.* **lang**[1]) (*v.* **hind, dalr**); *Indewell* 1395 × 1407, *Longindewell* 1395 × 1407 (*v.* **lang**[1]) (*v.* **wella**; prob. with **hind**); *le Infal'*, *atte Infal* 14 (1467 × 84) (*v.* **atte**) (*v.* **in**; with **fald** or **(ge)fall**); *Kettlebybrigge* p.1250 (1404) (*v.* **brycg**; Eye Kettleby adjoins to the east); *Ketilsschepine* m.13 (1404), *Ketilschipene* 14 (1467 × 84), *Ketilscipene* 1477 (e.16) (*v.* **scypen**; with the common ON pers.n. *Ketill*, an original by-name (cf. OIcel *ketill* 'a cauldron, a cauldron-shaped helmet'); note that the same pers.n. appears in the name of adjoining Eye Kettleby); *Kiwynge* 1395 × 1407, *Kywyng* 1407, *scortekaruinges* m.13 (1404), *scortekiruinges* p.1250 (1404) (*v.* **sc(e)ort**) (*v.* **kervinge**); *Kylnewong'* 1343 (c.1430), 1357 (c.1430), *Shortkylnwong'* 1340 (c.1430), 1395 × 1407, *Schortkilnewong'* 14 (1467 × 84) (*v.* **sc(e)ort**), *Stokkylnewong'* 14 (1467 × 84), 1477 (e.16) (*v.* **stocc**) (*v.* **cyln, vangr**); *lauedywong* p.1250 (1404), *(le)*

Ladywong 1381 Fine, 1382 Ipm, 1382 Cl, 14 (1467 × 84), 1395 × 1407, *le Ladywonge* 1430 Fine (*v.* **lavedi, vangr**; land prob. endowed for the upkeep of a chapel dedicated to Our Lady, the Blessed Virgin Mary); *lafrickethorn* p.1250 (1404) (*v.* **þorn**; either with **lāwerce, lāferce** 'the lark' or with the surn. *Laverick* derived as a by-name from it, *v.* Reaney *s.n.* Lark); *Laweson croft* 1395 × 1407 (*v.* **croft**; with the surn. *Lawson*); *le Ley Close* 1548 (*v.* **laie, clos(e)**); *literode* m.13 (1404) (*v.* **lȳtel, rod**[1]); *litlehil* p.1250 (1404), *Litlehull* 1395 × 1407 (*v.* **lȳtel, hyll**); *le littilcroft* m.13 (1404), *litilcroft, litlecroft* p.1250 (1404), *Litulcroft, Lytelcroft* 14 (1467 × 84) (*v.* **lȳtel, croft**); *longedele, longehedel'* m.13 (1404), *le longdele* p.1250 (1404) (*v.* **lang**[1], **deill**); *Long(e)furlong* m.13 (1404), 14 (1467 × 84) (*v.* **lang**[1], **furlang**); *Long(e)grene* 1395 × 1407, 1407 (*v.* **lang**[1], **grēne**[2]); *longkebithehee* m.13 (1404) (*v.* **lang**[2], **bī, þe, (ge)hæg**); *Longleys* 1407 (*v.* **lang**[1], **lǣs**); *Malthous* 1420 Ipm (*v.* **mealt-hūs**); *Manholme* m.13 (1404), p.1250 (1404), *Manholm* 1365 (c.1430), 14 (1467 × 84) bis, *Man(n)eholm* 14 (1467 × 84) bis, 1477 (e.16), *Mannholmnetherȝende* 1395 × 1407 (*v.* **neoðera, ende**), *Mannholmoverende* 1395 × 1407 (*v.* **uferra, ende**) (*v.* **(ge)mǣne, holmr**); *Marketgate* 1395 × 1407, *Marketgatewong* 1486 (*v.* **vangr**) (*v.* **market, gata**; the road to the market-place of Melton Mowbray, cf. Cheap End in Frisby on the Wreake); *le Medowgate, le Midowgate* 14 (1467 × 84), *Medowegate* 1477 (e.16) (*v.* **mǣd (mǣdwe** obl.sg.), **gata**); *Middilfurlong', Myddylfurlong'* 14 (1467 × 84), *Mydelfurlong, Mydulfurlong* 1477 (e.16) (*v.* **middel, furlang**); *le Midulthorp* 1400 (c.1430), *le Medilthorpe* 1412 AD, *middilthorpleys* m.13 (1404) (*v.* **lǣs**) (*v.* **middel, þorp**); *molendino de Kirkeby* p.1250 (1404) (with MLat *molendinum* 'a mill'); *atte Monekes* 1321 Misc (p) (*v.* **atte, munuc**; with reference to the Brothers of Kirby Bellars Priory); *Mouswell'* 14 (1467 × 84) bis, *Muswell* 1395 × 1407, *Mouswele* 1477 (e.16) (*v.* **mūs, wella**); *Mukwong* 1395 × 1407 (*v.* **muk, vangr**); *Newedoles* m.13 (1404), 1477 (e.16), *(le) Neudoles* p.1250 (1404), 1340 (c.1430) bis, *Newdol'* 14 (1467 × 84), *Newdoles* 14 (1467 × 84), 1477 (e.16) (*v.* **nīwe, dāl**); *Newdyke* 14 (1467 × 84) (*v.* **nīwe, dík**); *Newegrove* 1420 Ipm (*v.* **nīwe, grafa**[1]); *Nursery* 1708 (*v.* **nursery**); *Oterehelland* 1395 × 1407 (*v.* **ūterra, hyll, land**); *Paddecroft* m.13 (1404), *Paddoccroft* p.1250 (1404), *Paddokescroft(e)* 1381 Fine, 1382 Cl, 1382 Ipm, 1430 Fine, *Pad(d)ocke crofte* 1551 *Deed*, 1551, 1555 Pat (*v.* **croft**; either with the surn. *Paddock* or **padduc** from which it derives); *Peyslandes* 1357 (c.1430), *Peyslondis* 14 (1467 × 84) (*v.* **pise, land**); *Pinchepoil* m.13 (1404), *Pinchepol', Pynchepol* 14 (1467 × 84), *Netherpynchpole* 1395 × 1407 (*v.* **neoðera**) (*v.* **pinc, pōl**[1]; cf. Pinchpools, Ess 552); *Pipesdale* 1203 Fine, *Pippisdale* m.13 (1404), 14 (1467 × 84) bis, *Pippesdale* 14 (1467 × 84), 1395 × 1407, *Pypesdal* 1477 (e.16), *Hamer pippesdale* 1395 × 47 (*v.* **hamer** 'nearer home'), *Vttre pippesdale* 1395 × 1407 (*v.* **ūterra**), *homhalf' pipesdale* p.1250 (1404) (*v.* **hām** 'home', **half**), *huthalf' pipesdale* p.1250 (1404) (*v.* **ūt, half**), *pippisdalenethirende* m.13 (1404) (*v.* **neoðera, ende**) (*v.* **pīpe, dalr**); *Portisty* 14 (1467 × 84) (*v.* **port**[2], **stīg**; with reference to Melton Mowbray, cf. *Marketgate, supra*); *Quenildemilne* p.1250 (1404), *Quanemylnehade* 1407 (*v.* **hēafod**), *Quenemylnleys* 1407 bis (*v.* **lǣs**) (*v.* **myln**; the earliest form has the OE fem. pers.n. *Cwēnhild* as first el., which by 1407 has been reduced to **cwene** 'a woman'); *radecliue* m.13 (1404) (*v.* **rēad, clif**); *le Raton rowe* Edw 3 (c.1430) (*v.* **raton, rāw**); *Rauenoldland'* Edw 3 (c.1430) (*v.* **land**), *Rauenold pasture* 1365 (c.1430) (*v.* **pasture**) (cf. *Johannes Rauenold* 1365 (c.1430) and *Will' Rauenold* Edw 3 (c.1430) of Kirby); *Redehill* 1395 × 1407 (*v.* **rēad, hyll**); *Redyng* 14 (1467 × 84), 1477 (e.16), *Longeredyng', Longrydyng'* 14 (1467 × 84) (*v.* **lang**[1]), *Shorteredinghes* a.1250 (1404), *Shorte Redyng'* 1365 (c.1430) (*v.* **sc(e)ort**), *le Rydyng ouer the gate* 14 (1467 × 84) (*v.* **ofer**[3], **gata**), *Redyngegatte* 1365 (c.1430) (*v.* **gata**) (*v.* **ryding**); *Reydwelle* 14 (1467 × 84), 1477 (e.16) (*v.* **hrēod, wella**); *Reynerwell'* 14 (1467 × 84) (*v.* **wella**; either with the OFr pers.n. *Rainer/Reiner* or with its surn. reflex *Reyner*, *v.* Reaney *s.n.*); *Ridelwong* 1486 (*v.* **vangr**; with the surn. *Riddel*, cf. *Reginaldus Ridel* 1327 SR of Leics.); *Rigges* 14 (1467 × 84), *Riggesmedwe* m.13 (1404) (*v.* **mǣd** (**mǣdwe** obl.sg.)), *Riggisyke* 14 (1467 × 84), *Ryggesyk(e)* 14 (1467 × 84), 1477 (e.16) (*v.* **sík**), *Rygsyde* 14 (1467 × 84) (*v.* **sīde**) (*v.* **hrycg, hryggr**); *Riscroft* p.1250 (1404), *longeriscroft* m.13 (1404) (*v.* **lang**[1]) (*v.* **hrīs, croft**); *Ruchepole* 1477 (e.16) (*v.* **risc, pōl**[1]); *Ruschebuskes*, *Ruysshebuskes*, *Ruyschebuskys* 14 (1467 × 84), *Ruyschebuskes* 14 (1467 × 84), 1477 (e.16), *Rushebuskes* 1395 × 1407, *Ruischebuskes* 1477 (e.16) (*v.* **risc, buskr**); *Saltgate* p.1250 (1404), 1395 × 1407 bis (*v.* **salt**[1], **gata**; a salters' way); *Sandlondes* l.13 (1404), *Sandlandis*, *Sandelondis*, *Sandlond'*, *Sandlondis*, *Sondlondis* 14 (1467 × 84), *Sandeland'* 1395 × 1407, 1407, *Sandlandes*, *Sondelondys*, *Sonlondys* 1477 (e.16) (*v.* **sand, land**); *Sanpittes* 1407 (*v.* **sand-pytt**); *le Schelland*, *Schellond*, *Scheleland* 14 (1467 × 84), *Shelland* 1395 × 1407, *scelflondehole* m.13 (1404) (*v.* **hol**[1]) (*v.* **scelf, land**); *Scortegrene* p.1250 (1404) (*v.* **sc(e)ort, grēne**[2]); *Schortlandis* 14 (1467 × 84), *Schortlandes* 1477 (e.16) bis (*v.* **sc(e)ort, land**); *Sekemaneshous* m.13 (1404) (*v.* **sikeman, hūs**; referring to the infirmary building of Kirby Bellars Priory; the earliest OED citation for *sikeman* is dated c.1340); *Senholm(e)* m.13 (1404) bis, p.1250 (1404) bis, 1395 × 1407, 1407, *Senneholme* p.1250 (1404), *Seneholm* 14 (1467 × 84), *Saneholm* 14 (1467 × 84), 1477 (e.16), *Senholmisnetherhende* m.13 (1404) (*v.* **neoðera, ende**), *Senholmefurlonge* m.13 (1404), p.1250 (1404), *Senholmfurlong* 1395 × 1407 (*v.* **furlang**) (*v.* **sænna, senna, holmr**); *Seynt Mary hedland* 1407 (*v.* **hēafod-land**; the Abbey of St Mary de Pratis, Leicester, held land here); *Sheldisaker* 14 (1467 × 84) (*v.* **æcer**; either with **sceld** 'a shelter' or with the ME surn. *Sheld* (> ModE *Shield*), *v.* Reaney *s.n.* Shield); *Skelund* p.1250 (1404) bis (poss. a Scandinavianized form of *Schelland*, *supra*; otherwise *v.* **skial, lundr**); *Smalethornes* m.13 (1404), *Smalthornes* p.1250 (1404), 14 (1467 × 84), 1477 (e.16), *Smalethornis*, *Smalethornys* 14 (1467 × 84) (*v.* **smæl, þorn**); *Smithishakyr* m.13 (1404), *Smythisacre* 14 (1467 × 84) bis, 1477 (e.16), *Smithisakir* 14 (1467 × 84) (*v.* **smið, æcer**); *Souuesdale* p.1250 (1404) (*v.* **sōg**; with **dalr** or **deill**); *Sowthrowes* 14 (1467 × 84) (*v.* **sūð, vrá**); *Standard'* a.1250 (1404), *Standerd* 1357 (c.1430), *le Standerde* 1395 × 1407, *le Standard* 1407 (*v.* **standard**); *stanlond* p.1250 (1404), *standlandis* 14 (1467 × 84) (*v.* **stān, land**); *Stanyland'* 14 (1467 × 84) (*v.* **stānig, land**); *Steynhull* 1357 (c.1430), 1395 × 1407 (*v.* **steinn, hyll**); *stinesdale* m.13 (1404), *Stounisdale* 14 (1467 × 84) (with the ON pers.n. *Steinn* and prob. with **deill** rather than **dalr**); *Stoc(h)* m.13 (1404) bis, *Stok* p.1250 (1404), 14 (1467 × 84) (*v.* **stoc**); *Stocforlong'* 1340 (c.1430), *Stocfurlong* 14 (1467 × 84) bis, *Stockfurlong* 1395 × 1407, *Stokfurlong* 1395 × 1407, 1477 (e.16) (*v.* **stocc, furlang**); *Stocwellelane*, *Stokewelle lane* 1354 (c.1430) (*v.* **stocc, wella, lane**; alluding to a stream with a footbridge consisting of a tree trunk); *Stokhowe* 1395 × 1407 (*v.* **haugr**; either with **stoc** or **stocc**); *Stonyhyll* 14 (1467 × 84), 1477 (e.16) (*v.* **stānig, hyll**); *Stouesdale* 1357 (c.1430), (*super*) *Stovesdale* 1365 (c.1430) (*v.* **deill**; poss. with the ON pers.n. *Stúfr*); *Strowhades* 1357 (c.1430) (*v.* **strá, hēafod**); *le Styes* l.14 AD (*v.* **stig**); *sunderhaker* a.1250 (1404) (*v.* **sundor, æcer**); *surhoues* m.13 (1404), *surhowes* p.1250 (1404) (*v.* **sūr, haugr**); *Tasleclif* m.13 (1404), *Tasilclif* p.1250 (1404), *Tasilcliue* 14 (1467 × 84), 1477 (e.16), *Tasalclyf'* 14 (1467 × 84),

Tasclef 1395 × 1407 bis (*v.* **tǣsel, clif**); *le thickinc* m.13 (1404), *le thickyng*, *Thikking* p.1250 (1404), *Thykkyngdale medow* 1486 (*v.* **dalr, mǣd (mǣdwe** obl.sg.)) (*v.* **þicce**[1]; with **-ing**[2] or **eng**); (*le*) *Thirne* m.13 (1404), 14 (1467 × 84), 1395 × 1407, *le Thyrne* 14 (1467 × 84), 1477 (e.16), *Thyrnedeyle* m.13 (1404), *Thirndele* 14 (1467 × 84), *Thyrndele* 1477 (e.16), *Longthirndale* 1407 (*v.* **lang**[1]) (*v.* **deill**), *Thirndole*, *Thyrndole* 14 (1467 × 84) (*v.* **dāl**) (*v.* **þyrne, þyrnir**); *Thornybalke* 14 (1467 × 84), *Thornybalkewong* 1486 (*v.* **vangr**) (*v.* **þornig, balca**); *Thorpesgatte* 1357 (c.1430), *Thorpgate* 1395 × 1407, *Ouerthorpgate* 14 (1467 × 84), 1477 (e.16), *Ouirthorpisgate* 14 (1467 × 84) (*v.* **ofer**[3]) (*v.* **þorp, gata**); *Thyrnwong* 1486 (*v.* **þyrne, þyrnir, vangr**); *Toftes* 14 (1467 × 84), 1477 (e.16), *Tofts* 1395 × 1407 (*v.* **toft**); *Toukwong'*, *Towkwong'*, *Thowkwong'* 14 (1467 × 84), *Toukwong*, *Towkwong* 1477 (e.16) (*v.* **vangr**; with the surn. *Toke*, a reflex of the Anglo-Scand pers.n. *Tōka*, *Tōke* (ON *Tóki*), *v.* Reaney *s.n.*); *Twercliue* m.13 (1404), p.1250 (1404), *Thuerclif* p.1250 (1404) (*v.* **þverr, clif**; a furlong so named); *le Tunge* 14 (1467 × 84), *the tounge* 1477 (e.16) (*v.* **tunge**); *viam reg'* 1400 (c.1430) ('the king's highway', with MLat *via* 'a road' and *rex* (*regis* gen.sg.) 'a king'; with reference to Henry IV); *le Wade* 14 (1467 × 84), *atte Wade* 1477 (e.16) (*v.* **atte**) (*v.* **(ge)wæd**); *Wasteneyscroft* 1302 Ipm, *le Wasteneyescroft* Edw 1 (1380) Nichols, 1319 Dugd (*v.* **croft**; in the possession of *John de Wasteneys* 1302 Ipm); *Waterfurrowes* 1407 (*v.* **wæter, furh** and *the Waterfurrow(e)s* in Asfordby f.ns. (b)); *le Watermeade* 1548, 1556 (*v.* **wæter, mǣd**; referring to part of a system of irregation, *v.* Field 90-2); *Watermylle Close* 1548, *le Watermyll close* 1556 (*v.* **water-mylne, clos(e)**); *atte Welle* 1327 SR (p), 1342 (c.1430) (p) (*v.* **atte, wella**); *Westfeld(e)* 14 (1467 × 84), 1477 (e.16), *le Westefelde* 1548, *le Westfeld* 1556, (*in campo occident'* 1357 (c.1430), with MLat *campus* 'a field' and *occidentalis* 'western') (*v.* **west, feld**; one of the early great fields of the township); *le Westhorp* 1319 Dugd, 1354 (c.1430), *le Westthorpe* 1399 AD (*v.* **west, þorp**); *Westmedow(e)* 14 (1467 × 84), 1477 (e.16), *Westmedwe* 1477 (e.16) (*v.* **west, mǣd (mǣdwe** obl.sg.)); *Whetebergh'* 1357 (c.1430), 14 (1467 × 84), *Whatburowe* 1395 × 1407 (*v.* **hwǣte, berg**); *William corner dame Edeson(e)* 1319 Inqaqd, 1319 Pat (*v.* **corner, dame**, cf. *William Edesone* 1319 Inqaqd; the translated sources read 'a certain angle called William Edesone' and 'the angle of William Edesone' 1319 Inqaqd, 'to the corner which is called William corner dame Edeson' 1319 Pat); *le Wold(e)* 14 (1467 × 84), 1477 (e.16), (*in Waldis* m.13 (1404), *in Waldo* m.13 (1404), p.1250 (1404)) (*v.* **wald**); (*les*) *Wrangelandes* m.13 (1404), p.1250 (1404), *Wrangland'* m.13 (1404), 14 (1467 × 84), *Wranglondis* 14 (1467 × 84), *Wrangeland*, *Wrangelond* 1395 × 1407 (*v.* **wrang, vrangr, land**); *Wudegate* a.1250 (1404) (*v.* **wudu, gata**); *Wynd(e)mylnegate* 1357 (c.1430), 1365 (c.1430), *Wyndymylnegate* 1407 (*v.* **wind-mylne, gata**); *Wythowe* 14 (1467 × 84) (*v.* **hwīt, hvítr, haugr**).

Gaddesby

1. GADDESBY

Gadesbi 1086 DB (x3), *Gadesbie* 1086 ib, *Gadesbia* 1178 P, *Gadesby* c.1130 LeicSurv, 1322 Fine (p) *et passim* to 1502 *MiscAccts*, 1535 VE

Gaddesbi c.1130 LeicSurv, 1179 ChancR, 1206 P, *Gaddesbia* 1177 *ib*, *Gaddesby* 1263 *LCDeeds* bis, 1276 RH, 1278 RGrav *et freq*, *Gaddisby* 1209 × 35 RHug, 1510 *Rental*, *Gaddisbya* 13 *MiD* (p), *Gaddysby* Edw 1 (1449), 1342 (1449) *WoCart et passim* to 1363 (1449) *ib*, 1510, 1533 *Rental*, *Gadysby* 1502 *MiscAccts*, 1522 *Wyg*

Gadesberi 1200 P (p), 1201 ib (p), *Gadesbir'* 1201 ChancR (p)

Gatesbi 1169 P, *Gatesby* 1274 Cl, 1303 Pat, 1322 Fine (p), 1331 Pat

Gaddebi 1179, 1180, 1181, 1182 P, 1224 ClR, *Gaddeby* m.13 (1404) *Laz* (p)

Probably 'Gad's farmstead, village', *v.* **bȳ**. The ON pers.n. *Gaddr* (ODan *Gad*, OSwed *Gadd*) is an original by-name from ON *gaddr* 'a goad, a spur'. Fellows-Jensen (SSNEM 48) suggests that the first el. of Gaddesby may rather be the sb. *gaddr* transferred topographically to the 'spur of land' on which the settlement is located. However, its site lies on the south-facing escarpment of a long ridge which extends three miles to its west and roughly the same to its east, so that it is difficult to conceive of this physical feature as a hill spur.

The three 13th century spellings with *-beri/-bir'* do not indicate an earlier generic in *-byrig* (dat.sg. of *burh* 'a fortified place'), *v.* the discussion of the name of Asfordby.

BEESON'S BARN, with the surn. *Beeson*, *v.* Reaney *s.n.* BLACKSMITH'S SHOP (lost), *Blacksmiths Shop* 1847 *TA*, **blacksmith**, **sc(e)oppa**. BUNBURY FM, *Bunberry* 1625 *Terrier*, *Middle ~*, *Upper ~*, *Willamsons Bunbury* 1847 *TA*, *Bunbury Meadow* 1847 *ib*; earlier forms are needed, but prob. is 'reed hill', *v.* **bune**, **berg**. THE BUSHES, 1925 Kelly, *v.* **busc**. CARLTON LODGE. CHENEY ARMS (P.H.) (lost), *Cheney Arms* 1877 White, 1925 Kelly; cf. *Edward Hawkins Cheney* 1877 White of Gaddesby Hall, a principal landowner in the parish. COLES LODGE, with the surn. *Coles*, *v.* **loge**. DALE HILL, 1625 *Terrier*, 1737 PR, 1818, 1825 *Terrier*, 1847 *TA*, *v.* **dalr**. GADDESBY GRANGE, *v.* **grange**. GADDESBY HALL, 1831 Curtis, 1925 Kelly; on the site of *Paskehall* 1398 LAS, 1534 *Rental*, *Pask hall* 1561, 1572 LAS, *Pascke* ~ 1586 ib, *Paske* ~ 1592 ib, 1804 Nichols, 1815 Map, 1835 O, 1863, 1877 White, *v.* **hall**; with the surn. *Paske*, from ME *paske*, OFr *pasque* 'Easter', in turn from Hebrew *pesakh* 'a passing over', originally used as a pers.n. for someone born at Easter. GADDESBY LODGE, 1863, 1877 White, *v.* **loge**. GATE (P.H.) (lost), *Gate* 1846, 1863 White, *The Gate Public House* 1847 *TA*. GLEBE FM, *v.* **glebe**. HARBOROUGH COTTAGE, *Harbro' cottage* 1877 White, *v.* **cotage**. MALT SHOVEL (P.H.) (lost), *Malt Shovel* 1846, 1863 White, *The Malt Shovel Public House* 1847 *TA*; mine host *Henry Mason* 1846 White was a maltster and may have named the hostelry with reference to his profession. MANOR HO., *Manor House* 1863, 1877 White, *v.* **maner**. MESSENGER'S LODGE, *Messenger(s) Lodge* 1835 O, 1846 White, *v.* **loge**, cf. *Jas. Messenger, farmer*, resident in 1846 ib. NAPIER HO. OAKLANDS, *The Oaklands* 1925 Kelly. PARK HO., *Park House* 1877 White, 1925 Kelly, *v.* **park** and The Park in f.ns. (a). THE PINES. ROSE COTTAGE. ST LUKE'S CHURCH, *Church (St Luke)* 1925 Kelly; it is earlier recorded as *ecclesiam de Gaddesby* 1334 *Pat*, cf. *atte Kirke* 1377 LAS (p), *atte Kyrke* 1390 Pat (p), *v.* **atte, kirkja**. SPURR'S LODGE, with the surn. *Spurr*, *v.* **loge**. UNDERWOOD'S LODGE, 1835 O, *v.* **loge**; cf. *Wm. Underwood, farmer* 1846 White. WHEELWRIGHT'S SHOP (lost), *Wheelwrights Shop* 1847 *TA*, *v.* **whelewryght, sc(e)oppa**. WOODBINE COTTAGE.

FIELD-NAMES

Undated forms in (a) are 1847 *TA*; those dated 1797 and 1969 are *Surv*; 1818 and 1825 are *Terrier*. Forms throughout dated 1377, 1398, 1502, 1510, 1523, 1561, 1572, 1580, 1586 and 1592 are LAS; 1467 × 84 are *LTD*; 1477 (e.16) are *Charyte*; 1534 are *Rental*; 1625 are *Terrier*; 1627 are Ipm.

(a) The Acre, Three Acres, (the) Four ~, Six ~ 1847, Seven ~ 1847, 1969, (the) Ten ~, Top ~ ~, Bottom Eleven ~ 1847, Twelve ~, Thirteen ~, Sixteen ~ 1969, Nineteen ~, Twenty Acres 1847 (*v.* **æcer**); the Anglings (*v.* **angle, eng**); Ash Cl (*v.* **æsc**); Bottom ~ ~, Top ~ ~, Far ~ ~, First ~ ~, Barn Cl; Bell Bush (*Belbusk*, ~ *feild* 1625 (*v.* **feld**; one of the great fields of the township), *v.* **belle, busc, buskr**); Berry Cliff 1787 *TB*, 1797, Bury Cliff Hill 1818, 1825, Barrowcliffe Lane 1847 *TA*, Barrowcliffe Road 1798 *EnclA* (*Berrycliff(e)* c.1515 PR, 1625, cf. *High Berrycliff* *close* 1625, *v.* Barrowcliffe Spinney in Barsby *infra*); Big Fd 1969; The Bit, Lucerne Bit (Lucerne (*Medicago sativa*) was introduced into Britain as a fodder crop in the late 14th cent.) (*v.* **bit**); Bottom Mdw; Brewsters Cl 1969 (with the surn. *Brewster*); Brooksby Lane 1969 (Brooksby lies 2 miles to the north-west); Browns Cl 1847, Bottom ~ ~, Top Tom Brown's 1969; Bruces Cl (with the surn. *Bruce*); Bushy Fd 1969 (*v.* **busshi**); Buttlings Cl (perh. with a surn. *Buttling*, poss. a version of *Butlin* of which an early form *Butveleyn* occurs in neighbouring Northants. in 1429, *v.* Reaney *s.n.*; but note the presence of ling hereabouts as in The Lingens *infra*, so that **butte** with **lyng** may also be considered); Calf Cl 1847, 1969 (cf. *Calves Close* 1627, *v.* **calf**); Camp Fd 1969 (evidently referring to a military establishment, presum. of World War 2 date); Cemetery Fd 1969; First ~ ~, Second Church Lees (*v.* **leys** and St Luke's Church *supra*); Cow Cl; Cow Standing (*v.* **standing**); Cox's 1969 (the surn. *Cox* in the possessive case); Cross Gate Cl (*Crossgate*, *Crosgate furlong* 1625 (*v.* **furlang**), *v.* **cross, gata**); The Dale, First ~, Second ~, Third Dale 1847, Little Dales 1969, Dale Mdw 1847 (*v.* **dalr**); Draycott's Yard 1797, 1847 (*v.* **geard**; with the surn. *Draycott*); Far Cl; Far ~ ~, First Felsteads Cl (with the surn. *Felstead*); First Cl; The Gauls 1969, Goodalls Gauls 1847 (with the surn. *Goodall*), the Old Gauls, the Gauls Mdw 1847 (*v.* **galla**); Gravel Hole Cl (*v.* **gravel, hol**[1]); (the) Great Cl, Great Close Mdw (*the Great close* 1627, *v.* **grēat**); Bottom ~, Top Griff (*v.* **gryfja**); Highway (*v.* **hēah-weg**; a close thus named); Hollings Orchard (with the surn. *Hollings*); Far ~ ~, First Home Cl 1797, 1847, Middle ~ ~, Home Cl 1847 (*v.* **home**); The Hooks, Middle Hook (*v.* **hōc**); Bottom ~ ~, Middle ~ ~, Top Horse Leys (*v.* **hors, leys**); House Cl; Hovel Mdw 1847, 1969 (*v.* **hovel**); Huttins Mdw 1847, Huttons Mdw 1969, Huttins Nook 1847 (*v.* **nōk**) (with the surn. *Hutton*); Intake (*v.* **inntak**); Jessons Barn, Jessons Cl, Jessons Mdw (with the surn. *Jesson*); Kilbys Cl, Kilbys Mdw (with the surn. *Kilby* of a family originally from Kilby, 12 miles to the south-west, cf. *Thomas de Kylby* 1327 SR of Leics.); The Lancers 1969 (unexplained); Lawn Wall 1969; the Lees 1969, Little ~ ~, Over Lees (*v.* **uferra**), Nether Lees 1847 (*v.* **leys**); the Lingens 1847, 1969 (*v.* **lyng, eng**); Little Cl; Bottom ~ ~, Top Little Hill (*le Littelhull* 1398, cf. *Little hill furlong* 1625 (*v.* **furlang**), *v.* **lȳtel, hyll**); Top Little Mdw; Long Cl; Longlands, ~ Cl, Longlands Mdw, Five Acre Longlands (*v.* **æcer**) (*Langelond*(') 1467 × 84, 1477 (e.16), *v.* **lang**[1], **land**); Masons Cl (cf. *Masons farm* 1627 (*v.* **ferme**) and *Geoffrey Mason* 1627); the Meadow(s) 1847; Middle Cl; Far ~ ~, Near ~ ~, Great ~ ~, Upper Mill Cl 1847; Mill Fd 1969 (*the Mill feild* 1625, *v.* **feld**; one of the great fields); Mill Home (*v.* **holmr**); Mouldebanks 1787 *TB*, Mouldy Banks 1847 (cf. *Mouldy Bank Meadow* 1737, *v.* Mouldy Banks in Barsby f.ns. (a)); Muckhill Gate (*Muck-hill gate furlong* 1625 (*v.* **furlang**), *v.* **gata**; late forms, thus either with **muk, hyll** or **mycel, mikill, hyll**); New Cl; New Fd 1969; Ostir Ford 1798 *EnclA*, Oster ~ 1835 O, Ostor ~ 1863 (*v.* **eowestre**; **ford**); Bottom Paddock 1847, Middle ~, Top Paddock 1847, 1969, Miles' Paddock 1969 (with the surn. *Miles*) (*v.* **paddock**); Pages Cl 1847, Page's ~ 1969 (with the surn. *Page*); the Park, Bottom ~, Top Park (*the parke* 1559 Cor, cf. *Parke close* 1605 Ipm, *v.* **park**); Peach's Cl (with the surn. *Peach*); the Pikes (*v.* **pīc**); Pinfold (*the Pinfold* 1625, *v.* **pynd-fald**); (the) Pingle (*the Pingell* 1627, *v.* **pingel**); (the) Play Cl 1846 White, 1847 *TA*, 1863, 1877 White (*v.* **plega**; a place for games); Bottom ~ ~, Top ~ ~, First Ploughed Cl; Ploughed piece (*v.* **pece**); Pollard's Yard (*v.* **geard**; with the surn. *Pollard*); (the) Poor's Cl 1846 White, 1847 *TA*, 1863, 1877 White (*v.* **pouer(e)**; land dedicated to poor-law relief or charity, *v.* Field 191–3); Porter Bush (*v.* **busc**; with the surn. *Porter*); Reeves Cl, Reeves Bottom ~, Reeves Little Cl (cf. *John Reeve* 1847); Road Fd 1969; Round Hill 1969 (*the Round Hill* 1580, *v.* **round, hyll**); Great ~, Little Sandlands (*v.* **sand, land**); Second Cl; Seed Cl (*v.* **sǣd**; in f.ns., used of areas of sown grass); Shoulder of Mutton 1969 (a common modern f.n. used of a close shaped like a shoulder of mutton); (the) Slidings 1787 *TB*, 1798 *EnclA*, 1847 *TA*, Slydings 1825 (*the Slydings* 1625, *a close called Slydeings* c.1725 *Terrier*, *Slidings* c.1700, e.18, 1724 *ib*, *Slydings* 1745 *ib*; the first el. is from OE *slīdan* 'to slide, to slip', cf. OE *slide* 'sliding, slip' and OE *slidor* 'slippery; a slippery place'; poss. is a vbl.sb. use as 'a slippery place' or 'a steeply sloping place', *v.* **slidyng**; but a construction with **-ing**[2] or **eng** cannot be discounted, cf. the Anglings *supra*); the Slip 1969 (*v.* **slipe**); Smiths Mdw (cf. *John Smith* 1847); Spinney Cl (*v.* **spinney**); Swan Dale Hole 1818, 1825 (*Swinesdalehull*, *Swynesdalehull* 1467 × 84, *Swandale Hole* 1625, *Swine Dale Hole* 1737 PR, *v.* **swīn**[1], **svín, dalr, hyll**; it is poss. that the later forms relate to, but are not reflexes of the ME forms, thus *v.* **hol**[1]); the Syck (*v.* **sík**); Temple Cl (cf. *Templeland* 1502, 1523, *v.* **temple, land**; with reference to former land of the Knights Templars); Third Cl; Thorney Cl (1627, *Thorny Close* 1625, *v.* **þornig**); Little Thorns, Far Upper ~, Near Upper ~, Middle Upper Thorns, Far Nether ~, Near Nether Thorns (*v.* **þorn**); Three Cornered Cl (*v.* **three-cornered**); (the) Top Cl; Top Mdw; Top Town Cl, Top Town Close Mdw (*v.* **tūn**); Underwood Cl (*v.* Underwoods Lodge *supra*); Wheats Yard (*v.* **geard**; cf. *William Wheat* 1847).

(b) *Akirdik* 1467 × 84 (*v.* **æcer-dīc, dík**); *the Ashes* 1625 (*v.* **æsc**); *the Ash feild* 1625 (*v.* **æsc, feld**; one of the great fields of the township); (*in*) *Bandall* 1625 (*v.* **bēan**; with **dalr** or **deill**); *Banelonde* 1467 × 84 (*v.* **bēan, land**); *Baresbys farm* 1627 (*v.* **ferme**; held by *Will. Baresbye* 1627, whose family originally came from Barsby, only one mile to the south-east); *William Barnes hadland* 1625 (*v.* **hēafod-land**); *Beardscliffe* 1627 (*v.* **clif**; poss. with **brerd** 'rim, edge' or with the surn. *Beard* (*v.* Reaney *s.n.*), but earlier forms are needed); *Bell balk hades* 1625 (*v.* **belle, balca, hēafod** and Bell Bush *supra*); *Berkmore* 1523 (*v.* **berc, mōr**[1]); *Blackemore Leyes* 1534 (*v.* **blæc, mōr**[1], **lǣs**); *Blackland* 1534, *Blacklands* 1592 (*v.* **blæc, land**); *Blacks yard* 1625 (*v.* **geard**; with the surn. *Black*); *Blakesland* 1627 (*v.* **land**; this may belong with *Blackland*, *supra*, or contain the surn. *Black*); *Boreclose* 1477 (e.16) (*v.* **clos(e)**; either with **bār** 'a boar' or with the surn. *Bore* derived from it); *le Bosumhades* 1398 (*v.* **bōs (bōsum** dat.pl.), **hēafod**; *Beazams furlong* 1625 (*v.* **furlang**) may belong with the previous f.n., but note *Robert Bessom* 1625 of Gaddesby to whom this f.n. may rather relate); *Bradmerholelese* 1502 *MiscAccts* (*v.* **brād, mere**[1], **hol**[1], **lǣs**); *Over Bretland* 1625 (*v.* **uferra, breiðr, land**); *Brocfurlong'* 1467 × 84 bis, 1477 (e.16), *Brokfurlong'* 1467 × 84 (*v.* **brōc, furlang**); *Broclond* 1467 × 84 (*v.* **brōc, land**); *Bromholme lees* 1510 (*v.* **brōm, holmr, lǣs**); *the Brooke* 1625 (*v.* **brōc**); *John Burbage hadland* 1625 (*v.* **hēafod-land**; the *Burbage* family prob. came originally from the Leics. village of this name, 20 miles to the south-west); (*the*) *Cole close* 1580, 1627 (*v.* **clos(e)**; prob. with the surn. *Cole*, cf. Coles Lodge *supra*, but **cole** 'cabbage' is poss.); *Crosons farm* 1627 (*v.* **ferme**; with the surn. *Croson*, a late 16th and 17th cent. form of Croxton, *v.* South Croxton, the village 2 miles to the south from which this family presum. originally migrated); *Crow nest furlong* 1625 (*v.* **crāwe, nest, furlang**; note that *crow's nest* was sometimes used to denote the highest point in a district); *Freesby meere* 1625 (*v.* **(ge)mǣre**; with reference to Frisby on the Wreake which adjoins to the north); *Fulwelle*, *Folewell* 1467 × 84, *le Fulwell hull* 1398 (*v.* **hyll**) (*v.* **fūl, wella**); *the furr* *furlong* 1625 (*v.* **feor, furlang**); *Guylers close* 1627 (with the surn. *Guiler*, from OFr *guileor* 'a deceiver' (cf. *beguile*)); *Hempe yard* 1625 (*v.* **hemp-yard**); *Hodges farm* 1627 (*v.* **ferme**; in the possession of *Edw. Hodges* 1627); *holme closse* 1523 (*v.* **holmr, clos(e)**); *Hosulweclif* 1467 × 84 (*v.* **clif**; with the OE pers.n. *Ōswulf*); *Medelward* 1467 × 84 (*v.* **meðal, warth, ward**); *the Melland furlong* 1625, *Over Melland* 1625 (*v.* **uferra**), *the Nether Melland furlong* 1625 (*v.* **furlang**) (*v.* **land**; the first el. is poss. a reduced **meðal**, otherwise **myln**); *the Middle furlong* 1625 (*v.* **middel, furlang**; i.e. of *the Ash feild*); *Middle hades* 1625 (*v.* **middel, hēafod**); *the Mill* 1625 (*v.* **myln**); *molendino de Newbold, molendinum de Newboth* 1477 (e.16) (with MLat *molendinum* 'a mill' and referring to Newbold Folville *infra*); *Monke his land* 1534 (*v.* **land**; prob. *Monk* is here a surn. (*v.* Reaney *s.n.*), but note that the Abbey of St Mary de Pratis, Leicester, held land in Gaddesby, so that the sb. **munuc** (> *monke*) is conceivable); *Newball hedge* 1625 (*v.* **hecg**; a boundary marker of Newbold Folville *infra*); *Northsichehede* 1467 × 84 (*v.* **hēafod**), *Northsicheshende* 1467 × 84 (*v.* **ende**), *Northsikeward* 1467 × 84 (*v.* **warth, ward**) (*v.* **norð, sīc, sík**); the Over Close 1625 (*v.* **uferra**); *Owsley leyes* 1625 (*v.* **leys**), *Owsley sick* 1625 (*v.* **sík**) (*v.* **lēah**; perh. with the OE pers.n. *Ōswulf*, cf. *Hosulweclif, supra*; otherwise, *v.* **ōsle**); *Pennyard* 1627 (*v.* **geard**; either with the surn. *Penn* or with **penn**[2]); *Sandpit* 1625 (*v.* **sand-pytt**); *Steynho* 1467 × 84 (*v.* **stān, steinn, hōh**); *Stotfold(e)* 1467 × 84 (*v.* **stōd-fald**); *Stragdale, ~ leyes* 1625 (*v.* **leys**) (*v.* **dalr**; perh. with the Scand by-name *Strákr*); *le Thwerdoles* 1398, *Thewerdole, Thweredole* 1467 × 84 (*v.* **þverr, dāl**); *Thurne* 1467 × 84 (*v.* **þyrne**); *Wetfurrowes furlong* 1625 (*v.* **wēt, furh, furlang**); *Woldgatishede* 1467 × 84 (*v.* **hēafod**), *Woldgatishende* 1467 × 84 (*v.* **ende**) (*v.* **wald, gata**); *Woldward* 1467 × 84 (*v.* **wald, warth, ward** and the two preceding f.ns.; this is prob. a miscopied **Woldgatisward*, cf. the group of three f.ns. at *Northsichehede, supra*); *in the Wro(o)* 1377 (p), 1398 LAS (p), n.d. (1499) *WoCart* (p), *in le Wroo* 1439 *Wyg* (p) (*v.* **vrá**).

2. ASHBY FOLVILLE

Ascebi 1086 DB bis

Essebia c.1130 LeicSurv, e.Hy 2 Dane, l.12 (1449) *WoCart* bis, c.1200 Dane, *Essebi* e.13 (1449) *WoCart*, 1236 RGros, m.13 (1404) *Laz*, p.1250 (1449) *WoCart*, *Esseby* c.1180 (1449) *ib*, 1216 ClR, 1225 RHug *et freq* to 1294 *MiD*, 1303 (1449) *WoCart et passim* to 1342 Banco

Aessebi 1185 Templar

Eisseby c.1190 Nichols

Hesseby 1236 Fees, 1338 Pat, a.1350 (1449) *WoCart* (p)

Asseby p.1250 (1404) *Laz*, 1294 Coram, 1317 Ipm, 1318 (1449) *WoCart*

Assheby 1310 Fine, 1313 Banco, 1314 Ass *et freq* to 1500 AD, 1503 Banco *et passim* to 1541 MinAccts, 1553 Pat, *As(s)cheby* 1310 Ipm, 1316 (1449) *WoCart* (p) *et passim* to 1349 (1449) *ib*, 1351 BPR

Asshby 1316 (1449) *WoCart*, 1333 Inqaqd *et passim* to 1390 (1449), 1449 *WoCart*
Ashby(e) 1528 Visit, 1533 *Rental*, 1575 LEpis *et freq*

Affixes are variously added as:
~ *Fol(e)vill(e)*, ~ *Foleuyl(l)e*, ~ *Foluuil'* etc. 1232 RHug, 1236 RGros, 1243 Fees, Hy 3 *Crox*, 1294 *MiD*, 1310 Fine *et freq*
~ *Fol(l)well* 1526 Ct, 1528 Visit, 1535 VE *et passim* to 1609, 1612 LML, ~ *Fowlwell* 1541 MinAccts, ~ *Ful(l)well* 1540 ib, 1553 Pat, 1580 LEpis
~ *Fallowes* 18 Nichols, ~ *Follows* 1718 LML, ~ *on-the-Fallows* 1722 ib

'The farmstead, village where ash-trees grow', *v*. **æsc**, **bȳ**. The name is either a hybrid OE/Scand formation in origin or is the result of a Scandinavianization of an earlier English name. Note that the spellings in *Esse-* may be due to the influence of ON **eski** 'an ash-tree'.

Fulco de Foleuille held the manor early in the reign of Henry II (as in the p.n. form *Essebia Fulconis de Foleuilla* c.1200 Dane) and it remained in the family into the 14th century via such members as *Maroye de Foluille* c.1180 (1449) *WoCart*, *Willelmus de Foleuille* 1185 Templar, *Eustachius de Foluille* 1274 Pat, *Johannes de Folevyle* 1305 Hastings and *Johannes Folvyle* 1368 Pat. The family took its name from a place called Folleville in France, prob. that in Calvados, Normandy.

From early in the 16th century into the 17th century, the feudal surn. suffix became confused with the common stream-name *Fulwell* (OE *fūl-wella* 'foul or dirty stream'), while in the 18th century it was further confused with *Fallows* (ME *falou* 'ploughed land', later 'land left unploughed, fallow land').

NEWBOLD FOLVILLE (lost)

Niwebold 1086 DB
Neubold 1236 Fees, Hy 3 *Crox*, 1282 Banco *et passim* to 1390 (1449), 1449 *WoCart*, (~ *iuxta Gaddesby* 1282 Banco), (~ *iuxta Assheby Folevill* 1328 Pat), (~ *Folluill'* 1446 (1449) *WoCart*), *Neubolde* 1449 *ib*, 1453 Cl, (~ *Folvyll* 1453 ib)
Neubolt c.1130 LeicSurv, 1449 *WoCart*, (~ *Foluile* 1449 *ib*), *Newbolt* 1449 *ib*, (~ *Folluill* 1449 *ib*)
Newbold p.1250 (1449) *WoCart*, 1328 Pat *et passim* to 1535 VE, 1539 MinAccts

'The new building, the new dwelling', *v.* **nīwe, bold**. The manor was held by *Willelmus de Folevill'* 1236 Fees and by *Eust. de Foluille* c.1275 (1449) *WoCart*, *v.* Ashby Folville *supra*.

THE ALMSHOUSE, 1846, 1863 White; founded in 1673 by Francis, Lord Carington, for seven poor men, *v.* **almes-hous**. ASHBY FOLVILLE LODGE. ASHBY GRANGE, *v.* **grange**. ASHBY LODGE, 1846, 1863, 1877 White, *v.* **loge**. ASHBY PASTURES, *Ashby Pasture* 1787 *TB*, 1835 O, *The Pastures* 1925 Kelly, *v.* **pasture**. CARINGTON ARMS (P.H.), *Carington Arms* 1925 Kelly, CARINGTON SPINNEY, cf. *F.H. Carington Smith-Carington* 1925 ib, lord of the manor and major landowner. CHENEY ARMS (P.H.) (lost), *Cheney Arms* 1877 White, cf. *Edward H. Cheney* 1877 ib of Gaddesby Hall, a major landowner. HEADLAND HO., cf. *the Headland Close* 1762 *Reeve*, *v.* **hēafod-land**. JENNER'S LODGE (lost), 1863, 1877 White; with the surn. *Jenner*, *v.* **loge**. MALT SHOVEL (P.H.) (lost), *Maltshovel* 1863 White. MANOR HO., *Manor House* 1846, 1863 White, 1925 Kelly, *v.* **maner**. MILL FM, *Mill farm* 1925 Kelly, cf. *Ashby Mill* 1835 O, *v.* **myln**. OLD HALL, 1877 White, *v.* **hall**. POOL HO. ROYAL OAK (P.H.) (lost), *Royal Oak* 1846, 1863 White. ST MARY'S CHURCH, *Church (St Mary)* 1846, 1863, 1877 White, 1925 Kelly; it is earlier recorded as *ecclesie de Esseby* 1220 MHW, ~ *de Essebifolevill* 1236 RGros, *ecclesiam de Esseb' Folevill* 1236 ib, *ecclesie de Assheby Fol(e)vill* 1354, 1381 *Pat*, ~ *de Assheby Folvyle* 1389, 1398 *ib*. Note also *the Church Yard(e)* 1605, 1625, e.18, c.1725 *Terrier*, 1787 *TB*, *v.* **chirche-ȝeard**. STALLARD LODGE, with the surn. *Stallard*, *v.* **loge**. TITHEBARN FM (lost), *Tithebarn farm* 1877 White, *v.* **tēoða**. THE VICARAGE, 1877 White, 1925 Kelly; it is *the Viçcarage house* 1605 *Terrier*, *the Vicaridg(e) House* 1724, c.1725 *ib* and *the Vicars house* 1625 *ib*, *v.* **vikerage, vikere**.

FIELD-NAMES

Undated forms are 1847 *TA*; those dated 1787 are *TB*.

(a) Ashby Wood 1806 Map; the Barn Cl; Bottom Garden (*v.* **gardin**); Cox Holme (*v.* **holmr**; with the surn. *Cox*); the Cottagers Old Pasture 1825 *Terrier* (*v.* **cotager**) (1745 *ib*; it is *Ashby Coters Pastuer* e.18 *ib*, *Ashby Cotters Pasture* c.1725 *ib*, *v.* **cottere, pasture**); Debdale 1787, 1847, Far ~, Near ~, Great ~, Little ~, Top Debdale, Clifford's ~, Parker's Debdale (with the surns. *Clifford* and *Parker*) (*v.* **dēop, dalr**); Far Cl; The Gorse 1847, Haines Gorse 1806 Map (with the surn. *Haines*), Preston's Gorse (with the surn. *Preston*), First & Second Gorse, Far ~, Top Far ~, Bottom ~, Middle ~, Top Gorse, Bottom Old ~, Middle Old ~, Top Old Gorse (**wald** rather than **ald** is prob. here) (*v.* **gorst**); Bottom ~, Top Headland, Spinney Headland (*v.* **spinney**) (*v.* Headland Ho. *supra*); Hollow Cl (*v.* **holh** (**holwe** dat.sg.)); Home Cl (*v.* **home**); Hut Cl (*v.* **hut**); Langley's Cl (with the surn. *Langley*); Long Furlong (*v.* **furlang**); The Meadow; Middle Cl; Mill Cl & Windmill; Nether Cl; Nether Mdw; Noon's Cl (with the surn. *Noon*); First ~ ~, Third ~ ~, Over Part (*v.* **uferra**, **part**); Roundabout (*v.* **roundabout**; often signifying a group of trees encircled by cleared land, or else small pieces of land completely surrounded by trees); Springfield Mdw (*v.* Spring Fd in neighbouring South Croxton f.ns. (a)); Stanley's Cl (with the surn. *Stanley*); Stannage's Cl (with the surn. *Stannage*); Step Cl (perh. with **stæpe** 'a step', used of stepping stones; otherwise unexplained); Great ~ ~, Road Stump Cross, Stump Cross Mdw (*v.* **stump**, **cros**; a headless wayside cross); Top Cl; the Vicar's Cl 1787 (*v.* **vikere**); Washpit Cl (*v.* **wæsce**, **pytt**; referring to a sheep-dip); Williamson's Cl (with the surn. *Williamson*); Wood's Cl (with the surn. *Wood*).

3. BARSBY

Barnesbi 1086 DB bis, 1190, 1206 P, *Barnesbia* 1177 ib, *Barnesby* c.1130 LeicSurv, 1220 MHW, 1247 Abbr *et freq* to 1390 (1449) *WoCart*, 1402 *LCDeeds et passim* to 1502 *MiscAccts*, 1526 Ct, *Barnisby* c.1180 (1449) *WoCart* (p), c.1271 *Wyg* (p) *et passim* to 1294 *MiD*, 1327 SR, *Barnysby* 1449 *WoCart*

Bernisby c.1180 (1449) *WoCart*, 1275 AAS, 1275 IpmR, *Bernesby* 1342 (1449) *WoCart* (p), 1344 Ipm, 1502 *MiscAccts*

Barneby 1207 RFinib (p), 1224 ClR, 1276 RH, 1299 Ipm

Baresby(*e*) 1449 Fine, 1478 *Ct et passim* to c.1570 *Rental*, 1610 Speed, *Baresbee* 1553, 1554 Ct, *Baresbee alias Barnesbee* 1570 ib, *Barysby* c.1485 ECP, 1495 Ipm *et passim* to 1528 Visit, 1533 *Rental*

Barsby 1620, 1641 LML *et freq*

Probably 'Barn's farmstead, village', *v.* **bȳ**. The Scand pers.n. *Barn* is an original by-name from ON *barn* 'a child', *v.* SPNLY 48. Fellows-Jensen (SSNEM 35) suggests alternatively that rather than the pers.n., the first el. may be the sb. **barn** itself. Spellings in *Bern-* are due to the common interchange of *a* and *e* in AN.

BARROWCLIFFE SPINNEY, *Biriclyf*, *Bereclyf* 1467 × 84 *LTD*, *bereclif* 1601 *Terrier*, *Berricliff*(*e*) 1625, 1679, 1708, 1708 (18) *ib*, *Berryclifte* 1690 *ib*, *Bericliff* 1697 *ib*, *middle bereclif* 1601 *ib*, *highe bereclif* 1601 *ib*, *High Berricliffe* 1674 *ib*, *High Berry Clift* 1700 *ib*, *High Barrowcliff* 1798 *EnclA*, *Schortbericlif*, *Schortberyclyf* 1467 × 84 *LTD*, *Short*

Berricliff(e) 1708, 1708 (18) *Terrier* (*v.* **sc(e)ort**), *Long Berricliff(e)* 1708, 1708 (18) *ib*, cf. *Berricliff Flatt* 1708, 1708 (18) *ib* (*v.* **flat**), *Barrowcliffe Meadow* 1798 *EnclA*, 1847 *TA*, *v.* **berige**, **clif**, **spinney** and Barrowcliffe Fm in neighbouring Queniborough. BARSBY SPINNEY, *v.* **spinney**. BRUTNALL'S LODGE, cf. *Richard Brutnall, farmer* 1846 White, *v.* **loge**. PLOUGH (P.H.) (lost), *Plough* 1846, 1863 White. SHOULDER OF MUTTON (P.H.) (lost), *Shoulder of Mutton* 1846, 1863, 1877 White. WILLIAM IV (P.H.) (lost), *William IV* 1846, 1863 White, 1925 Kelly, *King William the Fourth* 1863 *Sale*, *King William IV* 1877 White.

FIELD-NAMES

Undated forms in (a) are 1798 *EnclA*; those dated 1863 are *Sale*. Forms throughout dated 1467 × 84 are *LTD*; 1601, 1605, 1625, c.1700, e.18, 1708, 1708 (18), 1709, 1724, c.1725 and 1745 are *Terrier*.

(a) Abbey Sick Furlong (*Abby sick(e)* 1601, 1625, c.1700, 1709, c.1725, 1745, *Abbey Sick* 1708, 1708 (18), *Abby sicke furlong* c.1700, c.1725, *Aby Sick forlongue* e.18 (*v.* **furlang**) (*v.* **abbaye**, **sík**; the Abbey of St Mary de Pratis, Leicester, held land here); Ashby Newbolds (a field neighbouring Newbold Folville *supra*); Backside Furlong (*v.* **bak-side**, **furlang**); Bawdland Hole (*v.* **hol**[1]) (*Bordland*, *Borland* 1708, 1708 (18), *Boreland Close* 1708, 1708 (18), *v.* **bord-land**); Breach Cl, Breach Furlong (*v.* **furlang**) (*v.* **brēc**); Broddles Lane (poss. with the surn. *Braddle*, *v.* Reaney *s.n.*); Buck Furs End (*v.* **ende**) (*buck furres* 1605, *Buck Furs* 1709, c.1725), Buck Furze Furlong (*Buckfors forlongue* e.18, *Buck Furs Furlong* 1724, 1745, *v.* **furlang**) (*v.* **bucca**, **fyrs**); Bunney Furlong (*v.* **furlang**; for the first word earlier forms are needed, but this may belong with *Banar lane eynd* in f.ns. (b)); Burn Wong Furlong (*v.* **furlang** and *Burne Wong* in adjacent South Croxton f.ns. (b)); Little ~ ~, Buss Sick, Buss Sick Close Furlong (*v.* **furlang**), Buss Sick Road (*Busseke* 1467 × 84, *Bussick(e)* 1605, 1625, 1709, c.1725, *Busick(e)* e.18, 1724, 1745, *Busick Furlong* c.1700 (*v.* **furlang**), *v.* **busc**, **sík**); Calabor Furlong (*Callaborrowe* 1605, 1625, *Kalaborrow* 1709, *Callyburrow furlong* c.1700 (*v.* **furlang**), *v.* **calu**, **berg**); Callis Cl (poss. with the surn. *Callis* (*v.* Reaney *s.n.*), cf. *Calles leays* in neighbouring South Croxton f.ns. (b)); Clifford's Lane (with the surn. *Clifford*); Coals Acre Furlong (*Coules acer* 1605, *Colles Acar* 1625, *Colesaker* e.18, *Cole aker* 1709, *Cole Akre* 1724, *Cole(s) Acre* c.1725, 1745, *Coles Acker Furlong* c.1700 (*v.* **furlang**), *v.* **æcer**; prob. with the surn. *Cole*, cf. Coles Lodge and perh. (*the*) *Cole Close* in Gaddesby f.ns. (b)); Cob Headland Furlong (*v.* **furlang**) (*Cob h(e)adland* e.18, 1708 (18), c.1725, cf. *Cobbe stile* 1625 (*v.* **stigel**, here in its sense 'a steep ascent'), *v.* **cobb(e)**, **hēafod-land**); the Cob Yard (*v.* **geard**; poss. refers to the sturdy horse known as 'a cob' (earliest OED citation 1818); otherwise *v.* **cobb(e)**); Crowthorne Furlong (*Crowthorn(e)* 1467 × 84, *Crothorn* 1709, *~ forlongue* e.18, *~ Furlong* 1724, c.1725, 1745 (*v.* **furlang**), cf. *Crowthorn Gate* 1708, 1708 (18) (*v.* **gata**), *v.* **crāwe**, **þorn**); East Croft Cl, East Croft Furlong (*v.* **furlang**) (*East Croft* 1570 Cor, *v.* **ēast**, **croft**);

East End Gate Furlong (*v.* **furlang**) (*Esturn*, *Eysturn* 1467 × 84, *Esterne gate* 1625 (*v.* **gata**), *v.* **ēast, þyrne, þyrnir**); Even Gate Hedge Furlong (*v.* **efen, gata, hecg, furlang**); Flag Pool Furlong (*v.* **flagge, pōl**[1], **furlang**); the Flatt (*the Flate* 1467 × 84, *v.* **flat**); Flithill, ~ Cl (*v.* **(ge)flit, hyll**); Fold Hill Furlong (*v.* **furlang**) (*Folehull* 1467 × 84, *fould hill* 1605, *Fold Hill* e.18, 1724, c.1725, 1745, *v.* **hyll**; either with **fald** or, less likely, **fola**); Forceland Sick Furlong (*v.* **land, sík, furlang**) (*atte frys* 1377 SR (p) (*v.* **atte**), *the fryse* 1467 × 84, *Hyfyrris* 1467 × 84 (*v.* **hēah**[1]), *v.* **fyrs**); Frontcliff Furlong (*Fruncliffe Furlong* c.1700, *frontclif forlongue* e.18, *Frontcliff Furlong* 1724, 1745, *v.* **furlang**), Front Cliff Sick (1708, 1708 (18), *Thruntley sicke* (sic) 1605, 1625, *v.* **sík**) (*v.* **front, clif**); Gaddesby Brook (*the bro(o)ke* 1605, 1625, *v.* **brōc**); Bottom ~ ~, Top Gaddesby Cl (Gaddesby adjoins to the north-west); Glebe Land (*v.* **glebe**); Great Paddock (*v.* **paddock**); Heandale Cl, Heandale Furlong (*v.* **furlang**) (*v.* **hegn, dalr**); Hoads Furlong (*v.* **hōd, furlang**); Home Cl 1863 (*v.* **home**); the Hooks (*v.* **hōc**); Kirdale Furlong (*Kirredale*, *Kyrredale* 1605, *Kirdale*, *Kyrdale* 1625, *Kerdale* 1708, 1708 (18), 1709, *Cerdall* 1745, *Cerdal forlongue* e.18, *Kerdale furlong* 1724, c.1725 (*v.* **furlang**), *v.* **kjarr**; with **dalr** or **deill**); Leicester Sick Furlong (*Leicester sick(e)* 1605, 1709, 1724, c.1725, 1745, *Leycester sicke* 1625, *Lester Sick forlongue* e.18 (*v.* **furlang**), *v.* Leicester Sick in neighbouring South Croxton f.ns. (a)); Little Sick Furlong (*littel ~*, *litle sick* 1709, *Little Sick(e)* 1708 (18), 1724, 1745, *Little Sick forlongue* e.18, *~ ~ furlong* c.1725 (*v.* **furlang**), *v.* **lȳtel, lítill, sík**); Longborough Furlong (*v.* **lang**[1], **berg, furlang** and Longborough Sick Furlong in South Croxton f.ns. (a)); Lustry Gate Furlong (sic) (*v.* **furlang**) (*Lusty Gate* 1709, 1724, 1745, *v.* Lustygate in South Croxton f.ns. (a)); Meadow Gate Furlong (c.1700, c.1725, *midowgate forlongue* e.18, *meadowe gate* 1605, *Medowe ~* 1625, *Meddow ~* 1709, *Meadow ~* 1724, 1745, *v.* **mǣd (mǣdwe** obl.sg.), **gata, furlang**); (the) Middle Fd (1625, 1708 (18), 1724, 1745, *Midulfelde* 1467 × 84, *the Myddle field of Baresbye* 1605, *the Midle Feild* c.1700, c.1725, *the midel field* e.18, *the Middel Feild* 1709, *v.* **middel, feld**; one of the great fields of the township); Mill Furlong (*v.* **myln, furlang**); Moordale (*Mordal* 1467 × 84, *Moredale* 1605, 1625, 1709, *Moor(e)dale* 1605, 1625, *v.* Moardale in South Croxton f.ns. (b)); Mouldy Banks (1709, *Molede Banks* c.1700, *Molde Banks* e.18, 1724, *Mouldebanks* 1745, *the South Moldey-Banks* c.1725, *v.* **mouldy, banke**); Nether End Lane (*v.* **neoðera, ende**); (the) Nether Fd (e.18, 1708, 1708 (18), 1724, 1745, *the Neither Feild* c.1700, 1709, *v.* **neoðera, feld**; one of the great fields, also called *North feild*); New Cl; Ozingdale Leys (*v.* **ōsle, dalr, leys**, cf. *Osindale*, Lei **2** 222); Paddecombs 1787 *TB*, Paddock Holme 1798 (*Padochholme* 1467 × 84 bis, *v.* **padduc, holmr**); Pasture Leys (*v.* **pasture, leys**); Pear Tree Lane (*v.* **pertre**); Queneborough Road (Queniborough lies 3 miles to the west); Ranglands Furlong (*v.* **wrang, vrangr, land, furlang**); Rawlinsons Willows (*v.* **wilig**; with the surn. *Rawlinson*); Rough Pit Furlong (*v.* **furlang**) (*Rowpytt* 1467 × 84, *v.* **rūh**[1], **pytt**); St James's Cl (presum. with reference to a chantry chapel since no local church is dedicated to St James, *v.* Field 240-42); Sandholes (*v.* **sand-hol**); Sandlands (*Sandland'* 1467 × 84, *Sand Lands* 1708, 1708 (18), *v.* **sand, land**); Long ~, Short Sauving (*Sawfen(ne)* 1625, *Sawfin* 1708, 1708 (18), *Salving* 1724, 1745, *Longesaltfen* 1467 × 84, *Longe Sawfen* 1605, *Longue sofin* e.18, *Long Soluing* 1709, *Long Salving* 1724, 1745 (*v.* **lang**[1]), *v.* **salt**[2], **fenn**); Screaves Furlong (1745, *Screaues forlongue* e.18, *v.* **scræf, furlang**; the first el. shows the influence of Scand *sk-*); Shelboard (*v.* **scofl-brǣdu**); Shortborough (*v.* **sc(e)ort, berg**); the Springfield Road (cf. *the springfield hedge* 1709, *v.* Spring Fd in neighbouring South Croxton f.ns. (b)); Stanner Furlong (*Over Stennarsse furlong* 1625 (*v*. **uferra**), *v*. **stān, steinn, furlang**; presum. with **ears**, but note *Steynho* 1467 × 84 in Gaddesby f.ns. (b) which may rather explain the second el.); Stoney Lands (*Stanelandes* 1467 × 84, *Stony Lands* 1708 (*v*. **stān, stānig, land**); Stormbrick Furlong (*v*. **furlang**; with a late reflex of *Stanbryg* in South Croxton f.ns. (b)); Long ~, Short Stubs, Stubs Cl (*Longstubbis* 1467 × 84 (*v*. **lang**[1]), *Stubbs* 1605, *Stubs* 1708, *Stubb* 1708, 1708 (18), *v*. **stubb**); Sword Wong (*Sywordwong* 1467 × 84, *Swad wonge forlongue* e.18, *Swadwong Furlong* 1724, c.1725, 1745 (*v*. **furlang**), *v*. **vangr**; either with the ME surn. *Siward* (> ModE *Seward*) or a pers.n. precursor, prob. ON *Sigvarðr* (ODan *Sigwarth*) or, less likely, OE *Sigeweard*, cf. *Siwordlong* in neighbouring South Croxton f.ns. (b)); Tafts Cl (*v*. **toft**); Tanners Cl (with the surn. *Tanner*); Thieving Furlong (*v*. **furlang**; a derogatory name for unproductive land, poss. originally from **þefa** 'brushwood, bramble'); Three Thorne Furlong (*v*. **furlang**) (1709, 1724, 1745, *three thornes* 1605, *thre(e) thorn* e.18, 1709, c.1725, *v*. **þrēo, þorn**), Three Thorne Head (*v*. **hēafod**); The Thurns (*Thyrne* 1467 × 84), Thurn Cl, Thurn Green (*v*. **grēne**[2]), Thurn Lane (*v*. **lane**), Thurn Sick Furlong (*v*. **furlang**) (*Thorn Sick* 1708, 1708 (18), ~ ~ *bottom* 1708, 1708 (18) (*v*. **botm**), *v*. **sík**), Thurnside (*Thorn Side* 1708, 1708 (18), ~ ~ *Hades* (*v*. **hēafod**), *v*. **sīde**) (*v*. **þyrne, þyrnir**; some later forms show replacement by **þorn**); Toardale Cl (*Todehole Close* 1627, *Toadhole* ~ 1708, 1708 (18)), Toardale Flatt (*v*. **flat**) (*Todehole* 1467 × 84, *toode hoole* 1625, *Toad hole* 1708, *Toadholes* 1708 (18), *v*. **tod-hole**); Twyford Road (Twyford adjoins to the south-east); the Upper Fd (1708, 1708 (18), 1724, 1745, *the over field called the East field* 1605 (*v*. **uferra**), *the Upper field called the East fielde* 1625, *the uper field* e.18, *the Upper Feild* 1709, c.1725, *v*. **upper, feld**; one of the great fields of the township); Waterfurrow Furlong (*v*. **wæter, furh, furlang** and *the Waterfurrow(e)s* in Asfordby f.ns. (b)); Wheathill Furlong (*Wheythull* 1467 × 84, *Whethill* 1708, 1708 (18), *Wrettel forlongue* e.18, ~ *Furlong* c.1725 (*v*. **furlang**)), Wheaten Dale Furlong (1724, 1745 (*v*. **furlang**), *le Whetyldale* 1422 Farnham, *Wheatendale* 1601 (prob. with **dalr** rather than **deill**)), (*v*. **hwǣte, hyll**).

(b) *Abdykis* 1467 × 84, *Abtikes* 1625, *Abticks* 1708, 1708(18), *Abtickes forlongue* e.18, *Abticks Furlong* 1724, c.1725, 1745 (*v*. **furlang**) (*v*. **dík**; the first el. is prob. a reduced **abbaye** with reference to the Abbey of St Mary de Pratis, Leicester; cf. Abbey Sick Furlong *supra*); *Ashby Hedge* 1605 (*v*. **hecg**; a boundary hedge), *Ashby Lane* 1625 (*v*. **lane**) (Ashby Folville adjoins to the north-east); *Ash Close* 1708, 1708 (18) (*v*. **æsc**); *badland* 1605, 1625 (*v*. **badde, land**); *Ballance* 1708, 1708 (18), 1724, 1745, *Great(e) Balland(e)* 1605, 1625, *Littel Ballance* c.1700, *Ballance Furlong* c.1700 (*v*. **furlang**), *Ballance hedge* c.1700 (*v*. **hecg**; a boundary hedge), *v*. **bēan, land**); *Banar lane eynd* 1467 × 84 (*v*. **lane-ende**; poss. with **baner** 'a banner, a flag' used of a landmark (*v*. VEPN *s.v.*) and cf. *Banars more* in Skeffington f.ns. (b)); *Barlyclife* 1467 × 84 (*v*. **bærlic, clif**); *Betwene the gates* 1467 × 84 (*v*. **betwēonan, þe, gata**; a furlong so called); *Brendwong* 1467 × 84 (*v*. **brend, vangr**); *Breyndysacr'* 1467 × 84 (*v*. **æcer**; the gen.sg. construction of the first el. suggests a surn. *Brend* (*v*. Reaney *s.n.*), formed from the pa.part. of OE *beornan* 'to burn', but **brend** used topographically of 'land cleared by burning' is also poss.); *Broadewong Furlong* c.1700 (*v*. **brād, vangr, furlang**); *Brounyngcroft* c.1180 (1449) *WoCart* (*v*. **croft**; either with the ME surn. *Brouning* (> ModE *Browning*), a reflex of the OE pers.n. *Brūning*, or with the pers.n. itself); *Bud Gate* 1708, 1708 (18) (*v*. **gata**; prob. with the surn. *Budd*, *v*. Reaney *s.n.*); *capella Barnesby* 1220 MHW (with MLat *capella* 'a chapel'); *Church way* 1625 (since there is no early church recorded for Barsby, this may refer to the parish church of nearby South Croxton; but note the chapel recorded in 1220); *Clauerdale* 1467 × 84 (*v.* **clāfre**; with **dalr** or **deill**); *Coccroft* 1467 × 84 (*v.* **croft**; either with **cocc**[1] or **cocc**[2], cf. *Cokkecroft*, Lei **2** 268); *Tho(mas) Cooks Yard end* 1708, 1708 (18) (*v.* **geard, ende**); *Copmore* 1467 × 84, 1625, *Cope Meer* 1708, 1708 (18) (*v.* **copp, mōr**[1]); *Crosse Lees* 1605, 1625, *Cross Leyes* 1724, *~ lays* 1745 (*v.* **cross, leys**); *Estfelde* 1467 × 84, *the East field(e)* 1605, 1625 (*v.* **ēast, feld**; one of the great fields); *Essicke* 1625, *East Sick* 1708, 1708 (18), 1709 (*v.* **ēast, sík**); *Mrs Eyton widowe her grounde* 1625 (*v.* **grund**; the *Eyton* family prob. came originally from Eaton, 12 miles to the north-east, *v.* Lei **2** 118 for early spellings of the p.n.); *Gadesbee meadowe* 1605, *Gadsbee medowe* 1625 (Gaddesby adjoins to the north-west); *William Gilsons Yard end* 1708, 1708 (18), *Gilsons yards end* 1708 (*v.* **geard, ende**); *Glodurwong* 1467 × 84 (*v.* **vangr**; poss. with OE **gleoda**/ON **gleða** 'a kite', but a surn. such as ME *Gladiere* (> ModE *Gladders*) from ME *gladere* 'one who gladdens' may be thought of; more forms are needed); *Gossick* c.1725 (*v.* **sík**; with **gōs** or **gorst**); *of the Halle* 1327 SR (p), *at Hall* 1322 ib (p) (*v.* **hall**); *High(e) Gate* 1605, 1625 *et passim* to 1745 (*v.* **hēah**[1], **gata**); *Kimberly's Yard land* 1745 (*v.* **yardland**; the *Kimberly* family was prob. originally from Kimberley, 24 miles to the north-west in Notts.); *the Knowle* 1605 (*v.* **cnoll**); *Litulclif*, *Litulclyffe* 1467 × 84 (*v.* **lȳtel, clif**); *Longe furlonge* 1605, 1625, *Longue forlongue* e.18, *Long furlong* c.1700, 1709, 1724, c.1725, 1745 (*v.* **lang**[1], **furlang**; in *the West field*); *Long Holm(e)* 1708, 1708 (18) (*v.* **holmr**); *Meyrsyk(e)* 1467 × 84 (*v.* **(ge)mǣre, sík**); *the nether end of the towne* 1625 (*v.* **neoðera, ende, tūn**); *Neytysheyde* 1467 × 84 (*v.* **nēat, hēafod**); *North feild* c.1725 (*v.* Nether Fd *supra*); *Nyngatis* 1467 × 84 (*v.* **nigon, gata**); *the Parsonage Close* 1606 Ipm, *the parsonage closse ende* 1605 (*v.* **ende**) (*v.* **personage**); *persons closse* 1625 (*v.* **persone, clos(e)**); *Reedmore* e.18 (*v.* **hrēod, mōr**[1]); *St Johns Leas* 1606 Ipm (*v.* **leys**; either with reference to land dedicated to St John's Church in adjoining South Croxton or to the site of Midsummer bonfires on St John's Day (24 June) or to former ownership by the Knights Hospitallers of St John (cf. Temple Cl in neighbouring Gaddesby)); *short furlonge* 1605, *Shorte forlonge* 1625 (*v.* **furlang**; in *the West field*); *ye Sick(e)* e.18, 1724, 1745 (*v.* **sík**; preceded by the definite article); *Spigellsti* e.18, *Spigelsty* 1724, c.1725, 1745 (*v.* **stīg**; an obscure first el., but perh. a forgotten **spitel** (in its sense 'a house of the Knights Hospitallers of St John') may be indicated; note *St Johns Leas*, *supra*); *Steynrows* 1467 × 84 (*v.* **steinn, vrá**); *Stonyslade* 1467 × 84 (*v.* **stānig, slæd**); *Strode Wong*, *~ ~ Meer* 1708, 1708 (18) (*v.* **strōd, vangr, (ge)mǣre**); *Tebbe Yard* 1570 CR (*v.* **geard**; with the surn. *Tebb*, a pet-form of *Tebbold* (Theobald), cf. *Joh' Tebbe* 1316 FA of Leics.); *Thorn Gate* 1708, 1708 (18) (*v.* **þorn, gata**); *Townsend* 1708, 1708 (18) (*v.* **ende**), *Town ground* e.18 (*v.* **grund**), *the towne meere* 1605 (*v.* **(ge)mǣre**), *the towne net pasture* 1605 (*v.* **nēat, pasture**), *Town side* 1709 (*v.* **sīde**) (*v.* **tūn**); *the Vickers Lay(e)s* e.18, c.1725 (*v.* **vikere, leys**); *Westfelde*, *Whestfelde* 1467 × 84, *the West field(e)* 1605, 1625 (*v.* **west, feld**; one of the great fields of the township); *West Sick Bottom* 1708, 1708 (18) (*v.* **sík, botm**); *Wheytlande*, *Wheytlandys* 1467 × 84 (*v.* **hwǣte, hveiti, land**); *Woodford* 1708, 1708 (18) (*v.* **wudu, ford**).

Grimston

1. GRIMSTON

Grimestone 1086 DB bis, 1166 RBE, Hy 2 Dugd, 1273 Banco, *Grimestona* c.1130 LeicSurv, *Grimeston* c.1130 ib, 1169 P *et passim* to 1295 *Deed* (freq), 13 *MiD*, 1311 Banco, *Grimmeston(e)* 1166 LN, 1276 RH, *Grimestun* Hy 2 Berkeley (p), *Grimistun* Hy 2 ib, *Grymeston* 1273, 1277 Banco *et freq* to 1426 ib, 1429 Fine *et passim* to1472 Hastings, 1559 Ipm

Grimston Hy 3 *Crox*, 1522 Deed, 1524 CoPleas *et passim* to 1610 Speed *et freq*, *Grymston(e)* 1326 Ipm, 1332 Pat *et passim* to 1453 *RTemple*, 1464 *Ct et freq* to 1541 MinAccts, 1553 Pat *et passim* to 1576 Saxton

Grymson 1537 MinAccts, 1537 BM, 1601, 1602 *Terrier*, *Grimson* c.1570 *Rental*, 1601 *Terrier*

'Grīm's farmstead, village', *v.* **tūn**. The ODan pers.n. *Grīm* (ON *Grímr*) is an original by-name that was often used of the god *Óðinn* in disguise (cf. OIcel *gríma* 'a mask'). The name was common in Norway and Iceland throughout the medieval period and was also frequent in Sweden and Denmark. The Anglo-Saxons used *Grīm* in the same way as a by-name for their god *Wōden*, a name which entered the OE pers.n. stock (*v.* Searle 268); but the Scand name is much more likely here. Note the 16th and 17th century forms in *-son* which show typical Leics. loss of *t* in the group *-ston*.

BARN FM. BLACK HORSE (P.H.), *Black Horse* 1846, 1863, 1877 White, 1925 Kelly. BLACK SWAN (P.H.) (lost), *Black Swan* 1846 White. GRIMSTON GAP, *v.* **gap**. GRIMSTON GORSE is *Gorse Cover* 1836 O, *v.* **gorst, cover(t)**. GRIMSTON TUNNEL, TUNNEL FM, TUNNEL PLANTATION, with reference to a railway tunnel. METHODIST CHAPEL. NOOK FM, *v.* **nōk**. PERKIN'S LANE, *Perkin Lane* 1766 *EnclA*, *v.* **lane**; with the surn. *Perkin*. ST JOHN'S CHURCH, *Church (St John)* 1846, 1863, 1877 White, 1925 Kelly; it is earlier recorded as a chapel in the groups *capellis de Cayham Grimeston et Caldewelle* 1220 MHW, *capellarum . . . de Gaddesby Kayham Grymeston . . . et Wykeham* 1328 *Pat*, ~ *de*

Gayddesby Cayham Grymstoune . . . et Wykam 1382 *ib* (with MLat *capella* 'a chapel'). Note also *the Church Yard* 1757 *Terrier*. WALTON FIELDS, 1925 Kelly. WEMBLEY HO., *Wembley house* 1925 Kelly; presum. named with reference to Wembley Park, London, the site of the British Empire Exhibition of 1924–25, for which Wembley Stadium was built 1922–23.

FIELD-NAMES

Undated forms in (a) are 1757 *Terrier*; those dated 1766 are *EnclA*.

(a) Asfordby Gate 1766 (*v*. **gata**; Asfordby lies 2 miles to the south-east); Barnetts Cl, ~ ~ Side (*v*. **sīde**) (with the surn. *Barnett*); Bean Thorn Furlong (*v*. **furlang**) (*v*. **þorn**, *banethorn'* in South Croxton f.ns. (b) and Beanthorne in Shoby f.ns. (a)); Bellers Lane 1766, Bellars Lane end (*v*. **lane**, **lane-ende**; with the surn. *Bellar*, *v*. Kirby Bellars); the Black half Acres (*v*. **blæc**, **half-aker**); Blakeman hill (with the surn. *Blakeman*, from the OE pers.n. *Blæcmann*, a by-name meaning 'a dark, swarthy man'); Brackindale Fd 1757, Brackendale ~ 1766 (*v*. **braken**, **dalr**; one of the great fields of the township); Brook(e) Cl 1766, the Brook furlong (*v*. **furlang**), the Brook leys, the Nether Brook leys (*v*. **leys**) (*v*. **brōc**); Cadewell Sick (*v*. **cald**, **wella**, **sík**); the Cow Pasture (*v*. **pasture**); the Cross Baulk 1813 *Deed* (*v*. **cross**, **balca**); Cuttings (*v*. **cutting**); Dalby Gate 1766 (*v*. **gata**; the road to Old Dalby which adjoins to the north-west); Deepdale 1757, Deepdale Fd 1757, 1766 (*v*. **feld**; one of the great fields) (*v*. **dēop**, **dalr**); the Earl of Aylesfords Land (*v*. **land** and cf. Lord Aylesford's Covert in Shoby *infra*); Farmer Leys (*v*. **leys**; either with the surn. *Farmer* or with **fermier**); Mr Grahams Cl, Mr Grayhams Land (*v*. **land**); Hemplock Nook (*v*. **hymlic**, **nōk**); Mr Hodgkins headland (*v*. **hēafod-land**); Holmcroft (*v*. **holmr**, **croft**); Thomas Kelhams Cl (the *Kelham* family presum. was originally from Kelham, 22 miles to the north-east in Notts.); Matthew Cl (with the surn. *Matthew*); the Meadows Cl 1766 (*v*. **mǣd (mǣdwe** obl.sg.)); the Mill Cl, (the) Mill Fd 1757, 1766 (*v*. **feld**; one of the great fields), the Mill hades (*v*. **hēafod**), the Mill Wong (*v*. **vangr**); New Covert 1806 Map (*v*. **cover(t)**); the Pasture 1766, the Pasture hedge 1757 (*v*. **pasture**); Pryor's Cl 1766 (with the surn. *Pryor*); the Pyne miln Cl (*pynne mylle* 1544 *ExchKR*, *Pyne mylle* c.1546 ECP, cf. *Pynemyll leys* 1616 Ipm (*v*. **leys**), *Pynemyll mead* 1616 ib (*v*. **mǣd**), *v*. **pynne-mylle**); Rush Bush Furlong (*v*. **risc**, **busc**, **furlang**); Saxelby Gate 1766 (*v*. **gata**), Saxulby Hedge (*v*. **hecg**; a township boundary hedge) (Saxelby adjoins to the south-east); Sholby Gate 1766 (*v*. **gata**), Sholby Lane 1766 (*v*. **lane**), Sholby Meer (*v*. **(ge)mǣre**) (Shoby adjoins to the south-west); the Stow (*v*. **stōw**); Swarflings (earlier forms are needed, but poss. is **swearð** 'greensward, grassland' with **land** (cf. *Cauckland* > *Cauckling* in Seagrave f.ns. (b)); the Three Cornered Cl (*v*. **three-cornered**); Henry Wards Land (*v*. **land**); Windmill Fd 1766 (the alternative name for Mill Fd *supra*; *v*. **wind-mylne**); Winterton Lane (*v*. **lane**; presum. with the surn. *Winterton*, since there is no evidence here for a *winter-tūn* 'farmstead used in winter'); Wood Furlong (*v*. **wudu**, **furlang**); The Wongs 1877 White (*v*. **vangr**).

(b) *othe grene* 1377 SR (p) (*v*. **þe**, **grēne**[2]); *atte Hall* 1377 SR (p) (*v*. **atte**, **hall**).

2. SAXELBY

Saxelbie 1086 DB, *Saxelby* 1219 RHug, 1228 *Rut*, 1209 × 35 RHug, 1250 Berkeley *et passim* to 1283, 1289 Banco *et freq*, *Saxelby* 1220 MHW, 1261 Cl (p)
Saxebia c.1130 LeicSurv
Saxilbi Hy 3 *Crox*, *Saxilby* 1259 RGrav, 1261 Cur, Hy 3 *Crox* (freq) *et freq* to 1393 Banco, 1428 FA *et passim* to 1541 CoPleas, 1610 Speed, *Saxilbee* 1610 LML
Saxulebi 1203 Fine bis, *Saxulby* 1450 ELiW, 1475 Banco *et passim* to 1550 AAS, 1576 LEpis, *Saxulbie* 1576, 1603 LibCl
Saxhilby 1473 *CCR*, *Saxhulby* 1539 *Deed*, *Sacshulby* 1539 MinAccts
Sowcelby c.1545 ECP, *Sauselbie* 1559 Pat

'Saxulf's farmstead, village', *v.* **bȳ**, cf. Saxilby, DLPN 106. The pers.n. *Saxulf* is ODan (ON *Saxulfr*).

BARNES HILL PLANTATION, cf. *Thomas Barnes, farmer* 1863 White. CHURCH LANE. GLEBE FM, *Glebe farm* 1877 White, 1925 Kelly, *v.* **glebe**. THE GRANGE, 1863 White, *v.* **grange**. GRIMSTON STATION. MAIN ST. MANOR HO., *Manor house* 1877 White, *v.* **maner**. MARRIOT'S WOOD, cf. *Thomas Marriott, farmer* 1863 White. THE RECTORY, 1877 White, 1925 Kelly, *the Rectory House* 1822 *Terrier*, *v.* **rectory**; cf. *the personage house* 1601 *ib*, *the Parsonage house* 1674, 1697 *ib et passim* to 1708 (18) *ib*, *v.* **personage**. ST PETER'S CHURCH, *Church (St Peter)* 1846, 1863, 1877 White, 1925 Kelly; it is earlier recorded as *ecclesiam de Saxelby* 1219 RHug, ~ *de Saxeleby* 1220 MHW. Note also *the Church and Churchyard* 1708, 1708 (18) *Terrier*. SAXELBY BARN. SAXELBYE PARK, 1925 Kelly, cf. *Park farm* 1925 ib, *v.* **park**. SAXELBY LODGE, ~ ~ FM, *v.* **loge**. SAXELBY NEW WOOD. SAXELBY PASTURES, *v.* **pasture**. SAXELBY TUNNEL, a railway tunnel. SAXELBY WOOD is *Saxelby Gorse* 1806 Map, 1836 O, *v.* **gorst**. STATION FM, *Station farm* 1925 Kelly, *v.* Grimston Station *supra*. SUMMER LEES PLANTATION, *v.* **sumor**, **leys**. TEN ACRE PLANTATION.

FIELD-NAMES

Undated forms in (a) are 1822 *Terrier*; 1757 are also *Terrier*. Forms throughout dated l.13 are *CRCart*; 1601, 1625, 1674, 1679, 1697, 1700, 1703, 1706, 1708 and 1708 (18) are *Terrier*.

(a) All Wong Cl (*v.* **vangr**) (cf. (*the*) *Hall Hedge* 1679, 1708, 1708 (18) (*v.* **hecg**), *v.* **hall**); Brook Cl (*the Brook* 1708, cf. *Brooke Furlonge* 1674 (*v.* **furlang**), *the Brookside* 1708, 1708 (18) (*v.* **sīde**), *v.* **brōc**); Dale Cl (*v.* **dalr**); Goss Cl (*the Gorse* 1679, cf. *goste ground* 1625 (*v.* **grund**), *deepe goste* 1625, *ye deepe gorse* 1674, *Deepgosse* 1679, 1697, 1700, 1703, 1706 (*v.* **dēop**), *Willm. Bonds gosse* 1674, *v.* **gorst**); Home Cl (*v.* **home**); Little Cl; Moor Ley Cl (*more leas*, ~ *leyes* 1625, *Moor Leyes* 1674, ~ *Leys* 1679, 1708 (18), ~ *Lays* 1708, *Moore layes* 1697, 1700, 1703, 1706, *v.* **mōr**[1], **leys**); Far ~ ~, Near Top Cl; Whart Ley Cl (*Whartlayes* 1697, *Whart(e)leyes* 1700, 1703, 1706, *v.* **þverr, þvert, leys**); Nether ~ ~, Upper Wilbourns Cl (with the surn. *Wilbourn* of a family originally from Welbourn, 26 miles to the north-east in Lincs.).

(b) *Asfordbie hedge* 1625 (*v.* **hecg**; a parish boundary), *Asfordby Meer* 1679 (*v.* **(ge)mǣre**) (Asfordby adjoins to the south-east); *Banlands* 1674, 1679, 1708, 1708 (18) (*v.* **bēan, land**); *Bonds Close* 1674, 1679 (cf. *Willm. Bond* 1674); *les Breches* 1289 Banco, *Brechis* l.13 (*v.* **brēc**); *bretland sicke* 1601 (*v.* **breiðr, land, sík**); *Brimblisdale* l.13 (*v.* **brēmel, brembel, dalr**); *Broadsick* 1697, 1700, 1703, 1706 (*v.* **brād, sík**); *the Colecart Road* 1703, 1706 (*v.* **col**[1], **carte**; as mineral coal appears not to have been mined at adjoining Asfordby until the 20th cent., it is to be assumed that the reference here is to charcoal, cf. the range of roads relating to **col-pytt** in Lei **2** 321; road-names with *Colecart* are frequent developments of those with *Colepit*); *Coleing* 1697, 1700, 1703, 1706, *Couling* 1757 (perh. **eng** with the ON pers.n. *Koli*, but earlier forms are needed); *the Common pasture* 1697, 1700 (*v.* **commun**), *the Cow Pasture* 1700, 1703 (*v.* **pasture**); *Dalby grounds* 1708, 1708 (18) (*v.* **grund**; land towards Old Dalby which adjoins to the north-west); *Depedale* l.13, *dep-dale* 1674, *Deepdale* 1679, 1708, 1708 (18), *Debdale* 1697, 1700, 1703, 1706, *Debdale Field* 1697, 1700, 1703, 1706 (*v.* **feld**; one of the great fields, also called *Mickledale Field*, *v. infra*), *debdall hill* 1601, *dep-dale hill* 1674, *Deepdale Hill* 1679, 1708, 1708 (18) (*v.* **dēop, dalr**); *Dikes end* 1674, 1679, 1708, 1708 (18) (*v.* **dík, ende**); *Esfordebidale* l.13 bis (*v.* **dalr**; Asfordby adjoins to the south-east); (*ye common balke called*) *gods-good balke* 1674, *Goddesgood Balk* 1679 (*v.* **balca**; *Goddesgood* is poss. a surn., cf. *Godesname*, *Godesgrace*, *Godeswowes* etc., *v.* Reaney *s.n.* Godsname, but this does not sit happily with its being a *common balke*); *Anth. Goodicary's house* 1708; *Gossegate Baulk(e)* 1700, 1706, (*the*) *Goosegate baulk* 1708, 1708 (18) (*v.* **gorst, gata, balca**); *greene-gate* 1674, *Greengate* 1679, 1708, 1708 (18), ~ *Baulke* 1697, 1700, 1703, 1706 (*v.* **balca**) (*v.* **grēne**[1], **gata**); *Grimpston hedges* 1625 (*v.* **hecg**; township boundary marker(s)), *Grimson meer* 1601, *Grimston Meer(e)* 1679, 1700 (*v.* **(ge)mǣre**) (Grimston adjoins to the north-west); *the Homestall* 1625, 1708, 1708 (18) (*v.* **hām-stall**; i.e. of *the Parsonage House*); *Imber Hill* 1674, 1679, 1708, 1708 (18) (earlier forms are needed; the surn. *Imber* is prob. (*v.* Reaney *s.n.*), but formally so is a reduced **hind-berige** 'a raspberry', cf. Imberhorne, Sx 332); *Jasper's Land* 1708 (*v.* **land**), *Jasper Simpson's Pingle* 1708 (*v.* **pingel**); *the kinges heigh waye* 1625 (*v.* **hēah-weg**; with reference to James I); *Letty-wonge* 1674, *Clety Wong* (sic) 1679, *Lety* ~ 1708, 1708 (18) (*v.* **vangr**; poss. with a surn. such as *Lettice* or *Lewty*, but note **hlēt** 'a share, a lot' which may rather occur here); *littel beck furlong* 1601, *Littlebeck furlong(e)* 1674, 1679, 1708, 1708 (18) (*v.* **lӯtel, lítill, bekkr, furlang**); *the Meer hedge* 1708, 1708 (18) (*v.* **(ge)mǣre, hecg**; a parish boundary hedge); *Micheldale* l.13, *mickell dall* 1601, *Michaeldale* (sic) 1697, 1700, 1706, *Mickledale* 1703, 1708, 1708 (18), *Micheldalehende* l.13 (*v.*

ende), *Mickeldall field* 1601, *Mickeldale feild* 1625, *Micledale Field* 1674, *Mycledale field* 1679, *Mickledale Field* 1708, 1708 (18) (*v*. **feld**; one of the great fields, also called *Debdale Field*, *supra*) (*v*. **micel**, **mikill**, **dalr**); (*the*) *mil(l)field* 1601, 1674, *Milne feild* 1625, *the Milne Field* 1708, 1708 (18), *Milln Hill Field* 1697, 1703, 1706, *Mill Hill Field* 1700 (*v*. **feld**; one of the great fields of the township), *mil(l)hill* 1601, *Mill Hill* 1679, 1703, *Milln hill* 1697, 1700, 1706, *Milne Hill* 1708, 1708 (18), ~ ~ *Furlong* 1708, 1708 (18) (*v*. **furlang**) (*v*. **myln**; referring to a windmill); *milhome* 1625, *Millhome* 1674, 1679, *Miln(e) Holme* 1708, 1708 (18) (*v*. **holmr**) (*v*. **myln**; referring to a watermill); *the Orchard* 1708; *the ouerthourt furlong* 1601, *ye overwhart furlonge* 1674, *ye Overthwart furlong* 1679, 1708, 1708 (18) (*v*. **furlang**), *the Overthwart Headland* 1708, 1708 (18) (*v*. **hēafod-land**) (*v*. **ofer-þwart**); *the owldes gate* 1601, *Woulds Gate* 1708, 1708 (18), *oulds gate furlonge* 1601, *Wouldsgate furlong* 1674, 1679, 1708, 1708 (18) (*v*. **furlang**) (*v*. **wald**, **gata**); *Parsonage Close* 1674 (*v*. **personage**); *the Parsons Lane* 1708, 1708 (18) (*v*. **persone**, **lane**); *the Pasture* 1625, 1703, 1706, 1708, 1708 (18) (*v*. **pasture**); *Pereclives* l.13 (*v*. **peru**, **clif**; with *peru* in the sense 'a pear-tree', the earliest cited usage in OED being c.1400); *the pinfould* 1601 (*v*. **pynd-fald**); *the Queens street* 1601 (*v*. **strǣt**; the principal highway, with reference to Elizabeth I); *Redland field* 1601, 1679, 1697, 1700, 1703, 1706, ~ *feild* 1625, *Redland Sick(e) field* 1674, 1708, 1708 (18) (*v*. **sík**) (*v*. **rēad**, **land**, **feld**; one of the great fields); *Sapehou* l.13 (*v*. **scēp**, **haugr**; with AN *s* for *sh*, cf. Sapcote in Sparkenhoe Hundred); *Shelboards* 1679, *Shelbreds furlong(e)* 1674, 1708, 1708 (18) (*v*. **furlang**) (*v*. **scofl-brǣdu**); *Jo. Simpson's Headley* 1708 (*v*. **headley**); *Sinam* 1697, 1700, 1703, 1706 (*v*. **sænna**, **senna**, **holmr**, **hamm**, cf. Sanham, Lei **2** 81 and *Synnomes*, Lei **2** 155); *Skonte brooke* 1601, *Skontbrook furlong* 1601, *Scontbrook* ~ 1679, 1708, 1708 (18), *Scantbrook* ~ 1708 (18) (*v*. **furlang**) (*v*. **skant** 'not abundant, scant' (from ON *skamt*), **brōc**; presum. referring to a small watercourse with a mediocre flow); (*the Highway called*) *the Streetway* 1708, 1708 (18) (*v*. **street-waie** and *the Queens street*, *supra*); *the Swans Nest* 1708, 1708 (18) (*v*. **swan**[1], **nest**; a small plot of grassland); *Tabern Hades* 1708, 1708 (18) (*v*. **hēafod**; with the surn. *Tabern*, metonymic for *Taberner*, a derivative of OFr *tabourner* 'to drum'); *Thurndale* 1697, 1700, 1703, 1706 (*v*. **þyrne**, **þyrnir**; with **dalr** or **deill**); *Tingoe* 1674, *Tingeo* 1679, *Tingo* 1708, 1708 (18) (*v*. **þing-haugr**; a moot-site beside *Redland field*, *supra*); *the Tyth Barn* 1700 (*v*. **tēoða**); *Wakah Wong* 1697, 1700, 1703, 1706 (*v*. **vangr**; the first word may be an early p.n., poss. with **wacu** 'a watch, a look-out' and a reduced **hōh** 'a spur of land', cf. Wakoe in Asfordby f.ns. (a); but note also **wācor** 'an osier, wicker'); *Wartnabe meer* 1601, 1625, ~ *meare* 1625, *Wartnaby Meer* 1679 (*v*. **(ge)mǣre**), *Wartnabie hedge* 1625, *Wartnaby Hedge* 1708, 1708 (18) (*v*. **hecg**; a township boundary hedge) (Wartnaby adjoins to the north-east); *weangate* 1601, *weane gate* 1625, *Waingate* 1679, *Wayngate* 1708, 1708 (18), *Waingate side* 1679, 1700, 1703, 1706 (*v*. **sīde**), *Wayngate upper furlong* 1708, 1708 (18) (*v*. **furlang**) (*v*. **wægn**, **gata**); *Welby Grounds* 1708, 1708 (18) (*v*. **grund**; Welby adjoins to the east); *Wildgoose meer* 1601 (*v*. **mere**[1]), *Wild Goose Meer(e) Furlong* 1708, 1708 (18) (*v*. **furlang**), *Wild-goos meer Leyes* 1674, *Wyld Goose Meer Leys* 1697 (*v*. **leys**), *Wild(e)goose nooke* 1697, 1700, 1703, 1706 (*v*. **nōk**) (*v*. **wilde-gōs**); *Witelondes* l.13 (*v*. **hwīt**, **land**); *Woolldales nooke* 1697, 1700, 1703, *Woollesdales nooke* 1706 (*v*. **wald**, **deill**, **nōk**); *Woolseters* 1601, *Wolsetters* 1625, *Woollsetters* 1697, 1700, 1706, *Woolsetters* 1703, *Hither Woolsetters* 1674, 1679, 1708, 1708 (18) (*v*. **hider**),

Woolsetter Lays 1708, *Woolesetter Leys* 1708 (18) (*v.* **leys**) (*v.* **wald**; the generic appears to be **sǽtr** 'a hill pasture, a shieling', a word usually appearing in northern England; but note **skáli** in nearby Shoby Scholes, also regularly with a northern provenance, both words being associated with Norwegian rather than with Danish settlers; OE *set* 'a place for animals, a fold' may appear to be a likelier possibility as the generic but does not explain the consistent *-er* spellings.

3. SHOBY

Seoldesberie 1086 DB
Siwaldebia c.1130 LeicSurv, *Siwaldebi* Hy 2 Dane, e.13, c.1240 Berkeley, *Siwaldeby* 1220 MHW, 1349 Nichols, *Sywaldeby* 1238, 1242 RGros *et passim* to c.1291 Tax, 1344 Pat
Siwoldebi c.1240 Berkeley (p), *Siwoldeby* 1247 Ass,1254 Val *et freq* to 1314, 1322 Hastings *et passim* to 1375 Banco, 1377 SR, *Sywoldeby* 1249 Cur, 1250 RGros *et freq* to 1373, 1379 Banco *et passim* to 1466, 1498 ib
Siwaldbi 1242 RGros, *Sywaldby* 1386 Fine, *Siwoldby* 1316 FA, *Sywoldby* 1374 Pat (p), 1383 Fine, 1510 LP, c.1545 ECP
Siwolby 1362 BPR, *Sywolby* 1465 Banco, 1559 Pat, *Sywalby* 1454 ib, 1465 Banco *et passim* to 1547 ECP
Sywouldeby 1531 ISLR, *Sywouldby* c.1545 ECP, *Sywowldbye* 1576 Saxton
Shouldby 1610 Speed, *Sholby* 1722 LML
Shoulby(e) c.1538, c.1546 ECP, *Showlby* 1544 Fine, *Shoulbie* 1580 *Fisher*, *Sholby* 1547 ECP, 1598 Fine *et passim* to 1614 LML, 1651 Fine, *Sholbie* 1601 Ipm, 1610 Fine, *Sholeby* 1604 SR
Showby 1507 Ipm, *Shoby* 1806 Map, 1811 Nichols, 1836 O *et freq*

'Sigvald's farmstead, village', *v.* **bȳ**. The pers.n. *Sigvald* is Scand, a reflex of *Sigvaldr*/*Sigvaldi*. The unique DB form of the p.n., with the generic as *-berie*, represents a Norman scribe's misrepresentation of *-bȳ* rather than an original OE *-byrig* (dat.sg. of *burh*) of an earlier Anglo-Saxon p.n., *v.* the discussion of the p.n. Asfordby.

LORD AYLESFORD'S COVERT, *v.* **cover(t)**; note *the Earl of Aylesford* 1846 White, lord of the manor. THE NURSERY, *v.* **nursery**. PRIORY FM, *Priory Farm* 1896 *Surv*; a fanciful name since there never was a priory here, but the farm is at the site of the remains of the early parish church which is recorded as *ecclesie de Siwaldeby* 1220 MHW, *ecclesiam* ~ ~, *ecclesie de Sywaldeby* 1238, 1242 RGros, 1344 *Pat*, *ecclesie de*

Sywoldeby 1250 RGros, ~ *de Siwoldeby* 1343 *Pat*. SCHOLES FM is *Shoby Wolds* 1836 O, *v*. **wald**. SHOBY COTTAGES. SHOBY HOUSE FM, *Shoby House* 1846 White, ~ ~ *Farm* 1896 *Surv*. SHOBY LODGE, ~ ~ FM. SHOBY SCHOLES, 1836 O, *le Scolles* 1544 *ExchKR*, *the Scolys* c.1546 ECP, *Shoby Scoles* 1806 Map, *v*. **skáli**.

FIELD-NAMES

Undated forms in (a) are 1896 *Surv*. Forms throughout dated 1544 are *ExchKR*; c.1545 are ECP; 1616 are Ipm.

(a) Barn Cl; Barnards Cl (1616; with the surn. *Barnard*); Great ~, Little Beanthorne (*v*. Bean Thorn Furlong in Grimston f.ns. (a) and *banethorn'* in South Croxton f.ns. (b)); Brook Cl, Brook Fd, Brook Leys (*v*. **leys**), Brook Mdw (*v*. **brōc**); Cow Close Stile 1766 *EnclA* (*v*. **stigel**); Cow Troops (*v*. **cū**, **þorp**); Dillimore (*v*. **mōr**[1]; the first el. may be a shortened form of *Daffydowndilly* 'the daffodil'); Dyke Fd (*v*. **dík**); Hawthorn Dale (*v*. **hagu-þorn**, **dalr**); The Meadow; Pool Croft (*v*. **pōl**[1], **croft**); Sheep Cot Cl (*v*. **scēp-cot**); Square Cl (with reference to shape); Top Mdw; Great ~ ~, Little Wood Cl (cf. *Oxe or Wood close* 1616, *v*. **oxa**, **wudu**, **clos(e)**).

(b) *le Clyff* 1544, *Clyffe* c.1545 (*v*. **clif**); *Foxeholes* a.1296 Hastings (*v*. **fox-hol**); (*le*) *Netherfeld* 1544, c.1545 (*v*. **neoðera**, **feld**; the only surviving name of a great field of the township); *Palecroft* 1616 (*v*. **pale**, **croft**); *le Parsons Closse* 1544 (*v*. **persone**, **clos(e)**); *le Sadleback* 1544 (*v*. **sadol**, **bæc**; describing the saddle-shaped profile of a ridge of land).

Hoby with Rotherby

1. HOBY

Hobie 1086 DB, *Hobi* 1183 P, l.12, Hy 2 Dane *et passim* to 1212 P (p), 1266 Pat (p), *Hoby* 1212 FF (p), 1216 ClR, 1220 Cur *et passim* to 1576 Saxton, 1610 Speed *et freq*

Houbia c.1130 LeicSurv bis, *Houbi* 1150 × 1200 *GarCh* (p), l.12 *GarCart* (p), 1203 P (p) *et passim* to 1326 Ipm, 1335 *Peake* (p), *Houby* 1209 Fine (p), 1224 RHug, 1236 Fees *et freq* to 1370, 1375 *Peake et passim* to 1453, 1454 *Comp*

Howby 1257 (Edw 1) *CroxR*, 1314 Hastings, 1336 *Peake* (p), 1412 PRep *et passim* to 1547 Pat, 1629 LML, *Howbie* 1580, 1581 LEpis

Howeby c.1291 Tax, 1352 BPR (p), 1367 Misc (p) *et passim* to 1438 *Peake*, 1471 Pat

'The farmstead, village at the headland', *v.* **hōh, bȳ**. The present village is sited at the foot of a great spur of land which abuts the river Wreake. Ekwall DEPN interprets Hoby as 'Hauk's bȳ', but his interpretation depends on the mistaken identification in ASWills of *Houcbig* 1066 × 68 with the Leics. Hoby. *Houcbig* is clearly in Lincs., possibly the lost *Houcbyg* listed in SPNLY 135.

ALL SAINTS' CHURCH, *Church (All Saints)* 1846, 1863, 1877 White, 1925 Kelly; it is earlier recorded as *ecclesiam de Hoby* a.1219 MHW, *ecclesia de Houby* 1407 *Pat*, *the Church* 1708, 1708 (18) *Terrier*. Note also *the Churchyard* 1605, 1708, 1708 (18) *ib*, *v.* **chirche-ȝeard**. AUSTEN DYKE, ~ ~ BRIDGE, *Oustrenges* 1322 Hastings, (*the*) *Osteringe* 1601 bis, 1605 bis, 1612 *Terrier*, *Ostringe* 1612 *ib*, *Hoby Ostring* 1625 *ib*, *Hoby Eastring* 18 *ib*, *Hoby Easting* 1745 *ib*, (*a meadow called*) *Hoby Eastings or Austring* 1708, 1708 (18) *ib*, (*the*) *Austrean* 1703, 1708, 1708 (18), 1730, 1745 *ib*, *Austran* 1745 *ib*, (*the*) *Austrian* 1912 *Sale*, cf. (*the*) *Austrean Meadow* 1708, 1708 (18), 1730, 1821 *Terrier*, 1846, 1863, 1877 White, *Austrian* ~ 1761 *EnclA*, *v.* **austr (austarr** comp.), **eng, dík**; the comparative is poss. here although the *r* is prob. intrusive, cf. the

Westerns in f.ns. (a); the dyke, the name of which appears to have been attracted to a local surn. *Austen* (cf. Austen's in f.ns. (a)), forms part of the parish boundary to the east. BLUE BELL INN, *Blue Bell* 1846, 1863, 1877 White, 1925 Kelly. CHANTRY HO., *Chantry house* 1925 Kelly, *v.* **chaunterie**; John Beler founded a chantry at Hoby after 1461 when he acquired the manor. ELM COTTAGE. THE ELMS, 1925 Kelly. GLEBE FM, *v.* **glebe**. THE GRANGE, 1925 Kelly, *v.* **grange**. HILL HO., *Hill house* 1877 White, 1925 Kelly. HOBY BARN. HOBY HO., *Hoby house* 1877 White. THE OLD MILL, *the Mill* 1708, 1708 (18) *Terrier*. THE RECTORY, 1877 White, *The Rectory House* 1821 *Terrier*, *v.* **rectory**; earlier is *the Parsonage hall* 1601 *ib* (*v.* **hall**), *the Parsonage Hoose* 1605 *ib*, ~ ~ *House* 1708, 1708 (18), 1730, 1745 *ib*, *v.* **personage**. RUTLAND ARMS (P.H.) (lost), *Rutland Arms* 1846, 1863, 1877 White, 1925 Kelly; with reference to the Duke of Rutland of Belvoir Castle, the county's senior peer. WASHSTONES LODGE, *Washstones* 1968 *Surv*; near to Washstones Bridge in Frisby on the Wreake.

FIELD-NAMES

Undated forms in (a) are 1968 *Surv*; those dated 1761 are *EnclA*, 1912 are *Sale*, 1919 are *Deed* and 1936 are *Terrier*. Forms throughout dated 1322 are Hastings; 1601, 1605, 1612, 1625, 1703, 1708, 1708 (18), 1730 and 1745 are *Terrier*.

(a) 4 Acre 1761, 1968, The 6 Acre 1912, 6 Acres 1968 (x2), First Six ~, Over Close Six Acres 1936 (*v.* **uferra**), 7 Acre (x2), 8 ~ (x2), Nine ~, 10 ~ 1936, 1968, 11 Acre, 12 Acres 1968 (*v.* **æcer**); Andison Cl, Far Andison Fd 1919, Addison Cl 1968 (*Alldersonne close* 1601, 1612, *Allderson* ~ 1605, *Alderson* ~ 1703, 1708, 1745, *Aldersons* ~ 1703, 1708, 1730, *Alderson's* ~ 1708, 1708 (18), *v.* **clos(e)**; originally with the surn. *Alderson*; *Oddison Close* 1760 Nichols prob. belongs here); Austin's Mdw 1919, Austen's 1968 (with the surn. *Austen/Austin*, cf. *John Austin* 1666 SR and *Henry Austin* 1679 *Terrier* of neighbouring Asfordby; the surn. appears to have influenced the form of Austen Dyke *supra*); Backwater Fd (*v.* **backwater**); Badger Hole (*v.* **badger, hol**[1]); Barn Cl 1936, 1968, Old Barn Cl 1919, 1936, New Barn Cl 1919, Far Old Barn Fd 1919, Far Barn, Second ~ ~, Barn Fd 1968; Barsby Mdw (Barsby lies over 4 miles to the south-east, so that the relationship of this meadow with that village is uncertain, but prob. *Barsby* is here a local surn. of a family originally from Barsby); Besson Nook Fd 1761 (cf. *Bessons close* 1601, 1605, 1612, 1703, 1708, 1708 (18), ~ ~ *Nook* 1730, 1745 (*v.* **nōk**); with the surn. *Besson*, a form of Beeson, *v.* Reaney *s.n.*); Big Cl; Lower ~ ~, Upper Black's Cl 1936, First ~, Second Black 1968 (with the surn. *Black*); The Brant 1912, Far ~, Middle ~, Flat Brant 1968 (*v.* **flatr**) (*le Brante* 1322, *the great(e) Brante* 1601, 1605, 1612, *the Great Brants* 1703, 1745, ~ ~ *Brents* 1703, ~ ~ *Breants* 1708, 1708 (18), 1730, *Litle*

Brante 1601, 1605, 1612, *the Little Brants* 1703, 1745, ~ ~ *Breants* 1708, 1730, *the hang(e)inge Brant* 1601, 1605, 1612 (*v.* **hangende**), *the Brante bottome* 1601, 1605, 1612, *the Brente Bottom* 1703, ~ *Breant* ~ 1708, 1708 (18), 1730, ~ *Brant* ~ 1745 (*v.* **botm**)), The Brants Barn 1835 O, Brents Pool Cl 1761 (*Brents Pool* 1703, *Breants* ~ 1708, 1708 (18), *Brants* ~ 1745, *v.* **pōl**[1]) (*v.* **brend** 'a place cleared by burning'); Brick Kiln Cl 1919 (*v.* **brike-kiln**); the Bridge Pieces 1760 Nichols (*v.* **pece**), Bridge Mdw 1936, Bridge Fd 1968; Bridle Road Fd (*v.* **brigdels**); Broad Plat 1761, 1968 (1708, 1745, *broad platte* 1601, *brode* ~ 1605, *broade* ~ 1605, 1612, *Broad Platt* 1703, 1708 (18)), Broad Plat Common 1761 (*v.* **commun**) (*v.* **brād, plat**); Brook Fd; Carts Cl, Carts Fd (with the surn. *Cart*, *v.* Reaney *s.n.*); Cattle's Cl 1919 (with the surn. *Cattle*, a diminutive of *Cat*, a short form of the OFr pers.n. *Catelin*(*e*) (Catherine)); Cheesecake Hill 1912, Cheesecake Mdw 1912, 1968 (*the Cheesecake* 1730, 1745, ~ ~ *Furlong* 1703, 1708 (18), 1730, *Chiscake furlong* 1745 (*v.* **furlang**), *v.* **cheesecake**); Church Piece 1761, 1968 (*v.* **pece** and All Saints' Church *supra*); Nether ~, Top Copley 1761, Copleys 1912, 1968, Top ~, Robinsons Copleys 1968 (with the surn. *Robinson*) (*v.* **copp, lēah**); Cottage Cl, Cottage Mdw (*v.* **cotage**); Cottagers Cl 1936 (*the Cottagers Close* 1708, 1708 (18), *Cottagers Close Nook* 1703, *the Cotagers Close Nook* 1745 (*v.* **nōk**)), Cottagers Mdw 1936 (*v.* **cotager**); Cross Hills (*v.* **cross**); the Cunnery 1760 Nichols (cf. *the connerye leas* 1601, *the Coneryes leyes* 1605, ~ *connegre* ~ 1612 (*v.* **leys**), *v.* **coningre**); Currer's Cl 1761 (with the surn. *Currer*, from OFr *courreour* 'a messenger'); Dings 1968, Bottom ~, Top Dings 1912 (*the Dinges* 1601, 1605, 1612, *the Dynges* 1601, *the Dings* 1708, 1708 (18), 1730, 1745, *the Ding Furlong* 1703, 1708, 1708 (18) (*v.* **furlang**), cf. *Abovedingesti* 1322 (*v.* **aboven**), *Underdingesti* 1322 (*v.* **under**), *v.* **stīg**; at the edge of the original parish bordering *Willoughes*/Ragdale; prob. with **þing**, referring to a moot-site); Dungeon Mdw 1936, Far ~, Near ~, Top Dungell 1968 (although *dungell* is a dial. form of *dungeon*, prob. here is a base **dyncge** 'manured land', with **hyll** 'a hill', cf. Dungehill Fm in Wymeswold); Felstead 1761, 1968 (with the surn. *Felstead*, cf. Felsteads Cl in Gaddesby f.ns. (a)); First Mdw 1936; The Flat (*the flatte* 1601, 1612, *v.* **flat**); Flowery Mount (self-explanatory); Foxley Gate 1968, ~ ~ Cl 1936 (*Foxley Gate* 1703, 1708, 1708 (18), 1745, *v.* **fox, lēah, gata**); Further Mdw 1936; Goodchilds (the surn. *Goodchild* in the possessive case); Gorse Sic (*Goss Sick* 1703, 1708, 1708 (18), 1730, 1745, *v.* **gorst, sík**); Grange Mdw (*v.* The Grange *supra*); Gravel Pit Cl 1936, Gravel Hole 1968 (*v.* **gravel, pytt, hol**[1]); Green Croft 1761, 1968 (*v.* **grēne**[1], **croft**); Hall Cl 1761, 1968 (*the hall close* 1601, ~ ~ ~ *ende* 1605, 1612 (*v.* **ende**), *v.* **hall**); Hazelwood (*v.* **hæsel, wudu**); Hemp Plick (*v.* **hænep, plek**); Henton's Fd 1912 (with the surn. *Henton* of a long-established family in Hoby, *v.* *William Hentons headland* 1601 in f.ns. (b)); Hennesey's (the surn. *Hennesey* in the possessive case); The Hill, Top Hill, Hill Fd; Holms 1968, Big ~, Little Holmes 1912, Holm Mdw 1762, 1968 (*le Holm* 1322, *Hobie holme* 1612, *Hoby* ~ 1625, *v.* **holmr**); Home Cl 1912, 1968, Little ~ ~, Long ~ ~ 1968, Needham's Home Cl 1912, 1968 (with the surn. *Needham*), First ~ ~, Second Home Fd 1968 (*v.* **home**); First Homestead (*v.* **hām-stede**); Hovel Fd (*v.* **hovel**); Lammas Cl 1761 (*v.* **lammas**); Land Cl (*v.* **land**; a close consolidating an unspecified number of 'lands' or selions of a former great field); The Leys (*v.* **leys**); Little Fd; Far ~, Road Little'un (*Litlinges* 1322, *Litle Inge* 1601, 1612, *Litle Ynge* 1605, cf. *Little Inn*(*e*) *Ditch* 1703, 1708 (18), 1730, 1745 (*v.* **dīc**), *Little Inne Ford* 1703, 1708, 1708 (18), 1730, *Little Inn Foard* 1745 (*v.* **ford**), *v.* **lȳtel, lítill, eng**); Long Mdw; Old Masters 1936, 1968 (the surn.

Masters in the possessive case, with **ald** or **wald**); Middle Fd (*the middle fiellde* 1601, ~ ~ *Field(e)* 1605, 1612 *et passim* to 1745, *v.* **feld**; one of the early great fields of the township); Mill Fd, Mill Mdw (*the Mill* 1708, 1708 (18), 1730, cf. *the Mill Lays* 1703, 1730, 1745, ~ ~ *Leys* 1708, 1708 (18) (*v.* **leys**), *the Mill Piece* 1708, ~ ~ *Peice* 1708 (18), 1730 (*v.* **pece**), *v.* **myln**); Moor's Beck 1761, The Moresback 1912 (*Moresbeck(e)* 1601, 1605, *Mooresbecke* 1601, 1605, 1612, *Moorsbeck* 1703, 1708, 1708 (18), 1730, 1745, *Moresbecfurlonges* 1322 Hastings (*v.* **furlang**), *v.* **mōr**[1], **mór**, **bekkr**); Needham's Mdw (with the surn. *Needham*); Nether Fd; First ~ ~ 1936, New Fd 1936, 1968, New Field Paddock 1968 (*v.* **paddock**) (*the new field* 1601, ~ ~ *fielde* 1605, 1612, ~ ~ *Field* 1703, 1730, *the new fielde hedge* 1605 (*v.* **hecg**), *v.* **nīwe, feld**); New Fds 1846 White, 1968 ((*the*) *New Fields* 1703, 1708, 1708 (18), 1730, 1745); New Land 1912, Newland 1968; the Paddock 1912, 1968, Pick's Paddock 1912 (cf. *Richard Pick* 1708) (*v.* **paddock**); Parris Cl 1912, 1968 (with the surn. *Parris*, *v.* Reaney *s.n.*); Parson's Cl 1761 (*the Parsons Close* 1703, 1708, 1708 (18), 1730, 1745, ~ *Parson's* ~ 1708, 1708 (18), *v.* **persone**); The Pasture 1912 (cf. *the cowe pasture* 1601, 1605, 1612, *v.* **pasture**); Pightles 1936 (*v.* **pightel**); Plantation Cl 1936 (*v.* **plantation**); Pond Cl; Priest's Wong 1761 (*le Prestwonges* 1322, *the priestes woonge* 1601, ~ ~ *wonge* 1605, 1612, *Priest(s) Wong* 1703, 1708, 1745, *Preists* ~ 1708 (18), cf. *Priestwong Headland* 1708, *Preists Wong* ~ 1708 (18), *Priests Wong Hedland* 1745 (*v.* **hēafod-land**), *v.* **prēost, vangr**); Ragdale Sic 1912 (*Ragdal(e) Sick* 1708, 1708 (18), 1745, *v.* **sík**; Ragdale adjoins to the north-west); Reservoir Fd; River Mdw; Robin Hood's Barn 1800 Nichols (a mound so named in a flat meadow near R. Wreake; *v.* M. R. Evans, '*Robynhill* or Robin Hood's Hills? Place-names and the evolution of the Robin Hood legends', JEPNS 30 (1997–98), 43–51); Robinson's (the surn. *Robinson* in the possessive case); Rough Mdw (*v.* **rūh**[1]); The Rushes (*v.* **risc**); Sanders 1761 (*v.* **sand, ears**; cf. *long sanders* in Hoton f.ns. (b)); Bottom ~ ~, Top Seven Leys 1912, Seven Leys 1968 (*v.* **leys**; when compounded with a numeral, *leys* represents grassland units of tenure corresponding to *lands* (i.e. selions or strips) similarly used of arable); Shed Cl 1936 (*v.* **shed**); Shoby Close East, ~ ~ West 1919, Shoby Nook 1919 (*v.* **nōk**) (Shoby adjoins to the north); Spinney Mdw (*v.* **spinney**); Stackyard Fd (*v.* **stak-ȝeard**); Surry Hill (with the surn. *Surry*, *v.* Reaney *s.n.*); Top Cl 1936; Upper Wong (*v.* **vangr**); The Warren (*v.* **wareine**); Water Mdw 1936 (part of an irrigation system, *v.* **wæter** and Field 90–1); Willow Cl 1936, Willows Mdw 1968 (*v.* **wilig** and the lost settlement of *Willoughes*, *infra*); the Westerns 1760 Nichols, West Ends 1761 (*the Westinges* 1601, 1605, *Westeinges* 1601, *Westynges* 1605, (*the*) *Westring(e)s* 1612, (*the*) *Westends* 1703, 1708, 1708 (18), 1730, *the Westons* 1745, *v.* **west, vestr, eng**); Wilkinson (the surn. *Wilkinson* used as a possessive); Woodgate (1703, 1708, 1708 (18), (*le*) *Wodegate* 1322, *v.* **wudu, gata**).

(b) *le accres* 1322 (*v.* **æcer**); *William Adlingtons piece* 1730 (*v.* **pece**; the *Adlington* family came originally from Allington (13th cent. spellings as *Adelington*, *v.* DLPN 2 *s.n.*), 24 miles to the north-east in Lincs.); *John Alsops Hedland* 1745 (*v.* **hēafod-land**); *Alwolmilnestede* 1322 (*v.* **mylne-stede**; with an OE pers.n., either *Ælfwald* or *Æðelwald* (> *Alwold* in DB)); *Utteralwolton* 1322 (recording a lost farmstead *Alwolton* (with prefixed **ūterra**), *v.* **tūn**; no doubt identifying the same individual as in the previous f.n.); *Aslande* 1605 (*v.* **æsc, land**); *Banecroftis* 1322, *Bancroft(e)* 1601, 1605, 1612, *Baincroft* 1708, 1708 (18), 1730, 1745 (*v.* **bēan, croft**); *Blakebanland* 1322 (*v.* **blæc**), *Mickilbanland*, *Mickilbanlond* 1322 (*v.* **micel, mikill**), *Banlondpit* 1322 (*v.* **pytt**), *Ballaunce stile* 1601, 1605, 1612 (*v.* **stīg**) (*v.*

bēan, land); *Barlie Water* 1601, 1605, 1612 (*v.* **bærlic, wæter**; an expanse of water or a stream beside which barley was grown); *Bihouerthwertmilnestede* 1322 (*v.* **bī, ofer-þwart, mylne-stede**); *Bonners Lane* 1703, 1708, 1708 (18), 1730, 1745 (*v.* **lane**; with the surn. *Bonner*); *Bordelond'* 1438 *Deed* (*v.* **bord-land**); *Bott Hole* 1703, 1708, 1708 (18), 1730, *Bot* ~ 1745 (*v.* **bot, hol**[1]); *Brandolfis acre* 1322, *Brandolfacrehauedes* 1322 (*v.* **hēafod**) (*v.* **æcer**; with the ON pers.n. *Brandulfr*); *le Breche* 1322 (*v.* **brēc**); *James Brettes headland*(*e*) 1601, 1605, 1612 (*v.* **hēafod-land**); *Breusters Close* 1703, *Brewsters* ~ 1708, 1708 (18), 1730, *Brewster* ~, *Bruster* ~ 1745 (with the surn. *Brewster*); *Brock*(*e*)*hill gate* 1601, *Brockhille* ~ 1601, 1605, *Brockhill* ~ 1605, 1612, 1730, *Brochill* ~ 1612, *Brockhil* ~ 1703, *Broccle* ~ 1703, 1708, 1708 (18), *Brockly* ~ 1745 (*v.* **brōc, hyll, gata** and Brook Hill in Rotherby f.ns.(a)); *le Broddole* 1322 bis, *the broad*(*e*) *doles* 1601, 1605, 1612 (*v.* **brād, dāl**); *the Bryers Woonge* 1601, *the briers wonge* 1605, ~ *bryers* ~ 1612, *Brier Wong* 1703, 1708, 1708 (18), 1730, *Briery Whong* 1745 (*v.* **brēr, brērig, vangr**); *Butcher Wong* 1708, *Butchers* ~ 1708 (18), 1745 (*v.* **vangr**; with the surn. *Butcher*); *Butterclifes* 1322 (*v.* **butere, clif**; referring to rich pasture which produced good butter); *the Butts* 1708 (18), 1745 (*v.* **butte**); *Calacre* 1322, *Hamircalacre* 1322 (*v.* **hamer**), *Outiyrcalacre* 1322 (*v.* **ūterra**), (*the*) *nether* ~, (*the*) *over Callakars* 1601, *the nether* ~, *the over Callacres* 1605, *nether* ~, *over colakers* 1612 (*v.* **neoðera, uferra**) (*v.* **cāl, æccr**); *Catwellefurlonges* 1322 (*v.* **cat(t), wella, furlang**); *the clea fiellde* 1601, *the Clay fielde* 1605, ~ *clea* ~ 1612, *the clay fielde towarde Thrussington* 1605, *the clea fielde towarde Thrushington* 1612 (Thrussington adjoins to the south-west), *the clea fielde towarde Keyme bridge* 1601, 1612, *the clay fielde towarde Keyme bridge* 1605 (*v. Kaimesbrigge, infra*), *the Clay Field next to* (*the*) *New Fields* 1703, 1708, 1708 (18), 1730, 1745, *the Middle Clay Field* 1703, 1708, 1708 (18), 1745 (*v.* **clǣg, feld**; 'the clay field' was one of the three early great fields of the township); (*the*) *Cliffe nooke* 1601, 1612, (~) *Clyffe* ~ 1605 (*v.* **clif, nōk**); *Colepitte gate* 1601, 1605, *colepit* ~ 1612 (*v.* **gata**), *Cole Pit Hill* 1708, *Colepitt* ~ 1708 (18), *Coalpit*~ 1745 (*v.* **col-pytt**; a place for the manufacture of charcoal); *Constable hades* 1601, 1605, 1612, 1703, 1708 (18), 1730, *Cunstable* ~ 1708, 1745 (*v.* **conestable, hēafod**); *Copping Nook* 1703, 1708, 1708 (18), *Coppice* ~ (sic) 1745 (*v.* **nōk**; with the surn. *Copping*, *v.* Reaney *s.n.*); *Cow*(*e*) *gate* 1601, 1605, 1612, *Cow Gate Hades* 1703, 1708, 1708 (18), 1730, 1745 (*v.* **hēafod**) (that a series of headlands abutted *Cow Gate* and the longevity of the name suggest that this is **cū, gata** 'the track along which cows are driven' rather than **cowgate** 'pasturage for a single cow'); *Crokedmedowe* 1322 (*v.* **croked, mǣd** (**mǣdwe** obl.sg.)); *Crokehou* 1322 (*v.* **haugr**; prob. with **crocc**, referring to a hill where pots were made, cf. *Crochou* in Barkby f.ns. (b)); *Daizy Nook* 1703, 1708, 1708 (18), *Daizay* ~, 1708 (18), *Dazy* ~ 1745 (*v.* **dægesēge, nōk**); *Dedhauedlond* 1322 (*v.* **dēad, hēafod-land**); *le Deuonde*, *le Deuondestrem* 1322 (*v.* **strēam**; a pre-English stream-name, presum. identical with R. Devon in Framland Hundred); *Doddesdic* 1322 (*v.* **dīc, dík**; either with the OE pers.n. *Dodd* or its surn. reflex); *Longedowedale* 1322 (*v.* **lang**[1]), *the nether* ~, *the over Dovedale* (*v.* **uferra**) 1601, 1605, 1612 (*v.* **dalr**; earlier forms are needed since it is uncertain whether these f.ns. record a pre-English stream-name as in Dovedale (Db 398–9) (and note the pre-English *Deuonde*, *supra*); however, a pers.n. OE *Dūfe*/ON *Dúfa* or a bird-name OE **dūfe**/ON **dúfa** may pertain; cf. *Nether douedale* in Cossington f.ns. (a)); *Nether* ~ ~, *Upper Down Hill* 1703, *Nether* ~ ~, *Upper Dought Hill* 1708, 1708 (18), 1730, *the nether* ~ ~, *upper Drought Hills* 1745 (unexplained; the forms are late and disparate, but the earliest form suggests an original **dūn**); *the Drain at the bottom of the Nether Pease Lands* 1703, 1708, 1730, ~ ~ ~ ~ ~ ~ *the Neather Paselands* 1745 (*v*. **drain** and *Peiselondes*, *infra*); *Dunnesdole* 1322, *Dunsedole* 1601, *Dunesdole* 1605, 1612 (*v*. **dāl**; either with the OE by-name *Dunn* (from OE *dunn* 'dark, swarthy') or with its surn. reflex); *Eastmore Reine* 1601, 1605, *Eastmore raigne* 1612, *Eastmorene* 1703, 1708, *East Morene* 1708 (18), 1730, 1745 (*v*. **ēast**, **mōr**[1], **rein**); *le Estbroc* 1322 (*v*. **ēast**, **brōc**); *le Estcroftis* 1322 (*v*. **ēast**, **croft**); *le Ferme* 1606 Ipm (*v*. **ferme**); *Flittelandes* 1322 (*v*. **(ge)flit**, **land**); *le Formedowes* 1322, *the Foremedowes* 1601, 1612 (*v*. **fore**, **mǣd** (**mǣdwe** obl.sg.)); (*the*) *Foxholes* 1703, 1708, 1708 (18), 1745 (*v*. **fox-hol**); *Foxhou* 1322, *Foxhowgonele* 1322 (*v*. **gonele**) (*v*. **fox**, **haugr**); *the Fullinge Mires* 1601, ~ ~ *myres* 1605, 1612, *Fulhill Mires* 1703, 1708, 1745, *Fulhil* ~ 1730 (*v*. **fulling**, **mýrr**; with these forms may belong *Fulwell Mires* 1703, 1708, 1730, having been attracted to *Fulwelle*- following); *Fulwellegate* 1322 bis (*v*. **gata**), *Fulwellemor* 1322 (*v*. **mōr**[1]) (*v*. **fūl**, **wella**); *Gamelisholm* 1322 (*v*. **holmr**; with the ON pers.n. *Gamall* (ODan *Gamal*)); *the Gating Baulk* 1708, 1708 (18) (*v*. **balca**; poss. with **gata**, **eng**); *Gerehow* 1322 (*v*. **haugr**; either with **geiri** 'triangular plot of land' or **geirr** 'a spear', also alluding to shape); *Glappi*[ ] 1322, (*the*) *Glapings* 1703, 1708, 1708 (18), 1745 (*v*. **glæppe**; poss. with **-ing**[2]); *le gores into rakedalebrockes* 1322 (*v*. **gāra** and *rakedalebrockes*, *infra*); *the Goss* 1703, 1708, 1708 (18), 1745, *the Goss Field* 1703, 1708, 1708 (18), 1730, 1745, *Goss Hades* 1708 (18) (*v*. **hēafod**), *the Goss Lays* 1730 (*v*. **leys**) (*v*. **gorst**); *le Gowiyl* 1322 (*v*. **goule**); *Greneslade* 1322, *Ovirgreneslade* 1322 (*v*. **ofer**[3]) (*v*. **grēne**[1], **slæd**); *Humfry*(*e*) *Gullsons headlande* 1601, 1605, *Humfrie Gullsons headland* 1612 (*v*. **hēafod-land**); *the hall baulke* 1601, 1612 (*v*. **balca**), *the Hall pieces* 1703, 1708, 1730 (*v*. **pece**) (*v*. **hall**); *the hanging furlonge* 1703, 1708, 1708 (18), ~ *Hangings* ~ 1745 (*v*. **furlang**), *the hanging lays* 1703, 1708, ~ ~ *Leys* 1708 (18), *the Hangings Lays* 1745 (*v*. **leys**) (*v*. **hangende**); *Longharepittes* 1322 (*v*. **lang**[1]), *Schortharepittes* 1322 (*v*. **sc(e)ort**), *the hare pittes* 1601, 1605, 1612, ~ ~ *Pitts* 1703, 1708 (18), ~ ~ *Pits* 1745 (*v*. **hār**[2], **pytt**); *le Hengondehul* 1322 (*v*. **hangende**, **hengjandi**, **hyll**); *Hennow* 1322, *Michelennow* 1322 (*v*. **micel**), *Middelhennow* 1322 (*v*. **middel**), *Henhouse* 1601, 1605, 1612, 1708, 1708 (18), 1730, *Hennowhauedes* 1322 (*v*. **hēafod**) (*v*. **henn**, **haugr**); *William Hentons headlande* 1601, 1612, *George Hentons Headland* 1703, 1708, 1708 (18), *William Henton Junior his headland* 1708 (*v*. **hēafod-land**), *William Henton Senior his Baulk* 1708 (*v*. **balca**); *Hilledoles* 1601, *the Hill Doles* 1605, 1612 (*v*. **hyll**, **dāl**); *le Hocdole* 1322 (*v*. **hōc**, **dāl**); *the Home* 1708 (18), 1730 (*v*. **holmr**); *the Homestall* 1605 (i.e. of *the Parsonage House*, *v*. The Rectory *supra*), *the Homestall of Thomas Brewande* 1605 (*v*. **hām-stall**); *Littelhows* 1322, *Litle hose* 1601, 1605, 1612 (*v*. **lȳtel**), *Long*(*e*) *hose* 1601, 1605, 1612, *the Long Hose* 1703, 1708, 1708 (18), 1745, *Short Hose* 1703, 1708, 1708 (18), 1730, 1745 (*v*. **haugr**; poss. originally **hōh** (**hōs** nom.pl.), cf. Hose, Lei **2** 99); *Ounderhounde croft* 1322 (*v*. **under**, **croft**; either with the OE/ON pers.n. *Hund* or its surn. reflex *Hound*; the sb. **hund** 'a hound, a dog' seems less likely in this compound); *atte Howe* 1332 SR (p), *at How*(*e*) 1377 ib (p) (*v*. **atte**, **haugr**); *le Hullys* 1322 (*v*. **hyll**); *Thomas James Headland* 1708, 1708 (18), *William James his Headland* 1708 (*v*. **hēafod-land**); *Kaimesbrigge* 1322, (*the*) *Keyme bridge* 1601, 1605, 1612, *Keyme bridge leas* 1601, ~ ~ *leyes* 1612 (*v*. **leys**) (poss. with OE **camb**/ON **kambr** 'a crest', ME **cayme** 'a bank or ridge of earth (along a ditch)' and **brycg**, but a surn. *Kaiham* of a family originally from Keyham (*q.v.*), 7 miles to the south, cannot be ruled out); *Katherines furlonge* 1601, 1605,

1612 (*v*. **furlang**; with the surn. *Katherin*, from the pers.n. *Katerin*, popular in the Middle Ages because of the legend of St Katherine of Alexandria); *Matth. Kings Headland* 1730 (*v*. **hēafod-land**); *Kitesnest* 1322, *the kites neste* 1601, 1612, *the kytes nest* 1605 (*v*. **cȳta, nest**); *Landmeresikfurlonges* 1322 (*v*. **land-(ge)mǣre, sík, furlang**); *the lenghthes* 1605, 1612, *the Lengths* 1703, 1708, 1708 (18), 1730, 1745 (*v*. **lengthe**); *the Litle Sicke* 1605 (*v*. **lȳtel, lítill, sík**); *le Longdoles* 1322, *the Longe Doles* 1601, 1605, 1612 (*v*. **lang**[1], **dāl**); *the Longe headlande* 1601, 1605, 1612, *the Long Headland(s)* 1703, 1708, 1708 (18), 1730, ~ ~ *Hedland* 1745 (*v*. **hēafod-land**); *Longelandes* 1322, *Nortlongelandes* 1322 (*v*. **norð**) (*v*. **lang**[1], **land**); *the Long Lays* 1703, 1708, 1730, ~ ~ *Leys* 1708 (18) (*v*. **leys**); *Manlandes* 1322, *Uttermanlandes* 1322 (*v*. **ūterra**) (*v*. **(ge)mǣne, land**); *Mannesmor* 1322 (*v*. **(ge)mǣnnes, mōr**[1]); *Mappes hille* 1601, 1612, *Mappes* ~ 1605, *Mopps*~ 1703, 1708, 1708 (18), *Marks or Mopps* ~ 1730, 1745 (with the surn. *Mapp* and poss. with an alternative **mearc**, cf. *le Merksfurlonges*, *infra*); *le Marlepit* 1322 (*v*. **marle-pytt**); *the Marshe* 1601, 1605, 1612 (*v*. **mersc**); *the Meadowe* 1708, *Medueplot* 1297 Banco (*v*. **plot**) (*v*. **mǣd** (**mǣdwe** obl.sg.)); *Meltongate* 1322, *Mellton gate* 1601, 1612, *Melton* ~ 1605, 1703, 1708, 1708 (18), 1730, 1745 (*v*. **gata**; the road to Melton Mowbray which lies 5 miles to the east); *le Merksfurlonges* 1322 (*v*. **mearc, furlang**); *Meriothul* 1322 (*v*. **hyll**; with the common north-eastern Leics. surn. *Marriott* (from *Mariot*, a diminutive of Mary)); *le Mickilbalke* 1322 (*v*. **micel, mikill, balca**); *le Mickeldole* 1322 (*v*. **micel, mikill, dāl**); *Mikelwonges* 1322 (*v*. **micel, mikill, vangr**); *Milkers Stile* 1703, 1708, 1708 (18), 1730, 1745 (*v*. **mylker, stīg**); *le Mor* 1322, *le Mordic* 1322 (*v*. **dīc, dík**), *Mordole* 1322 (*v*. **dāl**) (*v*. **mōr**[1]); *Mustardlond'* 1438 *Deed* (*v*. **mustard, land**); *the Narrow Sick* 1708, 1708 (18) (*v*. **nearu, sík**); *Hamerneudole* 1322 (*v*. **hamer, nīwe, dāl**); *the new close* 1612; *Nickacook wong* 1703, 1708, 1708 (18), 1730, 1745 (*v*. **vangr**; much earlier forms are needed, though in a water-side location, a folk memory of an Anglo-Saxon *nicor* 'a water-sprite' with *cocc* 'a hillock' may be thought of); *the Old Ford* 1703, 1708, 1708 (18); *Osbernmor* 1322 bis (*v*. **mōr**[1], **mór**; with the ON pers.n. *Ásbjǫrn* (> *Osbern* in DB)); *Ousterdale* 1322, *Hamerousterdale* 1322 (*v*. **hamer**), *Otterousterdale* 1322 (*v*. **ūterra**) (*v*. **austr** (**austarr** comp.), **dalr**; the comparative is poss. here although *-er-* may be intrusive); *Oxback Ditch* 1708, 1708 (18), 1730 (*v*. **oxa, bekkr, dīc**); *the Parsons Ground* 1708, 1708 (18) (*v*. **persone, grund**); (*the*) *Pear Tree Furlong* 1703, 1708, 1708 (18), *the Partree furlong* 1745 (*v*. **pertre, furlang**); *Peisefurlonges* 1322 (*v*. **pise, furlang**); *Peiselondes* 1322, *Nethirpeiselandes* 1322, *nether peaselandes* 1601, 1605, 1612, *the Nether Pease Lands* 1703, 1708, 1708 (18), 1730, 1745, *the Neather Paselands* 1745 (*v*. **neoðera**), *Ovirpeiselandes* 1322, *over peaselandes* 1601, 1605, 1612 (*v*. **uferra**), *Utterpeiselandes* 1322 (*v*. **ūterra**), *Peiselandhals* 1322, *peaseland(e) halfes* 1601, 1605, 1612 (*v*. **hals**) (*v*. **pise, land**); *Richard Picks baulk* 1703, 1708, 1708 (18), (*v*. **balca**), *James Pick's Headland* 1730 (*v*. **hēafod-land**); *Pinderemedowedole* 1322 (*v*. **pinder, mǣd** (**mǣdwe** obl.sg.), **dāl**); *Potwelle* 1322 (*v*. **wella**; either with **pot(t)** 'a pot', with reference to a spring with a pot for dispensing water, or with **potte** 'a deep hole'); *the priestes baulke(s)* 1601, 1605, 1612, ~ ~ *balkes* 1605, *the priest baulkes* 1612, *Priest Baulks* 1703, *Priests Baulk(s)* 1708, 1708 (18), 1730 (*v*. **prēost, balca**); *Quakefensike* 1322 (*v*. **quake, fenn, sík**); *Rakedalebro(o)ke* 1322 (*v*. **brōc**), *Rakedalemere* 1322 (*v*. **(ge)mǣre**) (Ragdale adjoins to the north-west); *le Rede* 1322, *le Hamerrede* 1322 (*v*. **hamer**), *le Otterrede* 1322 (*v*. **ūterra**), *the Reades* 1601, 1605, 1612, *the Reeds* 1703, *the Reads* 1708, 1730, *the Reids* 1745 (*v*. **hrēod**);

Riholm 1322, *Hameriholm* 1322 (*v.* **hamer**), *Utteriholm* 1322 (*v.* **ūterra**) (*v.* **ryge, holmr**); *Riolfhauedes* 1322 (*v.* **hēafod**; with the pers.n. *Ríulfr*, poss. an Anglo-Scand formation from *Ríkulfr*, *v.* SPNLY 219); *le Rischebuskes* 1322, *Hamerrischebuskes* 1322 (*v.* **hamer**) (*v.* **risc, buskr**); *the Round Hole* 1703, 1708, 1708 (18), 1730, 1745 (*v.* **round, hol**[1]); *Hamerroutes* 1322 (*v.* **hamer**), *Overroutes* 1322 (*v.* **ūferra**) (perh. with ON **hrúðr** 'scurf' used topographically of 'rough ground' or an unrecorded OE **rūt**, also 'rough ground' (*v.* Löfvenberg 171), cf. OE *rūhet* 'a place overgrown with brushwood, a piece of rough ground'); *Salterforde* 1322 (*v.* **saltere, ford**; with reference to a salt-way); *Salterswong* 1703, 1730, *Salter Wong* 1708, 1708 (18), *Hamersalterewonges* 1322 (*v.* **hamer**) (*v.* **saltere, vangr**); *the nether ~ ~, the over sande fiellde* 1601, *the Nether ~ ~, the Over Sande field(e)* 1605, 1612 (*v.* **uferra**), *the Sand Field* 1703, 1708, 1708 (18), *the sande fiellde towarde Keyme bridge* 1601, *the sand fielde towarde(s) Keyme bridge* 1605, 1612 (*v. Kaimesbrigge, supra*), *the Sand Field next Austrean* 1703, 1708, 1708 (18), 1730 (*v.* Austen Dyke *supra*), *the Sand Field next to (the) New Field(s)* 1703, 1708, 1708 (18), 1730, 1745 (*v.* **sand, feld**; 'the sand field' was one of the three early great fields of the township); *(the) Sand Pit(t) Hill* 1703, 1708, 1708 (18), 1730, 1745 (*v.* **sand-pytt**); *Scouilbrodes* 1322 (*v.* **scofl-brǣdu**); *Scrapholm* 1322 (*v.* **holmr**; with an ON pers.n., either *Skrápi* or, less likely, *Skrápr*); *Setcophul* 1322 (*v.* **set-copp, hyll**); *(the) shorte doles* 1601, 1605, *the Short Doles* 1612, 1708 (18), *~ ~ Dowls* 1703, 1708, 1730, 1745 (*v.* **dāl**); *the Shrubbs* 1708 (*v.* **scrubb**); *the Sixteens* 1708, 1708 (18) (a subdivision of *the Austrean* (*v.* Austen Dyke *supra*), presum. specifying 16 units of pasture); *Siwoldebyforthe* 1322 (*v.* **ford**), *Siwoldebymere* 1322 (*v.* **(ge)mǣre**), *Shobye brooke* 1601, *Shoollbie ~* 1605, *Sholbie ~* 1612 (*v.* **brōc**), *Shoulby Gate* 1703, 1708 (18), 1730, *Shouldby ~* 1745 (*v.* **gata**; also called *Shoulby Way* 1708, 1745, *v.* **weg**), *Shobie hedge* 1601, *Shoollbie ~* 1605, 1612, *Shoulby ~* 1703 (*v.* **hecg**; a township boundary marker) (Shoby adjoins to the north-east); *Hamerskeges* 1322 (*v.* **hamer**), *Otterskeges* 1322 (*v.* **ūterra**) (with ON **skegg** 'a beard', used topographically of something jutting out and covered with scrub); *Skeggedale* 1322, *Utterscheggedale* 1322 (*v.* **ūterra**), *Schegdale* 1703, 1708, 1708 (18), 1745, *Skegdale* 1708, *Shegdale* 1708 (18) (evidently with **skegg** as in the previous f.n.; prob. with **dalr** rather than **deill**); *le Sponges* 1322, *le Longsponges* 1322 (*v.* **lang**[1]) (*v.* **spang, spong**); *Standart* 1322 (*v.* **standard**); *Stocwellfurlonges* 1322 (*v.* **stocc, wella, furlang**; alluding to a stream crossed by a bridge consisting of a tree-trunk); *Schortstones* 1322, *shortestones* 1601, 1605, 1612, *Short Stones* 1703, 1708, 1708 (18), 1730 (*v.* **sc(e)ort**), *longestones* 1601, 1605, 1612, *Long Stones* 1703, 1708, 1708 (18), 1730 (*v.* **stān**); *Stondelues* 1322, *Stondelfnethirende* (*v.* **neoðera, ende**) (*v.* **stān-(ge)delf**); *the Stone Bridge* 1703, 1708, 1730; *Stonigate* 1322 (*v.* **stānig, gata**); *Stringham foorde* 1612, *~ ford* 1703, 1708, 1708 (18), 1730, 1745 (*v.* **streng, hamm, ford**; perh. describing a long, thin stretch of water-meadow or a string of such patches of meadow along a stream); *le Swathis* 1322, *the Swathedoles* 1601, 1605, 1612 (*v.* **dāl**) (*v.* **swathe**); *Swinholmes* 1322 (*v.* **swīn**[1], **svín, holmr**); *Tacwelle* 1322 (*v.* **wella**; either with an OE pers.n. *Tacca/Tæcca* or with **tacca/tacce** 'a young sheep'); *Tasilholm* 1322 (*v.* **tǣsel, holmr**); *Thacholm* 1322 (*v.* **þæc, þak, holmr**); *Thirnebothim* 1322, *the Thoorne bottome* 1601, 1612, *the Thorne bottom* 1605 (*v.* **þyrne, þorn, botm**); *Longthirndale* 1322 (*v.* **lang**[1], **þyrne, þyrnir, dalr**); *Thoretheoxeneworeslaine* 1322 ('where the oxen were slain', *v.* **oxa**; cf. *ubi Godwynesoxe moriebatur* 1343 ('where Godwine's ox died', Great Bowden, Gartree

Hundred) and *Thertheoxlaydede* 13 ('where the ox lay dead', Bk 259)); *le Thorn* 1322, *Tho(o)rne hades* 1601, 1605, 1612 (*v.* **hēafod**) (*v.* **þorn**); *Thorslos* (sic) 1322 (presum. the generic is **clos(e)**; with the Anglo-Scand pers.n. *Þōr*); *Thrushington Meadowes* 1601, *Thrussington meadowes* 1605, *Thrushington medowes* 1612, *Thrusing(e)ton mere* 1601, 1612, *Thrussington* ~ 1605 (*v.* **(ge)mǣre**) (Thrussington adjoins to the south-west); *the townesend(e)* 1605, 1612 (*v.* **ende**), *the Town Side* 1708, 1708 (18), 1745 (*v.* **sīde**) (*v.* **tūn**); *the Twellues* 1601, 1605, 1612, *the twellves* 1612, *the Twelves* 1708, *the Nether* ~, *the Upper Twelves* 1601, 1605, 1612, *the first Twellues* 1601, ~ ~ ~ *beneathe Brokesbie Mille* 1605, ~ ~ ~ *beneath Brookesbye mylle* 1612 (*v.* **myln**; Brooksby adjoins to the south), *the twellves at Barlie water* 1612 (*v. Barlie water, supra*) (*v.* **twelf**; with reference to various twelve units of agricultural land, presum. pasture, since *the Twellues* 1601 were part of *the Austrean*, as were *the Sixteens, supra*); *William Walkers piece* 1708, ~ ~ *peice* 1708 (18) (*v.* **pece**); *le Watreforowes* 1322 (*v.* **wæter**, **furh** and *the Waterfurrow(e)s* in Asfordby f.ns. (b)); *Wellefurlonges* 1322 (*v.* **wella, furlang**); *Willows Furlong* 1703, 1708, 1745 (*v.* **furlang**), *the Willowes hedge* 1601, 1605, 1612 (*v.* **hecg**; a boundary hedge), *the Willowes stile* 1601, 1605, 1612 (*v.* **stīg**) (all with reference to the lost settlement of *Willoughes, infra*); *Wlfinges* 1322, *Hamerwlfinges* 1322 (*v.* **hamer**) (*v.* **eng**; with the ON pers.n. *Úlfr* (ODan *Ulf*)); *Ovir the woldgate* 1322 (*v.* **ofer**[3]), *Woldgatesende* 1322 (*v.* **ende**) (*v.* **wald, gata**); *Hamerwonges* 1322 bis (*v.* **hamer, vangr**); *le Wrongelandes* 1322 (*v.* **wrang, vrangr, land**); *Hamirwyuelisbuskes* 1322 (*v.* **hamer**), *Otterwiuelisbuskes* 1322 (*v.* **ūterra**) (*v.* **buskr**; with a pers.n., either ON *Vífill* or OE *Wifel*); *Yocacre* 1322 (*v.* **geoc**[1], **æcer**).

2. ROTHERBY

Redebi 1086 DB

Rederbia c.1130 LeicSurv, *Rederbi* l.12, e.13 Dane, *Redrebi* c.1200 ib

Reidebi Hy 2 Dugd, *Reytherby* 1254 Val, 1299 Banco (p)

Retheresby e.13 Berkeley (p), *Rethesb'* 1220 MHW

Retherby 1206 Cur, 1221 Fine, 1221 Ass, 1236 Fees *et freq* to 1481 *Ct*, 1486 Ipm *et passim* to 1518 Visit, 1536 *RTemple*, *Rethirby* 1242, 1274 RGrav, *Rethurby* 1226 Fine, 1271 Cur, 1301 (1449) *WoCart et passim* to 1360 (1449) *ib*, 1377 SR

Ratherby 1487 Pat, 1506, 1507 Ipm, 1601 *Terrier*, *Ratherbie* 1582 LEpis, *Rathurby* 1576 LibCl, *Rathurbie* 1582 LEpis

Rotheby 1303 *MiD*, *Rotherby* 1253 × 58 RHug, 1266 Cur, 1316 FA *et passim* to 1579 LEpis, 1610 Speed *et freq*

'Hreiðar's farmstead, village', *v.* **bȳ**, cf. Rearsby *infra*. The ON pers.n. *Hreiðarr* (ODan *Rethar*) as the specific rather than the ON pers.n. *Hreiði* is indicated by the continuing presence of medial *r* and the surviving genitival forms in *-es-*. Some forms from the mid 13th cent. onwards show attraction to *rother*, a reflex of OE *hrȳðer* 'an ox, cattle'.

ALL SAINTS' CHURCH, *Church (All Saints)* 1846, 1863, 1877 White, 1925 Kelly; it is earlier recorded as *ecclesie de Retherb'* 1220 MHW, ~ ~ *Rotherby* 1344 *Pat*, *The Church* 1708, 1708 (18) *Terrier*. Note also *the Church Yard*, 1708, 1724, 1745, 1821 *ib*. THE HALL, 1846, 1863, 1877 White, *Rotherby Hall* 1831 Curtis, cf. *Sir Alexanderes Hall* 1612, 1625 *Terrier* (with reference to Sir Alexander Cave), *v.* **hall**. HIGHFIELDS FM, *the highe feilde* 1601 *Terrier*, ~ ~ *fielde* 1612 *ib*, ~ *high feild* 1625, 1674 *ib*, *High Field* 1806 Map, *v.* **hēah**[1], **feld**; one of the great fields of the township. Highfields Fm is on the site of *High Field Barn* 1835 O. MANOR HO., *Manor House* 1863, 1877 White, *The Manor* 1925 Kelly, *v.* **maner**. THE RECTORY is *the Rectory House* 1821 *Terrier*, *the Old Rectory* 1925 Kelly, *v.* **rectory**; earlier it is *the Mansion House* 1708, 1708 (18), 1724, 1745, 18 *Terrier*, *v.* **mansion-house**. ROTHERBY LODGE, 1835 O, *v.* **loge**. WHEATSHEAF (P.H.) (lost), *Wheat Sheaf* 1846 White.

FIELD-NAMES

Undated forms in (a) are 1846 *TA*; those dated 1968 are *Surv*. Forms throughout dated 1601, 1612, 1625, 1674, 1708, 1708 (18), 1724, 1745 and 18 are *Terrier*.

(a) 3 Acres, Bottom ~ ~, Middle ~ ~, Top ~ ~, 4 Acres, Far ~ ~, Near 5 Acres, 6 Acres, 8 Acres (*v.* **æcer**); Far ~ ~ ~, First ~ ~ ~, Middle Arable Hill Cl (*v.* **arable**); Ash Cl (*v.* **æsc**); Backwater Fd 1968 (*v.* **backwater**); Barn Cl 1846, 1968, Barn Close First Part, ~ ~ Second ~, ~ ~ Fifth ~, ~ ~ Sixth Part (*v.* **part**); Baulk 1968 (*v.* **balca**); Bottom ~ ~, Top ~ ~, Boultbee Cl (with the surn. *Boultbee*, *v.* Reaney *s.n.*); Brick Yards 1835 O, Brickyard Cl 1846, 1968 (*v.* **brike-yard**); Bridge Fd 1968 (cf. *the Bridge pieces* 1708, 1724, 1745, ~ ~ *peices* 1708 (18), 18, *v.* **pece**); Broading, ~ Mdw (*Broding*, *Broading* 1601, *Midle* ~, *Upper* ~, *Broaden* 1674, *broading dike* 1601, 1625, *brodinge* ~ 1612 (*v.* **dík**), *bro(a)dinge sicke* 1612, *broading sick* 1625 (*v.* **sík**) (*v.* **brād**, **eng**); Brook Cl 1846, Brook Hill 1846, Brook Mdw 1968; Brookesby Cl (*Brookesbie close* 1612; Brooksby adjoins to the west); Bull Piece (*v.* **bula**, **pece**); Charity Cl 1846, Charity 1968 (the Overseers of the Poor owned this close); First ~ ~, Second Coopers Cl, Coopers Close Third Part, ~ ~ Fourth ~, ~ ~ Fifth ~, ~ ~ Sixth Part 1846 (*v.* **part**), Nanny Cooper 1968 (all with the surn. *Cooper*); Cottage Cl 1846, 1968 (*v.* **cotage**); Cow Cl 1846, 1968 (*the Cow Close* 1674); Dirty Balk, ~ ~ Far Arable, ~ ~ First Arable, ~ ~ Middle Arable (*v.* **arable**), Bottom Dirty Balk (*v.* **dyrty**, **balca**); East Morends 1761 *EnclA*, East Moreens 1821 *Terrier*, Esmerines 1968 (*Eastmarine* 1708, 1708 (18), 1724, 1745, 18, *v.* *Eastmore Reine* in adjoining Hoby f.ns. (b); E. Meadowrain (sic) 1846 is presum. a garbled form of this f.n.); Far Mdw; Middle ~, Near Fatlands, Far ~ ~, Arable Fatlands (*v.* **arable**) (*fattlandes* 1601,

1625, *Fatlandes* 1612, *Great Fattlands* 1674, *v.* **fætt, land**); First Mdw; Gaddesby Lane Fd 1968 (Gaddesby lies 2 miles to the south-east); Glovers Cl 1846, First ~, Second Glovers 1968 (*Glover Close* 1674; *Will. Glover* is cited 1674); Goodchilds 1968 (the surn. *Goodchild* in the possessive case); Gravel Close Mdw 1968; Gravel Pit 1846 (*v.* **gravel, pytt**); Hall Fd 1968 (*v.* The Hall *supra*); Hansons Cl (with the surn. *Hanson*); Hazelwood Cl 1846, 1968, Little Hazelwood 1968 (*v.* **hæsel, wudu**); Great ~, High Fds, Great High Field Mdw (*v.* Highfields Fm *supra*); Hill Cl 1846, 1968; Home Cl 1846 (*the Home Close* 1674), Home Fd 1968 (*v.* **home**); Horse Cl (*the Horse Close* 1674); House Cl 1846, 1968; Wards Lammas Cl 1761 *EnclA*, 1846 (with the surn. *Ward*) (cf. *Wases Lammas Close* 1727 Nichols; with the surn. *Wase/Wass*) (*v.* **lammas**); Little Cl; Little Mdw; Little Paddock (*v.* **paddock**); L-shaped Fd 1968; Meadow Cl; Far ~ ~, Mill Mdw 1968; Bottom ~ ~ ~, Top New Laid Down 1968 (presum. with reference to recently sown grass); the Park Cl 1846, Park Fd 1968 (*v.* **park**); Pond Cl, Pond Mdw; Rabbit Hole 1846, 1968 (*v.* **hol**[1]), Top ~ ~, Rabbit Warrens 1761 *EnclA* (*v.* **wareine**) (*v.* **rabet**); Ram Paddock (*v.* **ramm, paddock**); Rotherby Wood 1806 ChAccts; Rough Cl (*the Rough Close* 1674), Rough Mdw (*v.* **rūh**[1]); the Slipe 1968 (*v.* **slipe**); Spinney Cl 1846, 1968 (*v.* **spinney**); Far ~ ~, Great ~ ~, Middle ~ ~, Near ~ ~, Nether Spring Cl (*ye Spring Close* 1674), Spring Mdw (*v.* **spring**[1]); Far ~, Near Ting-hill, Ting-hill Cl (*Tinge hill* 1612, 1625, *Tyngg Hill* 1674, *v.* **þing, hyll**, a moot-site; for additional forms, *v.* Frisby on the Wreake f.ns. (a) *s.n.* Ting Hills); Top Cl; Town Cl (*v.* **tūn**); Village Mdw (*v.* **village**); Wasses Cl (with the surn. *Wase/Wass*); Far ~ ~ ~, Near Water Mill Mdw (*v.* **water-mylne**).

(b) *Sir Alexanderes grene swarde* 1612 (*v.* **greensward**), *Sir Alex' headlande* 1612, *Sir Alexander* (*Cave*) *hadland* 1625 (*v.* **hēafod-land**), *Sir Alex' headlea* 1612, *Sir Alexander hadlea* 1625 (*v.* **headley**); *Mr Ashbies close* 1612, ~ ~ (*grasse*) *grounde* 1612 (*v.* **græs, grund**), ~ ~ *headlande* 1612 (*v.* **hēafod-land**), ~ ~ *headlea* 1612 (*v.* **headley**), ~ ~ *layes* 1612 (*v.* **leys**), *Mr Ashbies wonge* 1612 (*v.* **vangr**); *Mr Barnards land* 1674; *blackelandes* 1601 (*v.* **blæc, land**); *the leye of William Breet* 1601 (*v.* **ley**), *the medow of William Breet* 1601; *Brokesby hedge* 1601 (*v.* **hecg**; a township boundary marker, Brooksby adjoining to the south-west); *Burches Close* 1674 (*John Burch* is cited 1674); *the Burrowes* 1601, *the Burroughes* 1612, 1625 (*v.* **burgh**); *Cawdwell hades* 1601, *Caudwell haydes* 1612, 1625 (*v.* **cald, wella, hēafod**); *Clevers piece* 1708, ~ *peice* 1708 (18), *Cleavers Pieces* 1724, 1745 (*v.* **pece**; with the surn. *Cleaver*); *the Common Street* 1708 (*v.* **commun, strǣt**); *Cottagers meadow* 18, *Cottagers Pasture* 1708, 1708 (18), 1724 (*v.* **pasture**) (*v.* **cotager**); *the Cottiers Close* 1674, *the Cottiers Eaton Close* (sic) 1674 (the nature of *Eaton* here is obscure; it may record a lost farmstead (*v.* **tūn**), but more likely is **eating** 'the action of taking food', referring to grass available only for grazing and not for a hay crop, cf. Eating Cl in Great Dalby, Lei **2** 80), *Cottiers Meadowe* 1674 (*v.* **cottere**); *the Cow pasture* 1625, *the kowe paster*, ~ ~ ~ *heydes* 1612 (*v.* **hēafod**), ~ ~ ~ *layes* 1612 (*v.* **leys**) (*v.* **cū, pasture**); *the Crosse hill* 1601 (*v.* **cross**); *the East Hill Close* 1674; *fowre landes* 1612 (*v.* **fēower, land**; a group of selions conceived as a unit); *Frisby gate* 1601 (*v.* **gata**), *Frisbie haydes* 1612, *Frisbye* ~ 1625 (*v.* **hēafod**), *Frisbye mere* 1601, *Frisbie meare*, ~ *meere* 1612, *Frysbye meere* 1625, *Frisby Meare* 1674 (*v.* **(ge)mǣre**) (Frisby on the Wreake adjoins to the north-east); *Gadesby meere* 1601, *Gadsbie Meare* 1612, *Gadsbee meere* 1625 (*v.* **(ge)mǣre**; Gaddesby adjoins to the south-east); *Mr Will. Hartopps land* 1674; *hornetoft* 1601, ~ *furlong* 1625, *Horntoft furlonge* 1612 (*v.* **furlang**) (*v.* **horn, toft**); *knole haydes*

1612, *the nether ~ ~*, *the upper knolle hades* 1601, *the middle ~ ~*, *the nether knole haydes* 1612, *middle knole hades*, *neither knowle haydes* 1625 (*v*. **neoðera**) (*v*. **cnoll**, **hēafod**); *Mr Lanes close*, *~ ~ grass ground* 1625 (*v*. **græs**, **grund**), *Mr Lane hadland* 1625 (*v*. **hēafod-land**), *Mr Lanes hadlea* 1625 (*v*. **headley**), *~ ~ leas* 1625 (*v*. **leys**), *~ ~ woong* 1625 (*v*. **vangr**); *Langhdale* 1601, *Longdale* 1625, *Langdale ende* 1612 (*v*. **ende**), *Langedale sicke* 1612, *Longdale sick* 1625 (*v*. **sík**) (*v*. **lang**[1], **dalr**); *Leycestre way* 1612, *Lecester waye* 1625 (*v*. **weg**; the road to Leicester, 10 miles to the south-west); *the litle sick(e)* 1601, 1612, 1625 (*v*. **lȳtel**, **lítill**, **sík**); *(the) long(e) furlong(e)* 1601, 1612, 1625, *the longe furlonge haydes* 1612 (*v*. **hēafod**) (*v*. **lang**[1], **furlang**; in both High Fd and Middle Fd); *long rigges furland* (sic) 1612, *~ ~ furlong* 1625 (*v*. **hrycg**, **furlang**); *the lowe pasture* 1612 (*v*. **la(g)h**, **pasture**); *lowsy bushe* 1601, *Lousie bushe* 1612, *lowsie bush* 1625, *Lousie bushe haydes* 1612, *Lowsie bush haydes* 1625 (*v*. **hēafod**), *lowsy bush way* 1601 (*v*. **weg**) (*v*. **lowsy**, **busc**; poss. describing a piece of scrub infested by insects (but cf. also OE *lūs-þorn* 'a spindle-tree'), *v*. *Lousie Bush*, Lei **2** 49 and Lousy Bush, Lei **2** 92); *the marishe grounde* 1612, *the marrish ground* 1625 (*v*. **merisc**, **grund**; the older form of **mersc** is present here); *marlepittgate* 1601 (*v*. **gata**), *marlepitt heydes* 1612, *Marl pit haydes* 1625 (*v*. **hēafod**) (*v*. **marle-pytt**); *the medow(e) leas* 1612, 1625 (*v*. **leys**), *the medow side* 1601 (*v*. **sīde**) (*v*. **mǣd** (**mǣdwe** obl.sg.)); *(the) Mid(d)le feild* 1601, 1625, *~ ~ fielde* 1612 (*v*. **middel**, **feld**; one of the great fields of the township); *the midle high lea* 1625 (*v*. **middel**, **hēah**[1], **ley**); *the Mill Hill Close* 1674; *Thom' Mussons headlande* 1612, *John Musson hadland* 1625 (*v*. **hēafod-land**), *the land of Tho' Musson* 1601, *Mr Mussons land* 1674 (the *Musson* family was originally from Muston, 16 miles to the north-east, the surn. spelling showing typical Leics. loss in p.ns. of *t* in the group *-ston*); *the neates pasture* 1601 (*v*. **nēat**, **pasture**); *(the) Nether feild* 1601, 1625, *~ ~ fielde* 1612 (*v*. **neoðera**, **feld**; one of the great fields); *new closse hedge* 1601 (*v*. **clos(e)**); *the parsonage backside* 1601 (*v*. **bak-side**), *the personage land* 1674, *the Parsonedge Orcharde* 1612, *the parsonage orchard* 1625 (*v*. **orceard**) (*v*. **personage**); *the Parson(es) bushe* 1601, 1612, *the parsons bush* 1625 (*v*. **busc**), *the Parsons home Close* 1674 (*v*. **home**), *the Parsons further Close* 1674 (*v*. **persone**); *the Parting(e) grass(e)* 1601, 1612, 1625, *Parting grasse hades* 1612 (*v*. **hēafod**) (*v*. **parting**, **græs**; poss. alluding to allocation by lot, *v*. Field 23); *the pasture layes* 1612, 1625 (*v*. **pasture**, **leys**); *Pindars piece* 1708, 1724, *~ peice* 1708 (18), *Pindar's piece* 1745, *Pinders ~* 1821 (*v*. **pinder**, **pece**); *the Raine* 1601, *the Rayne* 1612, 1625 (*v*. **rein**); *at Ratherby Close gate* 1601 (*v*. **geat**; a furlong thus called), *Rotherbie close* 1612, 1625; *Redlandes* 1601, *Redland furlong(e)* 1612, 1625 (*v*. **furlang**) (*v*. **rēad**, **land**); *Row(e)burrough haydes* 1612, *Rowborough ~* 1625 (*v*. **rūh**[1], **berg**, **hēafod**); *the sande furlong* 1601 (*v*. **sand**, **furlang**); *the severall landes* 1612 (*v*. **severall**, **land**); *Shovell broad* 1601, *Shuvvle boarde furlonge* 1612, *Shovel board furlong* 1625 (*v*. **furlang**) (*v*. **scofl-brǣdu**); *(the) Streetway* 1601, *the Stre(e)teway* 1612, *the Street(e)waye* 1625 (*v*. **street-waie**); *great ~*, *litle toftsicke* 1601, *Tuffesicke* 1612, *Tufsick* 1625, *Tuffesicke furlong* 1612, *Tufsick ~* 1625 (*v*. **furlang**) (*v*. **toft**, **sík**); *the Topp of the hill* 1601, 1605 (*v*. **topp**; a furlong so called in the High Fd); *Mr Wage his close* 1625, *the land of Thomas Wage* 1601 (*v*. **land**); *the Walk mill meadowe* 1674 (*v*. **walke-milne**); *the waterfurrowes* 1601 (*v*. **wæter**, **furh** and *the Waterfurrow(e)s* in Asfordby f.ns. (b)); *the water leas* 1625 (*v*. **wæter**, **leys**; part of a system of irrigation, *v*. Field 90–1); *Mr Waze his land* 1674 (cf. *Wases Lammas Close*, *supra*).

3. BROOKSBY

Brochesbi 1086 DB bis, 1196 ChancR, 1197 × 1227 Hastings, *Brocchesbi* 1198 P

Brokesbya c.1130 LeicSurv, *Brockesby* 1123 × 47 QuR, 1202 Hastings, 1254 Val, *Brokesbi* 1197 P, 1207 GildR, *Brokesby* 1202 Fine, 1236, 1242 Fees, 1251 RGros *et freq* to 1510, 1514 LP *et passim* to 1547 Pat, 1610 Speed, (~ *super Wreke* 1296 Banco, ~ *super Wrethek* 1307 Ass), *Brokesbye* 1576 Saxton, *Brokesbie* 1577, 1580 LEpis, *Brokysby* 1517 DI, 1544, 1588 ISLR

Brokeby 1254 Pat

Broksby 1258 Ass, *Broxby* 1574, 1577 LEpis, *Broxbie* 1576 LibCl

Brookesbie 1610 LML, *Brooksby* 1835 O, 1842 Map *et freq*

Perhaps 'Brōk's farmstead, village', *v.* **bȳ**. Ekwall DEPN suggests that the p.n. is to be interpreted as 'the **bȳ** on the brook', referring to the river Wreake near to which the settlement is situated (hence affixes with MLat *super* 'on, upon'). However, the regular genitival forms may rather point to a Scand pers.n. as the specific; p.ns. in Leics. with OE *brōc* 'a brook' as the specific do not otherwise show genitival structure (as Nether Broughton in Framland Hundred and Broughton Astley in Guthlaxton Hundred). The spelling *Brokeby* 1254 is unique among some 150 other forms with the gen.sg. in the editor's collection. A Scand pers.n. *Brōk* would have been an original by-name from ON *brók* 'breeches'. The ON pers.n. *Brókki* is extant and may account for forms in *-cch-* and *-ck-*. Fellows-Jensen (SSNEM 39) ventures that an OE specific *brōc* may refer to a small stream which rises near Brooksby rather than to the river Wreake or alternatively, the specific may be an unrecorded ODan cognate *brōk* which appears to have been used in p.ns. in Denmark of 'a bog, a marsh'.

BROOKSBY GRANGE, 1925 Kelly, *v.* **grange**. BROOKSBY SPINNEY, *Brooksby Spinny* 1835 O, *v.* **spinney**. THE HALL, 1612 *Terrier*, 1846 White, *Brookesby Hall* 1846 ib, 1847 *TA*, 1863, 1877 White, *Brooksby* ~ 1925 Kelly, *v.* **hall**. ST MICHAEL'S CHURCH, *Church (St Michael)* 1846, 1863, 1877 White, 1925 Kelly; it is earlier recorded as *ecclesiam* ~ ~, *ecclesie de Brokesby* 1220 MHW, 1251 RGros, 1421 *Pat*.

FIELD-NAMES

Forms in (a) dated 1847 are *TA*, 1904 and 1935 are *Sale*, 1968 are *Surv*.

(a) 7 Acre 1935, 1968, Eight Acres Cl 1847, 9 Acres 1904, Hill nine acres 1847, 13 Acre 1935, 1968 (*v*. **æcer**); Barn Cl 1904, Second ~ ~, Third ~ ~ 1847; Barn Fd 1935, 1968; Bridge Mdw 1904, Lower ~ ~, Upper ~ ~ 1847; Brook Cl 1847, 1904, 1968; First ~ ~, Further Brook(e)sby Cl 1847, 1904; Brook(e)sby Pasture 1847, 1904 (*v*. **pasture**); Brooksby Station 1854 O (on the *Syston and Peterborough Branch Railway* 1854 ib); Butchers Cl 1847, 1904, Butchers Mdw 1904, First ~ ~, Further ~ ~ 1847 (with the surn. *Butcher*); Canal Mdw 1847 (with reference to a canalized reach of R. Wreake); the Car 1847 (*v*. **kjarr**); Charm Mdw 1847, 1904 (a complimentary name for easily-managed land); Cossacks Cl (with the surn. *Cusack*, *v*. Reaney *s.n.*); Cottage Cl 1847 (*v*. **cotage**); Cricket Fd 1968 (for the game of cricket); Far Cl 1847; Farm Fd 1968, Farm Institute Demonstration Plot 1968 (*v*. **plot**); First Cl 1904; First Piece 1904 (*v*. **pece**); Fox Burgh 1847 (*v*. **fox, burgh**; cf. Foxbury, Gl **4** 107); Further Cl 1847, 1904; Garden Mdw 1904 (*v*. **gardin**); Far ~ ~, Near Gorse Cl 1847 (*v*. **gorst**); Great Cl 1904; Great Mdw 1847, 1904; Hall Cl 1847 (*v*. The Hall *supra*); Hanging Mdw 1847, 1904 (*v*. **hangende**); First ~, Further ~, Great ~, Middle Hardmeats 1847, Further ~ ~, Great Hard Meads 1904, 1968 (*v*. **heard, mete**); Hentons Long Cl 1847, Hentons Piece 1847, 1904, 1968 (*v*. **pece**) (with the surn. *Henton*); High Fd 1847, 1904; Hill Cl 1847, 1904; Home Cl 1935, 1968 (*v*. **home**); Land Cl 1847, 1904, 1968, Land (Close) Mdw 1847, 1904 (*v*. **land**; enclosures consolidating unspecified numbers of selions or *lands* of a former great field); Long Mdw 1847, 1904, 1968; Lower Mdw 1847, 1904; Middle Cl 1847, 1904; Middle Fd 1847; Mill Cl 1904, Mill Mdw 1847, 1904, Mill Yard 1847 (*v*. **geard**) (*v*. **myln** and *Brookesbye mille*, *infra*); Near Cl 1847; Great Park 1904, Bottom ~, Top Park 1968, Park Orchard 1904 (*v*. **park**); First ~, Second ~, Further Pasture 1847, 1904, Pasture Cl 1904 (*v*. **pasture**); First ~, Second Piece 1847 (*v*. **pece**); Road Cl 1968; Rotherby Cl 1847, Rotherby Mdws 1904 (Rotherby adjoins to the north-east); Seeds Fd 1968 (*v*. **sǣd**; in f.ns., used of areas of sown grass); Shed Piece 1904 (*v*. **shed, pece**); Shire Mdw 1968 (this type of f.n. is usually found at a county boundary, but such cannot be the case here; perh. with the surn. *Shire* (*v*. Reaney *s.n.*) or alluding to the large, heavy draught horse known as a 'shire'); Spinney Fd 1968 (*v*. Brooksby Spinney *supra*); Storthe 1847 (*v*. **storð**); Thieves Cl, Thieves Mdw 1847 (many such names are derogatory for unproductive or otherwise unattractive land and may well have developed from OE **þefa** 'brushwood, bramble'); Thuns Cl 1904, 1968, Thuns Mdw 1904 (*v*. **þyrne**; these fields were Thieves Cl and Thieves Mdw in 1847); Top Mdw 1847, 1904; Townsend Cl 1847, 1904 (*v*. **tūn, ende**); Turnip Cl 1847 (*v*. **turnepe**); Turnpike Cl 1847, 1904 (*v*. **turnepike**); Waldrum Mdw 1847 (with the surn. *Waldrum*, *v*. Reaney *s.n.*); Willow Cl 1847, ~ ~ Mdw 1904 (*v*. **wilig**); Wreake Cl 1935, 1968 (beside R. Wreake).

(b) *Brookesbye mille* 1601 *Terrier*, ~ *mylle* 1612 *ib*, *Brokesbie Mille* 1605 *ib*, *Brokesbymilnegonele* 1322 Hastings (*v*. **gonele**) (*v*. **myln**); *ad fontem* 1259 Cur (p) (with MLat *fons* (*fontem* acc.sg.) 'a spring, a well'); *Michelwalda* 1343 Fine, 1346 Banco (*v*. **micel, wald**); *le Milnecroft* 1304 Banco (*v*. **myln, croft**).

4. RAGDALE

Ragendel(*e*) 1086 DB bis
Rachendale c.1130 LeicSurv, *Rakendale* 1166 RBE
Rachedal' c.1130 LeicSurv, *Rakedal*(*e*) 1220 MHW, 1243 Fees, 1254 Val *et passim* to 1285 Banco, 1294 OSut *et freq* to 1447 *Ferrers*, 1492 *Fisher et passim* to 1516 *Ferrers*, 1519 EpCB
Raggedal(*e*) 1243 Pat (p), 1262 Abbr, 1414 *Ferrers*, *Ragedale* 1428 FA
Ragdale 1428 FA, 1518 Visit *et passim* to 1580 *Fisher*, 1604 SR *et freq*

The first el. appears to be OE *hraca* 'a throat' used topographically in some such sense as 'a narrow passage'. Elements *s.v.* points out that *hraca* may be the source of dial. *rack* 'a narrow path' and *rake* 'a rough path, a narrow path up a ravine'. At Ragdale, a pinched dale rises northward from the wider Wreake Valley, giving access to the Roman road Margary 58a across the Wolds. Ragdale may perhaps be interpreted as 'the valley with a narrow passage or narrow pathway rising through it', *v.* **hraca** (**hracan** gen.sg.), **dæl**[1]. The rare, original OE *dæl* 'a valley' was here no doubt reinforced by ON **dalr** with the same meaning.

WILLOUGHES (lost)
Wilges 1086 DB, *Wiliges* Hy 1 Nichols, *Wileges* c.1130 LeicSurv, *Willeges* 1201 ChR
Wilewes c.1130 LeicSurv, 1375 Inqaqd, *Wylewes* 1285, 1343 Banco, 1365 Coram (p), *Wilwes* 1338 Banco, *Wyllwys* c.1347 Nichols, *Wilwys* 1422 AD
Wiléés (sic) 1166 LN, *Wileis* 1166 RBE, *Wylus* 1243 Fees
Wylhowe 1276 RH, *Wylhous* 1428 FA, *Willous* 1517 DI
Wilughes 1316 FA, *Wylughis* 1327 SR (p), *Wylughes* 1332 ib (p), 1375 IpmR, *Wilughis* 1445 Nichols, *Wyloughes* 1403 AD, 15 *Ferrers*, *Wilghes called also Willoughes* 1622 Burton, *Willoughes* 1846, 1863, 1877 White
Weloughes 1447 *Ferrers*, *Welughes* 1447 *ib*, *Wellowys* 1539 MinAccts
Wilowes 1390 Nichols, *Wylowes* 1397, 1402, 1404 *Ct*, *Willowes* 1397 Misc, 1403 Cl, 1492 *Fisher et passim* to 1580 *ib*, 1619 Fine, *Wyllowes* 1540, 1547, 1551, 1560 *Ct*, *Wilowys* 1424 AD, *Willows* 1513 *Ferrers*

'The willows', *v.* **wilig** (**wiligas** nom.pl.). By 1846 White, the name of the settlement survived as that of an estate in Ragdale. The original village lay between Ragdale and Hoby.

SIX HILLS

Seggeswalda a.1118 (s.a. 716) Flo, *Segeswalde* a.1118 (s.a. 755) ib, *Segesuuald* 1184 Selby, *Segheswald* l.12 *GarCart* bis, *Seggheswald* l.12 *ib*

Segeswold 1156 (1318) Ch, Hy 2 Dugd, *Seggiswold* Hy 2 ib, *Seggeswold* e.13 *GarCart*, 1290 Abbr, 1302 Ass, 1340 Ch

Segs Hill 1677 Thoroton, *Seggs Hill* 1701 *Terrier*, *Sex or Segs Hill* 1795 Nichols, 1806 Map, *Sex-hill* 1795 Nichols

Sixhill 1796 *EnclA*, *Six Hills* 1825 *Terrier*, 1835 O, 1846, 1877 White *et freq*

'Secgge's portion of the Wolds district', *v.* **wald**; with the OE pers.n. *Seccge*. Note the forms *Segehishou* and *Seggeshou* in adjoining Burton on the Wolds f.ns. (b) which no doubt refer to the same individual.

ALL SAINTS' CHURCH, *Church (All Saints)* 1846, 1863, 1877 White; it is earlier recorded as *ecclesiam* ~ ~, *ecclesie de Rakedale* 1220 MHW, 1406 *Ct*, 1406, 1407, 1411, 1415 *Pat*, *ecclesie parochialis de Rakedale* 1411 *ib*. RAGDALE HALL, 1925 Kelly, *Rakedale Hall* 1799 Nichols; it is *New Hall* 1846, 1863, 1877 White, *v.* **hall**. RAGDALE OLD HALL (lost), *Old Hall* 1846, 1863, 1877 White, *Ragdale Old Hall* 1925 Kelly, *v.* **hall**; demolished 1958. RAGDALE WOLDS FM, *Wold farm* 1863, 1877 White, *v.* **wald**. SPRINGFIELD FM. *v.* **spring**[1].

FIELD-NAMES

The undated forms in (a) are 1968 *Surv*.

(a) 8 ~, 10 ~, 14 Acre, 18 Acres, 20 Acre, 20 Acres (*v.* **æcer**); Ash Hill (*v.* **æsc**); Banky Fds (*v.* **banke**, **-ig**[3]); Barn Fd, Barn Mdw; Big Fd; Brook Fd; Clover Fd (*v.* **clāfre**; specifying a fodder crop); Dovecote (*v.* **dove-cot(e)**); First Fd; Hall Fd (*v.* Ragdale Hall *supra*); Home Fd (*v.* **home**); Hovel Fd (*v.* **hovel**); Hullocky (*v.* **hullok**, **-ig**[3]); Little Mdw; The March (*v.* **mersc**); Muckle Hills (*v.* **micel, mycel, mikill**); Narrow Fd (alluding to shape); The Normans (with the surn. *Norman* in the possessive case; cf. Little Normans in Frisby on the Wreake f.ns. (a)); The Oak (*v.* **āc**; a close containing such a tree); Park (*v.* **park**); The Ploughed Fd; Sand Fd (*v.* **sand**); Shoby Skales (adjacent to Shoby Scholes *q.v.*); Smith's Mdw (with the surn. *Smith*); Bottom ~ ~, Top Spinney Fd (*v.* **spinney**); Three Cornered Fd (*v.* **three-**

cornered); (The) Township 1798 Nichols, 1968 (*v.* **tounshipe**; according to Nichols, the site of *Willoughes*, cf. the Township in Hamilton f.ns. (a)); The Wales (two fields on the extreme western bounds of the parish; hence poss. an amused 'remoteness' name referring to the Principality, but *v.* Wales in Frisby on theWreake f.ns. (a)).

(b) *Bradedale* John Berkeley, *Braddale* l.Hy 2 ib, *Braddadale* Hy 2 ib (*v.* **brād**, **dalr**); *atte brigge* 1377 SR (p) (*v.* **atte**, **brycg**); *de Grene* 1397 *Ct* (p) (*v.* **grēne**[2]); *on le Hull* 1332 SR (p), *othe Hull* 1397 *Ct* (p) (*v.* **þe**, **hyll**); *Ragdale Barley field* 1708, 1708 (18) *Terrier*, ~ ~ ~ *hedge* 1703, 1708 (18), 1730, 1745 *ib* (*v.* **hecg**) (*v.* **bærlic**); *atte Welle* 1339 Pat (p) (*v.* **atte**, **wella**); *in le Wro* 1327 SR (p), *in the Wroo* 1395 *Ct* (p), 1397 *ib* (p) (*v.* **vrá**).

Hoton

HOTON

Hohtone 1086 DB
Holetone 1086 DB
Horton' c.1130 LeicSurv
Houtuna 1139 × 47 RegAnt (p), c.1180 (1411) Gilb, c.1200 Dane, *Houtun* l.12 *BHosp*, 1236 Fees, *Houtona* l.12 *GarCart*, c.1200 Dane, 1261 × 70 BM, (~ *iuxta Prestewald* 1261 × 70 ib), *Houton(')* l.12 *GarCart* (p), l.12 Dane, 1198 Fees, e.13 *GarCart et freq* to 1328 *MiD*, 1333 *GarCart et passim* to 1389, 1399 BM, (~ *iuxta Prestewold* 1369 Pat (p)), *Houtton* 1271 Ipm, 1292 ib (p)
Howeton c.1250, 1403 AD, 1451 Banco, (~ *iuxta Prestewald* c.1250 BM), *Howton* Hy 3 ib, 1377 SR (p) *et passim* to 1549 Pat, 1626 LML
Houghton 1370 Ipm, 1485 BM, 1630 LML, (~ *juxta Prestwould* 1630 ib), *Hoghton* 1375 Cl
Hotun' Hy 3 *Rut* (p), *Hooton'* 1258 Abbr, *Hotton* 1502 *MiscAccts*, 1541 MinAccts, *Hoton* 1539 Ipm, 1576 Saxton *et freq*, (~ *on-the-Hill* 1712 LML)

'The farmstead, village on the hill spur', *v.* **hōh, tūn**. Note the affixes with MLat *iuxta* 'next to' and *v.* Prestwold *infra*.

BARNSTAPLE HO., *Barnstaple house* 1877 White. BLACK-A-MOORS SPINNEY, *Blackmoor Spinny* 1836 O, *Blackamoore* 1871 *Plan*, *v.* **blæc, mōr**[1], **spinney**. THE COTTAGE. FAIRHOLME, 1925 Kelly. FALCON HO., *Falcon house* 1925 Kelly. FOX CROFT SPINNEY, *Fox Crafts* 1806 Map, *Fox Crofts* 1836 O, *Great ~ ~*, *Little ~ ~*, *Long ~ ~*, *Spinny Fox Croft* 1871 *Plan*, *v.* **fox, croft, spinney**. FURLONG'S BARN (2½"), cf. *the west long forlong* 1712 *Terrier*, *v.* **furlang**. GORSE FM, *the Gorse* 1759 *EnclA*, GORSE SPINNEY (2½") is *Hoton Spinney* 1806 Map, ~ *Spinny* 1836 O, 1871 *Plan* (*v.* **spinney**), cf. *Goss ground* 1735 *Map* (*v.* **grund**), *Goss Closes* 1793 *Deed*, *v.* **gorst**. HARTS FM. THE HOLLIES. HOLLYTREE HO., *Holly Tree house* 1877 White. HOTON HILLS, *Hoton Hill* 1806 Map, ~

Hills 1836 O, 1863, 1877 White, *Hooton hill* 1846 ib. HOTON HO., *Hoton house* 1877 White, 1925 Kelly. KING'S BRIDGE, KING'S BROOK is *the brucke* 1712 *Terrier*, *v.* **brōc**; with the surn. *King*. NEW COVERT, *v.* **cover(t)**. THE OLD PARSONAGE, 1925 Kelly, *v.* **personage**. PACKE ARMS INN, *Packe's Arms* 1846, 1863, 1877 White; *C.W. Packe* is lord of the manor 1846 ib. RIGGET'S SPINNEY, *Riggets Spinny* 1836 O, cf. *Rigget croft* 1871 *Plan* (*v.* **croft**), *v.* **riggett, spinney**; cf. Rickett's Spinney, Lei **2** 135. ST LEONARD'S CHURCH, *The Church* 1877 White; it is earlier recorded as *capellam de Houton* 1220 MHW (with MLat *capella* 'a chapel'). Note also *the Church yard* 1712, e.18 *Terrier*. VINE TERRACE.

FIELD-NAMES

Undated forms in (a) are 1871 *Plan*; 1760 are *EnclA* and 1793 are *Deed*. Forms throughout dated 1712 and e.18 are *Terrier*; 1735 are *Map*.

(a) Barn Cl; Bottom Acre (*v.* **æcer**); Far ~ ~, Near Bottom Cl; Bunlett, Bottom East ~, Bottom West Bunlett, West Top Bunlett (*v.* **bune, hlēt**); Calf Cl; Church Furlong (*v.* **furlang**), Nether Church Cl (*v.* St Leonard's Church *supra*); Churchmans Gorse (*v.* **gorst**; with the surn. *Churchman*, a reflex of OE *cyriceman* 'a custodian of a church'); Cow Cl; Croft (*v.* **croft**); East Cl; False Acres, Lacey's ~ ~, False Acre (*v.* **(ge)fall, æcer**; with the surn. *Lacey*); Far Cl; Fox Cl, Bottom Fox Furlong (*v.* **furlang**) (*v.* **fox**); Far ~ ~, Hill Cl 1871, Furrow Hill Cls 1793 (*v.* **furh**; poss. land scored with furrows for drainage); Home Cl (*v.* **home**); (the) Homestead 1793, 1871, Lane Homestead 1871 (*v.* **hām-stede**; the latter site has no trackway adjacent, so poss. with **leyne** 'a tract of arable land'); Hoton ~, Lings 1871, (the) Lings Common 1760 (*v.* **commun**) (cf. *atte Lynges* 1327 SR (p) (*v.* **atte**), *ling side* 1712 (*v.* **sīde**), *v.* **lyng**); House Cl, House Croft (*v.* **croft**), House Piece (*v.* **pece**); Lammas Cl (*v.* **lammas**); Little Cl; Little Mdw; Little Ewe Cl (*v.* **eowu**); Middle ~ ~, Top Long Furlong, Long Furlong Cl 1793, 1871, Long Furlong Mdw 1871 (*v.* **furlang**); Long Sick 1760 (cf. *long sick field* 1712, *v.* **sík**); Far ~ ~ ~, Long Side Cl, Long Side Mdw, Middle ~ ~, Top Long Side (*v.* **sīde**); Meadow (*the meadow* 1712), Meadow Side (*medow side* 1712, *v.* **sīde**); Middle Cl; Mill Hill Cl, Nether ~ ~, Mill Nook (*v.* **nōk**); Moonshine Cl (presum. a derogatory name for a close which appears promising but gives poor returns); Near Cl; the Pingle 1793 (*v.* **pingel**); the Pockets Mdw 1760, Socketts, ~ Cl (sic) 1871 (*v.* **poket**); Prestwold Lane End Shoot 1760 (*v.* **lane-ende, scēot**[3]; Prestwold adjoins to the south); Red Wong 1760 (*v.* **rēad, vangr**); Sanders (*long sanders* 1712, *v.* **sand, ears**); Sandhole, Middle Sandholes (*v.* **sand-hol**); the Sand Sick Cl 1793 (*the sand sick* 1712, *v.* **sand, sík**); Smallthorns, Bottom ~, Top Smallthorn (*smalthorns* 1712, *v.* **smæl, þorn**); Spitfire, ~ Cl (presum. a site where sparks flew, poss. a kiln or metal-working location); Dale ~ ~, Spring Cl (*v.* **dalr, spring**[1]); Sutters Cl (with the surn. *Sutters*, *v.* Reaney *s.n.*); Top Acre (*v.* **æcer**); Town Cl (*v.* **tūn**); Nether ~ ~, West ~ ~, Turnpike Cl, Bottom East ~ ~, Bottom West Turnpike Cl 1871, the Turnpike Road 1760 (*v.* **turnepike**); Water Furrows (*water *thorows* 1712, *v.* **wæter, furh** and *the Waterfurrow*(*e*)*s* in Asfordby f.ns. (b)); West Cl; Wimeswold Lower Cl (Wymeswold adjoins to the west).

(b) *bridely yate* 1712, *Bridle Gate Close* 1735 (*v.* **brigdels**, **gata**); *the common* 1712, *Hoton Common* 1735 (*v.* **commun**); *cots lane* 1712 (the road to Cotes which lies 1½ miles to the south-west); *great hedg* 1712 (*v.* **hecg**; presum. a major boundary marker); *John Kendalls close* 1712; *litel cot* 1712 (*v.* **lȳtel, cot**); *loughborow medow* 1712 (a meadow overlooking Loughborough which lies 3 miles to the south-west); *ye Middle feeld* e.18 (*v.* **middel, feld**; one of the great fields of the township, otherwise called *long sick field*, *v.* Long Sick *supra*); *miln yate* 1712 (*v.* **myln, gata**); *ye Nether feeld* e.18 (*v.* **neoðera, feld**; one of the great fields); *opher field* 1712, *ye Upper feeld* e.18 (*v.* **upper**, **feld**; one of the great fields); *Peg hill* 1712 (either with **pegge** 'a stump', perh. marking a boundary, or with the surn. *Pegg*); *the sick*(*e*) 1712, 1735 (*v.* **sík**); (*the*) *Tafts* 1712 (*v.* **toft**); *the nether* ~ ~, *the oper town leease* 1712 (*v.* **upper**) (*v.* **tūn, leys**); *the Well* 1712, *the Well field* 1712 (*v.* **feld**; one of the great fields, prob. to be identified with *ye Nether feeld*, *supra*) (*v.* **wella**); *Whitoths lane end* 1712 (*v.* **lane-ende**; with the surn. *Whitworth*).

Humberstone

Humberstone is now part of the Borough of Leicester.

HUMBERSTONE

Hvmerstane 1086 DB
Humberstan(e) c.1130 LeicSurv, Hy 2 Dugd, c.1150 BM *et passim* to l.13 *CRCart* bis, 1379, 1380 Pat, *Humbirstan'* l.13 *CRCart*, *Humbrestan'* Edw 1 *CroxR*, 1386 Hastings (p)
Humbrestein 1205 Cur (p), *Humbrestain* 1229 RHug bis, *Humb'stayn* c.1291 Tax
Humbristona 1190 × 1204 France, *Humbreston(e)* 1299 Ipm, 1338 Banco *et passim* to 1450, 1451 *Comp*, 1519 EpCB
Humberston(e) 1210 Cur, 1220 MHW *et passim* to 1294 Pat, 1306 *Hazlerigg* (freq) *et freq*, (~ *on-the-Hill* 1576 LEpis), *Humbirston'* 1359 *Rut* (p), 1374 *LCDeeds* (p), 1390 Misc, *Humburston(e)* 1373 *Rut* (p), 1377 *LCDeeds* (p), 1377 *Wyg* (p), 1419 Fine, 1459 *LCDeeds*

'Hūnbeorht's stone', *v.* **stān**. The township was named from a glacial erratic to the north of its site. It is uncertain whether the stone constituted a boundary marker for the Anglo-Saxon *Hūnbeorht*. It is the *Horston'* 1467 × 84 *LTD*, *Hooreston* 1601 *Terrier*, which may be interpreted as either 'the boundary stone' or simply 'the grey, hoar stone', *v.* **hār**^{2}, **stān** and Humber Stone *infra* for additional forms. Some 13th century spellings of the township's name show the influence of ON **steinn** 'a stone'.

BARKBY THORPE RD (BARKBY LANE 2½"), *Barkby Thorpe Road* 1789 *EnclA*; Barkby Thorpe adjoins to the north-west. BUSHBY BROOK, *the broke* 1601 *Terrier*, *the Brooke* 1638, 1698, 1712, 1724 *ib*, *the Brook* c.1730, 1742 *ib*; it is also *counsayle brooke* 1601 *ib*, *Counsel brooke* 1638 *ib*, *Counsell Brook(e)* 1698, 1712 *ib*, *Councell Brook* 1742 *ib*, *v.* **brōc** and Council Cl in f.ns. (a); Bushby lies 2 miles to the south-east. CHURCH FM, *v.* St Mary's Church *infra*. DALE HO. ELMS FM, ~ ~

COTTAGES, *the Elms* c.1730 *Terrier*, *v.* **elm**. FRANCIS DIXON LODGE. GIPSY LANE, *v.* **gipsy**. GRANGE LODGE, *v.* Humberstone Grange *infra*. GREEN LANE, *v.* **grēne**[1]. HAYNES RD, cf. *First ~ ~, Second Haynes' Close* 1861 *Plan*; with the surn. *Haynes*. HIGH MERES (2½") (lost), *the high meare* 1601, 1638 *Terrier*, *~ ~ Meer(e)* 1698, 1712, 1742 *ib*, *v.* **hēah**[1], **(ge)mǣre**; on the north-west boundary. HUMBER STONE is *Horston'* 1467 × 84 *LTD*, *Hooreston* 1601, 1698 *Terrier*, *Hoarestone* 1638 *ib*, *Horeston* 1658, 1712, 1724 *ib*, *Hoorstone* 1742 *ib* and *the great stone* 1671 *ib*; *v.* the discussion of the township's name *supra*. HUMBERSTONE FM, adjacent to Humber Stone. HUMBERSTONE GRANGE is *The Grange* 1877 White, *v.* **grange**. HUMBERSTONE HO. HUMBERSTONE MANOR is *Manor house* 1925 Kelly, *v.* **maner**. HUMBERSTONE PARK. KEYHAM LANE is *Keyham Road* 1789 *EnclA*; Keyham lies 3 miles to the east. MAIN ST is *the Common street* 1612 *Terrier*, *v.* **commun**. MANOR FM, *Manor farm* 1877 White, 1925 Kelly, *v.* Humberstone Manor *supra*. MARSTON RD, cf. *Marstuns gate* 1467 × 84 *LTD*, *v.* **gata** and Marston Mdw in f.ns (a). MELTON BROOK. NEW HUMBERSTONE. PAINTERS' ARMS (P.H.) (lost), *Painters' Arms* 1846 White. PLOUGH (P.H.) (lost), *Plough* 1846, 1863 White, *Old Plough* 1877 ib, *~ ~ Inn* 1925 Kelly. THE PORTWEY (sic), *(le) Portwey* 13 Nichols, 1467 × 84 *LTD*, *Portway* 1467 × 84 *ib*, *port waye* 1601 *Terrier*, *Port Way* 1638, 1698, 1712, 1724, 1742 *ib*, *v.* **port-weg**; the road to the market (town), i.e. Leicester; also styled *Portgate* 1467 × 84 *LTD*, *v.* **gata**. The present route is unrelated to the original and the name is a modern revival. QUAKESICK SPINNEY, *Quakesyke Spinney* 1870 *Sale*, *v.* **quake, sík, spinney** and *quakfyld sycke* in f.ns. (b). ST MARY'S CHURCH, *Church (St Mary)* 1846, 1863, 1877 White, 1925 Kelly; it is earlier recorded as *ecclesiam ~ ~, ecclesie de Humberston'* 1220 MHW, 1294, 1329 *Pat*, 1340 (c.1430), 1342 (c.1430), 1343 (c.1430) *KB*, *ecclesiam de Humberstan* 1241 RGros, and in the pairing *ecclesiarum de Evinton et Humberstane* 1318 *Pat*. Note also *the Church Yard* 1712 *Terrier*, 1789 *EnclA*, 1822 *Terrier*. SALTERSFORD RD, cf. *Saltersford Bridge* 1835 O, *v.* **saltere, ford**. SCRAPTOFT LANE, 1925 Kelly; it is *Scraptoffe gate* 1601 *Terrier*, *Scraptoft ~* 1612, 1638, 1698 *ib et passim* to 1890 *Plan*, *v.* **gata**; it is also *Scraptoft way* 1658 *Terrier* and *the Scraptoft Road* 1789 *EnclA*. STACK HOUSE FM (lost), *Stack House farm* 1877 White, *v.* **stakkr**, *Stakys* in f.ns. (b) and cf. Stackhouse, Ch **2** 69. STEINS LANE is *the Stean Road* 1890 *Plan*, *v.* Stean in f.ns. (a). THE TOWERS HOSPITAL. UPPINGHAM RD is *the Turnpike Road (from Leicester to Uppingham)* 1789 *EnclA*, 1822 *Terrier*, *v.* **turnepike**. THE VICARAGE, 1877 White, 1925 Kelly; it is *the Vicaridge House* 1712, 1724 *Terrier*, *~ Vicarage ~* 1822 *ib*, *v.* **vikerage**.

VICARAGE LANE. WIGLEY RD, 1890 *Plan*. WINDMILL (P.H.) (lost), *Windmill* 1846, 1863 White, ~ *Inn* 1877 ib, 1925 Kelly.

No early forms have been noted for the following Humberstone street-names: ABBOTS RD, ABBOTSFORD RD, AMYSON RD, ANEFORD RD, ARMADALE DRIVE, ARNCLIFFE RD, AUSTIN RISE, AVERIL AVE, BALE RD, BARBARA AVE, BECKETT RD, BRAYBROOKE RD, BRIGHTON RD, CARDINALS WALK, CARPE RD, CHESTNUT AVE, COLCHESTER RD, COLEMAN RD, COMPASS RD, DUDLEY AVE, DUNBAR RD, DUNHOLME RD, EASTBOURNE RD, EDGEHILL RD, ELMCROFT AVE, ESSEX RD, EXTON RD, FAIRFAX RD, FERN RISE, FREEMAN RD, GERVAS RD, GRANTHAM RD, GREENLAND DRIVE, HAMPDEN RD, HARTFIELD RD, HASTINGS RD, HAVENCREST DRIVE, HERTHUL RD, HUMBERSTONE DRIVE, HUNTINGDON RD, IRETON RD, KING EDWARD RD, LABURNUM RD, LAYTON RD, LEVERIC RD, LILAC AVE, LYDFORD RD, MALLORY PLACE, MARTIVAL, MERRIDALE RD, MORTON RD, NASEBY RD, NETHER HALL RD, NORTHFIELD RD, OCEAN RD, OVERTON RD, PADSTOW RD, THE PARKWAY, PEAKE RD, PERKYN RD, PETERS DRIVE, PINE TREE AVE, RADIANT RD, ST IVES RD, ST MARY'S AVE, SOMERS RD, STANLEY DRIVE, SWAINSON RD, TAILBY AVE, TAMAR RD, TENNIS COURT DRIVE, THURNCOURT RD, TOLCARN RD, TOMLIN RD, TRAFFORD RD, TURNER RD, UPPER HALL CL, VICTORIA RD, WINSLOW GREEN.

The following road-names are either lost or remain current only locally: *Agar's Lane* 1789 *EnclA* (cf. *Hannah Agar* 1789 *ib*); *Allsop's Lane* 1789 *EnclA* (cf. *Thomas Allsop* 1789 *ib*); *Ansty Lane* 1683, 1684 *Pochin* (Anstey lies 5 miles to the north-west); *Beeby Road* 1789 *EnclA* (Beeby lies 3 miles to the north-east); *Belgrave Road* 1789 *EnclA*, *Belgrave Gate* 1890 *Plan* (*v*. **gata**; Belgrave lies 2 miles to the north-west); *Bouchier Road* 1890 *Plan* (with the surn. *Bouchier*, *v*. Reaney *s.n.*); *the Church Lane* 1789 *EnclA*, 1822 *Terrier* (*v*. St Mary's Church *supra*); *Dalby's Lane* 1789 *EnclA* (with the surn. *Dalby* of a family originally either from Old Dalby, 11 miles to the north, or from Great ~, Little Dalby, 10 miles to the north-east); *Darbygate* 1467 × 84 *LTD*, 1658 *Terrier*, *Darby gate way* 1658 *ib* (*v*. **gata**; the road to Derby); *Evington Road* 1789 *EnclA* (Evington adjoins to the south-west); *Hartopp Road* 1890 *Plan* (with the surn. *Hartopp*); *Hawes's Lane* 1789 *EnclA* (cf. *Thomas Hawes* 1789 *ib*); *Laffelongs Road* 1890 *Plan* (*v*. Lafalong Cl in f.ns. (a)); *Leicester gate* 1601, 1698, 1712, 1724, 1742 *Terrier*, *Leicester Road* 1789 *EnclA* (*v*. **gata**; the road to Leicester); *Lewitt's Lane* 1789 *EnclA* (with the surn. *Lewitt*, cf. *Lewitt's House* 1789 *ib*); *the mylne waye* 1601 *Terrier*, (*the*)

Mill way 1638, 1698, 1712, 1742 *ib* (*v.* **myln, weg**; the track to the windmill in the North Fd); *Norman's Lane or Thurnby Road* 1789 *EnclA* (cf. *John Norman* 1789 *ib*; Thurnby lies 2 miles to the south-east); *Thurmaston Road* 1789 *EnclA* (Thurmaston lies 2 miles to the north-west); *Warner's Lane* 1789 *EnclA* (cf. *Thomas Warner* 1658 *Terrier*); *Wodegate* 1467 × 84 *LTD* (*v.* **wudu, gata**).

FIELD-NAMES

Forms in (a) dated 1788 are *Pochin*; 1789 are *EnclA*; 1822 are *Terrier*; 1830 are *Surv*; 1861, 1875, 1890 and 1919 are *Plan*; 1870 are *Sale*. Forms throughout dated 1467 × 84 are *LTD*; 1601, 1612, 1638, 1658, 1671, 1698, 1709, 1712, 1724, c.1730 and 1742 are *Terrier*; 1603 × 25, 1640, 1663, 1666, 1672, 1683 and 1684 are *Pochin*.

(a) Agar's Homestead 1789 (*v.* **hām-stede**; cf. *Hannah Agar* 1789); Bottom Cl 1875; Bottom Piece 1830 (*v.* **pece**); Bowman's Bush Furlong 1830 (*v.* **furlang**) (*bowman bushe* 1601, *Bowmans bush* 1638, 1698, 1712, *Bowman's* ~ 1742, *v.* **busc**; with the surn. *Bowman*); Big ~ ~, Little Bright's Cl 1870 (with the surn. *Bright*); Broad Mdw 1830 (*broadmedowe* 1612, *v.* **brād, mǣd (mǣdwe** obl.sg.)); the Brook 1789 (1612, *the Brooke* 1601, 1658, 1712, 1724, *v.* **brōc**; forming the northern boundary of the parish); Butt Leys 1789 (*v.* **butte, leys**); Council Cl 1788, 1789 (*counsayle* 1601, *Counsell* 1612, 1712, *Counsail* 1638, *Councell* 1742, *the Councell or the Councell Close* 1640, 1663, 1666, 1672, *the Councell Closes* 1683, 1684, cf. *counsayle layes* 1601, *Counsel leyes* 1638, 1698, *Counsell leys* 1712 (*v.* **leys**), *v.* **counsayl** (from OFr *conseil* 'consultation, deliberation'); evidently land subject to tenure by lot or to exploitation by agreement); Crabtre Furlong Cl 1830 (*the Crabtree furlong* c.1730, *v.* **crabtre, furlang**); the Cunnery 1789, the Coneygries 1822 (*the Great(e)* ~ ~, *the Little Conygree Close* 1603 × 25, 1666, *the Greate* ~ ~, *the Little Coningree Close* 1663, *the Great* ~ ~, *the Little Coneygrey Close* 1683, 1684, *the Conneygree furlonge* 1658, *Cunnery furlong* c.1730 (*v.* **furlang**), *the Cunnyngree meare* 1601, *the Cuningry Meer* 1638, *the Congree Meere* 1698, *Connigree Meer* 1712, *the Connagree mere* 1724, *Cunnigry Meere* 1742 (*v.* **(ge)mǣre**), *v.* **coningre**); Dalby Stile Furlong 1830 (*v.* **stig, furlang**; with the surn. *Dalby*, cf. *Dalby's Lane*, *supra*); Dock Wong 1919 (*v.* **docce, vangr**); Dove's Wong 1830 (*douewong* 1601, 1638, *Dove wonge* 1658, 1712, *Dove Wong* 1698, 1724, 1742, *Doves Wonge* c.1730 (*v.* **vangr**; prob. with the surn. *Dove*, *v.* Reaney *s.n.*; its source, the ON fem. pers.n. *Dúfa* (OE pers.n. *Dūfe*), is less likely); Elder Stump Furlong 1830 (*v.* **furlang**) (*Elderstob*, *Eldurstob* 1467 × 84, *elderstubbes* 1601, *Elder Stubbs* 1638, 1698, 1712, 1742, *v.* **ellern, stubb**); Flint Hills 1788 ((*the*) *flintinges* 1601, 1612, *flyntinges* 1601, (*the*) *Flintings* 1638, 1698, 1712, 1724, 1742, *the nether*~, *the over flintings* 1658 (*v.* **uferrra**), *v.* **flint**; with **-ing**^{2} or **eng**); Foot Road Cl 1830 (*v.* **foot-road**); Gravel Pit Cl 1830 (*v.* **gravel, pytt**); Great Cl 1875; Great Wong 1919 (*v.* **vangr**); East ~ ~, West Green Hill 1830 (*Grenhyll*, *Greynel* 1467 × 84, *greine hills* 1601, *greenhills*

1612, 1724, c.1730, *greenehill* 1638, 1698, *greenhill* 1712, 1724, 1742, *under greenhills* 1612 (a furlong so called), *greene hills furlonge* 1658 (*v.* **furlang**), *Greynel buskys* 1467 × 84 (*v.* **buskr**), *greine hyll slade* 1601, *Greenehill* ~ 1638, 1658, 1698, *Greenhill* ~ 1658, 1712, 1724, c.1730, 1742 (*v.* **slæd**), *v.* **hyll**; the first el. may well be **grein** rather than **grēne**[1]); Half Roods 1919 (*v.* **half, rōd**[3]); Hell Hole 1861 (c. 1730, *v.* **hell, hol**[1]; in f.ns., a frequent term of disparagement for uninviting ground, sometimes referring to damp hollows or to poor scrubland, *v.* Field 40); Hingings Furlong 1788 (*v.* **furlang**) (*Heyngyng'* bis, *Heynggyng'* 1467 × 84 bis, *Hingings* c.1730, *further* ~, *hither* ~, *hanging(e)s* 1601, 1638, 1698, 1712, 1742, *under hangings* 1712, 1742, *v.* **hangende, hengjandi**); Hollow Combs 1830 (1712, 1724, c.1730, *Hollow combes* 1601, 1638, 1698, 1742, ~ *comes* 1612, *Hollycombe Leys* c.1730 (*v.* **leys**), *v.* **holh, cumb**); Home Cl 1830 (*v.* **home**); Kilby's Cl 1789 (*Daniel Kilby* is cited 1789; the *Kilby* family came originally from the village of this name, 6 miles to the south); Lafalong Cl, Lafalong Furlong 1830 (*Lawfurlong* 1467 × 84, 1698, 1712, 1724, 1742, *Lawfurlands* 1601, 1712, 1742, *law ferlong* 1638, *Lawe furlongs furlonge* (sic) 1658, *Lawforland* 1698, *Lafferlong Furlong* c.1730, *hyther lawfurlands* 1601, *hither Lawforlands* 1698 (*v.* **hider**), *Schortlawfurlong'* 1467 × 84 (*v.* **sc(e)ort**), *Lawfurlong buskes*, *Lawfurlang' buskys* 1467 × 84, *Lawfurlands bushes* 1601, *Lawfurlong* ~ 1712, 1724, 1742, *Lafferlong* ~ c.1730 (*v.* **buskr, busc**), *Laufurlongfelde* 1467 × 84 (*v.* **feld**; one of the early great fields of the township), *v.* **la(g)h, furlang**); Little Piece 1830 (*v.* **pece**); Little Wong 1919 (*v.* **vangr**); Marston Mdw 1788, 1789 (*Merston'* 1467 × 84 bis, *ne(a)ther* ~, *over Marson* 1601, 1612, 1638, 1698, 1712, 1742, *neather* ~, *upper Marston* 1724, c.1730 (*v.* **neoðera, uferra**), *v.* **mersc, tūn**; note the typical Leics. 17th cent. loss of *t* in the group *-ston*; a lost settlement, *v.* Marston Rd *supra*); Mill Cl 1788 ((*the*) *myln close* 1601, (*the*) *Mill Close* 1638, 1666 *et passim* to 1742, *v.* **myln**; relating to a windmill north of the township); East ~ ~, West ~ ~, Nether Moor Leys 1830 (*the Mor* 1467 × 84, *Moreleys* 1467 × 84, *moore layes* 1601, *moorelees* 1612, *Moore Leys* 1638, c.1730, *Mooreleyes* 1698, *Moor Leys* 1712, 1742, *more lays* 1724, *Moore leys* (*short*) *furlonge* 1658 (*v.* **furlang**), *v.* **mōr**[1], **lǣs**); the Nether End Middle Fd 1789 (*the nether end of Humberston* 1658, 1742, *the neather end* 1742, *the neather ende fyld* 1601, *the Neather end feild* 1638, 1671, *the Neither end feilde* 1658, *the Netherend feild* 1666, *the Nether end Field* 1709) (*the nether end midlefeild* 1658, *the Middle Field in the neither end* 1698, *the Neather end Middle Feild* 1712, c.1730, *the middle feild in the neather end* 1724, 1742), Nether End North Fd 1789 (*the north fyld* 1601, ~ ~ *feild(e)* 1612, 1638, 1724, ~ ~ *Field* c.1730, *the nether end North feild* 1658, c.1730, *the North Field neather end* 1698, *the north feild in the neather end* 1724, 1742), the Nether End North Mdw 1788 ((*the*) *north meadow* 1601, 1671, 1698, 1712, 1742, *the Northe Meadowe* 1638, 1658, *the neather end North Meadow* 1658, 1712, *the north meadow in the neather end* 1742, cf. *Northmedowgate*, *Northmydowgate* 1467 × 84 (*v.* **gata**), *Northmedowgatesyde* 1467 × 84 (*v.* **sīde**), *North Meadow(e) Hill* 1638, 1658 *et passim* to 1742, *north middow hill* 1724, *North meadow hillside* 1638, 1698, 1712, 1742 (*v.* **sīde**), *v.* **norð, mǣd (mǣdwe** obl.sg.)), Nether End South Fd 1789 (*the South feild neither end* 1698, ~ ~ ~ *neather end* 1724, c.1730, *the South Neather End Feild* 1712) (cf. *the nether end west feild* 1658) (*v.* **neoðera, ende**); the Nether Orchard 1788; Newdales Furlong 1788 (*v.* **furlang**), the Noodles 1870 (*Newdal'* 1467 × 84, *Newdales* 1467 × 84, 1601, 1638 *et passim* to 1742, ~ *furlonge* 1658 (*v.* **furlang**), *v.* **nīwe, deill**); Pease Croft 1789 (*v.* **croft**), Pease Cl 1830 (*v.* **pise**); the

Pinfold 1789 (*v.* **pynd-fald**); Pitch Gaps 1919 (*v.* **piche, gap**); Pochins Wong 1830 (*v.* **vangr**; with the surn. *Pochin*); Quakesyke Mdw 1830 (*quaksick* 1612, *Quakesick* c.1730, *Quacksi(c)k furlonge* 1658 (*v.* **furlang**), *Quacksick furry(e) leys* 1658 (*v.* **fyrs, -ig**[3], **leys**), *Quacksick(e) gutter* 1638, 1658, 1724, *Quakesike* ~ 1698, 1712, *Quakesick Gutter* c.1730, 1742 (*v.* **goter**), *Quakesick(e) hill* 1638, 1698, 1712, 1742, *Quacksick partinge grasse* 1658 (*v.* **parting, græs**), *Quakesick Penn* c.1730 (*v.* **penn**[2]), cf. *Quakefeild* 1612, *quak feild furrs* 1612 (*v.* **fyrs**), *Quake fyld gutter* 1601 (*v.* **goter**), *Quakefyld hill* 1601, *Quakefeld(e) syke* 1467 × 84, *quakfyld sycke* 1601, *Quakefeild sick(e)* 1638, 1712, *Quakefield sick* 1742 (*v.* **sík**), *Quakefield side* 1698 (*v.* **sīde**) (*v.* **feld**; one of the early great fields), *Quacke feyne* 1467 × 84, *Quakefeynsyke* 1467 × 84 (*v.* **fenn, sík**), *v.* **quake**); Ravens Bush 1830 (1712, 1724, c.1730, *Rauens bush* 1601, 1638, *Raven* ~ 1698, *Raven's Bush* 1742 (*v.* **busc**; prob. with the surn. *Raven* rather than with its sources, the pers.ns. OE *Hræfn*/ON *Hrafn*; or else with the bird OE **hræfn**/ON **hrafn** 'a raven'); Rick Leys 1861 (*v.* **hrēac, leys** and *the Ricke place* in f.ns. (b)); Roads Cl 1830; Roborough Cl 1830 (*Rowbaro* 1467 × 84 bis, *Rowborow* 1601, 1638, 1712, 1724, *Rowburrow* 1612, *Rowborrough*, *Roughborrough* 1638, *Rowborough*, *Rowboroue*, *Rowborow(e)* 1698, *Rober*, *Roeborow* c.1730, *backeside Rowburrow* 1612, *the backside (of) Rowborow* 1712, 1724, 1742 (*v.* **bak-side**; a furlong thus called), *Rowbor(r)ough furlonge* 1658 (*v.* **furlang**), *Rowborrow syde* 1601, *Rowborough side* 1638, *Rowborow Side* 1742 (*v.* **sīde**), *Rowbarosyke* 1467 × 84 (*v.* **sík**), *v.* **rūh**[1], **berg**); Sand Hill 1789 (*Sand Hills* c.1730, *Sandhill furlonge* 1658 (*v.* **furlang**), *v.* **sand**); Seed Cl 1919 (*v.* **sǣd**; in f.ns. often used of areas of sown grass); Sibson's Cottage 1830 (with the surn. *Sibson* of a family originally from the village of this name, 23 miles to the west); Slade 1861 (*le Slade, the Slade* 1467 × 84), Slade Cl 1830 (cf. *Slademere*, *Slademore* 1467 × 84, *v.* **mere**[1], **mōr**[1]) (*v.* **slæd**); Bottom ~ ~, Top Long Slings 1861 (*Longslings* ~, *Longslyngs furlonge* 1658 (*v.* **furlang**), *v.* **sling**); South Mdw 1789 (*suthmede* Hy 3 *Crox*, *suthmedwe* Edw 1 *ib*, 1477 (e.16) *Charyte*, *the South meadow* 1671, *v.* **sūð, mǣd (mǣdwe** obl.sg.)); Stean 1919 (*Stayne* 1601, 1638, 1698, *Steane* 1698, 1712, 1742, *Staine* 1712, 1742, cf. *Stayne hedge* 1601 (*v.* **hecg**; a boundary hedge), Stean Gutter Furlong 1919 (*v.* **furlang**) (*stayne(s) gutter* 1601, 1638, *Staines gutter* 1698, 1742, *v.* **goter**), Steen Mdw 1830 (*Stayne meadow(e)* 1601, 1612, 1638, 1698, *Staine Meadow* 1712, 1742), Steens Cl 1830 (*v.* **steinn** and Steins Lane *supra*); Swan's Orchard 1789 (*Swans Orchard* 1683, 1684; cf. *John Swann* 1601); Thurmaston Gate 1861 (*v.* **gata**; Thurmaston lies 2½ miles to the north-west); Top Cl 1875; Upper End East Fd 1789 (*the over end or upper end* 1672 (*v.* **uferra**), *the Upper End* 1698, 1742, *the upper end feild* 1640, 1658, 1698), the Upper End South Fd 1789 (1698, 1712, 1742, *the South fyld* 1601, ~ ~ *feild* 1601, 1638, 1671, ~ ~ *Field* c.1730) (cf. *the Upper End Mill Feild* 1712, *the upper end field called the Milne Field* 1742 (*v.* **myln**), *the Upper End North Feild* 1698, 1712, 1742, *the North feild* 1671, *the Upper End North Meadow* 1712) (*v.* **upper, ende**); Widdowson's Cl 1789 (with the surn. *Widdowson*); Wissen Nook 1830 (*v.* **nōk**; prob. with a shortened form of the surn. *Widdowson*); The Workhouse 1789 (*v.* **workhouse**).

(b) *le Barnecroft* 1477 (e.16) *Charyte* (*v.* **bern, croft**); *Baulk Furlong* c.1730 (*v.* **balca, furlang**); *Bayles thing* 1555 Pat (*v.* **thing**; with the surn. *Bayles*, *v.* Reaney *s.n.*); *Belgraue hedge* 1601, 1638, *Belgrave* ~ 1612, 1658 *et passim* to 1742 (*v.* **hecg**; a parish boundary with Belgrave which adjoins to the north-west); *Bentlys backe side* 1698, *Bentleys backside* 1712, *Bentley's* ~ 1742 (*v.* **bak-side**), *Joseph Bentlys* *headland* 1698, *Jos. Bently's hadland*, *Bentleys* ~ 1712, *Bentley's* ~ 1742 (*v.* **hēafod-land**), *Bentlys penn* 1698, 1712, *Bentley's* ~ 1742 (*v.* **penn**[2]); *Blakemilde*, *Blakmylde*, *Blakmyled* 1467 × 84, *blackmyles* 1601, *Blakemiles* 1638, 1698, c.1730, *Blackmiles* 1712, 1724, 1742 (*v.* **blæc**, **mylde**); *Mr Booses laye* 1601 (*v.* **ley**); *breeches* 1612, *breach layes* 1601, *breechlees* 1612, *Breach leyes* 1638, 1671, 1698, ~ *leys* 1712, 1742 (*v.* **leys**) (*v.* **brēc**); *the bridge* 1601, 1612 *et passim* to 1742, ~ ~ *upon the common pasture* 1638, *the brydge upon the common pasture* 1601 (*v.* **brycg** and *the common pasture*, *infra*; the bridge lay to the north of the township); *Broadarses* 1601, 1712, 1742, *broad arsse* 1638, *Broadarse* 1698 (*v.* **brād**, **ears**); *Brokenback(e)s* 1601, 1638, 1698, 1712, *Brokenback* 1742, *broken backe furlonge* 1671 (*v.* **furlang**) (*v.* **brocen**, **bæc**; either a derogatory name for intractable land or referring to a ridge which had been broken up for cultivation); *Brokfurlong* 1467 × 84, (*the*) *Brooke furlonge* 1601, 1638, 1658, 1671, 1698, *Brook furlong* 1712, 1742 (*v.* **furlang**), *Broksyde* 1467 × 84 (*v.* **sīde**) (*v.* **brōc**); *the Bull peice* 1601, 1638, 1712, 1742, ~ ~ *peece* 1724 (*v.* **bula**, **pece**); *Wylliam Butterye hadland* 1601 (*v.* **hēafod-land**); *Calforthehey* 1467 × 84 (*v.* **ford**, **(ge)hæg**; the first el. could be **cald** or **calf** or **calu**); *Catts dirt Hadland* c.1730 (*v.* **drit**, **hēafod-land**; with the surn. *Catt*); *Mary Chamberlyns Lay* 1601 (*v.* **ley**), *Thomas Chamberlyns hadland* 1601, *Tho. Chamberlanes* ~ 1638 (*v.* **hēafod-land**); *Doctor Chippingdales hadland* 1601, 1638 (*v.* **hēafod-land**), ~ ~ *Ricke place* 1601 (*v.* **hrēac**, **place**) (Dr Chippingdale was a Prebendary of Lincoln Cathedral, *v.* Billson 167, 172); *Church Hadlands*, *Church Hadland Furlong* c.1730 (*v.* **furlang**) (*v.* **hēafod-land** and St Mary's Church *supra*); *Collwell hedge* 1612, ~ ~ *furlong(e)* 1658, c.1730, *Collinge hedge furlonge* 1671 (*v.* **hecg**, **furlang**; these names evidently refer to the same feature and presum. the first word is the surn. *Collwell*, *v.* Reaney *s.n.*); *the Common* 1612 (*v.* **commun**); *the Common pasture* 1601, 1638 *et passim* to 1742 (*v.* **commun**, **pasture**); *cowe gates* 1601, *Cowgate* 1638, 1698, *Cow Gate* 1712, 1742, *Cowgates furlonge* 1671 (*v.* **furlang**) (*v.* **cowgate** 'pasturage for a single cow'); *the Cow pasture* 1658, 1698 (*v.* **pasture**); (*the*) *Croft'* 1467 × 84, *Craftes* 1601, 1612, *Crafts* 1638, *Croft(e)s* 1638, 1698, 1712, c.1730, 1742, *Neither* ~ ~, *Over Crafts furlonge* 1658 (*v.* **neoðera**, **uferra**, **furlang**) (*v.* **croft**); *the Crooks* c.1730 (*v.* **krókr**); *Crosons hadland* 1601, 1638, ~ *headland* 1698, *Mr Crosons Hadland* 1712, 1742, *Croxtons headland* 1724, *Croson's hadland* 1742 (*v.* **hēafod-land**), *the Backside Mr Crosons Close* c.1730 (*v.* **bak-side**), *Mr Croson's Homestead* c.1730 (*v.* **hām-stede**), *Thomas Crosons yards end* 1658 (*v.* **geard**, **ende**) (a *Thomas Croson* is cited in 1601 and 1638; the *Croson/ Croxton* family prob. came originally from South Croxton, 4 miles to the north-east, rather than from Croxton Kerrial, 20 miles to the north-east in Framland Hundred; *v.* South Croxton for typical Leics. 17th cent. loss of *t* in p.ns. in the group *-ston* which the surn. exemplifies); *dale schyte* 1601 (*v.* **dalr**, **scyte**); *the Dalke* 1467 × 84, *the Dawke* 1638, 1698, *the dauke* 1712, 1724, *the Dawks* 1742, *the Dawckes furlonge* (*v.* **furlang**) (*v.* **dalk**); *Dallislade* 1638, 1698, 1742, *dallyslade* 1712 (*v.* **slæd**; earlier forms are needed for the first el.; if an early name, then the OE pers.n. *D(e)alla* is poss., but a late formation with the verb *dally* 'to flirt, to wanton' may allude to a lovers' trysting place); *Darby gate furlonge* 1658 (*v.* **furlang** and *Darbygate*, *supra*); *Dewell* 1601, 1638, *Dewells* 1712, *the backe syde of Dewell* 1601 (*v.* **bak-side**), *further* ~, *hyther dewell* 1601, *H(a)ither Dewell* 1638, 1698, 1712, 1742 (*v.* **hider**), *nether dewell*, ~ *duell* 1612, *great dewell furlonge* 1671 (*v.* **furlang**) (*v.* **dēaw**, **wella**); *above the Dikes* 1658, *the furlonge abutting on the Dike* 1658 (*v.* **dík**);

(*Beneath*) *the Ditch* 1712, 1724, c.1730, 1742 (*v.* **dīc**); *double hedges* 1601, (*the*) *Double hedge furlonge* 1658 (*v.* **furlang**) (*v.* **duble, hecg**; cf. (*a furlong called*) *against Double Hedges* in Sileby f.ns. (b)); *Dowsewong* 1467 × 84 (*v.* **douse, vangr**); *Dowwongus, Schortdowwongus* 1467 × 84 (*v.* **sc(e)ort**) (these forms may belong with the previous f.n., otherwise *v.* **vangr**; with either a first el. ME **dowe** 'dough' used to describe the nature of the enclosure's soil in wet conditions, or the surn. *Dow*(*e*), either a pet form of David (*v.* Reaney *s.n.*) or a nickname for a baker, cf. *Willielmus Dugh'* 1327 SR of Leics.); *drye layes* 1601, *dryleayes* 1612, *dry ley*(*e*)*s* 1638, 1698, 1712, 1724, *Dry*(*e*) *leys furlonge* 1658 (*v.* **furlang**) (*v.* **drȳge, leys**); *the east fyld called the mylnefyld* 1601, *the East feild* 1671 (*v. the Mylnfelde, infra*); *Evington fyld syde* 1601, *~ feild side* 1638, *E*(*a*)*vington field side* 1698, 1742 (*v.* **feld, sīde**; Evington adjoins to the south-west); *the Flatt* c.1730 (*v.* **flat**); *Flaxlond* 1467 × 84, *flaxeland* 1724, *Flaxlandbalk'* 1467 × 84, *flaxland balke* 1601, *flaxelande baulke* 1638, *Flaxen baulke* 1658, *Flaxton Baulk* (sic) c.1730 (*v.* **balca**) (*v.* **fleax, land**); *Flynty aboue the gate, Flynty be nethe the gate* 1467 × 84 (*v.* **aboven, benethe, gata**), *Flynty be nethe the wey* 1467 × 84 (*v.* **weg**) (*v.* **flinti**); *Fulwel, Fulwell', Fulweyle* 1467 × 84, *Fullwell*(*e*) 1612, 1712, *Fullwells* 1724, 1742, *Fulwell fyrrys* 1467 × 84 (*v.* **fyrs**), *Fulwelgate* 1467 × 84 (*v.* **gata**), *fulwell slade* 1601, 1638, *Fullwell ~* 1658, 1698 *et passim* to 1742 (*v.* **slæd**) (*v.* **fūl, wella**); *the Fulus* 1467 × 84, *the Fulls* 1601, 1612 *et passim* to 1742, *the fullus vnder the Croft'* 1467 × 84 (*v. the Croft', supra*) (*v.* **fūl**; the adj. is here used as a sb. in the plural); *Furry leyes furlonge* 1671 (*v.* **fyrs, -ig**[3]**, leys, furlang**); *Gauthernes hadland* 1601, *Gawthornes ~* 1638 (*v.* **hēafod-land**), *Gauthernes hadlaye* 1601 (*v.* **headley**) (*Thomas Gautherne* is cited 1601); *the goares* 1601, 1638, 1698, 1712, *the goores* 1724, *the gores furlonge* 1658, *the Goare Furlong* 1742 (*v.* **furlang**) (*v.* **gāra**); *Goose Nook*(*e*) 1683, 1684 (*v.* **gōs, nōk**); *the Gutter* 1638, 1698, 1712 (*v.* **goter**); *the Hadley Hade* (sic) c.1730 (*v.* **headley, hēafod**); *Little Hairston* c.1730, *Little Horston Hadland* c.1730 (*v.* **hēafod-land**) (*v.* **hār**[2]**, stān**; it is uncertain whether these f.ns. relate to Humber Stone); *the Hall* 1612, *the Hall land* 1658, *the Hall Meadows* 1658, *the hall sycke* 1601, *the Hall sick*(*e*) 1612, 1638, 1712, 1742 (*v.* **sík**), *the hall two yard lands* 1663, *~ ~ three ~ ~* 1666 (*v.* **yardland**) (*v.* **hall**); *hammelton hedge* 1601, *Hambleton ~* 1638, 1698, 1712, 1742 (*v.* **hecg**; a parish boundary marker), *hammelton hole* 1601, *Hamelton ~* 1612, *Hambleton ~* 1638, 1698, 1712, 1742 (*v.* **hol**[1]) (Hamilton adjoins to the north-east); *handsell* 1601, *Hansill* 1638, 1698, 1712, 1742, *Hansell furlonge* 1671 (*v.* **furlang**) (*v.* **hyll**; with the surn. *Hand*, *v.* Reaney *s.n.*); *Hardhurst* 1467 × 84 (*v.* **heard, hyrst**); *the Harp Leys* c.1730 (*v.* **hearpe, leys**; triangular units of grassland); *Harris leyes* 1638, 1698, *~ leys* 1712, 1742 (*v.* **leys**), *Harris penn* 1698, 1712, *~ pen* 1742 (*v.* **penn**[2]), *harris wyllowes* 1601 (*v.* **wilig**) (cf. *Thomas Harris* 1601, *John Harris* 1742); *hartclyffe* 1601, *Hartcliffe* 1612, 1638, 1698, 1712, 1742, *the backesyde of hartclyffe* 1601, *the Backside Hartcliffe* 1712, *the backside of Hartcliff* 1742 (*v.* **bak-side**), *Hartcliffe foote* 1612 (*v.* **fōt**) (*v.* **clif**; prob. with **heard, harðr** rather than with **heort**); *hauses hadland* 1601, *Hawes headland* 1698, *~ hadland* 1742 (*v.* **hēafod-land**; cf. *William Hause* 1601 and *William Hawes Churchwarden* 1698); *the hempe pyttes* 1601, *ye Hemppits* 1638, *Flempit*(*t*)*s* (sic) 1712, 1724, 1742 (*v.* **hænep, pytt**); *Hewet hadland, ~ hadlond* 1467 × 84 (*v.* **hīewet, hēafod-land**); *Mr Higgs Headland* 1698, *~ ~ Hadland* 1712, 1742 (*v.* **hēafod-land**), *Mr Higgs Rickplace* 1742 (*v.* **hrēac, place**); *the Homestall* 1612 (*v.* **hām-stall**); *the Homestead* 1712 (*v.* **hām-stede**; belonging to *the Vicaridge House*); *horeston* *furlonge* 1658 (*v.* **furlang** and Humber Stone *supra*); *Houghton furlonge* 1658 (*v.* **furlang**; with the surn. *Houghton* of a family prob. originally from Houghton on the Hill, 4 miles to the south-east); *howson close ende* 1601, *Howsons Close end* 1638 (*v.* **ende**), *howsens penne* 1601, *Howsons pen* 1638 (*v.* **penn**[2]) (with the surn. *Howson*, *v.* Reaney *s.n.*); *Johnsons Close* 1612, *Johnsons headland* 1698, ~ *Hadland* 1712, *Johnson's Hadland* 1742 (*v.* **hēafod-land**), *Johnson's leys* 1742 (*v.* **leys**) (with the surn. *Johnson*); *Ketylsacur*, *Keytylsacur* 1467 × 84, *Kettlesacre* 1601, 1638, 1698, 1712, c.1730, *Kettleacre* 1724, 1742, *Kettell's Acre* 1742, *Kettlesacre furlonge* 1658 (*v.* **furlang**) (*v.* **æcer**; with the ON pers.n. *Ketill*); *kinges hedge* 1601, *Kings* ~, 1698, 1712, 1724, *King's* ~ 1742, *Kings hedge furlonge* 1658, c.1730 (*v.* **furlang**) (*v.* **hecg**; with the surn. *King*); *the Kombys* 1467 × 84 (*v.* **cumb**); *Kyrk(e)hadlond'* 1467 × 84 (*v.* **kirkja, hēafod-land**); *kyrkdales* 1601, *Kirkdales* 1638, 1698, 1712, 1742, *Kirkedales furlonge* 1671 (*v.* **furlang**) (*v.* **kirkja, deill**) (*v.* St Mary's Church *supra*); *Langfurlong*, *Longfurlong'* 1467 × 84, *Long(e) furlong(e)* 1601, 1612 *et passim* to 1742, *longe furlonge leys* 1658 (*v.* **leys**) (*v.* **lang**[1], **furlang**; in the Nether End North Fd); *Mr Law's Hadland* 1712, *Laws headland* 1724 (*v.* **hēafod-land**); *ye Leyes* 1638, *the layes* 1698, *the Leys* 1712, 1742, *the Lays* 1724 (*v.* **leys**); *Litlemede* c.1240 Berkeley, *Lytul medo syde* 1467 × 84 (*v.* **sīde**) (*v.* **lȳtel, mǣd (mǣdwe** obl.sg.)); *Long Shoot* c.1730 (*v.* **scēot**[3]); (*on*) *Longton* 1612 (perh. a lost farmstead (*v.* **lang**[1], **tūn**), although the late spelling may disguise a name with **dūn** as the generic); *Lowton'* 1467 × 84 (*v.* **hlāw, tūn**; a lost farmstead); *lytleinges* 1601, *Littleling* 1638, *little ling* 1698, *Littleing* 1712, 1742, *Littling* 1742 (*v.* **lȳtel, lítill, eng**); (*in*) *Luffnam* c.1730 (this may be a very early name in **hām**; the first el. is the OE pers.n. *Luffa* in the possessive case (i.e. *Luffan*), cf. Luffenham, 18 miles to the east in Rutland and the lost *Luffewyke* (in Manton), 15 miles to the east, also in Rutland; the group may record the same Anglo-Saxon magnate (cf. *Wīgmund* of Wymeswold and Wymondham, 16 miles apart in north Leics.); if not a name with *hām* as the generic, then less likely **hamm**); *Mannsfyld slade* 1601, *Mansfeild* ~ 1658 (*v.* **slæd**), *Mansfeild Sick furlonge* 1658 (*v.* **sík, furlang**) (poss. with the surn. *Mansfield* of a family originally from the township of this name, 35 miles to the north in Notts.(note *John Mansfield* who was Mayor of Leicester in 1815 and its M.P. 1818–26, *v.* Mansfield St and the tavern-name Mansfield's Head, Lei **1** 48 and 132); but 'a field belonging to the community, a common field' (*v.* **(ge)mǣnnes, feld**) is poss. because of the early date of the name's compounding with *slæd*); *Mawnsell*, *Mawnsill* 1467 × 84 (*v.* **hyll**; the first el. is poss. the OE pers.n. *Mann*, with typical AN *aun* for *an*); *Maydens well* 1601, 1638, 1698, *Maidens* ~ 1712, *Maiden's* ~ 1742 (*v.* **mægden, wella**); *Midulfelde*, *Mydulfelde* 1467 × 84 (*v.* **middel, feld**; one of the early great fields); *the Mires* c.1730 (*v.* **mýrr**); *Money holes furlonge* 1671 (*v.* **hol**[1], **furlang**; poss. an allusion to the discovery of a coin hoard); *Moyses Close* 1640, 1663, 1666, 1683, 1684 (with the surn. *Moyse*); *the mylne* 1601, *the Mill* 1638, 1698, 1712, 1742, (*the*) *Mylnfelde* 1467 × 84, *the mylnefyld* 1601, *the ouer end feild called the milne feild* 1638, *the Milne Field* 1698 (*v.* **feld**; one of the early great fields of the township, referring to a windmill, *v. the ouer end feild*, *infra*), *the mylne meare* 1601, *the mil meere* 1638, (*the*) *Mill Meer(e)* 1698, 1712, 1742 (*v.* **mere**[1]), *the milne meddow* 1638 (*v.* **myln**); *the netherfeild* 1638, *the neather feild* 1698, 1712, ~ ~ *field* 1742 (*v.* **neoðera, feld**); (*the*) *Neather furlong(e)* 1601, 1638 *et passim* to 1742 (*v.* **neoðera, furlang**; i.e. of the North Fd); *the old milne hill* 1612 (*v.* **ald, myln**); *Omber layes* 1601, ~ *leyes* 1638, 1698, ~ *leys* 1712, 1742 (*v.* **leys**; with **omore**, prob. 'the bunting', cf. dial. *yellow-omber* 'the yellow-hammer', *v.* VEPN *s.v.* **amer**); *the ouer end feild* 1638, *the Over end Field* 1709 (*v.* **uferra, ende**); *the Parsonage Hadland* c.1730 (*v.* **personage, hēafod-land**); *the path waye at Symkyns Townes end* 1601, *the pathway at Simpkins townes end* 1638, ~ ~ *at Warners Townes end* 1698 (*v.* **pathwaye** and *the townes end, infra*); *the penns* 1658, *the Penn of Thomas Sutton* c.1730, *the Pen furlong* c.1730 (*v.* **furlang**) (*v.* **penn**[2]); *the Picks furlonge* 1658 (*v.* **pīc, furlang**); *the pitt* 1698, *Pytfurlong(e)* 1467 × 84, 1601, *Pit(t) furlong(e)* 1601, 1638 *et passim* to 1742 (*v.* **furlang**), *Pittleys* c.1730 (*v.* **leys**) (*v.* **pytt**); *the first* ~ ~, *the second plowe land* 1612, *the second ploughland* 1638, 1712, 1742, *the third plow(e) land* 1612, 1658, 1724, ~ ~ *ploughland* 1658, 1712, 1742, *the fifth ploughland* 1638, 1712, 1742, *the fift plowghland* 1658, *the sixth plowland*, ~ ~ *plough land* 1658 (*v.* **plōg(a)-land**); *presgraue hadland* 1601, *Presgraues* ~ 1638 (*v.* **hēafod-land**), *presgraues hadleye* 1601 (*v.* **headley**) (with the surn. *Presgrave* of a family originally from the lost village of *Prestgrave* in Neville Holt, 15 miles to the south-east); *Prior hadlaye* 1601, *prior headley* 1638, 1698, *Prior hadley* 1712, 1742, *pryor hadlaye end* 1601, *prior hadley end* (*v.* **ende**), *Prior hadley furlonge* 1671 (*v.* **furlang**) (*v.* **headley**; prob. with the surn. *Prior/Pryor*, although **prior** cannot be ruled out since Leicester Abbey once owned extensive lands here); *Quarell'* 1467 × 84 (*v.* **quarrelle**); *Rame Close or Rame Yard* 1603 × 25 (*v.* **ramm, clos(e), geard**); *Rangdales* 1601, 1612, *Wrangdales furlonge* 1658 (*v.* **furlang**) (*v.* **wrang, vrangr, deill**); *Ranglandes* 1601, *Ranglands* 1638, *Rangland* 1698, 1712, 1742, *Short Ranglands* 1601 (*v.* **wrang, vrangr, land**); *Rede, the Reyd(e)* 1467 × 84, *the Reades* 1601, 1612, 1638, 1698, *the Reads* 1638, 1712, 1724, *the Reeds* c.1730, *the Reads furlonge* 1658 (*v.* **furlang**) (*v.* **hrēod**); *Reddbank* 1612 (*v.* **banke**; with **hrēod** or **rēad**); *the Ricke place* 1601, 1638, 1698, ~ *Rycke* ~ 1601, *the Rick place* 1712, 1742 (*v.* **hrēac, place**); *Roebank Furlong* c.1730 (*v.* **rūh**[1], **banke, furlang**); *the Sallowes* 1601, 1612, 1638, *the Sallows* 1698, 1712, 1724, 1742, *Sallows furlonge* 1658 (*v.* **furlang**) (*v.* **salh**); *hadland Sancti Johannis* 1467 × 84 (*v.* **hēafod-land**), *Saynt Johns furlonge* 1658, *Saint Johns furlong* c.1730 (*v.* **furlang**; alluding either to land supporting a chapel dedicated to St John in the parish church or to land formerly owned by the Knights Hospitallers of St John); *Sandersons yard end* 1612 (*v.* **geard, ende**), *Saundersons back(e) syde* 1601, 1638 (*v.* **bak-side**), *Saundersons penne* 1601 (*v.* **penn**[2]) (with the surn. *Sa(u)nderson*); *Savages Close* 1698, *Savage's* ~ 1742, *Savages Close End* 1712 (*v.* **ende**) (with the surn. *Savage*); *Schortholmis, Schortholmus, Schortholmis aboue the gate, Schortholmus be nethe gate* 1467 × 84 (*v.* **aboven, benethe, gata**) (*v.* **sc(e)ort, holmr**); *Scraptoft way furlong* 1658 (*v.* **furlang** and Scraptoft Lane *supra*); *the screave leys* 1658 (*v.* **scræf, leys**); *Seytcoppis* 1467 × 84 (*v.* **set-copp**); *the short furlong above the high meare* 1601, 1638 (*v.* **furlang** and High Meres *supra*); *Short layes* 1601, ~ *ley(e)s* 1638, 1698, 1712, 1742, *the Shorte leys abuttinge on the bridge* 1658 (*v.* **leys**); *long* ~, *(the) short shouells* 1601, 1612, 1638, *Long* ~, *(the) Short Shovells* 1698, 1712, 1742, *Shouell Lees* 1612 (*v.* **leys**), *Longshowells furlonge* 1671 (*v.* **furlang**) (*v.* **scofl**; perh. land which had to be cultivated by shovel because of its awkwardness, or describing very narrow strips as with **scofl-brǣdu**, cf. *Scoueldale* in Burton on the Wolds f.ns (b)); *Stakys* 1467 × 84 (*v.* **stakkr**; perh. related to Stack House Fm *supra*); *Mr Suttons headland* 1698, ~ *hadland* 1712, *Mr Sutton's Hadland* 1742 (*v.* **hēafod-land**), *Mr Suttons headley* 1698, ~ ~ *hadley* 1712 (*v.* **headley**), *Mr Suttons Wonge* 1698, 1712, *Mr Sutton's Wong* 1742 (*v.* **vangr**); *swale layes* 1601, *Swale lees* 1612, ~ *leys* 1638, 1712, 1742, *Swales leys* 1658, *Swalelays* 1724, *Swale* *leys furlonge* 1658 (*v.* **furlang**) (*v.* **leys**; with the surn. *Swale* (from the ON fem. pers.n. *Svala*)); (*John*) *Swannes hadland* 1601, 1638 (*v.* **hēafod-land**), *Swannes Layes* 1601 (*v.* **leys**), *Swannes wong*(*e*) 1601, 1638 (*v.* **vangr**); *Swynstyse* 1467 × 84 (*v.* **swīn**[1], **stig**); *Symkins Close*, *Symkins land*, *Symkins Meadowe* 1658 (with the surn. *Simpkin*); *Tassells* 1601, 1612, 1638, 1698, 1712 (*v.* **tǣsel**); (*John*) *Taylers hadland* 1601, *Taylours* ~ 1638 (*v.* **hēafod-land**); *thornye meare* 1601, (*in*) *thornemeere* 1612, *Thorny meere* 1638, 1698, *Thorney Meer* 1712, 1742 (*v.* **þornig**, **(ge)mǣre**); *Thurmaston mere*, ~ *meyre*, *Thurmuston mere* 1467 × 84, *Thomerston meare* 1612, *Thurmaston Meare* 1658 (*v.* **(ge)mǣre**; Thurmaston adjoins to the north-west); *Toftes* 1467 × 84 (*v.* **toft**); *the Town*(*e*) *hadland* 1601, 1612 *et passim* to 1742, *the Town headland* 1698 (*v.* **tūn**, **hēafod-land**); *the Townes end* 1601, 1638, 1671, *the Towne end* 1698, *the Townsend* 1712, c.1730, 1742, *Simkins* ~ ~, *Symkyns Townes end* 1601, *Simpkins* ~ ~, *Sympkins townes end* 1638, *Warners Townes end* 1698, 1742 (with the surns. *Simpkin* and *Warner*) (*v.* **tūn**, **ende**); *two furlong*(*e*)*s and one* 1601, 1612, 1712, *two furlongs* 1638, 1671, 1712 (*v.* **furlang**); *the Vicaridge Hadland* c.1730 (*v.* **hēafod-land**), *the Vickeridge land* 1658, ~ *Vicaridge* ~ 1671, *the Viccaridge Ley* c.1730 (*v.* **ley**) (*v.* **vikerage**); *Walkers hadland* 1698, 1712, ~ *headland* 1724, *Walker's Hadland* 1742 (*v.* **hēafod-land**), *Walkers headley* 1698, ~ *Hadley* 1712 (*v.* **headley**) (with the surn. *Walker*); *the Wand' under the croft'* 1467 × 84, *Wands* 1658 (*v.* **vǫndr** and *the Croft'*, *supra*); (*Tho.*) *Warners Close end* 1698, 1712, *Warner's* ~ ~ 1724 (*v.* **ende**), *Thomas Warners land* 1658, ~ ~ *Hadland* 1712, 1724, *Warner's Hadland* 1742 (*v.* **hēafod-land**); *Waterforo'*, *Waterforose* 1467 × 84, *Waterthorrowes furlonge* 1658, *water thorowes* ~ 1671 (*v.* **furlang**) (*v.* **wæter**, **furh** and *the Waterfurrow*(*e*)*s* in Asfordby f.ns. (b)); *Wayne ford* 1601, *Waine* ~ 1638, 1712, *Wainsford* 1698 (*v.* **wægn**, **ford**); *wells close* 1601, *Wells penn* 1698, 1724, *Wells's* ~ 1742 (*v.* **penn**[2]) (with the surn. *Wells*); *the Whetefelde* 1467 × 84 (*v.* **hwǣte**, **feld**); *Wildes Close or Wildes Yard* 1603 × 25 (*v.* **geard**; with the surn. *Wilde*, cf. *Willielmus Wilde* 1177 P of Leics.); *William Wilsons Hadley* c.1730 (*v.* **headley**); *the windemilne* 1640 (*v.* **wind-mylne**); *Wolfrichwell* 13 Nichols (*v.* **wella**; with the OE pers.n. *Wulfrīc*); *Woodcocks close*, ~ *land* 1658 (with the surn. *Woodcock*); *Worths Pingle* 1658 (*v.* **pingel**; with the surn. *Worth*); *Wrongdoles* 1467 × 84 bis, *Rangdoles* 1601, 1638, 1698, 1712, *randoles* 1724, *Rangdoles furlonge* 1658 (*v.* **furlang**) (*v.* **wrang**, **dāl**); *le Wyllose* 1467 × 84, *the Willowes* 1658, *the Willows* c.1730 (*v.* **wilig**); *the Willow Trees* c.1730 (*v.* **wilig-trēow**).

Hungarton

1. HUNGARTON

Hvngretone 1086 DB, *Hungreton'* 1216 ClR, 1236, 1243 Fees, 1251 BPR, 1268 Pat

Hungerton(') c.1130 LeicSurv, Hy 2 Dugd, 1191, 1192 P *et freq* to 1390 Pat, 1405 AD *et passim* to 1576 Saxton, 1610 Speed, *Hungertona* Hy 2 Dugd, 1156 (1318) Ch, c.1240 AD (p), *Hung(g)ertone* 1228, 1231 RHug, c.1250 (1407) Gilb

Hongerton 1363 Ipm, 1411 *Rut*, 1540 Pat

Hungarton 1516 EpCB, 1518 Visit *et freq*

'The farmstead, village with unproductive land', *v.* **hungor, tūn**; a settlement whose inhabitants, because of its poor soils, could be prone to hunger in the worst years, cf. Hungerton, DLPN 68.

ASHBY ARMS (P.H.) (lost), *Ashby Arms* 1835 *Terrier*, 1846, 1863, 1877 White, 1925 Kelly; *W. W. Ashby* of Quenby Hall is lord of the manor 1846 White, cf. *Shukbrugh Ashby* (d. 1792) of this family, who rebuilt a large part of the village. BARLEY LEAS, 1968 *Surv*, *barly lease* 1605 *Terrier*, *Barley Leyes* 1625, 1625 (1671) *ib*, *Barly leyes* 1679 *ib*, *Barley Lays* c.1700, 1709 *ib*, ~ *leys* 1700 *ib*, cf. *Barley Leys Close* c.1830 *Map*, 1835 *Terrier*, *v.* **bærlic, leys**. BLACK BOY (P.H.), *The Black Boy (public house)* 1825 *Plan*, 1826 *Sale*, 1832 *Deed*, *Black Boy* 1863, 1877 White, 1925 Kelly. CHURCH LANE, *v.* St John the Baptist's Church *infra*. COLBAULK RD, *Coal Baulk* c.1830 *Map*, 1835 *Terrier*, *v.* **balca** and Colehill Cl in f.ns. (a). FOX HOLES SPINNEY is *Spinney Covert* 1806 *Map*, *Foxholes Covert* 1827 *ib* (*v.* **cover(t)**), *Fox hole Spinny* 1835 O (*v.* **spinney**), *foxholl'* Hy 7 *Terrier*, *Foxholes* 1601, 1625 (1671) *ib et passim* to 1709 *ib*, *foxe holes* 1612, 1625 *ib*, cf. *Fox Holes Close* c.1830 *Map*, 1835 *Terrier*, *v.* **fox-hol**. THE GRANGE, 1877 White, *v.* **grange**. HUNGARTON SPINNEYS. INKERMAN LODGE, *v.* **loge**; named from the Battle of Inkerman (1854) in the Crimean War, where the British defeated the Russians. MAIN ST. ST JOHN THE BAPTIST'S CHURCH, *Church (St John)* 1846, 1863, 1877 White, *Church (St John the Baptist)*

1925 Kelly; it is earlier recorded as *ecclesiam ~ ~*, *ecclesie de Hungerton* 1220 MHW, 1306, 1351 *Pat*, *ecclesia parochiali de Hungarton* 1549 *ib*. Note also *the Church yarde* 1605, 1625 *Terrier*, *the Churchyard* 1625 (1671), 1709, 1826 *ib*, *ye Churchyeard* 1679 *ib*, *v*. **chirche-ȝeard**. THE VICARAGE, 1877 White, 1925 Kelly; it is *the Vicaridge house* 1605, 1625, 1625 (1671), 1679 *Terrier*, *the Vicarage House* c.1700, 1709, 1826 *ib*, *v*. **vikerage**.

FIELD-NAMES

Undated forms in (a) are 1968 *Surv*; those dated 1752 and c.1830 are *Map*; 1825 and 1837 are *Plan*; 1826[1] are *Sale*; 1826[2] and 1835 are *Terrier*; 1832 are *Deed*. Forms throughout dated 1477 (e.16) are *Charyte*; Hy 7, 1605, 1612, 1625, 1625 (1671), 1679, 1700, c.1700 and 1709 are *Terrier*.

(a) Three Acre, Five ~, Six ~, Seven Acre 1968, the Eight Acres, the Nine Acres 1825, Top ~ ~, Nine Acre, Ten ~, Fourteen ~, Seventeen Acre 1968, the Eighteen Acres 1825, Twenty Six Acre 1968 (*v*. **æcer**); Abel Meer Cl c.1830, 1835 (*Hebwell meere* 1612, 1625 (1671), 1679, *Heb-well meere* 1625, *Ebwell meer* c.1700, 1709, *v*. **wella, mere**[1]; either with the OE pers.n. *Ebba* or with **eb** 'shallow'); Allotments (*v*. **allotment**); Barn Cl 1826[2], 1968; Beeby Fd (adjacent to the parish boundary of Beeby which adjoins to the north-west); Big Fd; Black Boy Fd (beside Black Boy (P.H.) *supra*); Blakesley's Cl, Blakesley's Mdw c.1830, 1835 (the *Blakesley* family was originally from the village of this name, 35 miles to the south in Northants.); Bridle Road Mdw (*v*. **brigdels**); Broad Flatt 1968, Broad Flat Cl c.1830, 1835, Broad Flatt Mdw 1968 (*v*. **brād, flat**); Broad Mdw c.1830, 1835; Brook Furlong c.1830, ~ ~ Cl 1835 (*the brooke furlong* 1612, 1625, 1625 (1671), (*the*) *Brook ~* 1679, 1700, c.1700, 1709, *v*. **brōc, furlang**); Bull Fd (*v*. **bula**); Burnt arse Leys c.1830, 1835 (*burnard lease* 1605, *Burndard Leyes* 1625, 1625 (1671), *Burndars ~* 1679, *v*. **leys**; with the surn. *Burnard* which according to Reaney *s.n.* is a compound of OFr *brun* and *hard*, originally a by-name for a person with brownish dark hair or complexion; there is later confusion with **ears**, used locally of a buttock-shaped hill-formation); Carvers Covert 1806 Map (*v*. **cover(t)**; with the surn. *Carver*); The Close; Coathills (*Cottehyll* Hy 7, *Coate hill* 1605, *Cotehill* 1612, *Cote Hill* 1625, 1625 (1671), 1679, *Courthil(l)* 1700, 1709, *v*. **cot, hyll**); Colehill Cl c.1830, 1835, Colehill side Cl c.1830, 1835, 1837 (*v*. **sīde**) (ostensibly with **cāl** 'cabbage', but these closes occupy the earlier *Cotehill* and their name may simply have arisen from a misreading of a faintly crossed manuscript *t* for *l* which was then perpetuated on 19th cent. estate plans); Cow Fd; Crane's Nest 1826[1] (*v*. **cran, nest**); Cricket Fd, Old Cricket Fd (both for the game of cricket); Dovecote Cl c.1830, 1835, Dove Cote 1968 (*v*. **dove-cot(e)**); Dowell's (the surn. *Dowell* in the possessive case, *v*. Reaney *s.n.*); Edwin's Cl (cf. *Stephen Edwin* 17 *Terrier* of Old Ingarsby *infra*); Far Cl 1826[1]; Far Sic (*v*. **sík**); Gilberts Cl c.1830, 1835 (with the surn. *Gilbert*); Glebe Lands (cf. *the Glebe*

House 1826[2], *v.* **glebe**); (the) Great Cl 1826[1], c.1830, 1835, 1968, Far Great ~, Middle Great ~ c.1830, 1835; the Great Mdw c.1830, 1835; (the) Bottom ~, (the) Top Green c.1830, 1835, 1968 (*the Greene* 1605, 1612, 1625, 1625 (1671), *the Green* 1679, 1700, c.1700, 1709, *v.* **grēne**[2]); Half Craft (sic) c.1830, 1835 (*haull crofte* Hy 7, *Hawcroft* 1605, 1679, *hall crofte* 1612, *Halcrofte* 1625, *Hallcroft* 1625 (1671), cf. *Halcroft Nooke* 1625, 1625 (1671), *Hawcroft nook(e)* 1625 (1671), 1679, *Half Croft Nook* (sic) 1700, 1709 (*v.* **nōk**), *v.* **hall, croft**); Hill Fd; Holland Dale c.1830 (1612, 1625, 1679, 1752, *Hollendale* 1605, cf. *the bottom of Hollandale* c.1700, 1709 (*v.* **botm**), *hollendale head* 1605, *Holland dale head* 1612, 1625 *et passim* to 1709 (*v.* **hēafod**); earlier are *Holowell dale nederende, Holow Well dalle ned'ende* Hy 7 (*v.* **neoðera, ende**), *Holowell dale ouerende* Hy 7 (*v.* **uferra, ende**), *Holowell tong'* Hy 7 (*v.* **tunge**)), Longside holland dale 1835 (*ye longside Hollandale* 1700, *the Long Side of Hollandale* 1709, cf. *the Short Side ~ ~* 1709 (*v.* **sīde**)) (it is uncertain whether *le holywell dall'* 1477 (e.16) belongs here; if so, then the origin of this complex of f.ns. is 'the valley of the holy well or spring', with **hālig, wella** and **dalr**, but if this unique form is the result of a monastic scribe's subjective reshaping of the name in Charyte's Rental, then we have simply the common 'stream running in a deep hollow', with **hol**[2], **wella** and **dalr**; but note *Ladywell sicke* in f.ns. (b)); Middle ~, Near ~, Upper Holme c.1830, 1835 (*the Holme* 1605, 1612, 1625, 1625 (1671), *ye Hoome* 1700, *the Home* c.1700, 1709, cf. *the Home field* 1700, c.1700, 1709 (*v.* **feld**; one of the great fields of the township, earlier *the East feild*), *Home furlong* c.1700, 1709 (*v.* **furlang**), *Holme gate* 1605, 1612, 1625, 1625 (1671), *Holm-gate* 1679, *Hoome gate* 1700, *Home ~* c.1700, 1709 (*v.* **gata**), *v.* **holmr**); Home Cl c.1830, 1835, 1837, 1968, (the) First ~ ~, (the) Second Home Cl 1825, 1832, Home Fd 1968 (*v.* **home**); Horse Fd; House Cl 1826[1]; Keyham Big Fd, Keyham Mdws (enclosures bordering Keyham which adjoins to the south-west); Lewin's Mdw (with the surn. *Lewin*, a reflex of the OE pers.n. *Lēofwine*); Little Cl; Upper Little Sick, Little Sick Cl c.1830, 1835 (*the little sicke* 1612, *v.* **sík**); Long Cl 1826[1]; Long sick c.1830, 1835, ~ Sic 1968 (*longe sicke* 1612, *Long Sicke* 1625, 1625 (1671), 1679, *Long Sick* 1700, c.1700, 1709, *v.* **sík**); (the) Middle Cl 1826[1], 1832; Muckleborough 1968, ~ Cl c.1830, 1835 (*Muckleborow(e)* 1605, *Muckleburrow(e)* 1612, 1625, 1679, *Muckleborrow* 1625 (1671), c.1700, *Mickhilborrow, Muckhillborrow* 1700, cf. *mukkulbarowmor'* Hy 7 (*v.* **mōr**[1]), *v.* **micil, mycel, mikill, berg**); the Near Cl 1826[1], 1832; Little ~ ~, Nether Noble Cl c.1830, 1835, 1837 (with the surn. *Noble*); Newton road piece 1835 (*v.* **pece**; Cold Newton adjoins to the south-east); Bottom ~, Paddock (*v.* **paddock**); Pathway Cl c.1830, 1835 (*over the path waye* 1625, *~ ~ Pathway* 1625 (1671), *the Path way* 1679, c.1700, 1709 (*v.* **pathwaye**; furlongs so called), cf. *Path Lands* 1625, 1625 (1671), 1679 (*v.* **pæð**)); Payne's (the surn. *Payne* in the possessive case); Pool(e) Leys c.1830, 1835 (*v.* **pōl**[1], **leys**); Railway Fd (adjoining a railway line); Reed Pool Covert 1806 Map (*v.* **hrēod, pōl**[1], **cover(t)**); Road Cl 1826[2], Road Fd 1968 (beside roadways); Rough Cl (*v.* **rūh**[1]); Sausmoor 1968, Sauce moor sick c.1830, 1835 (*sowsmer' syk* Hy 7, *sawremoore sick* 1605, *Sauremore sicke* 1612, *Saresmore sick, Saresmoor sicke* 1625, *Saresmore Sicke* 1625 (1671), *Sauce-more ~* 1679, *Saus(e)more Sick* c.1700, 1709, cf. *sowsmer' syk deyn* Hy 7 (*v.* **denu**), *v.* **mere**[1] 'wetland' (replaced by **mōr**[1], **mór** 'marshland'), **sík**; the repeated genitival forms of the first el. indicate the ON pers.n. *Sauðr* (a by-name from ON *sauðr* 'sheep') rather than ON *saurr* 'mud, sour ground' or *sauðr* itself, and wet ground would have been avoided by sheep farmers because of the incidence of liver fluke, cf. Sausthorpe, DLPN 106); Sherwood's Cl (with the surn. *Sherwood*); Stainsborough 1968, Stainborough Cl c.1830, 1835 (*steynbarow* Hy 7, *Steaneborrow* 1605, *Stainburrow* 1612 *Staynburrow* 1625, 1679, *Stainburrow* 1625 (1671), *Steanborrow* 1700, c.1700, 1709, *Steanebororrow furlonge* 1605, *Steanborrow Furlong* 1700, c.1700, 1709 (*v.* **furlang**), *v.* **steinn, berg**); Stone Bush 1968, ~ ~ Cl c.1830, 1835 (*Stone bushe* 1612, *v.* **stān, busc**; alluding to brushwood cover of stony ground); Three cornered Piece c.1830, 1835 (*v.* **three-cornered, pece**); Top Sic (*v.* **sík**); Town End 1968, Townsend Cl c.1830, 1835 (*the townes end* 1612, *v.* **tūn, ende**); Vicarage Mdw 1826[2] (*v.* **vikerage**); Wash Pit Yard (*v.* **wæsce, pytt, geard**; the site of a sheep-dip); Wells Cl 1826[1] (with the surn. *Wells*); The Wong c.1830, 1835 (*v.* **vangr**).

(b) *t'ram abbaț' leycestr'* Hy 7 ('the land of Leicester Abbey', with MLat *terra* and *abbatia*); *Ashby his hadland* 1605, *Mr Ashbies hadland* 1612 (*v.* **hēafod-land**; *George Ashbye* is cited 1605), *Mr Ashbyes hadling* (sic) 1612, ~ ~ *hadley* 1625, *Mr Ashbies Hadley* 1625 (1671), *Mr Ashbys Headley* 1679 (*v.* **headley**) (*v.* Ashby Arms (P.H.) *supra*); *babgraue crosse* Hy 7 (*v.* **cros**), *Badgrave hedge* 1605, *Bagraue* ~ 1612, *Bagrave* ~ 1625, 1625 (1671), *Baggrave* ~ 1700, c.1700 (*v.* **hecg**; a township boundary hedge), *babgraue mer'* Hy 7 (*v.* **(ge)mǣre**) (Baggrave adjoins to the north-east); *banlonde* Hy 7, *Bandlands* 1612, 1625 (1671), *bande landes* 1625, *Bande-lands* 1679, *schurtbanlonde*, *schurteballonte* Hy 7 (*v.* **sc(e)ort**), *bandlands furlonge* 1605 (*v.* **furlang**) (*v.* **bēan, land**); *Sir Roberte Banesters hadland* 1625, *Sir Robert Banisters* ~ 1625 (1671) (*v.* **hēafod-land**); *barleyhyll'* Hy 7 (*v.* **bærlic, hyll**); *bat(e)mor'* Hy 7, *Batemore* 1612, 1625 (1671), *bate moore* 1625, *Batemeere* 1679, *schurtbatemor'* Hy 7 (*v.* **sc(e)ort**) (*v.* **mōr**[1]; the first el. is poss. **beit** 'pasture' (in contrast to the common *Deadmore* 'infertile moorland', *v.* Ru 328 for examples), otherwise ME **bate** 'dispute' as in ModE *debate*, cf. *flytbarow*, *infra*); *Robert Bayleys Homestall* 1709 (*v.* **hām-stall**); *Beeby Hedge* 1625, 1625 (1671) (*v.* **hecg**; the township boundary hedge of Beeby which adjoins to the north-west); *Belland* 1477 (e.16) (*v.* **belle, land**); *(the) Bell Hadland* 1605, 1612 *et passim* to 1709, *Bel-hadland* 1625, *Bell-headland* 1679 (*v.* **belle, hēafod-land**); *betwene the hadlands* 1625, *between* ~ ~ c.1700, 1709, *between the Sicks* c.1700, 1709 (*v.* **hēafod-land, sík**; furlongs thus called); *Byshopp his yardes ende* 1605 (*v.* **geard, ende**; cf. *Steeven Bishopp* 1605), *Bishop(p)s Leyes* 1625, 1625 (1671), *Bishops Lays* c.1700, *Bishop's Leas* 1709 (*v.* **leys**); *blakehyll*, *blakhyll'* Hy 7 (*v.* **blæc, hyll**); *blakelond'* Hy 7, *blackland(e)s* 1605, 1612, 1625, 1679, *Blaklands* 1625 (1671), *Blakelands* c.1700, 1709, *Hyblaklond*, *hyblakelonde* Hy 7 (*v.* **hēah**[1]) (*v.* **blæc, land**); *Broadarses* 1709 (*v.* **brād, ears**); *broad plott leyes* 1612 (*v.* **brād, plot, leys**); *brokhyllsykke* Hy 7 (*v.* **brōc, hyll, sík**); *broklond'* Hy 7, *schortebroklond'* Hy 7 (*v.* **sc(e)ort**) (*v.* **brōc, land**); *Broçkwell foord* 1612, 1625, 1625 (1671), 1679 (*v.* **ford**), *Brockwell sicke* 1605, 1612, 1625, ~ *Sike* 1625 (1671), ~ *Sick* c.1700, 1709 (*v.* **sík**) (*v.* **wella**; perh. with the OE pers.n. *Broca* or with **brocc** 'a badger' rather than with **brōc** 'a brook' which would sit uneasily with *wella*; cf. Broxbourne, Hrt 219); *the brooke* 1605 (*v.* **brōc**); *Nan. Chamberlins Head-land* 1679 (*v.* **hēafod-land**); *(the) Church hadland(e)* 1612, 1625, 1625 (1671), 1679, ~ *headland* 1679 (*v.* **hēafod-land**), *Church meer(e)* 1612, 1625 *et passim* to 1709, ~ *Mear* 1700, c.1700, *Churchmear furlong* 1700, *Church Meer* ~ c.1700 (*v.* **furlang**) (*v.* **(ge)mǣre**) (*v.* St John the Baptist's Church *supra*); *(John) Clarkes hadland* 1605, 1612, 1625, 1625 (1671), *Clearks Headland* 1679 (*v.* **hēafod-land**); *Collins Headley* 1679 (*v.* **headley**; with the surn. *Collins*); *Comyn' balke* Hy 7 (*v.* **balca**), *Comyn' hadd'* Hy 7 (*v.* **hēafod**) (*v.* **commun**); *the howse of*

Richard Cooke 1612 (*v.* **hūs**); *coptehyll'* Hy 7 (*v.* **copped**[1], **hyll**); (*the*) *Crosse hedge* 1612, 1625, *Cross*(*e*) *Hedge or Beeby Hedge* 1625 (1671), 1679 (*v.* **cross** and *Beeby Hedge*, *supra*); *Dikefurlong* 1477 (e.16), *dykfurlong'* Hy 7, *dickfurlonge* 1605 (*v.* **dík**, **furlang**); *Dufhows croft* 1477 (e.16) (*v.* **dove-hous**, **croft**); *the East feild*(*e*) 1605, 1612, 1625 (1671), *the Easte Feilde*, *East field* 1679, (*in campo oriental'* Hy 7, with MLat *campus* 'a field' and *orientalis* 'eastern'), *v.* **ēast**, **feld**; one of the great fields of the township, also called *the Home field*, *v.* Holme *supra*); *the east meadow* 1605; *Farr dales* 1625 (1671) (*v.* **feor**, **deill**); *finall' gatte* Hy 7 (*v.* **finol**, **gata**); *flytbarow* Hy 7 (*v.* **(ge)flit**, **berg**); (*Roger*) *Gambles hadland* 1605, 1612 (*v.* **hēafod-land**); *godd' pytte*, *god' pytt* Hy 7 (*v.* **pytt**; the first el. appears to be **gōd**[2] 'good', perh. alluding to a fertile hollow, but neither the surn. *Good* nor (if this is a surviving early toponym) the OE pers.n. *Goda* can be ruled out); *gren gatte* Hy 7, (*a balke called*) *greengates* 1605 (*v.* **balca**), *greene gate* 1612, *grene gatte ned' ende* Hy 7 (*v.* **neoðera**, **ende**) (*v.* **grēne**[1], **gata**); *gr' gorr'* (sic) Hy 7 (*v.* **gāra**; the first el. is prob. **grēne**[1]); *hedbalke* Hy 7 (*v.* **hēafod**, **balca**); *holgat' furlong* 1546 AAS, *Holgate Furlonge* 1549 Pat (*v.* **hol**[2], **gata**, **furlang**); *the Hom*(*e*)*stall* 1605, 1709 (*v.* **hām-stall**; i.e. of *the Vicaridge house*, *v.* The Vicarage *supra*); *Hungarton More* n.d. Nichols (*v.* **mōr**[1]); *hyhol*(*l*)*me* Hy 7 (*v.* **hēah**[1], **holmr**); *Ingersby hedge* 1605, *Ingarsby*(*e*) ~ 1612, 1625, 1625 (1671), 1679 (*v.* **hecg**; a township boundary demarcation), *Ingersby way* 1605, c.1700, 1709, *Ingarsbe way*, *Ingaresbee waie* 1612, *Ingaresby waye* 1625, *Ingarsby way* 1625, 1679, 1700 (*v.* **weg**); earlier, the road is *Yngwarbygate* 1477 (e.16), *ynggursby gate*, *ynngursbygatte* Hy 7 (*v.* **gata**) (Old Ingarsby adjoins to the south); *against Keame Field* c.1700, 1709 (a furlong so called), *Keame meare* 1605, *Keaham* ~, *Keame meere* 1612 (*v.* **(ge)mǣre**; Keyham adjoins to the south-west); *Henry Kemp*(*e*)*s Hadland* 1625, 1625 (1671) (*v.* **hēafod-land**); *kilne dike meere* 1612, *Kil*(*l*)*dike meere* 1625, 1625 (1671), 1679, *Killdicke* ~, *Killdike* ~ 1700, *Kildike Mear* c.1700, ~ *Meer* 1709 (*v.* **cyln**, **dík**; poss. with **mere**[1] rather than **(ge)mǣre**); *the knowles* 1612 (*v.* **cnoll**); *kyrkewylows* Hy 7 (*v.* **kirkja**, **wilig** and St John the Baptist's Church *supra*); *Ladywell sicke* 1605 (*v.* **lavedi**, **wella**, **sík**; presum. a sacred spring dedicated to Our Lady, the Virgin Mary, and poss. to be identified with *le holywell*, *v.* Holland Dale in f.ns (a)); *the Leyes* 1625, 1625 (1671), 1679 (*v.* **leys**); *longlond'* Hy 7, *Longe Landes* 1625, *Longlands* 1625 (1671), 1679, *longlondel* Hy 7 (*v.* **deill**), *Long land side* 1612 (*v.* **sīde**) (*v.* **lang**[1], **land**); *lowsbygatte* Hy 7, *Loseby gate* 1605, *Lowesbie* ~ 1612 (*v.* **gata**; Lowesby lies 2 miles to the east); *lyttyldale* Hy 7 (*v.* **lȳtel**, **lítill**, **dalr**); *Marehill* 1477 (e.16), 1605, c.1700, 1709, *Marie hill* 1612, 1625, *Maryhill* 1625 (1671), 1679 (*v.* **(ge)mǣre**, **hyll**); *Masons Hadley* 1625, 1625 (1671) (*v.* **headley**; cf. *Tho. Mason* 1625); *the Middle Stint* 1625 (1671), 1679 (*v.* **stint**); *morlondeale* Hy 7 (*v.* **mōr**[1], **mór**, **land**, **deill**); *Myddulbarow* Hy 7, *Middleburrow*(*e*) 1605, 1612, *Middle borrowe furlonge* 1605 (*v.* **furlang**), *v.* **middel**, **berg**); *Myllyn' hyll* Hy 7 (*v.* **myln**, **hyll**); *the Nether Hook* 1700, c.1700, 1709 (*v.* **hōc**); (*the*) *Nether pen*(*n*) 1612, 1625, 1679, c.1700, 1709 (*v.* **penn**[2]); *Newton Hedge* 1700, c.1700, 1709 (*v.* **hecg**; a parish boundary marker), *Newton Streame* 1625, 1625 (1671) (*v.* **strēam**) (Cold Newton adjoins to the east); (*the*) *North feild*(*e*) 1605, 1612, 1625 (1671), ~ *feylde* 1625, ~ *Field* 1679, 1700, c.1700, 1709, (*in campo borial'* Hy 7, with MLat *campus* 'a field' and *borialis* 'northern'), *v.* **feld**; one of the great fields of the township); *Parkers Hadland* 1625, 1625 (1671) (*v.* **hēafod-land**; with the surn. *Parker*); *Penborrow nook* c.1700, *Penbrook Nook* (sic) 1709 (*v.* **penn**[2], **berg**, **nōk**; it is to be assumed that the 1709 form is unreliable); *the Pen end* 1625, 1625 (1671),

1679 (*v.* **ende**), *Pen furlong* 1625 (1671), c.1700, 1709 (*v.* **furlang**) (*v.* **penn**[2]); *Widdow Pikes Land* 1625 (1671) (*v.* **land**); (*the meadow called*) *the Poles* 1625, 1679, 1700, 1709 (*v.* **pole**; here a measurement of land, roughly 30 square yards (cf. *two poles of medow in the poles* 1612, *Two Poles of Grass ground in the Poles* 1709), *v.* OED *s.v.* pole, sb.[1], 3b, earliest citation 1637); *super portam viam* Hy 7 ('above the road to the market', with MLat *porta* 'a market'; a furlong so called, *v.* Portels Fm in adjacent Cold Newton and Porter's Lodge in Lowesby); *Pynfolde* Hy 7 (*v.* **pynd-fald**); *Quenbydale* Hy 7, 1605, 1625 (1671), 1679, 1700, c.1700, *Quenbie dale* 1612, 1625, *the* (*long*) *Side of Quenby Dale* c.1700, 1709 (*v.* **dalr, sīde**), *Quenbie hedge* 1612, *Quenby Hedg*(*e*) 1625, 1679, 1700, 1709 (*v.* **hecg**; a township boundary marker) (Quenby adjoins to the south-east); *roschell hend' sydde* Hy 7 (*v.* **ende, sīde**; the first word may be the surn. *Roskell* (a reflex of the ON pers.n. *Hrosskell*), but a toponym would rather be expected with *ende* (perh. **rysc** with **hyll** or **halh**, cf. *ryschealas* 840 × 852 (12) BCS 124 (S 79), and note *Rosgalls*, Lei **2** 244); additional forms are needed); *Sandy lands* 1605, 1679, *Sandie landes* 1612, *sande landes* 1625, *Sand Lands* 1625 (1671), *Sandlays* c.1700, *Sandy lays* 1709 (*v.* **sandig, sand, land**; in later forms, *lands* is replaced by **leys**); (*the*) *Sand pittes* 1605, 1612, 1625, ~ ~ *pitts* 1625 (1671), *Sand-pit* 1679 (*v.* **sand-pytt**); *schort londe*, *schurtlond*(*e*), *schurlonte* Hy 7 (*v.* **sc(e)ort, land**); *sculbrode* Hy 7 (*v.* **scofl-brǣdu**); *semer'wong* Hy 7 (*v.* **vangr**; prob. with the surn. *Seamer* (a reflex of either the OE pers.n. *Sǣmǣr* or OE *sēamere* 'a tailor')); *Sheepheard borde* 1605, *Sheepherds boord*(*s*) 1625, 1679, *Sheepheards Boords* 1625 (1671), *Sheapherdes boord hades* 1612 (*v.* **hēafod**) (*v.* **scēp-hirde, bord** and *Shepperd board*, Lei **2** 230; the f.n. appears to allude to good grazing for sheep); *Shorthasylis* 1535 VE (*v.* **sc(e)ort, hæsel**); *smallgatte* Hy 7 (*v.* **smæl, gata**); *smythesyke* Hy 7 (*v.* **smið, sík**); *Sneathes pen* 1625 (*v.* **penn**[2]; with the surn. *Sneath*); *snottybott'* Hy 7 (*v.* **snotte, snotty, botm**, cf. NFris *snottig* 'dirty, foul'; the adj. *snotty* 'viscous, slimy' is not recorded until 1657 OED); *nedd' soue*, *ouersoue* Hy 7 (*v.* **neoðera, uferra, sōg**); *steyse* Hy 7, *the styes* 1605, *the Sties* 1612, c.1700, 1709, *the middle styes* 1625, (*the*) *Middle Sties* c.1700, 1709 (*v.* **stig**); *stoue* Hy 7, *stowgatte* Hy 7 (*v.* **gata**) (*v.* **stōw**); *Francis Stubbes his close*, ~ *Stubbs his closse* 1612, *Stubb*(*i*)*s his hadland*, *Stubb*(*e*)*s hadland* 1605, 1612 (*v.* **hēafod-land**); *Syxhows* Hy 7, *Syxhowsyde* Hy 7 (*v.* **sīde**) (*v.* **six, haugr**); *messuagium Joh'is taylor* Hy 7 (with MLat *messuagium* 'a house, a holding'); *Math. Taylours Headland* 1679 (*v.* **hēafod-land**); *ned'thong*, *ouerthong* Hy 7 (*v.* **neoðera, uferra, þwang**); *thyrston' furlong* Hy 7 (*v.* **furlang**; either with the ON pers.n. *Þorsteinn* (ODan *Thorsten*) anglicized to OE *Þurstān* or, more likely, with its surn. reflex *Thurston*); *the tounges* 1605, *the tonges* 1612, 1625, 1625 (1671), *ye Tongues* 1679, *the Toungs* 1700, c.1700, 1709 (poss. with **tunge**, but these forms may belong with the earlier *ned'thong*, *ouerthong*, *supra*); *the Vicarage Close* 1700, c.1700, 1709 (*v.* **vikerage**); *Waterforows* Hy 7, (*the*) *Waterfurrows* 1605, 1700, c.1700, 1709, *the water furrowes* 1612 (*v.* **wæter, furh** and *the Waterfurrow*(*e*)*s* in Asfordby f.ns. (b)); *the Watering* 1700, c.1700, 1709 (*v.* **wateryng**); *Watkyn' hadlonte* Hy 7 (*v.* **hēafod-land**; with the surn. *Watkin* (from *Wat-kin*, a diminutive of Walter); *West barogh* Hy 7, *Westborrow* 1625 (1671), *Westburrow* 1679, *uestebarow ne'ende*, *uestebarow ouerende* Hy 7 (*v.* **neoðera, uferra, ende**), *v.* **west, berg**; it is uncertain whether the forms *nesborrow* 1605, *Nesburrow* 1612, 1625, *Nesbrough* c.1700, 1709 belong here, since all were in the North Fd, but if not, then *v.* **næss, nes, berg**); (*the*) *West feild* 1605, 1612, 1625 (1671), ~ ~ *feyld* 1625, ~ ~ *field* 1700, c.1700, 1709, (*in campo occidental'* Hy 7, with MLat *campus* 'a field' and *occidentalis* 'western'), *v.* **west, feld**; one of the great fields of the township); *Westeleys(e)* Hy 7, *West leyes* 1612, 1625, 1625 (1671), 1679, ~ *leys* 1700, *the West leas* c.1700, ~ ~ *lays* 1709 (*v.* **west, læs**); *West medow hadd'* Hy 7, *the west medow head* 1605 (*v.* **west, mǣd (mǣdwe** obl.sg.), **hēafod**); *the whorle sicke* 1605 (*v.* **hwerfel, hvirfill, sík**); *Wilsons Hadland* 1625, ~ *Headland* 1625 (1671) (*v.* **hēafod-land**; with the surn. *Wilson*); *Woodcockys lond* 1507 Nichols (*v.* **land**; with the surn. *Woodcock*); *Wrong' mer'* Hy 7 (*v.* **wrang, vrangr, (ge)mǣre**).

2. BAGGRAVE

Baggrave is a member of Gartree Hundred.

Badegraue 1086 DB, *Badesgraua* 1169 P
Balbegraue c.1130 LeicSurv, *Balbegrave* 1247 Abbr (p), l.13 CustRo, *Balbgrave* l.13 ib
Babbegraua 1177, 1178 P *et freq* to 1182 ib, *Babbegraue* 1199, 1200 ib *et passim* to 1281 *Peake* (p), 1294 *Wyg*, *Babbegrave* 1227 Fees, 1275 Hastings *et freq* to 1351 IpmR, 1352 Pat *et passim* to 1371 Cl, 1377 Pat
Babegraue 1190 P (p), Hy 3 *Crox* (p), *Babegraua* 1191 P (p), 1192 ib (p), 1193 ib (p), *Babegrave* 1262 Fine, 1286 Pat (p) *et passim* to 1344, 1372 Nichols
Babgrave 1299 Ipm, 1312 Banco *et passim* to 1385 Pat, 1402 FA, *Babgraue* 1352 *LCDeeds*, 1352 (1449) *WoCart*, 1478 *Ct*
Bagrave 1499, 1500 Ipm, 1507 Nichols, 1605 LML
Baggraue 1502 *MiscAccts*, 1576 Saxton, *Baggrave* 1502 Pat, 1507 Nichols, 1510 *Rental et freq*

Probably 'Babba's grove', *v.* **grāf**. This is a purely OE p.n. with what appears to be a masc. pers.n. *Babba* which is recorded independently on several occasions (*v.* Searle 78). Ekwall (DEPN *s.n.*) suggests that if the two forms with *d* are reliable, the pers.n. might rather be an otherwise unrecorded OE fem. pers.n. *Beaduburg*; but confusion with the OE masc. pers.n. *Badda* seems a likelier explanation for these spellings, and the unique gen.sg. formation *Badesgraua* may be discounted.

BAGGRAVE HALL, l.18 *Map*, 1835 O, 1846, 1863 White, 1925 Kelly; it is *the Hall* 1666 SR, *v.* **hall**. BAGGRAVE PARK. GEORGE'S SPINNEY, *v.* **spinney**, cf. *Georges Barn* 1945 *Sale*; adjacent to George's Spinney and with the surn. *George*. HALL SPINNEY, *v*. Baggrave Hall *supra*. HARTFIELD LODGE, *Hart Field* l.18 *Map*; cf. *Nether* ~, *Over Hart* 1625 *ib* (*v*. **neoðera, uferra**), *Hart Lands* 1968 *Surv*, *v*. **heard**, with the meaning 'hard to till'. NEW COVERT. PRINCE OF WALES COVERT, *v*. **cover(t)**. SOUTH LODGE. WATERLOO LODGE is *Waterloo farm* 1925 Kelly; named from the Battle of Waterloo, 1815. WATSON'S SPINNEY, *v*. **spinney**, cf. *Nether* ~ ~, *Over Watsons Close* 1625 *Map* (*v*. **neoðera, uferra**), *Watsons Close*, *Watsons Meadow* l.18 *ib*, *Barn* ~, *Far* ~, *Great Watson* 1968 *Surv*; with the surn. *Watson*.

FIELD-NAMES

In (a), forms dated 1752 and l.18 are *Map*; 1945 are *Sale*; 1968 are *Surv*. Forms throughout dated c.1505 are Nichols; 1625 are *Map*.

(a) Five Acre, Nine ~, Ten ~, Twelve ~, Fourteen ~, Fifteen ~, Twenty-five Acre 1968, Ten Acre Cl l.18 (*v*. **æcer**); Near & Far Baggrave Hooks 1945 (*v*. **hōc**); Little ~ ~, Barn Cl l.18, Barn Cl 1968; East Nether ~ ~, West Nether ~ ~, Upper Bear Cl (*v*. **bere**); Beaumonts Mdw l.18 (with the surn. *Beaumont*); Brick Kiln Cl 1968 (*v*. **brike-kiln**); Bulchers Mdw l.18 (with the surn. *Bulger*, *v*. Reaney *s.n.*); Carbridge Cl l.18, Carr Brigg Far Fd 1968 (*v*. Carr Bridge in Lowesby); (the) Conduits 1968 (*Condite Close* 1625, *v*. **cundite**); Cottage Cl 1968; Cottagers Cl l.18 (*v*. **cotager**); Crofts Mdw 1945 (either with **croft** or with the surn. *Croft*); the Cuckoo 1968 (poss. a close adjacent to woodland regularly frequented by the bird (*Cuculus canorus*), but some such names appear to denote fields which produce a markedly earlier harvest than their neighbours, *v*. Field 110); Fatlands Cls, Fatlands Mdw l.18, Little ~ ~, Middle ~ ~, Near Fat Lands 1968 (*v*. **fætt, land**); Gravel Hole 1968; Home Cl, Home Fd 1968 (*v*. **home**); Kings Mdw l.18 (cf. *the Kings close* c.1505 (*v*. **clos(e)**); with the surn. *King*, cf. *John King* 17 of adjacent Old Ingarsby); Kirtons Fd 1968 (with the surn. *Kirton*); Lewin Hooks 1752 (*v*. **hōc** and Lewin's Mdw in Hungarton f.ns. (a)); Lodge Cl, Lodge Close Mdw l.18 (cf. *Lodge meadowe* 1625, *v*. **loge**); Long Mdw l.18; Mayes Barn 1945 (with the surn. *Maye*, *v*. Reaney *s.n.*); New Mdw l.18; Oat Field Spinney 1835 O (*v*. **spinney**), North ~ ~, South Oat Fd 1968 (*Ote Feild* 1625, *v*. **āte**); the Ploughed Fd 1968; Ram Fd l.18 (cf. *Ramfeild Clos* 1625 (*v*. **clos(e)**), *Ramfeild Meadowe* 1625, *v*. **ramm, feld**); Richardson's Mdw l.18 (with the surn. *Richardson*); Road Fd 1968 (a roadside close); Nether Rough Cl 1945, Upper ~ ~ 1968 (*v*. **rūh**[1]); the Side Hills 1968 (*v*. **sīde**); Swans Nest 1752 (*v*. **swan**[1], **nest**; land beside Baggrave's northern boundary stream); Top Fd 1968; Top of Township l.18 (*v*. **topp**), Township Mdw l.18, The Townships 1968 (cf. *Tounship Close* 1625, *v*. **tounshipe**; the site of the deserted medieval village of Baggrave, cf. The Township in Hamilton f.ns. (a) and in Ragdale f.ns. (a)); Weatherstone Cl 1968 (poss. with the surn. *Weatherstone* which is extant; but this may rather be an earlier 'wether stone close' in a traditional sheep-farming area, describing an enclosure on stony ground, *v*. **weðer**, **stān**, cf. Weather Cl (x3) in Old Ingarsby *infra* and cf. *the Stone hoggs* *close* in Loddington f.ns. (b)); Wheat Cl l.18, Wheat Fd 1968 (*v.* **hwǣte**); Willow Sich l.18, ~ Sic 1968 (*Willow Cick* (sic) 1625, *v.* **wilig, sīc, sík**).

(b) *the Chapel yard* c.1505 (*v.* **chapel(e), geard**); *Cunny Grey* 1625 (*v.* **coningre**); *Mats meadowe* 1625 (with the surn. *Matt*, *v.* Reaney *s.n.*); *Mill holme* 1625 (*v.* **myln, holmr**; with reference to a water-mill; *Old Spiny* 1625 (*v.* **ald, spinney**); *Sand Closse* 1625 (*v.* **sand, clos(e)**); *Temple clos* c.1505 (*v.* **clos(e)**), *Templelands* c.1505 (*v.* **land**) (*v.* **temple**; with reference to former lands of the Knights Templars); *West Littelhil Fordole* c.1275 Hastings (*v.* **west, lȳtel, hyll, fore, dāl**).

3. OLD INGARSBY

Old Ingarsby is a member of Gartree Hundred.

Inuuaresbie 1086 DB
in Gerberie (sic) 1086 DB
Inguaresb' 1204 ClR, *Inguarisby* e.Hy 3 Hastings (p), *Inguerisbi* m.13 Nichols (p), *Higwerisby* p.1250 (1404) *Laz* (p), *Ingwaresby* 1279 Nichols (p)
Inguarebi 1177 P, 1210 Cur, *Inguaruibi* 1190 × 1204 France, *Ynguareby* 1278 Derby (p), *Ingwareby* 1205 ClR, 1236 Cur (p), 1262 Nichols (p), *Yngwarebi* 1210 Cur
Hingwardeby 1220 MHW, *Ingwardeby* 1249 Cur (p), 1278 Banco *et freq* to 1346 *RTemple* (p), 1376 *Dixie* (p), *Ingwardebey* 1306 *Ferrers* (p), *Ynguardeby* 1286 (1404) *Laz*, *Inguardebi* 1321 *Ferrers* (p), *Inguardeby* 1327 SR (p)
Yngwardisby p.1250 Nichols (p), *Ingwardisby* 1345 *LCDeeds* (p)
Ingwardby 1311 Cl (p), 1325 Inqaqd (p) *et passim* to 1535 VE, 1621 Fine
Ingwarby 1260 Cur, 1356 BurtonCart, 1445 Nichols, *Inguerby* 1286 ib (p), *Ingwerby* 1330 Hastings, *Yngwarby* 1339 Cl, 1353 Nichols
Ingarsby(e) 1535 VE, 1540 Pat, 1621 Fine, 1624 LML *et freq*, *Ingersby(e)* 1564 Nichols, 1604 SR, 1619 Fine
Old Ingersby 1835 O, *Old Ingarsby* 1846, 1863 White

'Ingwar's farmstead, village', *v.* **bȳ**. The pers.n. *Ingwar* is ODan (ON *Ingvarr*). The DB form *in Gerberie* is due to metanalysis, the initial *in* - of the name having been mistaken for the MLat prep. *in*. Its *-berie* spelling of the generic is erratic and does not indicate an earlier p.n. in *-byrig* (dat.sg. of OE *burh* 'a fortified place'), *v.* the discussions of Asfordby and neighbouring Quenby.

Ingarsby was depopulated in 1469 to make a monastic grange for the Abbey of St Mary de Pratis, Leicester. Its land, comprising some 1100 acres, was given over to sheep. The late prefix *Old* ~ distinguishes its site from that of New Ingarsby *infra*.

BOTANY BAY FOX COVERT is *Botany bay Cover* 1835 O, *v.* **cover(t)**; on the parish boundary, this is a transferred name for a remote piece of land and referring to the penal settlement established at Botany Bay in New South Wales, Australia, in 1788. CONDUIT SPINNEY, cf. *the Conduit Field, Conduit Meadow* 1918 *Sale*, *v.* **cundite**, **spinney**. HARWOOD NURSERIES, *v.* **nursery**. INGARSBY COTTAGES. INGARSBY HOLLOW, *Ingersby Hollow* 1835 O, *v.* **holh**. INGARSBY LANE. INGARSBY OLD HALL. MONK'S GRAVE, a large tumulus, poss. an early windmill mound. NEW INGARSBY, 1846, 1863 White, *New Ingersby* 1835 O. RAVENHEAD. REEDPOOL SPINNEY, cf. *Reed pool Meadow* 1918 *Sale*, *v.* **hrēod**, **pōl**[1]. THE WHITE HOUSE FM (INGARSBY LODGE 2½"), *Ingarsby Lodge* 1846, 1863 White; it is *Bates Lodge* 1835 O, with the surn. *Bates*, *v.* **loge**.

FIELD-NAMES

Undated forms in (a) are 1918 *Sale*; those dated 1940 are also *Sale*. Forms throughout dated 1540 are Pat, 1609 are Ipm and 17 are *Terrier*.

(a) Two Acres, Three Acre, the Five Acres (*v.* **æcer**); Allotment Gardens (*v.* **allotment**); Barn Mdw; Bennett's Mdw (with the surn. *Bennett*); Billesdon Cl (Billesdon adjoins to the south-east); Bowling Alley Cl (cf. *Bowling Alley meadows* 1609, *v.* **bowling-alley**); Clement's Mdw (with the surn. *Clement*, *v.* Reaney *s.n.*); Coplow Mdw (cf. *Coplowe pasture* 1540, *v.* **pasture**), New Coplow Six Acre (*v.* **æcer**) (cf. *Little Coplow* 17) (*v.* **copp**, **hlāw** and adjacent Billesdon Coplow in Gartree Hundred); Cow Cl (*le Coweclose* 1540, *the Cowe close* 1609, *the Cow Cloase* 17, *v.* **cū**, **clos(e)**); First Cl; Gamleys Mdw (prob. with the surn. *Gamble*, cf. Gamble's Fd in Quenby f.ns. (a)); Gravel Hole (*v.* **gravel**, **hol**[1]); the Great Cl, First ~ ~, Second Great Cl; the Great Mdw; Far ~ ~, First ~ ~, Hog Fd, Hogg Fd or Road Cl, Nether ~ ~ ~, Over Hogg Field Mdw (*v.* **uferra**) (*le Hoggefelde* 1540, *the hoggefields* 17, *v.* **hǫgg**, **feld**; one of the early great fields of the township); Lower ~ ~, House Cl, First ~ ~ ~, Second Upper House Cl, House Close Mdw; Lewis's Mdw 1918, 1940 (*Leaises meadow* 17; with the surn. *Lewis*); the Little Mdw; Far ~ ~, Near Lodge Cl, Lodge Close Mdw (*the Lodg Cloase* 17, *v.* Ingarsby Lodge *supra*); Far ~ ~, First ~ ~, Second ~ ~, Spring Merry Gate (*v.* **spring**[1]), Penn Merrygate, ~ ~ Mdw (*v.* **penn**[2]), Spinney Merrygate (*v.* **spinney**) (cf. *Merregate hill* 17, *v.* **gata**; it is uncertain whether these f.ns. relate to *Marehill* in Hungarton f.ns. (b) *supra*; if so, *v.* **(ge)mǣre**, but if not, *v.* **myry**); Middle Hole (*v.* **middel**, **hol**[1]); the Mill Dam (*v.* **damme**), Mill Field Mdw 1918, 1940 (*the mill* 17, *v.* **myln**); Pen Mdws (*v.* **penn**[2]);

Phipp's Mdw (with the surn. *Phipps*); Road Cl (a roadside field); Round Mdw (*v.* **round**; such enclosures are usually not circular; more often, they are are polygons); Lower ~, Mid ~, Upper Scabdale (*Scabdhill* 17, *v.* **hyll**; the first el. seems be ME **scabbed** 'having scabs', applied topographically to a hill with some such disfigured appearance); Spinney Cl (*v.* **spinney**); Squires Mdw (with the surn. *Squire*(*s*)); Further ~ ~, Hither Swan Style (*v.* **swān**[2]; with **stigel** in its sense 'a steep ascent'); First ~ ~, Second Top Cl; Weather Cl (x3) (*Weathers close* 1609, *v.* **weðer**); Willow Sic (*v.* **wilig**, **sík**).

(b) *Widdow Alleins ground* 17 (*v.* **grund**); *capellam de Hingwardeby* 1220 (with MLat *capella* 'a chapel'); *Crapalls meadow* 17 (poss. with the surn. *Cropwell* of a family originally from the village of this name, 18 miles to the north in Notts.); *Stephen Edwins house & Cloase* 17 (*v.* **clos(e)**); *Haliday grove* 1540 (*v.* **grāf**; with the surn. *Haliday*, *v.* Reaney *s.n.*); *Mr Herricks ground* 17 (*v.* **grund**); *le Horseclos* 1540, *the Horse close* 1609 (*v.* **hors**, **clos(e)**); *Houghton close* 1540, *~ ~ or Weathers close* 1609 (*v.* **clos(e)** and Weather Cl *supra*; Houghton on the Hill adjoins to the south-west); *John Kinges house* 17; *Leicester gate* 1609 (*v.* **gata**; the road to Leicester); *the little Ash close* 1609 (*v.* **æsc**); *Richard Loasbies Meadow* 17 (the *Loasby* family was originally from the village of Lowesby, 3 miles to the north-east); *le medowclose* 1540 (*v.* **mǣd** (**mǣdwe** obl.sg.), **clos(e)**); *le Midlefelde* 1540, *the Midlefeylde* 1609, *le Midlefelde grovett* 1540 (*v.* **grāfet**) (*v.* **middel**, **feld**; one of the early great fields); *le Millfeylde* 1609 (*v.* **feld**; one of the early great fields), *the Mill hill* 17 (*v.* **myln**); *the Milking close* 1609 (*v.* **milking**); *the Rammes close* 1609 (*v.* **ramm**); *Richard Sharpes house* 17; *George Taylers ground* 17 (*v.* **grund**); *Thorneby close* 1540 (*v.* **clos(e)**, *Thurneby feilde*, *Thurnbye feild* 1609 (*v.* **feld**; referring to Thurnby which adjoins to the south-west); *Ralph Toones Farme* 17 (*v.* **ferme**); *John Worths ground* 17, *Robert Worths grounds* (sic) 17 (*v.* **grund**); *le Wynmyll grovett* 1540 (*v.* **wind-mylne**, **grāfet** and *the Mill hill*, *supra*).

4. QUENBY

Qveneberie 1086 DB

Quenebia c.1130 LeicSurv, *Quenebya* Hy 3 *Crox*, *Quenebi* 1210 P (p), m.13 (1404) *Laz*, *Queneby* e.13 *Peake* (p), c.1225 Berkeley (p), 1230 Cur (p) *et freq* to 1384, 1396 Pat *et passim* to 1428 Nichols, 1477 (e.16) *Charyte*, *Quenib'* a.1250 (1404) *Laz*, *Quenyby* 1343 Ipm, 1389 Cor (p)

Quenesbi n.d. AD, *Quensby* 1384 Cl

Quenby 1237 Cur, 1260 Ass *et passim* to 1385 Banco, 1386 Cl *et freq*, *Qwenby* 1380 *Win*, 1393 Cl (p), 1416 ELiW

Perhaps 'the farmstead of the women', *v.* **kona** (**kvenna** gen.pl.), **bӯ**; i.e. a Scand **kvennaby*, cf. Whenby YN 30 and *Kvinneby* (Sweden), *v.* E. Hellquist, *De svenska ortnamnen på -by*, Göteborg (1918), 72. Ekwall's view (DEPN *s.n.*) that the DB form *Qveneberie* represents an earlier important Anglo-Saxon **Cwēnebyrig* 'the queen's manor', with *-byrig* > *-berie*, may be safely discounted since Leics. p.ns. in *burh* are formed with the nom.sg. *burh* rather than with its dat.sg. *byrig* (*v.* the discussion of the name Asfordby) and Queniborough, a rich and major vill, lies only five miles to the north-west. It is scarcely conceivable that two royal vills so close together would have been known by identical names. Quenby was relatively poor and insignificant, worth only a quarter of Queniborough by DB. It was depopulated in the 15th cent. by enclosure. It is noteworthy that its Anglo-Saxon neighbour was Hungarton on its poor soils and that both itself and nearby Ingarsby were given over to sheep in the 15th cent. rather than being maintained as arable estates.

A possible but less likely explanation of the p.n. is that the first el. is indeed OE **cwēn** 'a queen' and that an OE generic such as *þrop* 'outlying farmstead' or *stoc* 'dairy farm, cattle farm' has been replaced by Scand *bȳ* and that the settlement was an outlying dependent farmstead or cattle ranch of Queniborough.

QUENBY HALL, 1720 MagBrit, 1800 Nichols *et passim* to 1925 Kelly, *v.* **hall**. QUENBY LODGE, 1835 O, 1846, 1863 White, *v.* **loge**. QUENBY PARK, 1968 *Surv*, *v.* **park**.

FIELD-NAMES

Undated forms in (a) are c.1810 *Map*. Those dated 1918 are *Sale*, while those dated 1968 are *Surv*.

(a) Six Acre, Eleven Acres 1968, Ten ~ ~, Eighteen Acre Mdw c.1810 (*v.* **æcer**); Bridge Mdw ; Bushy Mdw (*v.* **busshi**); Colepitt Fd (*Colpytfeld* 1514 Ipm, *v.* **col-pytt**, **feld**; beside a place where charcoal was made); Coplow Wood (towards Billesdon Coplow in Gartree Hundred); Cross Leys (*v.* **cross**, **leys**); Dogkennel Mdw (*v.* **kenel**; with reference to kennels for hounds); Doctors Cl (*v.* **doctour**); Elliots Mdw (with the surn. *Elliot*); Feuks Cl (with the surn. *Fewkes*); First Fd 1968; Great ~ ~, Little Fog Fd (*v.* **fogge**); Gamble's Fd 1968 (with the surn. *Gamble* (from the ON pers.n. *Gamall*, an original by-name 'old')); Great Mdw; Hall Cl (*v.* Quenby Hall *supra*); Home Fd 1968 (*v.* **home**); Great ~ ~, Little Langleys (*v.* **lang**[1], **lēah**); Lewins Cl (*v.* Lewin's Mdw in Hungarton f.ns. (a)); Little Mdw c.1810, 1968; Mill Fd, Far ~ ~ ~, Near Mill Field Mdw (*v.* **myln** and *Queneby mylnes*, *infra*); Mott Fd, Mott Field Mdw c.1810, Big ~ ~, Little Mott Fd 1918 (*v.* **mote**; there is a moated site surviving here); Paddock (*v.* **paddock**); Paynes Cl c.1810, Payne's Mdw 1968 (with the surn. *Payne*); (the) Pineham c.1810, 1968 (poss. with **pine** and **hamm**, although late forms); Pingle (*v.* **pingel**); The Plain (*v.* **plain**); Pond Mdw 1918, 1968 (bordering a fish pond); Rough Fd 1968 (*v.* **rūh**[1]); Seed Fd 1968 (*v.* **sǣd**; in f.ns., often used of areas of sown grass); Shoulder of Mutton (a common f.n. alluding to shape); Stevens Cl (with the surn. *Steven*(*s*)); Taylors Hill, Taylors Mdw (cf. *George Taylers ground* in Old Ingarsby f.ns. (b) and *Math. Taylours Headland* in Hungarton); Toothill c.1810, Tootils 1968 (*v.* **tōt-hyll**; a survival from the early Anglo-Saxon period); Great Westhorne (*v.* **west**, **þorn**); Wood Mdw.

(b) *Quenby grovett* 1540 Pat (*v.* **grāfet**); *Queneby mylnes* 1428 Nichols, *Quenebemylnes*, *Quenebymylnes* 1477 (e.16) *Charyte* (*v.* **myln**).

Keyham

KEYHAM

Caiham 1086 DB, 1359 BPR, *Cayham* 1220 MHW, 1247 Ass (p), 1252 Fine *et freq* to 1362 *LCDeeds* (p), 1369 *Peake et passim* to 1491 *ShR*, 1504, 1507 Ipm
Cahiham c.1130 LeicSurv, *Kayeham* 1225 Cur
Kaiham 1199, 1200 P, 1233 Cur, 1279 BM, *Kayham* l.12 *Rut* (p), 1220 Cur, 1226 Fine *et freq* to 1414, 1428 *ShR et passim* to 1535 Ipm, 1570 *Rental*
Kayme 1502 *MiscAccts*, 1538 Ipm, 1541 MinAccts, *Keam*(*e*) 1576 Saxton, 1601 LibCl *et passim* to 1688, 1722 LML
Keyham 1517 Fine, 1535 VE *et passim* to 1604 SR *et freq*

A problematical name because of the interpretation of the first element. This must be some use or extension of use of OE *cǣg* 'a key'. A simple and reasonable explanation is that the specific is the OE pers.n. *Cǣga*, presum. an original by-name for a tall, thin man, a key-shaped fellow. (Pers.n. plus *hām* is a very common p.n. type in early English toponomy.) The alternative is the use of the sb. *cǣg*, but in which sense is here difficult to conceive. Keyham was no doubt an early estate on the line of a Roman road, an estate prob. previously a Romano-British land unit. OE *cǣg* in its literal sense 'a key', applied to something that could be locked, seems a particularly unuseful application in such a context. Ekwall DEPN *s.n.* Kew offers *cǣg* as transferred topographically to a projecting piece of land, something key-shaped. Keyham stands midway upon a long, thin ridge that stretches for 5 miles south-west from what later became the site of Barkby Thorpe towards Billesdon Coplow before turning back upon itself to the west in a conformation that remarkably resembles the keys and latch-lifters found in pagan Anglo-Saxon inhumation graves. The shape of the ridge is effectively displayed on the first edition map of the one-inch Ordnance Survey of 1835. But whether a feature of this size and extent would have been perceived as such a key-shape by Anglo-Saxons on the ground is very questionable. Therefore, either 'Cǣga's village, estate', or 'the village, estate on the key-shaped ridge (or even on the ridge called 'The Key')', *v.* **cǣg**, **hām**; but the interpretation with the OE pers.n. seems preferable.

ALL SAINTS' CHURCH, *The Church* 1797 *HighwayB*, 1877 White, *Church (All Saints)* 1925 Kelly. Note also *the Church Yard* 1757 *Terrier*, 1810 *HighwayB*, 1835 O, *the Old Churchyard* 1772 *EnclA*. A small church at Keyham is earlier recorded in the groups *capellis Cayham Grimeton et Caldewelle* 1220 MHW, *capellarum de Gaddesby Kayham et Wykeham* 1328 *Pat*, ~ *de Gayddesby Cayham et Wykam* 1382 *ib* (with MLat *capella* 'a chapel'). BLACKSMITH'S SHOP (lost), *Blacksmiths Shop* 1827 *Map*, v. **blacksmith**, **sc(e)oppa**. DOG AND GUN (P.H.), *Dog and Gun* 1846, 1863, 1877 White, 1925 Kelly. GLEBE FM, v. **glebe**. INGARSBY RD, Old Ingarsby adjoins to the south-east. KEYHAM BRIDGE, *the Bridge* 1805 *HighwayB*, cf. *Netherstone Bridge* 1772 *EnclA*. KEYHAM HIGH LEYS, *High Leys* 1772 *EnclA*, 1863 White, *High Lays* 1810 *HighwayB*, v. **hēah**[1], **leys**. MAIN ST is *the Town Street* 1772 *EnclA*, 1796 *HighwayB*, v. **tūn**. NETHER HALL, 1882 *Plan*, 1925 Kelly, v. **hall**. OLD HALL is *Keyham Hall* 1925 Kelly, cf. *Hall Lane* 1772 *EnclA*, 1819 *HighwayB*, *Hall Lain* (sic) 1817 *ib* (v. **lane**), v. **hall**. SNOWS LANE, 1796, 1797, 1819 *HighwayB*, *Snowlain* (sic) 1817 *ib*, v. **lane**; with the surn. *Snow*. WEST END FM, *the West End Farm* 1942 *Plan*, v. **ende**. WOODCOCK'S CHARITY SCHOOL (lost), *Woodcocks Charity School* 1827 *Map*.

FIELD-NAMES

Undated forms in (a) are 1827 *Map*. Those dated 1771 are *Map*, 1772 are *EnclA*; 1778, 1787, 1792, 1796, 1797, 1798, 1805, 1809, 1810, 1813, 1814, 1817, 1819 and 1832 are *HighwayB*; 1830 are *Surv*.

(a) Bastard Cl (v. **bastard**); Far ~, Near Blakelands 1830 (v. **blæc**, **land**); Bottom Headland 1830 (v. **hēafod-land**); Bottom Mdw; the Bridge Cl (v. Keyham Bridge *supra*); Mr Bunney's Land 1819, Bunney's Cl 1827 (the *Bunney* family no doubt originally came from the village of Bunny, 15 miles to the north-west in Notts.); Cats Hill (v. **cat(t)**); Church Hill 1832 (v. All Saints' Church *supra*); Clover Cl 1796 (v. **clāfre**; used as a fodder crop); Cramp Fd (v. **cramb**; cf. (the) Cramp Cl in Walton on the Wolds f.ns. (a)); Debdale Cl 1846, 1863, 1877 White (v. **dēop**, **dalr**); Derby Gate or Derby Gate Place 1772 (v. **place**) (v. **gata**; a plot of land or residence beside the old road to Derby); Dovecot Cl 1772 (v. **dove-cot(e)**); East Fd 1772 (v. **feld**; one of the great fields of the township); Far Mdw; the Flints (v. **flint**); Fludes Mdw (with the surn. *Flude*, v. Reaney *s.n.*); Fox holes 1796, Foxhole Leys (v. **leys**) (adjoining Foxholes Covert in Hungarton parish); Frisby Mdw, Frisby's Great Cl (with the surn. *Frisby* of a family originally from either Frisby (by Galby), 4 miles to the south-east, or from Frisby on the Wreake, 7 miles to the north-east); Grift Lane 1797, the Griftt Road (sic) 1817 (v. **gryfja**); the Gravil Hole 1787, 1809, 1814, the Gravil Pitt 1787,

1817, the gravel pit 1809 (*v.* **gravel**); Guilford Mdw, ~ Little Mdw, ~ Plough Fd (*v.* **plōg**) (with the common Leics. surn. *Guilford*); the Hall Pond 1809 (*v.* Old Hall *supra*); Headland Cl (*v.* **hēafod-land**); Heaps Lane 1796, Heaps Gate 1832 (with either **gata** or **geat**) (poss. with the surn. *Heap*, but this is not common in Leics.; otherwise *v.* **hēap**); High Street (*v.* **hēah**[1], **strǣt**; with reference to a minor Roman road); the Holme (*v.* **holmr**); (the) Home Cl (*v.* **home**); the Horse Pond 1814; House Cl 1830; the Houghton Gate 1814, Houghton Gate Cl 1778 (*v.* **gata**; Houghton on the Hill lies 2 miles to the south-east); Mr Hubbards Cl 1796, Mr Hubbards Gate 1797 (*v.* **geat**); the Hungarton Cl, the Little Hungarton Mdw 1827, Hungarton Gate 1797 (*v.* **gata**) (Hungarton adjoins to the north-east); Kings Cl, Kings Little Cl, First ~ ~, Second Kings Mdw, Kings Orchard (cf. *John King* of neighbouring Old Ingarsby); the Leys (*v.* **leys**); the Long Cl; Low Street (*v.* **la(g)h**, **strǣt** and High Street *supra*); The Meadow 1830; Middle Hill; Mr Moles's Yard 1796 (*v.* **geard**); Morder Hill 1827, Morter hill brig 1792 (*v.* **brycg**, **bryggja**), Morden Hill Mdw (sic) 1827 (*v.* **morter**; evidently a site where mortar's raw materials were excavated); Muckle Brinks (*v.* **micel**, **mycel**, **mikill**, **brink**); the New Cl; North Fd 1772 (*v.* **feld**; one of the great fields); the Orchard; Old Penn 1797, Pen Cl (*v.* **penn**[2]); the Pool 1797; Mr Pywells Bridge 1778, ~ ~ Cartway 1798 (*v.* **cart-waie**); Rye Cl (*v.* **ryge**); the Salters Closae 1778 (*v.* **saltere**, **clos(e)**; the parish lay on a medieval salters' way which used the route of a minor Roman road, *v.* High Street *supra*); Seed Cl, Seed Hill (*v.* **sǣd**; often used in f.ns. for areas of sown grass); Selby Corner (*v.* **corner**), Mr Selbys Hedge, Mr Selbys Orchard, ~ ~ ~ Corner, Mr Selbys Well (*v.* **wella**), all 1797; the Sough 1797, the Suff 1810 (*v.* **sōg**); South Fd 1772 (*v.* **feld**; one of the great fields); Suttons 1st ~, Suttons 2nd Cl 1827 (with the surn. *Sutton*); Big ~ ~, Little Top Cl; Top Mdw; the Tythes 1771 (*v.* **tēoða**); Water Hill (*v.* **wæter**; in proximity to the northern stream of the parish); Websters Mdw (with the surn. *Webster*); West Pond; Wildbores Paddock (*v.* **paddock**; with the surn. *Wildbore*); Workhouse Piece (*v.* **workhouse**, **pece**); Mr Windsor's Gravel Pit 1813, Mr Woodford's Gravil pit 1778 (*v.* **gravel**, **pytt**; these are perh. to be identified with the Gravil Hole *supra*).

(b) *Welleberche* 1477 (e.16) *Charyte* (*v.* **wella**; presum. with metathesized **brēc**).

Launde

Launde is described in White 1846 and 1863 as an extra-parochial liberty and included in East Goscote Hundred. Kelly 1925 notes that it was 'formerly extra-parochial, now a parish'.

LAUNDE

Landa c.1160 Dane, 1163, 1164 P *et freq* to 1478 *Peake*, 1482 AD *et passim* to 1530 Visit, 1535 VE, *la Landa* 1166 RBE, 1179, 1180 P *et freq* to 1190, 1191 ib
Lande 1166 LN, Hy 2 *AllS*, 1200 Cur (p), 1398 Pat, 1428 FA, *la Lande* 1210 P, 1220 Cur 1237, 1347 Cl
Land' 1202 Ass, 1231 RHug (p) *et passim* to 1249 Cl, 1269 For, *la Land'* 1198 Cur
la Launda 1333 Inqaqd
la Laund(e) 1202 Ass, 1243 Fees, 1248 Ch *et passim* to 1409, 1483 Cl, *Laund(e)* 1267 Cur, 1301 Abbr, 1306 Pat *et freq*
Lawnd(e) 1482 AD, 1501 Ipm, 1536 AAS, 1551 Ipm, 16 *Terrier*

'The woodland glade; the open space in woodland', *v.* **launde**. ME *launde* is from OFr *lande* 'a glade, woodland pasture'. The word appears in MLat as *landa* and *launda* 'a forest glade'. OFr, MLat and ME forms are represented here in the recorded spellings.

LAUNDE ABBEY

Launde Abbey 1586 *Plan*, 1846, 1863, 1877 White, 1925 Kelly, *Lawnde Abbey* 1617 LML, *Laund Abby* 1728 *Rental*, *Laund Abbey* 1824 O
priorie de Launde 1319, 1406 *Pat*, *priorie de la Launde* 1339 *ib*
monasteri de Launde 1397 *Pat*
ecclesiam conventualem de Landa 1319 *Pat*, *ecclesie Sancti Johannis Baptiste Launde* 1452 *ib*

Never an abbey but a priory for Augustinian Canons founded 1119 × 1125 by Richard Bassett, its church was dedicated to St John the Baptist. At the Dissolution, the priory became the property of Thomas Cromwell whose family built a mansion on the ruins. Note MLat *prioria* 'a priory', MLat *monasterium* 'a monastery' and MLat *conventualis* 'conventual, belonging to a religious convent', *v.* **abbaye**.

ABBEY FM is *Launde Lodge* 1824 O, *v.* **loge**. BROOK FM. BROOM'S FM is *Brooms Lodge* 1824 O; with the surn. *Broom*, *v.* **loge**. HILL FM (LAUNDE LODGE 2½") is *Launde Wood Lodge* 1824 O, *v.* **loge** and Launde Big Wood. LAUNDE BIG WOOD is *Lawnde Wood* Eliz 1 DKR, *Laund ~*, *Lawnd wood* 1669 *Rental*, *Lawne wood* 17 *ib*, *Laund Wood* 1806 Map, 1824 O; earlier it is *Westewoode* 1539 Deed, *Westwood* 1541 ib, 1604 Nichols, *Laund West Wood* 1800 ib, *v.* **west, wudu**. LAUNDE PARK, *Launde Parke* 1539 Deed, *Laund Parke* 1604 Nichols, *Lau'd park* 1610 Speed, *Laund Park* 1824 O, (*parcum de Landa* 1375 Nichols), *v.* **park**. LAUNDE PARK WOOD, *Laund Park Wood* 1806 Map. LAUNDE WOOD FM. PARK WOOD FM is *Keepers Lodge* 1824 O, *v.* **keeper, loge**.

FIELD-NAMES

Forms dated 1539 and 1541 are Nichols; 17 are *Clay*; 1728 are *Rental*.

(b) *Atkins closs* 17, *~ Close* 1728 (*v.* **clos(e)**; with the surn. *Atkins*); *Beadles three closes* 17 (with the surn. *Beadle*, from OE *bydel* 'a beadle', cf. *Ailsi le Bedell'* 1175 P of Leics.); *Burfeld* 1539, *Burfytt close alias Le Burfeeld* 1541, *the Burfeild* 17, *Burrfield* 1728 (*v.* **burh, feld** and 'The Burgh' discussed in Whatborough; one of the great fields of the township); *Chapell yard* 1728 (*v.* **chapel(e), geard**; the present chapel constitutes the erstwhile chancel of the priory church of St John the Baptist); *Coppetre* 1218 Nichols bis, *Copptre* Hy 3 **ib**, *Coptre* Hy 3 ib, 1269 For (*v.* **copped**², **trēow**); *Cummaneswodesyke* 1247, c.1250 Nichols (*v.* **wudu, sík**; the first el. may be the OBret pers.n. *Cunmin* or a later reflex *Cummin* (giving the surn. *Cummin(s)*, *v.* Reaney *s.n.*)); *the twoo Cuneryes* 17, *Cunnery* 1728 (*v.* **coningre**); *the Dames* 17, *Damms* 1728 (*v.* **damme**); *East meadow* 1728; *Estfeld* 1539, *Estefe(e)ld* 1541, *the Est feild* 17 (*v.* **ēast, feld**; one of the great fields); (*the*) *Gravell Pit Close* 1727, 1728 *Reeve* (*v.* **gravel, pytt**); *Holebec* Hy 2 Dugd, *Holebroc* 1162 × 66 *AllS*, c.1250, Hy 3 Nichols, *Holbroke* 1247, c.1250 ib, *Holbroc* c.1250 ib (*v.* **hol**², **brōc**; the earliest form shows Scand **bekkr**); *the Home* 17 (*v.* **holmr**); *Hors(s)e Close* 1539, 1541 (*v.* **hors, clos(e)**); *the two Horse crafts* 17, *Lower ~ ~*, *Upper Horse Croft* 1728 (*v.* **hors, croft**); *Hussiffe Close* 1728 (*v.* **huswyf** 'mistress of a family, wife of a householder'); *Lantern yerd* 1539, *the Laund towne yard* 17 (*v.* **geard**; these forms presum. belong together, but it is difficult to decide which carries more weight; if the earlier, then with ME **lanterne** 'a lantern', but even here it is uncertain whether the reference was to a permanent light to direct travellers (say) to the priory or whether to an architectural feature of a newly-built mansion after the Dissolution of the monasteries (*v.* OED *s.v.* lantern sb. 4); but if the 17th cent. form is significant (is this a rationalization of an ill-remembered name?), then with **tūn** in its sense 'village, estate'); *the Mill* 17, *Milwong* 1539, *Le Myllewong* 1541, *Mill Wong* 1728 (*v.* **vangr**), *Mylfeld* 1539, *Le Myllefelde* 1541, *the Far Milfeild*, *the Hither mill feild* 17, *Great ~ ~*, *Mill Field* 1728 (*v.* **feld**; one of the great fields) (*v.* **myln**); *More close* 1539, *Le Moreclose* 1541, *the Moore close* 17 (*v.* **mōr**[1], **clos(e)**); *le New(e)close* 1539, 1541 (*v.* **nīwe, clos(e)**); *the Newfeild* 17 (*v.* **nīwe, feld**); *Parckeers close* 17 (presum. with **parkere** 'a parker, a park-keeper' rather than its surn. reflex *Parker*; note the early Launde Park *supra*); *Pitt Close* 1728 (*v.* **pytt**); *Poters meadow* (sic) 1728 (with the surn. *Potter*; otherwise with its source, ME **pottere** 'a pot-maker'); *Le Pryours Close* 1541 (*v.* **prior, clos(e)**); *Reddysyke* 1540 Deed (*v.* **hrēodig, sík**); *Redegate* Hy 2, 1247 Nichols, *Redgate* 1247, a.1250, c.1250 ib (*v.* **gata**; either with **hrēod** or **rēad** or, less likely, **rǣde**); *Shepecote yarde* 1541, *the Sheepcoate yard* 17, *Sheep Coat yard* 1728 (*v.* **scēp-cot, geard**); *Steans Home Stead* 1728 (*v.* **hām-stede**; with the surn. *Stean*); *Swifts close* 17, *Swifts meadow* 1728 (with the surn. *Swift*); *Thomas Taylors close* 1539, 1541 (*v.* **clos(e)**); *Whadborowgh Newclose* 1541 (*v.* **nīwe, clos(e)**; adjoining Whatborough; perh. to be identified with *le New(e)close*, *supra*).

Loddington

LODDINGTON

Lvdintone 1086 DB, *Ludinton'* c.1130 LeicSurv, 1206 P (p) *et passim* to 1253 Cl, 1265 Misc (p)
Ludington 1248 Ch, l.13 CustRo
Lodinton' c.1125 Dugd, c.1130 LeicSurv, Hy 2 Dugd *et passim* to 1274 RGrav (p), 1332 Cl, *Lodintona* Hy 1 Dugd, 1330 Nichols, *Lodintone* 1166 RBE, 1220 MHW, *Lodenton* 1237 RGros, *Lodynton* 1346 Pap, 1349 Inqaqd, 1350 Pat
Lodington' c.1130 LeicSurv, 1208 FF *et passim* to 1349 *LCDeeds* (p), 1350 *Peake*, *Lodingthon'* l.13 *ib*, *Lodyngton'* c.1291 Tax, 1294 Coram *et freq* to 1446 *Wyg*, 1448 *Peake et passim* to 1535 VE, 1541 Dugd, *Loddington* 1551 Ipm, 1576 Saxton, 1610 Speed *et freq*

'The village, estate associated with or called after a man named Luda', *v.* **-ingtūn** and Cossington *supra*. The pers.n. *Luda* is OE.

BELTON RD, Belton in Rutland lies 2 miles to the south-east. BLACKSMITH'S SHOP (lost), *Blacksmiths Shop* 1847 *TA*, *v.* **blacksmith**, **sc(e)oppa**. BUTLERS COTTAGE, with the surn. *Butler*, cf. Butlers cunnery in f.ns (a) and *Butlers close* in f.ns. (b). COPTHILL FM is *Copt Hill House Farm* 1863 White; *Copt hill* 1669 *Rental*, 1847 *TA*, *Coptill* 17 *Rental*, *v.* **copped**[1], **hyll**. HALL FM, *Hall farm* 1925 Kelly, *v.* Loddington Hall *infra*. HOLLY COTTAGE. HORSEPOOLS FM, poss. with a rationalized form of Horshold in f.ns. (a); otherwise *v.* **hors**, **pōl**[1]. LAUNDE COTTAGE lies towards Launde *supra*. LODDINGTON HALL, 1846, 1863, 1877 White, 1925 Kelly, *Lodington* ~ 1800, 1804 Nichols; it is *the Mannor House* 1669 *Rental* (*v.* **maner**), *v.* **hall**. LODDINGTON HO., *Loddington house* 1925 Kelly. LODDINGTON LANE. LODDINGTON LODGE (lost), *le Lodge* 1539 *Deed*, *Lodington Lodge* 1824 O, *Loddington* ~ 1846 White, 1851, 1861 Census, *v.* **loge**. LODDINGTON MILL, 1851, 1861 Census, *the Mill* 1669 *Rental*, *Lodington Mill* 1824 O, *v.* **myln**. LODDINGTON REDDISH, *Reddish* 1604 Nichols; it is *Reddish Wood* 1663 *Deed*, 1800 Nichols,

1846 White, 1847 *TA*, 1850 *Surv*, 1863, 1877 White, *Redish Wood* 1824 O and *Loddington Wood* 1800 Map; prob. 'the reedy place', *v.* **hrēod**, **-isc**. The Reddish lies along Eye Brook. MANOR FM, *v.* **maner** and Loddington Hall *supra*. OXEY CROSS ROADS, OXEY FM, *v.* Oxey in f.ns. (a). ROUND HILL SPINNEY is *Wilsons Spinney* 1824 O, *v.* **spinney**; with the surn. *Wilson*. ST MICHAEL'S CHURCH, *Church (St Michael)* 1846, 1863, 1877 White, *Church (St Michael and All Angels)* 1925 Kelly; it is earlier recorded as *ecclesie de Lodington* 1220 MHW, ~ *de Lodinton* 1235 RGros, ~ *de Lodenton* 1237 ib, ~ *de Lodyngton* 1334 *Pat*, *the Church* 1674, 1708, 1708 (18) *Terrier*. Note also *the Church Yard* 1708, 1708 (18) *ib*. SCHOOL FM (SCHOOL 2½"). THE VICARAGE, 1861 Census, 1877 White; cf. *the Vicaridge house* 1674, 1686, 1690 *Terrier et passim* to 1724 *ib*, ~ *Vicarage* ~ 1708 (18) *ib*, 1847 *TA* and *the Parsonage House* 1762 *Terrier*, *v.* **vikerage**, **personage**. WOOD LANE, adjacent to Loddington Reddish and leading to Tugby Wood.

The following houses with appurtenances are recorded in 1669 *Rental*: *William Brownes house & close*; *George Burbidges house & homestead*, *Thomas Burbidges house & Homestead* (the *Burbidge* family was no doubt originally from Burbage, 22 miles to the south-west); *Mr Chapmans house*; *Fairechilds house & homestead*; *Groocockes house & Homestead*; *Bartholmew Ilsons house & Homested* (the *Illson* family was originally from Illston on the Hill, 5 miles to the north-east; p.n. forms for Illston which show typical Leics. loss of *t* in the group *-ston* occur from the earlier 16th cent.); *Rich. Jenkinsons house & Homestead*; *Humphrey Marshalls house & close*; *Edward Seaman house & homestead* (*v.* **hām-stede**).

FIELD-NAMES

Undated forms in (a) are 1847 *TA*; forms dated 1797 and c.1850 are *Surv*. Forms throughout dated Hy 2 and Hy 3 are *AllS*; 1274 are RGrav; 1539 and 1663 are *Deed*; 1669 and 17 are *Rental*; 1674, 1686, 1690, 1697, 1700, 1703, 1708, 1708 (18), 1718, 1721 and 1724 are *Terrier*.

(a) Two acres, Ten ~, Fifteen ~, Eighteen Acres (*v.* **æcer**); Allen's holmes 1847, Allen ~ c.1850 (*v.* **holmr**; *Thomas Allen* is cited 1847); Apple tree wong (*Apletree wong* 1669, *Appletree wonge* 17, cf. *Appletree close* 1539 (*v.* **clos(e)**), *v.* **æppel-trēow**, **vangr**); Ashborow 1847, Ashbarrow c.1850 (*Ashborough* 1663, *Ashborrough* 17, *Ashboro* 1708, 1708 (18), *Ashborough Close* 17, *Ashboro Gate* 1708, 1708 (18) (*v.* **gata**), *Ashboro hill* 1708, 1708 (18), *v.* **æsc**, **berg**); Avenue Cl (*v.* **avenue**); Back

Mdw (*v.* **back**); Bakers Mdw (with the surn. *Baker*); Bare bushes 1847, Barebushes or Brownsover Cl c.1850 (*v.* **bær, busc**; presum. with reference to scrub which had died off; *v.* Brownsover Cl *infra*); Barrow Hill 1824 O (1669, 17, *the Barrow Hill* 1669), Lower ~ ~, Upper Barrow Hill 1847 (17) (*v.* **berg**; it is poss. that tumuli are alluded to since this parish borders the early territorial unit which became Rutland, *v.* Ru xvi–xix); The Belt (*v.* **belt**); Black lands (*v.* **blæc, land**); Brick kiln leys (*v.* **leys**) (cf. *Brickilne Close* 17, *v.* **brike-kiln**); Brook Cl (*the Brooke* 1663, cf. *Brook mead* 1669 (*v.* **mǣd**); with reference to Eye Brook); Broom's Cl (*Charles Broom Snr and Jnr* and *Philip Broom* are cited 1847); Brownsover Cl c.1850 (presum. this is 'Brown's upper close', *v.* **uferra**, with the surn. *Brown*; *v.* Bare bushes *supra* and note *William Brown* 1669 *Rental*); Butcher's Cl (*Tobias Butcher* is cited 1847); Crodens Calboro (with the surn. *Croden*), Far ~, Great ~, Nether ~, Over Calboro (*v.* **uferra**), Nether ~ ~, Over Calboro Mdw 1797, 1847 (*the Coldborowes* 1669, cf. *Coldborowes Close* 17, *v.* **cald, berg**); Cherrytree Cl 1847, c.1850 (cf. *Cheretree lease* 1669 (*v.* **leys**), *v.* **cherietree**); (the) Conduit Cl 1800 Nichols, 1846 White, 1847 *TA*, 1863, 1877 White (*v.* **cundite**; a source of water formerly piped to Launde Abbey); Copt hill Mdw (*v.* Copthill Fm *supra*); Crabtree Cl 1847, c.1850 (cf. *the Crabbtree Hill Close* 17, *Crabtree hill* 1669, *v.* **crabtre**); Croxendale 1847, c.1850 (1663, *v.* **dalr**; earlier forms are needed to explain the first el.); Burbidges ~, Butlers ~ (with the surns. *Burbidge* and *Butler*), Great ~, Milking Cunnery (*v.* **milking**) (*le Conyngry* 1539, *the Conygree*, *Conygrees* 17, *the three Connygrees* 1669, cf. (*ye*) *Conygree hill* 17, *v.* **coningre** and note *Thomas Burbidge* 1847); Dixie's yard (*v.* **geard**; with the surn. *Dixie*); Dry skins (poss. refers to a location for part of the process of tanning hides, *v.* **skinn** and cf. Skin Pit Fd, Ch **3** 184); Green Fairchild's Cl (*v.* **grēne**[1]) (*Fairechildes close* 1669, cf. *Fairchildes meadow* 1669; with the surn. *Fairchild*); Far Cl; Farm Cl (*v.* **ferme**); First ~ ~, Big ~ ~, Little Glebe Cl (*v.* **glebe**); Gravel pits ((*the*) *Gravellpitt*(*e*) 1663, *v.* **gravel, pytt**); Green gate (1708, 1708 (18), *Grenegate* 1274, *the Greene Gate* 1669, *Broughtons Greene Gate* 17 (with the surn. *Broughton*)), Lower Green gate (*Nether Green Gate* 17, *v.* **neoðera**) (*v.* **grēne**[1], **gata**); Groococks Cl 1847, c.1850 (with the surn. *Groocock*); Hawthorn Hill (*v.* **hagu-þorn**); Home Cl 1847, c.1850, Reeves Home Cl 1847 (with the surn. *Reeve*(*s*)) (*v.* **home**); Horshold seek (*Old ~ ~*, *Horshold Seeke* 17, *v.* **hors, hald**[1], **sík**; *-hold* may poss. disguise **wald**, but wold country is otherwise unrepresented in this parish's f.ns., *v.* spellings for Prestwold *infra*); Joes Cl 1847, Joe's Cl or Mill Lane Mdw c.1850 (with the pers.n. *Joe* (from Joseph)); Lammas Cl 1847, ~ ~ or Mdw c.1850 (*v.* **lammas**); Land Cl 1847, c.1850, Green lands Cl 1847 (*v.* **grēne**[1]) (*v.* **land**; closes containing unspecified numbers of 'lands' or selions of a former great field); Limekilns (described as pasture in 1847; *Limekilns* 1708, 1708 (18), cf. *the Lyme Kilne close* 17, *Limekill Furlong* 1708, 1708 (18) (*v.* **furlang**), *v.* **lim-kilne**); Little end (*v.* **ende**); Little Mdw; Loddington Holt 1800, 1806 Map, Lodington ~ 1824 O (cf. *the Holt Marsh* 1663 (*v.* **mersc**), *v.* **holt**; prob. another name for Loddington Reddish); Loddington Rise 1806 Map, Long Rice 1847, c.1850 (*the Long Rise* 1663, *v.* **rise**); Little ~ ~, Long Cl (*Long close* 1669); Lount (*v.* **lundr**); Mill dam 1847, c.1850 (*v.* **damme**), Mill Holmes 1847, c.1850 (*the Mill Holmes* 1663, 1669, *v.* **holmr**), Mill Mdw 1847, c.1850, Mill Lane Mdw c.1850 (*v.* Joe's Cl *supra*) (*v.* **myln**); the Moors (*v.* **mōr**[1]); Mossendue's Cl (with the surn. *Mossendue*); Nether Mdw 1847, c.1850; Oak Holme 1847, c.1850 (*the Oakham* 1663, *v.* **āc, hamm, holmr**); Over Mdw 1847, c.1850 (*v.* **uferra**); Over yard (*v.* **uferra, geard**); Oxey,

~ Mdw, Nether Oxey, ~ ~ Mdw 1797, 1847, Oxey Drift 1847, c.1850 (*v.* **drift**) (*the Oxayes* 1669, *the Oxeye* 1708, 1708 (18), *the two Oxhayes Closes* 17, *v.* **oxa, (ge)hæg**); Paddock (*v.* **paddock**); Park (*parcum . . . de Lodinton* Hy 2) (*v.* **park**); Parsons nook (*v.* **persone, nōk**); Pye thorne (*v.* **pie, þorn**); the Quillets 1847, c.1850 (*v.* **quillet(t)**); Rainy Mdw (*v.* **rein**); Nether ~, Upper Reddish 1847, c.1850 (*v.* Loddington Reddish *supra*); Redlands 1847, c.1850 (*v.* **rēad, land**); Row Mdw 1847, c.1850 (*the Rows meadow* 1663, *v.* **vrá**); Far Sandhills ((*the*) *Sandalls* 1669, 17, *v.* **sand, hyll**); Sharpes Cl 1847, c.1850, Sharpes Mdw 1847, c.1850 (with the surn. *Sharpe*); Shellacres Cl (cf. *Rich. Shellaker* 1669); Bridge Stiltons (*Brigge Stilton* 1669, *v.* **brycg**), Bushy Stiltons (*Bushe Stilton* 1669, *v.* **busshi**), Far ~, Great ~, Lawrences Stiltons (with the surn. *Lawrence*), Shillacres Stiltons (cf. *Rich. Shellakers Stilton* 1669), Stilton's Mdw (*Stiltons* 1539 Nichols, *Old Stiltons* 17, ~ *Stilton* 1708, 1708 (18), *New Stilton* 1669, 1708, 1708 (18), *New Stiltons Close* 17, *Richard Johnsons house Stilton* 1669, *Stilton end* 1669, 1708, 1708 (18) (*v.* **ende**), *Stilton field* 1700, 1703, 1708, 1708 (18) (*v.* **feld**; one of the great fields of the township), 'the farmstead at the steep ascent', *v.* **stigel, tūn**; a lost settlement to the south-east of Loddington); Stocking Dike c.1850 (1663, *Stockindick* 1663, *v.* **stoccing, dík**); Stone pit Mdw (*v.* **stān-pytt**); Swine bridge (*Swinth brige* 17, *v.* **brycg**; the first el. is prob. **swin**[2] 'a channel' rather than **swīn**[1] 'a pig', cf. Swines Bridge Mdw in Cossington f.ns. (a)); Syson's nook 1847, Sysons ~ c.1850 (*v.* **nōk**; with the surn. *Syson* of a family originally from Syston, 12 miles to the north-west; spellings of the village name show loss of *t* in the group *-ston* from the beginning of the 17th cent.); Tarveys ~, Tarvey's Cl (the surn. is prob. *Turvey*); Townend ~, Townsend Cl, Town end homestead (*v.* **hām-stede**) (*v.* **tūn, ende**); Upper Cl 1847, c.1850; Bottom ~ ~, Top ~ ~, Way Cl (*v.* **weg**); The Waste (*v.* **waste**); Nether ~, Wood Cl 1847, Nether Wood Cl or Stocking Dike c.1850 (*v.* Stocking Dike *supra*).

(b) *Ashgate* 1375 Nichols (*v.* **æsc, gata**); *Blackborough Seeke* 1663 (*v.* **blæc, berg**); *Brockhill* 1708, 1708 (18) (*v.* **brōc, hyll**; but note that such a late form may conceal an earlier **brocc-hol**); *George Brushfields land end* 1708, 1708 (18); *John Bucks hadley* 1708, ~ ~ *headley* 1708 (18) (*v.* **headley**); *John Bulls land* 1708, *Thomas Bulls Lands* 1708, 1708 (18) (*v.* **land**); *the Widdow Burbidge Close* 1663; (*the*) *Church Close* 1669, 1674 *et passim* to 1721, *the Church Ley(e)s* 1708, 1708 (18) (*v.* **leys**), (*the*) *Church Moor(e)* 1669, 1708, 1708 (18) (*v.* **mōr**[1]), *the Church Sick* 1708, 1708 (18) (*v.* **sík**), *Church Wonge* 1663 (*v.* **vangr**) (*v.* St Michael's Church *supra*); *Clerkyswellebrukys* 1274 RGrav bis (*v.* **clerc, wella, brōc**); *Lawrence Collings leyes* 1708 (*v.* **leys**); *the Common Pasture* 1700 (*v.* **commun, pasture**); (*the*) *Constable way* 1708, 1708 (18) (*v.* **conestable, weg**); *atte crofte* 1377 SR (p) (*v.* **atte, croft**); *the Drift* 1708, 1708 (18) (*v.* **drift**); *Faire pasture* 1669 (*v.* **fæger, pasture**); *William Greens Close* 1669; (*the*) *Hall Close* 1663, 1674 *et passim* to 1708 (18), 1721, *the Hall Grounds* 1708, 1708 (18) (*v.* **grund**) (*v.* Loddington Hall *supra*); *Little ~ ~, Upper Hallatton Balke* 1663, *the two Hallerton Balkes* 1669 (*v.* **balca**; with the surn. *Hallaton* of a family originally from the village of this name, 4 miles to the south); *Helot(e)cros* Hy 2, Hy 3 (*v.* **cros**; poss. with the OFr pers.n. *Heliot* (from OFr *Élie-ot*, a diminutive of Elias), *v.* Reaney *s.n.* Eliot); *super le Hil* 1274 RGrav (p) (*v.* **hyll**); *the Hom(e)stall* 1686, 1690 *et passim* to 1724 (*v.* **hām-stall**; belonging to *the Vicaridge house*, *v.* The Vicarage *supra*); *the Homeste(a)d* 1674, 17 (*v.* **hām-stede**); *Horson Hill* 1708, 1708 (18), *Horsen hill Close* 1708, *Horson ~ ~* 1708 (18) (*v.* **hār**[2], **stān**; a hill bearing a stone marking the parish boundary); *the longe House Close*

1663; *George Jermins Close* 1708, *George Jermins Ley(e)* 1708, 1708 (18) (*v.* **ley**), *Francis Jermins Ley(e)s* 1708, 1708 (18) (*v.* **leys**), *Francis Jermins Land* 1708 (*v.* **land**); *the Lane* 1708 (18); *Laund field* 1700, 1703, 1708 (*v.* **feld**; one of the great fields, adjoining Launde to the north); *Lees* 1539 (*v.* **lǣs**); *the Ley of John Goodrich* 1708, 1708 (18) (*v.* **ley**); *Little Dale Hill* 1708, (*the*) *Little Dale seeke* (*next home*) 17, 1708 (*v.* **sík, holmr**) (*v.* **dalr**); *Lodghill* 17 (*v.* Loddington Lodge *supra*); *Everard Marstons Leyes* 1708, ~ *Marston's Leys* 1708 (18) (*v.* **leys**); *the Mill Close* 1663 (*v.* Loddington Mill *supra*); *Robert Palmers Land* 1708 (18) (*v.* **land**); *the Pasture* 1708 (*v.* **pasture**); *Pickman Barrs* 1708, 1708 (18) (with the surn. *Pickman* and **barre** 'a bar, a barrier'; the reference may be to land at a gate or barrier to woodland, but the original sense of *barre* was 'a long piece (of something)' and this sense may have been transferred to a long, narrow piece of land); *Riddish field* 1700, 1703, 1708, 1708 (18) (*v.* **feld**; one of the great fields of the township towards Loddington Reddish *supra*); *Thomas Sharpes Leyes* 1708, ~ *Sharp's Leys* 1708 (18) (*v.* **leys**); *Stereswod* 1375 Nichols (*v.* **wudu**; the first el. may be the ME surn. *Ster* (cf. *Gaufridius Ster* 1209 P and *Robertus le Steer* 1296 SR, from OE *stēor* 'a steer'), but note also the OE pers.n. *Ster(r)* (*v.* Searle 431) and the ON pers.n. *Styrr* (ODan *Styr*) (*v.* Feilitzen 377)); *the Stone hoggs Close* 1663 (*v.* **hogg**; a stone-fenced enclosure, presum. for young sheep, cf. *John Swan Sherrhoges close*, *infra*; otherwise for pigs); *the Street(e)* 1686, 1690, 1697, 1708 (*v.* **strǣt**; the principal thoroughfare of the township); *John Swan Sherrhoges close* 1669 (*v.* **hogg**; alluding to lambs after their first shearing, cf. Shear Hogs Cl in Illston on the Hill (Gartree Hundred), *v.* Field 120); *le Syke* 1274 RGrav (*v.* **sík**); *Tith Medow* 1708 (*v.* **tēoða**); *the Town Me(a)dow* 1708, 1708 (18) (*v.* **tūn**); *Richard Vills Ley(e)s* 1708, 1708 (18) (*v.* **leys**); *West End Brook* 1708 (*v.* **ende**; a stream which runs from north to south to the immediate west of the village); *the Wood Close* 1708 (adjoining Loddington Reddish *supra*).

Lowesby

LOWESBY

Glowesbi (sic) 1086 DB
Lousebia c.1130 LeicSurv, *Lousebi* 1184 P, e.13 (1404) *Laz*, 1232 RHug, c.1250 (1404) *Laz*, *Louseby* 1200 Dugd, 1220 MHW, 1229, 1232 RHug *et freq* to 1364 *Wyg* (p), 1404 *Laz et passim* to 1445 Nichols, 1446 Banco, *Lousebya* 1209 × 19 RHug, *Lowseby* 1315 *AllS*, 1440 Fine, *Lowceby* 1412 FA
Losebi e.Hy 2 Dane, *Loseb(e)ia* Hy 2 Dugd, 1178 × 84 (1328) Ch
Lousby John (1404), 1265 Nichols *et passim* to 1332 SR (p), 1352 Nichols, *Lowsby* 1468 Pat, 1518 Visit
Lowesby 1241 RGros, 1265 Misc *et passim* to 1435 *Comp*, 1438 *Peake et freq*, *Louesby* 1261 RGrav bis, 1491 BM
Lawcebye 1562 AAS, *Lawisbie* 1580 LEpis
Loasebie 1606 LML, *Loaseby* 1609 ib, *Loasby(e)* 1612, 1628 ib, *Loseby(e)* 1576 Saxton 1610 Speed

Possibly 'Lauss's or Lausi's farmstead, village', *v.* **bȳ**. The specific appears to be a Scand by-name such as *Lauss/Lausi* 'loose-living'. A by-name *Løs* is recorded in Denmark in 1298 (DgP II 710) and there was also an OScand by-name *Løse* (XenLid 103). Ekwall DEPN suggests that the specific may be OScand **lausa* 'a slope' which is found in Scand p.ns. as *-lösa/-löse*, but Janzén has shown that the element was no longer being used in p.n. formation at the time of the Scand settlements in England (*v. Names* **5** 97 and SSNEM 58).

ALL SAINTS' CHURCH, *Church (All Saints)* 1846, 1863, 1877 White, 1925 Kelly; it is earlier recorded as *ecclesie de Lousebeya* 1209 × 19 RHug, ~ *de Louseby* 1220 MHW, 1352 *Pat*, ~ *de Lowesby* 1241 RGros, *ecclesia de Lowesbye* 1554 *Pat*. Note also *the churchyarde* 1612 *Terrier*, *the Church yard* 1674, 1697, 1821 *ib*, *v.* **chirche-ȝeard**. CARR BRIDGE, ~ ~ SPINNEY, *Carbridge* l.18 *Map*, *Carr Bridge* l.18 *Surv*, *Car Bridge* 1835 O, *Carr Brigg* 1968 *Surv*, *v.* **brycg**, **bryggja**; the first word may be **kjarr** 'wet ground (especially that overgrown with brushwood)', but more likely is the surn. *Carr* derived from it, cf. *Edward Wills Carr*, rector of Lowesby 1775–93, and *Thomas Carr, farmer* 1877 White, cf. Lewin Bridge in Ratcliffe on the Wreake. CAUDALE FIELD FM, *Farr ~ ~*, *Great Cawdwell Field* 1763 *Deed*, *Caudle Field* 1763 *Terrier*, *Caudale ~* 1763 *ib*, 1783 *Deed*, 1969 *Surv*, *Cawdell ~* 1863 White, *v.* **cald, wella, feld**; prob. one of the great fields of the township. The farmstead is *Loseby Lodge* 1835 O (*v.* **loge**), *Cauldwell farm* 1877 White. THE CEDARS. CHURCH HILL, *v.* All Saints' Church *supra*. DUN'S LANE FM, cf. *Dun's Lane Cottage* 1846, 1863, 1877 White, *v.* **lane, cotage**; with the surn. *Dun(n)*, *v.* Reaney *s.n.* JOHN O' GAUNT is *John o' Gaunts Cover* 1863 White, *v.* **cover(t)**; a fox covert, cf. John o' Gaunt Fm and John o' Gaunt Viaduct in neighbouring Twyford. LOWESBY GRANGE, 1863, 1877 White, *v.* **grange**; it is *Austin's Lodge* 1824 O, *v.* **loge**; with the surn. *Austin*. LOWESBY HALL, l.18 *Surv*, 1821 *Terrier*, 1846, 1863, 1877 White, 1925 Kelly, *Loseby Hall* 1795 Nichols; it is *the Mansion house* 1783 *Deed* (*v.* **mansion-house**), *v.* **hall**. LOWESBY HALL FM is *The Farm* 1835 O. LOWESBY PARK, *the Park* 1763 *Terrier*, 1763, 1783 *Deed*, l.18 *Surv*, *v.* **park**. LOWESBY STATION. MAREFIELD LANE, Marefield lying 1½ miles to the east. MELTON RD, the road to Melton Mowbray which is situated 7 miles to the north-east. PARK RD, *v.* Lowesby Park *supra*. PORTER'S LODGE (2½"), *The Porters Lodge* 1835 O, *v.* **loge**. *Porter* is presum. a reduction of *Porthill* l.18 *Map*, an early market site (*v.* **port**[2], **hyll**) also represented by Portels Fm in neighbouring Cold Newton. Porter's Lodge is at a cross-roads on the crest of a hill, the road from the north-east Roman in origin, remembered in adjacent Streethill (*v.* Streethill Fm *infra*), and which is recorded in neighbouring Hungarton in the late 15th cent. as *portam viam* 'the road to the market'. The lodge is also known locally as *Thimble Hall* 1969 *Surv*, a term of affection for this little cottage orné, gothicized in 1816 by Sir Frederick Fowke of Lowesby Hall. SOUTH LODGE, 1863, 1877 White, *v.* **loge**. STATION COTTAGES. STREETHILL FM, *Streat hill alias Street hill* 1584 Ipm, *Street hill* 1610 ib, 1641 Nichols, 1752 *Map*, 1763 *Deed*, 1835 O, 1846 White; the farm site is *Streethill Lodge* 1698 LeicW (*v.* **loge**), *Street Hill House* 1752 *Map*, *Street-hill farm* 1877 White; a minor Roman road (*le Strete* 1396 Pat) crosses the hill here, *v.* **strǣt, hyll**. TWYFORD RD, Twyford lying 1½ miles to the north. THE VICARAGE, 1877 White; it is *the Vicaridge House* 1612, 1674 *Terrier*, *~ ~ Howse* 1625 *ib*, *v.* **vikerage**.

FIELD-NAMES

Undated forms in (a) are 1969 *Surv*; those dated 1763^1 are *Terrier*; 1763^2, 1781, 1783, 1847 and 1849 are *Deed*; l.18 are *Surv*.

(a) Three Acre, Four ~, Five ~, Six ~, Eleven ~, Twelve ~, Fourteen ~, Eighteen Acre (*v.* **æcer**); Back Fd (*v.* **back**); The Bank (*v.* **banke**); Barn Cl 1763^1, Barn Mdw 1763^1, l.18, 1849; Barnes Cl (with the surn. *Barnes*); Bents (either the surn. *Bent* in the possessive case or **beonet**); Berridges Cl 1763^2 (with the surn. *Berridge*); Big Mdw; Birch Cl (*v.* **birce**); Bottom Mdw; Bridge Cl (*v.* Carr Bridge *supra*); Brook Cl (*v.* **brōc**); Burrow Lane l.18 (*v.* **burgh, lane**); 1st ~ ~, 2nd Bush Cl (*v.* **busc**); Bushey Cl or Farr hill 1763^2 (*v.* **busshi** and Farr hill *infra*); Carbridge Cl 1763^2, Car Bridge Mdw 1763^1 (*v.* Carr Bridge *supra*); Chattles Mdw 1763^1, Chittle's Cl l.18 (with the surn. *Chettle*, a reflex of the Anglo-Scand pers.n. *Cytel* (from ON *Ketill*)); Church Cl 1763^1, Church Close Mdw 1763^1, l.18 (*v.* All Saints' Church *supra*); Clover Cl 1763^1, 1763^2, l.18, 1969 (*v.* **clāfre**; used as a fodder crop); Cocked Hat (an enclosure shaped like a tricorne hat); Cotchers Cl 1763^1, l.18, Cottyers ~ 1763^2 (*v.* **cottere**); Cover Fd (*v.* **cover(t)**); Cow Cl, Cow Fds, Cow Meadow Cl; Cresswell Cl 1763^2 (*v.* **cærse, wella**); Crew Yard 1763^2 (*v.* **crew-yard**; its earliest citation in OED is for 1778); Crook Cl, Crook Close Mdw 1763^1 (*v.* **krókr**); Crooked Cl 1763^2 (*Croked close* 1543 *Farn*, *v.* **croked, clos(e)**); Dairy Cl l.18, 1969 (*v.* **deierie**); Digman Cl 1763^1 (with the surn. *Digman*, *v.* Reaney *s.n.*); Dixon's Mdw (with the surn. *Dixon*); the Dove Coat 1783 (*v.* **dove-cot(e)**); the Dovehouse 1763^2 (*v.* **dove-hous**); Fat Cl (*v.* **fætt**; alluding to rich land); Feeding Fd (*v.* **feeding**; a field of superior grazing for cattle); Frisby Mdw (with the surn. *Frisby* of a family originally either from Frisby (by Galby), 4 miles to the south-west, or from Frisby on the Wreake, 7 miles to the north-west); Goldings Cl 1763^2 (with the surn. *Golding*, a reflex of the late OE pers.n. *Golding*); Gravell Hill 1763^2, Gravel Hole 1969, Gravel Pits 1763^1, 1969, ~ Pitts 1783, Gravel Pit Cl l.18, 1849 (*v.* **gravel**); Great ~, Little Hillockey 1763^1, Hillick a Close (sic) 1763^2 (*v.* **hylloc, -ig**^{3}); Home Cl, Top ~ ~, Home Fd (*v.* **home**); Homestead 1763^2 (*v.* **hām-stede**); (the) Horse Cl 1763^1, 1763^2; House and Parlour 1763^1 (*v.* **parlur**); Hovel Cl, Hovel Mdw (*v.* **hovel**); Kesteen's Cottage Fd, ~ Nether Fd (with the surn. *Kesteen*, a reduced form of Kesteven); Leatherlands Mdw (with the surn. *Leatherland*); Linish Cl (beside railway lines); Little Mdw 1763^2, l.18; Little ~ ~, Middle Lowesby Cl 1763^1, 1783, Great Lowesby Cl 1763^1, 1783, 1849; the Meer 1763^1 (*v.* **mere**^{1}); the Little Millfield 1763^2 (*v.* **myln**); Mowings Cl l.18 (*v.* **mowing**; a close in which grass was grown for hay); Mushroom Fd (in which mushrooms abounded); Nether Fd 1763^1, l.18, Far ~, Near ~, Home Netherfield 1763^2 (*v.* **home**) (*v.* **neoðera, feld**; prob. originally one of the great fields of the township); New Mdw 1763^1; Oak Cl (*v.* **āc**; presum. distinguished by a lone oak-tree); Old Mdw (with **ald** or **wald**, *v. the Upper and Nether Woldes* in f.ns. (b)); Peach Cl 1763^1 (with the surn. *Peach*); Peakes Cl l.18 (with the surn. *Peake*); Pecks Mdw 1763^1, 1763^2, Peck's ~ 1849 (with the surn. *Peck*); Pick Pockets One and Two (humorous derogatory names for two unprofitable fields); Pig House Fd; Plowd Cl 1763^1 (i.e. *ploughed*); Pole's Cl (with the surn. *Pole*, *v.* Reaney *s.n.*); Pool Yard 1763^1, l.18, Pool Yards 1969 (*v.* **pōl**^{1}, **geard**); Porthill Great Mdw, ~ Leys 1763^2 (*v.* **leys**) (*v.* Porter's Lodge *supra* and Portels Fm in neighbouring Cold Newton parish);

(a plot of ground called) the Pottery 1849, Lowesby Pottery 1846 White (*v.* **potterye**); Roadside Cl; the Seeds l.18, Big ~, Little Seeds, Seed Fds, Little Seed Fd 1969 (*v.* **sǣd**; often used in f.ns. of areas of sown grass); Sentry Cl (with the surn. *Sentry*, from ME *seintuarie* 'a shrine', *v.* Reaney *s.n.*); Shelter Hedge (presum. with reference to a windbreak, poss. for cattle); Smithsons Paddock (*v.* **paddock**; with the surn. *Smithson*); South Fd; (the) Spinnies l.18, the Little Spinney 1763[2], Spinney Mdw 1969 (*v.* **spinney**); Spring Cl (*v.* **spring**[1]); Stackups (*v.* **stakkr**; a stack-yard); Station Fd (*v.* Lowesby Station *supra*); Streethill Cls 1763[2] (*v.* Streethill Fm *supra*); Lower ~, Top Suttons (with the surn. *Sutton* in the possessive case); the Wash Pit 1781, Wash Pits 1969, Wash Pit Cl 1763[1], l.18, Wash Pit Fd 1969, Wash Pit Mdw 1763[1], 1781 (*v.* **wæsce, pytt**; with reference to a sheep-dip); Well Cl 1763[1], l.18 (*v.* **wella**); the Willow Beds 1763[2] (*v.* **wilig, bedd**).

(b) *Debdale Wong* 1705 Nichols (*v.* **dēop, dalr, vangr**); *ad fontem* 1327 SR (p) (with MLat *fons* (*fontem* acc.sg.) 'a spring'; note Spring Cl *supra*); *les Glebe Lands* 1554 Nichols, *les Gleab Landes* 1602 ib (*v.* **glebe, land**); *the homestall* 1612 *Terrier* (*v.* **hām-stall**; i.e. belonging to *the Vicaridge House*); *Lous*(*e*)*bywode* 1247, c.1250 Nichols (*v.* **wudu**); *Lyng close* 1543 *Farn* (*v.* **lyng, clos(e)**); *New Close* 1705 Nichols; *Sowcer Wonge* 1533 × 44 ChancP (*v.* **vangr**; prob. with the surn. *Sauser*, from OFr *saucier* 'a maker of sauces'; but note ME *sowcer* 'a dish in which sauces were placed on the table' > ModE *saucer*, so that it is poss. that the sb. was transferred topographically to a saucer-shaped depression in the ground); *the Vicaridge Close* 1612 *Terrier* (*v.* **vikerage**); *the Upper and Nether Woldes* 1630 Ipm (*v.* **wald**).

Cold Newton

COLD NEWTON

Niwetone 1086 DB bis
Neuton' c.1130 LeicSurv, 12 Dugd, 1220 RHug *et freq* to 1334 Pat, 1336 Ass *et passim* to 1554 Fine, 1558 Ipm, *Neutone* 1232 RHug, 1250 × 99 (1404), l.13 (1404) *Laz*, *Neutona* a.1250 (1404) *ib* (p) bis, m.13 (1404) *ib*, 1262 BM, 13 (1404) *Laz*, *Neutun* 1236 Fees, *Neutunia* a.1250 (1404) *Laz* (p)
Newinton' a.1250 (1404) *Laz* bis
Neweton(e) 1274 Banco, 1434 Fine, 1442 BM
Newton 1405 AD, 1428 FA *et passim* to 1555, 1567 Fine *et freq*

Affixes are variously added as:
~ *Burdet(t)* 1242 Fees, 1276 Banco *et passim* to 1500, 1514 Ipm *et freq* to 1610 Speed, ~ *Burditt* 1671 *Deed*
~ *iuxta Louseby* a.1250 (1404) *Laz*, 1274 Banco, l.13 (1404) *Laz*, 1389 BM
Tylton ~ 1544 Nichols
~ *Marmion* 1563 Nichols, 1588 *Conant*, 1671 *Deed*, ~ *Marmyon* 1567 Fine
Marmyons ~ 1671 *Deed*
Cold(e) ~ 1279, 1288 Ass *et passim* to 1437 Banco, 1554 Fine *et freq*

'The new farmstead', *v.* **nīwe** (**nīwan** wk.obl.), **tūn**; later described as 'cold' because of its exposed, bleak situation, *v.* **cald**. *Willelmus Burdet* held one knight's fee here in 1236 Fees. *Willielmus Marmion* held land and tenements in the township in 1271 Fine. That the affix ~ *Marmion* appears only from the later 16th cent. may be due to antiquarian rather than to popular usage. Both Lowesby and Tilton adjoin Cold Newton. The occasional form *Newinton'* is from **nīwan**, the wk.obl. case of **nīwe**.

COLD NEWTON GRANGE, *Newton Grange alias Le Spittell alias Le Spittell Grange alias Le Spittell Hills* 1539 Nichols, *Newton Grange alias le Spitle graunge alias Spittle Hill* 1554 Pat, *Newton Grange alias le Spittle or Spittle grange or Spittle hilles* 1575 Ipm, *Newton Grange alias le Spitle or Spittle grange or Spittle hilles* 1588 ib, *v.* **grange**, **spitel**, **hyll**; the grange was an outlier of the leper Hospital of St Lazarus in Burton Lazars, *v.* Lei **2** 63. COLD NEWTON LODGE, 1877 White, *v.* **loge**. DIAMOND SPINNEY, alluding to shape. ENDERBYS LANE, with the surn. *Enderby* of a family originally from the village of this name, 12 miles to the south-west. HAMNER'S LODGE FM, *Hamners Lodge* 1835 O, *v.* **loge**; with the surn. *Hamner*. HIGHFIELD FM, *Highfield Farm* 1863, 1877 White; *the Hyefeld* 1543 *Farn*, (*the*) *High Field* 1763 *Terrier*, 1763 *Deed*, l.18 *Surv*, *v.* **hēah**[1], **feld**; one of the great fields of the township. HUNGARTON RD, leading to Hungarton, 2 miles to the north-west. LORD MORTON'S COVERT, *v.* **cover(t)**. MAIN ST. MANOR HO., *Manor House* 1835 O, 1846, 1863, 1877 White, 1925 Kelly, *Capital Messuage or Scyte of the Mannor of Cold Newton* 1671 *Deed*, *v.* **maner**. PORTELS FM is *Portel farm* 1877 White; it is *Porthills Lodge* 1835 O, *Port Hill Lodge* 1846, 1863 White (*v.* **loge**), *v.* **port**[2], **hyll** and Porter's Lodge in Lowesby *supra*. SKEG HILL, *Skeghill* 1616 Misc, cf. *Skeyghhill close* 1623 Ipm, *v.* **skegg** 'a beard', used topographically of something jutting out and poss. covered with scrub, cf. *Hamerskeges* and *Skeggedale* in Hoby f.ns. (b). SLUDGE HALL (HILL HO. 2½"), *the Hill House* 1835 O, *Sludge hall* 1925 Kelly; the first word may indeed be ModE *sludge* 'mud, mire, ooze', and if so, this is an ironical toponym for a poor site; perh. cf. Frog Hall which occurs frequently. But the name may rather relate to the unexplained Sledge Spinney in Little Dalby, *v.* Lei **2** 85. SLUDGE HALL FM, SLUDGE HALL HILL. SPRINGFIELD HILL, 1846, 1863, 1877 White, *v.* **spring**[1]. STONE PIT LODGE (lost), *Stone Pit Lodge* 1846, 1863 White, *v.* **stān-pytt**, **loge**. WHITE'S BARN.

FIELD-NAMES

Undated forms in (a) are 1969 *Surv*; those dated 1763 are *Terrier*, l.18 are *Surv*, c.1810 are *Map*, 1842 are *TA*, 1847 and 1849 are *Deed* and 1863 are *Sale*. Forms throughout dated e.13 (1404), a.1250 (1404), m.13 (1404), p.1250 (1404) and l.13 (1404) are *Laz*; 1544, 1705 and 1720 are Nichols; 1588 and 1623 are Ipm; 1613 and 1671 are *Deed*; 1616 are Misc.

(a) Two Acres, Six ~, Seven Acre 1969, Eight Acres or New Mdw 1863, Eleven Acre 1969, (the) Fourteen Acres 1842, 1863, Sixteen ~ 1863, Eighteen Acres 1842, 1863 (*v.* **æcer**); the Allottment Ground 1849 (*v.* **grund**), Allotment Fd 1969 (*v.* **allotment**); Ash Cl (1623, *the Ash Close or Burbage Close* 1671, *v.* **æsc**; *Burbage* is the surn. of a family originally from Burbage, 19 miles to the south-west); Banky (*v.* **banke**, **-ig**[3]); Barn Close No.1, ~ ~ No.2 1863, Barn Cl, Barn Mdw 1969; Best or Home Cl 1863, Best Cl 1969 (a complimentary name for a very fertile enclosure, *v.* **best** and Home Cl *infra*); Brackland (*Breklands close* 1623, *v.* **bræc**[1], **land**); Top ~, Breach 1863 (*la Breache* 1616, *Breach close* 1623, *v.* **brēc**); the Brickyard 1847, 1849, Potteries Brickyard Fd 1969 (*v.* **brike-yard** and the Pottery in adjoining Lowesby f.ns. (a)); Chapel Fd (*le close near the chappell* 1623, (*capellam de Neuton* 1220 MHW, with MLat *capella* 'a chapel'), *v.* **chapel(e)**); Cliffords Mdw (with the surn. *Clifford*); Corner Bit 1863 (*v.* **corner**, **bit**); Middle ~ ~, Nether ~ ~, Upper Cottage Cl 1842 (*v.* **cotage**); Cow Cl, Cow Fd; Curtis Cl (with the surn. *Curtis*); Denshaws Cl c.1810, Denshire ~ 1842 (the surn. *Denshire* occurs c.1850 and is presum. a reduced form of Devonshire; a surn. *Denshaw* is not recorded); Diamond Cl (adjoining Diamond Spinney *supra*); Dock Hill (*v.* **docce**); Dunkirk Mdw (no doubt with reference to the Duke of York's unsuccessful siege of Dunkirk in 1793 and thus a name suggesting misfortune, with overtones of remoteness and difficulty of management); Elm Cl 1763, l.18, Elm Close Mdw 1763 (*v.* **elm**); Fallow Cl 1763, l.18 (*v.* **falg**); Far(r) Hill, Far Hill Mdw 1763; Far Mdw; the Folley 1842, the Folly 1863 (*v.* **folie**; by 1863, a name given to a meadow, but such names were originally accorded to mock ruins in landscaped parks and later applied to hill-top plantations which were thought to resemble such structures, *v.* Field 58); Footpath Plantation; Fulbacks, Great ~ ~, Little Fulback Mdw c.1810 (*Fullbeck* 1613, *Fulbecke close* 1616, *v.* **fūl**, **bekkr**); Gorse Hill (*v.* **gorst**); Gravel Pit 1863 (*v.* **gravel**); Great Cl 1863, Nether ~ ~ ~ ~, Upper Far Side Great Cl 1842 (*v.* **sīde**); Great Mdw c.1810, 1868; Hall Cl (*Nether ~ ~*, *Over hall close* 1623 (*v.* **uferra**), *v.* **hall**); High Field Mdw (*v.* Highfield Fm *supra*); High Leys 1763, l.18 (*High Lea close* 1616, *~ ley ~* 1623, 1671, *v.* **hēah**[1], **ley**, **leys**); Hill Acres (*v.* **æcer**); Home Cl 1863, Home Fd, Bottom Home Paddock (*v.* **paddock**) (*v.* **home**); Horse Pasture (*v.* **pasture**); House Cl 1863, House Mdw c.1810, House Paddock (*v.* **paddock**); Lane 1763, Lane Mdw l.18 (cf. *in the lane* 1377 SR (p), *v.* **lane**); Lissomes or Chapel Fd (with the surn. *Lissom* in the possessive case, *v.* Chapel Fd *supra*); Little Mdw c.1810, 1969; Long Mdw; Lowesby Cl 1763, 1969, Little ~ ~ 1969 (Lowesby adjoins to the north); The Meadow 1842, New ~, Old ~, Top Mdw 1863; New Cl; New Mdw 1863 (*v.* Eight Acres *supra*); Newton Hills 1846 White, The Hills 1969; Orchard Cl; Ornaments (unexplained); Paddock (*v.* **paddock**); Payne's Mdw (with the surn. *Payne*); Peak's Mdw (with the surn. *Peak(e)*); Plough Cl 1842, 1863, Spinney Plough Fd (*v.* **spinney**) (*v.* **plōg**); Portal No.1, ~ No.2, Portel, ~ Old Mdw 1763 (cf. *Porthill Close* 1616, *porthill feld* 1533 × 40 ChancP (*v.* **feld**; one of the great fields of the township), *v.* Portels Fm *supra* and Porter's Lodge in Lowesby); Primrose Hill (a hill upon which primroses abound, *v.* **primerose**); S. Bend (a close with a boundary or boundaries of this configuration); Far ~, Bottom ~, Top Seeds, First ~ ~, Second Top Seeds (*v.* **sǣd**; used in f.ns. for areas of sown grass); Sheepcote Leys 1863 (*Sheepcote leyes* 1623, *Sheepcoateleyes* 1671, *v.* **scēp-cot**, **leys**); the Slang (*v.* **slang**); Somerby Mdw (with the surn. *Somerby* of a family originally from the village of this name, 4 miles to the north-east); Stackyard l.18, 1969 (*v.* **stak-ȝeard**); Stone Pitts

1877 White, Big ~ ~ ~, Top Stone Pit Cl 1842, 1863, Little ~ ~ ~ 1863 (*Stonepit Closes* 1720, *v.* Stone Pit Lodge *supra*); Three-cornered Fd (*v.* **three-cornered**); Top Fd; the Top Mdw 1842; Wigleys Cl, Wigleys Mdw c.1810 (with the surn. *Wigley*); Wildbores, Wildbore's Pasture (*v.* **pasture**; with the surn. *Wildbore*); the Big Wolds (*v.* **wald**).

(b) *Ashbies or Fulbecke close* 1616 (with the surn. *Ashby*, *v.* Fulbacks in f.ns. (a)); *Banelond* a.1250 (1404), *Bradebanlond'* p.1250 (1404) (*v.* **brād**) (*v.* **bēan, land**); *Benchcroft close* 1623 (*v.* **benc, croft**); *benkes* e.13 (1404) (either **benkr** or **benc** (with Scand influence)); *Biridole* l.13 (1404) (*v.* **berige, dāl**); *Blakemilde* e.13 (1404), a.1250 (1404) (*v.* **blæc, mylde**); *Blindewelledole* a.1250 (1404) (*v.* **blind, wella, dāl**); *Bradedale* p.1250 (1404) (*v.* **brād, dalr**); *langebrand', shortbrand'* a.1250 (1404) (*v.* **brand, lang**[1], **sc(e)ort**); *Bretland* p.1250 (1404), *Breatland* 1616 (*v.* **breiðr, land**); *Brewhouse close* 1623 (*v.* **brew-hous**); *Broadhill close* 1616 (*v.* **brād, hyll**); *Burnemedue* p.1250 (1404) (*v.* **mǣd (mǣdwe** obl.sg.); either with **burna** or with either of the cognates OE **bryne**/ON **bruni** metathesized); *Burbage Close* 1671 (*v.* Ash Cl in f.ns. (a)); *Caldewelle* e.13 (1404), a.1250 (1404), *Caldewellemedue* l.13 (1404) (*v.* **mǣd (mǣdwe** obl.sg.) (*v.* **cald, wella**); *Coplowe hill close* 1613 (*v.* **copp, hlāw**); *Croftfurlong* p.1250 (1404) (*v.* **croft, furlang**); *Crosfurlang* a.1250 (1404) (*v.* **cross, furlang**); *Crossebeck close* 1623 (*v.* **cross, bekkr**); *Culurewang'* a.1250 (1404) (*v.* **culfre, vangr**); *Dovecote close* 1616 (*v.* **dove-cot(e)**); *le Dovehouse close* 1623 bis (*v.* **dove-hous**); *bosci de Foxoles* m.13 (1404) (with MLat *boscus* 'a wood'), *Foxholes* p.1250 (1404) (*v.* **fox-hol**); *frithelund* e.13 (1404) (*v.* **lundr**; with **frið** 'protection' or **friðen** 'protected, secure' and describing either a small fenced-in wood or a sacred grove, one offering sanctuary); *Frisbys close* 1616 (with the surn. *Frisby* of a family originally either from Frisby (by Galby), 4 miles to the south-west or from Frisby on the Wreake, 7 miles to the north); *fulewelle* e.13 (1404) (*v.* **fūl, wella**); *Gorebrodewong* p.1250 (1404) (*v.* **gorebrode, vangr**); *Gosewong* m.13 (1404) (*v.* **gōs, vangr**); *Gowborn close* 1623 (poss. with the surn. *Golbo(u)rn* (*v.* Reaney *s.n.*), but this belongs principally to the Cheshire/Lancs. area and may be thought out of place here at this date; if a topographical name, then 'the stream where the marsh marigold abounds', *v.* **golde, burna**); *grenedole* e.13 (1404), *Grenedale* a.1250 (1404) (these forms may well belong together, thus *v.* **grēne**[1], **dāl**; in the later form, **deill** may have replaced the generic, otherwise *v.* **dalr**); *Hardhill* e.13 (1404), *hardhil* a.1250 (1404), *hardehil* m.13 (1404) bis (*v.* **heard, hyll**; a hill with soil hard to till); *Hill furlong* 1623, 1671 (*v.* **furlang**); *holewelhil* e.13 (1404), *holewellehil* a.1250 (1404), p.1250 (1404) (*v.* **hol**[2], **wella, hyll**); *Houphing* p.1250 (1404) (poss. **hopping**; but an original long vowel is suggested in the first syllable, hence perh. **hōp**[2] with the suffix **-ing**[2]); *Hulwestergate* m.13 (1404) (*v.* **hulfestre, gata**); *Jordanes house* 1671 (occupied by *Hugh Jordan* in 1671); *kirkehil* e.13 (1404), *kirkehill'* a.1250 (1404) (*v.* **kirkja, hyll**; note that in the 13th cent., Cold Newton had only a chapel, *v.* Chapel Fd in f.ns. (a)); *langdale* a.1250 (1404), *litlelangedale* a.1250 (1404) (*v.* **lȳtel**) (*v.* **lang**[1], **dalr**); *haielangland, heielangeland* a.1250 (1404), *heilonghelond* p.1250 (1404) (*v.* **hēah**[1]), *witelangeland* a.1250 (1404), *witelonghelond* p.1250 (1404) (*v.* **hwīt**) (*v.* **lang**[1], **land**); *le longebosche* p.1250 (1404) (*v.* **lang**[1], **busc**); *Marshall(s) Close* 1623, 1671 (with the surn. *Marshall*); *Meduebreche* p.1250 (1404) (*v.* **mǣd (mǣdwe** obl.sg.), **brēc**); (*bosci de*) *Menelund* a.1250 (1404), m.13 (1404), p.1250 (1404) (with MLat *boscus* 'a wood'), *menelunt sike* m.13(1404) (*v.* **sík**) (*v.* **(ge)mǣne, lundr**);

Porteford' p.1250 (1404) (*v.* **ford**), *Portsike* p.1250 (1404) (*v.* **sík**) (*v.* **port**[2] and Portels Fm *supra*); *quartreacres* a.1250 (1404) (*v.* **quarter, æcer**); *Radecliffe close* 1616 (prob. with the surn. *Radcliffe* of a family originally from Ratcliffe on the Wreake, 8 miles to the north-west); *Redgreȝ* a.1250 (1404) (*v.* **hrēod, græs**; presum. a piece of grassland containing clumps of reed); (*bosco que vocatur*) *Salou* m.13 (1404), p.1250 (1404) (with MLat *boscus* 'a wood', *v.* **salh**; it is uncertain whether the *ou* of the toponym represents **hōh** or **haugr** or a miscopied plural **Salous*); *Sandpitt leyes* 1623, 1671 (*v.* **sand-pytt, leys**); *Shepecote close* 1616 (*v.* **scēp-cot**); *Spittle Close* 1705, *Spytell felde*, *~ feild* 1544 (*v.* **feld**; one of the great fields) (*v.* **spitel** and Cold Newton Grange *supra*); *Staffhopps* 1616, *Stafhopps close* 1623 (*v.* **stæf, hop**[1]; poss. alluding to a plot of land marked out by posts in a marshy area); *Steinclif* m.13 (1404), p.1250 (1404), *Steincliff, Steyncliff* 1544 (*v.* **steinn, clif**); *Steyning* 1544 (*v.* **steinn, eng**); *Sturges close* 1616, 1623, 1671 (with the surn. *Sturges*, *v.* Reaney *s.n.*); *Suthclif* a.1250 (1404) (*v.* **sūð, clif**); (*bosci de*) *Swinelond'* m.13 (1404), l.13 (1404) (with MLat *boscus* 'a wood'), *suinelund, suenelund, Suinelound* p.1250 (1404) (*v.* **swīn**[1], **svín, lundr**; referring to a wood where pigs were fed on mast); *Thuruerdesdole* p.1250 (1404) (*v.* **dāl**; with the ON pers.n. *Þórvarðr*); *Trumpeshou* p.1250 (1404) (*v.* **hōh, haugr**; the first el. is prob. the OE pers.n. *Trump* (as in Trumpington, Ca 91), perh. cf. Sw *trumpe* 'a surly person', but note also the ME surn. *Trumpe* (> ModE *Trump*), a metonymic for *Trumper* (OFr *trumpeur* 'a trumpeter')); *Tugeland'* p.1250 (1404) (*v.* **land**; perh. with an OE pers.n. *Tucga*); *uplandes* a.1250 (1404), *uplondis* m.13 (1404) (*v.* **up, land**); *utlant* m.13 (1404) (*v.* **ūt, land**); *Watirland* m.13 (1404) (*v.* **wæter, land**); *le Welleclif* p.1250 (1404) (*v.* **wella, clif**); *Wlfholes, Ulfholes, Vlfholis* a.1250 (1404), *Wulfolis* m.13 (1404), *Wolfeholes, Wolfholes, Wolfholis* p.1250 (1404) (*v.* **wulf, hol**[1]; evidently referring to wolf-traps, the more usual compound being *wulf-pytt*); *Wrights close* 1616 (with the surn. *Wright*); *yerdgatehil* p.1250 (1404) (*v.* **gerd, gata, hyll**, describing a road marked off by stakes, cf. *gyrdweg* 956 (13) BCS 955 (S 621)).

East Norton

EAST NORTON

Nortone 1086 DB, 1277 Hastings, 1308 Ipm, *Nortona* 1184 CartAnt, Hy 2 Dugd
Nortuna Hy 1 Dugd, *Nortun* 1236 Fees
North' 1233 Fees
Norton(') c.1130 LeicSurv, 1184 CartAnt, Hy 2 Dugd, 1212 Fine *et freq*

Affixes are variously added as:
~ *Ricard'* 1242 Fees
~ *iuxta Haloughton* 1317 Banco
~ *beside Gawdeby* 1499 *Wyg*
Est ~ 1271 Fine, 1308 Ipm *et freq* to 1541 MinAccts, 1557 Fine, *East* ~ 1604 SR, 1626 LML *et freq*

'The north farmstead, village', *v.* **norð**, **tūn**. It was usually described as 'east' to distinguish it from King's Norton (alias West Norton), *v.* **ēast**. The parish abuts Hallaton and Goadby. *Ricardus de Norton* is cited as holding the manor in 1236 Fees.

ALL SAINTS' CHURCH, *Church (All Saints)* 1846, 1863, 1877 White, 1925 Kelly; its predecessor is recorded as *capellam Norton* 1220 MHW (with MLat *capella* 'a chapel'). CAP'S SPINNEY, with the surn. *Capp*. CHURCH LANE, *v.* All Saints' Church *supra*. CRACKBOTTLE LODGE, ~ RD, ~ SPINNEY. EAST NORTON HALL, 1925 Kelly, *the Hall* 1728 *Deed*, *v.* **hall**. EAST NORTON STATION, cf. *Station Wharf* 1925 Kelly, *v.* **hwearf**; the station was on the former *Melton Mowbray and Market Harborough Railway* 1877 White. FIDDLERS GREEN, *Fidlers Green* 1839 *TA*, *v.* **grēne**[2]; prob. with the surn. *Fiddler*, but otherwise with its source ME **fithelere** 'one who plays the fiddle'. FINCHLEY BRIDGE, 1801 Map, 1846, 1863, 1877 White; earlier it is *Fynchefordebrig* 1375 Nichols, *Fynchefordebrigge* 1376 *For*, cf. *Finchesford'* 1227 ClR, *Fincheford* 1266, 1269 *For*, Hy 3 Nichols and *atte brigge* 1377 SR (p), *atte brugge*

1377 ib (p) (*v.* **atte**); originally 'ford frequented by finches' and later 'the bridge at *Fincheford*', *v.* **finc**, **ford**, **brycg**. The modern form *Finchley* may be a corruption of the older name or may represent an unrecorded Finchley nearby. GRANGE SPINNEY is beside Keythorpe Grange *infra*. HALL FM, *v.* East Norton Hall *supra*. HARDY'S GUNSEL, cf. *John Hardy, farmer* 1863 White and *v.* Big ~, Little Gunsel in adjacent Tugby and Keythorpe parish. KEYTHORPE GRANGE, 1925 Kelly, *The Grange* 1846, 1863 White, *atte Graunge* 1386 Cl (p) (*v.* **atte**), *v.* **grange**; Keythorpe adjoins to the west. MANOR HO., *Manor House* 1846, 1863, 1877 White, *v.* **maner**. MOOR HILL. NORTH PARK. RAM'S HEAD SPINNEY, *Ramshead or Ramshill* 1797 *Surv*, *Ram Head* 1824 O, *Ramshead* 1839 *TA*, *v.* **ramm**, **hēafod**; the precursor of the spinney is *Ramswood* 1674, 1690 *Terrier et freq* to 1721 *ib*, 1784 Nichols, *v.* **wudu**. STATION COTTAGES, *v.* East Norton Station *supra*. WALNUT FM. WESLEYAN CHAPEL. WHITE BULL (P.H.) (lost), *Bull Inn* 1839 *TA*, *White Bull* 1846, 1863 White, 1925 Kelly, *White Bull Inn* 1877 White.

FIELD-NAMES

Undated forms in (a) are 1839 *TA*; 1780 and 1789 are *Deed*; 1797 are *Surv*. Throughout, forms dated 1653 are Nichols; 1690, 1701 and 1728 are *Deed*.

(a) the Four Acre Mdw, the Ten ~, (the) Twelve ~, the Twenty Acres, the Twenty Acre Plantation, Thirty Acres (*v.* **æcer**); Allens Cl (1728), Allens Mdw (with the surn. *Allen*); Ash Plantation (*v.* **æsc**); Atkin's Cl 1797 (with the surn. *Atkin(s)*); Banks Cl (either with **banke** or with the surn. *Banks*); Beans Cl (prob. with **bēan** since *Bean* was not a Leics. surn. at this date); Blind boys Cl (poss. named from a horse); Blythe's Cl (cf. *Hannah Blythe* 1839); the Middle Breach Cl, Far ~ ~, Near Breach Mdw (cf. *Breach Field* 1653, *v.* **brēc**, **feld**; one of the great fields of the township); Brooke Cl (cf. *the Brookfield* 1701, *v.* **brōc**, **feld**; one of the great fields); Broughton's Cl 1797, 1839 (with the surn. *Broughton*); Bucks Cl, Bottom Bucks Mdw (with the common Leics. surn. *Buck*); Butts Cl (*v.* **butte**; on the parish boundary); Calf Lairs, the Calf Lairs Plantation (*v.* **calf**, **lair**); (the) Cow Cl 1797, 1839; Cow Pastures 1846, 1863, 1877 White (*v.* **pasture**); Dafts Cl (with the surn. *Daft*); First Mdw; Fulwell (*Fulwell close*, *Fulwell meadow* 1690, *v.* **fūl**, **wella**); the Glebe (*v.* **glebe**); Goss Covert (*v.* **gorst**, **cover(t)**); Gravel Pit Cl 1797, Gravel Hole Cl 1839 (*v.* **gravel**); Great Cl 1797, 1839, Great Close Mdw, Great Close Plantation 1839; Green Leys 1797, 1839 (*v.* **grēne**[1], **leys**); Hall Cl (*v.* East Norton Hall *supra*); Harringworth Poors Cl (*v.* **pouer(e)**; land endowed to provide funds for the poor of Harringworth which lies 8 miles to the south-east in Northants.); Holcombs (poss. the surn. *Holcomb* in the possessive case; otherwise 'deep valley', *v.* **hol**[2], **cumb**, cf. Hollow Combs in Humberstone f.ns. (a) and Reaney *s.n.* Holcomb); Holliwell (*v.*

hol[2], **wella**); Home Cl (1728, *v.* **home**); the Homestead (*v.* **hām-stede**); Knights Cl (1728; with the surn. *Knight*); the Land Cl, the Nether ~ ~, the Upper Land Cl (*v.* **land**; closes comprising unspecified numbers of 'lands' or selions of a former great field); Bottom ~ ~, Top Lane Cl, Lane Close Mdw (*v.* **lane**); Leonards Cl 1797, 1839 (with the surn. *Leonard*); the Meadow 1789; Mill Leys (*v.* **myln**, **leys**); Neats Gate (1728, *v.* **nēat**, **gata**); Nether Cl; the Nether Mdw; the New Mdw; Far ~ ~, First ~ ~, Norton Cl (*Norton Close* 16 *Rental*, *v.* **clos(e)**); Norton Poor's Land (*v.* **pouer(e)**; land endowed to provide funds for the relief of the parish poor of Norton, cf. Harringworth Poors Cl *supra*); Oat Cl 1789, the Oats Cl 1839 (*v.* **āte**); the Old Mdw; Old Road Piece (*v.* **pece**); the Over Mdw (*v.* **uferra**); Pages Mdw (with the surn. *Page*); the Parlour End 1780 (*v.* **parlur**, **ende**); Peakes Cl (with the surn. *Peake*); the Pen Yard (*v.* **penn**[2], **geard**); Pinfold Cl (*v.* **pynd-fald**); the Pingle (*v.* **pingel**); Ploughed Cl; Poors Piece (*v.* **pouer(e)**, **pece**; land endowed to provide funds for the parish poor of Norton); Rag(g)s Cl 1797, 1839 (with the surn. *Ragg*); Ramshead Cl, Second ~ ~, Ramshead Mdw (*v.* Ram's Head Spinney *supra*); the Rickstead Cl, ~ ~ Mdw, Cabin Rickstead (*v.* **cabin**) (*v.* **rickstead**); the Rossage, Rossage Cl, ~ Mdw (obscure; earlier forms are needed); (the) Rushy Cl 1797, 1839 (*v.* **riscig**); Second Mdw; Stone-pit Six Acres 1797 (*v.* **æcer**), Stone Pit Cl 1839 (*v.* **stān-pytt**); Thistley Cl (*v.* **thist(e)ly**); Top Cl; the Townend Cl 1789, Towns-end Cl 1797, Second ~ ~, Third ~ ~, Townsend Cl 1839 (*v.* **tūn**, **ende**); Turnpike Plantation (*v.* **turnepike**); (the) Verges, the Bottom ~, the Little Verges, Other Little Verges (*the Verges* 1623 ChancP, *Verges or Verges grove* 1625 Ipm (*v.* **grāf**), *v.* **verge**; these closes were at the western extremity of the parish); the West Orchard; Wildmans Mdw (with the surn. *Wildman*); Willow Bank Mdw (*v.* **wilig**, **banke**); the Woods Mdw (*v.* **wudu**).

(b) *Bissopescroft* 1477 (e.16) *Charyte* (*v.* **croft**; with the surn. *Bishop*); *Braunston Close* 1653 (with the surn. *Braunston* of a family prob. originally from Braunstone, 14 miles to the west); *the Bridge Close* 1701 (*v.* Finchley Bridge *supra*); *Buckwell Close* 1653 (presum. contains an early spring- or stream-name since Buckwell is not a Leics. surn., *v.* **bucca**, **wella**; the parish lay at the edge of early woodland); *Coles Close* 1728 (with the surn. *Cole*); *High Meadow Close* 1653; *Lower Freewood* 1690 (*v.* **frēo**, **wudu**; woodland in which commoners enjoyed certain rights, such as wood-gathering, cf. The Freewards, Ru 147-8); *the 3 Neather Ends* 1701 (*v.* **neoðera**, **ende**; closes so called); *Okeholme Close* 1653 (*v.* **āc**, **holmr**); *Peaseland Close* 1653 (*v.* **pise**, **land**).

Prestwold

PRESTWOLD

Presteuuald 1086 DB, *Prestewald(e)* 1158 France, 1177 Nichols, l.12 *GarCart* (freq) *et passim* to 1251 *BHosp*, 1254 Cl, *Prestewalda* 1175 × 81 RegAnt, Hy 2 Dane, *Prestewalt* l.12 ib, *Prestewaud'* 1211 P, 1235 RGros

Prestwald 1175 × 81 RegAnt, c.1200 Dane bis *et passim* to c.1291 Tax, 1340 Ch, *Prestwalda* c.1200 Dane, c.1200 (1411) Gilb, *Prestwalt* l.12 Dane, John BM, e.13 Berkeley (p), *Prestwaud* 1242 Fees, 1243 Cl, 1253 Pap

Prestewolde 1086 DB, *Prestewold'* l.12 *GarCart* bis, e.Hy 3 Berkeley, Hy 3 *Crox et passim* to 1349 *Wyg* (p), 1369 Pat

Prestwold 1253 Cur, 1271 Abbr, Hy 3 *Crox*, 1285 *Wyg et passim* to 1314 *GarCart*, 1322 *MiD et freq*, *Prestwolde* 1316, 1326 Pat *et passim* to 1543 *RTemple*, 1604 SR

Prestwode 1502 *MiscAccts*, *Prystwoode alias Prestwolde* 1539 *Deed*, *Prestwoold* 1533 Pat, *Prestwould* 1611 LML, *Prestwoud* 1620 ib

Presthold 1674 *Terrier*

'The portion of the Wolds district endowed for the support of priests', *v.* **prēost (prēosta** gen.pl.), **wald**. Income from livestock and woodland on this area of the wold country would have been permanently endowed by a wealthy magnate for the support of a community of priests who ministered intermittently at various churches built in different parts of his estates.

Spellings with *-waud* for *-wald* are due to AN influence.

BACK LANE, *v.* **back**. BIG LING SPINNEY is *the Lings* 1836 O, *Lings* 1871 *Plan*, *v.* **lyng**. BONSER'S SPINNEY, cf. *Bonsers Lings* 1871 *Plan*, *v.* **lyng**; with the surn. *Bonser*. COTES TOLL BAR, cf. *Tollgate Close* 1871 *Plan*, *v.* **toll-bar**, **toll-gate**; Cotes adjoins to the west. DALES SPINNEY (2½") is *The Dale Plantation* 1836 O, *v.* **dalr**. HOME FM is *Hall farm* 1877 White, *v.* Prestwold Hall *infra*. HOTON SPINNEY, towards Hoton which adjoins to the north. ICEHOUSE PLANTATION, 1836 O; beside the Hall's icehouse. LITTLE LING SPINNEY, *v.* **lyng**. MERE HILL, *Merehull'* 1212 Nichols, *Meer Hill* 1871 *Plan*, *le mere de Prestewold'* Edw 1 *Harl*, *v.* **(ge)mǣre, hyll**. MERE HILL COTTAGES. MERE HILL SPINNEY, *Mare Hill Spinney* 1806 Map, *Meer-hill Spinny* 1836 O, *v.* **spinney** and Mere Hill *supra*. OLD WOOD is *Meadow Plantation* 1836 O. PARK PLANTATION. PRESTWOLD HALL, 1829 *Plan*, 1846, 1863 White, 1872 *Plan*, 1877 White, 1925 Kelly, *Prestwould Hall* 1800 Nichols, *v.* **hall**. PRESTWOLD PARK. ROOKERY PLANTATION, *v.* **rookery**. ST ANDREW'S CHURCH, *Church (St Andrews)* 1846, 1863, 1877 White, *the Parish Church of Presthold* 1674 *Terrier*; it is earlier recorded as *ecclesiam* ~ ~, *ecclesie de Prestwald* 1220 MHW, 1241 RGros, *ecclesie de Prestewaud* 1235 ib, ~ *de Prestwolde* 1316 *Pat*, and in the group *ecclesiarum de Buckmynster Prestwolde et Sancta Maria Leicestre* 1558 *ib*. Note also *Prestwold Churchyard* 1850 *TA*.

FIELD-NAMES

Undated forms in (a) are 1871 *Plan*. Forms throughout dated Hy 3, Edw 1, l.13 and e.14 are *Harl*; 1735 are *Plan*.

(a) Four Acres (*v.* **æcer**); Bonsers Cl (with the surn. *Bonser*, cf. Bonser's Spinney *supra*); East ~ ~, West Clover Cl (*v.* **clāfre**; used as a fodder crop); Conygree Leys 1769 Nichols (*v.* **coningre, leys**); Corn Cl (*v.* **corn**[1]); Cotts Cl, Cotts Mdw (prob. with **cot** and with reference to neighbouring Cotes; *Cott* is not a Leics. surn.); Cow Cl (1735); Dale Cl (*Dayle Close* 1735, *v.* **dalr**); Ewe Cl (*Yoo Close* (sic) 1735, *v.* **eowu**); Gills Mdw (with the surn. *Gill*); Glovers Homestead (1735, *v.* **hām-stede**; with the surn. *Glover*); Gravel pit Cl (*v.* **gravel**); East ~ ~, West Great Grounds (*v.* **grund**); Hall Cl (*v.* Prestwold Hall *supra*); Hardy's Cl (*Harde's Close* 1735; with the surn. *Hardy*); Homestead (*v.* **hām-stede**); House Cl; Hydes Cl (with the surn. *Hyde*); The Lawn (*v.* **launde**); Far ~, Middle ~, Near Lings, Great ~ ~, Near ~ ~, Top Far Lings (*v.* **lyng**); Little Mdw; Long Mdw; Marshalls Cl (with the surn. *Marshall*); Middle Cl; Nether Cl; New Cl; Northsick Mdw (1735, *v.* **sík**); Over Cl (*v.* **uferra**); Parsons Cl (*v.* **persone**); Slash (*v.* **slash**); Three Cornered Cl (*v.* **three-cornered**); Town end Cl (*v.* **tūn, ende**); Waites Cl (with the surn. *Waite(s)*); First ~ ~, North ~ ~, South Warren Cl (*Warren Close* 1735), Warren Fd (*v.* **wareine**).

(b) *Barrets Close* 1735 (with the surn. *Barrett*); *Dayle Meadow* 1735 (*v.* **dalr**); *Fox Close* 1735 (*v.* **fox**); *Gares* 13 Nichols (*v.* **gāra**); *Gildehow* e.14, *Gildhow* n.d. AD (*v.* **gylde, haugr**); *Glovers lings* 1735 (*v.* **lyng**; with the surn. *Glover*); *de Grena* Hy 3 (p), *de la grene* Edw 1 (p), l.13 (p), *on the Grene* 1357 Pat (p) (*v.* **grēne**[2]); *Martholes* Hy 3 (*v.* **mearð, hol**[1]); *Meadow Close* 1735; *Mill Field* 1735 (*v.* **myln**); *North Sick Close* 1735, *North Sick Lay Close* 1871 (*v.* **ley**) (*v.* **sík**); *South Close* 1735; *le Stygate* n.d. AD (*v.* **sty-gate**); *West Close* 1735; *Wrongelandes* Hy 3, *le Wronglandes* Hy 3, Edw 1, *le Wrong Londes* e.14 (*v.* **wrang, vrangr, land**).

Queniborough

QUENIBOROUGH

Cvinbvrg 1086 DB

Queniburg' c.1130 LeicSurv, l.12 *GarCart*, e.13 *BHosp* (p) *et passim* to 1271 *RTemple*, 1286 *LCDeed* (p), *Queniburgo* l.12 *GarCart*, *Queniburc* l.12 *ib* (p), 1199 FF, 1212 *GarCart*, 1227 GildR (p), 13 *GarCh* (p), *Queniburgh* 1226 Fine, 1259 Cur *et freq* to 1361 *LCDeeds* (p), 1379 Ass *et passim* to 1517 Ipm, 1533 Fine, *Queniborowe* 1377 SR, 1540 Fine

Queneburhcht 1156 (1318) Ch (p), *Queneburch* Hy 2 Dugd (p), *Queneburg* 1258 RHug, *Queneborou* 1272 Ipm

Quenyburg' Hy 2 Dugd (p), 1403 Pat, 1409 PRep, *Quenyburgh* 1301 Ch, 1303 Pat (p) *et passim* to 1510 Rental, 1540 Ipm, *Quenybourgh* 1361 ib, 1362 BPR

Quenburgh' Hy 2 Dugd (p), *Quenburg'* 1254 Val, 1263 RGrav

Quenigburg' 1220 MHW, 1258 RHug, 1339 Selby, *Quenigborc* 1242 Fees, *Quenygburgh* 1327 SR

Queingburc 1233 Fees, *Queingbur'* 1241 RGros, *Queingburg'* 1241 ib, 1253 Cur

Queningburc 1236 Fees, *Queningburg'* 1252 GildR (p), 1258 Selby (freq) *et passim* to 1282, 1339 ib, *Queningburgh'* 1332 *LCh*, 1339 Selby, *Quenyngburgh'* 1274 Banco, c.1291 Tax *et passim* to 1434 Selby, 1459 Moulton, *Quenyngbor'* 1299 Ipm, *Quenyngbourgh* 1361 ib, *Quenyngbrugh* 1520 *Deed*, *Queningborow(e)* 1569 LeicW, 1576 LibCl, *Quinningborow* 1616 LML

Quenesborgh 1436 Pat, *Quenesburgh* 1502 Ipm, *Quenesbyrgh* 1506 ib

Queneburrogh 1506 Ipm, *Queneborough(e)* 1513 LP, 1536, 1546 AAS, 1548 Ex-Rel, *Queneborowe* 1541 MiscAccts, 1546 AAS, 1549 Pat, 1550 *Deed*, *Quenebrough* 1546 AAS, 1550 Pat

Quennyborow(e) 1523 AAS, 1528 Visit, 1529, 1533 AAS, *Quenyboroughe* 1535 VE, *Quenyborowe* 1535 ib, 1604 SR, *Quenyboro* 1576 Saxton

Quen(n)iborowe 1542 *RTemple*, 1542 Fine, 1607, 1613 LML, *Queniboro* 1610 Speed, *Queniburrough* 1641 LML, *Queniborough* 1706 ib *et freq*

'The queen's manor', *v.* **cwēn, burh**. Note the occasional later forms which have been accorded a masc. gen.sg. in *-es*, as in Quenby.

BARROWCLIFFE FM, *Berricliff(e)* 1682 *Surv*, 1699 *Terrier*, c.1785, 1788 *Surv*, *Bury clif* 1686 *ib*, *Berrye Cliffe* 1690 *ib*, *Berriclife* l.17 *Terrier*, *Berrycliff(e)* 1699 *ib*, 1744 *Rental*, *Barrow Cliff* 1806 Map, 1925 Kelly, *Barrowcliffe Farm* 1870 *Sale*, *v.* **berige, clif** and Barrowcliffe Spinney in neighbouring Barsby. BIGGS LODGE, *v.* **loge**; cf. *Mrs Jane Biggs, farmer* 1925 Kelly, *Thomas Biggs, farmer* 1925 ib. BRITANNIA (P.H.), *Britannia* 1846, 1863, 1877 White, 1925 Kelly. CHENEY HO., *v.* Cheney Arms (P.H.) in adjoining Gaddesby. CHESTNUT VILLA. THE COPPICE, 1877 White, 1925 Kelly, *v.* **copis**. THE FIRS. HILL COTTAGE. THE HOMESTEAD, 1925 Kelly, *v.* **hām-stede**. HORSE AND GROOM (P.H.), *Horse and Groom* 1877 White, 1925 Kelly. HORSE AND JOCKEY (P.H.) (lost), *Horse and Jockey* 1846, 1863 White. MANOR FM, *Manor farm* 1925 Kelly, *v.* **maner**. METHODIST CHAPEL. NEW HALL, 1846, 1863 White; it is *Queniborough Hall* 1925 Kelly, 1929 *Sale*, *v.* **hall**. NEW QUENIBOROUGH. NEW ZEALAND LANE (local), a 'remoteness' name for a lane towards the edge of the parish. OAK HO. OLD HALL, 1846, 1863, 1877 White, 1925 Kelly, *the Hall* l.17 *Terrier*; a later 17th cent. building, but an earlier hall is recorded in *atte Halle* 1377 SR (p) (*v.* **atte**), *v.* **hall**. QUENIBOROUGH BROOK, 1745 *Terrier*, 1835 O, *Quenyborow broke* 1467 × 84 *LTD*, *Queniborrow(e) brook(e)* 1601, 1625 *et passim* to 1712 *Terrier*, *the Brooke* 1690 *Surv*, 1699 *Terrier*, *the Brook* 1785, 1788 *Surv*, *v.* **brōc**. QUENIBOROUGH COTTAGE (2½"), cf. *The Cottage farm* 1925 Kelly; the site is called *Dunkirk* 1835 O, this presum. a 'remoteness' name for a location at the extreme edge of the parish. QUENIBOROUGH LODGE, 1835 O, 1877 White, 1925 Kelly, *v.* **loge**. RIDGEMERE LANE is *the Ridg Waye* l.17 *Terrier*, *the Ridgeway* c.1785, 1788 *Surv*, 1835 O, *v.* **hrycg, weg**; an ancient trackway and the boundary (**(ge)mǣre**) between Queniborough and Barkby (*q.v.* for earlier forms). ST MARY'S CHURCH, *Church (St Mary)* 1846, 1863, 1877 White, 1925 Kelly; it is earlier recorded as *ecclesie de Quenigburg'* 1220 MHW, ~ *de Queniburg* 1238 RGros, ~ *de Queingbur'* 1241 ib, *ecclesia de Queneburg* 1253 × 58 RTAL, *ecclesie de Quenyngburgh* 1341, 1403, 1420 *Pat*. THE VICARAGE, 1925 Kelly; it is *the Vicaridge Howse* 1601 *Terrier*, ~ ~ *House* 1625 *ib*, *v.* **vikerage**. WETHERLEY HO. (WETHERBY HO. 2½").

WILLIAM IV (P.H.) (lost), *William IV* 1846, 1863 White.

FIELD-NAMES

Forms in (a) dated c.1785, 1788, 1790 and 1793 are *Surv*; 1870 are *Sale*. Throughout, forms dated 1260, 1254 × 80 and 1434 are Selby; e.14 (1467 × 84) and 1467 × 84 are *LTD*; 1477 (e.16) are *Charyte*; 1561 (1700) and 1744 are *Rental*; 1601, 1612, 1625, l.17, 1699 and 1708 (18) are *Terrier*; 1682, 1682 (1791), 1686, 1690 and 1704 are *Surv*.

(a) Acre Land Furlong 1788 (*v*. **land**, **furlang**), Three Acres, The Twelve Acres (*v*. **æcer**); Almond Cl 1744, Almonds ~ 1790 (with the surn. *Almond*, a reflex of either the OE pers.n. *Æðelmund* or *Ealhmund*); Ash(e) Fd c.1785, 1788 (*Asefelde* 1561 (1700), *(the) Ash(e) Feild(e)* 1682, 1686, l.17, *~ Field* 1682 (1791), 1690, 1699, 1704, 1744, *v*. **æsc**, **feld**); Ash Hill 1790 (1682, l.17, 1699, 1744, *Ashe Hill* 1690), Ashe Hill Furlong c.1785, 1788 (*Ash hill Fur'* 1686, *v*. **furlang**) (*v*. **æsc**); Bankroofs 1790 (*Bangrass* 1699, *Banggrofts* 1744), Bancroft Bauk 1788 (*Bancrafte baulke* l.17, *Bangroft Baulk* 1744, *v*. **balca**), Bancroft Furlong 1788 (*Bangraue Fur'* 1682, *Bangrave ~* 1686, cf. *Bangroues gate furlonge* 1690 (*v*. **gata**), *v*. **furlang**) (*v*. **bēan**, **croft**); Barley Whom Gap 1790 (*v*. **bærlic**, **holmr**, **gap**); Barn Cl 1870; Beanford Furlong 1788 (*v*. **furlang**) (*Bean(e) Ford* 1682, 1686, 1699, 1744, *Beane forde* 1690, *~ foarde* l.17; 'bean ford' (*v*. **bēan**, **ford**) is an unlikely name (although 'barley ford' is common), but the consistent upper case *B* surviving throughout 100 years argues against an early misread upper case *W* (which could be similar to *B*) and the repetition thereafter in copied documents (i.e. a poss. original **Weanford* 'waggon ford', *v*. **wægn**, **ford** and cf. *weangate* in Saxelby f.ns. (b), *Weans gate* in Asfordby f.ns. (b) and *Wayne ford* in Humberstone f.ns. (b)); surviving forms are late, so it is likelier that the name was originally **Beanthorn*, *v*. **bēan-þorn** and cf. *Banethorn'* in adjoining South Croxton f.ns. (b), Bean Thorn Furlong in Grimston f.ns. (a) and Great ~, Little Beanthorne in Shoby f.ns. (a)); Beaumont c.1785, 1788 (the common Leics. surn. *Beaumont*); Beeby Gate c.1785, 1788, 1790 (1682, 1686, 1699, 1744, *v*. **gata**), Beeby gate Baulk c.1785, ~ ~ Bauk 1788 (*v*. **balca**) (Beeby lies 2½ miles to the south-east); Beever hooks 1790 (*Beaver hooke* 1682, *Bever hook* 1686, *Beaver hookes* 1699, *Beevor Hooks* 1744, *v*. **beofor**, **hōc**); Bennetcliffe Furlong 1790 (*v*. **furlang**), Bennettcliffe Hedge 1790 (*v*. **hecg**; a boundary hedge) (prob. with the substitution of a local family surn. *Bennet(t)* for *Berri-* in *Berricliff* (*v*. Berricliff Fd *infra*), cf. *the Homestall of William Bennett* 1601, 1625 (*v*. **hām-stall**), *the ground of William Bennett* 1612 (*v*. **grund**), *Bennitts Close* 1682 (*Tho. Bennitt* cited 1682), *Mr Bennett close* 1686, 1690, *Bennetts Close* 1699, *George Bennets Close* l.17, *Mr Bennett Close end* 1690 (*v*. **ende**), *Thomas Bennett land*, *Willm. Bennet(t) land* 1690 (*v*. **land**)); Berricliff Fd c.1785, Berricliff Furlong 1788 (*Berricliffe fur'* 1682, *Bury-clif Fur'* 1686, *Berry Cliff(e) furlong* 1690, 1699, *Berriclif ~* l.17, *v*. **furlang**), Barrow-cliff Mdw 1793 (and cf. *Bericlife side* l.17, *v*. **sīde**) (*v*. Barrowcliffe Fm and Bennetcliffe *supra*); Black Ballance Furlong c.1785, 1788 (*Blackballance Fur'* 1686, *v*. **furlang**), Black Vallans 1790 (*le Nethereblakebanlond*, *le Ouerblakebanlond* e.14

(1467 × 84) (*v.* **neoðera, uferra**), *Blackballance* 1682, 1699, *v.* **blæc, bēan, land**); Blackmans Wong 1788, Blackney's ~ (sic) 1790 (*Blakemanneswong'* e.14 (1467 × 84), *Blackmans wonge* 1686, 1690, ~ *Wounge* l.17, ~ *Wong* 1744, cf. *Black Man Fur'* 1682, *Blackmans Furlong* 1699 (*v.* **furlang**), *v.* **vangr**; with the surn. *Blackman/ Blakeman*, reflex of the OE pers.n. *Blæcmann* 'dark, swarthy man'); (the Meadow called) Boonton, Boontoon, Boontown c.1785, (the Meadow called) Boonton or Abovetowne 1788, Boonton Cls, Boonton Mdws 1793 (*Bountoune* 1690, *Boone Towne* 1699, *Boonton* 1704, *Boon Town* 1744, *v.* **bufan, tūn**), Above the Towne c.1785, Above Town 1790 ((*the furlong*) *Aboue the Towne* 1682, 1690, *A Boue ye Town* 1686, *v.* **aboven, tūn**); Bord Land 1788 (*v.* **bord-land**); Bord Mdw 1788 (perh. with **bord**; but note the previous f.n. to which this may specifically relate); Bottom Mdw 1870; Brancliff furlong c.1785, 1788 (*Branclif* e.14 (1467 × 84), *Brancliff(e)* 1690, 1699, 1744, *the Top of Bran Cliffe* 1690 (*v.* **topp**), *Brinkley Fur'* (sic) 1682, *Brankley Fur'* (sic) 1686 (*v.* **furlang**), cf. *Branclifgate* e.14 (1467 × 84) (*v.* **gata**), *v.* **brant, clif** and Brancliff Furlong in adjacent South Croxton f.ns. (a)); the Breach East & West Furlong c.1785, 1788 (*v.* **furlang**) (*Breach* 1699, *v.* **brēc**); Bridge-hook 1788, Brigg Hook 1790, Bridge-hook Furlong c.1785, 1790 (*v.* **furlang**) (*Bridge hook(e)* 1682, 1686, 1744, *Brig Hooke* 1690, 1699, *Brigghooks* l.17 (*v.* **brycg, bryggja, hōc**); (the) Brook Furlong c.1785, 1788, 1790 (l.17, 1699, 1744, *le Brokfurlong* e.14 (1467 × 84), *Broke Fur'* 1682, 1686, *Brooke furlong* 1690 (*v.* **furlang**), cf. *the Brooke side* l.17 (*v.* **sīde**); with reference to Queniborough Brook *supra*); Browns Mdw c.1785 (with the surn. *Brown*); Butcher head 1790 (1744, *Butcher had(e)s* 1682, 1686, *v.* **hēafod**), Butcher-hedge Furlong c.1785, 1788 (*Butchers Hedge* 1699, *v.* **hecg**, a boundary hedge) (with the surn. *Butcher*); Cluegate c.1785, Clugate 1788, Clewgut 1790 (*Clewgate* 1682, 1699, *Cluegate* 1686, cf. *Cluegate side* l.17 (*v.* **sīde**)), Clugate Furlong c.1785, 1788 (*Clue gate furlonge* 1690, *v.* **furlang**) (*v.* **clōh, gata**); Cockram Willow(e)s Furlong c.1785, 1788 (*v.* **furlang**) (*Cockram Willow(e)s* 1699, l.17, *v.* **wilig**; with the surn. *Cockram*, *v.* Reaney *s.n.*); Copthorn(e) Furlong 1788, 1790 (*Copthorn* e.14 (1467 × 84), *Crapp Thorne Fur'* 1682, *Cropthorn Fur'* 1686, *Copthorne furlong* 1690 (*v.* **furlang**)), Copthorne Goss c.1785, Copthorn Ghoss 1788 (*v.* **gorst**) (*v.* **copped**[2], **þorn**); the Corn Clay Fds 1793 (*v.* **corn**[1], **clǣg**); (the) Cowpasture c.1785, 1788 (*v.* **pasture**); Crabtree 1790 (*v.* **crabtre**); Debdale 1790 (1744, *Depedale* e.14 (1467 × 84), *Deepdale* 1682, 1686, cf. *Depedalegate* e.14 (1467 × 84) (*v.* **gata**), *Depedale Close* l.17), Debdale Tongue c.1785, 1788 (1699, *v.* **tunge**), the Long Debdale Leys c.1785, 1788 (*v.* **leys**), Long Debden 1790 (*Long Debdale* 1699) (*v.* **dēop, dalr**); Denford c.1785, 1788 (l.17, *v.* **ford**; prob. with **derne** rather than with **denu**); Dick Furlong c.1785, 1788 (l.17, *le Dikefurlong'* e.14 (1467 × 84), *Dicke fur'* 1690, *v.* **dík, furlang**); the Drinking Piece c.1785, 1788, 1790 (*the Drin(c)king peice* 1690, 1699, 1744, *the Drinking peece* l.17 (*v.* **drinkinge, pece**; a place for watering cattle); Dry Leighs 1790 (*v.* **drȳge, leys**); the Fair Mdw 1790 (*the Farr meadowe* 1744, *v.* **feor**); Foulpoole 1788, Fowl Poole 1790 (*Fulpol* e.14 (1467 × 84), *Fowlepoole* 1682, 1686, 1699, *Fowlpool* l.17, 1744), Foulpool(e) Leys c.1785, 1788 (*v.* **leys**) (*v.* **fūl, pōl**[1]); Furze Lands 1793 (*v.* **fyrs, land**); Gadsby Ash 1790 (1686, 1699, *Gaddesby Ash* 1682, *Gaddsbye Ashe* l.17, *Gadsbee Ashe furlonge* 1690 (*v.* **furlang**) (*v.* **æsc**)), Gadsby Cl 1790 (1699), Gatsby Closing 1790 (*v.* **closing**) (Gaddesby adjoins to the east); the Gleab Headley c.1785, ~ ~ Hadley 1788 (*v.* **headley**) (*the Gleebe* 1699, cf. *the Gleebe hadland* 1699 (*v.* **hēafod-land**), *v.* **glebe**); Godyar Hades c.1785, 1788 (*Gowgerr hades* 1682, *Gouger*

~ 1686, *Godyard* ~ 1690, *Gorgier* ~ 1699, *Goddard* ~ (sic) l.17, *v.* **hēafod**; with the surn. *Goodger/Gudger*, a late development of *Goodyear*, *v.* Reaney *s.n.*); the Goss Leys c.1785, Gorse ~ 1870 (*v.* **gorst, leys**); Gravelhole 1790 (*v.* **gravel, hol**[1]); the Great Goss c.1785, ~ ~ Ghoss 1788 (*the Great Goss* 1699, cf. *Great Gosse Furlong* 1682, *Great gorse Fur'* 1686 (*v.* **furlang**), *v.* **gorst**); the Green Cow-pasture c.1785 (*the Greene* 1699, *v.* **grēne**[2]); Greens Furlong c.1785, Greenes ~ 1788 (*Greenes Fur'* 1682, *Greens* ~ 1686, *v.* **furlang**; either with the surn. *Green* or with **grēne**[2]); Green Yard 1793 (*v.* **geard**; with **grēne**[1] or **grēne**[2]); Hallams ~, Halloms Cl c.1785, Hallam(s) Cl 1788 (*Allam Close* 1682, *Allum* ~ 1686, *Allome* ~ 1690, *Mr Alloms Close* 1699 (*Samuell Allome*, ~ *Allum* is cited 1690), cf. *Alloms hadland* 1699 (*v.* **hēafod-land**), *Alloms hedge* 1699 (*v.* **hecg**; a boundary hedge)); Hall Cl 1793, Hall Flatt 1788 (*v.* **flat**), the Hall Goss Flatt 1788 (*v.* **gorst**), Hall Land 1788 (*the Hall Land* 1708 (18), *v.* **land**, cf. *the Hall demeanes* l.17, *v.* **demeyn**), Hall Leys 1788 (*v.* **leys**) (*v.* Old Hall *supra*); (the) Hayfield c.1785, 1788, 1790 (1682 (1791), 1699, 1704, 1744, *Heyfelde* 1561 (1700), (*the*) *Hayhill Field* 1682, 1690, ~ *Feild* 1686, *the Heyfeilde* l.17, *v.* **hēg, feld**); Headland Furlong 1790 (*v.* **hēafod-land, furlang**); Hew Close Leighs 1790 (*v.* **leys**; prob. with the surn. *Hew*, *v.* Reaney *s.n.*); Holes Wong 1788 (*v.* **vangr**) (*Holes* e.14 (1467 × 84), cf. *Holesslade* e.14 (1467 × 84) (*v.* **slæd**), *Holes Close* 1744, *v.* **hol**[1]); Holmes Cl, Holmes Hill 1790 (prob. with **holmr** but the surn. *Holmes* is poss.); Home Paddock 1790 (*v.* **home, paddock**); Horse Hinderlands c.1785, Horshinderlands 1788, Huss Hinderlands 1790 (*Horse hinderland* 1682, *Horsehenderlands* 1686, *Horshinderlandes* l.17, *Osshinderlands* 1699, cf. *Horse hender leyes* 1690 (*v.* **leys**), *v.* **hors, hinder, land**); Hovel Sick c.1785, 1788, 1790 (*v.* **hovel, sík**); Lady Orchard 1793 (*v.* **lavedi**; here either alluding to a female proprietor or to a dowager); Leicester Road c.1785, 1788 (*Leicester Way* 1690; early Leicester lay 6 miles to the south-west); the Leighs 1790, ~ Leys 1793 (*the Leyes* 1690, ~ *Leys* 1744, *v.* **leys**); Ley Furlong c.1785 (*v.* **ley, furlang**); (the) Low Mdw c.1785, 1788, 1793 (1704, *v.* **la(g)h**); Marlepit(t)s c.1785, the Marlpitts 1788 (*v.* **marle-pytt**); Marston Bush 1788 (*Marsons Bush* 1744, *v.* **busc** and cf. *Thomas Marson* 1690; the surn. *Mars(t)on* was that of a family prob. originally from Potters Marston, 14 miles to the south-west, loss of *t* in the group *-ston* being typical in 17th cent. Leics. names); Masons Had Land 1788 (*v.* **hēafod-land**; with the surn. *Mason*); the Meadow 1788, 1790, the Mead 1790 (*the Meadow* 1682, 1686, *the meddow* l.17, *v.* **mǣd (mǣdwe** obl.sg.)); Meadowside Furlong 1788 (*v.* **sīde**) (cf. *Meadowe furlonge* 1690, *v.* **furlang**); the Mear c.1785, 1788, the Meer 1790 (*le Meere* 1434, *the meare* 1612, 1690, *the Meere* 1699, l.17, *the Meer* 1744), Mear Leys c.1785, 1788 (*Meare leyes* 1682, *Mear leys* 1686, *Meere leyes* l.17, ~ *Lays* 1699, *v.* **leys**) (either with **mere**[1] or **(ge)mǣre**); (the) Middle Fd c.1785, 1788, 1790 (1699, 1704, *Middelfeild(e)* 1561 (1700), l.17, *Midle Feild* 1686, ~ *Field* 1690, *Middle Feild* 1744, *v.* **middel, feld**; one of the later great fields of the township); Midland, ~ Goss 1790 (*v.* **gorst**) (*v.* **mid, middel, land**); the Mill 1790 (1744), the Mill Furlong 1790 (*v.* **furlang**), the Mill Goss c.1785, 1788, ~ ~ Ghoss 1788 (*v.* **gorst**) (*v.* **myln**); Mouldy Banks 1870 (*v.* **mouldy, banke**); Muckheaps Furlong c.1785, 1788 (*v.* **muk, hēap, furlang** and Snellso *infra*); (the) Muckhills 1790 (*Muck Hills* 1744, *v.* **muk**; presum. referring to middens, as does the previous f.n.); Nettlebed Furlong 1788 (*v.* **furlang**) (1686, *Nettlebed* 1699, *v.* **netel(e), bedd**); Newbridge 1788 (*v.* **nīwe, brycg**); New Close Leys c.1785, 1788 (*v.* **leys**) (*New Close* 1682, 1744, cf. *New Close Fur'* 1686 (*v.* **furlang**)); Norman's Cl 1790 (*Norman Close* 1682, 1686, *Normans* ~ 1699,

1744), Norman's Close Furlong 1790 (*Norman Close Furlong* 1682, *Normand* ~ ~ 1686, *v.* **furlang**) (with the surn. *Norman*); Normanton Cl, ~ ~ Short Furlong c.1785, 1788 (*v.* **sc(e)ort, furlang**; presum. with the surn. *Normanton* since there are no early forms to indicate a lost farmstead of this name (*v.* Normanton (Lei **2** 41) from which the family may have originally come)); Old Cl 1790 (1744, *v.* **ald**); Old Wall c.1785, 1788 (*v.* **ald, wall**); Pease Land Leys 1788 (*le Peyselande*, *le Lyttelpeyslond* e.14 (1467 × 84) (*v.* **lȳtel**), *Peaselands* 1682, 1686, 1744, *Peaseland leyes* 1690, *Pesan Lays* 1699 (*v.* **leys**), *v.* **pise, land**); Plank Furlong 1788 (*v.* **planke, furlang**); (the) Port Road c.1785, 1788 (*Port way* 1682, 1686, 1690, 1699, cf. *Portway side* l.17 (*v.* **sīde**), *v.* **port-weg**); Raisby Closing 1790 (*v.* **closing**; Rearsby adjoins to the north); Ranglands 1790 (1699), Wranglands 1790 (l.17, 1744, *le Wranglond'* e.14 (1467 × 84)), Ranglands Furlong c.1785, 1788 (*Wronglands furlonge* 1690, *v.* **furlang**) (*v.* **wrang, vrangr, land**); Redlands c.1785, 1788, 1790 (1690, 1699, l.17, 1744, *le Redelondes* e.14 (1467 × 84), *Reddlands* l.17), Redlands Furlong c.1785, 1788 (*Redlands Fur'* 1682, 1686, *v.* **furlang**) (*v.* **rēad, land**); Reed Lands 1790 (may belong with Redlands *supra*, otherwise *v.* **hrēod**); Rickstade 1788 (*v.* **rickstead**); Ridgeways 1790 (*le Riggeweies*, *le Rigweyes* e.14 (1467 × 84), *the Ridgeways* 1699), the Long Ridgeway c.1785, 1788 (*Long ridgway* 1699), Siston Ridgway c.1785, Syston Ridgeway 1788 (*Syston Ridge waye* 1690, *Syson Ridgeway* 1699, *Siston Ridgway* l.17; Syston adjoins to the south-west) (Ridgemere Lane *supra* appears to have had a branch into Syston, cf. a furlong called *betweene Ridgways*, *between the Ridgeways* 1699, *v.* **hrycg, weg**); Routholme c.1785, 1788 (*le Routholme* e.14 (1467 × 84), *Routeholme* 1434, *Rutholm*, *Rowholme* 1477 (e.16), *Rowtholme*, *Routsome* l.17, *Routham* 1686, 1699, *Rowtham* 1699 (*v.* **holmr**; the first el. may be ON **hrúðr** 'scurf' used topographically of 'rough ground', or an unrecorded OE **rūt** also with the meaning 'rough ground' (*v.* Löfvenberg 171), cf. OE *rūhet* 'a place overgrown with brushwood, a piece of rough ground'; Professor Richard Coates suggests as an alternative ON *rauðr* 'red', note Redlands *supra*, *v. Rowtam* in adjoining Rearsby f.ns. (b)); Great Sandfield c.1785, 1788 (*Sand Feild* 1682, ~ *Field* 1686, *Sandy field* 1682 (1791), (*the*) *Great(e) Sand Field* 1690, 1699, 1704, 1744, ~ ~ ~ *feilde* l.17), (the) Little Sandfield c.1785, 1788 (1699, 1704, 1744, *the little Sand feilde* l.17, *the litle Sand Field* 1690), the Corn Sand Fds 1793 (*v.* **corn**[1]) (*v.* **sand, feld**); Shil(l)gates Furlong c.1785, 1788 (*v.* **furlang**) (*Shilgate* l.17, *v.* **scylfe, gata**); Siseham Mear (sic) 1790 (*v.* **(ge)mǣre**; the boundary with Syston which adjoins to the south-west, *v.* Syston pitt *infra*); the Slade 1788 (*v.* **slæd**); Smallbrook(e) c.1785, 1788, 1790 (*Smalbroke* e.14 (1467 × 84), *Smalbrooke* l.17, *Smallbrook* 1699, 1744), Small Brook Furlong c.1785, 1788 (*Smallbrooke Fur'* 1682, *Smallbrough Fur'* (sic) 1686, *Smale brooke furlonge* 1690, *v.* **furlang**) (*v.* **smæl, brōc**); Snellso or Muckheaps Furlong c.1785, 1788 (*Snelleshou* e.14 (1467 × 84), *v.* **haugr**; with either the OE pers.n. *Snell* (from OE *snell* 'smart, active, bold') or with the ON pers.n. *Snjallr* (an original by-name, cf. OIcel *snjallr* 'excellent, valiant, well-spoken'), each giving the surn. reflex *Snell*; if with the OE pers.n., *haugr* may have replaced an earlier OE **hōh**; *v.* Muckheaps Furlong *supra*); South end Mdw 1788 (*v.* **ende**); Syston pitt c.1785, Siseham Pit (sic) 1790 (*v.* **pytt**; Syston adjoins to the south-west); Stepping Stones 1790 (*v.* **stepping-stone**); the Thack 1790 (1744, *the Thacke* 1690, *Thack* 1699, cf. *Thack meadow* 1682, 1686), the Thack Butts 1790 (*v.* **butte**) (*v.* **þæc, þak**); High Thorn(e)y c.1785, 1788, 1790 (*Thirnhou* e.14 (1467 × 84), *High Thornhill* 1682, 1686, *High Thurne* 1699, cf. *Thorney side* 1690, *Thurney Side*, ~ *Syde* 1744 (*v.* **sīd**)),

High Thorn(e)y Furlong c.1785, 1788, 1790 (*Hie Thorney Furlong* 1690, *v.* **furlang**), Thorney Slade 1790 (*High* ~ ~, *Thurney Slaide* 1744, *v.* **slæd**) (*v.* **þyrne, þyrnir, haugr**; later forms are influenced by **þorn** and **hyll**); Tol Grass Lands 1793 (*v.* **toll**; presum. requiring a payment for pasturage etc.); Town Leys 1788 (*v.* **tūn, leys**); Trouleway c.1785, 1788, Trole Way 1790 (*Trowle way* 1686, *v.* **trēow, wella, weg**; cf. Trowell, Nt 153); the Turn Pike 1790 (*v.* **turnepike**); Upper Furlong c.1785, 1788; the Upper Stigh c.1785, 1788 (*v.* **stig**); Viccars Sty Furlong c.1785, Viccarsty ~ 1788 (*v.* **vikere, stig**); Wad Acre(s) Furlong c.1785, 1788 (*le Wadeaker* e.14 (1467 × 84), *Wadacres* 1690, *Wadacre* l.17, *v.* **(ge)wæd, æcer**); Watsons piece 1788 (*v.* **pece**; with the surn. *Watson*); Wayne way 1788 (*Weane way* 1699, *v.* **wægn, weg**); Whinney Ley c.1785, 1788, Winney ~ 1790 (*v.* **whinny, ley**); Wire willows 1788 (*v.* **wer, wilig**; *v. Weyre welus* in adjoining Rearsby f.ns. (b)).

(b) *Aldefelde* e.14 (1467 × 84), *Aldefeldsyke* 1434 (*v.* **sík**) (*v.* **ald, feld**); *Aleyn Brigge* e.14 (1467 × 84) (*v.* **brycg**; with the surn. *Alleyn*, a reflex of an OFr pers.n. *Alain/Alein*); *Barkebygate* e.14 (1467 × 84) (*v.* **gata**), *Barkbyhauedlond* e.14 (1467 × 84) (*v.* **hēafod-land**) (Barkby adjoins to the south); *Barsbye Baulke* 1744 (*v.* **balca**), *Barsby meere* 1699 (*v.* **(ge)mǣre**) (Barsby adjoins to the east); *Batewong* e.14 (1467 × 84) (*v.* **vangr**; with the surn. *Bate* (from the pers.n. *Bate*, a pet-form of Bartholomew)); *the Beast Pasture* 1682, *ye Beast pastur* 1686 (*v.* **beste, pasture**); *Bedehou* e.14 (1467 × 84) (*v.* **haugr**; the first el. is either the OE pers.n. *Bēda* or its ME surn. reflex *Bede* (ModE *Beade*, *Beed*); ON **haugr** may have modified or replaced OE **hōh**); *Benethebrygg'* e.14 (1467 × 84) (a furlong thus called, *v.* **benethe, brycg**); *Eueritt Bird land* 1690 (*v.* **land**); *Blind Pool* 1744 (*v.* **blind, pōl**[1]); *Broxbye acre cloase* l.17 (*v.* **æcer, clos(e)**; with the surn. *Brooksby* of a family originally from the village of this name, 3 miles to the north-west); *Caldewelle* e.14 (1467 × 84), *Caudle* 1699, *Schortcaldewelle* e.14 (1467 × 84), *Shorte Cawdwell* l.17, *Short Caudle* 1699 (*v.* **sc(e)ort**), *Long Caudle* 1699, *Caudle Brook* 1699 (*v.* **cald, wella**); *campus borial' versus Rerisby et Gaddisby* e.14 (1467 × 84) (with MLat *campus* 'a field' and *borialis* 'north, northern'; one of the early great fields of the township adjacent to Rearsby and Gaddesby which lie to the north and east respectively); *Mr Caves ground* l.17 (*v.* **grund**); *the Church hadland* 1699 (*v.* **hēafod-land** and St Mary's Church *supra*); *le Clifgate* e.14 (1467 × 84) (*v.* **clif, gata**); *Between the Closeing* 1682, ~ *ye Closin* 1686 (a furlong thus called, *v.* **closing**); *the common* 1690, *the commons* 1690 bis, *the Common Laine* 1601, ~ ~ *Layne* 1625 (*v.* **lane**), *the Common meere* l.17 (*v.* **(ge)mǣre**), *the common pasture* 1690 (*v.* **pasture**) (*v.* **commun**; in these names used both as a sb. and as an adj.); *the Connyborrowe* 1690 (*v.* **coni, burgh**); *the Corner* 1690 (*v.* **corner**); *Cotes Close* 1699 (either with the surn. *Cote(s)* or with **cot** in its later pl. form); *Croxtonemore* e.14 (1467 × 84) (*v.* **mōr**[1]), *Croston feylde side* l.17 (*v.* **feld, sīde**), *Croson Meere* 1699 (*v.* **(ge)mǣre**) (South Croxton adjoins to the south-east); *Downaclease* 1699 (*v.* **donoke, leys**); *Estfeld versus Croxton* e.14 (1467 × 84) (*v.* **ēast, feld**; one of the early great fields, this lying towards South Croxton which adjoins to the south-east); *Estlondus* e.14 (1467 × 84) (*v.* **ēast, land**); *Ferredoles* 1477 (e.16) (*v.* **feor, dāl**); *Fordolus* 1477 (e.16) (*v.* **fore, dāl**); *the Fore meadowe* 1690, 1744 (*v.* **fore**); *le Fostretewong'* e.14 (1467 × 84) (*v.* **foss**[1], **strǣt, vangr**; an enclosure lying towards Fosse Way); *Gaddesbymedewe* e.14 (1467 × 84), *Gadsbee meadowe* 1690, *Gaddesbye meddow* l.17 (*v.* **mǣd (mǣdwe** obl.sg.); beside Gaddesby parish which adjoins to the east); *Godushowhend* 1477 (e.16) (*v.* **ende**; the first el. is prob. the OE pers.n. *God*, a pet-form of one of the names in *God-*, rather than *god* 'a heathen god' (cf. Gadsey, Bd 63), with OE **hōh** influenced by or replaced by ON **haugr**); *le Gorebrode* e.14 (1467 × 84) (*v.* **gorebrode**); *le Gutterefurlong* e.14 (1467 × 84) (*v.* **goter, furlang**); *le Halsonderlond* e.14 (1467 × 84) (*v.* **hall, sundor-land**); *Tho. Hardes Farme* 1682, *Tho. Hardys farm* 1682 (1791) (*v.* **ferme**); *le Harpe* e.14 (1467 × 84) (*v.* **hearpe**); *Hawkins Close* 1699 (with the surn. *Hawkins*); *Hay hill* 1690, *Hey* ~ l.17 (*v.* **hēg**); *le Holegate* e.14 (1467 × 84) (*v.* **hol²**, **gata**); *le Holland* e.14 (1467 × 84), *Holland* l.17 (*v.* **hol²**, **land**); *le Holubalc* e.14 (1467 × 84) (*v.* **holh, balca**); *the Home Close* 1699 (*v.* **home**); *the Homestall* 1601, 1625 (*v.* **hām-stall**; belonging to *the Vicaridge Howse*); *Humbirstongate* e.14 (1467 × 84) (*v.* **gata**; Humberstone lies 4 miles to the south-west); *Hyllesend* e.14 (1467 × 84) (*v.* **hyll, ende**); *le Inwonges* e.14 (1467 × 84) (*v.* **in, vangr**); *John Jonson land* 1690 (*v.* **land**); *Anthony Kellam land* 1690 (*v.* **land**; the *Kellam* family came originally from Kelham, 28 miles to the north-east in Notts.); *John Kilbee land* 1690, (*Widdow*) *Kilbys Farme*, *Anne Kilby wid. her Farme* 1699 (*v.* **ferme**) (the *Kilby* family came originally from the village of this name, 11 miles to the south); *Langedoles* 1477 (e.16) (*v.* **lang¹**, **dāl**); *Langedyk'* e.14 (1467 × 84) (*v.* **lang¹**, **dík**); *le Netherlangfurlong'* e.14 (1467 × 84) (*v.* **neoðera**), *le Medewelangfurlong'* e.14 (1467 × 84) (*v.* **mǣd** (**mǣdwe** obl.sg.)) (*v.* **lang¹**, **furlang**); *Lang(e)pol* e.14 (1467 × 84) (*v.* **lang¹**, **pōl¹**); *le Longesmale* (sic) e.14 (1467 × 84) (*v.* **lang¹**, **smæl**; with *smæl* used as a sb., presum. meaning 'a narrow piece of land'); *Long ley(e)s Fur'* 1682, 1686 (*v.* **leys, furlang**); *the Topp of the Meare* 1690, *the Top of the Meere* l.17 (*v.* **topp**; a furlong so called), *Mear(e) Fur'* 1682, 1686 (*v.* **furlang**) (*v.* **(ge)mǣre**); *Meare Willowes* 1682, *Mear Willows* 1686 (*v.* **wilig**; poss. with **mere¹** rather than with **(ge)mǣre**; note Wire willows in f.ns. (a), also with reference to a major pond); *le Medewfurlong'* 14 (1467 × 84), *Meadow Fur'* 1686 (*v.* **furlang**), *le Medow gate* e.14 (1467 × 84) (*v.* **gata**) (*v.* **mǣd** (**mǣdwe** obl.sg.)); *Melton foarde* l.17 (*v.* **ford**; on the road to Melton Mowbray which lies 8 miles to the north-east); *le Mersche* e.14 (1467 × 84) (*v.* **mersc**); *the Middle hedge* 1744 (with **hecg** or **edisc**); Mill hill 1682, 1686, *le Milne Wharf* e.14 (1467 × 84) (*v.* **hwearf**) (*v.* **myln**); *Mukslade* e.14 (1467 × 84), *Muckslade* l.17 (*v.* **muk, slæd**); *the Orchyard end* 1690 (*v.* **ende**), *Orchard corner* 1699, l.17 (*v.* **corner**) (*v.* **orceard**); *le Ouirhay* e.14 (1467 × 84) (*v.* **uferra, (ge)hæg**); *Oxholm* 1477 (e.16) (*v.* **oxa, holmr**); *Padocusholm* 1477 (e.16) (*v.* **padduc, holmr**); *the Parsonage grounde* 1612 (*v.* **grund**), *the Parsonage land* 1690 (*v.* **land**), *the Parsonage orchard* 1601, 1625 (*v.* **orceard**) (*v.* **personage**); *Pinchewang'* 1254 × 80 (*v.* **vangr**; either with the surn. *Pinch* (cf. *Hugo Pinch* 1190 of Lincs.) or with **pinca** 'a finch'); *Pinfold Green(e)* 1682, 1686, 1690, 1744 (*v.* **pynd-fald, grēne²**); *Pollidam close* (sic) 1699, *Pollard Home Close* 1744 (*v.* **home**), *Pollard Wonge* 1690, ~ *Wounge* l.17, *Pollard Wonge Close* 1690 (*v.* **vangr**) (with the surn. *Pollard*); *Prastland leyes* l.17 (*v.* **leys**; with the surn. *Priestland*); *Raresby Broom(e)* 1699 (*v.* **brōm**), *Raresby meere* 1699 (*v.* **(ge)mǣre**), *Raisby Road* 1744 (Rearsby adjoins to the north); *Between the Ridges* 1682, ~ *ye Riges* 1686 (*v.* **hrycg**; a furlong thus called, cf. a furlong called *between the Ridgeways*, *v.* Ridgeways in f.ns. (a) which may refer to the same feature); *le Riewong'* e.14 (1467 × 84), *le Ryewongpit'* e.14 (1467 × 84) (*v.* **pytt**) (*v.* **ryge, vangr**); *Rigslade* e.14 (1467 × 84) (*v.* **hrycg, hryggr, slæd**); *the Nether Roode* 1690 (*v.* **rōd³**); *the Round hole* 1699 (*v.* **round, hol¹**); *Magna* ~, *Parva Ryefeilde* 1561 (1700) (*v.* **ryge, feld**); *le Schortebreche*, *Schortbreche* e.14 (1467 × 84) (*v.* **sc(e)ort, brēc**); *the Shorte furlong* 1690 (*v.* **furlang**); *Shrubbs* 1699 (*v.* **scrubb**); *Willm. Skeath land* 1690 (*v.* **land**);

Smaldolus 1477 (e.16) (*v.* **smæl, dāl**); *Smereberwe, Smereberwehil* e.14 (1467 × 84) (*v.* **hyll**) (*v.* **smeoru, smjǫr, berg** and Smallborough in Barkby f.ns. (a)); *Mr Smith land* 1690 (*v.* **land**); *South feilde* 1467 × 84 (*v.* **sūð, feld**; one of the early great fields of the township); *Sower ~, Sowre Hookes* 1690, *Sower hooks* l.17, *Sower ~, Sowre hooke* 1699, *Sour Hook* 1744 (*v.* **sūr, hōc**); *Spitelcroft* 1260 (*v.* **spitel, croft**; cf. *terra hospitalis Sancti Johannis* e.14 (1467 × 84); the land was that of the Hospital of St John in Leicester, *v.* Lei **1** 93); *Standilwong'* e.14 (1467 × 84) (*v.* **hyll, vangr**; poss. with **stand**, but the *d* could be intrusive, hence with **stān**); *Stainfordforthesike* (sic) e.14 (1467 × 84) (*v.* **sík**), *Stanworthford* 1477 (e.16) (these presum. belong together; originally 'ford at the stone enclosure', *v.* **stān, worð, ford**, with the influence of Scand **steinn** in the earlier form); *Stainlond* e.14 (1467 × 84), *the Stone land* 1690 (*v.* **steinn, stān, land**); *Stapelfurlong'* e.14 (1467 × 84) (*v.* **stapol, furlang**); *le Steyes, le Styes* e.14 (1467 × 84) (*v.* **stig**); *the Stone* 1690 (*v.* **stān**; prob. a boundary marker); *Syston feilde side* l.17 (*v.* **feld, sīde**; Syston adjoins to the south-west); *John Taylor land* 1690 (*v.* **land**); *Thornepoole* 1699 (*v.* **þorn, pōl**[1]); *Willm. Thorpe land* 1690 (*v.* **land**), *(William) Thorps Farm(e)* 1699 (*v.* **ferme**); *Threhowes* e.14 (1467 × 84) (*v.* **þrēo, haugr**); *Town(e)s end* 1682, 1686, 1699, *Towne end Fur'* 1682, 1686 (*v.* **furlang**) (*v.* **tūn, ende**); *the Towne hadland* 1699 (*v.* **hēafod-land**), *the Towne Streete* 1601, 1625 (*v.* **strǣt**) (*v.* **tūn**); *Tythemedowe* 1477 (e.16) (*v.* **tēoða, mǣd** (**mǣdwe** obl.sg.)); *Widdowe Ward land* 1690 (*v.* **land**); *le Watergall* e.14 (1467 × 84), *Watergalls* 1699 (*v.* **wæter, galla**); *le Welle* e.14 (1467 × 84), *Vnder the Well* 1690, *Under well* 1699 (a furlong so called, *v.* **under**) (*v.* **wella**); *Werueldik'* e.14 (1467 × 84) (*v.* **hwerfel, hvirfill, dík**; cf. *Weruel s.n.* Warblong in Asfordby f.ns. (a)); *Westfelde* e.14 (1467 × 84) (*v.* **west, feld**; one of the early great fields); *Westlond* e.14 (1467 × 84) (*v.* **west, land**); *Wetforow'* e.14 (1467 × 84) (*v.* **wēt, furh**); *Wethybuscus* 1477 (e.16) (*v.* **wīðig, busc, buskr**); *White had(e)s* 1682, 1686 (*v.* **hēafod**; either with **hwīt** or, less likely, the surn. *White*; in eModE, *white* 'infertile' is contrasted with *black* 'fertile'); *Wilgercroft* e.14 (1467 × 84) (*v.* **croft**; with the ON pers.n. *Ulfgeirr*, prob. influenced by the OE cognate pers.n. *Wulgār*); *John Wikinson land, Morris Wilkinson land* 1690 (*v.* **land**); *Willowbedd Fur'* 1682 (*v.* **wilig, bedd, furlang**); *Willow Tree Ford* 1744 (*v.* **wilig-trēow, ford**); *Wright Close, ~ ~ end* 1690 (*v.* **ende**) (with the surn. *Wright*).

Ratcliffe on the Wreake

RATCLIFFE ON THE WREAKE

Radeclive 1086 DB, 1166 LN, 1220 MHW *et passim* to 1316 FA, 1322 Pat, *Radecliue* 1196 ChancR, 1332 *LCh* (p), *Radecliua* 1259 *Deed*, *Radeclyue* 1327 SR, *Radeclyve* 1260 Cur, 1285 FA *et passim* to 1315 Inqaqd, 1375 AD

Radecleve 1253 × 58 RHug, c.1291 Tax

Radeclif(') 1332 SR, 1379 Ass, 1403 AD, 15 *Ferrers*, *Radecliff(')* 1360 Coram, 1396 *Ferrers*, 1407 *RTemple*, *Radeclyf* 1365 Coram, 1368 Misc (p) *et passim* to 1412 *RTemple*, 1432 Pat, *Radeclyff(')* 1378 Banco, 1396 *Ferrers*, 1399 Banco, *Radeclyffe* 1403, 1412, 1416 ib

Raddecliff(') 1424 *Ferrers*, 1426 (1449) *WoCart*, *Raddeclyf* 1426 (1449) *ib*, 1428 AAS

Raddeclyff(') 1431, 1447 *Ferrers*

Radclif(f) 1285 Banco, 1360 Coram, 1378 Banco, 1502 Ipm, 1577 LEpis, *Radcliffe* 1326 Pat, *Radclyf* 1377 SR, 1424 AD, *Radclyff(e)* 1368 Banco, 14 *Ferrers et passim* to 1543 AAS, 1547 Pat

Radclyve 1311 Banco, 1360 Cl

Ratcliff(e) 1415, 1424 Banco, 1456 *MiD et passim* to 1604 SR, 1610 Speed *et freq*, *Ratclyff(')* 1424, 1434 Banco *et passim* to 1486 *Ferrers*, 1487 *Fisher et freq* to 1553 Pat, 1576 Saxton, *Ratclyf* 1492 *Fisher*, 1506 Ipm, *Ratclif* 1515 *LCh*

Rotclefe 1447 *RTemple* bis

Affixes are added as:

~ *Burdet* 1242 Fees, 1262 Ass

~ *super* (*le*) *Wrethek*, ~ *super Wre*(*y*)*ke* etc. 1259 *Deed*, 1293 Pat *et passim* to 1360 Cl, 1407 *RTemple et freq* to 1699 LML

~ *Surwrek* 1326 Pat, ~ *sur Wreyk'* 1396 *Ferrers*

~ *opon Wrethek* 1456 *MiD*, ~ *opon Wreyk* 1486 *Ferrers*, ~ *uppon the Wreake* 1612 *Terrier*

'The red cliff', *v.* **rēad**, **clif**. The township, which stands beside the river Wreake, takes its name from the red marl cliff here. *Willelmus Burdet* held the manor in 1242 Fees, while *Alexander Burdet* is still associated with it in 1428 FA.

Note MLat *super*, AFr *sur* and OE **uppan**, all with the meaning 'on, upon', in the formation of the affixes.

CLIFFE HO., *Cliffe house* 1925 Kelly, *the Clyff(e)* 1601, 1625, 1708 *Terrier*, *the Cliffe* 1612, 1674, 1708 (18) *ib*, *v.* **clif**. FOX AND GOOSE (P.H.) (lost), *Fox and Goose* 1863 White. LEWIN BRIDGE, 1806 Map, 1835 O, 1846, 1863 White, *Lewen Bridge* 1590 Nichols, *Luin* ~ 1635 *Surv*, *v.* **brycg**; with the surn. *Lewin*, a reflex of the OE pers.n. *Lēofwine*. LONGLANDS FM, *Lang(e)landes* 1601, 1612 *Terrier*, *Long(e)landes* 1601, 1612, 1625 *ib*, *Longlands* 1625, 1674, 1679, 1708, 1708 (18) *ib*, c.1790 *Plan*, 1837 *Valuation*, *v.* **lang**[1], **land**. NORTH'S LODGE, cf. *Charles North, farmer and bricklayer* 1846 White, *v.* **loge**. THE PRIORY. RATCLIFFE BARN. RATCLIFFE HALL, 1831 Curtis, 1846, 1863, 1877 White, 1925 Kelly, *v.* **hall**. RATCLIFFE MILL, 1877 White, 1925 Kelly, *the Mill* 1708, 1708 (18). RIVERDALE. ST BOTOLPH'S CHURCH, *the Church* 1708, 1708 (18) *Terrier*, *Church (St Botolph)* 1846, 1863, 1877 White, 1925 Kelly; it is earlier recorded as *ecclesie de Radeclive* 1220 MHW, 1242 RGros, *ecclesia parochiali* 1549 *Pat*. Note also *the Churchyard* 1708, 1708 (18) *Terrier*. SHIPLEY HILL, 1837 *Valuation*, 1846, 1863, 1877 White, 1925 Kelly, *Shiply Hill* c.1790 *Plan*, *v.* **lēah**; it is uncertain whether *Shipley* is a late reflex of *Sharpley* in f.ns. (b); if not, its first el. is **scēp** 'sheep'. SPINNEY FM. THE VICARAGE, cf. *the Vicarage House* 1601, 1625, 1708, 1708 (18), ~ *Vicaridge* ~ 1674, 1679, *v.* **vikerage**; cf. *the Old Rectory* 1925 Kelly and *the Rectory* 1925 ib, *v.* **rectory**. WREAKE HOUSE FM is *Wreak House* 1863, 1877 White, named from R. Wreake.

FIELD-NAMES

Undated forms in (a) are c.1790 *Plan*; 1837 are *Valuation*. Forms throughout dated 1601, 1612, 1625, 1674, 1679, 1690, 1693, 1700, 1703, 1708 and 1708 (18) are *Terrier*.

(a) Ash Fd (*v.* **æsc**); Bagerleys (the surn. *Baggerley* in the possessive case; cf. *Bess Baggerleys* 1810 in Charley, West Goscote Hundred, recording land owned by Elizabeth Baggerley and *v.* Reaney *s.n.* Baggarley); Balk Hill (*Balke hill* 1601, 1612, 1674, *Baulke* ~ 1625, 1690, *Baulk* ~ 1708, 1708 (18), *v.* **balca**); Second ~ ~, Barn Cl

1837; Bauks 1837 (*v.* **balca**); Branslet (*Banslade* 1601, 1612, 1625, 1708, 1708 (18), *Branslade* 1674, *v.* **bēan, slæd**); Brick-hill Cl 1837 (*v.* **brike-kiln**); Bretts Cl (with the surn. *Brett*); Brockley Hill, Brockly-hill furlong (*v.* **furlang**) (*v.* **brōc, lēah**); Church Headland (*Church hadland* 1708, *v.* **hēafod-land** and St Botolph's Church *supra*); Long Circles, ~ ~ Furlong, Short Circles Furlong (*v.* **furlang**) (*Shirkles* 1601, 1708, *Shirkels* 1625, *Shyrkyls* 1674, *Sykills* 1690, *Sturkles* 1708 (18), *Long Shirkles* 1601, 1625, 1708, 1708 (18), ~ *Shrilkes* 1612, ~ *Sirkills* 1679, 1690; earlier forms are needed, but this is poss. to be compared with Shericles in Peckleton, Sparkenhoe Hundred (*Sherakehilles*, *Sheracles* 1553, *v.* **scīr**[1], **āc, hyll**) which was a Hundred moot-site (*v.* Barrie Cox, 'Leicestershire moot-sites: the place-name evidence', *Transactions of the Leicestershire Archaeological and Historical Society* 47 (1971–72), 14–21); this location in the Nether Fd of Ratcliffe beside the Fosse Way may be the place where Ralph Basset held a court of the king's thanes on 30 November 1124 and hanged 44 thieves, *v.* ASC E 1124); Cliff furlong (*v.* **furlang**), Cliff Hill c.1790, 1837 (*v.* Cliffe Ho. *supra*); Coal-cart Way, Lower ~ ~ ~ ~, Upper Coal cart way furlong (*v.* **furlang**) (*v.* **col**[1], **carte, weg**; such names often reflect the manufacture of charcoal, but as this name appears also in Rearsby, which adjoins to the east, the poss. transportation of mineral coal may be considered); Colleborough Lane (*v.* **berg**; either with **calu** or **cald**); Cope Lane (poss. with **copp** 'the top of a hill', in dial. 'a ridge of earth, an embankment', but more likely with the surn. *Cope*); Crow Legs Furlong (*v.* **furlang**) (*Crolegges* 1601, *Croledges* 1612, *Crowledges* 1625, 1708, 1708 (18), *Crouleggs* 1675, *Crowleggs* 1679, 1690; ambiguous, since the generic could be **leggr** 'a leg' which, with **crāwe** 'a crow', may have described the shape of selions in a particular furlong (cf. *dogleg*), but the 1612, 1625 forms indicate the more likely **legge** 'a ledge, a ridge of earth'; formally, the first el. could also be OE **crōh**[2] or its ON cognate **krá**, both meaning 'a nook, a corner of land'); Dams-end Furlong c.1790 (*v.* **furlang**), Dams-end Lays c.1790 (*v.* **leys**), Dam ends meadow (sic) 1837 (*Dammes end*(*e*) 1601, 1612, 1625, 1674, 1679, *Damms end* 1690, 1708, 1708 (18), *v.* **damme, ende**); Dick half-acre Furlong (*v.* **dík, half-aker, furlang**); Dovecot Cl 1837 (*v.* **dove-cot(e)**); East Lands (1708, 1708 (18), *Estlandes* 1612, 1625, *v.* **ēast, land**); Elbow Pieces (*v.* **elbowe, pece**); Feriter Leys (*v.* **ferreter, leys**; Reaney *s.n.* Ferreter cites Walter *le Furettour* 1318 Cl as evidence of a precursor for a modern surn. Ferreter, but such a surn. does not occur in the entire British census of 1881); Lord Ferrers Home Cl (*v.* **home**); Flax Leys (1708, 1708 (18); earlier *flaxelande leyes* 1601, *the flaxeland leis* 1612, *flax land leies* 1625, *Flaxland lease* 1674, ~ *Leyes* 1679, *v.* **fleax, land, leys**); Fleet Cl (1708), Fleet Leys (1708, 1708 (18), *Fleete leyes* 1601, *fleet layes* 1612, *Flyte leyes* 1625, ~ *layes* 1674, *Fleet Leyes* 1679, *v.* **flēot, leys**); Foss Furlong (*the Foss*(*e*) *furlong*(*e*) 1601, 1612 *et passim* to 1708 (18) (*v.* **furlang**), cf. *Foss Hades* 1708, 1708 (18) (*v.* **hēafod**); beside Fosse Way which is recorded locally as *the fosse waye* 1601, 1612, *the Foss*(*e*) *way* 1625, 1674, 1679, 1708, *v.* **foss**[1] 'a ditch', with reference to the Roman drainage ditches running beside the ancient metalled road); Mr Freeman's Mdw 1837; Goose Nook c.1790, 1837, 1708, 1708 (18), *Gouse Nooke* 1601, *Goose* ~ 1612, 1625, 1674, 1679, *v.* **gōs, nōk**); Great Mdw 1837; Furlong at the Heart of the Field (*v.* **furlang**; in Nether Fd); High Lands 1837 (*v.* **hēah**[1], **land**); High Leys (*v.* **hēah**[1], **leys**); Hill Leys (*the hill* 1625, *v.* **leys**); Hollow Way (*v.* **hol**[2], **weg**); Holmes (*le Holm* 1612 Ipm, *v.* **holmr**); Hung Furlong (*v.* **furlang**), Hung Leys (1708, *Hung layes* 1674, *Hang Leys* 1708 (18) (*v.* **leys**), cf. *hunglandes* 1612, *honglandes*, *hanglands* 1625,

Hunglands 1679, 1690, 1708, *Honglands* 1679, 1690 (*v.* **land**) (with the pa.part. **hung** of the verb 'to hang', used as an adj. in the sense 'steeply sloping'); Knaptthorn (*v.* **cnæpp, þorn**); Lenard Acre (*Leonarde acres* 1601, *Leonard Acre* 1612, 1625 *et passim* to 1708 (18), *v.* **æcer**; with the common Leics. surn. *Leonard*, a reflex of the OGer pers.n. *Leonhard* 'lion-bold'); Lewing Home (*v.* **holmr**; with the surn. *Lewin*, cf. Lewin Bridge *supra*); Linthwaits Head-Land (*v.* **hēafod-land**; with the surn. *Linthwaite*); Little Cl; Long Cl; Long Nook (*v.* **nōk**); Martin's Lane (with the surn. *Martin*); Bottom ~ ~ ~, Top of the Meadow, Meadow Furlong (*v.* **furlang**) (*the Medowe* 1601, 1612, 1674, *the Meadow* 1679); Little ~ ~, Over Meer (*v.* **uferra**), Nether Meer, ~ ~ Leys (*v.* **leys**), Top of the Meer, Meer Furlong (*v.* **furlang**) c.1790, Meer Cl 1837 (*v.* **(ge)mǣre**); Middle Fd (1708 (18), *the Midle fielde* 1601, 1612, *the Myddle fielde* 1625, *the Midle feilde* 1674, *the Middle Feild* 1679, 1708, *v.* **middel, feld**; one of the great fields of the township); Mill Cl, Mill Leys (*v.* **leys** and Ratcliffe Mill *supra*); Mill Stone Furlong (*v.* **milne-stone, furlang**); Moor Bush (*v.* **busc**), Moorhead Leys (*v.* **hēafod, leys**) (*the Mores* 1601, 1612, 1675, *the Moores* 1625, 1690, *the Moors* 1708, 1708 (18), *v.* **mōr**[1]); Mount Pleasant 1806 Map (a common minor name, usually having a favourable meaning, but sometimes used ironically); Needham's Lane (with the surn. *Needham*); Nether Cl; Nether Fd (1708, 1708 (18), *the neither fielde* 1601, *the Nether fielde* 1612, 1625, ~ ~ *feild* 1674, 1679, *v.* **neoðera, feld**; one of the great fields); New Cl; Ratcliffe Cl 1837; Ratcliffe Garden 1837 *Valuation*, 1863 White (*v.* **gardin**); Red Gore, ~ ~ Foot (*v.* **fōt**) (*Red goar* 1708, 1708 (18), *v.* **rēad, gāra**); Road Cl 1837; Rod Hill (either with **rod**[1] 'a clearing' or **rōd**[3] 'a rood of land'); Great Royborough (*Ryborowe* 1601, *Rybowrowe* 1612, *Rieborowe* 1625, *Rieb(o)rough* 1674, 1679, *Ryborrow* 1690, *Great Ryburrow* 1708), Little Royborough (*Lytle Ryborowe* 1601, ~ *Rybowrowe* 1612, *Lyttle Riebowrowe* 1625, *Litle Riebrough* 1674, *Little Rieborough* 1679, ~ *Ryborrow* 1690 (*v.* **lȳtel**), cf. *Ryborow(e) hades* 1601, 1625, *Rieb(o)rough* ~ 1674, 1679, *Rieborrow* ~ 1690 (*v.* **hēafod**)) (*v.* **ryge, berg**); Sandy Leys 1837, Long ~ ~, Short Sandy Leys, Long Sandy Leys Furlong (*v.* **furlang**) c.1790 (*v.* **sandig, leys**); Sarson's Lane (with the surn. *Sarson*; note its earlier form in *Oliverus Sarazin* 12 Dane of Leics.); Sharp's Headland (*v.* **hēafod-land**; with the surn. *Sharp*); Sheep Common (*v.* **commun**); Shiplyhill Furlong c.1790 (*v.* **furlang**), Shipley hill meadow 1837 (*v.* Shipley Hill *supra*); Short Hundred (1601, 1674, 1679, 1708, *Shorte Hundred* 1625, *v.* **sc(e)ort, hundred**; in Nether Fd, it is uncertain to what *hundred* refers; poss. 100 selions, but also poss. is a local moot-site, *v.* Circles *supra*; earlier forms are needed); Farther Sike (*the further Sicke* 1601, 1612, 1625, 1679, 1690, *ye further Sick* 1674, *the farther Sick* 1708, 1708 (18), *v.* **furðra**), Middle Sike, Furlong between the Sikes (*betwixt the Sickes* 1601, *betweęn(e) the Sick(e)s* 1612, 1625 *et passim* to 1708, *v.* **betwixt, betwēonan**) (*v.* **sík**); Spinney Cl 1837 (*v.* **spinney**); Sun Hill (cf. *the furlong(e) named ageanst the Soone* 1601, 1612, (*the furlong(e) named*) *against the Sunne* 1625, 1679, *Against the soone* 1674, ~ ~ *Sun* 1690, *v.* **ageynst, sunne**; alluding to ground which caught the best of the sunshine); Sweden Furlong (*v.* **furlang**) (*Swithey* 1601, *Swithen* 1612, 1625, 1674, *Swythen* 1708, *v.* **sviðinn**); Far Top Cl 1837; Tup Cl (*Tubcloase* 1612, *Tubb Close* 1708, *Tubecloase ende* 1601, *Toubę Closse end* 1625, ~ *Close* ~ 1674, 1679 (*v.* **ende**), *v.* **clos(e)**; either with the surn. *Tubb* (a reflex of the ON, ODan pers.n. *Tubbi*) or, less likely, with **tup**); Tythe Piece (*v.* **pece**) (cf. *the Teyth dowle* 1601, 1674, ~ *Teith* ~ 1612, ~ *Tythe* ~ 1625, *the Teyth doule* 1674, *the Tyth dole* 1679, *v.* **tēoða, dāl**); Upper Fd (*the field(e) toward(e)s*

Thrussington 1601, 1625, 1708, 1708 (18), *the Heier fielde or the fielde towardes Thrussington* 1612, *v.* **hēr(r)a, feld**; one of the great fields, Thrussington adjoining to the north-east); Vicarage Furlong (*v.* **vikerage, furlang**; in c.1775, sited beside The Vicarage *supra*); Little ~ ~, Water Leys (*Water Leies* 1612, ~ *Leyes* 1625, 1679, ~ *layes* 1674, ~ *Leys* 1708, 1708 (18)), Water Leys Furlong (*v.* **furlang**) (*v.* **wæter, leys**; with reference to R. Wreake and an irrigation system, *v.* Field 90); Wood-Gate Furlong (*v.* **furlang**), Wood-Gate Leys (*v.* **leys**) (*Woodgate* 1601, 1612 *et passim* to 1708 (18), *v.* **wudu, gata**); White Close Stile (*v.* **stigel**; with **hwīt**, poss. in its later dial. sense 'dry pasture'); Worm Hill c.1790, 1837 (1708 (18), *Wormowe* 1601, 1612, *Woormowe* 1625, *Wornowe* 1679, 1690, *Whormehill* 1674, *v.* **wyrm, haugr**; the Scand generic may have influenced or replaced OE **hōh**, but was itself later replaced by English **hyll**).

(b) *the beastes pasture* 1625 (*v.* **beste, pasture**); *Braknell buske* 1601, *Bracknell* ~, 1612, 1625 (*v.* **buskr**), *Bracknell balke* 1674, 1679, 1690 (*v.* **balca**), *Bracknell hill* 1708, *Bracknehill* 1708 (18) (*v.* **braken, hyll**); *Henrie Burbages hadlande* 1612, *Henry Burbage hadland* 1625 (*v.* **hēafod-land**); the *Burbage* family prob. came originally from the township of this name, 18 miles to the south-west); *the Common ground(e)* 1601, 1625 *et passim* to 1708 (18) (*v.* **commun, grund**); *Cosington Ashes* 1601, 1625, 1679, ~ *asshes* 1612, *Coussington Ashes* 1674, *Cossington* ~ 1708 (18) (*v.* **æsc**), *Cosington meer* 1601, 1612, 1625, 1679, *Cossington meare* 1674, ~ *Meer* 1708, 1708 (18) (*v.* **(ge)mǣre**) (Cossington adjoins to the west); *the Cow Pasture* 1679, 1708 (*v.* **pasture**); *Elderstubbes* 1601, 1612, 1625, *Elderstubs* 1674, *Elderstubbs* 1679, 1690, *Elder Stubs* 1708 (*v.* **ellern, stubb**); *the Lord Ferrers ground* 1679 (*v.* **grund**), ~ ~ ~ *hadland* 1679 (*v.* **hēafod-land**); *flaxelandes* 1601, *flaxlandes* 1612, 1625, *Flax Lands* 1708, 1708 (18) (*v.* **fleax, land** and Flax Leys *supra*); *furleis* 1612, *forrleyes* 1674, *Farleys* 1708 (*v.* **feor, leys**); *Hassowe* 1601, 1612, 1625, 1674, 1679, *Hassow* 1708, 1708 (18) (*v.* **hǣs, haugr**; the Scand generic may have influenced or replaced OE **hōh**); *John Haynes grownd* 1679 (*v.* **grund**), *John Heane his hadland* 1625, *John Haynes Hadland* 1674, 1679, *Robert Heans Hadland* 1708, ~ ~ *Headland* 1708 (18) (*v.* **hēafod-land**), *John Haynes Sid(e)land* 1674, 1679, 1690, *Robert Heans sideland* 1708 (*v.* **sīde, land**), *John Heane his sydeley* 1625 (*v.* **sīde, ley**); *the Homestall* 1708 (18) (*v.* **hām-stall**; belonging to *the Vicarage House*); *the homesteed* 1612 (*v.* **hām-stede**); *Robert Kylbies hadland* 1601, *Robert Kilbies hadlande* 1612, *Robert Kilbye his hadland* 1625, *Kilbys hadland* 1679, 1690 (*v.* **hēafod-land**; the *Kilby* family came originally from the village of this name, 12 miles to the south); *(John) Leas Hadland* 1674, 1679 (*v.* **hēafod-land**), *Leas land* 1679 (*v.* **land**); *My Lords (grass) hadland* 1708 (*v.* **græs, hēafod-land**; with reference to Lord Ferrers); *Narowelandes* 1601, *Narowlandes* 1612, *Narrow(e)lands* 1624, 1674, 1679, 1690, 1708 (*v.* **nearu, land**); *the neates pasture* 1601, 1612, *the Neats Pasture* 1625, ~ *neat* ~ 1674 (*v.* **nēat, pasture**); *the neither furlonge* 1601, 1612, *the nether furlong* 1625, 1674, 1679 (*v.* **neoðera, furlang**; i.e. of Nether Fd); *the Pitts* 1708 (18), *Pitthades* 1601, 1612, 1679, 1708, 1708 (18), *Pytthades* 1625, *Pitts hades* 1674 (*v.* **hēafod**), *the Pitt stints* 1708 (*v.* **stint**) (*v.* **pytt**); *the Rane* 1601, *the Ranes* 1674, *the Raynes* 1679, 1690, *(the) Rain hollows* 1708, 1708 (18) (*v.* **holh**) (*v.* **rein**); *Sand Lands* 1708 (*v.* **sand, land**); *Sharplegate* 1625, 1674, 1679, *Sharpley gate* 1708, 1708 (18), *v.* **scearp, lēah, gata** and Shipley Hill *supra*); *Mr Sherleys hadland* 1612, *Sir Henry Shirleyes* ~ 1625, *Sir Robert Shirley hadland* 1674 (*v.* **hēafod-land**); *Storers piece* 1612 Ipm (*v.* **pece**; with the surn.

Storer); *the sty* 1601 (*v*. **stig**); *atte Style* 1332 SR (p) (*v*. **atte**, **stigel**); *Styles croft* 1617 Ipm (*v*. **croft**; prob. with the surn. *Styles*, otherwise **stigel**); *the Styntes* 1601, 1612, 1625, *the stintes* 1612, *the Stynts* 1625, 1674, 1679, 1690, *the Stints* 1708, 1708 (18) (*v*. **stint**); *Thrussington Meer(e)* 1601, 1612 *et passim* to 1708 (18), *Thrusington mere* 1674 (*v*. **(ge)mǣre**), *Thrussington way(e)* 1601, 1612 *et passim* to 1708 (18), *Thrussingeton Waye* 1612, *Thrusington way* 1674 (*v*. **weg**) (Thrussington adjoins to the north-east); *the towne fielde* 1625, *the Town feild* 1674, 1708 (18) (*v*. **feld**), *the towne gresse hadland(e)* 1612, 1674, *the Towne Grasse Hadland* 1679 (*v*. **græs**), *the towne hadland(e)* 1601, 1612 *et passim* to 1708, *ye Town Hadland* 1674, *the Town Headland* 1708 (18), *the towne hadlande ende* 1601, 1612, 1625 (*v*. **ende**) (*v*. **hēafod-land**), *the towne street* 1601, 1612, 1625, *the Town Street* 1708, 1708 (18) (*v*. **strǣt**) (*v*. **tūn**); *the vicarage cloase* 1601, 1612, ~ ~ *closse* 1625, *the Vicaridge Close* 1674, 1679, *the Vicarrage Closs* 1690 (*v*. **clos(e)**), *the vicarage yarde* 1601, 1612, 1625, *the Vicaridge Yard* 1674, 1679, *the Vicarage* ~ 1708 (18) (*v*. **geard**) (*v*. **vikerage**); *waterforowes* 1601 (*v*. **wæter**, **furh** and *the waterfurrow(e)s* in Asfordby f.ns. (b)); *Mr Wells's hadland* 1708, ~ ~ *Headland* 1708 (18) (*v*. **hēafod-land**); *Wenie clyffe* 1601, *Waenie* ~ 1612, *Whenie clyffe* 1625, *Whinney Cliff(e)* 1679, 1708 (18), *Whiney Cliffe* 1690, *Whinny Cliff* 1708 (*v*. **whinny**, **clif**); *wranglandes* 1601, 1612, 1625, *Wranglands* 1690, 1708, 1708 (18) (*v*. **wrang**, **vrangr**, **land**); *in the Wylughes* 1327 SR (p) (*v*. **wilig**); *yardes ende* 1601, (*the*) *Yards end* 1625, 1708 (*v*. **geard**, **ende**).

Rearsby

REARSBY

Redresbi 1086 DB

Reresbi 1086 DB, 1166 LN, *Reresby* 1166 RBE, 1220 MHW, 1225 RHug *et passim* to 1243 Fees, 1247 Fine *et freq* to 1508, 1509 *Rut et passim* to 1535 VE, 1539 MinAccts, *Reresbie* 1546 AAS, 1549 Pat, 1574 LEpis, *Rerisby* 1235 RGros, 1242 Fees, 1259 GildR (p) *et freq* to 1357 *Wyg*, 1362 *LCDeeds* (p) *et passim* to 1487 Pat, 1500 Will, *Rerysby* Edw 1 Derby, 1324 Ass *et passim* to 1402 Pat, 1474 Banco

Resebi c.1130 LeicSurv, *Resebia* c.1130 ib

Resby 1397 Misc, *Reysby* 1481 *Ct*, *Reasby(e)* 1576 Saxton, 1610 Speed

Rearesby 1590, 1604 SR

Raresby 1687, 1688 LML, *Raersby* 1717, 1719 ib, *Raisby* 1744 *Rental*, 1790 *Surv*, *Rasby* c.1775 *Plan*

Rearsby 1835 O, 1846 White *et freq*

'Hreiðar's farmstead, village', *v.* **bȳ**, cf. Rotherby *supra*. The pers.n. *Hreiðarr* is ON (ODan *Rethar*). Two affixes are recorded: ~ *Chaumberleing* 1242 Fees and ~ *en le Mere* 1372 Pat. Ralph Chamberlain held the manor in the reign of John and the family continued in possession until the reign of Henry VI (1422–61). But note the manor of Rearsby is still called *Chaumberlayns* 1486 Ipm and *Chamberleyns maner* 1506 ib, *v.* **maner**. The land on which Rearsby stands is low-lying in the Wreake basin. A major stream flows through the village into the river. The surrounding area was evidently once marshy, hence ~ *en le Mere*, with **mere**[1] in its sense 'wetland'.

BEESON'S BARN, cf. *Robt. and Wm. Beeson, farmers* 1846 White. BENSKIN'S BARN, cf. *John and Wm. Benskin, farmers* 1846 White. BLACK POOL. BLEAK MOOR, *Blakmor'* 1467 × 84 *LTD*, *blakemore* 1601 *Terrier*, *Blackmoor(e)* 1625, 1675, 1679 *et passim* to 1709 (18) *ib*, *Blackmore* 1648, 1712 *ib*, *Blakemoor* 1671 *Deed*, 1762 *EnclA*, *Blakmoor*

1745 *Terrier*, (*the*) *Great Bleakmoor* 1876 *Sale*, 1968 *Surv*, *v.* **mōr**[1], **mór**; with **blæc** or, less likely, **bleikr**. BROOK HO. (local), *Brook house* 1877 White, 1925 Kelly, *v.* **brōc**. BROOM LODGE is the site of *The Broom Barn* 1835 O, *v.* **brōm**. CHURCH LEYS, 1731 *Terrier*, 1762 *EnclA*, 1925 Kelly, 1968 *Surv*, *v.* **leys** and St Michael's Church *infra*. GRANVILLE HO. (local), *Granville house* 1925 Kelly. HORSE AND GROOM (P.H.), *Horse and Groom* 1846, 1863, 1877 White, 1925 Kelly. MANOR HO., *Manor house* 1877 White, 1925 Kelly, *v.* **maner**. METHODIST CHAPEL. THE OLD HALL, 1925 Kelly, *The Hall* 1877 White, *v.* **hall**. REARSBY GRANGE, 1934 *Sale*, 1968 *Surv*, *v.* **grange**. REARSBY HO., *Rearsby house* 1846, 1863, 1877 White, 1925 Kelly. REARSBY LODGE. REARSBY MILL, 1835 O, *the Mylne* 1467 × 84 *LTD*, *Rasby Mill* c.1775 *Plan*; it is *the Watermill* 1789 (1815) *EnclA* (*v.* **water-mylne**), *v.* **myln**. REARSBY STATION, 1835 O; on the former *Syston and Peterborough Branch Railway* 1835 ib. REARSBY WHARF LODGE (lost), *Rearsby Wharf Lodge* 1835 O, *v.* **hwearf, loge**. THE RECTORY, cf. *the Parsonage House* 1625, 1679 *et passim* to 1745 *Terrier v.* **personage**, RECTORY FM. ROSE AND CROWN (P.H.) (lost), *Rose and Crown* 1846 White. ST MICHAEL'S CHURCH, *Church (St Michael)* 1846, 1863, 1877 White, 1925 Kelly; it is earlier recorded as *ecclesiam* ~ ~, *ecclesie de Reresby* 1220 MHW, 1237 RGros, 1318 *Pat*, ~ *de Rerisby* 1327 *ib*. Note also *the Church Yard* 1852 *TA*. WHEEL (P.H.), *Wheel* 1846, 1877 White, 1925 Kelly, *Wheel Inn* 1863 White.

FIELD-NAMES

Undated forms in (a) are 1968 *Surv*; those dated 1762 are *EnclA*; 1826 are *Surv*; 1828 are *Terrier*; 1837 are *Valuation*; 1852 are *TA*; 1863 are *Deed*; 1876 are *Sale*. Forms throughout dated 1467 × 84 are *LTD*; those dated 1601, 1612, 1625, 1648, 1675, 1679, 1700, 1703, 1709, 1709 (18), 1712, 1731 and 1745 are *Terrier*; 1647, 1671 and 1678 are *Deed*.

(a) Four Acre, Six Acres, Seven ~, Eight ~, Nine Acre 1968, Ten Acre 1876, 1968, Eleven Acres or First Cl 1968 (*v.* **æcer**); The Arbor 1762 (1679, 1700, 1703, 1709, 1712, 1731, 1745, *the harbor* 1601, 1612, *the harbour* 1625, *the Arbour* 1648, 1709 (18), *v.* **erber**); Austins 1837, 1968 (the surn. *Austin* in the possessive case); Bancroft (1601, 1612, 1625 *et freq* to 1745, cf. *Bancroft bauk(e)* 1601, ~ *bawlke* 1612, ~ *baulke* 1675, 1679 *et passim* to 1712, *Bankroft Baulk* 1709 (18), 1745, *Bancrofts baulke* 1625, ~ *balke* 1648 (*v.* **balca**), *Bancroft doole* 1467 × 84 (*v.* **dāl**), *Bancroft furlong* 1675, 1679 *et passim* to 1745 (*v.* **furlang**), *Bancroft Leys* 1731 (*v.* **leys**)), Bancroft Mdw 1762 (1648, 1675 *et passim* to 1745, *Bancroft mydow* 1467 × 84, ~ *Med(d)ow* 1601, 1612, 1625, *the East Bancroft Meadow* 1745 (*v.* **mǣd** (**mǣdwe** obl.sg.), cf. *Bancroft Meadow Gate* 1712, 1745, *the Meadow Gate* 1700, 1703 (*v*. **gata**)) (*v*. **bēan, croft**); Barn Cl 1826, 1876, Second Barn Cl 1837, 1968, Top Barn 1968; Far Bastards 1837, First ~, Little ~, Long Bastards 1968 (*v*. **bastard**); Beavery Nook (beside R.Wreake, *v*. **beavery, nōk**); Beeson's Barn Fd (*v*. Beeson's Barn *supra*); Benskin's Fds, Benskin's Paddock (*v*. **paddock**) (*v*. Benskin's Barn *supra*); Blakemoor Spinneys 1761 Nichols (*v*. **spinney**), Bleakmoor Mdw 1837, 1876, 1968, Big ~, Little ~, Road Bleakmoor 1968 (*v*. Bleak Moor *supra*); the Big Mdw; Bog Lane Fd (*v*. **bog**); Bottom Cl 1837, 1876; Bready Wong 1762, 1837 (*Brytiwongis* 1467 × 84, *Brediwonges* 1601, 1612, *Bredywonges* 1612, 1648, *Brady wonges* 1648, *Breeding Wongs* (sic) 1731; also known as *Broadwonges* 1625, 1675, 1679, 1703, 1712, *Broad Wongs* 1675, 1703 *et passim* to 1745, *v*. **breiðr, vangr**; the first el. later varies with **brād**); Brick Fd (*v*. **bryke**); Brick Kiln Cl 1837, 1876, Brick Kiln Fd 1968 (*v*. **brike-kiln**); the Broad mere 1828 (*Brodemere, Brawde meyre* 1467 × 84, *broad(e) meare* 1601, 1612, 1648, *broad meere* 1625, *(the) Broad Meer* 1675, 1679 *et passim* to 1745, *v*. **brād**; with **(ge)mǣre** or **mere**[1]); Brook Cl (*the Brooke* 1612, 1625, 1675, *v*. **brōc**; beside Queniborough Brook *q.v.*); Upper Broom 1826, Broom Fd 1968 (1731) (cf. *the brome furlonge* 1601, *the broome furlong(e)* 1612, 1625, 1675, 1712 (*v*. **furlang**), *brome lees* 1601, 1612, *Broome leas* 1625, *(the) Broom(e) Leyes* 1675, 1700, 1703, 1709, *the Nether ~ ~, Over Broome leyes* 1648 (*v*. **uferra**), *Nether ~ ~, Upper Broom(e) Leyes* 1648, 1675, 1700, 1703, 1709, 1712, *Nether ~ ~, Upper Broom Leys* 1709 (18), 1745, *Below Broom Leys, Beyond Broom Leys* 1731 (furlongs so called), *the Broome leyes close* 1648, *Broomleys Close* 1731 (*v*. **leys**), *v*. **brōm** and Broom Lodge *supra*); Bottom ~, Top Bullocks (with the surn. *Bullock* in the possessive case); Church Lane Cl 1837, 1876, Church Leys 1837 (*v*. **leys**) (*v*. St Michael's Church *supra*); Common Plat 1826 (1731, *the commen plat* 1601, *Common Platt* 1648, 1745, *the Comon Plott* 1625, 1675, 1709, *Common Plott* 1679, 1700, 1703, 1709 (18), *v*. **commun, plat, plot**); Convent or Garlands Fd (poss. a memory of land here which was owned by Leicester Abbey; *v*. **convent**, which was not restricted in early usage to female religious communities, and *v*. Garlands Fd *infra*); Coopers Barn 1835 O (with the surn. *Cooper*); Corner Fd (*v*. **corner**); Cottage Fd; Cow Cl 1826, 1968, Second ~ ~ 1968; Cow Pasture 1762 (*v*. **pasture**); Cricket Fd (for the game of cricket); Cungen Mdw 1762 (*Cungie, Congie* 1601, *Congeye* 1612, *Cunsey* 1625, 1675, *Cunsing* 1648, *Cunsey or Cunsing* 1700, *Cungie medow* 1601, *Cunsey Meadow* 1678, 1679, 1745, *the Meadow called Cunsey* 1703, 1709, 1709 (18), 1712, 1745, *Cunsey hedge* 1675, 1700, *Cunsey meadow hedge* 1703, 1709, 1709 (18), 1712, 1745 (*v*. **hecg**), *Congie gap* 1612, *Cunsey gapp* 1625 (*v*. **gap**); obscure — and earlier forms are needed, the value of the *g* in the earliest surviving spellings being problematical; if an ancient name, then **cung** 'a hill' with **ēg** may be thought of, especially in a wetlands area, while a debased **coningre** must be very doubtful in view of its survival in the following f.n. group); Old Cunnery 1826 (*the Conygare* 1467 × 84, *the old cuningrye* 1601, *~ ~ cuningrie* 1612, *the ould Cuningrey* 1625, *the Old Coningrey* 1675, 1700, 1703, 1709, 1709 (18), *~ ~ Conyngrey* 1679, *the Old Coningrey or Conery* 1712, *the Old Conery* 1745, *the old Cuningrey wonge* 1648 (*v*. **vangr**), *the Cuningrye hedge* 1612 (*v*. **hecg**), *the Cuningrey side* 1625 (*v*. **sīde**)), Cunnery Cl 1837, 1876, 1968 (*Cuningrey Close* 1648, *the Coningrey Close* 1675, 1700, 1709, 1709 (18), *the Coningrey or Conery Close* 1712, 1745), Nether ~ ~, Upper Cunnery Mdw 1826 (*v*. **coningre**); Big ~ ~, Little Dale (*the Dale* 1467 × 84), Dale Cl 1826 *Surv*, 1846, 1863, 1877 White (*the*

Dale close 1648, ~ ~ *closes* 1675, 1679 *et passim* to 1745, *the Dale close end* 1648 (*v.* **ende**)), Dale Mdw 1837, Dales Fd 1762 (*the Dale field* 1601, 1612 *et passim* to 1745, ~ ~ *feild*(*e*) 1625, 1648, 1675, 1679, *v.* **feld**; one of the great fields of the township) (*v.* **dalr**); Dent's Cl 1837 (with the surn. *Dent*); Doddingthorne Mdw 1762, 1837 (*Dodyngton'* 1467 × 84, *Doddingthorn*(*e*) 1601, 1612 *et passim* to 1700, *Dodingthorpe* (sic) 1684 bis, *Doddingthorne medow* 1601, *Dod*(*d*)*ingthorn*(*e*) *meadow* 1678, 1679 *et passim* to 1745, *Doddington Thorn Meadow* 1709 (18); *Doddington* was poss. the Anglo-Saxon name of the settlement preceding Rearsby, either 'farmstead, estate called after or associated with a man called Dod(d)a', *v.* **-ingtūn** (cf. nearby Cossington), or less likely, 'farmstead belonging to Dod(d)ing', *v.* **tūn** and Feilitzen 225); Lower ~ ~, Drome Fd (with a shortened form of *aerodrome*, the field lying adjacent to Rearsby Airfield); East Mdw 1762 (*Est medow*, ~ *Midowe* 1467 × 84, *the East Med*(*d*)*ow* 1601, 1625, ~ ~ *Meadow*(*e*) 1648, 1675 *et passim* to 1745, *v.* **ēast, mǣd (mǣdwe** obl.sg.)); Eastern Leys (*v.* **leys**); Ephraim Leys 1826 (*v.* **leys**; *Ephraim* is a Hebrew pers.n., poss. used as a surn. here, although there is no record of its presence as a surn. in the East Midlands in the 1881 census); Eye Spie or Dent's Cl 1837, High Spie 1968 (perh. a humorous allusion to R. Eye, the earlier name for the whole of R. Wreake, *v. Eyfurlong'* in f.ns. (b) and Dent's Cl *supra*); Far Cl 1852; Far Mdw; First Cl 1876; First Mdw; Foster's Cl (with the surn. *Foster*); Frazier's or Wharf Mdw 1876 (with the surn. *Frazier*, *v.* Wharf Mdw *infra*); Garlands Fd (poss.with the surn. *Garland*, but this is rare in Leics.; whether the f.n. relates rather to *Garleygate*, *infra*, is uncertain ; *v.* Convent *supra*); Glebe Fd, Glebe Farm Fd (*v.* **glebe**); Gold Hill 1837 (either with the surn. *Gold*, or with **gold** if referring to the discovery of treasure, or with **golde** if alluding to the notable presence of marigolds or other yellow flowers; however, the usual spelling of the surn. in Leics. is *Gould*); Gooseholme 1762, 1837 (1625, 1678, 1679, 1700, 1712, *gosehome* 1601, 1612, *Goosholme* 1675, *Gooseholm* 1709, *the Goose-Holm* 1709 (18)), Gooseholm Mdw 1828 (*v.* **gōs, holmr**); Goss Cl 1826 (*v.* **gorst**); Gravel Pit(t) Cl 1837, 1876 (*v.* **pytt**), Gravel Stones 1968 (*v.* **gravel**); (the) Great Mdw 1837, 1876; Greenacre Cl 1846, 1863, 1877 White (*v.* **grēne**[1], **æcer**; *Greenacre* was not a 19th cent. Leics. surn.); Hames Cl (cf. *Joseph Hames* 1852); Hampson's Fds (with the surn. *Hampson*); Hay Furlong Leys 1762 (1731, 1745, *Hey furlong leyes* 1648, *Hay Furlong Leyes* 1675, 1679 *et passim* to 1712, cf. *nether heyfurlonge leyes* 1648, *v.* **hēg, furlang, leys**); Hill Cl 1826; Hilly Cl, Hilly Fd; Hollow Tongue 1826, 1837, 1968 (*Holotong'* 1467 × 84, *hollowtonge* 1601, 1625, *Hollow Tongue* 1675, 1679 *et passim* to 1745, *Hollowtong* 1700, *v.* **holh, tunge**); Home Cl or Cunnery Cl 1876, Home Cl or The Park or Cunnery Cl 1968 (*v.* Cunnery Cl *supra* and The Park *infra*), Home Fd 1968 (*v.* **home**); Hopkins' Wharf 1846 White (*v.* **hwearf**; with the surn. *Hopkins*); Horse Cl; Horse Pool Cl 1762, 1826 (*the hors*(*e*)*pole* 1601, 1625, 1648, *Horspool* 1731, *the over* ~ ~ (*v.* **uferra**), *the nether horse poole* 1648, *Thrussington Hors*(*e*)*poole* 1700, 1703, 1709, 1712 (Thrussington adjoins to the north, beyond R. Wreake), cf. (*the*) *Horsepool*(*e*) *furlong* 1675, 1679 *et passim* to 1745 (*v.* **furlang**), *v.* **hors, pōl**[1]); Hut Cl 1837, Hut or Simpson Cl 1876 (*v.* **hut** and Simpson Cl *infra*); Kirby Cl 1876, Kirby's Mdw 1968 (with the surn. *Kirby* of a family perh. originally from Kirby Bellars, 5 miles to the north-east); Lane Cl 1852 (*v.* **lane**); Long Mdw; Big Masons (with the surn. *Mason* in the possessive case); Middle Cl 1852; Middle Fd (*Mydylfelde* 1467 × 84, *v.* **middel, feld**; one of the early great fields); Middle Platt or Pingle 1826 (*v.* **plat, pingel**); Milestone Fd (*v.* **mīl-stān**); Mill Cl 1762, 1837 (*the*

Mill Close 1648, *Mill Closes* 1745, cf. *Millclose Leys* 1731 (*v.* **leys**)), Mill Fd 1968, Mill Piece 1837 (*v.* **pece**) (cf. *the milne bawlke* 1601 (*v.* **balca**), *the milne furlonge* 1601, 1612, 1625, *the Myll furlong* 1648, 1675, (*the*) *Mill furlong* 1679, 1700 *et passim* to 1745 (*v.* **furlang**), *Millne hylle* 1467 × 84, *the milne hill* 1601, *Millne hill* 1648 (*v.* **hyll**; a windmill site), *the Millhill furlonge* 1648, *the Millne wonge* 1648 (*v.* **vangr**)) (*v.* **myln**); Mill Willows Cl 1863 (this 19th cent. form is prob. based upon a reduced *milner willoes* 1601, 1612, *Milner willowes* 1625, 1675, *Miller Willowes* 1700, 1703, ~ *Willows* 1709, 1712, 1745, *v.* **wilig**; with the surn. *Milner/Miller*, cf. *Thomas Milner* 1601 and *Millers land* in f.ns. (b)); Little Moor 1968, Moore Cl 1876 (*the moare* 1612, *the Moore* 1625, 1648, *the Moor* 1675, 1712), (the) Moor Head 1837, 1876 (1731, *the Moore head* 1612, 1625, 1648, cf. *the Moor(e)head Furlong* 1675, 1679 *et passim* to 1745, *v.* **hēafod, furlang**) (*v.* **mōr**[1]); the Munchings (ostensibly a late jocular name for good grazing, but note that Leicester Abbey held land here, so **munuc** with **eng** may be thought of, despite a lack of early evidence); Mushroom Fd (a close in which mushrooms abounded); Bottom ~ ~, Far ~ ~, Long No Clock, No Clock Barn (cf. *le Naccok* 1342 in Walton on Thames (Sr) and *Nattokes* 1271 in Greatworth (Nth), *v.* **nattock**, Nth lii *s.n.* Naddocks and O 459 *s.v.*); Norman's Cl (*Normans close* 1601, 1709 *et passim* to 1745, cf. *Normans clos(s)e hedge* 1625, 1675 (*v.* **hecg**), *Normans Close style* 1648 (*v.* **stigel**), with the surn. *Norman*); Oak Cl 1762 ((*the*) *Oak(e) Close* 1675, 1679 *et passim* to 1745, *the Oke Close* 1712, cf. *the Oke close hedge* 1601, 1612, *the Oakes Close hedge* 1625 (*v.* **hecg**), *v.* **āc**); the Paddock (*v.* **paddock**); The Park (*v.* **park** and Home Cl *supra*); The Parlour (*v.* **parlur**); Parson's Cl (*v.* **persone**); Peaseland Hook 1762, 1837 (*Peyslond'*, *Undur peyslandis* 1467 × 84 (*v.* **under**), *Peaseland howke* 1601, *Peas(e)land Hook(e)* 1601, 1612 *et passim* to 1745 (*v.* **hōc**), cf. *Peasland Hooke furlong* 1675 (*v.* **furlang**), *Peas(e)land Hook(e) Meadow* 1678, 1679 *et passim* to 1745, *v.* **pise, land**); Piggery Fd (either with **piggery** or with a refashioned *Beavery*, since this is the location of Beavery Nook *supra*); (The) Pingle 1826, 1876, 1968 (*the Pingle* 1679, 1703 *et passim* to 1745, cf. *the Pingle Hedge* 1675, 1679 *et passim* to1745 (*v.* **hecg**), *the Pingle Leyes* 1675, *Pingle Leys* 1731 (*v.* **leys**), *v.* **pingel**); Little Ploughed Fd 1863; Poors Cls 1837, the Poor's Cl 1846, 1863, 1877 White, Poors Cl 1968 (*v.* **pouer(e)**; closes endowed for relief of the parish poor); Preston's or Presson's Mdw 1762 (*Persyng'* 1467 × 84, *Pressinges* 1601, 1648, 1675, *Pressings* 1625, 1679 *et passim* to 1745, *Pressings Meadow* 1678, 1679 *et passim* to 1745 (*v.* **eng**; either with the surn. *Perse* or its OFr pers.n. source *Piers*, *v.* Reaney *s.n.* Perse); Railway Fd (beside the former *Syston and Peterborough Branch Railway* 1835 O); Rearsby Turnpike Cl (*v.* **turnepike**); Redlands 1837, 1968 (1675, 1700 *et passim* to 1745, *redlandes* 1601, 1612, cf. *Redlands furlong* 1679 (*v.* **furlang**), *v.* **rēad, land**); Road Cl; Rough Cl (*v.* **rūh**[1]); Rushey Fd, Rushey Mdw (*v.* **riscig**); Rye Cl 1837, 1968 (*v.* **ryge**); S. Fd or Mdw (with a boundary shaped like the letter S); Second Sand Cl 1837 (*v.* **sand**); Old Seeds (*v.* **sǣd**; in f.ns., often used of areas of sown grass); Shaws Cl 1782, Top Shaws 1837 (with the surn. *Shaw* in the possessive case); Simpson Cl 1876 (with the surn. *Simpson*, *v.* Hut Cl *supra*); the Slang (*v.* **slang**); Spinney Cl 1837, 1968 (*v.* **spinney**); Station Fd (*v.* Rearsby Station *supra*); the Stonards (*v.* **stān**; poss. the modern reflex of *Stonowe* in f.ns. (b) (cf. *braso* > *braseardes* in f.ns. (b)) or *Stonhades*, *infra*); Stone Cl; Stone Heap or Gold Hill 1837 (*v.* **hēap** and Gold Hill *supra*); Stone Hedge Leys 1762, 1826 (if *hedge* here is not a reflex of **edisc**, then this is a later style for *Stone hade Leys* 1731 (*v.* **leys**), *Stonhades*

1601, *Stone hades* 1625, 1648, 1679, *~ ~ furlong* 1675, 1700 *et passim* to 1745 (*v.* **furlang**), *v.* **stān, hēafod**); Stonehill Cl (*v. Stonowe* in f.ns. (b)); Stoney Leys 1837, 1968 (*v.* **stānig, leys**); High Thorns 1826 (*the Thornes* 1601, 1625 *et passim* to 1700, (*the*) *High thornes* 1703, 1712, ~ ~ *Thorns* 1709, 1709 (18), 1731, 1745), Short Thorns 1826 (1709, 1709 (18), 1731, 1745, *Schortthorn'* 1467 × 84, (*the*) *Shorte thorne* 1601, 1625, 1648, 1675, 1700, (*the*) *Short thornes* 1679, 1703, 1712, *v.* **sc(e)ort**) (*v.* **þorn**); Three cornered Fd 1837, 1968 (*v.* **three-cornered**); Town End Cl 1826, 1837, Towns End 1968, Town's End Furlong 1762 (*v.* **furlang**) (*Townes end* 1648, *Town End* 1731, *v.* **tūn, ende**); Town Street 1762 (*v.* **tūn, strǣt**); Warren Cl 1762 (*v.* **wareine**); Water Furrows 1837, 1968 (1731, *waterthroroes, waterthrowrois* 1601, *waterthrowes* 1601, 1612, *Waterfurrowes* 1625, 1648, 1675, cf. *Waterfurrowes furlong* 1675, 1679, 1703, 1709, *Waterfurrows* ~ 1700, 1709 (18), 1712, 1745 (*v.* **furlang**), *Water furrowes hedge* 1648 (*v.* **hecg**), *v.* **wæter, furh** and *the Waterfurrow(e)s* in Asfordby f.ns. (b)); Wharf Cl 1837, 1876, Wharf Mdw 1837, 1876, 1968, Little Wharf 1968 (*v.* **hwearf**); Wilson's Cl, Top Wilsons (with the surn. *Wilson*); the Woodhouse's Homestead 1762 (*v.* **hām-stede**; cf. *Mr William Woodhouse* 1709).

(b) *Acres Well* 1601, 1612 *et passim* to 1745 (*v.* **æcer, wella**); *Three Acres* 1601, 1612 *et passim* to 1712 (*v.* **æcer**; a meadow so called); *Jasper Astells Close, Jasper Astells ground* 1703, *the late Jasper Astells ground* 1709 (*v.* **grund**), *Jasper Astells land* 1703, 1709 (18) (*v.* **land**); *Bastard Leas* 1731 (*v.* **bastard, leys** and Bastards in f.ns. (a)); *Bennetts bush* 1648 (*v.* **busc**; with the surn. *Bennett*); *Mr Benskins Close, Mr Benskins land* 1745 (*v.* **land**); *Blakehyrst* 1467 × 84 (*v.* **blæc, hyrst**); *Blakemorehylle* 1467 × 84, *Blackmoor(e) hill* 1625, 1675 *et passim* to 1709, *Black more hill* 1712, *Blakemoor* ~ 1745, *Blakemoor Leys* 1731 (*v.* **leys**) (*v.* Bleak Moor *supra*); *Brakenowe, Braknow* 1467 × 84 (*v.* **braken, haugr**); *Schort braso* 1467 × 84 (*v.* **sc(e)ort**), *Long bracers* 1601, 1625, 1679, *Long braseards* 1612, *Long Braziers* 1731, *Long Bracers furlong* 1700, 1703, 1709, 1712, *Long Braziers* ~ 1745 (*v.* **furlang**) (*v.* **haugr**; poss. with the ON pers.n. *Breiðr*, an original by-name meaning 'the broad one', *v.* SPNLY 64 and cf. Braceby, LPN 18); *Mr Bretts hedge* 1648 (*v.* **hecg**; a property boundary); *the Broad water* 1601, 1612, 1625 (presum. later called *the great water* 1648, *v.* **brād, wæter**); *Brookesby Close hedge* 1625, 1675, *Bruxbie hedge* 1601 (*v.* **hecg**; a parish boundary marker), *Brookesby hedge corner* 1648 (*v.* **corner**), *Broxby mere* 1467 × 84 (*v.* **(ge)mǣre**) (Brooksby adjoins to the north-east); (*the Foure*) *Bush wonges* 1679, 1712, *the 4 ~ ~, the Four Bush Wongs* 1700, 1703, 1709, 1745 (*v.* **busc, vangr**); *Chamberlins ground* 1625, *Mr Chamberlains* ~ 1703, 1709, 1709 (18) (*v.* **grund**), *Mr Chamberlaines hadland* 1712 (*v.* **hēafod-land**), *Mr Chamberlain(e)s land* 1700, 1703, 1712 (*v.* **land**); *Chickin home* 1601, *Chicken* ~ 1612, *Chickinholme* 1625, *Chickenholm(e)* 1675, 1679 *et passim* to 1745, *Chickeneholm* 1700 (*v.* **cīcen, holmr**); *the Church headland* 1601, *the Churche hadlond* 1612, *the Church Hadland* 1625, 1675 *et passim* to 1745 (*v.* **hēafod-land** and St Michael's Church *supra*); *Cley Cleaves* 1679, 1700, 1712, *Clay* ~ 1709 (*v.* **clǣg, clif**); *the Cley felde* 1467 × 84, *the Great Cley(e) field* (*towardes Queniborrow*) 1601, 1612, *the Great Cley Feild* 1625, *the Cleyfelde towarde Brokysby* 1467 × 84, *the Litle cley feild towardes Bruxbie* 1612, *the Little Clay feild* (*towardes Brookesbye*) 1625, 1648, 1675, 1679, *the Lit(t)le Clay field* 1700, 1703, 1709, 1712, 1745 (*v.* **clǣg, feld**; Queniborough adjoins to the south and Brooksby to the north-east; whether originally one great 'field with clay soil' is uncertain); *the Cole Cart* *way* 1679, 1700, 1709, 1731, ~ *Coal* ~ ~ 1712, 1745 (*v.* **col**[1], **carte**, **weg**; the name also appears in neighbouring Ratcliffe on the Wreake so that, rather than charcoal, the transport of mineral coal may be considered); *Cobdall' furlong* 1467 × 84, *litle* ~, *copdale* 1601, *great* ~, *short copdale* 1612, *great* ~, *little Cobdale* 1625, *Long* ~, *Short Cobdale* 1648, 1675 *et passim* to 1745, *Long* ~, *Short Cobdel* 1731 (*v.* **deill**; prob. either with the ON pers.n. *Kobbi* or with the ME surn. *Cobbe* (ModE *Cobb*), *v.* Reaney *s.n.*; OE **cobb(e)** 'a round lump', topographically 'a mound, a hillock' seems less likely); *the conie platt furlong* 1601 (*v.* **coni**, **plat**, **furlang**); *Wm. Cookes Land* 1700 (*v.* **land**); *Mayster Cotons closse* 1467 × 84 (*v.* **clos(e)**), *Cotons Maner* 1506 Ipm (*v.* **maner**), *Cottons wonge* 1601 (*v.* **vangr**) (cf. *Thomas Coton* 1467 × 84 and a poss. son *Thomas Coton* 1506 Ipm); *Cow Lane* 1731; *Cutt wonge* 1648, *Cuttwong close* 1675, 1700, 1731 (*v.* **vangr**; prob. with **cutte** 'a water channel' since the surn. *Cutt*, from the pet-form of Cuthbert, does not occur in the East Midlands); *Doleston* 1601, 1612, 1625, 1648, *Dolestone furlong* 1675, 1679 *et passim* to 1745 (*v.* **furlang**) (*v.* **dāl**, **stān**; presum a major boundary marker); *the Elmes* 1679, 1700, 1703, 1709, 1712, *the Elms* 1709 (18), 1745 (*v.* **elm**); *Eyfurlong'* 1467 × 84, *efferlonge leas* 1601, *Efurrlong leyes*, *Eyfurrlong* ~ 1625 (*v.* **leys**; either with reference to R.Eye which was the earlier name for R.Wreake along its whole course, or with **ēa** 'river, stream', alluding to the large watercourse which runs through the township); *Mr Falkners hadland* 1679 (*v.* **hēafod-land**); *Foxholes* 1648 (*v.* **fox-hol**); *Garleygate* 1467 × 84, *Garligate* 1648, 1700, ~ *furlong* 1712, 1745 (*v.* **furlang**), *Garleygatsyde*, *Garelegatesyde* 1467 × 84, *Garligate syde* 1601, 1612, ~ *side* 1625, 1648 *et passim* to 1725 (*v.* **sīde**) (*v.* **gata**; the first el. is prob. **gārlēac**, here used of wild garlic); *the Greene* 1679, *the Green* 1700, *the Green or Tenters* 1703, 1709, 1709 (18), 1712, *the Green Tenters* (sic) 1745 (*v.* **grēne**[2] and *Tenters*, *infra*); *the hart(e) furres* 1612, 1625, *the hart furrowes*, *the hard furres* 1648, *Hard furris furlong* 1675, *Hard furze(s)* ~ (sic) 1679, 1700, *Hard Furres* ~ 1703, *Hard Furrs* ~ 1709, 1731, *Hartfurres* ~ 1712, *Hartsfurres furlong* 1745 (*v.* **furlang**) (*v.* **furh**; prob. with **heard** 'hard' and referring to difficult tillage); *Hendike* 1601, 1612, 1648, (*the*) *Henditch* 1625, 1648 *et passim* to 1745 (*v.* **henn**, **dík**, **dīc**; the English generic eventually replacing the Scand); *Heywards acre* 1648 (*v.* **æcer**; either with **hei-ward** 'an officer in charge of fences and enclosures' or its surn. reflex *Heyward*); *the High bushes* 1648 (*v.* **hēah**[1], **busc**); *the highe furlonge* 1601, *the High furlong* 1625, 1648 *et passim* to 1745, (*the*) *High furlong(e) feilde* 1648, 1675, (*the*) *High furlong Field* 1648, 1679 *et passim* to 1745 (*v.* **feld**) (*v.* **hēah**[1], **furlang**); *the highe hades* 1601 (*v.* **hēah**[1], **hēafod**); *the high way baulke* 1625 (*v.* **hēah-weg**, **balca**); *the Hole* 1648 (*v.* **hol**[1]); *the homsteed* 1612 (*v.* **hām-stede**); *Mr Hubberts hadland* 1675, 1679, 1700, *Mrs Hubberts* ~ 1703, 1709, 1712 (*v.* **hēafod-land**), *Mrs Hubberts land* 1703, 1709 (*v.* **land**); *Hydurswath* 1467 × 84 (*v.* **hider**, **swathe**); *Inglandes lees* 1601, 1612, *Englands leas* 1625, ~ *Leyes* 1648, 1675 *et passim* to 1712, ~ *Leys* 1709 (18), 1745 (*v.* **leys**; with the common Leics. surn. *England*); *Jessons Hedge* 1712, 1745 (*v.* **hecg**; with the surn. *Jesson*); *Knaves holme* 1648 (*v.* **cnafa**, **holmr**); *the knole*, *the knoole* 1601, *the knowle* 1612, 1625 (*v.* **cnoll**); *Lady Wonge* 1467 × 84, 1625, 1648, ~ *Wong* 1675, 1679 *et passim* to 1745 (*v.* **lavedi**, **vangr**; prob. referring to land endowed for the upkeep of a chapel dedicated to Our Lady, the Blessed Virgin Mary); *leceter way* 1601, *leiceter way*, *leicetre waye* 1612, *Leicester way* 1625, 1648, 1731, *lecetre way furlonge* 1601, *Leicester way furlong* 1675, 1679 *et passim* to 1745 (*v.* **furlang**) (*v.* **weg**; the road to Leicester, 7 miles to the south-west); *the litle furlong* 1648 (*v.* **lȳtel**,

furlang); *the longe* 1601 (*v.* **lang**[2]; cf. *the short*(*e*), *infra*); *Longwong'* 1467 × 84, *the Longe wonge* 1648, *Long Wong* 1679, 1700, 1712, 1745, *long wong end* 1612 (*v.* **ende**), *Long Wong furlong* 1625, 1675, 1703, 1709 (*v.* **furlang**) (*v.* **lang**[1], **vangr**); *Marlepytwong'* 1467 × 84 (*v.* **marle-pytt, vangr**); *the medow* 1601, *the meddow* 1612, 1625 (*v.* **mǣd** (**mǣdwe** obl.sg.)); *Millers land* 1700, 1703, 1712 (*v.* **land**; with the surn. *Miller*, cf. Mill Willows Cl in f.ns. (a)); *William Mouldsworthes hadland* 1648 (*v.* **hēafod-land**); *Mydull furlong'* 1467 × 84 (*v.* **middel, furlang**; i.e. of *Cleyfelde*); *the New*(*e*) *Close* 1601, 1625, 1648, ~ ~ ~ *side* 1648 (*v.* **sīde**); *Newfelde* 1467 × 84, *the New feild*(*e*) 1601, 1625, 1648, 1675, 1679, ~ ~ *Field* 1700, 1703 *et passim* to 1745 (*v.* **nīwe, feld**); (*the*) *New Hedge* 1601, 1612 *et passim* to 1745 (*v.* **hecg**); *Mr Nobles ground* 1709 (*v.* **grund**), *Mr Nobles land* 1712 (*v.* **land**); *the Nooke peece* 1648 (*v.* **nōk, pece**); *Mr Ortons ground* 1675 (*v.* **grund**), *Mr Ortons hadland* 1679 (*v.* **hēafod-land**); *the Parsonage garden* 1712, *the Parsonage Home-stall* 1709 (18) (*v.* **hām-stall**), *the Parsonage yard* 1679, 1700, 1703 (*v.* **geard**), ~ ~ ~ *or Homestall* 1709 (*v.* **personage**); *the peartre close* 1612, (*the*) *Peartree Close* 1625, 1675 *et passim* to 1712, *the Pairtree Close* 1745 (*v.* **pertre**); *the Pikes* 1712 (*v.* **pīc**); *the Pike wonge* 1648 (*v.* **pīc, vangr**); *the Poole Close* 1648 (*v.* **pōl**[1]); *Pykwelle thorn'* 1467 × 84 (*v.* **pīc, wella, þorn**, cf. Pickwell, Lei **2** 240); *Queniborrow bridge* 1601, *Queniborrow medow* 1601, ~ *meddow* 1625, ~ *meadow* 1675, 1700, 1703, *Queenborrow* ~ 1709 (18), *Queniborough meadow* 1745, *Quenyboro meyre* 1467 × 84, *Queniborrow meare* 1648 (*v.* (**ge**)**mǣre**) (Queniborough adjoins to the south); *Quynsyng'* 1467 × 84 (*v.* **eng**; the first el. is poss. the ME surn. *Quyne* (from OFr *quin* 'a monkey'), *v.* Reaney *s.n.* Quin and cf. the construction of *Persyng'* (*v.* Presson's Mdw in f.ns. (a))); *Ratcliff close* 1603 Ipm, 1745, *Ratcliffe holme* 1675 (*v.* **holmr**), *ratliffe lane* (sic) 1601, *Ratcliffe Lane* 1675, 1679, 1700, 1703, 1709, 1712, *Rattcliff* ~ 1745 (Ratcliffe on the Wreake adjoins to the west); *Rearsbie medow* 1601; *Richardsons close*, *Richardsons ground* 1703, 1709, 1712, (*Mr*) *Richardsons Hadland* 1648, 1700, 1703, 1712 (*v.* **hēafod-land**), *Richardsons Hadley* 1709, ~ *Headley* 1709 (18), *Richardsons land* 1700, 1703, 1709, 1712 (*v.* **land**); *the Rick yard* 1648 (*v.* **reke-yard**), *the old rickstead* 1648 (*v.* **rickstead**); (*the*) *Round hill* 1625, 1675, *the Round hill furlong* 1675 (*v.* **furlang**) (*v.* **round**); *Rowtam* 1612, 1625, *Rowtham* 1675, 1745, *Routum* 1731, *Rowtham Leyes* 1700, 1703, 1712, ~ *Leys* 1709 (*v.* **leys**) (*v.* Routholme in adjoining Queniborough f.ns. (a) which no doubt records the same feature); *Mr Rudings Headland* 1745 (*v.* **hēafod-land**), *Mr Rudings Land* 1745 (*v.* **land**); *Rusebuske* 1467 × 84, *Rush Bush* 1625, 1648 *et passim* to 1745 (*v.* **risc, buskr, busc**; cf. *Rush Bush* in Scalford, *v.* Lei **2** 216); *the Ryefelde towarde Quenyboro* 1467 × 84, *the Ryefelde towarde Ratclyfe* 1467 × 84, *the great rye field*(*e*) 1601, 1612, *the litle rye filde* 1601, ~ ~ ~ *field* 1612 (*v.* **ryge, feld**; Queniborough adjoins to the south and Ratcliffe on the Wreake to the west; whether originally one great 'rye field' is uncertain); (*Mr*) *Sacheverells Close* 1700, 1703, 1712, *Sacheveralls Close* 1745, *Secheuerells headlande* 1601, *Mr Sacheverells hadland* 1648 (*v.* **hēafod-land**), *Mr James Sacheverells Land* 1712 (*v.* **land**), *Secheverels oke close* 1601 (*v.* **āc, clos**(**e**) and Oak Cl in f.ns. (a)); *the Salters Close* 1648 (*v.* **saltere**; Rearsby lay on a medieval saltway which ran south of R. Wreake from Kirby Bellars (with a branch across the river at Asfordby) to meet the Fosse Way north of Thurmaston); *the dead sand*(*e*) 1601 (*v.* **dēad, sand**; prob. with reference to infertile soil rather than to a site of a violent death or to the discovery of human bones); *the Great*(*e*) *Sand*(*e*) *Feild*(*e*) 1601, 1648, 1675, 1679, *the Great Sand Field* 1700, 1703 *et passim* to 1745, ~ ~ *Sandy Feild* 1625, *the Litle Sand*(*e*) *Feild*(*e*) 1601, 1648, 1675, 1679, *the Little Sand Field* 1700, 1703 *et passim* to 1745, ~ ~ *Sandy Feild* 1625 (*v*. **sand, sandig, feld**); *the short*(*e*) 1601, 1612, 1625 (*v*. **sc(e)ort**; the adj. is used as a sb. for 'a short piece of land', cf. *the longe, supra*); *the Short furlong* 1675, 1700, 1703, 1712, 1745 (*v*. **furlang**; poss. the same piece of land as that of the previous f.n.); *the Sladd* 1601, 1675 *et passim* to 1712, *the Slad* 1612, 1731, 1745, *the Slade* 1625, 1709 (18), *the Slade wonge* 1648 (*v*. **vangr**) (*v*. **slæd**); *the Spryng' at Rusebuske* 1467 × 84 (*v*. **spring**[1] and *Rusebuske, supra*); *Stonowe* 1467 × 84 (*v*. **stān, haugr** and the Stonards in f.ns. (a)); *Stony More* 1648 (*v*. **stānig, mōr**[1]); *the Swannysneste* 1467 × 84 (*v*. **swan**[1], **nest**); *Swarth furlong* 1467 × 84, *the swarth furlonge* 1601, (*the*) *Swath furlong*(*e*) 1625, 1648 *et passim* to 1745 (*v*. **furlang**) (*v*. **sweart, svartr**); *Tenters* 1703, 1709, 1712, 1745 (*v*. **tentour** and *the Greene, supra*); *Teynebrygis, Teynybrigges, Tynbryges* 1467 × 84, *Tenbrigges* 1601, 1612, 1675 (*v*. **tēn, brycg**; a sequence of ten causeways across marshy ground seems to be alluded to here); *Thevissti* 1467 × 84 (*v*. **þēof, stīg**); *the Thorny balkes* 1648 (*v*. **þornig, balca**); *Thrushington brigge* 1601, ~ *Bridge* 1648, *Thrussington Bridge* 1625, 1675 *et passim* to 1745 (*v*. **brycg**; crosses R. Wreake), *Thrushington Lane* 1612, *Thrussington* ~ 1700, 1709 *et passim* to 1745 (*v*. **lane**), *Thrushington Lane End* 1648, 1731 (*v*. **ende, lane-ende**) (Thrussington adjoins to the north); *the Towne close* 1648, *the Backside of the Town* 1679, 1700 *et passim* to 1745 (*v*. **bak-side**), *Town Side* 1731 (*v*. **sīde**) (*v*. **tūn**); *Trunsowhyll* 1467 × 84 (*v*. **trun, sōg, hyll**); *the Tyth Barn* 1679, 1700 (*v*. **tēoða**); *Bywades, by Wadys, Hydurbywadis* (*v*. **hider**), *Furbywadis* (*v*. **feor**) 1467 × 84 (*v*. **bī, (ge)wæd**; furlongs so called); *the Wash ditch* 1675 (*v*. **wæsce, dīc**; presum. a sheep-dip, cf. ModEdial **wash-dyke**); *Weyre welus* 1467 × 84, *wear willoes* 1612, *Wear Willowes* 1625, 1675, 1679, 1703, ~ *Willows* 1700, 1709, 1712, 1745 (*v*. **wer, wilig**; prob. the Wire willows (1788) recorded in adjoining Queniborough); *Mr Whittaphes hadland* 1625 (*v*. **hēafod-land**), *Mr Whitaphes pingle* 1648 (*v*. **pingel**); *the wind mill* 1601 (*v*. **wind-mylne**); *the Wongs* 1745 (*v*. **vangr**); *Mr Woodhouse his close* 1712, *Mr Woodhouse headland* 1745 (*v*. **hēafod-land**); *Wyllows* 1467 × 84 (*v*. **wilig**).

Seagrave

SEAGRAVE

Setgraue 1086 DB, 1167 × 70 *Rut* (p), l.12 *GarCart* (freq), 1199 MemR (p), *Setgrave* c.1180 Nichols (p), 1208 Cur (p) *et passim* to 1243 Fees (p), 1265 Nichols (p)
Sethgrava Hy 2 Berkeley (p), *Sethgravia* Hy 2 ib (p), *Sethgraue* l.12 *GarCart* (p)
Sedgrave 1156 (1318) Ch, Hy 2 Dugd, l.12 Dane (p) *et passim* to 1226, 1227 Pat *et freq* to 1278 Cl (p), 1279 Hastings (p), 1428 FA (p), *Sedgrava* l.Hy 2 Berkeley (p), l.12 ib, *Sedgraue* l.12 *GarCart* (p), 1218 RegAnt, 1235 (1404) *Laz* (p), 1250 Fine (p)
Satgrave 1086 DB, e.13 Berkeley (p) bis, e.Hy 3 ib (p) bis, *Satgraua* Hy 2 Dane (p), *Satgraue* 13 *ShR* (p)
Sadgrave 1184 Berkeley (p), l.12 Hy 2 ib (p) *et passim* to c.1225 ib (p), e.Hy 3 Hastings, *Sadgraue* 1190 AC (p), *Sadgrava* e.13 Berkeley (p)
Sagrave l.Hy 2 Berkeley (p), 1204 ChR, 1204 RegAnt, *Sagraua* 1193 P (p), l.12 Dane, *Sagraue* 1194 P (p), 1195 ib (p)
Segrave 1086 DB, 1201 OblR, 1204 RegAnt *et passim* to 1233 Ch (p), 1234 Pat *et freq* to 1583 LEpis, 1610 Speed, *Segraue* c.1130 LeicSurv, 1197 P, 1200 ib *et freq* to 1386, 1392 *MiD et passim* to 1518 Visit, 1576 Saxton, *Segraua* 1183, 1184 P *et passim* to 1199 ib (p), 1204 RegAnt, *Segrava* l.Hy 2 Berkeley, c.1200 *Sloane*, 1249 Pat (p)
Seygrave 1279 RGrav (p), 1285 FA (p), 1535 VE, 1540 MinAccts
Seagraue 1207 P (p), 1211 ib (p), *Seagrave* c.1240 Berkeley (p), 1620 LML *et freq*

This is a topographical name of Old English origin. The generic is most probably *grāf* 'a grove' rather than *græf* 'a ditch'. Spellings with medial *th*, *t* and *d* favour *sēað* 'a pit, a pool' as the specific, but formally *set* 'a fold for farm animals' is also possible as the first element, though given the transient nature of a fold, less likely. It should be noted also that *set* normally appears in place-names as the generic. A satisfying interpretation of the name is 'the grove near the pool', *v.* **sēað**, **grāf**. There is a large pool beside a stream at SK 623174 and adjacent to the pool are earthworks which presumably are the remains of medieval settlement.

ALL SAINTS' CHURCH, *the Church* 1709 (18) *Terrier*, *Church (All Saints)* 1846, 1863, 1877 White, 1925 Kelly; it is earlier recorded as *ecclesie Segravie* 1220 MHW, *ecclesiam* ~ ~, *ecclesie de Segraue* 1247 RGros, 1266, 1268, 1344 *Pat*. Note also *the Church Yard* 1709, 1709 (18) *Terrier*. BERRYCOTT LANE is *Berrye gate* 1601 *Terrier*, *Berrygate* 1625, 1709 *ib et passim* to 1750 *ib*, *Berygate* 1697 *ib*, *v.* **berige**, **gata**. BIG LANE. BUNKER HILL FM, *Bunker Hill Farm* 1919 *Sale*, *Bunker's Hill* 1863, 1877 White, 1925 Kelly; named from the Battle of Bunker Hill (1775) in the American War of Independence where British victory failed to break the colonists' siege of Boston. BUTCHER'S LANE, with the surn. *Butcher*. CHURCH GATE, *v.* **gata** and All Saints' Church *supra*. CONERY LANE, *the Cunnigree* 1601, 1625 *Terrier*, ~ *Conigre* 1638 *ib*, *ye Coniegree*, ~ *Coniegrey* 1674 *ib*, *the Cunegray* 1697 *ib*, ~ *Conygree* 1709, 1709 (18) *ib*, ~ *Cunigray* 1724, 1745, 1750 *ib*, *Conery* 1969 *Surv*, *v.* **coningre**. FISHPOOL BROOK is *Walton Brook(e)* 1601, 1625 *Terrier et passim* to 1750 *ib*, ~ *Broock* 1697 *ib*, *v.* **brōc**; the parish boundary with Walton on the Wolds which adjoins to the north-west. GIPSY LANE, *v.* **gipsy**. GORSE LANE, cf. *the Gorse* 1760 Nichols, *v.* **gorst**. HALL FM, *Hall farm* 1925, *v.* **hall**. KING ST. THE LODGE, 1877 White, *v.* **loge**. MOUNT PLEASANT FM, Mount Pleasant is for the most part a complimentary name for a location, but occasionally may be bestowed ironically. MUCKLE GATE LANE is *Mucklegate* 1601, 1625 *Terrier et passim* to 1750 *ib*, *Muckilgate* 1697 *ib*, *Muckelgate* 1697, 1724, 1745 *ib*, *Muclegate* 1750 *ib*, 1969 *Surv*, *v.* **micel**, **mycel**, **mikill**, **gata**. NEW YORK FM, a common 'remoteness' name for a site far from the village, but note *Bunker Hill* above which may relate the name of New York Farm also to the period of the American War of Independence. NORTH FM. NORTH HILL FM, *North Hill Farm* 1919 *Sale*, *North Hill* 1697, 1724, 1745, 1750 *Terrier*, 1877 White. THE OAKS. OLD WHITE SWAN (P.H.) (lost), *Old White Swan* 1925 Kelly. PARK HILL, ~ ~ LANE, PARKLEIGH, cf. *The Park* 1967 *Surv*, *v.* **park**. PAUDY LANE, *v.* Barrow upon Soar *s.n.* QUORN HUNT KENNELS. THE RECTORY, 1877 White, 1925 Kelly, *v.* **rectory**; earlier is *the Parsonage House* 1709, 1745 *Terrier*, *v.* **personage**. SEAGRAVE GRANGE FM, *Seagrave Grange* 1925 Kelly, *v.* **grange**. SEAGRAVE WOLDS, 1835 O, (*in*) *Waldis de Segraue* 13, 1352 *MiD*, *Waldes* 1362 *ib*, *the Ouldes* 1601, 1674, 1745 *Terrier*, *the Oldes* 1625, 1638, 1697 *ib*, *the Oulds* 1709 *ib*, *the Olds* 1724 *ib*, *the Woulds* 1750 *ib*, *v*. **wald**. SWAN ST, cf. Old White Swan *supra* and Swan with Two Necks *infra*. SWAN WITH TWO NECKS (P.H.) (lost), *Swan with Two Necks* 1846, 1863, 1877 White, *v*. Barrie Cox, *English Inn and Tavern Names* (Nottingham 1994), 39. WHITE HỌRSE (P.H.), *White Horse* 1846, 1863 White, 1925 Kelly, *Old White Horse* 1877 White.

FIELD-NAMES

Undated forms in (a) are 1969 *Surv*. Forms throughout dated 1228 are Ch; a.1241 are Nichols; 13, 1318, 1327, 1338, 1345, 1352, 1362, 1371 and 1392 are *MiD*; 1581, 1601, 1625, 1638, 1674, 1697, 1709, 1709 (18), 1724, 1745 and 1750 are *Terrier*.

(a) Three Acre, Three half ~, Four ~, Five ~, Six ~, the Eight ~, the Nine Acre (*v*. **æcer**); Back Fd, Far ~ ~ ~, 1st Back Lane Fd (*v*. **back**); Middle ~ ~, Barn Cl, Barn Fd, Barn Paddock (*v*. **paddock**); Far ~, Middle ~, Near Barrow (*v*. **berg**); Berrygate Cl (cf. *Berry*(*e*) *gate furlonge* 1601, 1625, *Berri*(*e*)*gate furlong*(*e*) 1638, 1674, *Berry Gate Furlong* 1709 (18), *v*. **furlang** and Berrycott Lane *supra*); Big Fd; Bottom Fd, Bottom Mdws; Brink Cl, Brink Fd (*Brincke Feilde* 1581, 1601, *Brinke feilde* 1625, 1638, *Brinke field* 1674, 1724, 1750, *~ feeld* 1697, *Brink feild* 1709, *~ Field* 1709 (18), 1745, *v*. **feld**; one of the great fields of the township), Brink Hill (1638, 1709, 1709 (18), *Brinck ~* 1601, *Brinke ~* 1625, 1674) (*v*. **brink**); Over the brook (cf. *the brook furlong*(*e*) 1601, 1638, 1674, *the Brook Furlong* 1709, 1709 (18), *v*. **furlang**) (*v*. **brōc**); Bulls Fd (with the surn. *Bull*); Bush Cl (*v*. **busc**); Cawdles (*Cawdewell* 1601, *Cawdwell* 1625, 1674, 1709, 1709 (18), *Caudwell* 1638, *the Cawdles* 1750, cf. *Cawdewell Springe* 1601, 1625, *Cawdwell Spring* 1709 (*v*. **spring**[1]), *the Caudal*(*l*)*s forde* 1697, 1724, *the Caudles Ford* 1745 (*v*. **ford**), *v*. **cald**, **wella**); Coalpit (*v*. **col-pytt**; a place where charcoal was made); Upper ~ ~, Cow Cl, First ~ ~, Second Cow Fd, the Cow Pasture (*v*. **pasture**); Crineries (poss. a metathesized plural form of *Conery*, *v*. Conery Lane *supra*); the Croft (*v*. **croft**); Crosslands (*v*. **cross**, **land**); Dams Cl (*v*. **damme**); Nan Dennis Parlour (*v*. **parlur**; with the surn. *Dennis*); Far Cl; Finch Ades (*Finchette hades furlonge* 1601, 1625 (*v*. **furlang**), *Fintchit hades* 1638, *Finchet ~* 1674, *Finchit ~* 1697, 1724, *Finchate ~* 1709, *Finchhad ~* 1745, *Finched hades* 1750, *v*. **hēafod**; the first word of surviving forms to 1750 may be spellings of Fineshade, the name of a priory in Northants. (*v*. Nth 164) which certainly held lands outside its county, as in North Luffenham (*Fincett Land* 1710, Ru 264), but any such possessions that may have been held by this priory in Seagrave are not recorded and nor is there evidence for the p.n. Fineshade having developed as a surn. reflex; an original 'headland frequented by finches' (*v*. **finc**, **hēafod**) is poss. if *Finchette*/ *Finched* conceals an earlier *hēafod*, later duplicated; alternatively, *Finchet*(*te*)/*Finchit* may be a British survival, with PrW **fin* 'end, boundary' and PrW **cę̄d* 'a wood', hence 'the woodland at the boundary'; perh. cf. *Trunchit* in f.ns. (b) as a further British survival here); Five cornered Fd; Far ~, First ~, Middle Fosse (cf. *the Fosse furlonge* 1601, *Foss furlong* 1674 (*v*. **furlang**), *the Foss*(*e*) *hades* 1638, 1724 (*v*.

hēafod); adjoining the Fosse Way which is recorded in this parish as *the Fosse* 1601, 1625, 1674, 1709, *the Foss* 1709, 1724, 1745, 1750); Frecks Fd (with the surn. *Freck*, a reflex of OE *freca* 'warrior', *v.* Reaney *s.n.* Freak); Garden Fd (*v.* **gardin**); Gorse Barn Fds (*v.* **gorst**); the Hardsick (*v.* **heard, sík**); the Hills 1760 Nichols, Hill Fd 1969 (cf. *de le Hul* 13 (p), *v.* **hyll**); Home Cl, Home Fd (*v.* **home**); 1st ~, 2nd Homestead (*v.* **hām-stede**); Horse Cl; Horsebush Cl (cf. *horsecroe bushe furlonge* 1601, *Horscrow bush furlonge* 1625, *Horsecrow Bush Furlong* 1709, 1709 (18) (*v.* **furlang**), *Horscobush Leays* 1697, ~ *Lays* 1724, 1745, ~ *Leys* 1750 (*v.* **leys**), *v.* **hors, crōh**[2], **busc**); Far ~, Near ~, Goss Hovel (*v.* **gorst**), Hovel Fd (*v.* **hovel**); Back ~, (*v.* **back**), Big ~, Middle Husses (with the surn. *Huss* in the possessive case; a *Thomas Huss* was born in Seagrave in 1858 (1881 Census)); Kennel Fd (*v.* **kenel**; adjacent to the Quorn Hunt Kennels); Kettles (the surn. *Kettle* in the possessive case; the surn. is a reflex of the ON pers.n. *Ketill*); Kilby's Hovel Fd (*v.* **hovel**; with the surn. *Kilby* of a family originally from the village of this name, 14 miles to the south); Lady Fd (*v.* **lavedi**); Lamins Cl (with the surn. *Lam(m)in*, from *Lamb-in*, a diminutive of *Lamb* (Lambert), *v.* Reaney *s.n.*); Old Lane Fd; Leeches (the surn. *Leech* in the possessive case; a reflex of OE *lǣce* 'a physician'); Lime Kiln (*v.* **lim-kilne**); Linnet Hill (either with the common Leics. surn. *Linnett* or with the songbird **linet**); Little Fd, Little Mdw; South ~, Top Long (*v.* **lang**[2]); the Long Cls, Long Fd (*v.* **lang**[1]); the Meadows; 1st ~, 2nd Melborough, Melber Cl (*Melborow* 1745, *Melbarrow* 1750, *Little melbarrowe* 1638, *Litel Melborow* 1694, *Little Melborough* 1724, ~ *Melborrow* 1749, ~ *Melborow* 1750, *Long Melborow* 1697, 1750, ~ *Melborough* 1724, ~ *Melbarrow* 1745, cf. *Melburre furlonge* 1601, 1625, *Melbur Furlong* 1674, 1709, 1709 (18), *Melborow forlong* 1697, *Melburre hill furlonge* 1601, 1625, *melber hill* ~ 1638, *Mellber hill Furlong* 1674 (*v.* **furlang**)), Far ~ ~, Melbourne Sich (*v.* **sīc**) (*Melburre Sicke* 1601, 1625, *Melbur* ~ 1625, 1674, *Melber sick* 1697, *Melbur Sike* 1709, *v.* **sík**) (*v.* **berg**; earlier forms are needed to identify the first el., but **mǣl**[2] 'speech' (with reference to a moot-site) or **myln** 'a mill' are likeliest; note also, however, OE (Angl) **mēl** 'a cross', since early examples of hills with crosses are recorded at Maldon (Essex) and Meldon (Northumberland) among others); Middle Fd; Middle Patch (*v.* **patche**); Mill Cl (cf. *the Mill hades* 1638, 1674, 1745, 1750, *Milhades* 1697, *the Millne Hades* 1724, *ne(a)ther mill* ~ 1601, *Nether mill hades* 1638, 1674, 1709, 1709 (18), *v.* **myln, hēafod**); the Orchard, Orchard Fd; (the) Paddock (*v.* **paddock**); Coopers Park (with the surn. *Cooper*), Home Park (*v.* **home**), Little ~ ~, Park Mdw (*v.* Park Hill *supra*); The Plains 1760 Nichols (*the Plaine* 1697, *the Plain* 1724, 1745, 1750, *v.* **plain**); Plough Cl (*v.* **plōg**); Pond Cl; Bottom ~, Top Riddles (with the surn. *Riddle* in the possessive case, cf. *Reginaldus Ridel* 1327 SR of Leics.); Rough Mdw (*v.* **rūh**[1]); Big ~ ~, Little Seagrave Sick (*v.* **sík**); Sewage Mdw (self-explanatory); Little Slang (*v.* **slang**); Slip (*v.* **slipe**); Smiths (the surn. *Smith* in the possessive case); Square Cl (*v.* **squar(e)**); Stack Cl (*v.* **stakkr**); Stutchbury (the surn. *Stutchbury* of a family originally from the village of this name, 45 miles to the south in Northants. (*v.* Nth 58)); Far ~ ~, Near Top Cl, Little Top Cl or Top Pringle (sic) (*v.* **pingel**), Top Fd; Walton's (either the surn. *Walton* in the possessive case or a field at the boundary with Walton on the Wolds which adjoins to the north-west); Wells (the surn. *Wells* in the possessive case); Westons Fd (with the surn. *Weston*); Wiches Fd 1760 (*v.* **wice**); the Wild Boars (sic) (the surn. *Wildbore* in the possessive case); Close above Windmill, Far ~ ~, Near Windmill Cl, Windmill Pingle (*v.* **pingel**) (*v.* **wind-mylne**); Big ~, Little Wisterbrook

(*Wistoftbrooke* 13, *Whistoe brooke* 1601, 1625, *Whistow* ~ 1638, *Whitsters brook* 1674, *Whistobrucke* 1697, *Whistow Brook* 1709, *Whistobrook(e)* 1724, 1750, *Wistobrook(e)* 1745, 1750, cf. *Whistobrooke fowre roades* 1638 (*v.* **fēower**, **rōd**³), *v.* **brōc** and *Wistoft* in f.ns. (b)).

(b) *Ansley* 1697, 1724, 1745, 1750 (*v.* **lēah**), *Ansleye Feilde* 1581, 1601, *Ansley fe(e)ild* 1625, 1697, *Anslye Feilde* 1638, *Ansley Field* 1674, 1709 *et passim* to 1750 (*v.* **feld**; one of the great fields of the township), *Ansleye gate* 1601, *Anslea* ~ 1625, *Annsly* ~ 1638, *Annsley gate*, *Anslegate*, *Ansl(e)ygate* 1724, *Ansleygate* 1674, 1697 *et passim* to 1750 (*v.* **gata**), *Ansley(e) gate furlonge* 1601, 1625, 1709, *Ansligate furlonge* 1638 (*v.* **furlang**), *Ansicke* 1601, *Annsicke* 1625, 1638, 1724, *Annesicke* 1638, 1674, *Annsick* 1697, *Ansike* 1709, *An(n)sick(e)* 1745, 1750 (*v.* **sík**), *Ann Sicke Head* 1724, *Ansick(e)* ~ 1745, 1750 (*v.* **hēafod**), *Ansick head furlonge* 1625, *Ansikehead Furlong* 1709, 1709 (18) (*v.* **furlang**), *Ansicke well* 1601, *Annsicke* ~ 1625, 1638, *Annesicke* ~ 1674, *Ansike* ~ 1709, *Ansick well* 1709 (18) (*v.* **wella**), *Anstilsike* 1325, 1326 Ipm (*v.* **sík**) (the 1601 forms *Ansleye* and *Ansicke* suggest an unrecorded OE pers.n. *Ān* as the first el. of each (cf. Annesley, Nt 112), but the much earlier form *Anstilsike* presum. belongs with them and thus *Ans-* may be a reduction of *Anstil-*, either an original **ānsetl** 'a hermitage' (cf. Ansley, Wa 75) or **ānsethyll* 'hill with the isolated fold' (*v.* **ān**, **(ge)set**, **hyll**)); *Barlicroft* 1228, a.1241 Nichols (*v.* **bærlic**, **croft**); *Bardolflane* 1352 (*v.* **lane**; with either the pers.n. or the surn. *Bardolph*, reflexes of the OGer pers.n. *Bartholf*); *the beastes pasture* 1601, 1674, ~ *Beasts* ~ 1625, 1745, ~ *Beast* ~ 1638, 1709, 1750 (*v.* **beste**, **pasture**); *Berrye brooke* 1601, 1638, 1674, *Berry* ~ 1625, 1724, 1745, *Berrie brooke* 1674, *Barybrucke*, *Berybruck* 1697, *Berry Brook* 1709, *Barry* ~ 1709 (18), *Bery brooke* 1750, *Berrye brooke close* 1601, *Berry brooke closse* 1625, ~ ~ *close* 1674, *Berrye brooke furlonge* 1601, 1625, 1638, *Bury Brooke* ~ 1625, *Berrie brooke* ~ 1674, *Berry Brook Furlong* 1709 (*v.* **furlang**), *Berrye brooke leas* 1601, 1625, *Berybruck leays* 1697, *Berrybrook Leas* 1709, ~ *Leys* 1709 (18), 1750, *Berry Brook(e) lays* 1724, 1745 (*v.* **leys**) (*v.* **berige**, **brōc**); *Berry-gate Furlong* 1709 (*v.* **furlang**), *Berry gate Layes* 1724, *Berrygate lays* 1745, ~ *leys* 1750 (*v.* **leys**) (*v.* Berrycott Lane *supra*); *blakelandes* 1601, *Blacklands* 1625, 1709, 1709 (18), *Blakelands* 1674, 1697, 1724, 1750, *Blaklands* 1745, *Blakelands Furlonge* 1638 (*v.* **furlang**) (*v.* **blæc**, **land**); *John Blunts hadleye* 1638 (*v.* **headley**); *Boardes hill* 1601, 1638, 1674, *Boards* ~ 1625, 1709 (18), *Board's* ~ 1709 (either with the surn. *Board* (very rare in Leics.) or more likely a reduced style of *Shepperd board* (*v.* Lei **2** 230), alluding to good grazing (for sheep)); *Brantcroft* 13 (*v.* **brant**, **croft**); *Bringsike* 13 (*v.* **sík**), *Brinke forlonge* 1724, *Brink furlong* 1745, *Brinke forlong* 1750 (*v.* **furlang**) (*v.* Brink Fd *supra*); *Broad Baulke* 1697, 1724, ~ *Balk* 1745, ~ *baulk* 1750 (*v.* **balca**); *a le brok* 13 (p), *a le brouk* 13 (p) (*v.* **brōc**); *Brownsons Closs* 1724, *Brownsords* ~ 1745, 1750 (*v.* **clos(e)**; originally with the surn. *Brownson*, later confused with the surn. *Brownsword*, *v.* Reaney *s.nn.*); *Bryntle* 13 (*v.* **brend**, **lēah**); *Burnesicke* 1601, 1625, 1638, *Bourne sicke* 1674, *Bourn Sike* 1709, *Boanesick*, *Boansicke* 1724, *Bonesick* 1745, 1750 (*v.* **sík**; either with **burna** 'a stream' or with **bryne/bruni**, cognates, both meaning '(a place cleared by) burning'; the feature also occurs in adjoining Sileby); *Butlays* 1697, 1724, 1745, *Butt lays* 1724, 1745, ~ *Leys* 1750 (*v.* **butte**, **leys**); *le Calkelandsike* 13, *Long(e) Cawkelande sicke* 1601, 1625, *the two Cawklande sickes* 1601, (*the*) *Caukeland sick(e)* 1638, 1674, 1697, *Cauckland Sicke* 1638, 1674, 1745, (*the*) *Cauckland Sickes* 1697, 1724, *Long Cawkeland Sike* 1709, 1709 (18), *Cawkeland*

calc, land, sík); *the Closing* 1697, 1724, 1750, *the Clossing* 1745 (*v.* **closing**); *Corbits leasow* 1674 (*v.* **lǣs** (**lǣswe** gen.sg., dat.sg.); with the surn. *Corbitt/ Corbett*); *Corbye leas* 1601, 1625, *Corby Leas* 1709, ~ *Leys* 1709 (18) (*v.* **leys**; with the surn. *Corby* of a family originally from a village of this name, either that 24 miles to the north-east in Lincs., or that 24 miles to the south-east in Northants.); *Cosington Sick* 1697, ~ *Sike* 1709, *Cossington Sike* 1709 (18), *Cussington sicke* 1724, *Cusin(g)ton Sick* 1745, 1750, *Cosington sicke furlonge* 1601, 1625, *Cossington* ~ 1638, 1674 (*v.* **furlang**) (*v.* **sík**; Seagrave shares a short boundary with Cossington to the south); *Cotcliffe hill* 1638, 1674, *Cotliffe hill furlong(e)* 1601, 1625, *Cotcliff(e) Hill* ~ 1709, 1709 (18) (*v.* **furlang**) (*v.* **cot, clif, hyll**); *Crooesick* 1724, *Crow Sick* 1745, 1750 (*v.* **sík**; either with **crōh**[2] or **crāwe**); *le Crosfurlong* 1318, (*the*) *Crosse furlonge* 1601, 1625, ~ *furlong* 1674, *Cross furlong(e)* 1709, 1709 (18), 1745, 1750, ~ *forlong* 1724 (*v.* **cross, furlang**; in *Ansleye Feilde*); *Cumberlea sicke* 1601, 1625, *Cumberly(e)* ~ 1638, 1697, *Cumberley Sick(e)* 1674, 1697, 1724, *Cumberlea Sike* 1709, *Cumberly Sick* 1745, 1750 (*v.* **sík**), *Cumberley hill* 1697, *Cumberly* ~, 1697, 1724, 1745, 1750 (*v.* **lēah**; the first el. is no doubt **Cumbre** 'the British', cf. *Comberdale* in neighbouring Wymeswold; note the adjoining Walton on the Wolds (with **walh** 'a Briton') and also in Seagrave the poss. Brit topographical names *Finchet(te)* (*v.* Finch Ades *supra*) and *Trunchit*, *infra*; evidently a small area of RB survival); *Dicegate* 1638, 1674, 1697, 1724, 1745, 1750, *Disegate* 1697 (*v.* **gata**; earlier forms are needed to explain the first el.; while a Scand pers.n. *Dís/Dísa* (Lind 61) is formally poss., as is the surn. *Dice* (*v.* Reaney *s.n.*), neither is satisfactory in a rural context compounded with *gata*); *elrenestub* 13, *Elderstupe hades* 1697, *Elderstubhades* 1724, 1745, 1750 (*v.* **hēafod**) (*v.* **ellern, stubb**); *Matt Eltons Closs* 1697, *Matthew Eltons* ~ 1724, *Eltons Closs* 1750 (*v.* **clos(e)**); *the Est Sick(e)s* 1724, 1745, *the East Sicks* 1750 (*v.* **ēast, sík**); *fatlande sickes* 1601, *the fatland* ~ 1625, (*the*) *Fattland* ~ 1674, 1724, *Fatland Sikes* 1709, 1709 (18), ~ *sicks* 1745, 1750, *Fatland sicke* 1638, 1724, *Fattland* ~ 1674, *Fatland sick* 1697, 1745, 1750, *little fatland(e) sicke* 1601, 1638, *Litle* ~ ~ 1625, *Little Fattland* ~ 1674, *Litel fatland sick* 1697, ~ ~ *Sike* 1709 (18), *Fatland Sick Close* 1697, *Fattlandsicke Closs* 1724, *Fatland sick* ~ 1745, 1750 (*v.* **clos(e)**) (*v.* **fætt, land, sík**); *Matthew Feildings hadley* 1638 (*v.* **headley**); *Flaxlands* 1709 (*v.* **fleax, land**); *the flaxleyes* 1638, *Flaxlays* 1697, 1724, 1745, *Flaxleys* 1709 (18), 1750, *ye flax leasowes* 1674 (*v.* **lǣs** (**lǣswe** gen.sg., dat.sg.)) (*v.* **fleax, leys**); *the Foss(e) hades* 1674, 1745, *the Ne(a)ther Foss hades* 1697, 1724, 1745, ~ *Nather* ~ ~ 1750 (*v.* **neoðera**) (*v.* **hēafod**; butting on the Fosse Way which constitutes the eastern boundary of the parish); *le fouleforye* 13, *le foulforye* 1318 bis (*v.* **fūl, furh**); *John Gambles Hadley* 1674 (*v.* **headley**), *John Gambles Homestead* 1724, 1745, 1750 (*v.* **hām-stede**) (the surn. *Gamble* is a reflex of the ON pers.n. *Gamall*, an original by-name meaning 'old'); *atte gate* 1327 SR (p) (*v.* **atte, gata**); *Golding Bank(e)* 1697, 1724, *Golden* ~ 1709,1745, 1750 (*v.* **golden, banke**; presum. a place growing with golden flowers); *le grene* 1352, *la Grene de Segraue* 1392, *a la grene* 13 (p), *de la grene* 13 (p), *atte grene* 13 (p) (*v.* **atte**) (*v.* **grēne**[2]); *Haghorne furlonge* 1638, *Hagghorne Furlong* 1674 (*v.* **furlang**; poss. with **hǫgg, horn** rather than with **hagu-þorn/hag-þorn**, since in the latter case the loss of *þ* (> *th*) would be unusual and spellings of *Haw-* would normally have been expected); *Haliwell* a.1241 (*v.* **hālig, wella**); *Hall lays Closs* 1724, 1745 (*v.* **leys, clos(e)**), *ye Hall sideling* 1674 (*v.* **sīdling**) (*v.* **hall**); *Hochavedland(s)* 1228, a.1241 (*v.* **hōc, hēafod-land**); *Hogcraft, Hogcrafte bushes* 1638, *Hoggecroft* ~ 1674 (*v.* **busc**), *Hogcraft furlonge* 1638,

Hoggecroft Furlong 1674 (*v.* **furlang**), *Hoggecroft leasowes* 1674 (*v.* **lǣs (lǣswe** gen.sg., dat.sg.)) (*v.* **hogg, croft**); *holdal* 13, *Hodell sick*(*e*) 1601, 1625, *Far*(*re*) ~ ~, *Hodale sicke* 1638, 1674 (*v.* **feor**), *Hodel*(*l*) *Sike* 1709, 1709 (18), *the Hodale Sicks* 1697, 1750, *the Hodalls Sickes* 1724, *the Hodal Sicks* 1745 (*v.* **sík**) (*v.* **hol**[2], **dalr**); *Holebroc* 1228 (*v.* **hol**[2], **brōc**); *Houghtons Close* 1601, 1638, ~ *Closse* 1625, *Nicholas Houghtons close* 1674, ~ ~ *closs* 1697 (*v.* **clos(e)**), *Nicholas Houghtons hadland* 1638, 1674 (*v.* **hēafod-land**), *Nicholas Houghtons hadley* 1638, 1674 (*v.* **headley**), *Houghton's Orchard* 1709, 1709 (18) (cf. *Ann Houghton* 1709); *Hubbard's House* 1709, *Hubbert's* ~ 1709 (18); *Hufton bushe furlonge* 1601, 1625 (*v.* **busc, furlang**; the surn. *Hufton* may be an earlier version of *Houghton*, *v.* Reaney *s.n.* Hufton and *Houghtons Close*, *supra*); *Hurdlegate Bush* 1724, 1745, 1750 (*v.* **busc, gata**; *Hurdle-* may belong with *holdal*, *supra*, otherwise *v.* **hyrdel**, alluding to a road marked off by hurdles or moveable fencing); *Johnson's Barn* 1709, *Johnsons Close* 1601, ~ *Closs*(*e*) 1625, 1724, 1745, *Widow Johnsons Closs* 1697, *Johnson's Close* 1709, *Johnson Closs* 1750 (*v.* **clos(e)**), *Johnson's House* 1709, *Johnsons yarde* 1601, *Johnson's Yard* 1709 (*v.* **geard**) (all in the possession of *Widow Johnson* in 1709); *King Dike* 1724, 1745, 1750 (*v.* **dík**; with the surn. *King*); *the Knowls* 1697 (*v.* **cnoll**); *George Lanes Yard* 1638 (*v.* **geard**); *Litleberwe* a.1241, *Little Barrow*(*e*) *hedge* 1601, 1674, 1709, *litle barrow hedge* 1625 (*v.* **hecg**), *Litel Barrow nooucke* 1697, *Littlebarrow knuck* 1724, 1745, ~ *Nook* 1750 (*v.* **nōk**), *Litle Berwesike* a.1241, *Littilborousike* 1325, *Lyttelburghsike* 1326 (*v.* **sík**) (*v.* **lӯtel, lítill, berg**); *Long Hill* 1724, 1745, 1750; *le longlandis* 13, *le Longgelandes* 1327, *longe landes* 1601, *longelands* 1625, *Longlands* 1638, 1674 *et passim* to 1750 (*v.* **lang**[1], **land**); *le longeweluerode* 13 (*v.* **lang**[1], **wilig**; with **rod**[1] or **rōd**[3]); *Loves Close* 1674, *Georg Loues yarde* 1625, *George Loves yard* 1674 (*v.* **geard**); *ye meere balke* 1674, *the Meare Baulke* 1697 (*v.* **(ge)mǣre, balca**); *Middle Doles* 1697, 1724, 1745, 1750 (*v.* **dāl**); *Muchelcroft* a.1241, 13 (*v.* **micel, mycel, croft**); *Muckledoles* 1601, 1625, 1709, 1745, *Muckildoles* 1697, *Muckelldols* 1724, *Mucle doles* 1750 (*v.* **micel, mycel, mikill, dāl**); *Mucklegate Furlong*(*e*) 1638, 1674 (*v.* **furlang** and Muckle Gate Lane); *Murburre hill* 1601, 1625, *Murbar* ~ 1638, *Murber* ~ 1674, *Far* ~ ~, *Morbor hill* 1697, *Murbur* ~ 1709, *Marbur* ~ 1709 (18), *Morbar* ~ 1724, *Mulberry Hill* 1745, 1750, *Neather* ~ ~, *the Upper Murburre sicke* 1601, 1625, *Nether Morbar* ~, *Murbar* ~ 1638, *Nether* ~ ~, *Mulber sicke* 1674, *Morbor sick* 1697, *Nether* ~ ~, *Murbar Sike* 1709, *Morbar Sicke* 1724, *Mulberry Sick* 1745, 1750 (*v.* **sík**) (*v.* **mōr**[1], **mór, berg**; the occasional form is attracted to Melborough *supra*); *nagges peece* 1601, *Nagges peice* 1625, *Nags peece* 1638, *ye Nagges piece* 1674, *the Nag pece* 1697, *the Nag's Peice* 1709, *the Knag Pice* 1724, 1745, 1750 (*v.* **nagge, pece**); (*the*) *Neather Feild*(*e*) 1601, 1625, 1638, *the Nether feeilde* 1697, *Nether Field* 1709, 1709 (18), 1745, *Nather Fielde* 1750 (*v.* **neoðera, feld**; one of the great fields of the township); *le Neþerehauedis* 13 (*v.* **neoðera, hēafod**); *the New Closes* 1709; *John Norths hadley* 1638, 1674 (*v.* **headley**); *the Ouldes shrubbes* (*upon the Fosse*) 1601, 1674, *the Olds shrubbs upon the Fosse* 1625, *the Oulds Shrubbs* (*upon the Fosse*) 1709, 1709 (18) (*v.* **wald, scrubb**; with reference to the Fosse Way); *the Parsonage Gardens* 1709 (18), *the parsonage grass*(*e*) *hadeland*(*e*) 1601, 1625, 1709, ~ ~ *headland* 1745 (*v.* **græs, hēafod-land**), *the first parsonage land* 1601, 1625, 1674 (*v.* **land**) (*v.* **personage**); *Parson*(*s*) *Closs* 1745, 1750 (*v.* **clos(e)**), *the Parson*(*s*) (*grasse*) *hadley* 1638, 1674 (*v.* **græs, headley**) (*v.* **persone**); *the Pasture* 1709 (18) (*v.* **pasture**); *the pinfold* 1625, *pinfoulde bankes* 1601, *Pinfold*(*e*) ~ 1638, 1674 (*v.* **banke**) (*v.* **pynd-**

fald); *Prestold bushes* 1697 (*v.* **busc** and the following f.n.); *prestwellesike* 13, *Prestole sicke* 1601, *Prestwold* ~ 1625, 1674, *Prestolde* ~ 1638, *Prestwould sicke* 1674, *Prestold Sick*(*e*) 1697, 1724, 1745, 1750, *Prestole Sike* 1709, *Prestow* ~ 1709 (18) (*v.* **prēost, wella, sík**; the name of 'the priest's spring or stream' was here attracted to that of the township of Prestwold (*q.v.*), 4 miles to the north-west); (*sub fonte*) *Pudewell* a.1241, 13 (*v.* **wella**; with the OE pers.n. *Puda*; note MLat *fons* (*fonte* abl.sg.) 'a spring'); *Rangland* 1697, *Rangelande sicke* 1601, *Rangland sick*(*e*) 1638, 1674 *et passim* to 1750, ~ *Sike* 1709, 1709 (18) (*v.* **sík**), *Rangelande sicke furlonge* 1601, *Rangland sick furlonge* 1625, ~ *Sike Furlong* 1709 (*v.* **furlang**) (*v.* **wrang, vrangr, land**); *Thomas Reades Close* 1674; *Seuene Wong* 13 (*v.* **vangr**; in view of the evident RB survival in this area, the first word is very likely the pre-English stream-name *Severne*, *v.* Severn Acre in adjoining Walton on the Wolds f.ns. (a) and cf. Saffron Brook, Lei **1** 226 and R. Severn, RN 358); *ye Sixe lands* 1674, *the Six* ~ 1709, 1709 (18) (*v.* **six, land**); *John Smiths hadley* 1638, ~ *Smythes* ~ 1674 (*v.* **headley**), *John Smythes sidley* 1638 (*v.* **sīde, ley**); *Sow furlong* 1697, 1727, *South* ~ 1745 (*v.* **sūð, furlang**); *Thomas Stablefords hadland* 1638 (*v.* **hēafod-land**), *Stableford*(*s*) *hadley* 1638, 1678 (*v.* **headley**); *Standordfeld* 1345, *Standertfyld* 1371, *Standard Feilde* 1581, 1638, *Standart Feilde* 1601, *Standard Field* 1674, 1709 *et passim* to 1750, *Standerd Feeilde* 1697 (*v.* **feld**; one of the early great fields), *Standard gate* 1638, 1674 *et passim* to 1750, *Standerd* ~ 1697 (*v.* **gata**), *Standart hill furlonge* 1601, *Standard hill furlong*(*e*) 1625, 1638, 1674, 1709 (*v.* **furlang**) (*v.* **standard**); *Stayne Leas* 1709, ~ *Leys* 1709 (18), *Stayne leas furlonge* 1601, 1625, *Steaneleyes* ~ 1638, *Steanley furlong*(*e*) 1674 (*v.* **furlang**) (*v.* **steinn, leys**); *Stoe hill* 1601, 1625, *Stow* ~ 1638, 1674, 1745, *Stooe* ~ 1724, 1750 (*v.* **stōw**); *stoxclif* 13 (*v.* **stocc, clif**); (*the two*) *Swathland sickes* 1601, 1625, ~ *sicks* 1638, 1674, 1745, 1750, ~ *sikes* 1709 (*v.* **swathe, land, sík**); *Sylebie brooke* 1601, *Sylebye* ~ 1625, *Sileby*(*e*) ~ 1638, 1674, *Sileby brook* 1709, 1709 (18), *Sileby brucke forlong* 1697, *Silbybrooke forlong* 1724, *Sileby brook furlong* 1745, 1750 (*v.* **brōc, furlang**), *Sylebie meare* 1601, *Sylebye* ~ 1625, *Sileby meere* 1674, ~ *Mere* 1709, ~ *Meer* 1709 (18) (*v.* **(ge)mǣre**) (Sileby adjoins to the south-west); *Thomelyn* a.1241 (a virgate or yardland so called (20 or 30 acres)); the pers.n. *Thomelyn*, which is a double diminutive of *Thom* (Thomas), as *Thom-el-in*); *thornecraft lays* 1697, *Thornicraft* ~ 1724, *Thornicroft Lays* 1745, *Thornicroft Leys* 1750 (*v.* **leys**; with the local surn. *Thorneycroft*); *Thornheya* 1371 (*v.* **þorn, (ge)hæg**); *Thorn*(*e*) *end* 1724, 1745, 1750 (*v.* **þorn, ende**); *Virgata Thurger*, ~ *Tirga* a.1241 (with the ON pers.n. *Þorgeirr* (ODan *Thorger*) and MLat *virgata* 'a virgate or yardland' (20 or 30 acres)); *the furlong next to the Town*(*e*) 1674, 1709, 1709 (18) (*v.* **tūn**); *Trunchit hades* 1697, *Trunshit* ~ 1724, *Trunchad* ~ 1745, *Trunched hades* 1750 (*v.* **hēafod**) (*Trunchit* is poss. a British survival, with PrW **trūm* 'a nose, a promontory' and PrW **cę̄d* 'a wood', hence 'wood on the nose of land or the promontory', cf. Trunch in Norfolk (*Trunchet* 1086 DB) and cf. *Finchet*(*te*), a further poss. British survival in the parish, *v.* Finch Ades in f.ns (a)); *the tythe pece* 1601, ~ ~ *peice* 1625, 1709, ~ ~ *piece* 1674, *the Tith*(*e*) *peece* 1638, 1697, *the tyth pice* 1745, 1750 (*v.* **tēoða, pece**); *Robert Wakelings Closs* 1750 (*v.* **clos(e)**), *Richard Wakelands hadland* (sic) 1638, *John Wakelins* ~ 1697 (*v.* **hēafod-land**), *Wakelyn Hades* 1601, *Wakeland* ~ (sic) 1625, *Wakelin* ~ 1638, 1674, *Wakling Hades* 1697, 1724, 1745, 1750, *Ouer Wakelin hades* 1638, *Over Wakelyn* ~ 1709 (*v.* **uferra**), *Upper Wakelin hades* 1674 (*v.* **hēafod**) (cf. also *Ralph Wakelin* 1674; the surn. *Wakelin* is a reflex of the OFr pers.n. *Walchelin*);

Walton meare 1697, ~ ~ *forlong* 1724, ~ *Mear furlong(e)* 1745, 1750 (*v.* **furlang**) (*v.* **(ge)mǣre**; Walton on the Wolds adjoins to the north-west); *Waterfurrowes* 1638, 1674, *the Waterthorowes* 1697, *Water Furrows* 1709, *Water furrowes furlonge* 1601, 1625 (*v.* **furlang**) (*v.* **wæter**, **furh** and *the Waterfurrow(e)s* in Asfordby f.ns. (b)); *Welhil* 13, *Sortewellehul'* 13 (*v.* **sc(e)ort**) (*v.* **wella, hyll**); *Welsike* 13 (*v.* **wella, sík**); *the Well Yard* 1709 (18) (*v.* **wella**, **geard**; i.e. of *the Parsonage House*); *Westprestgate* 13 (*v.* **west, prēost, gata**); *Weteberusike* 13, *Wheatburre sicke* 1601, 1625, *Wheatebar* ~ 1638, *Wheatebur sicke* 1674, *Wheatbar Sick* 1697, *Wheatburr* ~ 1709, *Wheatbarr Sike* 1709, 1709 (18), *Wheatbarow Sicke* 1724, *Wheatbrow* ~ 1745, *Wheatborow Sick* 1750 (*v.* **hwǣte, berg, sík**); *Weynnylande* 13 (*v.* **whinny, land**); *Wistoft* 13, *Whistoe hill* 1601, 1625, *Whistow* ~ 1638, *Whitsters hill* 1674, *Hither Whistosicke* 1638, ~ *Whitsters sicke* 1674 (*v.* **hider**), *Upper Whistow sicke* 1638, ~ *Whitsters* ~ 1674, *Ouer Whistosick* 1697 (*v.* **uferra**), *Nether* ~ 1697 (*v.* **sík**) (*v.* **toft**; names compounded with *toft* as the generic are usually combined with either a pers.n. or a significant word; here is poss. either a Scand pers.n. *Vísi/Viss* or else **wisse** 'a marshy meadow'; the name appears to have been attracted to that of *Stoe hill*, *supra*; *v.* Wisterbrook in f.ns. (a)); *Wodhomes* 1601, 1625, *Wadhomes* 1638, *Woddholms* 1697, *Woodholmes* 1709, 1724, 1745, 1750 (*v.* **wād, holmr**); *Tho. Wyldes* ~ 1709, *Thomas Wildes Cottage* 1709 (18), *Thomas Wyldes hadley* 1638, 1674 (*v.* **headley**), *Thomas Wyldes Swath* 1674 (*v.* **swathe**).

Sileby

SILEBY

Siglesbie 1086 DB
Siglebi 1086 DB bis, 1190 × 1204 France, 1221 FineR, *Siglebia* c.1130 LeicSurv, *Sigleby* c.1130 ib, 1229 RHug, 1239 Ch, *Sygleby* 1229 RHug
Silesbi 1205 P, *Sylesby* 1255 Cl bis,1395 Pat, 1460 ISLR
Silebi 1207 P bis, *Sylebi* 1220 Fine, *Sileby* 1228 Ch, 1255 GildR (p) *et passim* to 1313, 1316 *LCDeeds et freq* to 1375 *ib* (p), 1377 Cl *et passim* to 1488 Pat, 1535 VE *et freq*, *Silebe* 1457 *Ct*, *Silebye* 1539 MinAccts, 1608 LML, *Syleby* 1220 MHW, 1252 Fees *et freq* to 1484 *Deed*, 1500 *Wyg*, 1522 *Ferrers et passim* to 1610 Speed
Syleby 1511 *RTemple*, *Syelbee* 1525 AD
Silby 1328 Banco, 1354 Cl, 1374 Banco, *Silbye* 1532 *RTemple*, *Sylby* 1353 Ipm, 1361 GauntReg *et passim* to 1508 *RTemple*, 1518 Visit, 1532 FF

'Sigulf's farmstead, village', *v.* **bȳ**. The ON pers.n. *Sigulfr* (OSwed *Sighulf*) is to be preferred as the specific to OE *Sigewulf*. The latter developed early to *Siulf*, *v.* Feilitzen 116 and Searle 426.

BACK LANE, 1760 *EnclA*, 1846, 1863, 1877 White, *v.* **back**. THE BANKS, 1846, 1863, 1877 White, *v.* **banke**. BARROW RD, *Barrow Road* 1760 *EnclA*, 1846, 1863, 1877 White, 1925 Kelly; Barrow upon Soar adjoins to the north-west. BELLE ISLE, 1835 O, 1846 White; this is *Isle Lodge* 1863 ib, *Belle Eye Lodge* (sic) 1877 ib, *v.* **loge**. Built after the Enclosure of 1760 and named from Belle Isle (Strait) in Canada, which featured in Wolfe's victorious campaign in the Seven Years War with France, *v.* Quebec Ho. and Hanover Fm *infra*. BROOK HO., *Brook house* 1925 Kelly, BROOK ST, *Brook Street* 1760 *EnclA*, 1846, 1863, 1877 White, 1925 Kelly, *the Brook* 1822 *Terrier*, *v.* **brōc**. CARPENTERS' ARMS (P.H.) (lost), *Carpenters Arms* 1771 *Deed*. CHARLES ST. CHARNWOOD HO. COSSINGTON RD, *Cossington Road* 1760 *EnclA*; it is *Cossington lane* 1846, 1863, 1877 White; Cossington adjoins to the south-east. DUKE OF

YORK (P.H.), (*the*) *Duke of York* 1846, 1863, 1877 White, 1925 Kelly. FIELD BARN. FOUNTAIN (P.H.) (lost), *Fountain* 1846, 1863 White, ~ *Inn* 1925 Kelly. THE GRANGE, 1925 Kelly, *v.* **grange**. THE HALL. HANOVER FM is *Hanover Lodge* 1846, 1863 White, *v.* **loge**. As with Belle Isle *supra* and Quebec Ho. *infra*, it was built after the Enclosure of 1760 and named in celebration of the reign of the Hanoverian King George II (died 1760) and the victorious *annus mirabilis* of 1759 for Britain in the Seven Years War with France. HIGHBURY. HIGHGATE LODGE, *v.* **loge** and Highgate Fd in f.ns. (a). HIGH ST, *High Street* 1846, 1863, 1877 White. HORSE AND TRUMPET (P.H.) (lost), *Horse and Trumpet* 1846, 1863, 1877 White, 1925 Kelly. KING ST, *King Street* 1846, 1863, 1877 White. MOUNTSORREL LANE is *Mountsorrel Road* 1760 *EnclA*, 1846, 1863 White; Mountsorrel adjoins to the south-west. PEAS HILL FM, *Pease Hill Farm* 1835 O, *Peasehill* 17 *Terrier*, *Pease Hill* 1760 *Map*, *v.* **pise**. PINFOLD, *v.* **pynd-fald**. PLOUGH (P.H.) (lost), *Plough* 1846, 1863 White, 1925 Kelly, *Old Plough* 1877 White. QUEBEC HO., *Quebec* ~ 1806 Map, *Quebeck House* 1846 White, *Quebec* 1835 O, 1877 White, *Quebec Lodge* 1863 ib (*v.* **loge**); built after the Enclosure of 1760 and named from Wolfe's victory at Quebec in the Seven Years war with France, *v.* Belle Isle and Hanover Fm *supra*. RAILWAY INN, 1846, 1877 White, *Railway Hotel* 1925 Kelly; Sileby was served by *the Midland Counties Railway* in 1846 White. Note *Sileby Station* 1835 O. RATCLIFFE RD, *the Ratcliff Road* 1760 *EnclA*; it is *Ratcliffe lane* 1877 White, Ratcliffe on the Wreake lying 2 miles to the south-east. RED LION (P.H.) (lost), *Red Lion* 1863 White, *Old Red Lion* 1877 ib, 1925 Kelly, ~ ~ ~ *Inn* 1920 *Sale*. ST MARY'S CHURCH, *the Church* 1709 *Terrier*, *Church (St Mary)* 1846, 1863, 1877 White, *Church (St Mary the Virgin)* 1925 Kelly; it is earlier recorded as *ecclesia de Syleby* 1220 MHW, *ecclesie de Sileby* 1361, 1362 *Pat*, *ecclesie parochialis de Syleby* 1447 *ib*. SEAGRAVE RD, (*the*) *Seagrave Road* 1760 *EnclA*, 1925 Kelly; it is *Seagrave lane* 1877 White. Seagrave adjoins to the north-east. SHEEPWASH, *the Sheep Wash* 1760 *EnclA*, *v.* **scēp-wæsce**. SILEBY LODGE, 1877 White, *v.* **loge**. SILEBY MILL (2½"), *Sileby Mill* 1782 *EnclA*, 1822 *Terrier*, 1835 O, ~ *mills* 1877 White, *Sileby Water Mill* 1822 *Terrier* (*v.* **water-mylne**), *v.* **myln**. THE VICARAGE, 1877 White, 1925 Kelly, *v.* **vikerage**. WESTFIELD, 1925 Kelly.

Note also: *Church Lane* 1760 *EnclA*, 1846, 1863, 1877 White (*v.* St Mary's Church *supra*); *East Lane* 1760 *EnclA*; *Elmfield Lane* 1925 Kelly; *Gate Lane* 1760 *EnclA* (*v.* **gata** and Old Gate Lane in neighbouring Thrussington); *Godfreys Lane* 1760 *EnclA* (with the surn.

Godfrey); *Parsons Lane* 1760 *EnclA* (cf. *Nicholas Parsons* 17 *Terrier*, *Tho. Parsons* 1760 *EnclA*); *Ratcliff Cross* 1760 *EnclA*, 1835 O (*v.* **cross**; a cross-roads towards Ratcliffe on the Wreake); *Swan street* 1877 White; *Wards Lane* 1760 *EnclA* (with the surn. *Ward*).

FIELD-NAMES

Undated forms in (a) are 1760 *EnclA*; forms dated 1761 are *Plan*. Forms throughout dated 1228 are Ch; 1325 and 1326 are Ipm; 17 and 1745 are *Terrier*; 1702, 1722 and 1731 are *Deed*.

(a) Acre Lands (*Acre Lands Platt* 1745 (*v.* **plat**), *v.* **æcer, land**); Ash Cl 1761 (*v.* **æsc**); the Backwater (*v.* **backwater**); Banks Common (*v.* **commun**), Upper Banks, Banks Furlong (*v.* **furlang**) (*v.* The Banks *supra*); Barnets Cl, Barnits Close Furlong (*Mr Barnards Close* 17, *a Furlong called Barnards Close* 1745; the surn. was originally *Barnard* rather than *Barnet*, but note that Reaney includes both as developments of the OFr pers.n. *Bernart* (OGer *Bernard*), *v.* **furlang**); Barrow Brook Furlong (*Barrows Brook furlong* 1745, *v.* **brōc, furlang**), Barrow Gap Furlong (*v.* **gap, furlang**) (Barrow upon Soar adjoins to the north-west); Bear Stakes (a location for bear-baiting, *v.* Field 247); Between Dykes ((*a Platt called*) *Betwixt Dikes* 1745 (*v.* **plat**), *v.* **betwixt, dík**); Between Gates (*Betwixt Gates* 1745, *v.* **betwixt, gata**; the name of a furlong); Blew Pits (1745, *v.* **blew, pytt**); Breach Hill, Breach Sty (*v.* **stīg**) (cf. *High Breach furlong* 1745 (*v.* **furlang**), *v.* **brēc**); Brook Fd 1761 (*v.* **brōc**); Burn Sick (cf. *Bourne Sick furlong* 1745 (*v.* **furlang**), *v.* **sík**; the first el. is either **burna** 'a stream' or one of the cognates **bryne/bruni** '(a place cleared by) burning'; note *Burnesicke* in adjoining Seagrave f.ns. (b)); Butchers Cls (with the surn. *Butcher*); Canby Sick Furlong (*Canby Sick*, ~ ~ *Furlong* 1745, *v.* **sík, furlang**), Little Canby Fd (1745), Over Canby Fd (*v.* **uferra**; *Upper Canby Field* 1745) (Canby appears to be a lost farmstead, *v.* **bȳ**; with the ON pers.n. *Kani*); Castle Hill 1761 (there is no evidence on the ground for any kind of fortification here; a possibility is a reduction of the surn. *Castledine*, *v.* *Castledines land* in f.ns. (b)); Church Headland Furlong (*v.* **hēafod-land, furlang** and St Mary's Church *supra*); Clay Fd 1761 (*v.* **clǣg**); the Clock Pieces (*v.* **pece**; as noted in the Enclosure Award of 1760, these were 'enjoyed by the said Parish Clerk as a satisfaction for his trouble in regulating and winding up the weights belonging to the Clock and Chymes of the said Parish Church of Sileby'); Clovengore Bault (*v.* **clofen, gāra, balca**); Cocks Bridge Pasture (*v.* **pasture**; poss. with the surn. *Cocks* since surns. sometimes occur in the names of bridges in Leics. (cf. Lewin Bridge in Ratcliffe on the Wreake), although the usual Leics. spelling of the surn. is *Cox*); the Common (*v.* **commun**); Cordel Sty (with **stīg** or **stig**) (*Caudwells* 17, *Cawdells furlong* 1745 (*v.* **furlang**), *v.* **cald, wella**); Cossington end 1877 White (*v.* **ende**), Cossington wolds 1877 ib (*v.* **wald**), Cussington Brook Furlong 1760 (*v.* **furlang**) (*Cussington Brooke* 17, *v.* **brōc**), Cussington Stone 1760 (*v.* **stān**; presum. a parish boundary marker) (Cossington adjoins to the south-east); Cow Cl 1761; Dale Cl 1761 (*v.* **dalr**); Deadman's Sty (*v.* **dede-man, stīg**); Dim(m)insdale (*Diminsdale Platt* 1745 (*v.* **plat**), *v.* **dimming, dalr** and Dimsdale in Frisby on the Wreake f.ns. (a)); Long Drab(b)s (*Long Drabs* 17, *v.* **drabbe** and The Drabble, Lei **2** 263); East Fd 1761; Far Fd 1761; Farthings (*v.* **fēorðung**); Felford Furlong (*v.* **furlang**) (*Felford Ford Platt* (sic) 1745 (*v.* **plat**), *v.* **ford**; the first el. is either **feld** or **felte**); Over ~ ~ (*v.* **uferra**), Flax Lands (*Flaxlands* 17, *v.* **fleax, land**); Frogg Hole (*Frog Hole or Barrows Brook furlong* 1745, *v.* **frogga, hol**[1] and Barrow Brook Furlong *supra*); Gateland Leys (*v.* **gata, land, leys**); Goose Green (*v.* **gōs, grēne**[2]); Greeden 1760, Greaden 1761, Greedon Furlong 1760 (*v.* **furlang**) (*Greedon* 1745; earlier forms are needed, but poss. 'the green hill or upland pasture', *v.* **grēne**[1], **dūn**); Green Sty (*atte Grenesty* 1327 SR (p) (*v.* **atte**), *Greene Stye* 17), Little Green Sty (*Little Greene Stye* 17) (*v.* **grēne**[1], **stīg**); the Hay Brook (*v.* **brōc**) (*le Haye* 1325, 1326, *the heay* 17, *the Hay* 1745), Hay Sty Furlong (*v.* **furlang**) (*a furlong called in ye Hay & Hay Stye* 1745, *v.* **stīg**) (*v.* **(ge)hæg**); Highgate Cl, Highgate Fd (1745, *v.* **feld**; one of the great fields), Highgate Furlong (*v.* **furlang**) (*v.* **hēah**[1], **gata**); High Sty, ~ ~ Furlong (*High Stye Furlong* 1745, *v.* **hēah**[1], **stīg, furlang**); Hingin Brinks (*v.* **hangende, brink**); Hithersike Bridge (*v.* **hider, sík**); Home Cl 1761 (*v.* **home**); Howgate Fd 1760 *EnclA*, 1822 *Terrier*, 1863 White (*How Gate*, ~ ~ *Field* 1745 (*v.* **feld**; one of the great fields), *v.* **haugr, gata**); Hundy Hill, Hundy Slade (*v.* **slæd**) (*v.* *Hundehoge* in neighbouring Cossington f.ns. (b)); Ilemoor, Ilemore Common (*v.* **commun**) (cf. *Ilemore hill furlong* 1745 (*v.* **furlang**), *v.* **mōr**[1]; prob. with **igil**, cf. I(s)lemoor Cls in Syston f.ns. (a)); Kings Closes Furlong (*v.* **furlang**; with the surn. *King*); Lammas Cl (1702, *Lamas Close* 1731, cf. *Lam(m)as ground* 1702, 1722, 1731 (*v.* **grund**), *v.* **lammas**); Latmore End (*v.* **mōr**[1], **ende**; earlier forms are needed to explain the first el.); Lampert Green 1761 (*v.* **grēne**[2]; with the surn. *Lampert*, a reflex of the OFr pers.n. *Lambert*); Little Barrow (*Litleberg* 1228, *Litelberue* 14, cf. *Litle Bergsic* 1228, *Litelberuesike* 14 (*v.* **sík**), *v.* **lȳtel, lítill, berg**); Little Mdw 1761; Long Lands (cf. (*a Platt called*) *Bottom of Long Lands* 1745 (*v.* **plat**), *v.* **lang**[1], **land**); Maiden Green 1761 (*v.* **mægden, grēne**[2]; a place where the village girls gathered); Marehouse furlong (*v.* **mareis, furlang**); Marsh (cf. *March Leys* 17 (*v.* **leys**), *March Platt* 1745 (*v.* **plat**), *v.* **mersc**); Meadow Ditch (*v.* **dīc**); Merry Ditch (*v.* **myry, dīc**); Nether ~ ~, Over Merry Wong (*v.* **uferra**) (*v.* **myry, vangr**); Mile End 1761 (*v.* **ende**; prob. with **myln** rather than **mīl**, cf. Nuball end *infra*); Mill Holme (*le Milneholm* 1325, 1326, (*Holmo molendini* 14, with MLat *holmus* 'a river meadow' and *molendinum* 'a mill'), *v.* **myln, holmr**); Nether Sty Furlong (*Nether Stye furlong* 1745, *v.* **stīg, furlang**); Northins 1761 (*the Northings* 17), (the) Short Northings 1760 (cf. *Long* ~ ~, *Short Northings Platt* 1745, *v.* **plat**) (*v.* **norð, eng**); Nuball end (*v.* **ende**; Nuball is a late form of Newbold, here an otherwise unrecorded habitation site, *v.* **nīwe, bold**); Open Wards Cl (*v.* **open**; with the surn. *Ward*, cf. *Wards Lane*, *supra*); (the) Parkes, Under the Parkes (*Under the Parks* 1745, *v.* **park**); Pauls Hedge (*v.* **hecg**; with the surn. *Paul*); Plane 1761 (*v.* **plain**); Redlands (*v.* **rēad, land**); Round Pasture (*v.* **round, pasture**); Royal Knowl Cl (*v.* **ryge, hyll, cnoll**); Sandpit Cls (*v.* **sand-pytt**); Segshill Sty (cf. *Seggs hill stye furlong* 1745, *v.* **stīg, furlang**; the track to Six Hills *q.v.*); Short Lands (*Shortlands* 17, *v.* **sc(e)ort, land**); Shrubb Sty (*Shrobs stye* 1745, *v.* **scrubb, stīg**); Sileby Mill Holm 1782 *EnclA* (*v.* **holmr** and Sileby Mill *supra*); Nether ~, Over Slades 1760 (*v.* **uferra**), Betwixt the Slades 1760 (*v.* **betwixt**; the name of a furlong), Slade Fd 1761 (*v.* **slæd**); Small Holmes (*v.* **holmr**); (the) South Fd 1760, 1761 (*v.* **sūð, feld**; one of the great fields of the township); Southins 1761 (*v.* **sūð, eng**; cf. Northins *supra*); Ston Mdw (*v.* **stān, stoned** and *the stone middow* in Knipton f.ns. (b), Lei **2** 19);

Stoney Lands (*Stony Lands* 17, ~ ~ *furlong* 1745 (*v.* **furlang**), *v.* **stānig, land**); Sunnell 1761 (*v.* **sunne, hyll**; land which caught the best of the sunshine); Thwart Lands (cf. *Whart Lands furlong* 1745 (*v.* **furlang**), *v.* **þverr** (**þvert** neut.), **land**); Townsend Cl 1761 (*the Townesend* 17, *v.* **tūn, ende**); Walton Gate Furlong (1754; note also *a furlong called Walton Gate betwixt the Closes* 1745 (*v.* **betwixt**), *v.* **gata, furlang**; Walton on the Wolds lies 2½ miles to the north-west); Water Ditch (*v.* **wæter, dīc**; poss. with free-flowing water in contrast to Merry Ditch 'the muddy ditch' *supra*, or else part of an irregation system); Water Furrow Furlong (*v.* **wæter, furh, furlang** and *the Waterfurrow(e)s* in Asfordby f.ns. (b)); Wheat Hill 1761 (*v.* **hwǣte**); Widness 1761 (*v.* **wīd, næss, nes**; presum. with reference to a headland formed by the channel of the river Soar); Wind Mill Hill (*v.* **wind-mylne**); Wood gate (cf. *Woodgate Furlong* 17, *v.* **furlang**), Woodgate Tongue (*v.* **tunge**) (*v.* **wudu, gata**).

(b) *Against Double Hedges* 1745 (*v.* **duble, hecg**; the name of a furlong, cf. *double hedges* in Humberstone f.ns. (b)); *Barlycroft* 14 (*v.* **bærlic, croft**); *Betwixt ye Closes* 17 (*v.* **betwixt**; the name of a furlong); *Bonacres* 17, *Bourn Acres* 1745 (*v.* **æcer** and Burn Sick in f.ns. (a)); *Braunsford Platt* 1745 (*v.* **ford, plat**; additional and earlier forms are needed to explain the first el. which could be an early OE stream-name **Brūn* 'the brown one' (cf. *Bronsforde* in Wye, KPN 246-7)); *Castledines land* 17 (*v.* **land**; with the surn. *Castledine*); *the Corn Mill* 1616 *Deed* (*v.* **corn**[1], **myln**); *Fordelis* 1325, *Fordelys* 1326 (*v.* **fore, deill**); *le Goris* 1325, *le Gorys* 1326 (*v.* **gāra**); *Hogston side* 17 (*v.* **sīde**; *Hogston* appears to be a lost early farmstead (*v.* **tūn**), with an OE pers.n. *Hogg* (cf. Hoggeston, Bk 67 and Hogsthorpe, DLPN 64); otherwise with **hogg**); *Longs furlong* 1745 (*v.* **lang**[2], **furlang**); *lympittes* 1325, *lymputes* 1326 (*v.* **lyme-pytt**); *Middletons land* 17 (*v.* **land**; with the surn. *Middleton*); *Moores grass hadland* 17 (*v.* **græs, hēafod-land**; with the surn. *Moore*); *George Ortons hadland* 17 (*v.* **hēafod-land**); *the Parsonage land* 17 (*v.* **personage, land**); *Nicholas Parsons his Land* 17 (*v.* **land**); *Pease hill furlong* 1745 (*v.* **furlang**), *Peasehill Stye* 17 (*v.* **stīg**) (*v.* Peas Hill Fm *supra*); *the rickes* 17 (*v.* **hrēac**); *the Shrubb feild* 17 (*v.* **scrubb, feld**; one of the great fields); *Six Roods* 1745 (*v.* **six, rōd**[3]; the name of a furlong); *South field Lays* 1745 (*v.* **leys** and South Fd *supra*); *Southholme Bank Platt* 1745 (*v.* **banke**), *Southholme Gap Platt* 1745 (*v.* **gap**), *Southholme Platt* 1745 (*v.* **plat**) (*v.* **sūð, holmr**); *the South Meadow* 17; *Under the Woulds* 1745 (*v.* **wald**; the name of a furlong); *the Wellbucke Feild* 17 (*v.* **wella, bekkr, feld**; one of the great fields); *Wheatlys Headland* 1745 (*v.* **hēafod-land**; with the surn. *Wheatley*); *Whinidoles* 14 (*v.* **whinny, dāl**); *Whity Bush furlong* 1745 (*v.* **wīðig, busc, furlang**; cf. *Wethybuscus* in Queniborough f.ns. (b)).

Skeffington

SKEFFINGTON

Sciftintone 1086 DB

Sceftinton' c.1130 LeicSurv, 1165 P (p) *et passim* to 1252 Fees, 1279 Coram (p), *Sceftintun'* 1226 Cur (p), c.1250 (1404) *Laz*

Sceftenton' c.1130 LeicSurv, *Skeftenton* 1220 MHW, 1280, 1282 Pat

Scheftinton' 1179, 1181 P *et freq* to c.1275 (1404) *Laz* (p), 1276 RH *et passim* to 1294 *MiD* (p), 1310 Ipm, *Scheftintonam* c.1160 Dane, *Scheftynton* 1274 RGrav

Scheftyngton' 1262 Ass (p), 1290 Inqaqd, 1317 *Rut*, *Schef(f)tington'* c.1250 (1404) *Laz*, l.13 *CRCart*, c.1292 *LCDeeds* (p), 1303 Pat, e.14 (1404) *Laz* (p)

Scaftintona 1177, 1178 ChancR, *Scaftinton'* 1187, 1191 P *et freq* to 1211, 1212 ib, *Scaftintone* 1224 RHug, *Schaftinton'* 1177, 1178, 1188 P

Scheffyngt(h)on' 1290 Inqaqd, 1381 SR (p), 1406 *Wyg*

Skeftintun' 1231 Cl, 1232 × 47 *Rut*, *Skeftinton'* 1209 For, 1219 Cur *et passim* to 1242 RGros (p), a.1250 (1404) *Laz et freq* to 1293 *LCDeeds* (p), 1300 *ib* (p) *et passim* to 1316, 1363 *RTemple*, *Skeftintone* l.13 *Peake* (p), *Skeftynton* 1258 Ch, 1309 Ipm *et passim* to 1338, 1356 Pat, *Skeftyntona* c.1306 *Wyg* (p)

Skeftington' 1230 P, 1247 Fees, 1248 *Rut* (p) *et freq* to 1327 *ib* (p), 1332 *RTemple* (p) *et passim* to 1344 Ass (p), 1372 Banco (p), *Skeftincton'* Hy 3 *Crox*, Edw 1 *CroxR*, *Skeftinkton'* 1311 *Rut* (p), *Skeftyngton'* 1277 Banco (p), 1281 Ass (p) *et passim* to 1316 *Peake* (p), 1317 Ipm *et freq* to 1348 Pat (p), 1369 Ipm

Skef(f)inton 1261 Cur, 1324 QuR, 1350 Pat, *Skef(f)ynton* 1345 ib (p), 1349 Inqaqd *et passim* to 1428 FA, 1478 Pat

Skef(f)yngton' 1327 SR, 1328 Banco *et passim* to 1409 *LCh*, 1440 Pat, 1472 *Peake*, *Skeffington* 1452 Banco, 1613 LML *et freq*

Skeuyngton' 1411 (1473) *Wyg*, 1473 *CCR*, *Skevyngton* 1434 Pat, 1471 *Hazlerigg et passim* to 1539, 1541 MinAccts, *Skevington* 1519 EpCB, 1520 *Rental et passim* to 1533 AAS, 1718 LML, *Skeauinton* Saxton

'The village, estate associated with or called after a man named Sceaft', *v.* **-ingtūn**. The initial consonant *Sh-* of the OE pers.n. *Sceaft* was subsequently Scandinavianized to *Sk-*.

BROWN'S WOOD, cf. *Browns Leys* 1773 *EnclA*, *v.* **leys**; cf. also *John Brown, farmer* 1863 White. THE CEDARS, cf. *Cedars Farm* 1924 *Sale*. CROW WOOD, *v.* **crāwe**. FOX AND HOUNDS (P.H.), *Fox and Hounds* 1846, 1863, 1877 White, 1925 Kelly. GAP COTTAGES, *v.* Skeffington Gap *infra*. GLEBE FM, *ye Gleebe* 1708 *Terrier*, *v.* **glebe**. HOMESTEAD FM, *Homested* e.19 *Plan*, *v.* **hām-stede**. HOOTHILL SLANG, *v.* **slang**, HOOTHILL WOOD, 1800 Nichols, 1824 O, *Hoothills* 1708, 1708 (18) *Terrier*, *Hoothill* 1773 *EnclA*, cf. *Hoot Hill Gate* 1773 *ib* (*v.* **gata**); from **tōt-hyll** 'a look-out hill'. KENNEL COTTAGE, *v.* **kenel**; the hounds of the Fernie Hunt were housed here. LITTLE SKEFFINGTON. MAIN ST. MELTON RD. NEW COTTAGES. NEW PLANTATION. OLD COTTAGE FM. PRIEST HILL is *Prestwode hyll'* 1467 × 84 *LTD*, *Priestwood Hill* 1824 O (*v.* **hyll**), *Priestwood* 1708, 18 *Terrier*, *Preistwood* 1708 (18) *ib*, *v.* **prēost, wudu**; woodland endowed for support of the parish priest. THE RECTORY, 1877 White, 1925 Kelly, *v.* **rectory**. ST THOMAS BECKET'S CHURCH, *the Church* 1708, 1708 (18) *Terrier*, *Church (St Thomas-à-Becket)* 1846, 1863, 1877 White, 1925 Kelly; it is earlier recorded as *ecclesie de Skeftenton* 1220 MHW, 1282 *Pat*, *ecclesiam* ~ ~, *ecclesie de Skeftinton* 1243 RGros, 1281 *Pat*, *ecclesiarum de Skeftynton et Cotesbache* 1356 *ib*. SKEFFINGTON GAP, 1877 White, *v.* **gap**. SKEFFINGTON GAP FM is the location of *George Inn* 1824 O. SKEFFINGTON GLEBE RD, *v.* Glebe Fm *supra*. SKEFFINGTON HALL, 1800 Nichols, 1863, 1877 White, 1925 Kelly, *The Hall* 1806 Map, 1846, 1863 White, *v.* **hall**. SKEFFINGTON LODGE FM, cf. *the Lodge* 1877 White, *Lodge Farm* 1939 *Sale*, *v.* **loge**. SKEFFINGTON VALE, 1859 *Sale*, 1877 White, *v.* **val**; it is *Skeffington Lodge* 1815 Nichols, 1824 O, *v.* **loge**. SKEFFINGTON WOOD, 1806 Map; earlier it is *Great Wood* 1800 Nichols. SOUTH FARTHING, *v.* **fēorðung**. UPPINGHAM RD. VALE COTTAGE, cf. *Vale house* 1925 Kelly, *v.* Skeffington Vale *supra*. WELLHEAD, *v.* **wella, hēafod**. WELSH MYERS, *Walchemore* 1467 × 84 *LTD*, *Welchmore* 1625 *Terrier*, *Welsh Moor* 1708, 1708 (18) *ib*, *Welch-Mire* 18 *ib*, *v.* **wælisc, mōr**[1]. WHITE LODGE. WOOD FM.

FIELD-NAMES

Undated forms in (a) are 1773 *EnclA*; those dated 1800 are Nichols, e.19 are *Plan* and 1824 are O. Forms throughout dated Hy 3 are *Crox*, 1290 are Ch, l.13 are *CRCart*, 13 are Nichols, Edw 1 are *CroxR*, 1467 × 84 are *LTD*, 1625, 1708, 1708 (18) and 18 are *Terrier*.

(a) Four ~, Six Acres e.19 (*v.* **æcer**); Long ~ ~, Short Beanhill Furlong (*v.* **bēan, hyll, furlang**); Bishops Lane (with the surn. *Bishop*); Branthill Fd (*v.* **brant, hyll**); Brockwell e.19 (*v.* **wella**; with either **brocc** or **brōc**); Bromes wood 1800, 1824 (cf. *George Brome* 1715 Nichols); the Bull Hook (*v.* **bula, hōc**); Butterpot Lane (*v.* **butere**, with **pot(t)** or **potte**; the precise implications of this name are uncertain since it may indicate a lane leading to a *Butterpot* (a complimentary name for good land) or it may rather describe a lane with yellow clay mire in wet conditions); Copner Bridge, Copner Hill Leys (*v.* **leys**) (ostensibly with the rare surn. *Copner* (a reflex of OE *cōpenere* 'a lover'), but there is no record of this in the East Midlands; an OE toponym such as **Coppanōra* 'Coppa's flat-topped hill' (with **ōra**[1]) may be postulated, but earlier forms are needed); Cullorns Ford (*v.* **ford**; with the surn. *Cullon*); Dedford (*v.* **dēad**; perh. a ford across still water or the site of a death; however, this may rather be a garbled version of the early *Deydmore* in f.ns. (b)); Dirty Lane (*v.* **dyrty**); Eagland Wood 1800, 1824 (*Eykelond* 1280 Misc bis, *v.* **eik, land**); Foxton Hill Headland (*v.* **hēafod-land**; with the surn. *Foxton* of a family poss. originally from the village of this name, 8 miles to the south-west in Gartree Hundred); the Gravel Pitts (*Gravelpittes* 1467 × 84, *Gravelpitt* 1625, cf. *Gravelpythyll'* 1467 × 84 (*v.* **hyll**), *v.* **gravel, pytt**); Hawkshill Spinney (*v.* **hafoc, hyll, spinney**); Hinger Spinney (*v.* **hangra, spinney**); Hobroke Hill (*v.* **hol**[2], **brōc**); Home Cl e.19 (*v.* **home**); Horningold Furlong (*v.* **furlang**; the village of Horninghold lies 5 miles to the south-east in Gartree Hundred, but no surn. deriving from it is recorded to explain such an attachment to this furlong; a poss. explanation is that the whole of the high land between Skeffington and Horninghold once bore the name *Horning(e)wald*, perh. 'woodland on the horn-shaped heights' (*v.* **horning, wald**); the township name Horninghold will be discussed at greater length in the Gartree Hundred volume to follow, but note *Brentingeswold* in f.ns (b) which confirms a range of wold country in this area); Lunsdale e.19 (cf. *Lundesbroc* Hy 3, 1290 (freq), *lundisbroc'* Hy 3 bis, *Lundesbrock* 13, *Lowndysbrok'* 1467 × 84 (*v.* **brōc**), *v.* **lundr, dalr**); Manybush wood 1800 (*Manibuskes* Hy 3, 1290 (freq), 13, *Manybuskys*, *Manybusse* 1467 × 84, cf. *Manibushegate* 1281 Banco (*v.* **gata**), *Manibuskesike* 1290 (*v.* **sík**), *v.* **manig, busc, buskr**); Mill Ditch Furlong (*v.* **dīc**), Mill Hill Furlong (*v.* **furlang**) (the forms may refer both to a watermill and to a windmill); Nether Ground e.19 (*v.* **grund**); New Cl e.19; Reaves Cl e.19 (with the surn. *Reaves/Reeves*); Round Cl (in modern f.ns. describing fields not necessarily circular, but equilateral or irregular polygons rather than oblong); Rowlow Fd (prob. **rūh**[1] with **hlāw**); Smith Hill Cl (either with the surn. *Smith* or with **smið**); the Stamford Road (Stamford lies 18 miles to the east); Magna ~ ~, Parva Warren's Holm e.19 (*Warinisholm* Hy 3, l.13, 13, Edw 1, *Warinesholm(e)* 1290 bis, *Warensholme* 1467 × 84, *Warrensholme* 1625 (*v.* **holmr**; the early forms and genitival structure indicate the AFr pers.n. *Warin* as the first el. rather than the surn. *Warren* or **wareine**); Wheat Hill Hades (*v.* **hēafod**), Wheat Hill Lane (earlier the hill is *Weteberue* Edw 1, *v.* **hwǣte, hveiti, berg**); the Wood Cl 1800 (1708, 1708 (18)).

(b) *Adlokwell' syke* 1467 × 84 (*v.* **wella, sík**; with an OE pers.n., either *Æðellāc* or *Ēadlāc*, cf. Allexton *supra*); *Andreslund* 13, Edw 1, *Andrislund* 13, *Anderland Hades* 18, *~ heads* 1708, *Anderlands heads* 1708 (18) (*v.* **hēafod**) (*v.* **lundr**; with a pers.n., prob. ODan *Andor* (ON *Arnþórr*) or, less likely but formally poss., OE *Andrēas* (cf. *Andreskirk* in Breedon on the Hill, West Goscote Hundred)); *Arlandsyke*, *Arlondsyke* 1467 × 84 (*v.* **á** (**ár** gen.sg.), **land**, **sík**); *the ash tree* 1625 (*v.* **æsc**); *Banars* ~, *Banerys more* 1467 × 84 (*v.* **mōr**[1]; poss. with **baner** 'a banner, a flag' used topographically of a (high) landmark (*v.* VEPN *s.v.*) or, less likely, with reference to the use of banners as a feature of medieval processions for the blessing of the fields (*v.* Field 232); cf. *Banar lane eynd* in Barsby f.ns. (b)); *Beggars bush* 1625, 1708, 18 (*v.* **beggere**, **busc**; a recurring f.n. which appears to denote poor or unproductive land (cf. EDD *beggar* 'to impoverish land, to exhaust soil of nutrients')); *Bellewellesik* 1290 (*v.* **wella**; the first el. is either an OE pers.n. *Bella* or **belle** 'a knoll'); *Blakwelslade* 1467 × 84 (*v.* **blæc**, **wella**, **slæd**); *Bracundalhyll'* 1467 × 84 (*v.* **braken**, **dalr**, **hyll**); *Brakon'*, *the Brakon* 1467 × 84 (*v.* **braken**); *Branteslandis* 1290 (*v.* **land**; the genitival structure points to the OE pers.n. *Brant* as first el. rather than to **brant** 'steep'); *Brechlahil* 1290 (*v.* **brēc**, **lēah**, **hyll**); *Brendedalehil* Hy 3, 1290, *Brendendalehil*, *Brendindalehil* 1290, *Brendalehil* 13 (*v.* **brend**, **dalr**, **hyll**); *Brentingeswong'* l.13, *Brentingwong* 1290 (*v.* **vangr**), *Brentingiswolde* 13, Edw 1 (*v.* **wald** and note Horningold in f.ns. (a)) (with the OE pers.n. *Brenting*); *Brocesheuid* Hy 3, *Brokesheved* 13 (*v.* **brōc**, **hēafod**); *Brocholes* Hy 3, 13, *Brokhols* 1467 × 84 (*v.* **brocc-hol**); *Brodyngis*, *Brodyngys* 1467 × 84 (*v.* **brād**, **eng**); *the Bushes* 1625 (*v.* **busc**); *Butfurlong'* 1467 × 84 (*v.* **butte**, **furlang**); *Buttleas hedge* 1625 (*v.* **butte**, **leys**, **hecg**); *Caluero* 1467 × 84 (*v.* **calf** (**calfra** gen.pl.), **hōh**); *the Church hadland* 1625 (*v.* **hēafod-land** and St Thomas Becket's Church *supra*); *Cleyhyll* 1467 × 84 (*v.* **clǣg**, **hyll**); *Clipthorngate* 1290, *Clipthorn' gate* 1467 × 84 (*v.* **gata**), *Clypson way* 1625, *Clipsum* ~ 1708, *Clipsam* ~ 18 (*v.* **weg**) (*v.* **þorn**; with a pers.n. such as *Clip*, that of a 10th cent. moneyer (*v.* ZEN 55) or its source ON *Klyppr*, or in view of a lack of genitival *s* in the early forms, ODan *Klippi*; note also the otherwise unrecorded OE pers.n. *Cylp* (with metathesis) in Clipsham, Ru 80); *Clipthorntoftes* 1290 (*v.* **toft** and the preceding f.n.); *Coldeford* Hy 3, 13 (*v.* **cald**, **ford**); *Cowgate* 1467 × 84 (*v.* **cū**, **gata**, **cowgate**; it is uncertain how early dial. *cowgate* 'pasturage for a single cow' was in use); *Craftes close* 1625, *Crofts Close* 1708, 18, *Crafts hedge* 1625 (*v.* **hecg**) (prob. with the surn. *Crofts* (the usual Leics. form) rather than **croft**); *Crokislundeswong'* Hy 3, 13, *Croklundeswong* 1290, *Croclindeswong'* l.13, 13, Edw 1 (*v.* **lundr**, **vangr**; with the ODan pers.n. *Krōk*); *Crossegate* 1290 bis (*v.* **gata**; prob. with **cross** rather than **cros**, but note two standing crosses *infra*); *Crosselandis*, *Crosselandys* 1467 × 84, *Crosslands* 1708, 1708 (18), 18 (*v.* **cross**, **land**); *ad crucem Margarete* 1467 × 84 (with MLat *ad* 'at, near', *crux* (*crucem* acc.sg.) 'a cross' and the pers.n. *Margaret* (OFr *Marguérite*); presum. the name of a furlong); *cruce de Sceftinton'* p.1250 (1404) *Laz* (with MLat *crux* (*cruce* abl.sg.) 'a cross'; the township's major standing cross); *Thomas Dalbeys grasse* 1625 (*v.* **græs**); *Dedmanysgraue* 1467 × 84 (*v.* **dede-man**, **græf**; a poss. reference to a pagan Anglo-Saxon inhumation burial site); *Depedale* Hy 3, *Debdale*, *Dybdal* 1467 × 84, *Debdalhylle* 1467 × 84 (*v.* **hyll**), *Depedale more* 13 (*v.* **mōr**[1]) (*v.* **dēop**, **dalr**); *Dewelstreme* 1467 × 84 (*v.* **dēaw**, **wella**, **strēam**); *Deydmore* 1467 × 84 (*v.* **dēad**, **mōr**[1]; quite a common f.n., prob. indicating infertile wasteland); *the Deynys* 1467 × 84 (*v.* **denu**); *Eastland* 1708, *Estlondsyke* 1467 × 84 (*v.* **sík**) (*v.* **ēast**, **land**); *Ellerenestubbe* 1290 (*v.* **ellern**, **stubb**); *Elsteyn* 1467 × 84 (*v.* **stān**, **steinn**; with an OE pers.n. *Ella* or *Eli*); *Elsted* 1625, 18, *Elstead* 18, *Eastead* 1708, 1708 (18), *Ealstead*, *Easthead* 1708 (18) (it is uncertain whether this is a late garbled version of the previous ME f.n.; if not, then *v.* **stede**, with the same OE pers.n.); *Endris* Hy 3, 1290 bis, 13, *Enderis* 1290, *Endris Ford* 18, *Enderis Foard* 1708, *Endoris Foord* 1708 (18) (*v.* **ford**), *Endersheyde* 1467 × 84 (*v.* **hēafod**), *Endryslund* 1290 (*v.* **lundr**; note that this form may belong rather with *Andrislund*, *supra*), *Endris Way* 18, *Enderis* ~ 1708, 1708 (18) (*v.* **ende, hrīs**); *Eske* 1467 × 84 bis, *Eskis* 1708, 1708 (18) (*v.* **eski**); *Eskelund'* Hy 3, 13, *Eskelond* 1290 (*v.* **eski, lundr**); *Estberuesik* 1290 (*v.* **ēast, berg, sík**); *Estmor* 1290 (*v.* **ēast, mōr**[1]); *Fayr(e)wellecroft* Hy 3, 13 (*v.* **croft**), *Fairwellefeld* 1290, *Feyrewelfelde* 1467 × 84 (*v.* **feld**), *Fayrwellehil* Hy 3, *Fayrewelle hill* 13 (*v.* **hyll**) (*v.* **fæger, wella**; cf. Farewell (St)); *Fishpoole yard* 1606 Ipm (*v.* **fisc-pōl, geard**); *Flintideles* Hy 3, 13 (*v.* **deill**), *Flyntydole* 1467 × 84 (*v.* **dāl**) (*v.* **flinti**); *Flatmedo(w)*, *Flat mydo*, *Flate mydow*, *Flatmydowsyde* 1467 × 84 (*v.* **sīde**) (*v.* **flatr, mǣd (mǣdwe** obl.sg.)); *Gibsons hill* 18 (with the surn. *Gibson*); *Gothewode* 1467 × 84 (*v.* **wudu**; with the OE pers.n. *Gōda*, with *th* for *d* due to Scand influence); *grangie abbatis de Croxton'* 1467 × 84 (with MLat *grangia* 'a grange' and *abbas* (*abbatis* gen.sg.) 'an abbot'; with reference to Croxton Abbey in Croxton Kerrial, founded originally in 1162 as a priory of Premonstratensian Canons, *v.* Lei **2** 103), *the Grange Close* 1708 (18), *the Grange Wood* 1715 Nichols, (*the*) *Grange Wood Close* 1708 *Terrier*, 1712 DKR, 1715 Nichols (*v.* **grange**); *Gren* 1467 × 84, *le Grene* 1477 (e.16) *Charyte* (*v.* **grēne**[2]); *Grundlees*, *Grundles* 1290 (*v.* **grund, lǣs**; *grund* is here poss. the ON word in its sense 'a plain; a flat grass-grown plot of ground'); *Haesike* 1290 (*v.* **(ge)hæg, sík**); *Haldeynisbroch* Hy 3, 13 (*v.* **brōc**; with the Anglo-Scand pers.n. *Halfdene* (ODan *Halfdan*) 'half Danish'); *Hall land* 1625 (*v.* **hall**); *Hanmul*, *Hanmulmore* 1467 × 84 (*v.* **mōr**[1]), *Hanmulwell* 1467 × 84 (*v.* **wella**) (*v.* **myln**; either with the OE pers.n. *Hana* or with **hān** 'a rock, a (boundary) stone'); *Hawsyke* 1467 × 84 (*v.* **haga**[1], **sík**; it is prob. that this f.n. is a variation of *Haesike*, *supra*); *Heytlund* Hy 3, *Heydlund* 13 (*v.* **hēhðu, lundr**); *Heynorstorth* 1290 (*v.* **storð**; poss. compounded with OE **hēan-ofre* '(at) the high ridge', *v.* **hēah**[1] **(hēan** wk.obl.), **ofer**[2], cf. Heanor, Db 469; but the second el. could rather be **ōra**[1]); *Hobyswonge* 1467 × 84 (*v.* **vangr**; presum. with the surn. *Hoby* of a family originally from the village of this name, 10 miles to the north-west, although this would be an early instance of such migration; a lost farmstead here also of this name is poss.); *Holegate* 1290, *Holgate flanke* 1467 × 84 (*v.* **flanke**, in the transferred sense 'the side of something'; earliest OED citation in this sense 1624, *v.* OED *s.v.* flank, 5), *Holegatehyll'* 1467 × 84 (*v.* **hyll**) (*v.* **hol**[2], **gata**); *Horspolgate* Hy 3, 1290, 13 (*v.* **hors, pōl**[1], **gata**); *Hougwod* 1290 (*v.* **haugr, wudu**); *Houme* 13, *Holme* 1467 × 84 (*v.* **holmr**); *Hunistonisholm* Hy 3, 1290 (*v.* **holmr**; either prefixed by 'Hūn's farmstead' (*v.* **tūn**) or by 'Hūn's boundary-stone' (*v.* **stān**), the pers.n. *Hūn* being OE; the spelling *Humberstonisholm* 13 appears in Nichols, but this is presum. his misreading of *Hunistonisholm*, a surn. derived from the village of Humberstone some 5 miles to the west being unlikely at this date); *the Lane end* 1708, 1708 (18) (*v.* **lane-ende**); *Langborowong'* 1467 × 84 (*v.* **lang**[1], **berg, vangr**); *Liteldale* Hy 3, 13, *Lituldal*, *Lyteldale*, *Lytuldal* 1467 × 84, *Litledale* 1625, 1708, *Little Dale* 1708 (18), 18, *Liteldalgate* 1467 × 84 (*v.* **gata**), *Lytuldale heyde* 1467 × 84 (*v.* **hēafod**) (*v.* **lȳtel, lítill, dalr**); *Litelhaye* Hy 3, 1290, 13, *Littelhaye* 1290, *Litilhae* Hy 3 bis, 13, *Lytulhawe* 1467 × 84, *Lytulhawforth*, *Lytullehawforthe* 1467 × 84 (*v.* **ford**) (*v.* **lȳtel, (ge)hæg, haga**[1] and note the comment on *Hawsyke*, *supra*); *Londesdale* 1467 × 84 (*v.* **dalr**; prob. with **lundr**); *Longedalelund* Hy 3, 13 (*v.* **lang**[1], **dalr, lundr**); *Lundesbroc* Hy 3, 1290 (freq), *Lundisbroc'* Hy 3 bis, *Lundesbrock* 13, *Lowndysbrok'*

1467 × 84 (*v.* **lundr, brōc**); *atte Medewe* 1327 SR (p) (*v.* **atte**), *of the Medowe* 1377 ib (p), *Mydo croft'* 1467 × 84 (*v.* **croft**), *the Meadowe close* 1625 (*v.* **mǣd (mǣdwe** obl.sg.)); *Middelholm* 1290 (*v.* **middel, holmr**); *the Middle field*, ~ *Myddle* ~ 1625; *the Mill* 1625, *Mill bushes* 1625 (*v.* **busc**), *the Mylnefelde* 1467 × 84, (*the*) *Mill field* 1625, 1708, 1708 (18), 18 (*v.* **feld**; one of the early great fields of the township), *Milnfurlong* 1467 × 84 (*v.* **furlang**), *Mylnehole* 1467 × 84, (*the*) *Mill hole* 1625, 1708, 1708 (18), 18 (*v.* **hol**[1]), *Milnehyll* 1467 × 84 (*v.* **hyll**), (*the*) *Mill Sick* 1708, 18 (*v.* **sík**), *Miln(e)wey* 1467 × 84, (*the*) *Mill way* 1625, 1708, 18 (*v.* **weg**) (*v.* **myln**; it appears that the village had both watermill and windmill, note *Milnehyll* and *Water mill*, *infra*); *Mowsholme* 1467 × 84 (*v.* **mūs, mús, holmr**); *Nether ende* 1625 (*v.* **neoðera, ende**); *the netherfield* 1625; *Nettilholm* 1290 (*v.* **netel(e), holmr**); *the new close* 1625, *New Close* 1708, 1708 (18); *Northe fielde* 1625 (*the*) *North field* 1625, 1708, 1708 (18), 18 (*v.* **feld**; one of the great fields of the township); *Northmedwe* Hy 3 bis, 1290 bis, l.13, *Northmedewe* 1290, 13, *Northmedue* 13, Edw 1, *Normedewe* 13, *North Meadow* 1625, 1708, 18 (*v.* **norð, mǣd (mǣdwe** obl.sg.)); *þe opon' woddes* 1467 × 84 (*v.* **þe, open, wudu**; an area of unenclosed woodland); *Orchardleyes* 1467 × 84, *Orchard Leas* 1708, ~ *Leys* 1708 (18), *Orchard Leas Close* 1708, 18, ~ *Leys* ~ 1708 (18), *Orchard leys hedge* 1625 (*v.* **hecg**) (*v.* **orceard, lǣs**); *the over hedge* 1625 (*v.* **uferra, hecg**); *Overtwart the Way* 1625 (*v.* **ofer-þwart, weg**; a furlong so called); *the Parsons yards end* 1625 (*v.* **persone, geard, ende**); *Peyslande* 1467 × 84, *Peaseland* 1625, *Peyslande flank'* 1467 × 84 (*v.* **flanke** and *Holgate flanke*, *supra*), *Peas(e)land Sick* 1708, 18, *Pease Land Sike* 1708 (18) (*v.* **sík**), *Peyslond' streme* 1467 × 84 (*v.* **strēam**), *Esterpeseland* 1290 (*v.* **ēasterra**) (*v.* **pise, land**); *Peytheweyt syke* 1467 × 84 (*v.* **pise, þveit, sík**); *Phiscur acur* 1467 × 84 (*v.* **æcer**; the first el. is a reflex of OE **fiscere** 'a fisherman', poss. influenced by its ON cognate **fiskari**, but perh. used here as the surn. *Fisher* (note that *fiscere* was used also in OE for 'the kingfisher')); *Priests sicke* 1625 (*v.* **prēost, sík**); *Priestwood Sick* 1708, 18, *Preistwood* ~ 1708 (18) (*v.* **sík** and Priest Hill *supra*); *Prior(s) slade* 1625, *Priers* ~ 1708, *Pryers* ~ 1708 (18) (*v.* **prior, slæd**; with reference to the Prior of Croxton (Kerrial); the house was a priory before becoming an abbey, *v. grangie abbatis de Croxton'*, *supra*); *Randulfwde* l.13, *Randulfwode* 13, *Randulswde* Edw 1 (*v.* **wudu**; either with the OFr pers.n. *Randulf* (< ON *Rannulfr*) or with its surn. reflex, eventually giving ModE *Randolph*); *Redmore* 1290, *Rydmore*, *Redmorestrem* 1467 × 84 (*v.* **strēam**) (*v.* **hrēod, mōr**[1]); *Reygn midow hylle* 1467 × 84 (*v.* **hyll**), *Reygn mydow syke* 1467 × 84 (*v.* **sík**) (*v.* **rein, mǣd (mǣdwe** obl.sg.)); *Riggeweyegate* 1290 (*v.* **hrycg, weg, gata**; part of the upland route from Allexton in the south-east of the Hundred to its moot-site in Barkby parish); *Rodeb'ge* Hy 3, *Rodeburge* 13 (*v.* **berg**; either with **rod**[1] or **rōd**[3]); *Roluiston broc* Hy 3, 1290, *Rolluiston broc* 13, (*riuulum de Rolston'* 1467 × 84, with MLat *rivulus* 'a stream') (*v.* **brōc**; Rolleston in Gartree Hundred adjoins to the south-west); *Rogewode* 1467 × 84 (*v.* **rūh**[1], **wudu**); *Rowwardis* 1467 × 84, *Raweshill* 1625, *Rowers hill* 1708, 1708 (18), 18, *Rovers* ~ 1708, *Rouers* ~ 1708 (18) (*v.* **hyll**) (*v.* **rūh**[1], **warth, ward**); *Ryeland* 1290, *rylandis* 1467 × 84 (*v.* **ryge, land**); *Sandpitt hill* 1625, 1708, 18 (*v.* **sand-pytt**); *Scoretoft*, *Schoretoft* 1290, *Scortoft* 13 (*v.* **scor(a), toft**); *Scrybestreme* 1467 × 84 (*v.* **scrybb, strēam**); *le Shetewong* 1290 (*v.* **vangr**; either with **scēat** or with **scite**); *Shirremilneholm* 1281 Banco (*v.* **myln, holmr**; the first el. is OE *scīr*, but in which sense is unclear; if in its use as 'an administrative district, a small district with independent privileges and jurisdiction' (*v.* **scīr**[1]), then such a district is unrecorded and not obvious here; since the mill with its holme is obviously a watermill, then *scīr* may be in this case a stream-name, i.e. 'the bright one', hence *v*. **scīr**[2]); *Skotgate* 1290, *Scotgate* 13 (*v*. **skot, gata**); *Sling meadow hill* 1625, *Sling Meadow Sick* 1708, 18 (*v*. **sík**) (*v*. **sling**); *Snapis* 1290 (*v*. **snape**); *the Sowthfelde* 1467 × 84 (*v*. **sūð, feld**; one of the early great fields of the township); *Sowtlondecroft'* 1467 × 84 (*v*. **sūð, land, croft**); *Spakysdale* 1467 × 84, *Speakdale* 1708, 1708 (18) (*v*. **dalr**), *Spake slade* 18 (*v*. **slæd**) (with the ON pers.n. *Spakr*); *Stainsgate* Hy 3, 13, *Staingate* 1290 (*v*. **steinn, gata**); *Star ende* 1625 (*v*. **star, ende**); *Stochil* 1290, *Stoksele* 1467 × 84, *Stokishilforth* 1290 (*v*. **ford**), *Stokselgate* 1467 × 84 (*v*. **gata**), *Stokselwey* 1467 × 84 (*v*. **weg**), *Stokselsyke* 1467 × 84 (*v*. **sík**) (*v*. **hyll**; prob. with **stocc** rather than with **stoc**); *the Strete* 1467 × 84, *Stretewong* Hy 3 bis, 13 (*v*. **vangr**) (*v*. **strǣt**; no doubt a Roman road running south from the ford at Melton Mowbray and perh. an earlier name for *Stainsgate, supra*); *Stretton gate* 1467 × 84 (*v*. **gata**; Stretton lies 5 miles to the south-west in Gartree Hundred); *Succewels* 1467 × 84 (*v*. **succa, wella**); *Swanildepol* Hy 3, *Swanilpol* 13 (*v*. **pōl**[1]; with the ON fem. pers.n. *Svanhildr*); *Swetesyke* 1467 × 84 bis, *Sweete sicke* 1625, *Sweet sick* 1708, 18 (*v*. **swēte, sík**); *thorinhil* Hy 3, *Thornhil* 1290 bis, *Thornil hill* (sic) 13 (*v*. **þorn, hyll**); *Thorscroppis* 1290 bis (*v*. **crop(p)**; either with the Anglo-Scand pers.n. *Þórr* (*Þōr*) or with the Scand pers.n. *Þórir*, *v*. SPNLY 295 and 307 *s.nn.*); *Tilton footway* 1708, 1708 (18), 18 (*v*. **fote-waye**), *Tilton hill* 1625, 1708, *Tilton way* 1708 (18) (Tilton adjoins to the north); *Tipperiscroft* 1290, *Tipperscroft* l.13, *Tippiscroft* 13 (*v*. **croft**), *Tipperscheld'* Edw 1, *Tippescheld* 13 (*v*. **sceld**) (with the occupational surn. *Tipper* 'a maker of and/or fitter of metal tips', prob. arrowheads, *v*. Reaney *s.n.*); *the Upper Close* 1625; *of the vale* 1377 SR (p) (*v*. **val** and Skeffington Vale *supra*); *le Wassingford* 1280 Misc, *Waschyngforth* 1467 × 84 (*v*. **waschyng, ford**; it is uncertain whether the ME vbl.sb. *waschyng* refers here to sheep-washing or to clothes laundering); *Water mill* 1625, *Water Mill Trofe* 1708, ~ ~ *Troffe* 1708 (18), ~ ~ *Trough* 18 (*v*. **trog**) (*v*. **water-mylne**); *Waturforoys* 1467 × 84 (*v*. **wæter, furh** and *the Waterfurrow(e)s* in Asfordby f.ns. (b)); *le Westfelde vocat' the Mylnefelde* 1467 × 84 (*v*. **west, feld** and *the Mylnefelde, supra*); *Westmor* 1290 (*v*. **west, mōr**[1]); *Wodefelde* 1467 × 84, *Woodfield* 1625, 1708, *the Wood feild* 1708 (18) (*v*. **wudu, feld**; one of the great fields); *Wodegate* 1290 bis, *Wodgate* 1467 × 84 (*v*. **gata**), *Wod(e)wey* 1467 × 84 (*v*. **weg**) (*v*. **wudu**); *Wronglondis* 1467 × 84, *Ranglandes* 1625, *Wranglands* 1708, 1708 (18) (*v*. **wrang, vrangr, land**); *Wyngargore* 1467 × 84 (*v*. **gāra**; with the OE pers.n. *Winegār*); *Wynterthornis* 1467 × 84 (*v*. **þorn**; either with **winter**[1], referring to thorn-scrub used only in the winter season's husbandry, or with the surn. *Winter*, a reflex of the OE pers.ns. *Winter/Wintra*); *Wyothebroche* Hy 3, *Wyotebroche* 1290, *Wyothebrocke* 13 (*v*. **wīðig, brōc**).

Syston

SYSTON

Sitestone 1086 DB
Sithestun' 1201 Cur, *Sitheston'* 1207 P, 1232 Fine *et passim* to 1277 Cl, 1282 Pat *et freq* to 1370 *Wyg*, 1374 *LCDeeds* (p) *et passim* to 1631, 1632 LML, *Sithestone* 1277 Hastings, *Sithiston(e)* 1205 RotNorm, 1277 Hastings, 1316 FA, 1251 Ch, *Sytheston'* 1220 MHW, 1247 Fees *et passim* to 1276 × 91 *RTemple*, 1297 Coram *et freq* to 1391 *Wyg* (p), 1392 Pat *et passim* to 1534 *RTemple*, 1561 LeicW, *Sythestone* 1231 RHug, 1540 Fine
Sithston 1535 VE, 1630 LML, *Seithston* 1580 LeicW
Sideston' 1204 ClR, 1205 P, 1257 Ch, *Sidestone* 1220 RHug, *Sydeston'* 1229 Cl, 1251 Fees, 1264 Cl
Sieston c.1130 LeicSurv, 1540 MinAccts, 1549 Pat, *Syiston* 1271 Ipm, *Syeston'* 1411 ELiW, 1411 PRep *et passim* to 1548 Ex-Rel, 1558 Ipm, *Seiston* 1549 Pat, 1576 LibCl, *Seyston* 1558 *Pat*
Siston 1329 Ipm, 1380 *LCDeeds* (p), 1614 LML, 1647, 1689 *MiscAccts*, *Syston* 1338, 1339 Pat *et passim* to 1536, 1546 AAS *et freq*
Sison 1601 *Terrier*, 1622 Burton, 1635 *Surv*, *Syson* 1635 *ib*

The first el. is an OE pers.n. showing early shortening, such as *Sigehǣð* or *Sigefrið*, compounded with **tūn** 'a farmstead, a village'. The 17th cent. spellings *Sison/Syson* have typical Leics. loss of *t* from the group *-ston* which occurs from the 16th cent. onwards. Three 13th cent. forms with *-stan* spellings are attributed to this township: *Sithestan* 1254 Val, 1290 OSut and *Sydestan* c.1291 Tax. These are all from ecclesiastical records and presum. reflect scribal confusion with spellings for the Lincs. Syston some 27 miles to the north-east in the same diocese, whose generic is OE *stān* 'a stone', *v.* DLPN 122 *s.n.*

ALBERT ST, named in honour of Albert of Saxe-Coburg-Gotha who married Queen Victoria in 1840 and became Prince Consort in 1857. Note the *Queen Victoria* in Inns and Taverns *infra*. ARCHDALE ST,

Archdale street 1925 Kelly. BARKBY LANE, 1778 *EnclA*; it is *Barkby road* 1877 White, 1925 Kelly, Barkby adjoining to the south-east. BATH ST, *Bath street* 1846, 1863, 1877 White, 1925 Kelly. BROAD ST, *Broad street* 1925 Kelly. BROOK SIDE, 1925 Kelly; it is *Brook Bank* 1877 White, *v.* **banke**, BROOK ST, *Brook street* 1846, 1863, 1877 White, 1925 Kelly, cf. *ye brooke lane* 1673 *Ct*, *Brook Lane* 1778 *EnclA*, *v.* **brōc**; with reference to Barkby Brook. CHAPEL ST, *Chapel street* 1846, 1863, 1877 White. CROSS ST, *v.* **cross**; once part of an early footpath running at an angle to the pattern of later town development. GOOD'S LANE, *Goodes lane* 1925 Kelly, cf. *Mary Goode* 1877 White, resident in Syston. THE GREEN, 1846, 1863, 1877 White, 1925 Kelly, *ye common greene* 1673 *Ct* (*v.* **commun**), *v.* **grēne**[2]. HIGH ST, *High street* 1846, 1863, 1877 White, 1925 Kelly; it is *the Town Street* 1778 *EnclA*, *v.* **tūn**. LEICESTER RD, *Leicester road* 1846, 1863, 1877 White; it is *Leicester Way* 1778 *EnclA*, the 18th cent. Borough of Leicester lying 5 miles to the south-west. THE LIMES. LODGE FM. MASSINGHAM, 1925 Kelly. MEADOW LANE, 1925 Kelly; leading to *the Great Meadow* 1778 *EnclA*. MELTON RD, *Melton road* 1846, 1863, 1877 White, Melton Mowbray lying some 9 miles to the north-east. MILLSTONE LANE, *v.* **milne-stone**, cf. Millstone Lane, Lei **1** 50. NORTH ST. PONTYLUE FM. ROUND HILL, 1835 O, 1925 Kelly; describing shape. ST PETER'S CHURCH, *the Parishe Churche* 17 *Terrier*, *the Church* 1709, 1709 (18) *ib*, *the Parish Church* 1778 *EnclA*, *Church (St Peter)* 1846, 1863 White, 1925 Kelly; it is earlier recorded as *ecclesie de Sytheston* 1220 MHW, *ecclesiam* ~ ~, *ecclesie de Sitheston* 1323, 1361, 1378 *Pat* and in the group *ecclesiarum de Buckmynster Seyston et Sancte Maria Leicestre* 1558 *ib*. Note also *the Church Yard* 1605, 1697 *Terrier et passim* to 1778 *EnclA*, *v.* **chirche-ȝeard**. ST PETER'S ST, *St Peter street* 1925 Kelly; named from St Peter's Church *supra*. SANDFORD RD. SCHOOL ST is *School lane* 1877 White. SOUTH END TERRACE, *v.* **ende**. SOUTHFIELD LODGE, 1925 Kelly (*v.* **loge**), *the South Field* 1778 *EnclA*, *v.* **sūð**, **feld**; one of the great fields of the township. STATION RD (local), *Station road* 1877 White; note *Syston Station* 1835 O at which *the Syston and Peterborough Railway* 1846 White commenced; it was opened to Melton Mowbray in 1846. SYSTON LODGE, cf. *Syston Lodge Farm* 1889 *Sale*, *v.* **loge**. SYSTON MILLS, *Sytheston milnes* 1596 *Rental*, *Sison miln* 1601 *Surv*, *Siston Mill(s)* 1647 ChAccts, 1666 *Surv*, 1689 ChAccts, *Syeston Mill* 1709 ib, *Siston Mill* 1730 ib, *Syston Mill(s)* 1751, 1772 ib *et passim* to 1835 O, *Syston Water Mill* 1778 *EnclA*, *Water Mill* 1863 White, (*molendini de Sytheston* 1276 × 91 *RTemple*, with MLat *molendinum* 'a mill'), *v.* **myln**, **water-mylne**. TENTERCROFT AVE, presum. preserving an early f.n., *v.* **tentour**, **croft**.

TURN ST, *Turn street* 1877 White, 1925 Kelly; it is *Turnagain lane* 1778 *EnclA*, 1846, 1863 White; no doubt a lane with a dead-end. UNIVERSITY FM, alluding to the University of Oxford. Of the living of the parish church with its nine acres of glebe, *the University of Oxford have the Impropriation and receive the Tithes* 1709 *Terrier*. THE VICARAGE, 1877 White, 1925 Kelly; it is *the Vicarage House* 1605, 1709, 1709 (18) *Terrier*, *the Vicaridge house* 17 *ib*, *v*. **vikerage**. WANLIP RD, *Wanlip road* 1877 White, 1925 Kelly, Wanlip adjoining to the west. WELLINGTON ST. WEST ST, *West street* 1925 Kelly.

INNS AND TAVERNS

BLACK MOOR'S HEAD (lost), *Black moor's Head* 1846 White. BLACK SWAN (lost), *The Black Swan* 1778 *EnclA*. BLUE BELL (lost), *Blue Bell* 1846, 1863, 1877 White, *Bell Inn* 1925 Kelly, 1927 *Sale*. BULL'S HEAD (lost), *Bull's Head* 1846, 1863, 1877 White. FOX AND HOUNDS, 1846, 1863, 1877 White. GATE is *The Gate Hangs Well* 1925 Kelly. HOPE AND ANCHOR, 1846, 1863 White, 1925 Kelly; beside the Grand Union Canal. MIDLAND RAILWAY is *Midland Counties Arms* 1846, 1863 White, *Midland Arms* 1877 ib; named with reference to the nearby *Midland Counties Railway* 1854 O, *Midland Railway* 1863, 1877 White. PEACOCK (lost), *Peacock* 1846 White. QUEEN VICTORIA, 1877 White, 1925 Kelly. WHITE SWAN (lost), *White Swan Inn* 1846, 1863 White, *White Swan* 1877 ib.

FIELD-NAMES

Undated forms in (a) are 1778 *EnclA*; those dated 1870 are *Sale*. Forms throughout dated 1605, 1658, 1674, 1697, 17, 1700, 1704, 1709 and 1709 (18) are *Terrier*.

(a) (Waste Ground called) The Banks (cf. *Broken Banks* 1697, 1700, 1704, 1709, 1709 (18), *v*. **banke**; prob. with **brocen**, but **braken** is poss.); Barkby Brook (*the Brook(e)* 1674, 1709, 1709 (18), *v*. **brōc**), Barkby Holt 1870 (*v*. **holt**) (Barkby adjoins to the south-east); Barkby Wharf 1835 O (*v*. **hwearf**; on *Leicester Canal* 1835 ib (now Grand Union Canal) but in Syston parish); Bare Pool Cl (*v*. **bær**, **pōl**[1]); Bow Bridge (*v*. **boga**); Breach Cls (*v*. **brēc**); Brook Cl (*v*. Barkby Brook *supra*); Butchers Cross Cl (*v*. **cross**; with the surn. *Butcher*); Charles's Cls (with the surn. *Charles*); Church Lane (*v*. St Peter's Church *supra*); Cramp Lane 1846, 1863 (prob. with the surn. *Cramp*, but **cramb** is poss.); Crow Holm Cl (*v*. **crāwe**, **holmr**); the Far Part (*v*. **feor**, **part**); Flatt End (*the Flat end* 1600 Nichols, *the Flattern* (sic) 1605 ib, *v*. **flat**,

ende); the Fore Mdw (*v*. **fore**); Fox Covert 1870 (*v*. **fox, cover(t)**); Franks's Cl (with the surn. *Franks*); Goose Nook, ~ ~ Lane (*v*. **gōs, nōk**); Gorse Covert 1870 (*v*. **gorst, cover(t)**); Holt Cl 1870 (*v*. Barkby Holt *supra*); Humberston Hook (*Humberston Hooke* 1658, *v*. **hōc**; with the surn. *Humberston* of a family originally from Humberstone, 3½ miles to the south); I(s)lemoor Cls (*v*. **igil, igli** 'a leech'; originally prob. with **mere**[1] 'a pool', later replaced by **mōr**[1], **mór**, cf. Ilemoor in Sileby f.ns. (a)); Langer Leys (*v*. **lang**[1], **gāra, leys**, cf. Langar, Nt 227); the Leasures (*v*. **lǣs** (**lǣswe** gen.sg., dat.sg.)); Leicester Way Cl; Littl(e)ing Cl (*v*. **lȳtel, lítill, eng**); the Long Cl; Long West Leys (*v*. **leys**); the Middle Fd (1709, 1709 (18), *the Middle Feild* 1697, 1700, 1704, *v*. **middel, feld**; one of the great fields of the township); Mill Holm Cl (*v*. **myln, holmr**); the Great ~, the Little Moor, the Red Moor (*v*. **hrēod**) (*v*. **mōr**[1]); (the) New Bridge; the North Fd (prob. the name of one of the early great fields); Northings Bridge, Northings Cls (*v*. **norð, eng**); the Old Way (either with **ald** or **wald**; note the Woult *infra*); Over Ridge Cl (*v*. **uferra, hrycg**); Parr's Cl (with the surn. *Parr*); Pippin Thorn Lane (*v*. **þorn**; with the surn. *Pippin*, a reflex of the OFr pers.n. *Pipin/Pepin*, cf. *Radulfus Pipin* 1086 DB, who held land in Goadby Marwood, 13 miles to the north-east in Framland Hundred and *Reginaldus Peppin* 1205 Cur, also of Leics.); the Pit Bridge (*v*. **pytt**); Plough Cl 1870 (*v*. **plōg**); Rough Leys Cl(s) (*v*. **rūh**[1], **leys**); Round Hill Cl 1826 *Pochin* (*v*. Round Hill *supra*); Swithorn ~, Swythorn Cl (either with **sviðinn** or with the compound **sviða, þorn**); Syson's Cl (with a 17th cent. form of the village name, but one which may be a surn. developed from the p.n.); Syston Bridge 1846, 1863, 1877 White, Syston Windmill 1877 ib (*v*. **wind-mylne**); Thief Lane Cl (either with **þefa** 'brushwood' or with **þēof** 'a thief'; note *Thevissti* in nearby Rearsby, of which this lane may be a continuation); Thurney Cl (*v*. **þyrne, -ig**[3]); Tithe Pieces 1777 Nichols (*v*. **tēoða, pece**); Tookeys Garden (*v*. **gardin**; a close in the possession of *John Tookey* 1778); Town end Cl(s) (cf. *Siston Townes end* 1673 *Ct*, *v*. **tūn, ende**); Turnpike Road (*v*. **turnepike**); Water Furrows Cls (*v*. **wæter, furh** and *the Waterfurrow(e)s* in Asfordby f.ns. (b)); Water Holm or Mill Holm Cl (*v*. **wæter, holmr** and Mill Holm Cl *supra*); Well Wong Cl (*v*. **wella, vangr**); Wheat holme, Wheatholm Cls (*v*. **hwǣte, holmr**); Windmill Cl(s) (*v*. Syston Windmill *supra*); Wool leys Cl (*v*. **wald, leys**); the Woult, the Little Woult, the Woult Fd (*v*. **wald**).

(b) *the Cow Pasture* 1674, 1709, 1709 (18) (*v*. **pasture**); *the Homestall* 1605, 1709, 1709 (18) (*v*. **hām-stall**; belonging to *the Vicarage house*); *the Homestall of William Flecher* 1605 (*v*. **hām-stall**); *Leicester Field* 1697, 1709, 1709 (18), ~ *Feild* 1700, 1704 (*v*. **feld**; one of the great fields, that towards Leicester and known later as the South Fd, *v*. Southfield Lodge *supra*); *the Old Mill Furlong* 1674 (*v*. **ald, myln, furlang**); *Slash* 1697, 1700, 1704, 1709 (*v*. **slash** 'a long and deep cut', here poss. transferred to a topographical feature; but note also dial. *slashy* 'miry' and, surviving in American English, *slash* 'a piece of wet or swampy ground overgrown with bushes', *v*. OED *s.v*. sb. 3); *Somer Leys* 1697, 1709 (18), ~ *Lays* 1709 (*v*. **sumor, leys**; pastures that would be either flooded or very muddy for much of the year and therefore of use limited to summer).

Thrussington

THRUSSINGTON

Tvrstanestone 1086 DB, *Turstanestona* c.1130 LeicSurv, *Turstaneston(e)* 1202 Ass (p), 1232 RHug, *Turstaniston'* 1175 P

Tursteineston' 1175 ChancR, l.Hy 2 Berkeley, 1202 Ass (p), 1206 Cur, *Tursteinestun* Ric 1 BM, *Tursteinestuna* c.1200 Dane, *Turstenestona* 1316 Cl

Tursteinton c.1200 Hastings (p), e.13 Berkeley (p) (freq), c.1240 ib (p), *Tursteintona* e.13 ib (p), *Tursteinetun* e.13 ib (p)

Turstantone 1224 RHug

Thursteinest' e.13 (1449) *WoCart* (p), *Thursteineston* John Berkeley (p), *Thursteinistun* c.1240 ib (p)

Thursteinton c.1240 Berkeley (p), *Thurstainton* 1239 Cur, 1247 Abbr

Thurstaneston(e) 1220 MHW, 1224, 1232 RHug, 1233 Fees, 1242 Cur

Thurstanton' 1209 × 35 RHug, 1236 Fees, 1239 RGros *et freq* to 1314 Hastings, 1327 Fine *et passim* to 1539 MinAccts, 1553 Pat, *Thurstinton'* 1242 Fees, 1294 Pat, 1299 Ipm, *Thurstynton* 1347 Pat, 1350 Ipm *et passim* to 1369 GildR, 1379 Ass

Thorstanston 1316 Pat

Thorstanton' 1282 *Rut* (p), *Þorstanton'* 1282 (e.15), l.13 (e.15) *BelCartB*

Thurstington 1319 Banco, 1325 Ipm *et passim* to 1342 GilDR (p), 1346 BM, *Thurstyngton* 1327 Fine, 1345 GildR (p) *et passim* to 1361 *LCDeeds* (p), 1428 FA

Thrustyncton' 1367 *LCDeeds* (p)

Thursyngton' 1360 Coram, 1362 Ipm *et passim* to 1492 *RTemple*, 1506 Ipm, *Thurssyngton'* 1447 *RTemple*, *Thursington* 1461 ISLR, 1487 Pat *et passim* to 1518 Visit, 1585 LibCl

Thrussyngton 1382 Cl, 1385 *LCDeeds* (p) *et passim* to 1534 *RTemple*, 1540 MinAccts, *Thrussington* 1502 Ipm, 1518 Fine *et passim* to 1603 LibCl, 1610 Speed *et freq*, *Thrushin(g)ton* 1601, 1648 *Terrier*

'Þorstein's farmstead, village', *v.* **tūn**. The common ON pers.n. *Þorsteinn* (ODan *Thursten*, OSwed *Þorsten*) had its second el. anglicized as early as DB by the substitution of cognate OE *-stān* for ON *-steinn*. For detailed discussion of the pers.n. *Þorsteinn*, *v.* SPNLY 313–17.

BLUE BOAR (P.H.) (lost), *Blue Boar* 1846, 1863, 1877 White. BLUE LION (P.H.), *Blue Lion* 1846, 1863, 1877 White, 1925 Kelly. BRIDGELAND FM, cf. *First ~ ~, Bridgeland Close* 1837 *Valuation*, *v.* **brycg**, **land**. CHURCH LANE, *v.* Holy Trinity Church *infra*. GRANGE COTTAGE, *v.* Thrussington Grange *infra*. HOLY TRINITY CHURCH is *Thrushinton churche* 1601 *Terrier*, *Thrussington Church* 1625, 1648 *ib et passim* to 1745 *ib*, *Church (Holy Trinity)* 1846, 1863, 1877 White, 1925 Kelly; it is earlier recorded as *ecclesie de Thurstaneston* 1220 MHW, *ecclesiam de Thurstanton* 1239 RGros, *ecclesie de Thurstinton* 1294 *Pat*, *ecclesiarum de Thurstanton et Norton Diseny* 1309 *ib*. JERICHO LODGE, *v.* **loge**; a 'remoteness' name for this site at a distant edge of the parish from the township. LEOPARD'S HEAD (P.H.) (lost), *le Libbarts head* 1639 Ipm; *libbard* is an archaic variant of *leopard*. THE MANOR (local), *v.* **maner**. OLD GATE LANE is *the Old gate* 1625 *Terrier*, *Oldgate Road* 1789 (1815) *EnclA*, *Woldgate Lane* 1835 O, *v.* **wald**, **gata**. OX BROOK, 1835 O, *v.* **oxa**, **brōc**. RAGDALE WOOD lies on the parish boundary adjacent to Ragdale Hall *q.v.* STAR (P.H.), (*the*) *Star Inn* 1837 *Valuation*, 1877 White, *Star* 1846, 1863 White, 1925 Kelly. THRUSSINGTON GRANGE, 1800 Nichols, 1835 O, *v.* **grange**. THRUSSINGTON LODGE (x2), cf. *Johnsons lodge* 1837 *Valuation*, *Proudmans lodge* 1837 *ib*; with the surns. *Johnson* and *Proudman*, *v.* **loge**. THRUSSINGTON MILL, *Thrusington myll* 1601 *Terrier*, *Thrushington Mill* 1648 *ib*, *the Mill* 1674, 1690 *ib et passim* to 1703 *ib*, (*molendinum de Thurstaneston* 1242, with MLat *molendinum* 'a mill'), *v.* **myln**. THRUSSINGTON WOLDS GORSE (*v.* **gorst**) is *Manor Covert* 1806 Map (*v.* **cover(t)** and The Manor *supra*), *Thursington Woulds* 1806 ib, *Thrussington Wolds* 1815 ib, 1835 O, *v.* **wald**. THE VICARAGE, 1877 White, 1925 Kelly; earlier is *the Vicaridg(e) house* 1674, 1693, 1697, 1700, 1703 *Terrier*, *the Vicarage House* 1781 *ib*, 1789 (1815) *EnclA*, 1821 *Terrier*, *v.* **vikerage**.

FIELD-NAMES

Undated forms in (a) are 1837 *Valuation*; those dated 1789 (1815) are *EnclA*, while 1821 are *Terrier*. Forms throughout dated l.Hy 2 are Berkeley; 1601, 1625, 1674, 1679, 1690, 1693, 1697, 1700, 1703, 1708 and 1708 (18) are *Terrier*; 1609, 1615, 1637 and 1639 are Ipm.

(a) the Ten ~, the Fourteen Acres (*v.* **æcer**); Angel Cl (*Angell close* 1639; either with **angle** 'an angle, a corner' or with the common surn. *Angel(l)*, an original by-name from OFr *angele* 'messenger, angel', but this is otherwise unrecorded in the East Midlands); Ash Hill (*v.* **æsc**); Far ~ ~, Top ~ ~, Barn Cl; Barsby's Cl (cf. *Mark Barsby* 1700, 1703; the *Barsby* family came originally from the village of this name, 4 miles to the south-east); the Bastards 1837, Grange Bastards 1789 (1815) (*v.* Thrussington Grange *supra*), Bastard Cl (*v.* **bastard**; used of fields of abnormal shape or low yield); the Bellringing Cl (endowed land for the payment of bellringers in the parish church); Birds Cl, Birds Mdw (with the surn. *Bird*); Lower ~ ~, Black Roods, Black Roods or Hovel Cl (*v.* **blæc, rōd**[3] and Hovel Cl *infra*); Bogg Cl (*v.* **bog**); Far ~ ~, First ~ ~, Bottom Cl; First ~ ~, Second ~ ~, Brick-kiln Cl, Brick-kiln Mdw (*v.* **brike-kiln**); Brick-Yard (*v.* **brike-yard**); Brookhouses Cl (with the surn. *Brookhouse*); the Buntrill (*Bunter hill* 1601, 1679, 1697, 1700, *Bunters* ~ 1625, *Bunther* ~ 1674, *Bunterill hill* (sic) 1690, *Buntril Hill* (sic) 1708, cf. *Bunther Hill close* 1674, *v.* **hyll**; prob. with the surn. *Bunter*, from ME *bunter* 'a maker or user of sieves' (ME *bunte* 'a sieve'), but this is otherwise unrecorded in the East Midlands); Busk Wong (*v.* **buskr, vangr**); Chamberlains or Gravel Pitt Cl (with the surn. *Chamberlain*, *v.* Gravel Pitt Cl *infra*); the Little ~, the Great Chissel (*v.* **cisel**); Church headland (1700, 1708, *the church hadland* 1601, 1679, *Church headelande* 1625, *the Church-head-land* 1693, 1697, 1703, cf. *Church-hadland Furlong* 1690 (*v.* **furlang**), *v.* **hēafod-land** and Holy Trinity Church *supra*); Coal Pitt Cl 1837, Coal Pit Leys 1789 (1815), 1821, Top ~ ~ ~ ~, Coal Pit Leys Cl 1837 (*v.* **leys**) (*v.* **col-pytt**; a place where charcoal was made); Dent's Cl, Dent's Orchard (with the surn. *Dent*); Dob Headland (1693, 1697, 1700, 1703, 1708, *dolbe hadland* 1601, *dob headlande* 1625, *Dobb hadland* 1674, *Dobhadland* 1679, 1690, *v.* **hēafod-land**; the first word is either the surn. *Dobb* (from a pet-form of Robert) or from an early spelling of the surn. *Dalby* (cf. *Willielmus Dolbe* 1327 SR of Leics.) of a family in origin from either Great Dalby, Little Dalby or Old Dalby, all villages within a 6 miles radius of Thrussington); Doubledays Cl (with the surn. *Doubleday*, cf. *Willielmus Dubilday* 14 AD of Leics.); Lower ~ ~, Upper ~ ~, Far Cl, Far Mdw (*v.* **feor**); Ferneley's Cl, Ferneley's Old Gate Cl (*v.* Old Gate Lane *supra*) (cf. *John Ferneley* 1837); First Cl (cf. Second Cl *infra*); Bottom Fosse Cl (beside the Roman road Fosse Way); Fowl Sick (*fould sicke* 1601, *Foulesicke* 1625, *Full sicke* 1674, *Foulsicke* 1690, *Foul-seek* 1693, 1697, 1700, 1703, *Foulseck* 1700 bis, *Foul Sick* 1708, 1708 (18), cf. *Foul-Seek lays* 1703 (*v.* **leys**), *v.* **fūl, sík**); Fox's Lane 1789 (1815) (with the surn. *Fox*); Field ~, Hall ~, Top Garden (*v.* **feld, hall, gardin**); Gossy Cl (*v.* **gorstig**); Gravel Pitt Cl (*v.* **gravel, pytt** and Chamberlains *supra*); Graves' First ~, Graves' Second ~, Graves' Third Cl, Graves' Third Top Cl, Graves' Fourth Top Cl, Graves' Holme (*v.* **holmr**), Graves' Mdw, Graves' Orchard (with the surn. *Graves*); Great Mdw 1789 (1815), 1837 (*the great meadowe* 1625); Half Moon Cl (an enclosure of crescentic shape); Harp(s) Cl 1789 (1815), 1837 ((*a place called*) *the Harpes* 1601, 1625, *the Harps* 1693, 1697, 1700, 1703, *Harp(e)s close* 1674, 1679, 1690, 1708, *v.* **hearpe**; used of triangular pieces of land); Hebbs Cl (with the surn. *Hebb*, in origin a short form of the pers.n. *Hebert* (from Herbert); Hens and Chickens (poss. alludes to the birdsfoot trefoil (*Lotus corniculatus*), *v.* Field 71); Hoby Fd 1789 (1815) (*the Field towards Hoby* 1674, 1679, 1693, 1694, *the Field next Hoby* 1690, *v.* **feld**; one of the great fields of the township, also called *ye East field towards Hoby* 1700, *v. the Easte feild* in f.ns. (b)), Hoby Gate 1789 (1815) (*v.* **gata**), First Hoby Road Cl 1837 (cf.

Hoby-way 1697) (Hoby adjoins to the north-east); Hollings Cl (with the surn. *Hollings*); the Holmes 1789 (1815), Holme 1837 (*the Holmes* 1615, *v.* **holmr**); the Home Allotment 1821 (*v.* **allotment**), Home Cl, the Home Farm 1837 (*v.* **home**); the Bottom ~, the Top ~, Homestead (*v.* **hām-stede**); Honey Pot (a name which may be complimentary, referring to good land or derogatory, alluding to sticky soil); Blacks ~ ~ (with the surn. *Black*), Far ~ ~, Second ~ ~, Third ~ ~, House Cl, the House Wong (*v.* **vangr**); Hovel Cl, Hovel Mdw (*v.* **hovel**); Jordan's Cl, Jordan's Middle ~, Jordan's Top Cl, Jordan's Thorns (*v.* **þorn**) (with the surn. *Jordan*; from the name of the Holy Land's River Jordan, originally used as a pers.n. by returning crusaders who brought home its water for the baptism of their children); Lammas Cl (*v.* **lammas**); Launsdale (poss. with **launde** or **lundr** with **dalr**, but earlier forms are needed); the Little Mdw 1789 (1815); First ~ ~, Second ~ ~, Long Cl, Long Mdw; Loughborough Way Cl 1789 (1815) (*Loughborough Waye* 1625, ~ *Way* 1693, 1697, 1700, 1703; Loughborough lies 8 miles to the north-west); Loughbro' Hill Cl, Loughbro' Wheat Cl (cf. *Loughborough lande* 1625, *Loughborow land* 1674, 1690, *land belonging to Loughborough Bridges* 1700, 1703, *Mark Barsby's Loughborough lays* 1703 (*v.* **leys** and Barsby's Cl *supra*); all lands endowed for the maintenance of the bridges across R. Soar immediately north of Loughborough); (the) Manor Piece (*v.* **pece** and The Manor *supra*); Far ~, First ~, Second ~, Third Manslain (earlier forms are needed; the site of a fatality is poss., but so is the compound **(ge)mǣnnes** 'common land' with **leyne** 'a tract of arable land'); Marl Pitt, ~ ~ Cl (cf. *Marlpitt furlong* 1674, 1679, *Marlpit* ~ 1700, 1703 (*v.* **furlang**), *v.* **marle-pytt**); Marson's Lane 1789 (1815) (with the surn. *Marson* of a family which may well originally have come from Potters Marston (spellings in *Marson* from the early 17th cent.), 15 miles to the south-west in Sparkenhoe Hundred); Middle Cl; Middle Fd 1789 (1815) (1693, 1697, 1700, 1703, 1708, *the mydle feilde* 1601, *the Midle feild* 1625, *the Midle Field* 1674, 1679, 1690, *v.* **middel**, **feld**; one of the great fields of the township); Far ~ ~, First Mill Furlong ((*the*) *Mill Furlong* 1679, 1690, *v.* **furlang**), the Mill Holme 1789 (1815) (*v.* **holmr**) (*v.* **myln**); Miry Wong, ~ ~ Spinney (*v.* **spinney**) (*v.* **myry**, **vangr**); Moor Brook (1708 (18), *Morebrook* 1601, 1697, 1700, 1703, *Moore Brook* 1625, 1690, *Moar Brook* 1708, *v.* **mōr**[1], **brōc**); Morley's Mdw (with the surn. *Morley*); Muck Pitt (*v.* **muk**, **pytt**); Navigation Piece (*v.* **pece**; beside a canalized reach of R. Wreake); New Cl 1789 (1815); Nineteen Lands (*v.* **land**; a close consisting of 19 selions or 'lands' of a former great field); First ~ ~ ~, Second ~ ~ ~, Third ~ ~ ~, Top Old Gate Cl (*v.* Old Gate Lane *supra*); the Orchard; Otterdale, ~ Mdw (*Otterdale* 1601, 1625 *et passim* to 1703, *v.* **oter**, **dalr**); Outwards & Homewards, ~ ~ ~ Mdw (presum. closes adjacent to the township); Oxback brook Cl (this form appears to be compounded with both Scand **bekkr** and OE **brōc**, *v.* Ox Brook *supra*); Oxen holes (*v.* **oxa**; ostensibly with **hol**[1], but this late form may disguise **dāl**, cf. *le Oxdoles* in Wymeswold f.ns. (b)); Pale Cl (1609, *Peale close* 1637, *v.* **pale**); Pettifors Cl (with the surn. *Pettifor*, *v.* Reaney *s.n.*); Randalls Paddock (*v.* **paddock**; with the surn. *Randall*, earlier *Randel*, a diminutive of *Rand* (from Randolph)); Rang Back (*v.* **wrang**, **vrangr**; prob. with **bekkr**, cf. Oxback brook *supra*); Ratcliffe Fd 1789 (1815) (1708, 1708 (18), *the field toward(s) Ratcliff* (*super Wreak*) 1674, 1679, 1693, 1697, *the Field Next Ratcliff* 1690; one of the great fields, *v.* **feld** and *the Weste feilde* in f.ns. (b)); Far ~ ~, First ~ ~, Second ~ ~, Morley's ~ ~ (with the surn. *Morley*); Sand Fd ((*the*) *Sand Field* 1700, 1703, 1708, *the Sand*(*s*) 1693, 1697, 1700, *v.* **sand**); Sand Pitt Cl (*v.* **sand-pytt**); Sandy Leys 1837, ~ ~ Furlong 1789 (1815) (*v.* **furlang**) (*v.* **sandig, leys**); Seagrave Road Cl (Seagrave adjoins to the north-west); Second Cl (cf. First Cl *supra*); Seed Cl, Bottom ~ ~, Top Seeded Cl (*v.* **sǣd**; often used in f.ns. of closes with sown grass); First ~ ~, Second Sheep cote (*Sheep Coat* 1708, 1708 (18), *v.* **scēp-cot**); Shobries Cl (sic) (prob. with the surn. *Shoby* of a family originally from the village of this name, 4 miles to the north-east; otherwise with a much reduced **scofl-brǣdu**); First ~ ~, Second Sibson's Cl (with the surn. *Sibson* of a family originally from the village of this name, 21 miles to the south-west in Sparkenhoe Hundred); Slade Leys (*v.* **slæd, leys**); Slither Wong (*v.* **slidor, vangr**); Spinney Cl (*v.* **spinney**); Long Stripes, ~ ~ Mdw (*v.* **strīp**); Sun Hill, ~ ~ Cl (*sunne hill* 1625, *Sun Hill* 1674, 1679 *et passim* to 1708 (18), cf. *Sunhill furlong* 1700, 1703 (*v.* **furlang**), *v.* **sunne**; alluding to ground which caught the best of the sun); Bottom ~, Top Thackholms (*Thackhoome* 1674, *Thackholme* 1679, *Thackum* 1708, 1708 (18), cf. *Thack(h)am close* 1700, 1703, *Thack(h)am corner* 1625, 1697, 1700, 1703 (*v.* **corner**), *Thackham hedge* 1625, *Thackholme* ~ 1690 (*v.* **hecg**), *v.* **þæc, þak, hamm, holmr**; this may be an original OE **þæc-hamm* which has been Scandinavianized); Thorny Cl (*v.* **þornig**); the Top Cl, Far ~ ~, First ~ ~, Second ~ ~, Top Cl, Blacks ~ ~, Hollings Top Cl (with the surns. *Black* and *Hollings*); Top field farm; Town end Cl (*the Townes ende* 1601, *v.* **tūn, ende**); the Town Street 1789 (1815) (*v.* **tūn, strǣt**); Tween Stiles (*v.* **betwēonan, stīg**; a furlong thus called); Water Cl 1789 (1815), 1837 (1637, *v.* **wæter**); the Lower ~, the Upper Woulds 1789 (1815), the Hut Wolds (*v.* **hut**), the Long Wolds, Wolds Cl, the Wolds Mdw 1837 (*ye Woulds* 1703, *v.* **wald**); Wood against Mill; First ~, Second Woodgate (*Woodgate* 1625, 1693, 1697, 1700, 1703, *Woodgate way* 1674 (*v.* **weg**), cf. *Woodgate furlong* 1690 (*v.* **furlang**), *Woodgate heads* 1693, 1697, 1700, 1703 (*v.* **hēafod**), *v.* **wudu, gata**); Woollertons Cl (with the surn. *Woollerton*; the family prob. originally came from Wollaton, 16 miles to the north-east in Notts.); Wraryback Furlong 1789 (1815) (*v.* **bekkr, furlang**; perh. with **wōrig** 'winding').

(b) *Back Lane* 1742 *Deed* (*v.* **back**); *Mark Barsby's lays* 1700 (*v.* **leys** and Barsby's Cl *supra*); *Bessons* ~ 1674, *Beesons close* 1679, *Bessons* ~ 1674, *Beesons hadland* 1679 (*v.* **hēafod-land**) (with the surn. *Beeson*, *v.* Reaney *s.n.*); *the brinkes* 1601, *the Brinckes* 1625, (*ye*) *Brinks* 1693, 1697, 1708, *brinkes furlong* 1674, (*the*) *Brink(s) furlong* 1679, 1690, 1700 (*v.* **furlang**), *the brincke holes* 1625 (*v.* **hol**[1]) (*v.* **brink**); *the Broken lands* 1625 (*v.* **brocen, land**); *Brokesbys land* 1625 (*v.* **land**; although Brooksby adjoins to the east, a surn. derived from it may be present here); *Burrowseek* 1700, 1703 (*v.* **berg, sík** and *Litlborough sicke*, *infra*); (*near*) *Castldines gate* 1690 (*v.* **geat**; with the surn. *Castledine*); *the Easte feild* 1625, *ye East field towards Hoby* 1700, (*the*) *East Field* 1703, 1708, 1708 (18) (*v.* **ēast, feld**; one of the great fields, *v.* Hoby Fd *supra*); *Freemans land* 1615 (with the surn. *Freeman*); *the hall* 1601, *the Hall furres* 1625, *ye Hall-furs* 1693, 1697, *Hall Furrs* 1708 (with **furh** or **fyrs**, but ambiguous; *v.* *Wales furlong*, *infra*), *Upper hall furr pingle* 1690, *the Hall fur pingle* 1693, 1700, 1703, *ye Hall-furr-pingle* 1697 (*v.* **feor, pingel**) (*v.* **hall**); *Hoby new close hedge* 1601 (*v.* **hecg**), *Hoby way pingle* 1690, 1693, 1697 (*v.* **weg, pingel**) (Hoby adjoins to the north-east); *Lambecotehou* l.Hy 2 (*v.* **lamb, cot, haugr**); *Litleborough sicke* 1625, *Littlborrow sick* 1674, *Littleborough sicke* 1679, *Littleburrow sicke* 1690, *Littleborough seek* 1693, *Littleburrow* ~ 1697, 1700, 1703 (*v.* **lȳtel, lítill, berg, sík**); *ye Meadow* (*by ye Mill*) 1693, 1697, 1700, 1703; *the Mill furlong* 1708 (*v.* **furlang**), *le Mill house* 1609 (*v.* **myln**); *Millners close* 1690, *Milners* ~ 1700 (with the surn. *Milner*, cf. *Thomas Milner* 1601 *Terrier* of adjacent Rearsby);

(*ye*) *New-field-hedg*(*e*) 1693, 1697, 1700, 1703, *the Newefield hedg* 1700 (*v*. **hecg**), *New-field-side* 1693, 1697 (*v*. **sīde**); *Newman furlong* 1674, 1679 (*v*. **furlang**; with the surn. *Newman*); *the north feilde* 1601 (*v*. **norð**, **feld**; one of the early great fields, replaced by *the Easte feild*, *supra*); *Oxdale* 1553 Pat, 1615 Ipm, 1619 Fine (*v*. **oxa**, **dalr**); *Ratcliffe waye* 1601, *Ratcliff way* 1690, *Ratcliff high way* 1674, 1679, *ye High Way* (*to Radcliff*) 1693, 1697, 1703 (*v*. **weg**, **hēah-weg**), *Ratcliffe gate* 1625 (*v*. **gata**), *Ratcliffe* ~, *Ratclyffe meere* 1601, *Ratcliffe meare* 1625, *Ratcliff mear* 1674, 1679, *Radcliff Mear* 1693, *Ratcliff*(*e*) *Meer* 1708 (*v*. **(ge)mǣre**) (Ratcliffe on the Wreake adjoins to the south-west); *Rodeley leyes* 1601, *Rothley leas* 1625, *Rhodely-lays* 1700, 1703, *Rhodl*(*e*)*y Leys* 1708 (*v*. **leys**; poss. with the surn. *Rodeley/Rothley* of a family originally from the village of Rothley, 5 miles to the south-west in West Goscote Hundred; spellings of the place-name with *Rode*- occur principally from the later 13th cent. through to the 18th cent., *v*. Reaney *s.n.* Rothley); *Round close* 1609, 1637 (*v*. **round**; in later f.ns. describing fields not necessarily circular, but equilateral rather than oblong or irregular polygons); (*ye*) *Short Hedge* 1690, 1693, 1697, ~ ~ *Hedges* 1700, 1703, 1708 (*v*. **hecg**); *the South feilde* 1601 (*v*. **sūð**, **feld**; one of the earlier great fields, replaced by *the West feilde*, *infra*); *Tho. Storers close* 1674; *Swallow dale* 1601, 1625, 1693, 1697 (*v*. **swalg**, **dalr**); *Thre Howes* l.Hy 2, *Threhowes* 13 Nichols, *the Thrawes* 1601 (*v*. **þrēo**, **haugr**); *Thrussington Meer* 1690 (*v*. **(ge)mǣre**); *ye towne hadland* 1674 (*v*. **tūn**, **hēafod-land**); *the Vicars Springes* 1625, *Vicars Springs* 1674, 1679, 1690, (*the*) *Vicar's Springs* 1693, 1697, 1700, 1703, *Vicar Springs* 1708, 1708 (18) (*v*. **vikere**, **spring**[1]; described in the terriers as a piece of grass ground); *Wales furlong* 1674, 1679, *Whales fur* 1700, *Wales Furr* (sic) 1708 (*v*. **furlang**; prob. with the surn. *Wale* or *Wales*, cf. *Wale's Yard*, Lei **1** 175); *the Weste feilde* 1625, (*ye*) *West field* (*towards Radcliff super Wreak*) 1700, 1703, 1708, 1708 (18) (*v*. **west**, **feld** and Ratcliffe Fd *supra*; one of the great fields of the township from c.1625 onwards).

Thurmaston

THURMASTON

Tvmodestone 1086 DB bis, *Turmodestona* 1156 (1318) Ch, 1190 × 1204 France, *Turmodeston'* 1175 ChancR (p), 1176 P (p), 1192 ib *et passim* to a.1250 (1404), c.1250 (1404) *Laz* (p), *Turmodesthon*(*a*) c.1200 *Sloane*, *Tur*(*e*)*modestun'* 1199 Cur (p), 1201 P, *Turmodiston'* 1175 P (p), c.1250 (1404) *Laz* (p)

Tormodestuna 1107 Dugd, *Tormodestonæ* s.a. 1081 (c.1131) Ord

Turmundeston' 1210 P (p), *Thurmondestone* c.1250 (1404) *Laz* (p), *Thurmondiston'* c.1250 (1404) *ib* (p)

Thormodeston' c.1130 LeicSurv

Thurmodeston' c.1130 LeicSurv, 1191 P, 1215 RegAnt *et freq* to 1270 Cur, c.1275 (1404) *Laz* (p) *et passim* to 1318, 1340 Ch, *Thurmodestun* 1215 RegAnt, *Thurmodiston'* c.1250 *LCDeeds* (p), p.1250 (1404) *Laz* (p), 1284 *RTemple* (p)

Thurmeston' 1203 RegAnt, 1280 Misc (p), 1283 *MiD et freq* to 1380 *LCDeeds* (p), 1392 *MiD*, 1394 ELiW, *Thurmistona* c.1250 (1404) *Laz* (p)

Thormeston 1289, 1399 Pat, *Thormaston* 1304, 1420, 1553 ib

Thurmenstone 1314 *GarCart*, *Thurmanston* 1340 Ch

Thurmaston 1326 Ipm, 1340 Ch, 1346 *LCDeeds et passim* to 1464 *Wyg*, 1486 Ipm *et freq*

Thrumaston 1537 MinAccts, 1606, 1721 LML, *Thromaston* 1546 AAS, 1554 Ex-Rel, 1595 *Rental et passim* to 1612 *MiscAccts*, 1679 LML

Thromerson 1609 *Merton*

'Þormóðr's village', *v.* **tūn**. The common ON pers.n. *Þormóðr* is found also in Norway, Iceland, Sweden, Denmark and Normandy, *v.* SPNLY 311. In a few 13th and 14th cent. spellings for Thurmaston, the pers.n. of the specific has been attracted to the ON pers.n. *Þormundr*. Note metathesis of the specific in some 16th, 17th and 18th cent. forms and the typical 17th cent. Leics. loss of *t* in the group *-ston*.

A large pagan Anglo-Saxon cremation cemetery has been discovered here, no doubt that of an important early settlement at this site.

BLACK HORSE (P.H.) (lost), *Black Horse* 1846, 1863, 1877 White, 1925 Kelly. BOAT (P.H.) (lost), *Boat* 1846, 1863 White, *Boat Inn* 1877 ib. BROOK ST, *Brook street* 1925 Kelly. CHURCH ST is *Kyrkgate* 1320 × 40 (1467 × 84) *LTD*, v. **kirkja**, **gata**. COLBY LODGE (2½"), COLBY RD, *Colby* 1320 × 40 (1467 × 84) *LTD* bis, *Colbie* 1650 *Terrier*, *Coleby* 1672 *ib*, 'Koli's farmstead', v. **bȳ**, with the ON pers.n. *Koli*; its site was prob. that of the lodge. GARDEN ST, cf. *Garden Close* 1861 *Plan*, v. **gardin**. THE GRANGE, 1925 Kelly, v. **grange**. HARROW (P.H.), *Harrow* 1846, 1863 White, *Harrow Inn* 1877 ib, 1925 Kelly. HIGHWAY RD, cf. *Highway Farm* 1814 *Deed* and *Syston Highway Close* 1784, 1786, 1796, 1812 *ib*, v. **hēah-weg**; Syston adjoins to the north. HUMBERSTONE LANE, 1925 Kelly; early Humberstone lay 2½ miles to the south-east. MANOR RD, cf. *Manor house* 1877 White, 1925 Kelly, v. **maner**. METHODIST CHAPEL. THE MILL, MILL LANE, cf. *the Mill Close* 1660 *Terrier*, 1707, 1726, 1773, 1826 *Deed*, v. **myln**. PLOUGH (P.H.) (lost), *Plough* 1846, 1863 White, *Old Plough* 1877 ib, *Plough Inn* 1877 ib. RED HILL LANE, *Redhill* 1655, 1660 *Terrier*, *Big* ~ ~, *Little Red Hill* 1870 *Sale*, v. **rēad**, **hyll**; alluding to the colour of the soil. ST JOHN THE EVANGELIST'S CHURCH, a 13th cent. structure in ruins, with only the west gable surviving. Presum. *capellam de Thurmodeston* 1220 MHW (with MLat *capella* 'a chapel') refers to this building, as do *the Chappel* (*of Thurmaston in the parish of Belgrave*) 1708 (18) *Terrier* and *the Chappel(l) house* 1707, 1726, 1733, 1826 *Deed*, v. **chapel(e)**. ST MICHAEL'S CHURCH, *Church (St Michael)* 1863, 1877 White, 1925 Kelly; in origin a 14th cent. edifice, refashioned in 1848. STONEHAM HO., v. *Stonholm* in f.ns. (b). STONELEIGH. THURMASTON HALL, 1925 Kelly; cf. *Old Hall* 1925 ib, *atte Hall* 1320 × 40 (1467 × 84) *LTD* (p), *At(t)hehall* 1477 (e.16) *Charyte* (p) (v. **atte**), v. **hall**. THURMASTON LODGE, 1835 O, *The Lodge* 1863 White, v. **loge**. UNICORN ST, cf. *Unicorn* 1846, 1863 White, *Unicorn Inn* 1925 Kelly, *Unicorn and Star* 1877 White. THE VICARAGE, 1925 Kelly, v. **vikerage**. WHITE HART (P.H.), *White Hart* 1846, 1863, 1877 White, 1925 Kelly.

No early forms have been noted for the following Thurmaston street-names: ALEXANDER ST, BARKBY THORPE RD, BEACON AVE, BEECHWOOD AVE, BRADGATE AVE, CAMPBELL AVE, CANAL ST, CHARNWOOD AVE, CHECKLAND RD, CHURCH HILL RD, DALE DRIVE, DOROTHY AVE, DOVEDALE RD, FERNDALE RD, FESTIVAL AVE, FOREST AVE, LONSDALE RD, MAPLE RD, MARGARET CL, MELTON RD, NEWARK RD, NORTHDOWN DRIVE, PARKDALE RD, ROSENDEN AVE, RUTLAND DRIVE, SANDIACRE DRIVE, SILVERDALE DRIVE, SOUTHDOWN DRIVE,

SPENCER AVE, WESTDOWN DRIVE, WHARF ST, WINSTER DRIVE.

FIELD-NAMES

Forms in (a) dated 1762 are Nichols; 1763 are *EnclA*; 1784, 1796, 1812, 1814, 1823, 1826 and 1896 are *Deed*; 1821 are *Terrier*; 1861 are *Plan*; 1870 are *Sale*. Forms throughout dated 1320 × 40 (1467 × 84) and 1467 × 84 are *LTD*; 1477 (e.16) are *Charyte*; 1635 are *Merton*; c.1635, 1655, 1658, 1660 and 1700 are *Terrier*; 1707, 1726, 1733 and 1786 are *Deed*.

(a) First ~ ~, Second Six Acres, the Ten Acres 1861 (*v.* **æcer**); Far ~ ~, Barn Cl 1870; Bastard Ley Cl 1784, 1786, 1812 (*John Burbages Bastard Ley Close* 1655, (*the*) *Basterd Lay close* 1660), the Back of Bastard Ley Cl 1784, 1786, 1796, 1812 (*v.* **back**) (*v.* **bastard, ley**); the Belle Holme 1763 (*Belleholm* 1320 × 40 (1467 × 84), *Belholm*(*e*), *Belleholme* 1477 (e.16), *Beleholme* 1502 *MiscAccts*, *Belholme* 1523 LAS, *Bellholme* 1609 Ipm, *v.* **belle, holmr**); Bull Piece 1763 (1725 DKR, *v.* **bula, pece**); Calves Water 1763 (*v.* **calf, wæter**); the Chappell Cl 1726, 1733, Chappel ~ 1826 (*v.* **chapel**(**e**) and St John the Evangelist's Church *supra*); Church Fd 1726, 1733, 1763, 1826 (*Kyrkefelde* 1320 × 40 (1467 × 84), *Kyrkfeld* 1467 × 84 (*v.* **kirkja**), *the Church feild* 1665, 1660, *v.* **feld**; one of the great fields of the township), Church Leys 1763 (*v.* **leys**) (*v.* St John the Evangelist's Church and St Michael's Church *supra*); the Clays 1861 (*v.* **clǣg**); Claycliff Fd 1763 (*Cleyclif*, *Cleyclyf* 1467 × 84, *Long Claycliffe* 1655, *Middle Cleaclift* 1660, *Short Cleacliffe* 1655, ~ *Cleaclift* 1660, *v.* **clǣg, clif**); Cooper's Leys (*v.* **leys**; with the surn. *Cooper*); East Mdw 1763, 1861 (*le Estmedow* 1320 × 40 (1467 × 87), *the East Meadow* 1658, cf. *Estmedugate*, *Estmedwgate* 1320 × 40 (1467 × 84) (*v.* **gata**) (*v.* **ēast, mǣd** (**mǣdwe** obl.sg.)); Far Cl 1870, Far Fd 1861, the Far Pasture 1812 (*v.* **pasture**; part of Thurmaston Pasture *infra*); Fox Holes 1861 (*Foxholes* 1320 × 40 (1467 × 84), *v.* **fox-hol**); Freeborough 1786, 1796, 1812 (*v.* **frēo**; poss. with **bearu** rather than with **berg**, since the notion of freedom from charge suggests woodland where wood could be gathered without penalty); Gutridge's Farm 1846 (with the surn. *Gutridge*, *v.* Reaney *s.n.*); Hamilton Brook 1763 (Hamilton lies in Barkby Thorpe parish which adjoins to the south-east); High Mere 1896 (*v.* **(ge)mǣre**); Hill Cl 1784, 1786, 1796, 1812 (*the Hill Close* 1660); Hincks' Cl, Hincks' Mdw 1861 (with the surn. *Hincks*; either a reflex of the OE pers.n. *Hynca* or of the OE by-name *Hinca* 'the limper' (cf. *hellehinca* 'hell-limper, devil' as in *Andreas* 1173)); Home Cl 1861 (*v.* **home**); Hovel Cl 1861 (*v.* **hovel**); Humberstone Gate Cl 1861 (*v.* **gata** and Humberstone Lane *supra*); Kate's Parlour 1861 (*v.* **parlur**; either with the pers.n. *Kate*, a pet-form of Katherine, or with the surn. *Kate*, a reflex of the ON pers.n. *Káti* (ODan *Kati*), an original by-name meaning 'merry, glad'); Lammas Cls 1763, 1784, 1796, 1812 (*v.* **lammas**); the Langworth Mdw 1762 (*Langwath* 1467 × 84, 1477 (e.16) bis, *Langworth* 1655, 1660, *Langwith Mead* 1635, ~ *meadow* c.1635 (*v.* **mǣd** (**mǣdwe** obl.sg.), cf. *Langworth lane end* 1655, 1660 (*v.* **lane-ende**), *v.* **lang**[1], **vað**); Leicester Fd 1763, Leicester Road Cl 1861 (at the south-western edge of the parish); Long Cl 1861; Long Nook Mdw 1812 (*v.* **nōk**); North-West ~ ~, South-East ~ ~, Middle Fd 1763; Mill Fd 1763; the

Moor, Moor Cls 1763 (*v.* **mōr**[1]); the Nest Mdw 1762 (*Nesse* 1320 × 40 (1467 × 84) bis, 1477 (e.16), *Nest* 1660, cf. *Nessedik'* 1467 × 84 (*v.* **dík**), *Neast hooke* 1635 (*v.* **hōc**), *v.* **næss, nes**); Nether Mdw 1763; the North End 1784, 1786 *et passim* to 1821 (1700, 1707, 1726, 1733, *North Thorpe otherwise called the North End of Thurmeston* 1700, *v.* **ende**, cf. the South End *infra* and *v.* *Northorpe* in f.ns. (b)); Oak Coppice 1870 (*v.* **copis**); Penfold 1763 (*le Pynfold* 1320 × 40 (1467 × 84), 1467 × 84), Pinfold Furlong 1826 (1655, 1660, 1726, 1733, *v.* **furlang**) (*v.* **pynd-fald**); Redhill Cl 1784, 1796, 1812 (*v.* Red Hill Lane *supra*); Sand Cls 1784, 1786, East ~ ~, West Sand Cl 1812, Sand Fd 1763, Sand Field Cl 1861 (*v.* **sand**); the South End 1812, 1823 (*v.* **ende**; cf. the North End *supra*); Souther Dole Mdw 1784, 1786, 1796, Southward Dole 1784, 1786, 1796, ~ ~ Mdw 1812 (*v.* **southward**) (*Souterdole* 1320 × 40 (1467 × 84), *Sowterdolys* 1467 × 84 bis, *Sowterdoles* 1655, *v.* **sūðer, dāl**); the Southward Pasture 1812 (*v.* **southward, pasture**; part of Thurmaston Pasture *infra*); Spinney Cl 1870 (*v.* **spinney**); *the Swifts Pasture* 1812 (*v.* **pasture**; most likely with the surn. *Swift* rather than with the bird **swift**; part of Thurmaston Pasture *infra*); Tenter Leys 1763 (*v.* **tentour, leys**); Thurmaston Mdw 1784, 1786, 1796 (*Thromaston meadowe* 1546 AAS, *v.* **mǣd (mǣdwe** obl.sg.)); Thurmaston Pasture 1784, 1786, 1812, the Pasture 1763, Top Pasture 1812 (*v.* **pasture**); Townsend Cl 1763 (*v.* **tūn, ende**); (the) Windmill Cl 1784, 1786, 1796, 1812 (*the Winde Mill* 1660, *v.* **wind-mylne**); the Wygmore Sets 1861 (*v.* **(ge)set**; poss. with the common f.n. *Wigmore* (*v.* **wigga, mōr**[1]) where *wigga* may be interpreted as 'that which moves', the compound perh. a term descriptive of marshy land, *v.* Brk **3** 916).

(b) *Abouethedike*, *Abouethedyk'* 1320 × 40 (1467 × 84) (*v.* **aboven, þe, dík**; a furlong so called); *Abouethekirke* 1320 × 40 (1467 × 84) (*v.* **aboven, þe, kirkja**; a furlong thus called); *Ankewong'* 1320 × 40 (1467 × 84) (*v.* **vangr**; poss. with the surn. *Anke*, from a short form of ON pers.ns. in *Arn-* such as *Arngeirr*, *Arngrímr*); *Annotesbuttes* 1320 × 40 (1467 × 84) (*v.* **butte**; the ME fem. pers.n. *Annot* (*Ann-ot*), a diminutive of *Ann*, a pet-form of *Annes* (Agnes), gave rise to the surn. *Annot* by 1327, *v.* Reaney *s.n.* Annott); *Appeltrestubbe* 1320 × 40 (1467 × 84) (*v.* **æppel-trēow, stubb**); *Atteston* 1320 × 40 (1467 × 84) (*v.* **atte, stān**; a furlong beside a boundary marker or other noteworthy stone); (*the closes called*) *the back sides* 1660 (*v.* **bak-side**); *Balihauedlond'* 1320 × 40 (1467 × 84) (*v.* **hēafod-land**; either with the ME surn. *Baly*, a reflex of **baillif** 'a bailiff' or with the sb. itself); *le Balk* 1320 × 40 (1467 × 84) (*v.* **balca**); *Banerodys* 1467 × 84 (*v.* **bēan, rōd**[3]); *Banland* 1320 × 40 (1467 × 84) (*v.* **bēan, land**); *Bark(e)by furlong* 1655, 1660 (*v.* **furlang**), *Barkbygate* 1320 × 40 (1467 × 84), *Barkeby gate* 1655 (*v.* **gata**), *Barkeby way* 1655 (*v.* **weg**) (Barkby adjoins to the east); *Batelston'*, *Batilston'* 1320 × 40 (1467 × 84) (this may represent a late farmstead with **tūn** and the ME pers.n. *Batel* in the possessive case (cf. *Batelistwaite*, YW **7** 302) or even this pers.n. with **stān** 'a stone' as a boundary marker; but note the possibility of **bataille** 'battle' used of a legal conflict, again with **stān**, recording some sort of boundary dispute); *Benethebroke(s)* 1320 × 40 (1467 × 84) (*v.* **beneoðan, þe, brōc**; a furlong thus called); *Blakberd fyrrys* 1467 × 84, *Blackbeard Furs* 1660 (*v.* **fyrs**; with the ME surn. *Blakeberd* (> ModE *Blackbird*), from OE *blæc* and *beard* 'black beard'); *Blodhow* bis, *Blodhowfeld* (*v.* **feld**), *Blodhowgate* bis (*v.* **gata**), all 1320 × 40 (1467 × 84) (*v.* **blōd, haugr**; the implications are uncertain, but colour may poss. be referred to (cf. Red Hill *supra* of which this may be an earlier name)); *Boroland* 1467 × 84 (*v.* **land**; more spellings are needed to identify the first el., but **burgh** 'a burrow' seems likelier than **burh**);

le Brademares 1320 × 40 (1467 × 84) (*v.* **brād**, **mareis**); *Brakenrodis* 1320 × 40 (1467 × 84) (*v.* **braken**; with **rod**[1] or **rōd**[3]); *Brakrodis* bis, *Brakrodys*, *Brakrod'* 1467 × 84 (poss. shortened forms of the previous f.n.; otherwise **bracu** with **rod**[1] or **rōd**[3]); *atte Breche*, *le Breche* 1320 × 40 (1467 × 84) (*v.* **atte**, **brēc**); *Brentclyf* 1320 × 40 (1467 × 84), *Brenclyf*, *Branclif*, *Branclyf* 1467 × 84, *Brentcliffelde als. Kyrkefelde* 1320 × 40 (1467 × 84) (*v.* **feld** and Church Fd *supra*) (*v.* **clif**; with **brant** or **brend**); *the Broad Headland* 1655 (*v.* **hēafod-land**); *Brodmedow* 1477 (e.16) (*v.* **brād**, **mǣd** (**mǣdwe** obl.sg.)); *Brodwong* 1467 × 84, 1477 (e.16), *Broadwong* 1655, 1660, ~ *end* 1655 (*v.* **ende**) (*v.* **brād**, **vangr**); *Brouneshull'*, *Browneshull'* 1320 × 40 (1467 × 84), *Brownsel*, *Brownsyl* 1467 × 84 (*v.* **hyll**; prob. with the ME surn. *Broun/Browne* (> ModE *Brown*); but a pers.n., either OE *Brūn* or ON *Brúnn*, or even a nickname from OFr *brun* 'brown' of hair or complexion is poss.); *atte Brigge*, *atte Brygge* 1320 × 40 (1467 × 84) (*v.* **atte**, **brycg**); *Burnecroft* 1320 × 40 (1467 × 84) (*v.* **croft**; with **bryne** or **bruni**); *Burnetcroft* 1655, 1660 (*v.* **croft**; this f.n. may belong with the previous name, but if not, then with the surn. *Burnet*, from OFr *burnete/brunette*, a diminutive of OFr *brun* 'brown', used of hair or complexion, cf. Burnett Hills in neighbouring Barkby f.ns. (a)); *Burstalforth* 1320 × 40 (1467 × 84) (*v.* **ford**; Birstall lies across R. Soar to the west); *the Cheescake* 1655 (*v.* **cheesecake**); *Clipstherne* 1477 (e.16) (*v.* **þyrne**, **þyrnir**; with a pers.n. such as *Clip*, the name of a 10th cent. moneyer (*v.* ZEN 55) or its source ON *Klyppr*; note also the otherwise unrecorded OE pers.n. *Cylp* (with metathesis) in Clipsham, Ru 80 and cf. *Clipthorngate/Clipthorntoftes* in Skeffington f.ns. (b)); *Clottiland'*, *Clottislandes* 1320 × 40 (1467 × 84) (*v.* **clot(t)**, **-ig**[3], **land**); *Cokkiscomb* 1320 × 40 (1467 × 84) (the earliest OED citation for a *cockscomb* is c.1400 (*cokkes comb*) and this concept may have been transferred to describe a topographical feature; otherwise *v.* **cocc**[2], **cumb**); *Colbyslade* 1320 × 40 (1467 × 84) (*v.* **slæd** and Colby Lodge *supra*); *Dalby medowe* 1320 × 40 (1467 × 87) (*v.* **mǣd** (**mǣdwe** obl.sg.); prob. with the surn. *Dalby* of a family originally from one of the nearby villages called Great~, Little ~, Old Dalby, cf. *Willielmus Dolbe* 1327 SR of Leics.); *the Dale close* 1655, 1660 (*v.* **dalr**); *le Dales* 1320 × 40 (1467 × 84), *þe Dalys*, *Dayls* 1467 × 84, *the Dales* 1655, *the Dales feild* 1655, 1660 (*v.* **feld**) (*v.* **deill**); *Edimar'* 1320 × 40 (1467 × 84) (the generic may be an abbreviated *-mares* (< **mareis**, cf. *le Brademares*, *Gudemares*, *Litelmares* and also *Longmaresende* in this parish) or **marr**[1]; more forms are needed to identify the first el., although **ēðe** 'wasteland' is poss.); *Ernotelandes*, *Ernotelondes* 1320 × 40 (1467 × 84) (*v.* **land**; either with the OFr pers.n. *Ernaut* or with its ME surn. reflex *Ernot*, *v.* Reaney *s.n.* Arnot); *Fishers House* 1660, 1707, 1726, 1733 (with the surn. *Fisher*); *in to Fosse* 1320 × 40 (1467 × 84) (*v.* **foss**[1]; an early reference to the Fosse Way); *Foxlandes* 1320 × 40 (1467 × 84) (*v.* **fox**, **land**); *Frysbek'* 1467 × 84 bis (*v.* **fyrs**, **bekkr**); *Fulforthe* 1320 × 40 (1467 × 84), *Fulford well hadland* 1660 (*v.* **wella**, **hēafod-land**) (*v.* **fūl**, **ford**); *Greynedegates* 1320 × 40 (1467 × 84) bis (*v.* **grein**, **hēafod**, **gata**); *Grimesacr'* 1320 × 40 (1467 × 84) (*v.* **æcer**; either with the ON pers.n. *Grímr* (ODan *Grīm*) or with its surn. reflex *Grime(s)*); *Griwong* 1320 × 40 (1467 × 84) (*v.* **vangr**; the first el. is prob. a surn. since *wong* is freq. compounded in this way, poss. ME *Grei* (< *grǣg* 'grey', i.e. 'grey-haired') > ModE *Gray*; but additional forms are needed); *the Grype* 1467 × 84 (*v.* **gryppe**); *Gudemares* 1320 × 40 (1467 × 84) (*v.* **gōd**[2], **mareis**; perh. to be contrasted with *Edimar'*, *supra*); *Halywell herne* 1467 × 84 (*v.* **hālig**, **wella**, **hyrne**); *Harberts close* 1655, 1660, *Harberts hadland* 1655 (*v.* **hēafod-land**) (cf. *Robert Harbert* 1655); *Harwell* 1467

× 84 ('boundary stream', *v.* **hār**[2], **wella**); (*a furlong called*) *Hell* 1655, 1660, *Hell hedge* 1655, 1660 (*v.* **hecg**) (poss. with **hell** used as a term of contempt for land difficult to cultivate; otherwise *v.* **hyll**); (*le*) *Holegrift*, *Holgrift'* 1320 × 40 (1467 × 84) (*v.* **hol**[1], **gryfja**); *Holm* 1477 (e.16) (*v.* **holmr**); *Honyaker* 1477 (e.16), *Hunnyacre* 1467 × 84 (*v.* **hunig, æcer**); *atte how* (p), *atte the how* (p) (sic) 1320 × 40 (1467 × 84) (*v.* **atte, haugr**); *Humberstonmere* 1320 × 40 (1467 × 84) (*v.* **(ge)mǣre**; Humberstone adjoins to the south-east); *Hundou* 1320 × 40 (1467 × 84) (*v.* **hund, hundr, haugr**); *Hungerfelde* 1320 × 40 (1467 × 84) (*v.* **hungor, feld**; one of the early great fields of the township); *Hunger hill* 1655 (*v.* **hungor**); *le Hurst* 1477 (e.16) (*v.* **hyrst**); *over Innhams* 1655, *ouer inhams* 1660 (*v.* **uferra, innām**); *Langlandes*, *Longlandes* 1320 × 40 (1467 × 84), *Langlandys*, *Longlandis*, *Longlandys* 1467 × 84, *Langelondes*, *le Longlondes* 1477 (e.16) (*v.* **lang**[1], **land**); *les Limstalles*, *Lymstallis* 1320 × 40 (1467 × 84), *Limestalende* 1477 (e.16) (*v.* **ende**) (*v.* **līm, stall**); *Litelmares* 1320 × 40 (1467 × 84), *Little Mear(e)s* 1726, 1733 (*v.* **lȳtel, mareis**); *Little Meadow* 1726; *Longholm(e)* (*v.* **lang**[1], **holmr**); *Longmaresende* 1320 × 40 (1467 × 84) (*v.* **lang**[1], **mareis, ende**); (*the*) *Longrake* 1320 × 40 (1467 × 84), 1477 (e.16) (*v.* **lang**[1], **rake**); *Luq'stoa* 1190 × 1204 France (*v.* **stōw**; either with the OE pers.n. *Luca* or with *Lucas*, the learned form of Luke; a lost site near Thurmaston); *Maynihows* 1320 × 40 (1467 × 84) (*v.* **manig, haugr**); *the meadow gate* 1655 (*v.* **gata**); *the Modyr and the Chylde* 1467 × 84 (*v.* **mōdor, cild**; in *Kyrkefelde* (*v.* Church Fd *supra*); it is uncertain to what kind of feature this name was attached, although the name of a messuage may be ruled out (*v.* Barrie Cox, *English Inn and Tavern Names* (1994), 8-12 and 80-84)); *le Mylnecroft* 1477 (e.16) (*v.* **myln, croft**); *the neather end feild* 1660 (*v.* **neoðera, ende**); *Northaye* 1477 (e.16) (*v.* **norð, (ge)hæg**); *le Northfeld'* 1320 × 40 (1467 × 84), *Northefelde* 1467 × 84 bis (*v.* **norð, feld**; one of the early great fields of the township); *Northorpe* 1298 Nichols, *Northorp* 1298 ib, 1320 × 40 (1467 × 84) *LTD*, 1349, 1351 *Wyg*, 1360 Nichols, 1477 (e.16) *Charyte, Northorp' in Thurmeston* 1477 (e.16), *Northorpfeld* 1477 (e.16) (*v.* **feld**; poss. to be identified with *le Northfeld'*, *supra*), *Northorpmore* 1477 (e.16) (*v.* **mōr**[1], **mór**) (*v.* **norð, þorp**); *ouerfurlong* 1477 (e.16) (*v.* **uferra, furlang**); *Ouergong* 1320 × 40 (1467 × 84) (*v.* **gang, gangr**; with **ofer**[3] or **uferra**); *the Pit Aker* 1660 (*v.* **pytt, æcer**); *the First ~, the Second ~, the Third ~, the Fifth Plowland* 1655, *the Secound ~, the Fourth ~, the Sixth plow Land* 1660 (*v.* **plōg(a)-land**); *Portfelde* 1320 × 40 (1467 × 84) (*v.* **port**[2], **feld**; one of the early great fields, this lying towards Leicester, cf. Leicester Fd *supra*); *le Portstrete* 1320 × 40 (1467 × 84) (*v.* **port**[2], **strǣt**; another name for the Fosse Way en route to Leicester); *Pynslade* 1467 × 84 (*v.* **pynd, slæd**); *Redeforth* 1320 × 40 (1467 × 84) (*v.* **hrēod, ford**); *le Rederodes* 1320 × 40 (1467 × 84) (*v.* **rōd**[3]; with **hrēod** or **rēad**); *Rishlandes* 1320 × 40 (1467 × 84) (*v.* **risc, land**); (*le*) *Ryefurlong* 1320 × 40 (1467 × 84), 1477 (e.16) (*v.* **ryge, furlang**); *Sadelback* 1320 × 40 (1467 × 84) (*v.* **sadol, bæc**; a ridge so called); *Saltergate* 1320 × 40 (1467 × 84) (freq) (*v.* **saltere, gata**); *Sampson Croft* 1320 × 40 (1467 × 84) (*v.* **croft**, either with the OFr pers.n. *Samson* or with its surn. reflex); *the Sand hadland* (*v.* **hēafod-land**), (*the*) *Sandhill* 1655, 1660 (*v.* **sand**); *Schirdiccotes* 1320 × 40 (1467 × 84) bis (*v.* **dīc, dík, cot**; with **scīr**[1] or **scīr**[2]); *le Schorthorngate* 1320 × 40 (1467 × 84) (*v.* **sc(e)ort, þorn, gata**); *Sewisthorpe* 1534 Nichols (*v.* **þorp**; with the OE pers.n. *Sǣwīg*); *Seyntmaremedow* 1477 (e.16) (*v.* **mǣd (mǣdwe** obl.sg.); no doubt the property of the Abbey of St Mary de Pratis, Leicester); *Sheffeild(s) close* 1655, 1660, *Sheffields Close* 1660, 1707, *Sheffeildes yardland*

1660, *Sheffields* ~ 1660, 1707 (*v.* **yardland**) (with the surn. *Sheffield*); *Smalmedow* 1320 × 40 (1467 × 84) (*v.* **smæl, mǣd (mǣdwe** obl.sg.)); *le Smalrodes* 1320 × 40 (1467 × 84) (*v.* **smæl, rōd**[3]); *Sowthfelde* 1467 × 84 bis (*v.* **sūð, feld**; one of the early great fields, presum. to be identified with *Portfelde, supra*); *Spencers meadow* 1660 (with the surn. *Spencer*); *Stanylandes, Stonylandes* 1320 × 40 (1467 × 84), *Stonylandis* 1467 × 84, *farther Stoney Lands* 1660, *hither Stony lands* 1655 (*v.* **farther, hider**) (*v.* **stānig, land**); *Stocfurlong', Stokfurlong'* 1320 × 40 (1467 × 84) (*v.* **furlang**; the following f.n. suggests locally **stocc** rather than **stoc** as the first el.); (*bosco de*) *Stokkyng* 1477 (e.16) (*v.* **stoccing**; with MLat *boscus* 'a wood'); *Stonholm* 1320 × 40 (1467 × 84) (*v.* **stān, holmr**; Stoneham *supra* may be a late reflex of this f.n); *Syreshamdikys, Syreshamdyk'* 1320 × 40 (1467 × 84), *Syreshamdikesheued* 1320 × 40 (1467 × 84) (*v.* **hēafod**) (*v.* **hamm, dík**; with the OE pers.n. *Sigehere*, cf. Syresham, Nth 59); *Syston meare* 1655, *Siston* ~ 1660 (*v.* **(ge)mǣre**; Syston adjoins to the north); *le Thirne* 1320 × 40 (1467 × 84) (*v.* **þyrne**); *Thirnhow, Thornhow* 1320 × 40 (1467 × 84) (*v.* **haugr**; with **þyrne, þyrnir, þorn**); *Thorpgate* 1320 × 40 (1467 × 84), *Thorpe hedge* 1655 (*v.* **hecg**; a parish boundary), *Thorpe highway* 1644 (*v.* **hēah-weg**), ~ *way* 1660 (Barkby Thorpe adjoins to the south-east); *Thromaston mylnes* 1595 *Rental*, 1612 ChAccts, *Thurmaston Mills* 1689, 1730 ib *et passim* to 1750 ib, (*molendinum de Thurmeston* 1477 (e.16), with MLat *molendinum* 'a mill') (*v.* **myln**); *Thurmodesthorpe* n.d. Nichols (*v.* **þorp**; with the ON pers.n. *Þormóðr* as in Thurmaston, presum. that of the same overlord); *le tithemedowe in Belleholm* 1320 × 40 (1467 × 84) (*v.* **tēoða, mǣd (mǣdwe** obl.sg.) and the Belle Holme *supra*); *Tounhull* 1320 × 40 (1467 × 84) (*v.* **tūn, hyll**); *Tutbury furze* 1655, *Tutberry Furs* 1660 (*v.* **fyrs**; Tutbury Priory held a grange at Wymondham, 16 miles to the north-east (*v.* Lei **2** xiii and 287), but its presence in Thurmaston is otherwise unrecorded); *the Two Lays Close* 1655, 1660 (*v.* **leys**; a close comprising two former units of grassland); *Under Onelip* 1660 (a furlong so called, Wanlip lying across R. Soar to the north-west); *the Watergalls* 1655, *the Water galles* 1660 (*v.* **wæter, galla**); *Henry Watts his hedge* 1655; *Wetlond* 1320 × 40 (1467 × 84) (*v.* **wēt, land**); *Wheatbutt layes*, ~ *Leys* 1660, *Wheat But Leys* 1707 (*v.* **butte, leys**; either with **hwǣte** or **wēt**); *Whitacres* 1660 (*v.* **hwīt, æcer**); *Whitlandes, Schort Whytelandes* 1320 × 40 (1467 × 84) (*v.* **sc(e)ort**) (*v.* **hwīt, land**); *le Whytemarlepitt, le Witemarlepit* 1320 × 40 (1467 × 84) (*v.* **hwīt, marle-pytt**); *Williamwro* 1320 × 40 (1467 × 84) (*v.* **vrá**; either with the OFr pers.n. *William* or its surn. reflex); *in le Willeus* (p), *in les Willowheis* (p), *in le Willows* (p), *in le Willughes* (p), *in le Wylowhes* (p), all 1320 × 40 (1467 × 84) (*v.* **wilig**); *Wodegate* 1320 × 40 (1467 × 84) (*v.* **wudu, gata**); *le Wong* 1320 × 40 (1467 × 84), 1477 (e.16), (*the*) *Wong* 1467 × 84, *the Wonges* 1660, *the Wong on top of the hill* 1655, *the hither Wong close* 1655 (*v.* **hider**), *the Wong feild* 1655 (*v.* **feld**) (*v.* **vangr**); *Wulfitewell, Wulfiotewell* 1320 × 40 (1467 × 84) (*v.* **wella**; with the OE pers.n. *Wulfgēat*); *Wythibusforlong'* 1320 × 40 (1467 × 84) (*v.* **wīðig, busc, furlang**); *Wyn(n)ywong'* 1320 × 40 (1467 × 84) (*v.* **whinny, vangr**).

Tilton

1. TILTON (~ ON THE HILL 1" O.S.)

Tillintone 1086 DB
Tiletone 1086 DB bis
Tilton(') c.1130 LeicSurv, 1163 P (p), 1166, 1167 ib *et freq*, (~ *Diggeby* 1242 Fees), *Tiltona* 1165, 1167 P *et passim* to l.13 (1404), 1298 (1404) *Laz*, *Tiltone* e.13 (1404) *ib*, 1209 × 35 RGros, 1236 GildR (p), e.14 (1404) *Laz*, *Tiltun* 1210 GildR, 1231 Ch, 1236 Fees, *Tylton(')* 1231, 1233 Cl, 1254 Val *et freq* to 1473 *CCR*, 1502 *MiscAccts et passim* to 1576 LEpis, 1604 SR, *Tyltone* 1301 Hastings (p), 1339 Pat
Tilton on the Hill 1688 LML, 1830 Moule

'Tila's farmstead, village', *v.* **tūn**. The masc. pers.n. *Tila* is OE. *Tillintone* of 1086 DB retains the gen.sg. of the specific as *-in-* (< *-an-*). *Robertus de Diggeby* held the manor in 1322, 1324 Cl.

BACK RD, *v.* **back**. DIGBY FM, cf. *Digby lane* 1641 *Surv*, *v.* **lane**, with the surn. *Digby*; the monuments of John Digby (d. 1269) and Sir Everard Digby (d.1509) are in the parish church. HYDE LODGE RD. LEICESTER RD is *Lecester way* 1641 *Surv*; Leicester lies 10 miles to the west. LODDINGTON RD, Loddington adjoining to the south-west. MAIN ST is *the Streete* 1601 *Terrier*, *the Towne Street* 1641 *Surv* (*v.* **tūn**), *v.* **strǣt**. MANOR HO., *the Mannour house* 1641 *Surv*, *Manor House* 1846, 1863 White, 1925 Kelly, *v.* **maner**. MAREFIELD LANE is *Marfield Road* 1807 *Surv*; Marefield adjoins to the north. MELTON RD, (*the*) *Melton Road* 1807 *Surv*, 1839 *EnclA*; Melton Mowbray lies 8 miles to the north. METHODIST CHAPEL, *the Methodist Chapel* 1839 *TA*. MILL HO., cf. *Tilton windmilne* 1586 *Plan*, *the Wind Mill* 1641 *Terrier*, *ye Windmill* 1647 *Rental*, *Tilton Mill* 1863 White, *v.* **wind-mylne**. OAKHAM RD, *the Oakham Road* 1839 *EnclA*; Oakham (Ru) lies 8 miles to the north-east. RED LODGE FM, RED LODGE RD, *Red lodge* 1925 Kelly, *v.* **loge**. ROBIN-A-TIPTOE FM, *Robin-a-Tiptoe farm* 1925 Kelly; it is *Wildbore's Lodge*

1824 O, *v.* **loge**; with the surn. *Wildbore* (originally a nickname 'wild-boar' from OE *bār*). ROBIN-A-TIPTOE HILL, *Robin a Tipto(e)* 1586 *Plan*, 1708 (18), 1709 *Terrier*, 1815 Nichols, *Robin a Tiptoes* 1641 *Surv*, 1799 Nichols, 1806 Map, 1824 O, 1839 *TA*, *Robin on Tiptoe* 1839 *ib*, *Tiptoe* 1968 *Surv*; with a Leics. name for *Robin Goodfellow*, 'the drudging goblin', who threshes corn and does domestic chores whilst the farmer and his household are asleep, hence *a-Tiptoe*, *on Tiptoe*. In the East Riding of Yorks., he is known as *Robin Roundcap*, *v.* E. M. Wright, *Rustic Speech and Folk-Lore* (Oxford 1913), 201 and B. Dickins, 'Yorkshire Hobs', *Transactions of the Yorkshire Dialect Society*, vii, 19-22. Whether this hill-name conceals an earlier *Tiplow* (*v.* Big Tiplow Mdw in f.ns. (a)) is uncertain. RODHILL FM, *Redehyl* 1399 *AllS*, *Redde hill* 1586 *Plan*, *Red(d) hill* 1609 *AllS*, *Red Hill* 1839 *TA*, *Rodhills* 1845 *ib*, *Rodhill* 1968 *Surv*, *v.* **rēad, hyll**. ROSE AND CROWN (P.H.), *Rose and Crown* 1839 *TA*, 1846, 1863, 1877 White, 1925 Kelly. ST PETER'S CHURCH, *the Church* 1641 *Surv*, 1708 (18), 1709 *Terrier*, *Church (St Peter)* 1846, 1863, 1877 White, 1925 Kelly; it is earlier recorded as *ecclesie de Tilton* 1220 MHW, 1238 RGros and in the groups *ecclesias de Hallstedde et Tylton* 1553 *Pat*, *ecclesiarum de Buckmynster Tilton Halsted et Sancta Maria Leicestre* 1558 *ib*. Note also *the Churchyard* 1697, 1708 (18), 1709 *Terrier*. SYKES SPINNEY, cf. *Thomas Sykes* 1839 *TA*, *James Sikes, farmer* 1846 White, *J. P. Sikes, major landowner* 1877 ib. TILTON GRANGE, 1863, 1877 White, 1925 Kelly, *v.* **grange**. TILTON WOOD, 1806 Map, 1824 O, 1839 *TA*; it is *(the) Great Wood* 1641 *Surv*, 1647 *Rental*, 1839 *TA*. TRYON SPINNEY, with the surn. *Tryon*; not a Leics. surn., but cf. the Tryon family resident in nearby Hambleton (Ru) since at least 17 *Conant*. THE VICARAGE, 1877 White, 1925 Kelly, cf. *the Vicarage House* 1606, 1674, 1697 *Terrier et passim* to 1709 *ib*, *the Vicaridge House* 1641 *Surv*, *v.* **vikerage**. WOOD FM, beside Tilton Wood *supra*.

FIELD-NAMES

Undated forms in (a) are 1968 *Surv*; those dated 1839 are *TA*. Forms throughout dated 1586 are *Plan*; 1606, 1703, 1708 (18) and 1709 are *Terrier*; 1632 are *Conant*; 1641 are *Surv*; 1644 are *Clay*; 1647 are *Rental*.

(a) Two Acre, Four Acres, Five Acre 1968, Six Acres, Six Acre Mdw 1839, Seven Acre 1968, Seven Acre Mdw 1839, Ten Acre Fd, Fourteen Acre, 14-Acre Fd, Eighteen Acre, 18-Acre Fd, Twenty Acre Mdw, 26-Acres 1968 (*v.* **æcer**); Allotment Fd (*v.* **allotment**); Arable Cl, Arable Six Acre (*v.* **æcer**) (*v.* **arable**); Bacon's Mdw (with the surn. *Bacon*); Banky Cl 1839 (*the Bank Close* 1641, *Banks closse* 1647, *v.* **banke, -ig**[3]); Barn Fd; First ~ ~, Second Barnes' Fd (with the surn. *Barnes*); Bells Cl 1839, Little ~ ~, Bell's Cl 1968 (poss. land originally endowed for the provision and maintenance of church bells and ropes or for payment of bellringers; otherwise with the surn. *Bell*, cf. Bells furlong in Halstead f.ns. (a)); the Big Fd; Black Hovel Fd, Black Shed Fd (poss. the same field, *v.* **hovel, shed**); Blunts Part 1839 (*v.* **part**) (cf. *Blunts Close* 1641; with the surn. *Blunt*); Bolsters Mdw 1839 (1647, *Boulsters Meadow* 1641; perh. with **bolstre** 'a padding, a cushion' transferred fancifully to a meadow with clumps of coarse grass; otherwise with the surn. *Bo(u)lster*, although this is not otherwise recorded as an East Midlands surn.); Bottom Mdw 1839, 1968; Far ~, First Brinks 1839 ((*the*) *Brinks* 1641, 1647, 1703, 1708 (18), 1709, *v.* **brink**); Brook Cl 1839, Brooky or Brook Mdw (*v.* **brōc, -ig**[3]); Bullifants Cl 1839 is Bullison's Cl (sic) 1968, Bullifants Mdw 1839 is Elephant's Cl (sic) 1968 (with the surn. *Bullivant* (from OFr *bon enfant* 'good child')); Bungalow Fd; Caravan Fd (alluding to a trailer home or a site for trailer homes); Centre Fd (also called Middle Fd); Church Cl (*v.* St Peter's Church *supra*); Clay Hole 1839 (*v.* **clǣg, hol**[1]); Cooks Yard 1839 (*v.* **geard**; with the surn. *Cook*); New ~ ~, Old Cottage Fd; Cow Cl 1839, 1968; Cowshed Fd; Croft 1839, The Croft 1925 Kelly (*v.* **croft**); the Dam 1839, Dambank 1839, 1968 (*v.* **banke**) (*v.* **damme**); Davids Cl 1839, David's ~ 1968 (with the surn. *David*, found in Leics. records as early as *Robertus David* 1276 RH; from Hebrew *David* 'a friend'); Donkey Fd (a close for the nurturing and protection of donkeys); Downhill Way 1968 is Town Hill Way 1839 (*v.* **tūn**); Elephant's Cl (*v.* Bullifants Cl *supra*); Nether ~, Over End 1839 (*v.* **neoðera, uferra, ende**); First Part 1839 (*v.* **part**); the Flat (*v.* **flat**); Flat Mdw 1839, 1968 (prob. with **flat** rather than with **flatr**); Footway Cl 1839, Footway Mdw 1839 is Footroad Mdw 1968 (*v.* **fote-waye, foot-road**); Fowl House Fd (*v.* **fowl-house**); Frisby's Cl, Frisby's Mdw 1839 (with the surn. *Frisby* of a family prob. originally from either Frisby (by Galby), 4 miles to the south-west or Frisby on the Wreake, 8 miles to the north-west); Gibbs Cl 1839 (with the surn. *Gibb(s)*, a reflex of the pers.n. *Gibb*, a pet-form of Gilbert); Gravel Hole Fd 1968, Gravel Pit, ~ ~ Cl 1839, Gravel Pit Fd 1968 (*v.* **gravel, hol**[1], **pytt**); Graveyard Cl (the site of the burial of cattle carcases after an outbreak of foot-and-mouth disease); Halfords Lands, Big ~, Little Halfords (with the surn. *Halford*); Half Yard Land, ~ ~ ~ Mdw, Freemans Half Yard Land 1839 (with the surn. *Freeman*) (*v.* **yardland**); Little Haugh Wood, ~ Haw ~ 1839 ((*the*) *Little Hall Wood*, *the little Halwoord Close* 1641, *Little Haw close* 1647; prob. with **haga**[1] rather than with **hall**); Hensons Yard 1839 (*v.* **geard**; with the surn. *Henson*); Bottom ~, Top Herberts (with the surn. *Herbert* in the possessive case); Hill Fd; Hill Sick, ~ ~ End 1839 (*v.* **ende**) (*v.* **sík**); Hollands Cl 1839 (with the surn. *Holland*); Big ~ ~, Home Cl 1839 (*the Home Close(s)* 1641, 1703), Home Fd, Home Field Paddock (*v.* **paddock**) (*v.* **home**); Horse Part 1839 (*v.* **part**), Horse Pastures (*v.* **pasture**); Hovel Cl, Hovel Yard 1839 (*v.* **geard**) (*v.* **hovel**); Great ~, Little Howback 1839, Hump Back (sic) 1968, Houback or Houbank Hill 1799, 1800 Nichols, Howbank Hill 1846, 1863, 1877 White, 1925 Kelly, (*Holebeck* 1586, *Holback* 1647, *Hobecks* 1703, *the Hobacks* 1708 (18), 1709, cf. *Holback Close* 1632, *Hobeck Meadowe* 1632, *Holbeck Meadow* 1641, *Hobeck Pasture* 1632, *Holbeck Pasture*, *Holbeck al' Robin a Tiptoes Pasture* 1641 (*v.* **pasture**), *v.* **hol**[2], **bekkr** and Robin-a-Tiptoe Hill *supra*); Intake 1839 (*v.* **inntak**); Jennys Cl 1839, Jennings Cl (sic) 1968, Jennys Mdw 1839 (prob. with the pers.n. *Jenny* (a pet-form of both Janet and Jennifer) in the possessive case;

the surn. *Jennis* is unrecorded in the East Midlands); Lane Mdw 1839 (*v.* **lane**); Leesons Cl 1839, 1968, Leesons Mdw 1839, Bottom Leeson's 1968 (with the surn. *Leeson*); Little Bit 1839, ~ Bits 1968 (*v.* **bit**); Little Mead 1839, ~ Meadow 1968 (*v.* **mǣd**); Little Pasture 1839 (*v.* **pasture**); Little Wood 1839; Long Mdw; Far ~, First or Near Lounds (*v.* **lundr**); Lowesby Mdw (Lowesby adjoins to the north-west); Lucerne Fd (lucerne (*Medicago sativa*) was introduced into Britain as a fodder crop in the late 14th cent.); Manions (the surn. *Mannion* in the possessive case, *v.* Reaney *s.n.*); Manor House Garden 1839 (*v.* **gardin** and Manor Ho. *supra*); Mantons over part 1839 (*v.* **uferra**, **part**; with the surn. *Manton* of a family poss. originally from the village of this name, 8 miles to the east in Ru); Marefield Hill (Marefield adjoins to the north); Middle Close East, ~ ~ West 1839 (*the Middle Close* 1632, 1641, 1647); Middle Fd; Middle Part 1839 (*v.* **part**); Mill Spot 1839 (*v.* **myln, spotte**); Mires (*v.* **mýrr**); the Mushroom Fd (a field where mushrooms abound); Nether Cl 1839; Nether Fd 1824 O; Nettle Hill 1839 (*v.* **netel(e)**); New Cl 1839 (1632, 1641 *et passim* to1709); (the) New Mdw 1839; No Mans Land (*v.* **nān mann**, **land**); No Name (a close thus called); the Nooks 1839 (*v.* **nōk**); Old Mdw 1839, 1968; Old Quarry, Old Ironstone Quarry Fd (*the Quarrey* 1586, *v.* **quarrere**); Old Wood 1839; Bottom ~ ~, Top 1000 yards; the Orchard 1839; Ortons Middle ~, Ortons Nether Part 1839 (*v.* **part**); the Osiery Beds, Osiery Beds Fd (*v.* **osiery, bedd**); the Paddock, Back Paddock (*v.* **back**), Everard's Paddock, Harrison's Paddock (with the surns. *Everard, Harrison*), Lambing Paddock (*v.* **lambing**), Smith's Paddock (with the surn. *Smith*) (*v.* **paddock**); Paradise (*v.* **paradise**); the Park (*v.* **park**); Great ~, Little Pasture 1839 (*v.* **pasture**); Pinfold Fd 1824 O, Pinfold 1968 (*v.* **pynd-fald**); Plough Cl, Plough Piece 1839 (*v.* **pece**) (*v.* **plōg**); Old Ploughed Cl 1839, (the) Old Ploughed Fd 1968; Pontons Mdw 1839, 1968 (with the surn. *Ponton*); Poor Cl (*v.* **pouer(e)**; a charitable endowment for the benefit of the parish poor); the Prairie (*v.* **prairie**); Pub Fd 1968 is Rose and Crown Croft 1839 (*v.* **croft** and Rose and Crown (P.H.) *supra*); Railway Cutting (land beside this railway feature); Resborrow, the Risborough 1839 (*boscus de Riseberwe* 1266 For, *boscum qui vocatur Riseberwe* 1269 ib (with MLat *boscus* 'a wood'), *Risebergh* 1297 Banco, *Rearesborow* 1647, *Ryseburrow Hill* 1497 *Farnham*, *Raisborough Close* 1632, *Resborrow Close* 1641, *Ryseburrow Hill close* 1644, *v.* **hrīs, hrís, berg**); Road Cl; Rolts Mdw 1839 (with the surn. *Rolt*, a reflex of the ON pers.n. *Hróaldr* (ODan *Roald*)); Nether ~ ~, Over Rough Mdw 1839 (*v.* **uferra**) (*v.* **rūh**[1]); Little ~ ~, Round Hill 1839 (*v.* **round**); the Seeds 1839, Herbert Seeds 1968 (with the surn. *Herbert*), Little Seeds 1839, 1968, Old Seeds 1968 (*v.* **sǣd**; in f.ns., often alluding to areas of sown grass); Bottom ~ ~, Top Sharps Cl 1839, Little ~, Sharps 1968 (with the surn. *Sharp*); Sheep layers 1839 (*v.* **lair**); Shepherds House 1839 (*v.* **scēp-hirde**); Shield's Fds (with the surn. *Shield*); Short Wood 1839 (1641, 1708 (18), 1709, *v.* **sc(e)ort**); Big ~, Little Slades (*v.* **slæd**); Slang (*v.* **slang**); Slip (*v.* **slipe**); Spring Cl (*v.* **spring**[1]); Stablefords (the surn. *Stableford* in the possessive case); Stallions Fd (*v.* **stallion**); Far ~, Steans, Steans Mdw 1839 (either with the surn. *Stean* or with **steinn**); Stone Pits (*v.* **stān-pytt**); Sykes Mdw 1839 (cf. Sykes Spinney *supra*); High Thorns 1839, ~ Thorn 1968, High Thorn Mdw 1839 (*East* ~, *North* ~, *West Hythorne* 1647, *v.* **hēah**[1], **þorn**); Tim's Fd (either with the pers.n. *Tim*, the pet-form of Timothy, or with the surn. *Timms*, a reflex of the OE pers.n. *Tima*); Big Tiplow Mdw 1839 (prob. with a garbled *Tiptoe*, *v.* Robin-a-Tiptoe Hill *supra*, but *Tiplow* may be the earlier hill-name, with **hlāw** and an OE pers.n., *Tippa* or *Tibba*); Top Mdw 1839, 1968; Top Spot 1839 (*v.* **spotte**); Town Cl 1839 ((*the*) *Towne Close* 1641, 1647, *v.* **tūn**); Townsend (*v.* **tūn, ende**); Triangle (a three-cornered close); Valley Fd (*v.* **valeie**); Big ~, Long Wadland 1839 (*Wadlands* 1641, *Wadland* 1708 (18), 1709, *v.* **wād, land**); Wash Pit Yard 1839 (*v.* **wæsce, pytt, geard**; the location of a sheep-dip); Websters Cl 1839 (with the surn. *Webster*); Whatborough Leys 1839 (*v.* **leys**; Whatborough adjoins to the north-east); Woodfield Cl, Bottom ~ ~, Top Woodfield Mdw, Nether Wood Fd 1839 (*v.* **wudu, feld**); Wood Mdw; Palmers ~ ~, Taylors Yard Land 1839 (*v.* **yardland**; with the surns. *Palmer* and *Taylor*).

(b) *Mr Abell Barkers grounds* 1641 (*v.* **grund**); *Bankett Close* 1632 (*v.* **banke, -ett(e)**; this may belong with Banky Cl in f.ns (a)); *Beeby's Yard* 1708 (18), 1709 (*v.* **geard**; with the surn. *Beeby* of a family originally from the village of this name, 5 miles to the north-west); *Willm. Bennitts house* 1647; *Bilsdon Common* 1641 (*v.* **commun**; Billesdon adjoins to the south-west); *atte Brigge* 1327 SR (p), *atte Brigg* 1332 ib (p), *atte Brigh* 1332 ib (p), (*ad pontem* 1377 ib (p); with MLat *pons* (*pontem* acc.sg.) 'a bridge'), *v.* **atte, brycg**); *Burtons homestead* 1708 (18), 1709, *Butlers homestead* 1708 (18) (*v.* **hām-stede**; with the surns. *Burton* and *Butler*); *Clarks yard* 1709 (*v.* **geard**; with the surn. *Clark*); *the Corne Close* 1641 (*v.* **corn**[1]); *the Cottiers Close* 1641 (*v.* **cottere**); (*ad*) *crucem de Tilton* 1227 ClR (p) (with MLat *crux* (*crucem* acc.sg.) 'a cross'; an early standing cross survives near the parish church); *Dauis land* 1647 (*v.* **land**; with the surn. *Davis*); *the East Close* 1641; *Fancoates Close* 1641 (with the surn. *Fancott/Fancourt*); *the Farm*(*e*) *Yard* 1708 (18), 1709 (*v.* **farmyard**; the earliest OED citation for this is dated 1748); (*ad*) *fontem de Tilton* 1225 GildR (p) (with MLat *fons* (*fontem* acc.sg.) 'a well, a spring'); *Great Meadowe* 1632; *Great Wood close* 1632, *the great Wood Meadow Close* 1641 (*v.* Tilton Wood *supra*); *Little Heiguh al's Little Acre* 1708 (18), 1709 (*v.* **æcer**); *the Homestall* 1606 (*v.* **hām-stall**; i.e. of *the Vicarage House*); *the Hooke* 1641, *the hookes* 1647 (*v.* **hōc**); *othe Hull* 1332 SR (p) (*v.* **þe, hyll**); *John James his House* 1641; *Daniell Keys Close* 1641; *the Malt mill* 1641 (*v.* **malte-mylne**); *the Meadow Close* 1641, *the Meadows* 1708 (18); *the North Close* 1641; *the Old Grounds* 1703 (*v.* **ald, grund**); *the Pasture Close* 1641, 1647, *The Pasture Meadow* 1641 (*v.* **pasture**); *pilartonwong'* Hy 3 *Crox* (*v.* **pīl-āte (pīl-ātan** nom.pl.) 'pill-oats', **vangr**); *Russells Close* 1641 (with the surn. *Russell*); *Slaters Close* 1641, 1708 (18), 1709 (with the surn. *Slater*); *Spencers homestead* 1708 (18) (*v.* **hām-stede**; with the surn. *Spencer*); *Swines-poole* 1647, *Swines-poole Meadow* 1641 (*v.* **pōl**[1]; prob. with **swīn**[1] rather than with **swin**[2], cf. Hog Pool in Halstead f.ns. (a)); *Tilton cowpwodis* 1467 × 84 *LTD* (*v.* **wudu**, poss. with **copp**; if with **cūpe** 'a basket', the implications are unclear); *Tylton waturmylne* 1467 × 84 *LTD* (*v.* **water-mylne**); *the West Close* 1641.

2. HALSTEAD

Elstede 1086 DB
Haldsted' 1230 P, 1230 ChancR (p), 1230 MemR (p), 1236 Cur (p), *Halt*(*e*)*sted* 1249 Pat (p), 1257 Pap
Hautsted' 1230 P (p)

Hallested(*e*) c.1130 LeicSurv, l.13 *CRCart* (p), Edw 1 *CroxR* (p) *et passim* to 1465 *AllS*, 1466 Pat, *Hallesteyde* 1315 *AllS*, *Halested'* 1198 GildR (p), 1242 P (p), 1276 RH, l.13 (1404) *Laz*
Halsted(*e*) 1209 Cur (p), e.13 *Peake*, 1227 GildR *et passim* to Hy 3 *Crox* (p) *et freq* to 1345 Inqaqd, 1384 *AllS et passim* to 1541 MinAccts, 1610 Speed, *Halsteda* 1167 P, *Halsteyde* 1305 *AllS*
Hausted(*e*) 1167 ChancR, 1200 Cur (p), 1242 P (p) *et passim* to 1316 Misc, 1328 Cl, *Hausteda* 1209 × 19 RHug (p), *Haustead* 1620 LML, *Haulstead* 1641 *Surv*
Hawstede 1351 *MiD* (p), *Hawstead* 1607 LAS

The two elements which constitute this name are OE (Angl) *hald* 'protection' (developing as ME *hald*, *hold* 'shelter, refuge') and OE *stede* 'a place, a site', thus giving a general sense 'a place of protection'. Halstead occupies a fine hilltop location, but whether this place of protection originally referred to a fortified settlement is uncertain. K. Sandred in his *English Place-Names in -stead* (1745) includes Halstead (Lei, Ess, K) and the etymologically identical Hawstead (Sf) in a group of ancient names whose generics in *stede* he interprets as 'pasture (probably enclosed)' and also perhaps 'enclosure (for other purposes besides pasturing)'. Ekwall DEPN *s.n.* Halstead explains the appellative as 'a place of shelter for cattle'. The Anglo-Saxons used *burh* to signify an inhabited stronghold, so perhaps we should look to this particular place of protection as one to do with animal husbandry in uncertain times and especially referring to pasturage. A reasonable explanation of the appellative would be 'a protected place for pasturing livestock', *v.* **hald**[1], **stede** and Ekwall Studies[2], 52.

Forms with *u* for *l* are due to AN influence. The rare spellings *Haustide* 1276 RH (p) and *Halstyd* 1469 *AllS* may contain OE *styde*, a secondary form of the generic *stede*.

COLBOROUGH HILL, *Calborowe* 1539 Nichols, *Cawborow* 1586 *Plan*, *Coleburrow* 1647 *Rental*, *Caldborough* 1839 *TA*, *Colborough* 1968 *Surv*, *Colborough Hill* 1824 O, *Colberer Hill* 1845 *TA*, *v.* **berg**; with **cald** or **calu**. HALSTEAD COTTAGES. HALSTEAD GRANGE, 1925 Kelly, *v.* **grange**. HALSTEAD HO., *Halstead House* 1863 White. HALSTEAD LODGE. LAUNDE RD, Launde adjoining to the East. SALISBURY ARMS (P.H.) (SALISBURY HOTEL 2½"), *Salisbury* 1925 Kelly. STANTON PLANTATION. STONE LODGE. TENNIS WOOD, cf. *Tennis Wood Field* 1968 *Surv*. TILTON STATION, cf. *Station Wharf* 1925 Kelly, *v.* **hwearf**. WHITE LODGE.

FIELD-NAMES

Undated forms in (a) are 1845 *TA*; those dated 1807 and 1968 are *Surv*, while 1839 are *EnclA*. Forms throughout dated 1305, 1367 and 1609 are *AllS*; 1586 are *Plan*; 1641 are *Surv*; 1647 are *Rental*; 1708 (18) and 1709 are *Terrier*.

(a) Five Acre Mdw 1845, Sixteen Acre Mdw 1807, 1845 (*v.* **æcer**); Atkins Road (with the surn. *Atkins*); Back o'the Barn (*v.* **back**), Barn Cl; Beldam Cl (1708 (18), 1709, *v.* **beldam** 'an aged woman, a grandmother', with reference to a female owner); Bells furlong 1807, 1845 (*v.* **furlang**; either with the surn. *Bell* or alluding to land endowed for the provision and maintenance of church bells and ropes or for the payment of bellringers, cf. Bells Cl in Tilton f.ns. (a)); the Bits (*v.* **bit**); Bogdale (*v.* **bog, dalr**); Bottom Fd 1807; Far ~, First Breach 1807 (*v.* **brēc**); Bridle Gate 1807 (*v.* **brigdels, gata**); Little ~ ~, New Brook Fd, Brook Mdw (*v.* **brōc**); Brooksby's Cl 1839, Brooksby Cl, Brooksby Close Mdw 1845, Brooksby 1968 (with the surn. *Brooksby* of a family originally from the village of this name, 8 miles to the north-west); Bull gate (*v.* **bullgate**); Bushy furlong 1807 (*v.* **furlang**), Bushy Fd 1845 (*v.* **busshi**); Calf Cl, Calf Mdw (*v.* **calf**); Causeway Cl (*v.* **caucie**); Cheesecake Bit 1807 (*v.* **cheesecake, bit**); Church Furlong 1807, 1845 (*v.* **furlang**), Church Land Hades 1807 (*v.* **land, hēafod**) (presum. with reference to St Peter's Church in Tilton, but note that a church is recorded for Halstead as late as 1558 *Pat*, *v.* St Peter's Church *supra*); Clay Furlong 1807, 1845 (*v.* **furlang**), Clay Hill 1845, Clay Hole 1845 (*v.* **hol**[1]) (*v.* **clǣg**); Nether ~, Over Colbro 1807 (*v.* **uferra**), Far ~, Near ~, Bottom ~, Top Colberer 1845, Far ~, Near Colborough 1968 (cf. *Colborrow Close* 1641), Middle ~ ~, Top Colberer Hill, Colberer Hill Mdw 1845, Caldborough Mdw 1839 (*Colborrow Meadow* 1641, *Coleburrow* ~ 1647) (*v.* Colborough Hill *supra*); Coltsfoot hole 1807 (*v.* **coltefote, hol**[1]; coltsfoot (*Tussilago farfara*), a common weed in clayey ground, is named from the shape of the leaves); Common Pasture (*v.* **commun, pasture**); Cottage Cl 1807 (*v.* **cotage**); Cow Cl; (the) Cow Pasture 1839, 1845, Halstead Cow Pasture 1839 (*v.* **pasture**); Mead Croft (*v.* **mǣd**), Near Croft Leys (*v.* **leys**) (*v.* **croft**); Curtis's or Tamworth Cl 1807 (*v.* Tamworth Cl *infra*), Little Curtis's Cl 1807 (with the surn. *Curtis*); Cumberland Cl (prob. with the surn. *Cumberland*; but note a range of these names in Framland Hundred (*v.* Lei **2** 144) where an alternative of **cumber** with **land** (hence 'ground encumbered with stocks or stones') is suggested, although a name commemorating the victory of the Duke of Cumberland at the Battle of Culloden Moor (1746) may also feature in some instances); Davids Cl, Davids Croft (*v.* **croft**) (with the surn. *David*, *v.* Davids Cl in Tilton f.ns. (a)); Great ~ ~, Little Nether End, Over End 1807, 1845, ~ ~ Cl 1839 (*v.* **uferra**) (*v.* **ende**); Fall Hill (*v.* **(ge)fall**); Far Mdw; Old ~ ~ ~, Foot Road Cl (*v.* **foot-road**); Fox Covert (*v.* **fox, cover(t)**); Garden End 1807 (*v.* **ende**), Garden Spot 1845 (*v.* **spotte**) (*v.* **gardin**); Gorse Mdw (*v.* **gorst**); Gravel Pit 1807 (*v.* **gravel, pytt**); Great Pasture (*v.* **pasture**); Hall Cl, Hall Close Mdw 1839 (*atte Hall* 1327 SR (p) (*v.* **atte**), ((*ad*) *aulam* 1332 ib (p); with MLat *aula* (*aulam* acc.sg.) 'a hall'), *the Hall* 1641), Hall Yard 1839, 1845, Bottom ~ ~, Top Hall Yard 1845 (*the Hall-Yard* 1708

(18), 1709, *v.* **geard**) (*v.* **hall**); Halstead Fd 1824 O (*Haustead field* 1641); South Hangings Side 1807 (*v.* **hangende, sīde**); Hardys Hollow (*v.* **holh**; with the surn. *Hardy*); Over the Hill 1807 (a furlong so called); Hog Pool 1807 (*v.* **hogg, pōl**[1] and *Swines-poole* in Tilton f.ns. (b)); Holt Foot Hill (*v.* **holt**; perh. with **fōt**, but this may rather contain a late form of *Holtforth* in f.ns. (b)); Holy Plat (sic) 1807 bis (*v.* **plat**; prob. with **holh** rather than with **hālig**); Far ~ ~, First ~ ~, Middle Horse Cl; House Cl; Hunting Brigg Cl (*v.* **huntinge, brycg, bryggja**); Lane Mdw 1807 (*v.* **lane**); Little Cl 1845, Little Fd 1807 *Surv*, 1824 O, 1839; Little Mdw; Loddington Baulk 1807 (*v.* **balca**; Loddington adjoins to the south-east); (the) Long Furlong 1807, 1839 (*v.* **furlang**); Long Mdw; the Loughborough Road 1839 (Loughborough lies 16 miles to the north-west); Great ~, Little Lound, Lound Cl, East ~ ~, West Lound Hollows (*v.* **holh**), Lound Road Cl (*Halsteade Lounde* 1586, *the Lound*, *the Lownde* 1609, cf. *the Lounde Lodge*1586 *Plan*, *Lodge House* 1671 LeicW (*v.* **loge** and Abbey Fm in Launde), *v.* **lundr**); Mallows Bush piece 1807 (the Shrub Mallow (*Hibiscus syriacus*) appears to be alluded to here, *v.* **mealwe, busc, pece**); Mannions 1807, Manions 1845 (the surn. *Mannion* in the possessive case, *v.* Reaney *s.n.*); Great ~ ~, Little Marefield Hill 1845, Marfield Road Piece 1807, 1845 (*v.* **pece**) (Marefield adjoins to the north); Marsick furlong 1807 (*v.* **furlang**), Marsyke Fd 1839, Middle ~, Nether ~, Upper Marsickpiece 1807 (*v.* **pece**), Little Marsick 1845 (*v.* **(ge)mǣre, sík**); Melcoff Hole 1807 (*v.* **hol**[1]; earlier forms are needed to explain the first word, but **meoluc** with **cofa** may be thought of); Melton Road furlong 1807 (*v.* **furlang**; Melton Mowbray lies 8 miles to the north); Middle Gate 1807 (*v.* **gata**); Middle Piece (*v.* **pece**); First ~ ~, Second Mill Cl 1845, Mill Fd 1839, 1845, Bottom Mill Fd 1845, Mill Spot 1807 (*v.* **spotte**); the Mires, Mires Cl (*v.* **mýrr**); Morter Pits 1807 (*v.* **morter, pytt**); Nether Cl; Nether Fd; New Fd, ~ ~ Mdw 1807; New Mdw; the Newbold Road 1839 (Newbold lies 1½ miles to the north-wast); Orchard Cl; Over Fd 1807, Little ~ ~, Over Mdw 1845 (*v.* **uferra**); Owston Mdw, Owston Road Cl (Owston lies 2 miles to the north-east); Pains Yard 1807 (*v.* **geard**; with the surn. *Pain*); Bottom ~, Over Paradise (*v.* **uferra**) (*the Paradize* 1609, *v.* **paradis**); Bottom Parsonage Croft (*v.* **personage, croft**); Parsons Cl (*v.* **persone**); Pasture Cl 1807, Pasture Lane 1839 (*v.* **lane**) (*v.* **pasture**); Bottom ~ ~, Pen Cl (*v.* **penn**[2]); (the) Pinfold 1807, 1839, Pinfold Fd 1839, Bottom ~ ~, Pinfold Hill 1845, ~ ~ Fd 1807 (*Pinfold Hill* 1609, *v.* **pynd-fald**); Far ~ ~, Near Ploughed Fd; Randles, Randalls Croft (*v.* **croft**) (cf. *William Randall* 1845); Red Rock Cl (*v.* **rēad, rokke**); Road Cl, ~ ~ Mdw 1845, Second ~ ~, Road Piece 1807 (*v.* **pece**), Road Plantation 1845); Rodhills, ~ Corner (*v.* **corner**) (*v.* Rodhill Fm in Tilton *supra*); Rough Cl, Little ~ ~ ~, Rough Close Hill (*v.* **rūh**[1]); the Salisbury, Near Salisbury 1968 (*v.* Salisbury Arms (P.H.) *supra*); Bottom ~, Far ~, Middle ~, Top Seeds (*v.* **sǣd**; in f.ns. often used of areas of sown grass); Shop Lane 1839 (*v.* **sc(e)oppa**); Sikes Corner (*v.* **corner** and Sykes Spinney in Tilton); Nether ~ ~, Simpsons Cl 1807, Simpsons Mdw 1845 (with the surn. *Simpson*); Great ~, Slade (cf. *Sladeleas*, *Slade Leyes* 1609, *v.* **leys**), Great ~ ~, Little Slade Fd, Slade Field Corner (*v.* **corner**) (*Sladefeild* 1609, *v.* **feld**) (*v.* **slæd**); Spinney Cl (*v.* **spinney**); the Spot (cf. *Spoute meadow* 1586, *Spott meadowe*, *Spott meadow(e) Feild*, *Spoutmeadowe feild*, *Spott alias Spoute meadowe feild*, *Spott alias Spowte meadowe feild* 1609, *v.* **mǣd (mǣdwe** obl.sg.), **feld**; whether originally with **spotte** or **spoute** is uncertain, since although *spoute* appears in the earliest form here, *spotte* occurs regularly in the later f.ns. of the parish, as in Garden Spot and Mill Spot *supra* and in Mill Spot and Top Spot in Tilton f.ns (a); alternatively, *spotte* may have replaced *spoute* in this instance); Spring Fold Bank (sic) 1807, 1845 (*Springe Poole banck* 1609 (*v.* **spring**[1], **pōl**[1], **banke**); Bottom ~ ~, Middle ~ ~, Top Stone Cl, Home Stone Cl (*v.* **home**) (*v.* **stān**); Stone Pit(s) 1807, 1845, Stonepit (Road) Piece 1807 (*v.* **pece**) (*v.* **stān-pytt**); Three Cornered Cl, Three Cornered Mdw (*v.* **three-cornered**); Tiplow Cl, Bottom ~ ~, Top Tiplow Mdw (*v.* Big Tiplow Mdw in Tilton f.ns. (a)); Toby's Yard 1807, Toby ~ 1845 (*v.* **geard**; prob. with the pers.n. *Toby*, an informal style of the Hebrew pers.n. Tobiah (Greek form Tobias), since as a surn., Toby appears not to occur in Leics.); Wad Cl (*v.* **wād**); Waggon Hovel Cl (*v.* **wægn, wag(g)on, hovel**); the Waste (*v.* **waste**); Willow Holt (*v.* **wilig, holt**); Windmill Croft (*v.* **wind-mylne, croft**); Wood End Cl (*v.* **ende**), Wood Nook Corner (*v.* **nōk, corner**); Wrights Road 1839 (with the surn. *Wright*).

(b) *Ashegate* 1609 (*v.* **æsc, gata**); *Balanslade* 1586, 1609, *Baland Slade* 1609 (*v.* **bēan, land, slæd**); *Brakendale, Bracondale, Further ~, Nether ~, Upper ~, Brakendales, Brakendale Sike* 1586, ~ *seek* 1609 (*v.* **sík**) (*v.* **braken, dalr**); *Brentethorne* 1586, *Brent(t)horne* 1609 (*v.* **brend, þorn**); *Coldelesb'rge* 1194 CurR (*v.* **berg**), *Cawdell Hill* 1586, 1609, *Caldwell* ~ 1609 bis (*v.* **cald, wella**; with **hyll** replacing **berg**); *atte Cros* 1327 SR (p), 1367 Banco (p) (*v.* **atte, cros**); *Curley dale* 1586, 1609, *Curlie dale, Curledale or Redhill, Curl(e)ydale or Reddhill* 1609 (*v.* **dalr** and Rodhill Fm in Tilton *supra*; the first el. is poss. **curlewe**); *Deepe dale* 1586, 1609, *Deepdale* 1609, ~ *Mouth* 1586 (*v.* **mūða**) (*v.* **dēop, dalr**); *ecclesias de Hallstedde et Tylton* 1553 *Pat*, *ecclesiarum de Buckmynster Tilton Halsted et Sancta Maria Leicestre* 1558 *ib* (with MLat *ecclesia* 'a church'; there is now no parish church at Halstead); *Gildenthorn* 1305, *Guilte Thorn, Guilthorne, Guiltthorne* 1609 (*v.* **gylden, þorn**); *Hall hades* 1586 (*v.* **hall, hēafod** and Hall Cl in f.ns. (a)); *Halstead Brook, Halsteed Brooke* 1609 (*v.* **brōc**); *Jonathan Hawkins's homestall* 1708 (18) (*v.* **hām-stall**); *Hennes neste* 1586, *Hennesnest, hennes neast* 1609 (*v.* **henn, nest**); *Holtforth* 1367, *Holt forde* 1586, *Holford* 1609, *Holtford furl'* 1586, *Holford furlong(e)* 1609 (*v.* **furlang**) (*v.* **holt, ford**); *Home bancke* 1586, *Holme Banck, Home banke* 1609 (*v.* **holmr, banke**); *Iewes Sike* 1586, *Jewes seeke, Jewes syke, Jowes seek* 1609 (*v.* **sík**; with the surn. *Jew*, *v.* Reaney *s.n.*); *the Kiln-Yard* 1708 (18) (*v.* **cyln, geard**); *Lambcọte dale* 1586, 1609 (*v.* **lamb, cot, dalr**); *Langborow hill* 1586, *Langburrow(e)* 1609, *Langborow hades* 1586 (*v.* **hēafod**) (*v.* **lang**[1], **berg**); *Loesby Spiney* 1586, *Loseby Spinney or Woode, Lousby Speenny or Woode, Lousbie Woode* 1609 (*v.* **spinney**; Lowesby adjoins to the north-west); *Medecroft* 1609, *Medcroftleys* 1609 (*v.* **leys**) (*v.* **mǣd, croft**); *Merfeild Meere* 1609 (*v.* **(ge)mǣre**; Marefield adjoins to the north); *Midleborow* 1586, *Middleburrowe* 1609 bis (*v.* **middel, berg**); *Middlemore hades* 1609 (*v.* **middel, mōr**[1], **hēafod**); *the milne damme* 1586, *the mill dam* 1609 (*v.* **myln, damme**); *Newton Wood* 1609 (Cold Newton adjoins to the west); *Oueston gate* 1586 (*v.* **gata**), *Ouston hedge* 1609 (*v.* **hecg**; a parish boundary marker), *Owston meere* 1609 (*v.* **(ge)mǣre**), *Oueston path* 1586 (*v.* **pæð**), *Oselweston Stone pittes* 1586 (*v.* **stān-pytt**) (Owston adjoins to the north-east; there is still an ironstone quarry towards this parish boundary); *Peres Crosse* 1609 (*v.* **cros**; either with the OFr pers.n. *Piers* or its surn. reflex, *v.* Reaney *s.n.* Pierce); *Smithe meadow* 1586, *Smithie* ~, *Smithe meadowe* 1609 (*v.* **smiððe, mǣd (mǣdwe** obl.sg.)); *Speares Close* 1609 (with the surn. *Speare(s)*); *Tamworth Close* 1609 (with the surn. *Tamworth*; note the early *Willielmus de Tamworth* 1262 RFL); *Tiptaffs Close* 1708 (18), *Tiptafts* ~ 1709 (with the local surn. *Tiptaft*); *Tristrams Close* 1609 (with the surn. *Tristram*, *v.* Reaney *s.n.*); *atte well* 1332 SR (p) (*v.* **atte, wella**); *Whateboroughe gate* 1586 (*v.* **gata**), *Whadborough* ~, *Whadburrowe hedge* 1609 (*v.* **hecg**; a parish boundary marker, Whatborough adjoining to the north-east); *Whitland*, ~ *hades* 1586, *Wheatland* ~, *Whetlande hades* 1609 (*v.* **hēafod**) (*v.* **hwǣte, hveiti, land**); *Woodgate* 1586, 1609 (*v.* **gata**), *Woodhead* 1609 (*v.* **hēafod**) (*v.* **wudu**).

Tugby and Keythorpe

1. TUGBY

Tochebi 1086 DB, 1167 P, 1184 CartAnt (p)
Tokebia c.1130 LeicSurv, 1179 P (p), *Tokebi* 1176 ib (p),1177 ib (p) *et freq* to 1193 ib (p), 1205 ChancR (p), *Tokeby* 1206 Cur (p), 1220 MHW, 1220 GildR *et passim* to 1294 *Wyg* (p), l.13 *CRCart et freq* to 1419 *Peake*, 1423 *LCh et passim* to 1550, 1551 *Peake*
Tokesby 1274 RGrav
Thocebi John Hastings (p), *Thokebi* John *Rut*, e.13 Nichols, 1228 Cl (p), *Thokebya* 1240 GildR (p), 1220 × 50 *RTemple* (p), *Thokeby* 1252 Fees (p), 1262 Fine (p), 1274 Ipm, *Thokebey* 13 *Peake*
Toukebi 1203 P (p), 1204 ib (p), 1205 ib (p), *Toukeby* 1257 Ch, 1274 Ass, 1364 Pat (p)
Tokby 1384 *Peake* bis, 1496 *LCh* bis, 1535 VE
Tukeby 1518 Visit, *Tukby* 1526 AAS, *Tuckby* 1710 LML
Tuggebye 1539 *LCh*, *Tougbye* 1550 *ib*
Tugby(*e*) 1519 EpCB, 1535 VE, 1540 MinAccts *et freq*

'Tóki's farmstead, village', *v*. **bȳ**. The specific is the ON pers.n. *Tóki* (ODan *Toki*, OSwed *Toke*). In DB, *Tochi* is recorded as holding Tugby as part of a larger estate TRE. Spellings with *th* for *t* are the result of AN orthographical interchange between the symbols *th* and *t* for etymological *t*. Also AN is *k* represented by *ch* before a front vowel.

BLACK HORSE (P.H.), *Black Horse* 1846, 1863, 1877 White, 1925 Kelly. BLACKSMITH'S SHOP (lost), *Blacksmiths Shop* 1797 *Surv*, *v*. **blacksmith**, **sc(e)oppa**. BRIERY LEYS SPINNEY, *Briery Leys* 1797 *Surv*, *v*. **brērig**, **leys**; it is *Rolleston Spinney* 1806 Map, ~ *Spinnies* 1824 O, *v*. **spinney**; Rolleston adjoins to the west. FISHPOOL SPINNEY, (*the*) *Fish Pool*(*e*) 1674, 1690 *Terrier et freq* to 1718, 1721 *ib*, *v*. **fisc-pōl**. FOX AND HOUNDS (P.H.), *Fox and Hounds* 1846, 1863, 1877 White, 1925 Kelly. BIG ~, LITTLE GUNSEL, *Gunsin* 1703 *Terrier*, *Gunshill* 1709 *ib*, *Guncills* 1797 *Surv*, *Neither Gunsicke* 1674 *Terrier*, ~ *Gunsing* 1690, 1697, 1712 *ib*, *Nether Gunsing* 1700, 1706, 1708 (18), 1718, 1721 *ib*, ~ *Gunsin* 1703 *ib*, ~ *Gunshill* 1709 *ib* (*v.* **neoðera**), *Gunsicke Furlong* 1674 *ib*, *Gunsing furland* (sic) 1690 *ib*, ~ *furlong* 1697, 1700 *ib et passim* to 1721 *ib* (*v.* **furlang**). With Hardy's Gunsel in adjoining East Norton, these are the names of three plantations which line a large spur of land, two of the plantations sloping down towards a stream which runs along its foot. The first el. of all the forms is the ON pers.n. *Gunnarr* in the possessive case, while the generic of the earliest pair is **sík** 'a piece of meadow along a stream'. It is uncertain whether *Gunsicke* and *Gunsing* from the outset referred to two different features (*Gunsing* with **eng** 'a meadow' as generic) or whether *eng* replaced the *sík* of an original *Gunsick*, *eng* itself being eventually replaced by *hill*. Although *Gunshill* is recorded by 1709, while *Gunsing* continues to 1721, it seems doubtful that *Gunshill* constituted an independent name rather than its being a refashioning by popular etymology. HALLATON RD, Hallaton lying 3 miles to the south-east. HARBROOK FM, *Hallbrooke* 1674, 1690, 1718, 1721 *Terrier*, *Hallbrook* 1697, 1706 *ib et passim* to 1715 *ib*, *Nether* ~, *Upper Hallbrook* 1700 *ib*, *Hawbrook* 1703 *ib*, *Harbrook* 1797 *Surv*, cf. *Hallbrooke Hill* 1674, 1690, 1721 *Terrier*, *Hallbrook* ~ 1697, 1700 *ib et passim* to 1718 *ib*, *Hawbrook* ~ 1703 *ib*, *Harbrook Hill* 1797 *Surv*, *v.* **hall**, **brōc**. HARRISON'S BARN, cf. *Thomas Harrison, farmer and grazier* 1877 White. HAZLERIGG FM, neighbouring Noseley was the manor of the *Hazlerigg* family and monuments in its church commemorate *Sir Thomas Heselrige* (d.1629), *Sir Arthur Heselrige* (d.1660), *Lady Heselrige* (d.1673) and *Sir Robert Heselrige* (d.1721). HOMESTEAD SPINNEY, *Nether* ~, *Homestead* 1797 *Surv*, *v.* **hām-stede**. MANOR FM, *v.* **maner**. MODEL FM. NETTLEHAM FM, prob. with **netel(e)**, **hamm**. ST THOMAS BECKET'S CHURCH, *Church (St Thomas-à-Becket)* 1846, 1863, 1877 White, 1925 Kelly; it is earlier recorded as *ecclesie de Tokeby* 1220 MHW, 1238 RGros, ~ *de Tokeb'* 1244 ib. Note also *the Churchyard*(*e*) 1674, 1697, 1721 *Terrier*, *the Church yeard* 1690 *ib*. SOUTHFIELDS. SPINNEY NOOK, *v.* **nōk**. TUGBY BUSHES, 1784 Nichols, 1824 O, *v.* **busc**. TUGBY WOOD, 1800 Map, 1824 O, *the Wood* 1797 *Surv*. VANE FM, *Vane Farm* 1943 *Sale*. THE VICARAGE, 1877 White, 1925 Kelly, cf. *the Vicaridge House* 1674, 1690 *Terrier et passim* to 1721 *ib*, ~ *Vicarage* ~ 1708 (18) *ib*, *v.* **vikerage**. WEST MAINS, 1925 Kelly, *v.* **(ge)mǣnnes** 'common land'. WOOD LANE.

FIELD-NAMES

Undated forms in (a) are 1797 *Surv*; those dated 1821 are *Terrier*. Forms throughout dated 1631 are *Conant*; those dated 1674, 1690, 1697, 1700, 1703, 1706, 1708 (18), 1709, 1712, 1715, 1718 and 1721 are *Terrier*.

(a) Twenty Acres (*v*. **æcer**); Barn Cl; Nether ~, Over Barchill 1821 (*v*. **uferra**) (*v*. **berc, hyll**); Barnett Leys (*v*. **leys**; with the surn. *Barnett*); Brakendale (*Brackendall(e)* 1674, 1697, *Brackendaill* 1690, *Brackendail(e)* 1690, 1697, 1706, *Brackendale* 1706, 1708 (18), *Nether Brackendale* 1703, 1712, *(ye) Netherside Brackendale* 1700, 1715, 1721, *the Neather side Brackendaile* 1709, *ye Nether side Brackindale* 1718, *Upperside Brackendale* 1700, 1703, *the Uper side Brackendaile* 1709, *ye Upperside Brackendall* 1712, *ye Upper side Brackendale* 1718, 1721 (*v*. **neoðera, upper, sīde**), *ye Uppermost side Brackendale* 1712 (*v*. **uppermoste**) (*v*. **braken**; prob. with **dalr** rather than **deill**); Carter's Cl (with the surn. *Carter*); Clover Cl (*v*. **clāfre**; a fodder crop enclosure); Cow Layer (*v*. **lair**); Dobbs Leys (*Doles Leyes* 1674, *the Dols leyes* 1690, *the Doles lese* 1697, *Dobs Leys* 1700, 1708 (18), 1712, *Dobbs Leyes* 1703, *Dobs leies* 1709, ~ *Leyes* 1706, 1715, ~ *Lays* 1718, 1721 (*v*. **dāl, leys**; it is uncertain whether the surn. *Dobbs* here is a renaming of the leys or is a misreading of *Doles* with subsequent repetition in the glebe terriers); Dykes Cl 1821 (*Dikes* 1674, 1690 *et freq* to 1721, *Ditches* 1709 (*v*. **dīc**), *v*. **dík**); Fishpool Cl (*v*. Fishpool Spinney *supra*); Gilbrodas 1821 (*Gill broad Arse* 1674, 1697, 1703, 1706, 1718, *Gilbroadarse* 1690, 1715, *Gyllbroadars(e)* 1700, 1712, *Gill Broadarse* 1708 (18), *Gilbradis* 1709, *Jill broadarse* 1721, *v*. **brād, ears**; a wide, buttock-shaped hill formation appears to have been afforded the pers.n. *Gill*, a pet-form of Gillian, presum. with jocular reference to a well-known local woman's posterior); Gravel Pits, Near ~ ~ ~, Gravel pit Cl (*v*. **gravel, pytt**); Great Cl; Great Pasture (*v*. **pasture**); Hall Fd (*v*. **hall**); Nether ~, Middle ~, Over Hanner (*v*. **uferra**) (unexplained since earlier forms are needed, but perh. with *Heynor* as in the *Heynorstorth* of adjacent Skeffington f.ns. (b)); Hogmores Cl (*v*. **hogg, mōr**[1]); Home Cl 1797, 1821 (*v*. **home**); Mill Cl (cf. *Mill Feild* 1674, 1690, 1697, 1708 (18), ~ *Field* 1700, 1718, 1721, *Milln Field* 1703, *Milfield* 1706, 1709, 1712, 1715, *v*. **myln, feld** and Tugby Mill *infra*; one of the great fields of the township); Norton Cottage Cl 1821 (East Norton adjoins to the east); Nosely Path (*v*. **pæð**; a close so called, Noseley lying 2 miles to the south-west); Over Pasture (*v*. **uferra**), Pasture Cl (*v*. **pasture**); Plowed Cl; Riggers (*Riggose* 1674, 1690, 1697, 1712, 1721, *Riggoos(e)* 1700, 1703, 1706, 1708 (18), 1715, *Righouse* 1709, *Riggous* 1718, *Under Riggoos(e)* 1700, 1703, 1706, 1708 (18), ~ *Righous* 1709, ~ *Riggose* 1712, ~ *Riggos* 1715, ~ *Rogose* 1718 (*v*. **under**), *v*. **hryggr**; prob with **haugr** (in the pl.)); Rolston Way (1674, *Roulston Way* 1690, 1700 *et freq* to 1721, *Roulson* ~ 1697, 1703, 1712, *Rowlston* ~ 1703, 1706, 1712, *v*. **weg**; Rolleston adjoins to the west); Scribb 1797, Scrib Cl 1821 (cf. *Scrib Feild* 1674, *Scribe field* 1690, 1709, *Scrib* ~ 1697, 1700 *et freq* to 1721 (*v*. **feld**; one of the great fields), *Scrib furlong* 1674, 1679 *et freq* to 1721, *Scribe* ~ 1690 (*v*. **furlang**), *v*. **scrybb** '(a place overgrown with) brushwood', with Scand *sk-*); Slade (*v*. **slæd**); Stearns Willows (*Staines Willows* 1674, 1706, 1718, 1721, *Stan(e)s* ~ 1690, 1697, 1709, *Stains* ~ 1690, 1708 (18), *Steynes* ~ 1700, 1703, 1706, 1708 (18), *Staynes* ~ 1712, *Steines* ~ 1715, *Staines Willow(s) Bank(e)* 1674, 1721, *Stans willous banke* 1690, ~ *Willow* ~ 1697, *Steynes willow bank* 1700, 1703, 1706, 1708 (18), *Staynes*

~ ~ 1712, *Steines* ~ ~ 1715, *Stains* ~ ~ 1718 (*v.* **banke**), *v.* **wilig**; with the surn. *Staines*, *v.* Reaney *s.n.*); Tongue Leys (*v.* **tunge, leys**); Townsend Cl, Towns-end Spinny (*v.* **spinney**) (*Townsend* 1706, 1708 (18), 1712, cf. *the Town(e) End furlong(e)* 1674, 1718, *(the) Towns end furlong* 1690, 1697, 1700, 1709, 1715, 1721 (*v.* **furlang**), *Townsend leys* 1703 (*v.* **leys**), *v.* **tūn, ende**); Tugby Mill 1824 O; Bottom of Wood (*v.* **botm**); Woodhouse Leys ((*the*) *Woodash* (sic) 1674, 1690 *et freq* to 1721, *Wood Ash Leyes* 1712 (*v.* **leys**), *v.* **wudu**; despite the earliest recorded forms of the generic, its original was no doubt **hūs**, of a well-documented compound).

(b) *Under Barrowe* 1674, 1721, ~ *Barrow* 1690, 1700 *et freq* to 1718 (*v.* **under, berg**); *Blackeue Sick(e)* 1674, 1690, *Blackowe sick* 1690, *Blackeo* ~ 1697, *Blackew* ~ 1700, 1706, 1708 (18), 1712, 1715, *Blackyew* ~ 1703, *Blacko* ~ 1709, *Blackewe* ~ 1718, *Blackwell* ~ (sic) 1721, *v.* **sík**; earlier forms are needed to explain the first word; a stream-name, with **blæc** and **ēa** 'a stream', the latter perh. influenced by French *eau* 'water' as in various Lincs. examples, appears unlikely but could account for its restyling as *Blackwell*; the surn. *Blackow(e)/Blackoe* is common in Lancs., but is otherwise unrecorded in Leics.); *Blakelands* 1674, 1690 *et freq* to 1721, *Blackeland* 1697, *Blacklands* 1709 (*v.* **blæc, land**); *Breading* 1674, 1690 *et freq* to 1721, *Breadings* 1690, 1709, *Breding* 1703, *Brading* 1718, *Breeding* 1721 (*v.* **breiðr, eng**); *atte Brigge* 1373 Pat (p), *atte Brygge* 14 (1449) *WoCart* (p) (*v.* **atte**), *Bridge Furlong* 1674, 1690 *et freq* to 1718 (*v.* **furlang**), *Butts bridge Furlong* 1721 (*v.* **butte**) (*v.* **brycg**); *Bullocke holme* 1674, *Ballock holme* 1690, 1697, 1706, 1712, ~ *home* 1700, 1715, *Bollock home* 1703, *Ballockholm* 1708 (18), *Ballackholme* 1709, *Ballocke holme* 1718, 1721 (*v.* **bulluc, holmr**); *the Corner street(e)* (sic) 1674, 1690, 1697 (*v.* **strǣt**; presum. originally *the Common street*, miscopied and so repeated in the parish glebe terriers); *Davies hedge* 1697 (*v.* **hecg**; a property boundary), *Davies Willows* 1690, 1697, 1709, 1718, 1721, *Davis* ~ 1700, 1703, 1706, 1708 (18), 1712, 1715, *Davys* ~ 1703, 1712 (*v.* **wilig**; with the surn. *Davies*); *Short Dole* 1674, 1697 *et freq* to 1721, ~ *Dols* 1690 (*v.* **dāl**); *Clement Dormans Rickstead* 1674, 1718, ~ ~ *Ricksted* 1697, 1700, 1703, 1709, 1712, *Dormans Rick Sted* 1706, ~ *Rickstead* 1708 (18), *Clem Dormans Rick Stead* 1715, *John Dormans Ricksted* 1690 (*v.* **rickstead**); *the Freehold (Land)* 1674, 1706, 1708 (18), *Tugby Freehold* 1674, *the Freeland* 1674, 1697, 1706, 1708 (18) (*v.* **frehold, frēo, land**); *Grifte Feild* 1674, *Grife field* 1690, *Griff(e)* ~ 1697, 1700 *et freq* to 1721 (*v.* **feld**; one of the great fields of the township), *Grifte End* 1674, *Grift(e)* ~ 1674, 1697 *et freq* to 1718, *Grife* ~ 1690, *Grif* ~ 1703 (*v.* **ende**), *Grife furlong* 1690, 1709, *Griffe* ~ 1697, 1718 (*v.* **furlang**), *Grifte Furrows* 1674, *Griff(e)* ~ 1700, 1703 *et freq* to 1721 (*v.* **furh**), *Griff hole* 1674, 1706, 1708 (18), 1712, 1715, *Griffe* ~ 1690, 1697, 1709, 1718, 1721, *Grif* ~ 1700, 1703 (*v.* **hol**[1]), *v.* **gryfja** 'a hole, a pit', dial. **griff** 'a small deep valley'); *Half rood furlong* 1706, 1708 (18), 1709, 1721 (*v.* **furlong**), *Half rood furrow(e)s* 1700, 1703 *et freq* to 1721, *Half road Furrows* 1718 (*v.* **furh**) (*v.* **half, rōd**[3]); *Harborrs Well* 1674, 1718, 1721, *Harbors* ~ 1690, 1697, 1700, 1706, 1708 (18), 1715, *Harbours* ~ 1703, 1712, *Harbert* ~ (sic) 1709 (*v.* **wella**; the possessive case suggests the surn. *Harbo(u)r*, otherwise with its source **herberȝe, herborouȝ** 'a shelter (for travellers)'); *the Harp(e)* 1674, 1690 *et freq* to 1721 (*v.* **hearpe**); *Henses stile* 1674, 1700, 1706, 1708 (18), 1718, 1721, *Henes* ~ 1690, *Hanses stile* 1697, *Henses style* 1703, 1712, *Hans stile* 1709, *Hensestyle* 1715 (*v.* **stigel**; with a surn., either *Hense* or *Hanse*); *the Homestead* 1674, 1718, 1721, *the Homested* 1690, 1697 (i.e. of *the Vicaridge House*, *v*. **hām-stede**); *Hungdalle* 1674 (*v*. **hung**, **dalr**; cf. Hung Furlong in Ratcliffe on the Wreake f.ns. (b)); *Nether* ~, *Hungerland(e)s* 1674, 1690 *et freq* to 1721 (*v*. **hungor**, **land**); *Keirkesland End* 1674, *Kerkes* ~ ~ 1697, 1709, *Kirks* ~ ~ 1700, 1718, *Kerks land end* 1703, 1706, 1708 (18), 1712, *Kirkesland end* 1715 (*v*. **land**, **ende**; either with the surn. *Kirk* or with **kirkja**); *Keithrope hedge* 1704, *Keythorp(e)* ~ 1690, 1700 *et freq* to 1721, *Keytharp(e)* ~ 1690, 1697 (*v*. **hecg**; a parish boundary marker), *Keythorp yate* 1703, *Keyhtorpe gate* 1709 (*v*. **gata**) (Keythorpe adjoins to the south-east); *the Kings high(e) way(e)* 1674, 1690, 1697 (*v*. **hēah-weg**; with reference to Charles II and William III); *Knosley Way* 1674, *Nosely* ~ 1690, 1700 *et freq* to 1721, *Noseley* ~ 1697 (*v*. **weg**; Noseley lies 2 miles to the south-west); *ye Lane Baulk* 1721 (*v*. **lane**, **balca**); *Leceister Way* 1674, *Leicester* ~ 1690, 1697 *et freq* to 1721, *Leister* ~ 1700 (*v*. **weg**; Leicester lies 11 miles to the west); *Littling* 1674, 1697 *et passim* to 1721, *Littleing* 1690, 1708 (18), 1718, *Littling Furlong* 1715 (*v*. **furlang**) (*v*. **lȳtel**, **lítill**, **eng**); *Lunsdall(e)* 1674, 1690, *Lunsdaill(e)* 1690, 1697, *Lunsdale* 1700, 1715, 1718, 1721, *Lunsdail(e)* 1706, 1709, *Lundsdale* 1706, 1708 (18), *(ye) East side Lunsdale* 1700, 1703, 1706, 1708 (18) (*v*. **sīde**), *Lunsdall Gutter* 1674, *Lunsdalle guter* 1690, 1697, *Lunsdal(e) Gutter* 1700, 1703 *et freq* to 1721, *Lunsdail(e) guter* 1709, *Lundsdale gutter* 1712 (*v*. **goter**) (*v*. **lundr**, **dalr**); *Mare Close Meadow*, *Mare Close Pasture* 1631 (*v*. **mare**, **pasture**; the forms prob. refer to the same feature); *Micklebarrow Sick* 1700 (*v*. **micel**, **mikill**, **berg**, **sík**); *Micklemoor(e) Sick(e)* 1674, 1690, 1708 (18), 1718, *Micklemore* ~ 1700, 1703 *et passim* to 1721 (*v*. **micel**, **mikill**, **mōr**[1], **mór**, **sík**); *Midlemoore sick* 1697, *midle more sick* 1709 (*v*. **middel**, **mōr**[1], **sík**); *Mill hill furlong* 1674, 1690 *et freq* to 1721, *(the) Milhill* ~ 1706, 1709, 1712, *Mil hil* ~ 1715 (*v*. **myln**, **hyll**, **furlang** and Tugby Mill in f.ns. (a)); *New Diche* 1674, ~ *Dick* 1690, 1697, ~ *Dich* 1700, 1703, 1706, 1709, ~ *Ditch* 1708 (18), 1712, 1715, 1718, ~ *Dike* 1721 (*v*. **dīc**, **dík**); *Norton Meire* 1674, 1697, ~ *Mere* 1700, 1712, ~ *Meer(e)* 1703, 1706 *et passim* to 1721, *Norton meare furlong* 1690, *the mear furlong* 1709 (*v*. **furlang**) (*v*. **(ge)mǣre**; East Norton adjoins to the east); *Paddocke Bush* 1674, *Paddocks* ~ 1697, 1718, 1721, *Padock* ~ 1700, *Paddock bush* 1703, 1706, 1708 (18), 1712, *Padocks bussh* 1709 (*v*. **busc**), *Paddocke Gutter* 1674, *Paddocks* ~ 1674, 1700, 1703, 1706, 1708 (18), 1721, *Paddock* ~ 1690, 1712, 1715, *Padduck(s) gutter* 1700, *Padocke(s) guter* 1709, *Paddoks* ~, *Paddockes Gutter* 1718 (*v*. **goter**) (the repeated possessive case of the first word suggests that it is the surn. *Paddock* (an original by-name from ME *paddok* 'a frog') rather than **paddock** 'a small field'); *ye Skittils* 1700, 1712, *Skittil(l)s* 1703, 1706, 1708 (18), *Sketles* 1709, *the Skittlys Furlong* 1674, *(ye) Skittles furlong* 1690, 1697, 1715, *ye Skittle furlong* 1718, 1721 (*v*. **furlang**) (poss. is a Scandinavianized **scytel**[2] 'unstable', perh. alluding to arable beside quakefen; or else a similarly modified **scyt(t)el**, **scyt(t)els** 'a bolt, a bar', referring to an enclosure that could be barred or bolted); *Swans lane end* 1690 (*v*. **lane-ende**; with the surn. *Swan*); *(the) Varges* 1674, 1697, 1709, 1712, 1715, *Vargies* 1690, 1706, 1708 (18), 1721, *(ye) Vargis* 1700, 1703, 1718 (*v*. **verge**); *the Vicaridge yard* 1712 (*v*. **vikerage**, **geard**); *Longe* ~ ~, *Shorte Watter Furrowes* 1674, *Long(e)* ~ ~, *Short(e) Water furrows* 1690, 1697 *et freq* to 1721 (*v*. **wæter**, **furh** and *the Waterfurrow(e)s* in Asfordby f.ns.(b)); *Wesson freehold* 1690 (*v*. **frehold**), *Wessons furlong(e)* 1674, 1700 *et freq* to 1721, *Wesson* ~ 1690, *Wesons* ~ 1697 (*v*. **furlang**) (cf. *John Wesson* 1690; the surn. with typical 17th cent. Leics. treatment of *Weston*); *(the) West Furrows* 1674, 1700 *et freq* to 1721 (*v*. **furh**); *Mr James Wilsons Rickstead* 1721 (*v*. **rickstead**).

2. KEYTHORPE

Keythorpe is a member of Gartree Hundred.

Cheitorp 1086 DB
Caitorp 1086 DB, *Caythorp(e)* 1242 Fees, a.1250 Nichols (p), 1274 Ass (p) *et passim* to 1540 MinAccts, 1538 × 44 ECP, *Cathorp* 1576 Saxton
Kaytorp' 1200 × 50 *Peake* (p), 1252 Cl (p), l.13 *CRCart* (p), 13 *Peake* (p), *Kaythorp(e)* 1260 Cl, 1262 Fine (p), Hy 3 *Hazlerigg* (p) *et passim* to 1344 (1449), 1353 (1449) *WoCart*
Keytorp' 1260 Cl (p), 1345 Pap (p), *Keythorp(e)* Hy 3 *Hazlerigg*, 1304 Pat, 1316 FA, 1322 *LCDeeds* (p), 1330 *Hazlerigg et freq*
Keuthorp' Hy 3 *Hazlerigg* (p)

Perhaps 'Keyia's or Keia's outlying farmstead', *v.* **þorp**. The pers.n. *Keyia* (side-form *Keia*) is Scand. Ekwall DEPN suggests OE *Cǣga* as the compounded pers.n., but this appears to be too early as a specific for *þorp*. Fellows-Jensen prefers as the specific a postulated OE *cǣg* 'a stone' (SSNEM 112). However, this does not reflect the location's drift geology and, as with the early OE pers.n. *Cǣga*, would sit unhappily with the later Scand *þorp*.

Keythorpe was a daughter settlement of Tugby.

COX'S CLOSE SPINNEY. HALLATON SPINNEYS, Hallaton adjoining to the south-east. HIGHFIELD SPINNEYS, *High Field* 1797 *Surv*, *v.* **hēah**[1], **feld**. HOME FM, *v.* **home**. ISSET'S LODGE, *Issets Lodge* 1824 O, *v.* **loge**; cf. *Hannah Issitt, tenant farmer* 1863 White. KEYTHORPE COURT, *v.* **court**. KEYTHORPE HALL, 1846, 1863, 1877 White, 1925 Kelly, *v.* **hall**. KEYTHORPE HALL FM (OLD KEYTHORPE 2½"). KEYTHORPE HO. KEYTHORPE LODGE FM (KEYTHORPE LODGE 2½"). KEYTHORPE PARK (EAST ~, MIDDLE ~, WEST PARK). KEYTHORPE SPINNEY. THE LAKE. LIMEKILN SPINNEY, *v.* **lim-kilne**. LONG SPINNEY. MOOR HILL SPINNEYS. RAVENS REST. ROSE COTTAGE FM. ROUND SPINNEY, *v.* **round**. SCOT'S LODGE (lost), *Scots Lodge* 1824 O, *v.* **loge**; with the surn. *Scot*.

FIELD-NAMES

Undated forms in (a) are 1797 *Surv*. Forms dated 1649 and 1652 are *Conant*, while those dated 1723 are Nichols.

(a) Four ~, Eight Acres (*v.* **æcer**); Ash Cl (*v.* **æsc**); Bennett's Cl (with the surn. *Bennett*); Breaky Part (*v.* **part**) (cf. *the Brackey Close* 1723, *v.* **braky**); Broad Mdw (cf. *Great Broadfield* 1723, *v.* **brād**); Cow Cl, ~ ~ Mdw; Cub Mdw (*v.* **cubb**); Far Mdw; First Mdw; Little High Fd, ~ ~ ~ Mdw (*v.* Highfield Spinneys *supra*); Long Cl; Middle Mdw; New Mdw (1723); Peas Cl, ~ ~ Mdw (*v.* **pise**); Quarters, Quarter Mdw (*v.* **quarter**); Town Cl (*v.* **tūn**).

(b) *the Horse Closes*, *the Horse Close Meadows* 1723; *Ould*(*e*) *Meadowe* 1649, 1652, *Old Meadow* 1723 (*v.* **ald**); *Tom's Close* 1723 (with the surn. *Tom*, from the pet-form of Thomas); *the Wood Ground* 1723 (*v.* **wudu, grund**).

Twyford and Thorpe

1. TWYFORD

Tuiuorde 1086 DB
Tuiford' 1162 × 70 *Rut* (p), 1179, 1180 P *et freq* to 1204, 1205 Cur, 1233 Cl, *Tuifort* Hy 2 Dane bis, *Tuyford* 1236 Fees, 1258 RHug
Thuiford' a.1250 (1404) *Laz* (p), *Thuifort* 1247 BM, *Thuyford* 1326 Ipm, *Thwiford'* 1201 P (p), 1202, 1203 ib, *Thwyford* 1234 Fees, 1346 Pat
Twiford 1184 Berkeley (p), 1195 P, 1196 ChancR, 1197 P *et freq* to 1247 Fine, 1248 Abbr *et passim* to 1340 IpmR, 1404 *Laz*, 1550 Pat *et freq* to 1581 LEpis, 1610 Speed, *Twifort* m.13 (1404) *Laz* (p), *Twyford(')* c.1130 LeicSurv, 1206 RFinib, 1220 MHW *et passim* to 1271 Fine, 1276 RH *et freq*, *Twyfford(e)* 1366 *Rut*, 1502 *MiscAccts et passim* to 1539 MinAccts, 1580 LEpis, *Twyforde* 1300 Ipm, 1385 Cl *et passim* to 1473 *CCR*, 1535 VE
Thwinford' 1204 RFinib

'The double ford', *v.* **twī-**, **ford**. The unique *Thwinford'* 1204 RFinib is formed with the OE adj. **twinn** 'double, two-fold' rather than with the usual OE prefix *twī-* 'double'. Spellings with *th* for *t* are the result of AN orthographical interchange between the symbols *th* and *t* for etymological *t*.

ALLOTMENT GARDENS, *Twyford Allotments* 1969 *Surv*, *v.* **allotment**. BURROUGH RD, Burrough on the Hill adjoining to the East. THE DAIRY FM. FREEZELAND LODGE, *Freeze Land* 1835 O, *v.* **fyrs**, **land**, **loge**. HIGHFIELD FM. IVY HO. JOHN O' GAUNT FM, JOHN O' GAUNT HOTEL (2½"), *John O' Gaunt hotel* 1925 Kelly. JOHN O' GAUNT VIADUCT, a 14-arch viaduct of the former Great Northern and London North Western Joint Railway, *v.* also John O' Gaunt, a fox covert in neighbouring Lowesby. John of Gaunt (d.1399) was a major landowner in Leics. His second wife, Constance of Castile, was buried in the Collegiate Church of the Annunciation of the Blessed Virgin Mary in The Newarke, Leicester (*v.* Lei **1** 101), of which only fragments remain. JUBILEE HO.

(2½"). KING ST. MANOR HO., *Manor house* 1877 White, *v.* **maner**. MAREFIELD LANE, Marefield adjoining to the south-east. PLOUGH (P.H.) (lost), *Plough* 1846, 1863 White, *Plough Inn* 1877 ib. SADDLE (P.H.), *Saddle* 1846, 1863 White, *Saddle Inn* 1877 ib, 1925 Kelly. ST ANDREW'S CHURCH, *Church (St Andrew)* 1846, 1863, 1877 White, 1925 Kelly; it is earlier recorded as *ecclesie de Twyford*(*e*) 1220 MHW, 1323 *Pat*, 1330 (c.1430), 1333 (c.1430) *KB*, 1412 *Pat*, 1412 (c.1430) *KB*. Note also *the Church yarde* 1612 *Terrier*, *v.* **chirche-ȝeard**. SPRINGFIELD, 1925 Kelly, *v.* **spring**[1]. STATION HILL, cf. *John o' Gaunt Station* 1951 Map; the railway line is now defunct. THIMBLE HALL RD, *v.* Porter's Lodge in neighbouring Lowesby. THREE HORSE SHOES (P.H.) (lost), *Three Horse Shoes* 1846, 1863, 1877 White, *Three Horseshoes* 1925 Kelly. THE WINDMILL (lost), *The Windmill* 1846, 1863 White, *v.* **wind-mylne**.

FIELD-NAMES

Undated forms in (a) are 1969 *Surv*. Those dated 1826 are *Terrier*, 1837 are *Map*, 1918 and 1937 are *Sale*. Forms throughout dated a.1250 (1404) are *Laz*, 1601, 1612, 1679, 1701 and 1708 (18) are *Terrier*.

(a) Three Acres 1969, Top Five ~, Top Six Acre 1918, Seven Acres 1969, the Eight ~ 1918, the Nine ~ 1969, the Eleven Acre 1918 (*v.* **æcer**); Ansondale 1918, Ansidale Cl 1937 (*v.* **dalr**; earlier forms are needed to explain *Anson-/Ansi-*); Ashby Road Cl 1918 (Ashby Folville adjoins to the north-west); Back Fd 1918 (*v.* **back**); Bannel sick Cl 1837 (*v.* **bēan, hyll, sík**); Barn Mdw; (the) Big Fd; Black Dyke 1826, ~ Dykes 1969 (*v.* **blæc, dík**); Bottom Fd; Bottom Mdw 1937, ~ Mdws 1969; Bridle Road Fd (*v.* **brigdels**); Far ~, Middle Broaders (*v.* **brād**, **ears**, cf. *Broadarses* in Humberstone and Hungarton f.ns. (b)); Bush Fd 1918 (*v.* **busc**); Caravan Fd (a mobile-home site); Causeway Baulk Cl 1937 (*v.* **caucie**, **balca**); Clan Banks (*v.* **banke**; prob. with **clǣne** 'clear of weeds'); Big ~ ~, Little Club Fd (poss. originally with **cubb**); Cook's Cl 1937 (with the surn. *Cook*); Corner Fd (*v.* **corner**); the Cricket Fd (for the game of cricket); Croddall hill Cl 1837 (*Crondale hille* a.1250 (1404), *v.* **cran, cron, dalr, hyll**); Crotton Gap 1918 (*v.* **gap**; with a local, late form of Croxton (South) which adjoins to the west); Dexters Cl 1837 (with the surn. *Dexter*); Docksey, Doxy (*v.* **docce**; poss. with **sík**, while **ēg** is less likely, but earlier forms are needed); Dove Hole (*v.* **dūfe, hol**[1], cf. Dove Hole Cl, ~ ~ Mdw in adjoining Burrough on the Hill, Lei **2** 233); Eaton's Fd (with the surn. *Eaton*); Far Side Cl 1918 (*v.* **sīde**); Front Fd 1918; the Gravel Hole 1969 (*v.* **hol**[1]), Gravel-pit Cl 1837 (*v.* **pytt**) (*v.* **gravel**); Great Cl; the Green Hill 1918, 1969, Bottom ~ ~, Top Green Hill 1918 (*v.* **grēne**[1]); Hen-holes 1837 (*v.* **henn, hol**[1] and Tear-sick *infra*); Hill Fd; Second ~ ~, Home Cl 1918, Home Fd 1969, Far ~ ~ 1918 (*v.* **home**); Far ~ ~, Horse Cl 1918; Houghton's Cl 1918 (with the surn. *Houghton*); House Cl 1918; Leicester Road Cl; Liner's Fd 1918 (with the surn. *Liner*; the usual Leics. form is *Lyner*); Little Mdw

1918; the Meadow; Middle Cl; Middle Fd; Mill Fd (*the Mill Feyld* 1701, *v.* **feld**); Mouse Dale Cl 1937 (*v.* **mūs, dalr**); North Dale Fd 1937 (*v.* **dalr**); Over the Brook Mdw 1918; the Paddock, Far ~, Home ~ (*v.* **home**), Middle Paddock (*v.* **paddock**); Parr-gate Cl 1837 (*v.* **pearr(e), gata**); the Bottom Plough Cl 1918 (*v.* **plōg**); Bottom ~ ~, Top Ploughed Fd 1918; the Pond Fd (*v.* **ponde**); First ~ ~ ~, Field over Railway (beside the now defunct lines of the former Great Northern and London North Western Joint Railway); Ranglands 1837, 1969 (*v.* **wrang, vrangr, land**); the Ridge Cl 1918 (*v.* **hrycg**); the First ~, the Second Riggett 1918, the Ricketts 1969 (*v.* **riggett**); Roman Trees (obscure; earlier forms are needed); the Rustalls (perh. 'rust-coloured spring', *v.* **rūst, wella**, cf. Rusthall (K), but again earlier forms are needed); Seed Cl 1918, Top Seeds 1969 (*v.* **sǣd**; often used in f.ns. for areas of sown grass); Shackell Mdw 1918, Bottom ~ ~, Top Shackell Headland 1918 (*v.* **hēafod-land**) (*v.* **scacol, shackle**); Shouldercoates 1826, Shoulder Coats 1969 (*v.* **sculdor** 'a shoulder', transferred topographically as 'the shoulder of a hill', **cot**); the Slade (*v.* **slæd**); the Slang (*v.* **slang**); Sough brook 1826 (*v.* **sōg, brōc**); Spinney Piece 1918 (*v.* **pece**), Spinney-side 1837 (*v.* **sīde**) (*v.* **spinney**); Stain Bridge 1826 (*v.* **steinn**); First ~ ~, Top Styes Cl (*v.* **stig**); Tear-sick or Hen-holes 1837 (*v.* **sík**; prob. with **tare** 'vetch' (*Vicia sativa* was grown for forage and for soil improvement), *v.* Hen-holes *supra*); Thimble Hall Fd (*v.* Porter's Lodge in neighbouring Lowesby); Three Corner Fd (*v.* **three-corner**); Top Fd; Twyford Hill; Viaduct Fd (*v.* John o' Gaunt Viaduct *supra*); Ward's Cl 1918 (with the surn. *Ward*); Weldon (perh. the surn. *Weldon* of a family originally from Weldon, 18 miles to the south-east in Northants., but if the survival of an early name, then *v.* **wella, dūn**); Willow Sick Cl 1837, Willow Stick Cl (sic), Bottom Willow Stick (sic) 1918 (*v.* **wilig, sík**).

(b) *Barlicholm*(*e*) a.1250 (1404) (*v.* **bærlic, holmr**); *le bryggefotte* 1486 AD (*v.* **brycg, fōt**); *the Common brooke* 1601, 1612 (*v.* **commun, brōc**); *Fulkilfurlong'* a.1250 (1404) (*v.* **hyll, furlang**; either with the OFr pers.n. *Fulco* or its surn. reflex *Fulk*, *v.* Reaney *s.n.*); *the Homestall* 1708 (18) (*v.* **hām-stall**; i.e. of *the Vicarage house*, *infra*); *Keldalegate*, *Keildalegate* a.1250 (1404) (*v.* **kelda, dalr, gata**); *Littlehilles* a.1250 (1404) (*v.* **lȳtel, hyll**); *Lyttlegreene* 1561 (1700) *Rental* (*v.* **lȳtel, grēne**[2]); *Mikeltungis* a.1250 (1404) (*v.* **micel, mikill, tunge**); (*the*) *Milne holme* 1601, 1612, *Mill* ~ 1679, 1701 (*v.* **myln, homr**); *Mydeldale* 1284 Ass (*v.* **middel, dalr**); *Peseclif* a.1250 (1404) (*v.* **pise, clif**); *Redegrese*, *Rede Greȝ* a.1250 (1404) (*v.* **hrēod, græs**); *Redespire* a.1250 (1404) bis (*v.* **hrēod, spīr**); *Smal*(*e*)*hilles* a.1250 (1404) (*v.* **smæl, hyll**); *Thirnedalehille* a.1250 (1404) (*v.* **þyrne, þyrnir, dalr, hyll**); *Toftes*, *Toftessike* a.1250 (1404) (*v.* **sík**) (*v.* **toft**); *the towne brooke* 1601 (*v.* **brōc**), *the towne Closynge* 1612 (*v.* **closing**), *the towne streete* 1601, 1612 (*v.* **strǣt**) (*v.* **tūn**); *the Vicarage house* 1601, 1612, ~ *Vickeridge* ~ 1701 (*v.* **vikerage**); (*the*) *Watermill lease* 1601, 1612 (*v.* **water-mylne, leys**).

2. THORPE SATCHVILLE

Torp' c.1141 Dugd, c.1160 BM, c.1180 (1449) *WoCart*, 1199 Cur (p), l.12, c.1200 Dane *et freq* to 1243 Fees, m.13 (1404), Hy 3 (1404) *Laz* (p)

Thorp(*e*) c.1130 LeicSurv, 1207 FF (p), 1227 Ch, 1234 Fees *et passim* to 1271 Abbr, Hy 3 *Crox et freq*, (~ *iuxta Twyford* 1324, 1325 Inqaqd, 1535 VE)

The feudal affix is added as:
~ *Secheville* 1262 Fine, ~ *Sechvile* 1284 Ass, ~ *Seccheville* 1295 Banco and with various spellings freq to date. Note 16th and 17th cent. forms, as ~ *Segefeld*(*e*) 1535 VE, 1550 Pat, ~ *Sachfe*(*i*)*ld* 1604 SR, 1610 Speed, ~ *Sechfeild* 1612 LML, ~ *Satchfield* 1626 ib etc.

'The outlying farmstead', *v*. **þorp**. This township was originally a daughter settlement of Twyford. The manor was held by *Radulfus de Secchevill'* in 1204 Cur and by *Gunnora de Secchevill'* in 1246 Ass. (The fem. pers.n. *Gunnora* is ODan *Gunnor* (ON *Gunnvǫr*) which is found in Normandy, *v*. SPNLY 118 and Feilitzen 278). The family came from Secqueville in Normandy. Popular etymology seems to have been at work on the feudal surn. in the 16th and 17th cents., supposing a topographical 'sedge field'.

ADAM'S GORSE, 1870 *Sale*, *Adam* ~ 1843 *TA*, *v*. **gorst**; with the surn. *Adam*. THE COTTAGES. THE ELMS. FOX (P.H.), *Fox* 1846 White, 1925 Kelly, *Fox Inn* 1877 White. THE HALL, 1846, 1863, 1877 White, *Thorpe Hall* 1831 Curtis, *v*. **hall**. THE HERMITAGE, cf. *Hermitage Farm* 1898 *Deed*, *v*. **ermitage**; but there is no evidence that this was an early religious site. MARKHAM HO., cf. *Markham House farm* 1925 Kelly. ST MICHAEL'S CHURCH, *Thorpe Church* 1826 *Plan*, *The Church* 1877 White, *Church (St Michael)* 1925 Kelly; an early ecclesiastical building here is recorded as *capellam de Torp* 1220 MHW, with MLat *capella* 'a chapel'. THORPE TRUSSELS, 1806 Map, 1835 O, *Thorpe Trussell* 1863 White, ~ *Trussel* 1925 Kelly, a fox covert of the Quorn Hunt; prob. with the common Leics. surn. *Trussell*, cf. *Robertus Trusel* 1195 P of Leics. and *John Trussel* 1395, 1415 Nichols, who held land in Drayton (Gartree Hundred), 14 miles to the south-east; less likely with the obsolete **trussell** 'a bundle', the source of the surn., perh. applied fancifully to a clump of trees. WHITE LODGE, 1925 Kelly, *v*. **loge**.

FIELD-NAMES

Undated forms in (a) are 1843 *TA*; those dated 1814 are *Deed*, 1826 are *Plan*, 1870 are *Sale* and 1969 are *Surv*. Forms throughout dated a.1180 (1449) are *WoCart*, Hy 3 are Dane, 1282 are *Deed*, 1561 (1700) and 1744 are *Rental*, 1682, 1745 and 18 are *Surv*.

(a) Two Acre 1969 (cf. *two ack(e)r close* 1682, 18, *2 Acres Close* 1744, 1745), Three Acre 1843 (cf. *ye three ack(e)r close* 1682, 18, *3 Acres Close* 1744, 1745), Four Acre 1843 (*v*. **æcer**); Adam's Gorse Cl 1870 (*v*. Adam's Gorse *supra*); Little ~ ~, Ashby's Wold (*v*. **wald**; with the surn. *Ashby*); Barn Cl 1826, 1843, 1870, Barn Mdw 1843; Berridges Cl (with the surn. *Berridge*); Best Cl (*v*. **best**; a complimentary name for very fertile land); Blore's Wold (*v*. **wald**; with the surn. *Blore*); Bogg Cl (*v*. **bog**); Bottom Cl; Bottom ~, Top Breakback 1843, Breakback 1969 (a derogatory name for intractable land); Great Brooks, ~ ~ Mdw (*v*. **brōc**); Upper Bull Dale Cl 1814 (*v*. **bula**, **dalr**); Far ~, Grass ~ (*v*. **græs**), Bundells (*le Bonydole* 1282, *v*. **dāl**, perh. with **bony** 'abounding in bones'; otherwise, *bony* in this sense is not recorded until a.1535 (OED), and *bony* 'pleasing to the sight' until 1552 (OED), cf. *Bony doles* in Cossington f.ns. (b)); the Bungalow Fd 1969; Bush Cl (*v*. **busc**); Calf Cl (*v*. **calf**); Chamberlains Cl 1826, 1843, Chamberlain's 1969 (with the surn. *Chamberlain*); Chapel Cl (*v*. **chapel(e)**; no late chapel is recorded for Thorpe Satchville, but *v*. St Michael's Church *supra*); Chaplin's 1969 (with the surn. *Chaplin* in the possessive case); Cheese-cake Cl (*v*. **cheesecake**); Clothman's Cl (with the surn. *Clothman*, *v*. Reaney *s.n.* Clothier); Cook's Cl 1969 (with the surn. *Cook*); Cowslip Mdw 1843, 1870 (*v*. **cū-sloppe**); Crabtree Cl (*v*. **crabtre**); Old Cricket Fd 1969 (for the game of cricket); First ~ ~, Second ~ ~ 1826, Cussington Hills 1969 (cf. *Cusingedale* 1246 Ass, *Cusindale* Edw 3 (c.1430) *KB*; *Cussington*, rather than representing an early **Cus(s)ingtūn* 'farmstead, village associated with a man named Cus(s)a' (with -**ingtūn**, cf. Cossington *supra*), may rather be in origin **Cus(s)andūn* 'Cus(s)a's hill' (with **dūn** and *Cus(s)an*, the possessive case of *Cus(s)a*), the notion of a hill-formation surviving in the modern name *Cussington Hills*, while the medieval forms with *-dale* are likelier to represent an earlier **Cus(s)andæl* 'Cus(s)a's valley' (with **dæl**[1] and *Cus(s)an*); since *Cusingedale* is an Assize Rolls form, and thus prob. not a spelling by a local scribe, it is very unlikely to be significant as indicating an early folk-name formation with *-inga-*, gen.sg. of *-ingas*, and meaning here 'the valley of the people of Cus(s)a'); Fir Dales, ~ ~ Mdw (*v*. **feor**, **deill**); Dennis's Wold (*v*. **wald**; with the surn. *Dennis*); Dove Bank 1826, 1843, ~ Banks 1969 (*v*. **dūfe**, **banke**); Eaton's 1969 (the surn. *Eaton* in the possessive case, cf. Eaton's Fd in Twyford f.ns. (a)); Eight o' Clock Cl 1969 (obscure); Far Cl; Far Hill; Far Mdw; First Mdw; Fisher's Hill (with the surn. *Fisher*); Fish pool Cl 1826, Fish Pool 1969 (*v*. **fisc-pōl**); Golf Links (for the game of golf); Gravel Hill 1843, Gravel Hole 1969, Gravel Pit Cl 1843 (*v*. **gravel**); (the) Great Cl; Hall's Cl (with the surn. *Hall*); Hearty Cl (*v*. **hearty**); Hill Cl; Far ~, Near Hollow 1826, 1843, the Hollows 1969 (*v*. **holh**); Home Cl 1826, Great ~ ~, Little Home Cl 1843, Home Fd 1969 (*v*. **home**); Horse Cl, ~ ~ Mdw; Hovel Cl 1843, 1969 (*v*. **hovel**); Humpback 1969 (alluding to the configuration of the field's surface); Insdale 1826 (with **dalr** or **deill**; earlier forms are needed to explain the first el.); Job's Fd 1969 (with the surn. *Job*, *v*. Reaney *s.n.*); Jorden's Cl (with the surn. *Jorden*, *v.* Jordan's Cl in Thrussington f.ns. (a)); Jump Fd 1969 (presum. a practising ground for equestrians); Kestin's Cl (with the common Leics. surn. *Kestin*, poss. a reduced Kesteven); Lane Cl 1826, 1843 (*v.* **lane**); Lee's Cl (with the surn. *Lee*); Linney's (Far) Cl (with the surn. *Linney*, a reflex of the OE fem. pers.n. *Lindgifu* 'shield-gift'); Far ~ ~, Long Cl; Long Mdw 1969; Manner's Cl (with the surn. *Manners*); Marl Pit, ~ ~ Cl, ~ ~ Fd 1969 (*v.* **marle-pytt**); Maypole Leys, ~ ~ Mdw (*v.* **leys**) (this may simply be land where the maypole was erected for May festivities, but note *le Mapeldole* 1282 in f.ns. (b) and thus the possibility of *mapel* > *maypole*); Middle Cl; Middle Ground 1814, 1843 (*v.* **grund**); Far ~ ~, Near Moll's Wold (*v.* **wald**; with the surn. *Moll*, from a pet-name for Mary); First Myres 1843, Myres Cl 1969 (poss. with the surn. *Myres* rather than with ON **mýrr** 'a marsh' from which it developed, but note *Quagmire Meadow* in f.ns. (b); the usual Leics. spelling of the surn. is *Myers*); New Mdw; New Piece (*v.* **pece**); Old Barn 1969; Old Mdw; Oswin's Cl, Oswin's Wold (*v.* **wald**) (with the surn. *Oswin*, a reflex of the OE pers.n. *Ōswine* 'god-friend'); Paddock 1843, 1969, Top ~ 1969 (*v.* **paddock**); Great ~, Little Padwell 1826, 1843, Bottom ~, Top Padwell 1969 (*v.* **wella**; with the OE pers.n. *Padda*, an original by-name from OE *padde* 'a toad', cf. *Padhull* 1313 Banco, *v.* **hyll**; with the same OE pers.n.); the Park 1969 (*v.* **park**); Parker's Wold (*v.* **wald**; cf. *William Parker* 1843); Best ~ (*v.* **best**), Middle Pestl(e)y 1826, 1843, Second ~, Third Pestly, Pestly Mdw 1826 (obscure; earlier forms are needed, but perh. **prēost**, **lēah** may be thought of); Pick's Mdw 1826, 1843 (with the surn. *Pick*); Pinfold Mdw 1843, Pinfold Slip 1969 (*v.* **slipe**) (*v.* **pynd-fald**); Ploughed Cl 1843, 1969; the Rickyard Fd 1969 (*v.* **reke-yard**); Rippin's Cl (with the surn. *Rippin*, common in Leics.); Road Cl; Sandpit 1969, ~ Cl 1843, 1969 (18, *Sandpitt Close* 1682), Sandpit Mdw 1843, 1969 (*v.* **sand-pytt**); Sandy Nook (*v.* **sandig, nōk**); Second Cl; Seed Fd 1969 (*v.* **sǣd**; in modern f.ns., often used of areas of sown grass); Slang Cl 1843, the Slang 1969 (*v.* **slang**); Slarry Cl 1826, Slurry, Sleary Cl 1969 (*v.* **slory**); Smellings (*v.* **smæl, eng**; cf. Smallings in Wymeswold f.ns. (a)); Spinney Fd 1969; Stockwell 1843, ~ Cl, ~ Mdw 1969 ('stream with a footbridge consisting of a tree-trunk', *v.* **stocc, wella**); Far ~, Near ~, First ~, Second Stokes Cl 1843, Stokes Fd 1969 (with the surn. *Stokes*); Strawberry Fd 1969 (*v.* **streberie**); Tally-ho Hill 1843, 1969, Tallyho Hill Cl 1870 (with the fox-hunting cry 'Tally-ho!'; the hill is beside Adam's Gorse, a fox-covert, hence presum. the site of the onset of many a chase); Thorpe Hill 1969; Thorpe Pasture 1824 O (*v.* **pasture**); Thorpe Would 1800 Nichols (*Walda de Torp'* c.1180 (1449), *Wald de Thorp* 1282, *v.* **wald**); Tin Hut Fd 1969 (*v.* **hut**); Top Cl; Tyre's Cl, Tyres Mdw 1969 (with the surn. *Tyres*); Village Hall Fd 1969; Wellfield 1969 (*v.* **wella**); Bottom ~ ~, Top White Mdw 1843, Bottom ~ ~, Top White's Mdw 1870 (with the surn. *White*); Will's Mdw (with the surn. *Wills*); Williamson's Cl (with the surn. *Williamson*); Wood Cl 1826, 1843, 1969, Far ~ ~, Near ~ ~ 1843 (*v.* **wudu**); Big ~, Far ~, Near Wold, Great ~, Little Wolds (*v.* **wald** and Thorpe Would *supra*).

(b) *Bincroft* 13 (1404) *Laz* (*v.* **binn, croft**); *Colley Grange* 1537 MinAccts, ~ *graunge* 1535 × 45, 1543 × 45 ib, cf. *de la Graunge* 1295 Banco (p) (*v.* **grange**; since there is no record of an ecclesiastical grange here, *Colley* may indicate a grange in private hands; the form of this surn. in Leics. is usually *Coley*, an original by-name from OE **colig* 'coal-black' and of people prob. meaning 'swarthy', and also poss. 'black-haired'); *Crowedale* c.1180 (1449) (*v.* **crāwe, dalr**); *Depedale* c.1180 (1449), 1282 (*v.* **dēop, dalr**); *Flentdole* c.1180 (1449) (*v.* **flint, dāl**); *Foreworde Wold* 1282 (*v.* **foreward, wald**); *othe Grene* 1327 SR (p) (*v.* **þe, grēne**[2]); *le Greyvedole* Hy 3, 1282 (*v.* **grǣfe, dāl**); *le Mapeldole* 1282 (*v.* **mapel, dāl**); *Northfeild* 1561 (1700) (*v.* **norð, feld**; one of the great fields of the township); *Quagmire Meadow* 1734 *Reeve* (*v.* **quagmire**); *Radgres* c.1180 (1449), *le rede gres* 1282 (*v.* **hrēod, græs** and *Redegrese* in Twyford f.ns. (b)); *Southfelde* 1561 (1700) (*v.* **sūð, feld**; one of the great fields); *Tunmannemedwe* Hy 3, 1282 (*v.* **tūn-mann, mǣd** (**mǣdwe** obl.sg.)); *atte Well* 1332 SR (p) (*v.* **atte, wella**); *Westfeild* 1561 (1700) (*v.* **west, feld**; one of the great fields); *atte Weye* 1332 SR (p) (*v.* **atte, weg**); *Wyllydowles* 1561 (1700) (*v.* **wilig, dāl**).

Walton on the Wolds

WALTON ON THE WOLDS

Waletone 1086 DB, 1222 RHug, *Waleton'* 1195 P, 1209 Cur, 1212 *GarCart et passim* to 1254 Val, 1258 RHug, *Waletun* l.12 *GarCart* bis, *Waletuna* l.12 *ib* (p) bis, *Walet'* l.12 *ib* (p), 1212 *ib*
Valetu' l.12 *GarCart* (p)
Waltun' m.13 *MiD*, *Walton*(') 1260, 1261 Cur, 1264 RGrav *et freq*, *Waltone* 1274 (1579), 1276 (1579) *LRoll*
Wauton' 1247 Abbr, 1253 (1449) *WoCart* (p), 1258 RHug, l.12, 13 *MiD*

Affixes are added as:
~ *de Wauz* 1270 RGrav
~ *super Waldas* 1354 Pat, ~ *super le Wolde* 1467, 1563 Nichols, ~ *super Woldes* 1537 Pat, ~ *sup' le Woulds* 1604 SR, ~ *sup' Olds* 1678 LML
~ *othe Wold'*, ~ *othe Wolld*(*e*) 1346 (15) *CCart*
~ *on le Wold*(*e*) 1415, 1464, 1467, 1475 *Pat*
~ *on the Wolds* 1604 LML, ~ *on the Woulds* 1631 ib
~ *Malore* 1386 Fine

'The farmstead, village of the British', *v.* **walh (wala** gen.pl.), **tūn**. Spellings with *u* for *l* are due to AN influence. In the common suffixes, OE (Angl) **wald** has developed its later meaning 'high ground cleared of woodland'. *Willielmus Malory*, ~ *Maulore* held the manor in 1384, 1386 Fine.

ANCHOR (P.H.), *Anchor* 1846, 1863, 1877 White, 1925 Kelly. ASH PLANTATION is *Walton Plantation* 1806 Map, 1836 O, *v.* **plantation**. BAILIFF'S COVERT, *v.* **cover(t)**; poss. with **bailiff**, since *Bailiff* is not a Leics. surn. (perh. cf. Constables Mdw in f.ns. (a) *infra* for another township official). BAULK LANE, *v.* Black Lane *infra*. BIG CLUMP, cf. *Big Clump Field* 1968 *Surv*, *v.* **clump**. BLACK LANE, e.18 *Terrier*, 1796 *EnclA*; this continues as Baulk Lane *supra*, hence *v.* **balca**. COTESWICK

FM. THE DENE. THE HAYS, *v.* **(ge)hæg**. HOMELEIGH, *Holmleigh* 1925 Kelly. THE HOMESTEAD, cf. *Oldham's Homestead* 1796 *EnclA*, *v.* **ham-stede**; with the surn. *Oldham*. LIME HOLE PLANTATION, cf. *Limepit Wong* 1700 *Terrier*, *v.* **lyme-pytt, vangr**. MANOR FM, *Manor farm* 1925 Kelly, *v.* Old Manor *infra*. MIDDLE FM. MIDDLE PLANTATION. NEW LANE. NORTH PLANTATION. OLD MANOR is *Manor house* 1925 Kelly, *v.* **maner**. THE RECTORY, 1877 White, 1925 Kelly, *Rectory House* 1825 *Terrier*, *v.* **rectory**; cf. *the Parsonidge house* 1700, e.18 *ib*, *v.* **personage**. THE ROOKERY, 1877 White, cf. *Rookery farm* 1925 Kelly, *v.* **rookery**. ST MARY'S CHURCH, *Church (St Mary)* 1846, 1863, 1877 White, 1925 Kelly; the earlier church (of St Bartholomew) is recorded as *ecclesia*(*m*) ~ ~, *ecclesie de Waleton* 1220 MHW, 1238, 1249 RGros, *ecclesie de Walton super Waldas* 1354 *Pat*, ~ *de Walton on le Wolde* 1415 *ib* and in the pair *ecclesiarum de Walton on le Wold et Cosyngton* 1464, 1467, 1475 *ib*. Note also *the Church yard* 1796 *EnclA*, 1825 *Terrier*. SHEEP-LE FM (sic), cf. (*the*) *Sheep Leys* 1796 *EnclA*, *v.* **scēp, leys**. SHITTLEWOOD'S BARN, cf. *John Shytylwood* 1524 SR, *Daniel Shittlewood* 1628 ib, *Francis Shuttlewood, farmer* 1846 White, *John Shuttlewood, farmer* 1877 ib. SMALL CLUMP, cf. Big Clump *supra*. TOP TOWN PLANTATION, *v.* **tūn**. WALTON BROOK, 1836 O, 1925 Kelly, *Walton Brooke* 1694 *Reeve*, *the Brooke* 1796 *EnclA*, e.18 *Terrier*, ((*in*) *torrentem de Waleton'* 1212 *GarCart*, with MLat *torrens* (*torrentem* acc.sg.) 'a fast-flowing stream'), *v.* **brōc**. WALTON GRANGE, 1908 *Sale*, *The Grange* 1877 White, *v.* **grange**. WALTON HOLME, *the Holme* e.18, 1825 *Terrier*, *v.* **holmr**. WALTON LODGE. WALTON THORNS, 1806, 1815 Map, 1836 O, 1925 Kelly, cf. *Walton Thorn Lodge* 1863 White (*v.* **loge**), *Walton Thorns Farm* 1928 *Deed*, *v.* **þorn**. WALTON TOP FM. WHITE LODGE FM.

FIELD-NAMES

Undated forms in (a) are 1968 *Surv*; those dated 1782 are *Surv*, 1796 are *EnclA* and 1825 are *Terrier*. Forms throughout dated 1614 are Ipm, while 1700 and e.18 are *Terrier*.

(a) Six Acre (*v.* **æcer**); Miss Andersons Fds; (the) Ash Cl 1796 (*v.* **æsc**); the Back Lane, Back Lane Cl 1796 (*v.* **back**); Barrow Nether Road 1796 (Barrow upon Soar adjoins to the south-west); Mr Bosworth's Headland 1782 (*v.* **hēafod-land**; the surn. *Bosworth* may be derived from either Husbands Bosworth or Market Bosworth, both Leics. townships); Bottom Fd; (the) Broomfield Cl 1796 (*Bromfield close*, ~ ~ *furlong* 1700, *Bromfeild close*, ~ ~ *furlong* e.18 (*v.* **furlang**), *v.* **brōm**); Bybarrow Fd 1796, 1825 (*Bibroughs* 1700, *Bybroughs* e.18, *Bibrough Field* 1700, *Bybrough Feild* e.18, *v.* **bī, berg**); Chapmans Fd (with the surn. *Chapman*); Mr Cheslyns Coppice 1782 (*v.* **copis**); Clarks Fd (with the surn. *Clark*); (the) Cock Cl 1796, 1825 (*v.* **cocc**[2]); Cockling Croft Fd 1796 (*Cogling croft* 1700, e.18, ~ ~ *field* 1700, ~ ~ *Feild* e.18, *v.* **croft**; poss. with the surn. *Cockling* (*v.* Reaney *s.n.*) which appears in Leics. as *Cocklin* (though rarely); a topographical name describing a small rounded hill (with **cogg** and **-ling**) may also be thought of, but earlier forms are needed); the Coney Cl 1796 (*v.* **coni**); Constables Mdw (the surn. *Constable* is rare in the county, thus perh. with **conestable**, a township official, cf. Bailiff's Covert *supra*); Coopers Mdw (with the surn. *Cooper*); the Cottage Croft 1796 (*v.* **croft**), the Cottage Fd 1968 (*v.* **cotage**); the Cow Cls 1796, 1825; Cowpens (*v.* **penn**[2]); (the) Cramp Cl 1796 (*v.* **cramb**); Debdale Cl 1796 (*Debdall* e.18, cf. *Debdall hedge* 1700 (*v.* **hecg**), *v.* **dēop, dalr**); Gambles Fd (with the surn. *Gamble*, a reflex of the ON pers.n. *Gamall*); Gravel Pit (*v.* **gravel**); Mr Hall's Land 1782 (*v.* **land**); Hardy's Cl (with the surn. *Hardy*); the Herring Shoot 1782 (*v.* **scēot**[3]; earlier forms are needed for *Herring*, but note Herring Cl in South Croxton f.ns. (a)); High Barn Cl 1782; Hoggin Hole (1700, *Short hogginhole* e.18, *v.* **hogging, hol**[1]); the Holme Mdw 1796 (cf. *ye Home Furlong* 1700 (*v.* **furlang**), *v.* **holmr** and Walton Holme *supra*); Home Fd (*v.* **home**); Horse Cl; the Horse Leys 1796 (*v.* **leys**); Hovel Fd (cf. *the houill close* e.18, *v.* **hovel**); Jacks Hole (*Jackanap(e)s hole* 1700, e.18, *v.* **jackanapes, hol**[1]); Keatings, Bottom ~, Top Keightlings (sic) (poss. with the surn. *Keating* in the possessive case); Little Cl; the Long Hedge 1782 ((*the*) *Long hedg* 1700), Long Hedge Headland 1782 (*v.* **hēafod-land**), the Long Hedge Shoot 1782 (*v.* **scēot**[3]); the Long Sike 1825 (*the Long sicke*(*e*) 1700, e.18), Long Sike Fd 1796 (*Long Sick feild* e.18) (*v.* **sík**); Loughborough Road 1796, 1825 (Loughborough lies 4 miles to the west); the Meadow; Middle Croft 1796, ~ Craft 1968 (*Middle croft* 1700, *Midlecroft* e.18, *v.* **middel, croft**); Middle Sand Fd (*v.* **sand**); Millbush (*v.* **myln, busc**); (the) Nether Cl 1796; Nether Fd 1782, 1796, 1825 (1700, (*le*) *Nether feild* 1614, e.18), Nether field Cl, (the) Nether field Road 1796; the Pasture 1796, 1825 (*v.* **pasture**); Packman Road 1796, 1825, Packmans ~ 1796 (*Packman way* e.18, *v.* **packeman, weg**); Pen Fd (*v.* **penn**[2]); the Pingle 1796 (*v.* **pingel**); Plaster Hill Fd (*v.* **plaster** and cf. Plaster Pit Barn in adjacent Burton on the Wolds); Polly Flinders Corner (*v.* **corner**; presum. with late reference to the nursery rhyme character Little Polly Flinders who 'sat among the cinders' and thus poss. the site of some early industrial waste (cf. the Slag *infra*); *flinders* are 'fragments, pieces', so that the association with Polly Flinders may have developed from the presence of such waste materials); Raven Cl 1796 (poss. with **hræfn** rather than with the surn. *Raven* (for which *v.* Reaney *s.n.*); perh. cf. Rancliff Wood in adjacent Burton on the Wolds); Robinsons Fds (with the surn. *Robinson*); Sandpit (*v.* **sand-pytt**); Scottie (unexplained; as a surn., *Scottie* is very rare, but poss. is a familiar form of the surn. *Scott*); Seagrave Road 1796 (Seagrave adjoins to the south-east); Severn Acre (*v.* **æcer**; poss. with a pre-English stream-name *Severne*, *v.* *Seuene Wong* in adjoining Seagrave f.ns. (b)); Sheepgate Cl 1792 Nichols, 1796 (*v.* **shepe-gate**); Sixhill Road 1796, Sixhills ~ 1825 (*v.* Six Hills); the Slag (sic) 1782 (presum. this is not in error for the Slade *infra*; perh. with **slagg**, *v.* Polly Flinders Corner *supra*, but note the ME adj. **slag** 'slippery with mud'); the Slade, Slade Fd 1782 (*v.* **slæd**); Smith Cl 1796, Smiths ~ 1968 (either with the surn. *Smith* or with **smið**); (the) Street Hill Fd 1796, 1825 (*Streethill* 1700, e.18, *v.* **strǣt**; with reference to the Roman road Margary 58a across the Wolds, continuing to Barrow upon Soar); Swine Hole (*v.* **swīn**[1], **hol**[1]); Top Fd; the Town Street 1796 (*v.*

tūn, strǣt); the Turnpike Road 1782 (*v.* **turnepike**); Tylers Corner (*v.* **corner**; with the surn. *Tyler*); Vestys Cl (with the surn. *Vesty*); Wagon Holes (*v.* **wægn, wag(g)on**; poss. with **hovel** rather than **hol**[1], cf. Waggon Hovel Cl in Halstead f.ns. (a)); Walton Dump Fd 1782 (either with **dump**[1], here alluding to a deep hole in the bed of the river Soar or to a deep depression in the ground (cf. Norw *dump* 'a pit, a pool', Dan dial. *dump* 'a natural depression in the earth'), or with **dump**[2] 'a place where refuse from a mine or quarry is deposited'); Walton Mdw; Walton New Covert 1806 Map (*v.* **cover(t)**); Walton Wolds 1836 O (*the Woulds* e.18), the Woulds Cl 1796 (*v.* **wald**); (the) Western Cl 1796, 1825, 1968 (*v.* **westerne**); Whitcrofts Fd (with the surn. *Whitcroft*).

(b) *ye Acars*, ~ *Acres* 1700, *the Acres* e.18, *the Acre furlong* e.18 (*v.* **furlang**) (*v.* **æcer**); *Barrough hedg* e.18 (*v.* **hecg**; the parish boundary with Barrow upon Soar which adjoins to the south-west); *Blunts hadland* e.18 (*v.* **hēafod-land**; with the surn. *Blunt*); *the Midle brook* e.18, *(the) Nether Brook(e)* 1700, e.18, *the Upper Brook* 1700, e.18 (presum. these are furlong names), *Brook furlong* 1700, *the broock furlong* e.18 (*v.* **furlang**) (*v.* **brōc**); *Buckland wong* 1700 (*v.* **vangr**; either with the surn. *Buckland* or with **bōc-land**, cf. *Bucklandes* in Normanton, Lei **2** 42); *Burton Balk* 1700, e.18 (*v.* **balca**), *Burton gate* 1700, e.18 (*v.* **gata**) (Burton on the Wolds adjoins to the north); *Cakelands* 1614, 1700, e.18 (*v.* **calc, land**; also present in adjoining Seagrave parish); *the Close furlong* 1700, e.18 (*v.* **clos(e), furlang**); *the Cow Pasture* e.18 (*v.* **pasture**); *the Cunnery End* 1700, e.18 (*v.* **coningre, ende**); *Dawson leas* e.18 (*v.* **leys**; with the surn. *Dawson*); *the Flash* e.18 (*v.* **flasshe**); *ye Flatt* 1700 (*v.* **flat**); *the furry close* e.18, *Furry close furlong* 1700 (*v.* **furlang**) (*v.* **fyrs, -ig**[3]); *the hall hades furlong* e.18 (*v.* **hall, hēafod, furlang**); *the holme furlong* e.18 (*v.* **holmr, furlang**); *Littleburgh Slade* 1700, *Little Brow slade* e.18 (*v.* **lȳtel, berg, slæd**); *ye Long furlong* 1700, e.18 (*v.* **furlang**); *the Midle Feild* e.18 (*v.* **middel, feld**); *Miln furlong* 1700 (*v.* **furlang**), *the Miln hades, the Milne heads* 1700 (*v.* **hēafod**) (*v.* **myln**); *ye Moore* 1700, *the More* e.18, *Moore Ditch* 1700 (*v.* **dīc**) (*v.* **mōr**[1]); *Parsons sicke* e.18 (*v.* **persone, sík**); *ye Paylehedge furlong* 1700, *the payle hedg furlong* e.18 (*v.* **pale, furlang**; the second el. may be **edisc** rather than **hecg**,); *Seagrave brucke* e.18 (*v.* **brōc**; Seagrave adjoins to the south-east); *the Sheepcoat close* 1700, *Sheepcote* ~ e.18 (*v.* **scēp-cot**); *Stonepit furlong* 1700 (*v.* **furlang**), *Ston(e)pit Leas* 1700, e.18 (*v.* **leys**) (*v.* **stān-pytt**); *Syleby Balk* 1700, *Silby baulke* e.18 (*v.* **balca**; Sileby parish lies beyond Seagrave parish, south of Walton on the Wolds, and thus has no boundary in common with Walton; there may have been unrecorded boundary adjustments hereabouts, but if not, then the f.n. must contain the surn. *Sileby* based on the township name); *ye Walkmill Nook* 1700 (*v.* **walke-milne, nōk**; this may be the *Walkemylnenoke* of adjoining Barrow upon Soar f.ns. (b)); *atte Welle* 1327 SR (p), 1333 Pat (p) (*v.* **atte, wella**); *Westons hadland* e.18 (*v.* **hēafod-land**; cf. *Anthony Weston* e.18); *Whinny Leas* 1700, e.18 (*v.* **whinny, leys**).

Whatborough

WHATBOROUGH

Wetberga, *Wetberge* 1086 DB, *Weteberue* l.13 *CRCart* (p)
Wateberga c.1130 LeicSurv, 1167 P *et passim* to 1182 ib (p), Hy2 *AllS*, *Wateberege* 1155 RBE, *Wateberg(e)* 1225 GildR, 1230 MemR *et freq* to 1267 *LCDeeds* (p), 1273 *Wyg et passim* to 1298, 1367 *AllS*, *Watebergh'* 1327 SR (p), 1351, 1397 *AllS*, *Wateberew* Hy 2 *ib*, 1238 Cl *et passim* to 1313, 1347 *AllS*, *Wateberu* 1312 *ib*, *Wateberwe* 1315 *ib*
What(e)berge Hy 2 *AllS*, 1220 Cur (p) *et passim* to Hy 3 Nichols, 1298 *AllS*, *Whatebergh* 1314 Coram, 1331 Cl (p) *et passim* to 1380 *AllS*, 1428 FA, *Whateberuw* Hy 2 *AllS*, *What(e)berew* Hy 3 Nichols, 1379 *AllS*, *Whatbarough* 1440, 1469, 1478 *ib*, *Whatbarowe* 1483 *ib*, 1507 Pat, *Whatborow(e)* 1525 *AllS*, 1535 VE, *Whatborough* 1478 Pat *et passim*
Whadbergh(e) 1386, 1396 *AllS*, (*le*) *Whadborowe* 1451 *ib*, 1539 Nichols, *Whadbarow* 1528 Visit, *Whadboro(u)gh* 1535 VE, 1539 Nichols, 1604 Fine, *Whadborowgh alias Wateborowgh* 1541 Nichols, *Whadborrough* 1674 *Terrier*
Weteburg(h) Hy 2 *AllS*, *Wetteburg'* e.13 *Wyg* (p), *W(h)ateburgh* 1328 Banco (p), 1384 *AllS*, *Wadburgh* 1451 *ib*, *Whaddeburgh* 1465 *ib*

'The hill where wheat is grown', *v.* **hwǣte, berg**. In the Domesday Survey, Whatborough is described as having three villagers, one freeman and eleven smallholders, while the Matriculus of Hugh de Welles of 1220 refers to a chapel here. No township survives on Whatborough Hill. It belonged to All Souls College, Oxford, after 1437 but was leased to Launde Priory, which by 1495 had wholly enclosed it for sheep pastures.

From the reign of Henry II, occasional spellings of the generic have been attracted to OE *burh* 'a fortified site'. It is interesting to note that immediately following the entry for Whatborough on folio 230, DB records that 1½ carucates of land *in Burgo* (i.e. 'in The Burgh') belong to Whatborough. W. G. Hoskins (*Essays in Leicestershire History*, 95–6) treats 'The Burgh' as a lost township between Whatborough and Launde.

Minor names relating to it such as *Burgthueit* 1162 × 66 *AllS* and *Burgness* Hy 3 Nichols occur from the 12th cent. onwards. Whether this was the original settlement to which 'the wheat hill' belonged is uncertain, but movement of the principal habitation site from 'The Burgh' to Whatborough in more secure times may have taken place.

WHATBOROUGH FM is presum. the site of *Whatborough Lodge* 1663 LeicW, *v.* **loge**. WHATBOROUGH HILL, *Whadborough Hill* 1831 Curtis. WHATBOROUGH RD is *Whatborough gate* 1586 *Plan*, *v.* **gata**.

FIELD-NAMES

Forms in (a) dated 1800 are Nichols. Forms throughout dated 1162 × 66, Hy 2[1], 1305, 1525 and 1609 are *AllS*; Hy 2[2] are Dugd; a.1250 and Hy 3 are Nichols; 1536 are AAS; 1586 are *Plan*; 1591 are *Deposition*; 16 are *Terrier*; 1620 are LAS.

(a) Brockburrow 1800 (*Brockborow*, *Brokebarowe* 1586, *Brockbergh* 1620, *v.* **brōc, berg**).

(b) *Black Thorn Leas* 1586 (*v.* **blæc-þorn, leys**); *Bruckburow close* 1591 (*v.* **clos(e)**), *Brockborow gate* 1586 (*v.* **gata**) (*v.* Brockburrow in f.ns. (a)); *Browning leaes* 1586 (*v.* **leys**; with the surn. *Browning*, a reflex of the OE pers.n. *Brūning*); *la Burgh* a.1250, *Burgness* Hy 3 (*v.* **næss**), *Burgthueit* 1162 × 66, Hy 2[1], *Burthett al's Burfytt al's Burfeilde* 1586 (*v.* **þveit**) (*v.* **burh** and the discussion of Whatborough *supra*); *capellas Watheberg' et Merdefeld* 1220 MHW (with MLat *capella* 'a chapel'; Whatborough was once a chapelry of Tilton on the Hill, while *Merdefeld* is neighbouring Marefield, 2 miles to the north-west); *the Doales* 1586 (*v.* **dāl**); *the Great Close* (*v.* **grēat, clos(e)**); *Heresmore* Hy 2[2] (*v.* **mōr**[1]; ostensibly with OE *here* 'an army', but very unlikely; note the following f.n.); *Herewardeswde* Hy 2[2] (*v.* **wudu**, with the OE pers.n. *Hereward*; the previous f.n. *Heresmore* may well be a garbled **Herewardesmore*, since the two f.ns. are from the same early source and *here* with *mōr* seems historically an unlikely combination); *Hole Crofte* 1586 (*v.* **hol**[1], **croft**); *Lighte hill* 1586 (*v.* **lēoht, hyll**); *Longeholme* 1305 (*v.* **lang**[1], **holmr**); *the Moore Close* 1586 (*v.* **mōr**[1], **clos(e)**); *the Newe Close* 1586 (*v.* **nīwe, clos(e)**); *Oke stile* 1586 (*v.* **āc, stigel**); *Rushe meadowe* 1586 (*v.* **risc, mǣd (mǣdwe** obl.sg.)); *Stanwelsyke* 1586 (*v.* **stān, wella, sík**); *Tyrle meadowe* 1586 (*v.* **tyrl** 'that which turns or rolls along', prob. a stream-name, cf. Tirle Brook, Gl **1** 13); *Whateboroughe Close or Pasture* 1586 (*v.* **pasture**), *Whadborow* ~ 1591, *Whadburrowe Close* 1609 (*v.* **clos(e)**), *Whadbarrowe close hedge* 1609 (*v.* **hecg**), *Whatbore Felde*, *Watbarowfelde* 16 (*v.* **felde**), *Whatbarow okys* 1525 (*v.* **āc**); *Withcocke gate* 1586 (*v.* **gata**; Withcote lies some 1½ miles to the east); *Wolsterne* 1586 (*v.* **þyrne**; with the OE pers.n. *Wulf*).

Wymeswold

WYMESWOLD

Wimvndeswald 1086 DB, *Wimundeswald* 1205, 1206, 1207 P, *Wymundeswald*(*e*) a.1183 Potter, 1209 x 35 RHug, 1316 Pat, *Wimvndeswale* 1086 DB

la Wymundeswald 1254 Misc

Wimvndewalle 1086 DB, *Wimundewald'* 1166 P (p), l.12 *GarCart* (freq), 1199 FF *et passim* to 1236 Fees, 13 *BHosp*, *Wymundewald'* 1198 Fees, 1220 MHW *et passim* to 1256 *MiD*, 1272 Cur, *Wymundwald* 1247 Ass, 1254 Val, 1316 Pat, *Wymund*(*e*)*waud* 1242 Fees, 1258 RHug, 1260 Ass, 1267 Lib

Wimundeswold' a.1183 Potter, 1212 Cur, *Wymundeswold*(*e*) 1261, 1268 Cur *et passim* to 1407 (15) *CCart*, 1428 FA, *Wymondeswold*(*e*) 1326 Cl (p), 1326 Pat (p), 1330 FA *et freq* to 1449 *RTemple*, 1456 *MiD et passim* to 1488, 1493 *ib*, *Wymundswold* 1247 Ass

Wymondesolde 1498 *MiD*, *Wymondisolde* 1500 *ib*

Wimundewold' Hy 2 *BHosp*, l.12 *GarCart*, e.13 *BHosp* (freq) *et passim* to 1346, 1349 Pap (p), *Wymundewold*(*e*) e.13 *BHosp*, 1212 *GarCart*, 1256 *MiD et freq* to 1359 Pat, 1362 Pap (p), *Wimondewold* 13 *BHosp*, *Wymondewold*(*e*) 1276, 1341, 1342 Cl, 1457 *Ct*, *Wimundwold* 1276 RH, *Wymundwold'* 1252 Fees, 1276 IpmR *et passim* to 1389 Coram, 1425 *MiD*, *Wymondwold*(*e*) 1307 Pat, 1316 FA, 1359, 1374 *MiD*

Wymeswold(*e*) 1406 Pat,1418 *Comp*, 1502 *MiscAccts et passim* to 1536, 1537 *RTemple et freq*, *Wymyswold* 1502 *MiscAccts*, 1538 *Deed*, 1541 MinAccts, *Wimeswold*(*e*) 1572, 1574 LEpis, 1576 LibCl, *Wymswold* 1550 Pat, 1555 *Ct*, *Wym*(*m*)*yswould* 1518 Visit, 1554 Ex-Rel, *Wymeswould* 1523 AAS, 1604 SR, *Wimyswould* 1526 AAS, *Wimeswoud* 1614, 1619 LML

Wymeshold 1519 EpCB, *Wymysolde* 1535 VE, *Wymsold*(*e*) 1536, 1538 *MiD*, 1549 Pat, *Wymysold* 1544 *MiD*, *Wymesolde* 1566 *Ct*

'Wīgmund's portion of the Wolds district', *v.* **wald**. The name refers to a sizeable area of wold country belonging to the Anglo-Saxon *Wīgmund*. The interesting 1254 form *la Wymundeswald* (with the OFr def.art. *la*, hence 'the wold country of Wīgmund') indicates that even by the middle of the 13th century, the emphasis was still on the land unit rather than on the habitation site which had developed within it. It is possible that Wīgmund was the same magnate who gave his name to the early estate of Wymondham, 15 miles to the east in Framland Hundred (*v.* Lei **2** 286), cf. Prestwold *supra*.

BAPTIST CHAPEL, built 1781 (on date-stone). BARN FM. BARRACK COTTAGES, *barrack* is sometimes a reflex of *berewīc* 'a barley farm, a grange, an outlying or demesne farm', but there are no early forms here to support this interpretation; more likely is **barrack** 'a temporary shelter, a rude hutment', referring to a building which preceded the cottages. BROOK ST, *Brooke Street* 1759 *EnclA*, (*the*) *Brook street* 1800 Nichols, 1863, 1877 White, 1915 Potter, 1925 Kelly, *v.* **brōc**. BULL'S HEAD (P.H.) (lost), *Bull's Head* 1846, 1863, 1877 White. CRIPWELL FM, *Cripwell farm* 1925 Kelly; poss. 'curling, winding stream' as in *Cripswell* in adjacent Willoughby on the Wolds (Nt 325) (*v.* **cyrps**, **wella**), although the surn. *Cripwell* belongs especially to southern Notts. and is also found in Leics. in the western Wolds villages in the 19th cent. DUNGEHILL FM, (*the*) *Dungeon* 1759 *EnclA*, 1877 White, *v.* **dyncge**, **hyll**, cf. Dungeon Mdw in Hoby f.ns. (a). EAST ST, *East street* 1863, 1877 White, 1925 Kelly, *~ ~ or Little End* 1915 Potter, *v.* **ende**. ELLER'S FM, *Ella's farm* 1925 Kelly, ELLER'S GORSE, *Ellas Gorse* 1836 O, *v.* **gorst**, cf. *Wm. Ella* 1846 White. THE ELMS, *Elm est* (*v.* **ēast**), *~ south*, *~ west* 1620 Terrier, *v.* **elm**. FAR ST, *Far street* 1863, 1877 White, 1915 Potter, 1925 Kelly. FIELD FM, *Field farm* 1925 Kelly, *v.* **feld**. FOX (P.H.) (lost), *Fox* 1846, 1863, 1877 White. GAMBER'S HILL LODGE, *Gambers Hill* 1944 *Sale*; it is *Granborough Hill* 1759 *EnclA*, *Granborough* 1915 Potter, *v.* **grēne**[1], **berg**, cf. Grandborough, Bk 134 and Wa 130. HIGHTHORN FM, *Highthorns* 1877 White, *v.* **hēah**[1], **þorn**. HOLMLEA, *Home Leys* 1759 *EnclA*, *Holm Lea* 1925 Kelly, *v.* **holmr**, **leys**. LONDON ST. MANOR HO., *The Manor House* 1863, 1877 White, *v.* **maner**. METHODIST CHAPEL. MILL COTTAGE, *v.* Old Windmill *infra*. MUSHILL FM, MUSHILL LANE, *Mushill* 1877 White, cf. *Muswell* 1543 Terrier, c.1625 *Terrier*, *v.* **mūs**, **wella**; *Mushill* is prob. a development of *Muswell*, cf. *fourwell* > *Fore-hill* in f.ns. (b) *infra*. NARROW LANE, *The Narrow Lane* 1836 O, *v.* **nearu**, **lane**, cf. Wide Lane *infra*. OLD WINDMILL, *the Wynd myll of Maister Robert Leake* 1601 *Terrier*, *ye*

Wind-Miln 1703 *ib*, *the Windmilne* e.18 *Surv*, *the Windmill* 1759 *EnclA*; also *the Mill* c.1700, 1704, 1709, 1712, 1724 *Terrier*, *the Milne* 1708 (18) *ib*, *Wimeswold Mill* 1836 O, *v.* **wind-mylne**, **myln**; note that two windmills are present in the parish in 1836 O. THE PEASLANDS, *Pease Lands* 1759 *EnclA*, *v.* **pise**, **land**. ROSE AND CROWN (P.H.) (lost), *Rose and Crown* 1877 White. ST MARY'S CHURCH, *the Church* 1708 (18) *Terrier*, *the Parish Church* 1759 *EnclA*, *Church (St Mary)* 1846, 1863, 1877 White, 1925 Kelly; it is earlier recorded as *ecclesie de Wymundewald* 1220 MHW, *ecclesia parochiali de Wymsolde* 1549 *Pat*, and in the groups *ecclesiarum de Norton Wymundeswald et Edwaldeston* 1316 *ib* and *ecclesias de Sedbargh . . . et Wymeswold* 1554 *ib*. Note also *the Churchyard* 1625, 1708 (18) *Terrier*, *v.* **chirche-ȝeard**. SHEEPWASH, *the Sheep Wash* 1759 *EnclA*, *v.* **scēp-wæsce**. SHOULDER OF MUTTON (P.H.) (lost), *Shoulder of Mutton* 1877 White. STOCKWELL, 1847, 1915 Potter, cf. *Stockwell street* 1863, 1877 White, 1925 Kelly; 'stream with a footbridge consisting of a tree-trunk', *v.* **stocc**, **wella**. STORKIT LANE, *Stalkott lane* 1703 *Terrier*, *Stalkett Lane* 1759 *EnclA*, *v.* **stall**, **cot**, **lane**. THREE CROWNS (P.H.), *Three Crowns* 1846, 1863, 1877 White, 1925 Kelly. TURNPOST FM, *Turnpost farm* 1925 Kelly; at a Y-junction of roads leading from the village; the compound *turnpost* is unrecorded in OED and EDD but may be a local alternative for *turnpike*. THE VICARAGE, 1877 White, 1925 Kelly; cf. *an house called the old vicaridge* 1625 *Terrier*, *the Old Vicarage* 1708 (18) *ib*, *v.* **vikerage**. WEST BANK, *v.* **banke**. WEST COTTAGE. WHITE HORSE (P.H.) (lost), *White Horse* 1877 White, 1925 Kelly. WIDE LANE is *The Great Lane* 1836 O, *v.* **grēat**, **lane**, cf. Narrow Lane *supra*. WILLOUGHBY GORSE, 1836 O, *v.* **gorst**; it is *Allsops Covert* 1806 Map, *v.* **cover(t)**, with the surn. *Allsop*; Willoughby on the Wolds in Notts. adjoins to the north-east. WINDMILL (P.H.), *Wind Mill* 1846 White, *Windmill* 1863 ib, *Windmill Tavern* 1877 ib, *Windmill Inn* 1925 Kelly. WINFIELD'S LANE, cf. *Wm. Winfield* 1846 White. WOLDS FM, *Wolds farm* 1925 Kelly, *v.* **wald**. WOODGATE HO., *Woodgate* 1543 Terrier, *v.* **wudu**, **gata**. WOODLAND COTTAGE. WYMESWOLD HALL, *the Hall* e.18 *Surv*, *v.* **hall**. WYMESWOLD LODGE, 1877 White, 1925 Kelly, *v.* **loge**.

The following road-names are either lost or remain current only locally:

Back Lane 1759 *EnclA*, *v.* **back**.
Bossy Gate, *~ ~ Road* 1759 *EnclA*, *v.* **gata** and *Bossehow-* in f.ns. (b).
Burton lane 1759 *EnclA*, 1877 White, *Burton Road* 1759 *EnclA*; Burton on the Wolds adjoins to the south.

Chapel bar 1877 White, 1925 Kelly, *v.* **chapel(e)**, **barre**; this may be a transferred street-name from nearby Nottingham which there records a medieval gateway to the old town (*v.* Nt 15). In Wymeswold, the name presum. relates in some sort to the Baptist Chapel.

Church Lane 1915 Potter, *v.* St Mary's Church *supra*.

Clay street 1925, cf. *the Clay* 1666 *Deed*, 1863, 1877 White, 1915 Potter, *v.* **clǣg**.

Innergate 1759 *EnclA*, *Inney Gate* 1971 *Surv*, *v.* **innar**, **gata**.

Littelende 1402 Cor, *Little End* 1759 *EnclA*, 1863, 1877 White, 1915 Potter, *the Little End of the Town* 1759 *EnclA*, *v.* **lȳtel**, **ende** and East St *supra*.

Loughborough Road 1759 *EnclA*; Loughborough lies 4½ miles to the south-west.

Marthegrevegate a.1183 (l.14) *Beau*, *v.* **gata**; an early local name for the Fosse Way en route to Belgrave (*q.v.*) whose original form contained *mearð* 'a marten or weasel' rather than *bel* 'beautiful'.

Mill Lane 1759 *EnclA*, *v.* Old Windmill *supra*.

(*the*) *Old Gate* 1759 *EnclA*, *Oldgate* 1971 *Surv*, *the Old Road* 1759 *EnclA*, *v.* **gata**; prob. with **wald** rather than with **ald**.

Remson gate 1543 Terrier (*v.* **gata**), *Rempston Way* 1601 *Terrier* (*v.* **weg**), *Rempston lane* 1601, 1700, c.1700, 1709, 1712, 1724 *ib*, *Rempson* ~ 1704 *ib*, *Remstone* ~1708 (18), *Rempston Road* 1759 *EnclA*, *Rempstone* ~ 1818, 1825 *Terrier*; Rempstone in Notts. adjoins to the north-west.

Saltestrete 1412 Cor, *Sawestrete*, *Sawstrete* 1543 Terrier, *Lyttell Sawstrete* 1543 ib (*v.* **lȳtel**), *v.* **salt**[1], **strǣt**; a salters' way, poss. the Roman road Margary 58a across the Wolds to Barrow upon Soar. It is uncertain whether *Lyttell Sawstrete* refers to a local branch from it (?Wide Lane *supra*). A salters' way may have led north-west via Wymeswold from the ford at Asfordby.

the Vale Road 1759 *EnclA*, *v.* **val**.

West End 1925 Kelly, *v.* **ende**.

Westwoldgate 1412 *Ct*, *West Wold gate* 1418 *Comp*, *v.* **west**, **wald**, **gata**.

Willoughby Road 1759 *EnclA*; Willoughby on the Wolds in Notts. adjoins to the north-east.

Wimeswold Town Street 1849 *TA*; it is *Townlane* 1620 Terrier, *v.* **tūn**, **strǣt**, **lane**.

the Woulds Lane 1759 *EnclA*, *Burton Woulds Lane* 1759 *ib*, *v.* **wald**; Burton on the Wolds adjoins to the south, with Burton Wolds to the south-east.

the Wysall Road 1759 *EnclA*, *Wysall lane* 1925 Kelly; note also *Wysall Foot Way* 1759 *EnclA*, *v*. **fote-waye**. Wysall in Notts. lies 2 miles to the north.

The following houses are recorded in e.18 *Surv*: *Wm. Baxters house*, *Ralfe Dudleys ~*, *Thomas Fewkes ~*, *Thomas Grundleys ~*, *Wm. Marshalls house*, *Wm. Phipps his house*, *Edward Plowrights ~*, *Thomas Wildeges house*.

FIELD-NAMES

Undated forms in (a) are 1759 *EnclA*; those dated 1818 and 1825 are *Terrier*, 1848 are *Plan*, 1849 are *TA*, 1915 are Potter and 1971 are *Surv*. Forms throughout dated Hy 2, e.13 and 13^2 are *BHosp*, a.1183 (l.14) are *Beau*, l.12 and 1212 are *GarCart*, 1256, 1293 and 1331 are *MiD*, 13^1 are Deed, 1389 and 1395 are Cor, 1412 are *Ct*, 1418 are *Comp*, c.1425 are *SW*, 1543 and 1620 are Terrier, 1601, 1625, c.1625, 1674, 1700, c.1700, 1703, 1704, 1708 (18), 1709, 1712 and 1724 are *Terrier*.

(a) Four ~, Six Acre, Bottom ~ ~, Top 7 ~, Nine ~, 12 ~, 15 Acre 1971 (*v*. **æcer**); Anthony Leys Cl (with the surn *Ley* in the possessive case); Arrow Fd 1759, 1915 (*Horrou* 1212, *Orrow* c.1425, *Harrowefeld* 1412, *Arrowfeild* 1620, *Arrowe feilde* c.1625, *v*. **feld**; one of the great fields of the township), Arrow Hill 1915 (poss. with **hærg** 'a heathen temple, a sacred grove'; the site is adjacent to *Vernemeto*(*n*) (Brit **nemeton* 'a sacred grove', with **uer* 'great'), a Romano-British settlement on the Fosse Way; note also *Cumberdale* in f.ns. (b) *infra* which indicates RB survival here); Ballow Woulds (*Ballowald* e.13, *Ballow wold* 13^1, cf. *Ballewaldebreche* 13^2, *Balhobreche* l.12, *Ballowebrechis* e.13, 13^1 (*v*. **brēc**), *v*. **ball, hōh, wald**); Band Lands 1759, 1971 (*Bandlandes* 1543, *Bandlands* 1674, *Ban-lands* 1700, cf. *Bandlande hades* c.1625 (*v*. **hēafod**), *v*. **bēan, land**); Barn Fds 1971; Barrats Cl 1759, 1818, 1825, Barrat Hades Furlong 1759 (*v*. **furlang**) (*Barrett hades* c.1625, *v*. **hēafod**; cf. *Will'm Barrett* c.1625); Bartle Croft (*Bartalcroft* 1418, *v*. **croft**; either with the pers.n. *Bartil*, a shortened form of *Bartilmew* (Bartholomew) or with its surn. reflex *Bartle*); the Bluebell 1971 (a field thus called, presum. where bluebells grew in profusion); the Bottom 1915 (*v*. **botm**); Little ~, Bowstrings 1971 (obscure; poss. a garbled form of **boosing** 'a cow shed, a cattle-stall' or descriptive of long selions lying across a bend in the boundary of a former great field, thus creating a D-shaped furlong); Break Lands 1971 (*v*. **bræc**^{1}, **land**); Broadridge Cl (*Brodridge* 1620, *v*. **brād, hrycg**); Browns land 1971 (*v*. **land**; with the surn. *Brown*); Budges Cl (cf. *Widow Budge* 1759); Butt Cl (*v*. **butte**); Chainacre Cl (*Chynakres* 1543, *v*. **cinu, æcer**); Chalk Hill 1971 (*v*. **calc**); William Charles's Cl; Clay Cl (*v*. **clǣg** and *Clay street*, *supra*); Cliffe Hill 1759, the Cliffs 1877 White (*le Cleff* 1412, *v*. **clif**); the Common Pasture (*v*. **commun**), (the) Cottage Pasture (*v*. **cotage**), the Cottagers

Pasture (*v.* **cotager**) (*v.* **pasture**); the Cow Layer 1759, Cowlair 1971 (*v.* **lair**); the Crafts or Goose Nest 1971 (*v.* **croft** and Goose Nest *infra*); Crow Hill Syke 1915 (*v.* **crāwe**, **sīk**); Cumberdale Furlong (*v.* **furlang**), Cumberdale Sick (*v.* **sík**), Cumberdale Watering (*v.* **wateryng**) (*Cumberdale* 1543, *Comberdale* c.1625, *forthersyde Comberdale*, *the hyther side Comberdale* c.1625 (*v.* **furðor**, **hider**, **sīde**), *v.* **Cumbre**, **dæl**[1]; evidence for RB survival in this area of the Wolds); the Cunnery Cl (*v.* **coningre**); Deadmans Grave 1759, 1971, 1st Dedmans (sic) 1971 (*deade mans grave* c.1625, *v.* **dede-man**, **græf**; poss. a pagan Anglo-Saxon inhumation site; a large Anglo-Saxon inhumation cemetery was excavated nearby beside the Fosse Way in the 1970s); Delph Cl (*v.* **(ge)delf**); the Dilks 1971 (poss. the common Leics. surn. *Dilks* in the possessive case or else a garbled pl. of **dík**; earlier forms are needed); Doctors Cl (*v.* **doctour**, cf. Doctors Cl in Cossington f.ns. (a)); Dog Kennel Cl (*v.* **kenel**; such names sometimes refer to the kennels in which hunting dogs were kept); Flaxland Cl (cf. *Flaxland hades* 1620 (*v.* **hēafod**), *v.* **fleax**, **land**); Goodmans Croft (*v.* **croft**; with the surn. *Goodman*, *v.* Reaney *s.n.*); Goose Foot Cl (*Gosefot* e.13, *Gosfote* 13[1], *Goose Foot* c.1700, 1703, 1708 (18), 1709, 1712, 1724, *ye Goose foot* 1704, *Gowsefote had* 1543 (*v.* **hēafod**), *Goosefoot furlong* 1674 (*v.* **furlang**); perh. 'the foot of the hill where geese are pastured', *v.* **gōs**, **fōt**, cf. in structure *Oxefotemor*, Ch **3** 96 n.1; but this may have been, rather, once *Gosecot*, the original moot-site of the undivided Goscote Wapentake, *v.* East Goscote Hundred and Introduction xiii); Goose Nest 1971 (if this is the very late survival of an early name, then perh. 'goose headland', *v.* **gōs**, **næss** and cf. *Gowsefote had*, *supra*; but alternatively a later version of Goose Foot *supra*); Gorse Barn 1971 (*v.* **gorst**); Granborough Hill Cl (*v.* Gamber's Hill Lodge *supra*); the Greens (*v.* **grēne**[2]); Hall Ask 1971 (*v.* **askr**), Hall Cl 1971, Hall Worm (sic) 1971 (this prob. with **vangr**, but otherwise with **wamb/womb** used topographically of 'a hollow') (*v.* Wymeswold Hall *supra*); Hallams Croft 1971 (*v.* **croft**; with the surn. *Hallam*); Hardacre 1971 (*hardaker* 1543, *Hard-Acre* c.1700, 1703, *Hardacres* 1708 (18), 1709, 1712, 1724), the Hardacre Fd 1759, 1818, 1825 (*Hardacer feld* c.1425, *Hardakerfelde* 1543, *Hardaker feild* 1625, *Hardeacre feild* c.1625, *Hardacre Feild(e)* 1674, 1700, 1704, ~ *Field* c.1700, 1703 *et passim* to 1724, *v.* **heard**, **æcer**, **feld**; one of the great fields); Heaning Fd, the Heanings (*heynyng* 1543, *v.* **hegning**); Hens and Chickens (a poss. allusion to the birdsfoot trefoil (*Lotus corniculatus*), *v.* Field 71); the Hills; Top ~ ~, Middle Home Cl 1971, Home Fd 1971 (*v.* **home**); Home Leys Cl (*v.* Holmlea *supra*); the Honeysuckle 1971 (*v.* **hunisuccle**; here prob. either a name for flowers of clover, esp. common red clover, or for woodbine (*Lonicera periclymenum*), *v.* Field 98 and *the Honey Suckles close* in adjacent Burton on the Wolds f.ns. (b); but note the Bluebell *supra*); Horse Pasture 1971 (*v.* **pasture**); Houndland Baulk (*v.* **land, balca**; either with **hund** or with the pers.n. *Hund* (found in both OE and ON)); Innergate Hedge (*v.* **hecg** and Innergate *supra*); Kiln Cl, ~ ~ Hedge (*v.* **hecg**) (*v.* **cyln**); the Lamas Cl (*v.* **lammas**); the Lilly Croft 1759, Lily Croft 1971, the Great Lilly Croft otherwise the Upper Lilly Croft 1759, Great ~ ~, Little Lilly Croft 1759, the Upper Lillycroft or Great Lillycroft 1818, 1825, Lower Lilly Croft 1848, Great or Upper Lilly Croft 1849 (*lylycroft* 1412, *v.* **croft**; with the surn. *Lilly* (cf. *Hugh Lily* 1275 of Lincs.), prob. from a pet-form of Elizabeth, *v.* Reaney *s.n.*); Little Furlong 1971 (*v.* **furlang**); Long Cl; Long Furlong 1971 (1543, *v.* **lang**[1], **furlang**); (the) Long Leys, the Long Leys Common (*v.* **commun**) (*v.* **leys**); the Marsh Drain (*v.* **mersc, drain**); Mill Fd 1971, Mill Lane End 1759 (*v.* *Mill Lane*, *supra* and **lane-ende**); Mill Hill Leys 1759 (*v.* **leys**) (*Milne hill* a.1183 (l.14), *milnehil* l.12, *v.* **myln, hyll**; a windmill site); Mushill Cls (cf. *Muswell furlonge* c.1625, *v.* **mūs, wella, furlang** and Mushill Fm, ~ Lane *supra*); the Nook 1925 Kelly (*v.* **nōk**); Old Hill 1759, Old Hills 1971 (*v.* **wald**); the Parks 1971 (*v.* **park**); Peaseborough Sick (*Pesebarogh'* 1418, *Peysbergh' syke* 1412, *Peesborow syck* 1620, *Peasebarrowe sicke* c.1625 (*v.* **sík**), cf. *Peesborow Lees* 1620 (*v.* **leys**), *v.* **pise, berg**); Potters Ford 1759, 1836 O, Big ~ ~, Little Potters Ford 1971 (*v.* **ford**; either with **pottere** or with its surn. reflex *Potter*, cf. *Gaufridius Poter* 1196 Cur of Leics.); Rabbit Warren 1971 (*v.* **rabet, wareine**); the Ramble (rivulet) 1831 Curtis, 1846 White (*v.* **rivulet**; this stream-name may derive from the verb *ramble* 'to wander in an aimless manner' or be a late, garbled form of **rynel** (ModEdial. *rundle*) 'a runnel, a rivulet'); Redbrink Cls (*v.* **brink**; prob. with **hrēod** rather than with **rēad**); Rempstone Sick (*v.* **sík**; Rempstone in Notts. adjoins to the north-west); the Road Piece (*v.* **pece**); Rough Cl 1971 (*v.* **rūh**[1]); Round Cl (*v.* **round**); Running Furrow (*Runnyng Forowe* 1543, *Runynge Furrowe* 1601, *Runnynge Thor(r)owe* c.1625, *v.* **rinnende, furh**; a major drainage ditch, cf. Running Furrow in Muston f.ns. (a), Lei **2** 37); Rushes Sick 1971, ~ ~ Gorse 1759 (*v.* **gorst**) (*Riskisike* a.1183 (l.14), *rushe* ~, *rushys sycke* 1543, *v.* **risc, sík**; the earliest form with ON *-sk-*); the Sallow Watering (*v.* **salh, wateryng**); Far ~, Hither Sick 1759, 1971, 1st Sick 1971 (*v.* **sík**); (the) Six Rood Furlong (*v.* **furlang**) (*Sischerude* 13[1], *v.* **six, rōd**[3]); Smallings 1971 (*Smalyng* 1418, 1543, *litelsmaling, Littilsumalingge* 13[2], *Lyttel Smaling* 13[1], *lytilsmallyng* 1412, cf. *Smalyngdoles* 1412 (*v.* **dāl**), *Smalingesike* e.13, *Smalinge Syke* 13[1], *Smallyngsyk'* 1412 (*v.* **sík**), *v.* **smæl, eng**); Sostridge Baulk (*v.* **balca**), Sostridge Cl (earlier forms are needed, but perh. with **soss** and **ric**, cf. Sossmoss, Ch **1** 97); Sties 1971 (*v.* **stig**); Stocking Gorse (*v.* **stoccing, gorst**); Stub Whong (*v.* **stubb, vangr**); Suth Cl (*v.* **sūð**); Thorp Cl 1971, Thorpe Fd 1759 (*Thorpe Felde* 1543, ~ *feild(e)* 1601, 1625, c.1625, 1674, 1700, 1704, *Thorp Field* c.1700, 1708 (18), 1712, 1714, *v.* **feld**; one of the great fields, lying towards Thorpe in the Glebe in Notts. which adjoins to the north); Town Cl 1759 (cf. *Townland* 1620, *v.* **land**), Bottom ~, Top ~, Townend 1971 (*v.* **ende**) (*v.* **tūn**); Turnpost, ~ Fd 1971 (*v.* Turnpost Fm *supra*); Waites Head Land (*v.* **hēafod-land**; with the surn. *Waite*, *v.* Reaney *s.n*); Waterland Leys (*v.* **leys**) (*Waterlandes* 1601, *Water-Lands* 1700, *Marwaterlandes* a.1183 (l.14) (*v.* **māra**), *Mykyl Waterlondeshend* a.1183 (l.14) (*v.* **micel, mikill, ende**), *Lyttel Waterland* 1543 (*v.* **lȳtel**), *v.* **wæter, land**); Waydall ~, Waydell Cl, Waydell Hedge 1759 (*v.* **hecg**), Little ~, Long ~, Wadle 1971 (*Whadale* 1543, 1601, 1674, 1700, 1704, *the Whadel* c.1700, *Whey-dale* 1709 (18), 1709, 1712, 1724, *Whadale Crosse* 1601 (*v.* **cros**), *Whadale furlong(e)* 1543, 1704, *Whey-dale-Furlong* 1703 (*v.* **furlang**), *v.* **hwǣg, dalr**); (the) West Fd 1759, 1818, 1825 (c.1700, 1703 *et passim* to 1724, *the West Felde* 1543, *the Weste Feilde* 1601, *the West feild* 1625, 1674, 1700, 1704, *v.* **west, feld**; one of the great fields of the township); Bottom ~, Top Wetlands 1971 (*v.* **wēt, land**); Widows Cl (*v.* **widuwe**; land providing an income for a widow, dower land); Willoughby Brook 1759 (*Wylougby broke* e.13 *MiD*, *v.* **brōc**), Willoughby Ford 1759 (*v.* **ford**), Willoughby Gorse 1836 O (*v.* **gorst**) (Willoughby on the Wolds in Notts. adjoins to the north-east); Willow Tree 1971 (*v.* **wilig-trēow**; a close containing such trees); Wisemoor Hill (*Whismer* ~, *Whistmer hill* c.1625, *v.* **wisse**; either with **mere**[1] in its sense 'wetland' or with **mōr**[1]); the Woulds 1759, (the) Wolds 1846, 1877 White (*Wolda de Wimendewold*, ~ ~ *Wymundewold'* e.13, *Waldis de Wymundewold* 1256, (*in*) *Waldo* 1293, *Wald* 1412, *lez Woldes* 1418, *the Woldes* 1543, c.1625, cf. *le Woldhull'* 1331, *Woldhill'* 1412,

Woldas hyll' 1418 (*v.* **hyll**), *Woldsyke* c.1425 (*v.* **sík**), *v.* **wald**); Wysall Lane Acre 1971 (*v.* **lane, æcer**; Wysall in Notts. lies 2 miles to the north).

(b) *Alfletford'* 1292 OSut (*v.* **ford**), *Alfleteþorn* 13[1], *Alfletethorn* 13[2] (*v.* **þorn**) (either with **alh** 'a heathen temple' and **flēot** 'a stream' (cf. *Alhfleot* 812 (9) BCS 341 (S 169), 815 (9) BCS 353 (S 178) or with the OE fem. pers.n. *Alflǣd* (from *Ælfflǣd*, *v.* Feilitzen 144); note the comments on Arrow Fd and Arrow Hill in f.ns. (a)); *averyll syck* 1543 (*v.* **hæfera, hafri, hyll, sík**); *barle marche* 1543 (*v.* **mersc**; presum. with **bærlic** 'barley', but hill sites are more usual for the growth of barley and wheat, perh. cf. *Barlie Water* in Hoby f.ns.(b)); *benell* 1543 (*v.* **bēan, hyll**); *Longbenelondichend* a.1183 (l.14) (*v.* **lang**[1], **bēan, land, dīc, dík, ende**); *Bishop croft* 1543 (*v.* **croft**; with the surn. *Bishop*); *blackelandes, blackeland sicke* c.1625 (*v.* **sík**) (*v.* **blæc, land**); *Blakewong* 1412, *Blak' Wong'* 1418 (*v.* **vangr**; either with **blæc**, alluding to the colour of the soil, or with the surn. *Black/Blake*, *v.* Reaney *s.n.*); *Bossehowhyll'* 1412, *Boshowehyll'* 1418 (*v.* **hyll**, an addition to the earlier **Bossehow* when the meaning of its generic (prob. originally OE **hōh** 'a spur of land' rather than ON **haugr** 'a hill') had been forgotten; the first el. may be the OE pers.n. *Bōsa*, cf. *Bosseland* in Kirby Bellars f.ns. (b)); *Branseford bridge* 1623 Nichols (*v.* **ford, brycg**; with the OE pers.n. *Brant*, the bridge no doubt replacing the ford); *Breches* c.1425 (*v.* **brēc**); (*upon*) *brere* 1543 (*v.* **brēr**); *Broade Rushe* c.1625 ('the wide rush bed', *v.* **brād, risc**); *Bromberga* l.12, *Nether Bromberghe* a.1183 (l.14) (*v.* **neoðera**), *hygh brombarowe* 1543 (*v.* **hēah**[1], **brōm, berg**); *Bulborow hill* 1620, *Bulbarowe ~*, *Bulbarrwe hill* c.1625 (*v.* **berg**; either with the OE pers.n. *Bula* or with **bula** 'a bull'); *the Colledge land* c.1625 (*v.* **college**; note that it is *the land of Trynyte Colledge in Cambridge* 1601, while *Trinitie Colledge in Cambridge is the patrone* 1625 (i.e. of the living of the parish church)); *le corf* 1418, *Corf furlong* 1543 (*v.* **furlang**) (*v.* **corf**); *Cramborow syck* 1620 (*v.* **cramb, berg, sík**); *Crofte hades* c.1625 (*v.* **croft, hēafod**); *Crombdale* 1543 (*v.* **cramb, dalr**); *Crosse wonge furlonge* 1601 (*v.* **vangr, furlang**; with **cross** or **cros** (note *Whadale Crosse*, *supra* and (*ad*) *Crucem Herberti* 13[2] (with MLat *crux* (*crucem* acc.sg.) 'a cross' and the OFr pers.n. *Herbert*)); *damasyn hadlands* 1543 (*v.* **damesyn, hēafod-land**); *depedale* 1418 (*v.* **dēop, dalr**); *fourwell hades* 1543, *forwell ~* 1601, *Forrold ~* 1674, *Forral ~* c.1700, *Fore-hill ~* 1703, 1708 (18), 1709, 1712, 1724, *ye Forrell hades* 1704 (*v.* **fēower, wella, hēafod**); *Ghonderesyke* e.13, *Gondere Syke* 13[1] (*v.* **gandra, sík**); *Green hill* 1630 Nichols, *Greenhilleland(e)*, *Grenelland* (*v.* **land**) (*v.* **grēne**[1], **hyll**); *the hall balke* 1543 (*v.* **balca** and Wymeswold Hall *supra*); *the Homestall* 1708 (18) (*v.* **hām-stall**; i.e. of *the Old Vicarage*); *Horrousicha* 1212 (*v.* **sīc, sík** and Arrow Fd *supra*); *hortebe aker* 1543 (*v.* **æcer**; the first word may be a surn. *Herteby*, from an early spelling of Harby (*v.* Lei **2** 93) which lies 10 miles to the north-east in Framland Hundred or, less likely, a lost **hjarðar-bý(r)* 'herd farm' (*v.* **hjǫrð (hjarðar** gen.sg.), **bȳ**); *Hosewong* 1293 (*v.* **vangr**; poss. with the surn. *Hose* (*v.* Reaney *s.n.*) or with **hos(s)** 'shoots, tendrils; brambles, thorns', but additional forms are needed); *hourlston* 1543, *Sort(e)holestanes* l.12 (*v.* **sc(e)ort**), *v.* **hol**[1], **stān**); *Hungerhyll* a.1183 (l.14) (*v.* **hungor, hyll**); *leke beddes* 1543 (*v.* **lēac, bedd**); *longeforlong'* 1412, *Long furlong* 1620, *Longfurlonge hauides* 13[1] (*v.* **hēafod**), *v.* **lang**[1], **furlang**); *lyllygate* 1620 (*v.* **gata**; with the surn. *Lilly*, cf. the Lilly Croft in f.ns. (a)); *Lynge Landes* c.1625 (*v.* **lyng, land**); *Martinhaw* a.1183 (l.14) (*v.* **haga**[1]; with the MLat pers.n. *Martin*); *Merestall'* e.13, *Mearstall* 13[1], *merestoles* 1543 (*v.* **mere-stall** and Ch **3** 158–9 for discussion of the compound); (*le*) *Middelfurlong* 13[1], 13[2] (*v.* **middel**,

furlang); *Middil Clif* e.13 (*v.* **middel, clif**); *Millewarde breche* 13[1] (*v.* **mylenweard, brēc**); *mylnehads* 1543 (*v.* **myln, hēafod**); *the New Close* 1630 Nichols; *le Oxdoles* 1412 (*v.* **oxa, dāl**); *the Pesefeld* c.1425 (*v.* **pise, feld**); *langepeselandes* l.12 (*v.* **lang**[1], **pise, land**); *Pesesike* e.13, 13[1] (*v.* **pise, sík**); *the Pingle* (*on ye Stalkott lane End*) 1703, 1704 (*v.* **pingel** and *Stalkott lane End, infra*); *Rem(i)ston sycke* 1543 (*v.* **sík**; Rempstone in Notts. adjoins to the north-west); *Robbe Wong* a.1183 (l.14) (*v.* **vangr**; presum. at this date with the pers.n. *Robbe* (a pet-form of Robert) rather than with its surn. reflex *Robb*); *Sortimore* 13[1] (*v.* **sc(e)ort, mōr**[1]); *Sparoughull* 1395 (*v.* **spearwa, hyll**); *ye Stalkott lane End* 1703 (*v.* **lane-ende** and Storkit Lane *supra*); *Stauntons land* 1543 (*v.* **land**; with the surn. *Staunton*); *Stouke Wong* 1543 (*v.* **vangr**; with the surn. *Stoke*); *strete hauedes* c.1425 (*v.* **strǣt, hēafod**; presum. with reference to the Roman road Fosse Way); *stylbecke* 1543 (*v.* **stille, bekkr**, i.e. 'quiet stream'; however, this may rather be 'boundary stream', with **skil**); *the Tenter furlong* 1674 (*v.* **furlang**), *the Tenters* c.1700, 1703 *et passim* to 1724 (*v.* **tentour**); *Thornelsyke* 1412 (*v.* **sík**), *Thornelwong'* 1412, 1418 (*v.* **vangr**) (*v.* **þorn, hyll**); *Thorpmere* e.13 (*v.* **(ge)mǣre**), *Thorppyt* 1543 (*v.* **pytt**), *Thorpsyke* e.13, 13[1], *Thorpseke* 1389 (*v.* **sík**), *Torphil* l.12 (*v.* **hyll**) (all with reference to Thorpe in the Glebe in Notts. which adjoins to the north); *the towne lande* 1601 (*v.* **tūn**); *Whetdalle* 1543 (*v.* **hwǣte, dalr**); *Willoughbie balke* 1601, *Willoughby Balk* 1704, ~ *Baulk* 1708 (18), 1709, 1712, 1724 (*v.* **balca**; Willoughby on the Wolds in Notts. adjoins to the north-east); *Wolstonwell'* l.12, *Wolstonwelsiche* Hy 2, *Wolstonwellesice*, *Wulstanwellesica* l.12, *Wolstonwellesike* e.13 bis, *Wolstonwelsyke* 13[1] (*v.* **sīc, sík**), *v.* **wella**; with the OE pers.n. *Wulfstān*); *Wymundedisch* e.13, 13[1], *Wymundeshedysch* 13[2] (*v.* **edisc**; with the OE pers.n. *Wīgmund*, as in the township name Wymeswold).

THE ELEMENTS, OTHER THAN PERSONAL NAMES, IN EAST GOSCOTE HUNDRED'S PLACE-NAMES, FIELD-NAMES AND STREAM-NAMES

This list includes the elements in uncompounded and compounded place-names, field-names and stream-names. The names quoted in each entry are arranged in alphabetical order, with no distinction between uncompounded and compounded names. Names which survive on modern maps and also lost major names are listed first, followed by a summary of the use of the elements in field-names and stream-names. Although a concise translation of each element is provided, for fuller discussion of its significance and use, reference should be made to *English Place-Name Elements* (EPNS, vols. 25 and 26, amended in JEPNS 1), *The Vocabulary of English Place-Names* (CENS, in progress), M. Gelling, *Place-Names in the Landscape*, 1984 and M. Gelling and A. Cole, *The Landscape of Place-Names*, 2000.

The elements are often given in an OE, ON or OFr form, but it should be remembered that many of these elements continued as common nouns in the English language and that many of the names in Leicestershire's East Goscote Hundred are of more recent origin than the periods represented by the lexical head-forms used. Many terms are included which are not listed in the above-mentioned volumes, but it has not been felt necessary to distinguish these. Those elements marked * are not independently recorded in the head-forms cited or are hypothetical reconstructions from the place-name evidence.

A field-name which is common to a series of townships is sometimes quoted in a form which may have alternative spellings in those townships and which may appear for an individual township in either list (a) or list (b), depending on date. Where this occurs, the particular list in which the field-name features is not specified.

á (**ár** gen.sg.) ON, 'a river, a stream'. ?*Arland Bush meare* (f.n. Barkby), *Arlandsyke* (f.n. Skeffington).

abbat OFr, ME, 'an abbot'. Abbot's Spinney. *Abbotispool* (f.n. Belgrave), *Abbottesmede* (f.n. Asfordby), *Abbotts Clos(s)e* (f.n. Barkby Thorpe).

abbaye ME, (OFr *abbaie*), 'an abbey'. Abbey Lane, Launde Abbey. *Abbey hedge* (f.n. Belgrave), Abbey Sick Furlong, *Abdykis* (f.ns. Barsby), *Abbye sicke* (f.n. South Croxton).

abbod OE, 'an abbot'. *Abedylsyke* (f.n. South Croxton).

aboven ME, **above** eModE, prep., 'above, over'. *Abouethebrok'* (f.n. Barkby), *Abouethedike*, *Abouethekirke* (f.ns. Thurmaston), *Abovedingesti* (f.n. Hoby), *Above Meadow*, *the Felde aboue the towne* (f.ns. Belgrave), *Above the Towne* (f.n. Queniborough), *Flynty aboue the gate*, *Schortholmis aboue the gate* (f.ns. Humberstone).

āc OE, 'an oak-tree'. ?Circles (f.n. Ratcliffe on the Wreake), the Oak (f.n. Ragdale), Oak Cl (f.n. Lowesby, Rearsby), Oak Holme (f.n. Loddington), *Okeholme Close* (f.n. East Norton), *Oke stile*, *Whatbarow okys* (f.ns. Whatborough), *Secheverels okeclose* (f.n. Rearsby), ?Wollax Wong (f.n. Barrow upon Soar).

æcer OE, 'a plot of cultivated land'; also 'an acre, a specified measure of ploughland', originally the unit which a yoke of oxen could plough in a day. The OE el. is generally indistinguishable from ON **akr** 'a plot of arable land'. Very freq. in f.ns.: as a simplex, e.g. *le accres* (Hoby), *lez Acres* (Barrow upon Soar), *the acres* (Beeby); with a numeral indicating size, e.g. *Fiuea(c)kres* (Barkby), *Twelfacres* (Welby); especially with an early pers.n. or its ME surn. reflex, e.g. *Brandolfisacre* (Hoby), *Ketylsacur* (Humberstone), *Osgoteacre*, *Rauensakir'* (South Croxton), *Oswoldacr'* (Cossington); with reference to location, e.g. *Neckacres* (Asfordby), Severn Acre (Walton on the Wolds), *sunderhaker* (Kirby Bellars), *le Woldacr'* (Cossington); to the nature of the soil, e.g. the Hardacre Fd (Wymeswold), Mow Macre Hill (Belgrave). Note Lady Acre (Barkby), *ladyacre* (Welby), prob. denoting land dedicated to Our Lady, the Blessed Virgin Mary.

æcer-dīc OE, perh. 'the ditch surrounding an arable plot' or 'the ditch marking the limit of ploughland'. Spellings with final *k* are due to Scandinavian influence. *Akirdik* (f.n. Gaddesby).

æhta OE, num., 'eight'. *Achterode* (f.n. Kirby Bellars).

æppel OE, 'an apple; an apple-tree'. *Apple Holme*, *Apple Yard* (f.ns. Cossington).

æppel-trēow OE, 'an apple-tree'. *le apiltrestub* (f.n. Cossington), *Appeltrestubbe* (f.n. Thurmaston), Apple tree wong (f.n. Loddington).

æsc OE, 'an ash-tree'. ?Asfordby, Ashby Folville. Freq. in f.ns.: signifying small stands of trees, e.g. *the As(s)hes* (Cossington, Gaddesby), Ash Hill (Queniborough, Thrussington), Ash Plantation (East Norton), *Cosington Ashes* (Ratcliffe on the Wreake); or boundary markers, e.g. *the ash tree* (Skeffington), Gadsby Ash (Queniborough), High Ash (South Croxton); identifying individual closes, e.g. Ash Cl (Barsby, Cossington, Gaddesby, Keythorpe, Cold Newton, Sileby), Ash Fd (Gaddesby, Queniborough, Ratcliffe on the Wreake); defining roads, e.g. *Ash(e)gate* (Halstead, Tilton). Spellings in *E-* may be owing to the influence of ON **eski** 'an ash-tree', e.g. *Esseberie* (Asfordby), *Essebi* (Ashby Folville), but an OE collective ***esce** 'a group of ash-trees' may also have existed.

æspe OE, 'an aspen-tree'. ?*Aspedic* (f.n. Welby).
ageynst ME, prep., 'facing, directly opposite'. *Against the Sunne* (f.n. Ratcliffe on the Wreake).
ald OE (Angl), adj., 'old, ancient; long-used; disused'. Common in f.ns.: especially describing land-units, e.g. *Aldefelde*, Old Cl (Queniborough), *the old Inclosure* (Cossington), Old Mdw (Asfordby), *Oldpark* (Belgrave), *Old Spiny* (Baggrave), *the ould woult close* (Barkby), Old Yard (South Croxton); or structures, e.g. *the old milne hill* (Humberstone), Old Wall (Queniborough). Note also *Aldeclif* (Kirby Bellars).
alh OE (Angl), 'a heathen temple'. ?*Alfletford'*, ?*Alfleteþorn* (f.ns. Wymeswold).
allotment ModE, 'a portion of land assigned to a particular individual', especially in names recording the redistribution of land at Enclosure: as in the Allottment Ground (f.n. Cold Newton), the Home Allotment (f.n. Thrussington); and later 'a small portion of land let out to an individual (e.g. by a town council) for cultivation', as in Allotments (f.n. Hungarton), The Allotments, Allotment Thurns (f.ns. South Croxton), Allotment Fd (f.n. Tilton), Allotment Gardens (f.n. Old Ingarsby, Twyford).
almes-hous ME, 'an almshouse, a house founded by a private charity for the reception and support of the aged poor'. The Almshouse.
almr ON, 'an elm-tree'. *at ye Allems* (f.n. Asfordby).
alor (alres gen.sg.) OE, 'an alder-tree'. *arlestub hades* (f.n. Asfordby).
ān OE, num., adj., 'one, single'; in p.ns., presum. used sometimes with the sense 'alone, isolated'. ?*Anstilsike* (f.n. Seagrave), *Oneclif* (f.n. Barrow upon Soar).
angle ME, 'an angle, a corner, a point of land'. ?Angel Cl (f.n. Thrussington), the Anglings (f.n. Gaddesby).
ānsetl OE, 'a hermitage'. ?*Anstilsike* (f.n. Seagrave).
arable ModE, adj., 'being or capable of being ploughed; fit for tillage'. Arable Cl (f.n. Tilton), Arable Fatlands, Arable Hill Cl, Dirty Balk Far Arable (f.ns. Rotherby).
askr ON, 'an ash-tree'. Hall Ask (f.n. Wymeswold).
āte OE, 'oats'. Oat Cl (f.n. East Norton), Oat Fd (f.n. Belgrave).
atte ME, prep. with masc. or neut. def.art., 'at the'. Common in f.ns. and often used for ME toponymic surns. Examples in f.ns. are: *Atteblakeforth* (Barkby), *atte fen*, *Attehorshow*, *atte Hulles in to þe gate*, *atte Wade* (Kirby Bellars), *atte pol sik ende* (Barkby Thorpe); toponymic surns. include *atte brygende*, *atte Grove* (Barrow upon Soar), *atte Grene* (Barkby Thorpe), *atte Welle* (Allexton).
austr (austarr comp.) ON, adj., '(to the) east'. Austen Dyke. *Ousterdale* (f.n. Hoby).
avenue ModE, 'a tree-lined approach'. Avenue Cl (f.n. Loddington).
back ModE, 'hindmost, lying behind'. Back Lane (Prestwold, Sileby), Back Rd. Back Fd (f.n. Twyford), *Back Lane* (Thrussington, Twyford), the Back Lane Cl (f.n. Walton on the Wolds), Back Mdw (f.n. Loddington).
backwater ModE, 'a pool or lagoon without current, lying more or less parallel to a river and fed from it at the lower end by a back-flow; water dammed back in the channel of a mill-race'. Back Water (f.n. Belgrave), the Backwater (f.n. Sileby), Backwater Fd (f.n. Hoby, Rotherby).
***badde** ME, adj., 'bad, worthless'. *badland* (f.n. Barsby).
badger ModE, 'a badger'. Badger Hole (f.n. Hoby).

bæc OE, **bakke** ME, 'a back, a ridge'. *Brokenback(e)s* (f.n. Humberstone), Saddleback (f.n. Asfordby), Saddle Backs (f.n. South Croxton), *Sadelback* (f.n. Thurmaston), *le Sadleback* (f.n. Shoby).

bær OE, adj., 'bare, without vegetation'. Bare bushes (f.n. Loddington), Bare Pool (f.n. Syston).

bærlic OE, **barli** ME, 'barley'. Barley Hill Ho., Barley Leas. *the Barley close* (f.n. Burton on the Wolds), *Barley Feild* (f.n. Cossington), *barleyhyll'* (f.n. Hungarton), Barley Leys (f.n. South Croxton), *Barlicholm(e)* (f.n. Twyford), *Barlicroft* (f.n. Seagrave), *Barliholme* (f.n. Barkby), *barle marche* (f.n. Wymeswold), Barley Whom Gap (f.n. Queniborough), *Barlie Water* (f.n. Hoby), *Barlyclife* (f.n. Barsby), *Barlycroft* (f.n. Sileby), *Ragdale Barley field* (f.n. Ragdale).

bæð OE, 'a bath'; topographically, it may have been used for 'a bathing-place' and of a place for cleaning wool. *Bathpol'* (f.n. Kirby Bellars).

baillif OFr, 'a bailiff, a steward'. ?Bailiff's Covert. ?*Balihauedlond'* (f.n. Thurmaston).

bak-side ME, 'property behind a dwelling; the back, the rear'. *backesyde of hartclyffe, the backe syde of Dewell, the Backside Mr Crosons Close, Bentlys backe side, Saundersons back(e) syde* (f.ns. Humberstone), Backside (f.n. Welby), Backside Furlong (f.n. Barsby), *the Backside of the Town* (f.n. Rearsby), *the back sides* (f.n. Thurmaston), *the parsonage backside* (f.n. Rotherby).

balca OE, 'a ridge, a bank; a ridge of unploughed land that marked the boundary between adjacent strips of a common field'. Baulk Lane, Cobaulk Rd. Freq. in f.ns.: often compounded with a surn., e.g. *Cheuerall Balk* (Asfordby), *Goddesgood Balk* (Saxelby), *Greenum baulke* (Cossington). Reference may be made to topographical features, e.g. *Arlong Bush balk* (Barkby), *Bell balk hades* (Gaddesby), *Gallowborrow(e) baulk(e)* (Barkby Thorpe); to size, e.g. *the great balke, ye litle Balk* (Asfordby); to fauna or flora, e.g. *Conebalk* (Belgrave), *Rush Balk* (Barkby), *Thorn(e)y Balk(e)* (Asfordby, Kirby Bellars), *the Willowes Baulk* (Barrow upon Soar).

***ball** OE, 'a ball'; topographically 'a rounded hill; a mound of earth set up as a boundary marker'. Ballow Woulds (f.n. Wymeswold).

bān OE, 'bone'. ?*Bonacres* (f.n. Cossington).

bane ME, 'poison'. ?*Banethorn'* (f.n. South Croxton), ?Beanford Furlong (f.n. Queniborough), ?Beanthorne (f.n. Shoby), ?Bean Thorn Furlong (f.n. Grimston). But *v.* ***bēan-þorn**.

baner OFr, **banere** ME, 'a banner, a flag', perh. used topographically of a (high) landmark. ?*Banar land eynd* (f.n. Barsby), ?*Banars more* (f.n. Skeffington).

banke ODan, **bank(e)** ME, 'a bank, the slope of a hill or ridge'. The Banks, West Bank. The Bank (f.n. Lowesby), Banks (f.n. Beeby), The Banks (f.n. Syston), Banky (f.n. Cold Newton), *Banky(e) Close* (f.n. Allexton), *Bankett Close*, Banky Cl, Dambank (f.ns. Tilton), Banky Fds (f.n. Ragdale), Dove Bank (f.n. Thorpe Satchville), *Golden Bank(e)* (f.n. Seagrave), Hillybanks (f.n. Kirby Bellars), *May Bankes Close* (f.n. Allexton), Mouldy Banks (f.n. Queniborough), Red Banks (f.n. Asfordby), *Reddbank* (f.n. Humberstone), *South thum banke* (f.n. Cossington), *Southholme Bank Platt* (f.n. Sileby), Spindle Banks (f.n. South Croxton), Spring Fold Bank (f.n. Halstead), Willow Bank Mdw (f.n. East Norton).

bār OE, 'a (wild) boar'. *Barschawe* (f.n. Belgrave), ?*Boreclose* (f.n. Gaddesby).

barn ON, 'a child, offspring'. ?Barsby.

barrack ModE, 'a barrack, a temporary shelter, a rude hutment'. Barrack Cottages.

barre OFr, 'a bar, a barrier'. *Chapel bar* (Wymeswold). *Pickman Barrs* (f.n. Loddington).

bastard OFr, adj., sb., 'bastard'; toponymically, used of fields of abnormal shape or poor yield and occasionally of selions of former great fields not completely swarded over. The Bastard (f.n. Cossington), Bastard Cl (f.n. Keyham), *Bastard Leas*, Bastards (f.ns. Rearsby), Bastard Ley Cl (f.n. Thurmaston), Bastards (f.n. Welby), the Bastards (f.n. Asfordby, Thrussington), *Glebe bastard Ley*, Moors Bastard (f.ns. South Croxton).

bataille OFr, 'battle'. ?*Batelston'* (f.n. Thurmaston).

bate ME, 'contention, strife'. ?*bat(e)mor'* (f.n. Hungarton).

bēan OE, 'the bean'. Burton Bandalls. Freq. in f.ns.: in the compound *bean-lands* (with various spellings in Barrow upon Soar, Barkby, Barsby, Cossington, South Croxton, Frisby on the Wreake, Gaddesby, Hungarton, Kirby Bellars, Cold Newton, Saxelby, Thurmaston, Wymeswold; cf. *Balanslade* (Halstead), *Banlondpit* (Hoby)); in *Bancroft* (with various spellings in Barrow upon Soar, Hoby, Kirby Bellars); in Beanhill (with various spellings in Barrow upon Soar, Belgrave, Skeffington, Twyford). Note also *Bandall* (Gaddesby), *Banerodys* (Thurmaston) and *Banslade* (Ratcliffe on the Wreake).

***bēan-þorn** OE, poss. an alternative name for 'gorse'; but *v.* **bane**. ?*Banethorn'* (f.n. South Croxton), ?Beanford Furlong (f.n. Queniborough), ?Beanthorne (f.n. Shoby), ?Bean Thorn Furlong (f.n. Grimston).

b(e)aru (b(e)arwe dat.sg.) OE, 'a small wood'. Barrow upon Soar. ?Freeborough (f.n. Thurmaston).

beavery ModE, 'a place in which beavers live'. Beavery Nook (f.n. Rearsby).

bedd OE, 'a bed, a plot where plants grow or are grown'. *leke beddes* (f.n. Wymeswold), Nettlebed Furlong, *Willowbedd Fur'* (f.ns. Queniborough), Osier Beds (f.n. Frisby on the Wreake), the Osiery Beds (f.n. Tilton), Reed Bed (f.n. Belgrave), the Willow Beds (f.n. Lowesby).

beggere ME, 'a beggar'; the common f.n. *Beggar's Bush* appears to denote poor or unproductive land (cf. EDD *beggar* 'to impoverish land, to exhaust soil of nutrients'). *Beggars bush* (f.n. Skeffington).

beit ON, 'pasture'. ?*bat(e)mor'* (f.n. Hungarton).

bekkr ON, 'a stream, a beck'. In f.ns., recurring are *Holbeck* (with various spellings in Asfordby, Frisby on the Wreake, Kirby Bellars, Launde, Tilton), *littel beck* (with various spellings in Asfordby, Frisby on the Wreake, Saxelby) and Oxback (Hoby, Thrussington). In East Goscote Hundred, *beck* > *back* often from the later 17th cent., as Fulbacks (Cold Newton), Howback (Tilton), *littleback* (Asfordby), Rang Back (Thrussington). In contrast to Framland Hundred, stream-names with ON *bekkr* are few (*v.* Lei **2** 311), outnumbered by those with OE *brōc* at a ratio of 1:3 and in names recorded only before 1500, at a ratio of 1:7. Only *Holbek* (Kirby Bellars), *Holebec* (Launde) and *Osebec* (Welby) are recorded before 1500, *v.* **brōc**.

bel[2] OFr, adj., 'fair, beautiful'. Belgrave.

beldam ME, 'a grandmother, a matron of advanced years'. ?Beldam Cl (f.n. Halstead).

belle OE, 'a bell'; may be used topographically in the sense 'bell-shaped', particularly of 'a bell-shaped hill, a knoll'. In f.ns., sometimes denotes land endowed for the upkeep of church bells. *Belleholme* (f.n. Belgrave, Kirby Bellars, Thurmaston), *Belland*, (*the*) *Bell Hadland* (f.ns. Hungarton), *Bell balk hades*, Bell Bush (f.ns. Gaddesby), ?*Belles close* (f.n. Cossington), ?*Bellewellesik* (f.n. Skeffington), ?*Belloue* (f.n. Kirby Bellars), *Bell peice* (f.n. Allexton), Bellpits (f.n. South Croxton).

belt ModE, 'a belt (of woodland), a screen of trees'. The Belt (f.n. Loddington).

benc OE, 'a bench', used topographically of 'a ledge, a terrace, a bank'. *Benchcroft close*, ?*benkes* (f.ns. Cold Newton).

benethe ME, prep., 'beneath, under, below'. *Benethebrygg'* (f.n. Queniborough), *be nethe the Merstals* (f.n. Cossington), *the Felde be nethe the Town* (f.n. Belgrave), *Flynty be nethe the gate*, *Schortholmus be nethe gate* (f.ns. Humberstone).

***benkr** ON, 'a bench', used topographically of 'a ledge, a terrace, a bank'. ?*benkes* (f.n. Cold Newton).

bēo OE, 'a bee'. Beeby.

beofor OE, 'a beaver'. Beever hooks (f.n. Queniborough).

berc OE (Angl), 'a birch-tree'. Barchill (f.n. Tugby), *Berkmore* (f.n. Gaddesby).

berg OE, 'a rounded hill, a mound, a burial mound', **berg** ON, 'a hill'. Whatborough; Bunbury Fm, Colborough Hill, Gamber's Hill Lodge. Freq. in f.ns.: as a simplex referring either to a hill or burial mounds upon a hill, e.g. Barrow Hill (Loddington), ?*Borow* (Cossington); compounded with an el. signifying a crop, e.g. Peaseborough (Wymeswold), Royborough (Ratcliffe on the Wreake), *Whetebergh'* (with various spellings in Cossington, Kirby Bellars, Seagrave, Skeffington), or wild flora, e.g. *Ashborow* (Loddington), Risborough (Tilton), *thurnebarrow hill* (Asfordby); with an el. indicating the size or shape of the hill, e.g. *Hyboro* (Cossington), *Litileberwe* (Barrow upon Soar), Longborough (Barsby), Muckleborough (Hungarton), Smallborough (Barkby); or the quality of its soil, e.g. *Malmberthorn* (Cossington), *Smereberwe* (Queniborough), Stainsborough (Hungarton); or its physical aspect, e.g. Blackborough (Loddington), Calabor (Barsby), Roborough (Humberstone); or its location, e.g. *Myddulbarow*, *West barogh* (Hungarton); occasionally with a pers.n., e.g. *Kettellbarrow* (Barkby).

berige OE, 'a berry'. Barrowcliffe Fm, Barrowcliffe Spinney, Berrycott Lane. *Berrye brooke* (Seagrave), *Biridole* (f.n. Cold Newton).

bern OE, 'a barn'. Barrow Barn. Barn Cl (f.n. Burton on the Wolds, Cossington, Kirby Bellars, Welby), *le Barnecroft* (f.n. Humberstone), *Barneȝarte* (f.n. Barrow upon Soar), *the Barne Plott* (f.n. Cossington), ?*Bernewonge* (f.n. Kirby Bellars).

***berse** ME, '?a hedge made with stakes; ?an enclosure'. ?*Parsey half Acre* (f.n. Asfordby).

best ModE, adj. 'best'. Best Cl (f.n. Beeby, Cold Newton, Thorpe Satchville), The Best Fd (f.n. Kirby Bellars), Best Mdw (f.n. Cossington).

beste OFr, 'a beast'; later 'livestock, cattle'. *Beaste gate* (Cossington), *the beastes pasture* (f.n. Ratcliffe on the Wreake, Seagrave), *the Beast Pasture* (f.n. Queniborough).

betwēonan OE, prep., 'between, amongst', usually in compound p.ns. with the elliptical sense 'the place between'. *Betwene the gates* (f.n. Barsby, Beeby, Kirby Bellars), *Betwynedeke* (f.n. Cossington), Furlong between the Sikes (f.n. Ratcliffe on the Wreake).

betwixt eModE, prep., 'between'; in p.ns., used as **betwēonan** *supra*. *Betwixt Dikes*, *Betwixt Gates* (f.ns. Sileby), *Betwixte the ditches* (f.n. Barrow upon Soar), *betwixt the Sickes* (f.n. Ratcliffe on the Wreake).

bī OE, prep. with dative, 'by, near'. *Bihouerthwertmilnestede* (f.n. Hoby), Byagate (f.n. Barkby), Bybarrow Fd (f.n. Walton on the Wolds), *Bywades* (f.n. Rearsby), *longkebithehee* (f.n. Kirby Bellars).

big ME, 'big, large'. Big Cl, Big Mdw (f.ns. Barkby).

bile OE, 'a bill, a beak', used topographically of a pointed projection. ?*Bille pasture* (f.n. Kirby Bellars).

bill OE, 'a bill, a sword', topographically 'a sharp ridge, a promontory'. ?*Bille pasture* (f.n. Kirby Bellars).

binn OE, 'a manger, a stall'. *Bincroft* (f.n. Thorpe Satchville).

birce OE, 'a birch-tree'. Birch Cl (f.n. Lowesby).

bit ModE, 'a small piece of land'. The Bit, Lucerne Bit (f.ns. Gaddesby), the Bits, Cheesecake bit (f.ns. Halstead), Digby's Bit (f.n. Beeby), Little Bit (f.n. Tilton), Mill Close Bit (f.n. Cossington).

blacksmith ModE, 'a blacksmith'. Blacksmith's Shop (Cossington, South Croxton, Gaddesby, Keyham, Loddington, Tugby).

blæc OE, **blak(e)** ME, **black** ModE, adj., 'black, dark-coloured, dark'; in eModE, also 'fertile' as against *white* 'infertile'. Black-a-Moors Spinney, ?Bleak Moor. Freq. in f.ns.: principally combined with an el. signifying soil, e.g. *Blackland* (with various spellings in Belgrave, Gaddesby, Hungarton, Keyham, Loddington, Rotherby and Seagrave), *Blakemilde* (Barkby, South Croxton, Kirby Bellars and Cold Newton), Blackmole (Asfordby); or with an el. meaning a hill or slope, e.g. *Blacclif* (Burton on the Wolds), *Blackborough* (Loddington), *blakehyll* (Hungarton). Note also *Blackemore* (Gaddesby), *Blackmiers* (Barkby), *Blakehyrst* (Rearsby), *Blakewonge* (Belgrave).

***blæc-þorn** OE, 'a blackthorn, a sloe-tree'. *Black Thorn Leas* (f.n. Whatborough).

blár ON, adj., 'dark, lead-coloured'; by extension as ME **blo**, 'cheerless, cold, exposed'. *bloepoole* (f.n. Asfordby).

bleikr ON, 'pale'; perh. also 'bleak'. ?Bleak Moor.

blew ME, adj., 'blue; dark-coloured'. Blew Pits.

blind OE, **blindr** ON, adj., 'blind'; topographically, 'concealed, overgrown'. *Blindewelledole* (f.n. Cold Newton), *Blind Pool* (f.n. Queniborough).

blōd OE, 'blood'; topographically, in some instances may refer to colour. *Blodhow* (f.n. Thurmaston).

bōc-land OE, 'land granted by charter'. ?*Buckland wong* (f.n. Walton on the Wolds).

bog ME, 'a bog', a marsh'. the Bog (f.n. Frisby on the Wreake), Bogdale (f.n. Halstead), Bogg Cl (f.n. Thorpe Satchville).

boga OE, 'a bow; an arch or arched bridge; something curved or bent (as a curved valley or river-bend)'. Bow Bridge (f.n. Syston), Bowers (f.n. Belgrave), Lambles (f.n. Cossington).

bold OE, 'a dwelling, a house'. Newbold Folville. Nuball end (f.n. Sileby).

bolstre ME, 'a cushion, a pad'. ?Bolsters Mdw (f.n. Tilton).

bōn ME, 'favour, gift; demand, requirement'; boon work was a service that a feudal lord required of his tenants. ?*Bonacres* (f.n. Cossington).

bond ME, adj., 'held by tenure of bond service'. ?*Bondehirne* (f.n. Asfordby).

bóndi ON, 'a peasant landowner'. ?*Bondehirne* (f.n. Asfordby).

bond-man ME, 'a husbandman, an unfree villager, a serf'. *Bondman medow* (f.n. Barrow upon Soar).

bony ME, adj., 'abounding in bones'. ?*Bony dolys* (f.n. Cossington), ?Bundells (f.n. Thorpe Satchville).

boosing ModE, 'a cow-shed, a cattle-stall'. ?Bowstrings (f.n. Wymeswold).

bord OE, 'a table, a board'; prob. also 'a border'. ?Bord Mdw (f.n. Queniborough), *Sheapheards borde* (f.n. South Croxton), *Sheepheard borde* (f.n. Hungarton).

borden ME, adj., 'made of boards or planks'. Boarden Bridge Mdw (f.n. Beeby).

bord-land ME, 'demesne land, land which supplied food for the lord's table'. Bawlands (f.n. Asfordby), Bawdland Hole (f.n. Barsby), *Bordelond'* (f.n. Hoby), Bord Land (f.n. Queniborough).

***bōs (bōsum** dat.pl.) OE, 'a cow-stall'. *Bossycke* (f.n. South Croxton), *le Bosumhades* (f.n. Gaddesby).

bot ME, 'a parasitical insect, a horse-fly'. *Bott Hole* (f.n. Hoby), ?*Langbothyl* (f.n. Cossington).

bōð ODan, 'a booth, a temporary shelter'. ?*Langbothyl* (f.n. Cossington).

botm OE, 'a bottom'; in p.ns. especially 'the floor of a valley'. the Bottom (f.n. Wymeswold), *Bottomes hedge*, *Bottoms*, Sarson's Nook Bottom (f.ns. Barkby), *the bottom of Hollandale*, *snottybott'* (f.ns. Hungarton), Bottom of Wood (f.n. Tugby), *the Brante bottome*, *Thirnebothim* (f.ns. Hoby), Brook Meadow Bottom, Home Close Bottom, Hooks Bottom (f.ns. Beeby), *Thorn Sick bottom*, *West Sick bottom* (f.ns. Barsby).

bottom ModE, adj., 'bottom, lowermost' (by extension from **botm**). Bottom Cl (f.n. Cossington, Welby), Bottom Gibsons Cl (f.n. Barkby), Bottom Six Hills (f.n. Barrow upon Soar).

bowling eModE, vb.sb., 'playing at bowls, the action of rolling a bowl'. Top Bowling Leys (f.n. Cossington).

bowling-alley eModE, 'an alley or long enclosure for playing at bowls or skittles'. Bowling Alley Cl (f.n. Old Ingarsby).

brād OE, adj., 'broad, spacious'. Bradgate Lane, Breadcroft. Common in f.ns.: e.g. *Bradegate*, *Bradewong*, *brodedol'*, *brodefoxholl'* (f.ns. Cossington), *Bradmerholelese* (f.n. Gaddesby), *Brodale*, *Brodescherd* (f.ns. Barkby), *Brodhome*, *Brodsike* (f.ns. South Croxton) etc.

bræc[1] OE, 'a brake, a thicket, brushwood'. Brackland (f.n. Cold Newton), Break Lands (f.n. Wymeswold), *Brecland(e)* (f.n. Kirby Bellars), *Brec(e)lond* (f.n. South Croxton), ?*Thackbracks* (f.n. Cossington).

brǣdu OE (Angl), 'breadth', **brode** ME, 'a broad stretch of land, a broad strip of land, a broad cultivated strip of a common field'. *Ratcliff(e) Broad* (f.n. Cossington), *Twelfrodisbrod(e)* (f.n. South Croxton).

braken ME, 'bracken, fern'. Brackindale Fd (f.n. Grimston), *Bracundalhyll'*, *the Brakon* (f.ns. Skeffington), *Braken* (f.n. South Croxton), *Brakendale* (f.n. Halstead, Tugby), *Brakenowe* (f.n. Rearsby), *Brakenrodis* (f.n. Thurmaston), *Braknell buske* (f.n. Ratcliffe on the Wreake).

braky ModE, adj., 'overgrown with brushwood or fern'. Breaky Part (f.n. Keythorpe).

brand OE, 'fire', used topographically of 'a place where burning has occurred'. Bran Hills. ?Brandbury (f.n. Cotes), Brandy Mdw (f.n. Kirby Bellars), *langebrand'*, *shortbrand* (f.ns. Cold Newton), ?*brantclos* (f.n. South Croxton).

brant OE, ***brant** ON, adj., 'steep, steep-sided'. Brancliff Furlong (f.n. South Croxton, Queniborough), ?Brandbury (f.n. Cotes), ?*brantclos* (f.n. South Croxton), *Brantclyf* (f.n. Barkby), *Brantcroft* (f.n. Seagrave), *Brantcroftdyke* (f.n. Kirby Bellars), Branthill Fd (f.n. Skeffington), ?*Brentclyf* (f.n. Thurmaston).

brēc OE (Angl), **breche** ME, 'a breaking; land broken up for cultivation, newly broken-in ploughland'. Common in f.ns.: as a simplex, e.g. *la Breache*, *le Breche* (with various spellings in Barkby, Barrow upon Soar, Belgrave, Cossington, South Croxton, Hoby, Cold Newton, Queniborough), *les Breches* (with various spellings in Humberstone, Saxelby, Wymeswold); occasionally with a qualifier, e.g. *le Schortebreche* (Queniborough); or with an indication of location, e.g. *Brecchou* (Kirby Bellars), *Brechlahil* (Skeffington), *Meduebreche* (Cold Newton); or of tenure or ownership, e.g. *Millewarde breche* (Wymeswold).

breiðr ON, adj., 'broad, spacious'. Bratlands (f.n. Belgrave), *brawater* (f.n. Asfordby), *Breading* (f.n. Tugby), Bready Wong (f.n. Rearsby), *Bretland* (f.n. Gaddesby, Cold Newton), *bretland sicke* (f.n. Saxelby).

***brēme** OE, 'broom, a place where broom grows'. *Bremehou* (f.n. Cossington).

brēmel, brembel OE, 'bramble, a blackberry-bush; the dog-rose'. *Brimblisdale* (f.n. Saxelby).

brend ME, pa.part., 'burnt'; in p.ns., usually 'cleared by burning'. *Brendedalehil* (f.n. Skeffington), *(le) Brendwong* (f.ns. Barsby, South Croxton), ?*Breyndys acr'* (f.n. Barsby), ?*Brentclyf* (f.n. Thurmaston), *Brentethorne* (f.n. Halstead), *Bruntes* (f.n. Beeby), *Bryntle* (f.n. Seagrave).

***brende** OE, 'a burnt place'. The Brant (f.n. Hoby).

brēr OE (Angl), 'a briar, a wild rose, a bramble'. *(upon) brere* (f.n. Wymeswold), *the Bryers Woonge* (f.n. Hoby).

brerd OE, 'a rim, a (topmost) edge'. ?*Beardscliffe* (f.n. Gaddesby).

***brērig** OE (Angl), adj., 'growing with or overgrown by briars'. Briery Leys Spinney. *Briery Whong* (f.n. Hoby).

brew-hous ME, 'a brewery, a drinking establishment'. *Brewhouse close* (f.n. Cold Newton), ?*Broweshouse* (Barrow upon Soar).

bridd OE, 'a bird'. *Birdlip* (f.n. Cossington).

brigdels OE, 'a bridle', used in the sense 'fit for a horse to pass', as in *bridle-way*. Bridle Gate (Halstead), Bridle Gate Cl (f.n. Beeby, Cotes, Hoton), Bridle Road Fd (f.n. Hoby, Kirby Bellars, Twyford), Bridle Road Mdw (f.n. Hungarton), Hoby Bridle Rd (Frisby on the Wreake).

brike-kiln ME, 'a brick-kiln'. Brick-hill Cl (f.n. Ratcliffe on the Wreake), Brickkilen Cl (f.n. Barkby), Brick Kiln Cl (f.n. Baggrave, South Croxton, Hoby, Rearsby, Thrussington), Brick kiln leys (f.n. Loddington).

brike-yard ME, 'a brick-works, a brick-field, a yard where bricks are made'. Brick-Yard (f.n. Thrussington), the Brickyard (f.n. Cold Newton), Brickyard Cl (f.n. Rotherby).

brink ODan, ME, 'a brink, the edge of a bank'. *the brinkes* (f.n. Thrussington), Brinks (f.n. Tilton), Brink Hill (f.n. Seagrave), High Brinks Cl (f.n. South Croxton), Hingin Brinks (f.n. Sileby), Muckle Brinks (f.n. Keyham), *the mylne brynke* (f.n. Barrow upon Soar), Redbrink Cls (f.n. Wymeswold).

brōc OE, 'a brook, a stream'. Barkby Brook, Brook Ho., Brook Lane, Brook St (Sileby, Wymeswold), Bushby Brook, Fishpool Brook, Harbrook Fm, King's ~, Ox ~, Queniborough ~, Walton Brook. Freq. in f.ns., esp. compounded with a settlement name and thus prob. identifying a more major watercourse, e.g. *Baggrave Brook* (South Croxton), *Rakedalebro(o)ke* (Hoby), *Wistoftbrooke* (Seagrave), *Wylougby Broke* (Wymeswold); common as a simplex, e.g. *le Brok'* (with various spellings in Barkby, Barrow upon Soar, Burton on the Wolds, Cossington, Gaddesby etc.); occasionally with a directional adj., e.g. *le Estbroc* (Hoby), *Sowbroke* (Beeby, South Croxton), *West brook* (Barkby). Note also the interesting *Monkesbroke* (Barrow upon Soar), *Skonte brooke* (Saxelby) and *Yenbrook* (South Croxton). In contrast to those in Framland Hundred (*v.* Lei **2** 315), East Goscote Hundred stream-names with OE *brōc* outnumber those with ON *bekkr* at a ratio of 3:1 and in names recorded only before 1500, at a ratio of 7:1, *v.* **bekkr**.

brocc OE, 'a badger'. ?Brockwell (f.n. Skeffington), ?*Brockwell sicke* (f.n. Hungarton).

brocc-hol OE, 'a badger hole, a sett'. *Brocholes* (f.n. Skeffington, Welby), Brockholes (f.n. Asfordby). Note that a late form *Brockhill* may sometimes disguise this compound.

brocen OE, pa.part., 'broken, broken-up'. *Brokenback(e)s* (f.n. Humberstone), ?*Broken Banks* (f.n. Syston), *the Broken lands* (f.n. Thrussington), *Brokenlond* (f.n. Barrow upon Soar).

brōm OE, 'broom'. Broom Lodge. *Bromberga* (f.n. Wymeswold), *Bromcliffe* (f.n. South Croxton), *Bromholme lees* (f.n. Gaddesby), Broomfield Cl (f.n. Walton on the Wolds), The Brummels (f.n. Kirby Bellars), *Raresby Broom(e)* (f.n. Queniborough), Upper Broom (f.n. Rearsby).

brū OE, 'an eyebrow'; topographically 'a hill-brow, a hill, a steep slope'. *Brotherne* (f.n. Kirby Bellars).

brún[2] ON, 'a brow, the edge of a hill'. First ~, Second Born (f.ns. Frisby on the Wreake).

bruni ON, 'burning; a place cleared by burning'. ?*Burnecroft* (f.n. Thurmaston), ?*Burnemedue* (f.n. Cold Newton), ?*Burnesicke* (f.n. Seagrave), ?*Burne Wong* (f.n. South Croxton), ?Burn Sick (f.n. Sileby), ?Burn Thorn (f.n. Beeby), ?Burn Wong Furlong (f.n. Barsby), *v.* **bryne**.

brycg OE, 'a bridge, a causeway'; in the Danelaw, the spellings of p.ns. with *brycg* are often influenced by ON **bryggja** 'a jetty, a quay'. Bridgeland Fm, Lewin Bridge. Sometimes prefixed by a settlement name, e.g. *Barewebrigg* (Barrow upon Soar), *Kettlebybrigge* (Kirby Bellars). Commonly compounded with OE *stān* 'stone' as *Stanbryg* (South Croxton), *the stone bryge* (Asfordby); occasionally with a pers.n. or surn., e.g. *Tuttebrugge* (Burton on the Wolds). Note the wooden construction of Boarden Bridge (Beeby).

***brȳd** OE, adj., 'surging'. ?Bridewell (f.n. Beeby).

bryggja ON, 'a landing-stage, a jetty, a quay', *v.* **brycg**.

bryke late ME, 'a brick'. Brick Fd (f.n. Rearsby).

bryne OE, 'burning; a place cleared by burning'. ?*Burnecroft* (f.n. Thurmaston), ?*Burnemedue* (f.n. Cold Newton), ?*Burnesicke* (f.n. Seagrave), ?*Burne Wong* (f.n. South Croxton), ?Burn Sick (f.n. Sileby), ?Burn Thorn (f.n. Beeby), ?Burn Wong Furlong (f.n. Barsby), *v.* **bruni**.

bucca OE, 'a buck, a male deer, a he-goat'. Buck Furs End (f.n. Barsby), *Buckpool* (f.n. Kirby Bellars), *Buckwell Close* (f.n. East Norton).

bufan OE, prep., 'above, over, on top of'. Boonton (f.n. Queniborough).

bula OE, 'a bull'. Common in f.ns.: ?*Bulborow hill* (Wymeswold), Bull Dale Cl (Thorpe Satchville), Bull Fd (Hungarton), Bull Heads (South Croxton), the Bull Hook (Skeffington), *the Bullins* (Kirby Bellars), *Bull leyes* (Barkby Thorpe), Bull Piece (Belgrave, Cossington, Humberstone, Rotherby, Thurmaston).

bullgate ModEdial., 'pasturage for a single bull'. Bull Gate (f.n. Halstead).

bulluc OE, 'a bullock'. *Bullocke holme* (f.n. Tugby), Bullock Yard (f.n. Cotes).

bune OE, 'a reed'. ?Bunbury Fm. Bunlett (f.n. Hoton).

***bur-blade** ME, prob. the name of a plant; poss. a compound of ME *burre* 'burdock' and *blæd* 'a leaf'. *Burbladehyl* (f.n. Cossington), *Burblad(e)syk* (f.n. Belgrave).

burgh OE, **borow** ME, 'a burrow'. ?*Boroland* (f.n. Thurmaston), *the Burrowes* (f.n. Rotherby), Burrow Lane (f.n. Lowesby), *the Connyborrowe* (f.n. Queniborough), Fox Burgh (f.n. Brooksby).

burh OE, 'a fortified place; a pre-English earthwork; an Anglo-Saxon fortification; a fortified house or manor'. Queniborough. *Burfeld* (f.n. Launde), *la Burgh* (f.n. Whatborough), *Goldsburgh* (f.n. Kirby Bellars).

burh-tūn OE, 'a fort enclosure; a farmstead with a palisade'. Burton on the Wolds.

burna OE, 'a stream'. ?*Burnemedue*, ?*Gowborn close* (f.ns. Cold Newton), Holborne (f.n. Barrow upon Soar).

busc OE, **bush** ME, 'a bush, a thicket, ground covered with shrubs'. The Bushes, Tugby Bushes. Freq. in f.ns.: with a surn. indicating ownership, e.g. Bowman's Bush (Humberstone), *Mr Lumners bush* (Cossington), Marston Bush (Queniborough), Porter Bush (Gaddesby); prefixed by a locational el. or minor p.n., e.g. East Meadow Bushes (Belgrave), *Hogcrafte bushes*, *Hurdlegate Bush* (Seagrave), Moor Bush (Ratcliffe on the Wreake); with an el. defining the nature of the shrubs/thicket, e.g. Rush Bush Furlong (Grimston), *Wythibusforlong'* (Thurmaston). Note the important Moota Bush (f.n. Barkby).

buskr ON, 'a bush, a thicket'. Common in f.ns.: *Belbusk* (Gaddesby), *Braknell buske* (Ratcliffe on the Wreake), Busk Wong (Thrussington), *Greynel buskys* (Humberstone), *Hamirwyuelisbuskes* (Hoby), *Horseydelbuske*, *Thickebusk* (Cossington), *Manibuskes* (Skeffington), *Rischebusk'* (with various spellings in Barkby, Hoby, Kirby Bellars, Rearsby), *Sendebusk*, *Swetebuske* (South Croxton).

busshi ME, adj., 'growing with bushes'. *the Bushey close* (f.n. with various spellings in Burton on the Wolds, Cossington, Lowesby), Bushy Fd (f.n. Gaddesby), Bushy furlong (f.n. Halstead), Bushy Mdw (f.n. Quenby), Bushy Stiltons (f.n. Loddington).

but OFr, 'an archery butt'. Flagstaff Butts. ?*the butt lane* (Barkby).

butere OE, 'butter'; often referring to rich pasture which yielded good butter. *Butterclifes* (f.n. Hoby), Butterpot Lane (Skeffington).

butte ME, 'a short strip of arable land'. *Annotesbuttes*, *Wheatbutt layes* (f.ns. Thurmaston), *Butfurlong'*, *Buttleas hedge* (f.ns. Skeffington), *Butlays* (f.n. Seagrave), *Butt Close* (f.n. Cossington), Butt Cl (f.n. Wymeswold), ?*the butt lane* (Barkby), Butt leys (f.n. Humberstone), Buttlings Cl (f.n. Gaddesby), *the Butts* (f.n. Hoby), *Butts bridge Furlong* (f.n. Tugby), Butts Cl (f.n. East Norton), *Grundisbutts* (f.n. South Croxton), *Smithisbuttes* (f.n. Barrow upon Soar), *Soure Butts* (f.n. Barkby Thorpe), the Thack Butts (f.n. Queniborough).

bȳ ODan, 'a farmstead, a village'. Asfordby, Ashby Folville, Barkby, Barsby, Beeby, Brooksby, Frisby on the Wreake, Gaddesby, Hoby, Old Ingarsby, Lowesby, Quenby, Rearsby, Rotherby, Saxelby, Shoby, Sileby, Tugby, Welby. *Canby* (f.n.

Sileby), *Colby* (f.n. Thurmaston), ?*hortebe aker* (f.n. Wymeswold).

byden OE, 'a vessel, a tub'; topographically, 'a hollow'. *Bydwell* (f.n. Barrow upon Soar).

bȳre OE, 'a byre, a cowshed'. *Westhorpbirimedow(e)* (f.n. Barkby).

cǣg OE, 'a key'; poss. used topographically of a key-shaped hill-formation. ?Keyham.

cærse OE, 'cress, watercress'. Cresswell Cl (f.n. Lowesby).

cabin ModE, 'a cabin'. Cabin Rickstead (f.n. East Norton).

cāl OE, **kál** ON, **cale, cole** ME, 'rape, cole, cabbage'. *Calacre* (f.n. Hoby), *Cawland*, *Chalhoum*, *Colhille* (f.ns. Kirby Bellars).

calc OE, 'chalk, limestone'. Chalkpit Fm, Chalk Pool Hill. *Cakelands* (f.n. Walton on the Wolds), *le Calkelandsike* (f.n. Seagrave), *Calkhill'* (f.n. Cossington), *Calkland* (f.n. Kirby Bellars), *Cawkells* (f.n. Barkby Thorpe), Chalk Hill (f.n. Wymeswold).

cald OE (Angl), **kaldr** ON, **cald, cold** ME, adj., 'cold; exposed, wind-swept'. Cold Newton; Caudale Field Fm, ?Colborough Hill. Cadewell Sick (f.n. Grimston), Calboro (f.n. Loddington), *Caldewelle* (f.n. Cold Newton, Queniborough), *Caldewellesyke* (f.n. Barrow upon Soar), Cawdles (f.n. Seagrave), *Cawdwell hades* (f.n. Rotherby), *Coldelesb'rge* (f.n. Halstead), ?Colleborough Lane (Ratcliffe on the Wreake), Cordel Sty (f.n. Sileby).

calenge OFr, ME, 'challenge, dispute; land in dispute'. *la Chaleng'* (f.n. Barrow upon Soar), *Kalengewong'* (f.n. South Croxton).

calf (**calfra** gen.pl.) OE, 'a calf'. Calf Cl (f.n. Beeby, Gaddesby, Halstead, Thorpe Satchville, Welby), *Calfdale* (f.n. Barkby), *Calf holme* (f.n. Asfordby, Kirby Bellars), Calf Lairs (f.n. East Norton), *Calvercroft* (f.n. Kirby Bellars), *Caluero* (f.n. Skeffington), Calves Water (f.n. Thurmaston).

calu OE, adj., 'bare, lacking in vegetation'. ?Colborough Hill. Calabor Furlong (f.n. Barsby), *Caleberg* (f.n. Barkby Thorpe), ?Colleborough Lane (Ratcliffe on the Wreake), ?*Gallow Hill* (f.n. Barkby).

camp OE, 'open land'. Camp Cl (f.n. Belgrave).

carpenter ME, 'an artificer in wood'. Carpenter's Shop.

carte ME, 'a cart'. *the Coalcart Road* (Saxelby), *the Cole Cart Way* (Ratcliffe on the Wreake, Rearsby).

cart-waie ME, 'a way along which a cart can be driven'; later 'a rough road on a farm, passable by a heavy cart'. Mr Pywells Cartway (Keyham).

cat(t) OE, 'a cat', **catte** OE, 'a she-cat'. ?Catsick Hill, ?Catsick Lane. *Catlyf* (f.n. Frisby on the Wreake), Cats Hill (f.n. Keyham), *Cattishou* (f.n. Kirby Bellars), *Catwelle furlonges* (f.n. Hoby).

caucie ONFr, **cauce, cause** ME, 'an embankment or dam, a raised way across marshy ground or along a dyke; a (raised) paved way'. *le Cawsey* (Barrow upon Soar), Causeway Baulk Cl (f.n. Twyford), Causeway Cl (f.n. Halstead).

cayme ME, 'a bank or ridge of earth (along a ditch)', from OE *camb*, ON *kambr* 'a comb, a crest'. ?*Kaimesbrigge* (f.n. Hoby).

cēap OE, 'a market'. Cheap End.

ceaster OE, 'an old fortification; a Roman site'. Middle ~, Road Chesters (f.ns. Frisby on the Wreake).

chapel(e) OFr, ME, 'a chapel'. Chapel bar (Wymeswold), *the Chappel(l) house* (Thurmaston). Chapel Cl (f.n. Thorpe Satchville), Chapel Fd (f.n. Cold Newton), *the Chapel yard* (f.n. Baggrave), *Chapell yard* (f.n. Launde), the Chappell Cl (f.n. Thurmaston).

chaunterie ME, 'a chantry'. Chantry Ho.

cheesecake ModE, 'a tart, usually made with eggs and cheese'; applied topographically to a wedge-shaped field in humorous reference to a portion of such a confection. *the Cheescake* (f.n. Thurmaston), *Cheescake nook* (f.n. Cossington), Cheesecake bit (f.n. Halstead), Cheese-cake Cl (f.n. Thorpe Satchville), Cheesecake Hill, Cheesecake Mdw (f.ns. Hoby).

cherietree ME, 'a cherry-tree'. Cherrytree Cl (f.n. Loddington).

chirche-ȝeard ME, 'a church-yard'. Freq., earlier instances being *the Church Yard(e)* (belonging to the parish churches of Cossington (1564), Hungarton (1601), Ashby Folville, Beeby, Hoby, Syston (1605), Lowesby, Twyford (1612)).

cīcen OE, 'a chicken'. *The Chickines* (f.n. Barrow upon Soar), *(the) Chicken wong(e)* (f.n. Asfordby), *Chickinholme* (f.n. Rearsby).

cild OE, 'a child, a boy'. *the Modyr and the Chylde* (f.n. Thurmaston).

cinu OE, 'a fissure, a ravine'. Chine Ho. Chainacre Cl (f.n. Wymeswold).

cirice OE, 'a church'. (Parish churches with their various dedications are not listed.) Church Headland Furlong (f.n. South Croxton).

cisel OE, 'gravel'. the Great Chissel (f.n. Thrussington).

clǣg OE, 'clay, clayey soil'. *Clay street* (Wymeswold). *Clay field*, Cleay Cliff (f.ns. Barkby), Clay Lands (f.n. Belgrave), *the clea fiellde* (f.n. Hoby), *Clefoxholl'*, *le Cleyclif*, *Cleyclos* (f.ns. Cossington), *the Cley felde*, *Cley Cleaves* (f.ns. Rearsby), the Corn Clay Fds (f.n. Queniborough).

clǣne OE, adj., 'clean, clear of weeds'. ?Clan Banks (f.n. Twyford).

clāfre OE, 'clover'. *Clauerdale* (f.n. Barsby), Clover Cl (f.n. Barkby, Beeby, Belgrave, Keyham, Lowesby, Prestwold, Tugby), Clover Fd (f.n. Ragdale).

clapere ME, 'a warren'. Clapperdale Furlong, Clapperdale Leys (f.ns. South Croxton).

clerc OE, OFr, 'a cleric'. *Clerkyswellebrukys* (f.n. Loddington).

cley-pytt ME, 'a clay-pit'. Bottom ~, Top Claypits (f.ns. Frisby on the Wreake).

clif OE, 'a cliff, a bank, a steep hillside'. Ratcliffe on the Wreake; Barrowcliffe, Barrowcliffe Fm, Barrowcliffe Spinney, The Cliff, Cliff Hill, Cliff Ho., Rancliff Wood, Strancliffe. Freq. in f.ns.: with an el. identifying a crop, e.g. *Barlyclife* (Barsby), *Perecliues* (Saxelby) or wild flora, e.g. *Bromcliffe* (South Croxton), *Tasleclif* (Kirby Bellars), *Thurnclyf* (Barkby), *Wenie clyffe* (Ratcliffe on the Wreake); or with an el. indicating shape, e.g. *Branclyf*, *Longclif* (Barkby), *Hyclyf* (Cossington); or wild fauna, e.g. *Catlyf* (Frisby on the Wreake), *Hartclif* (with various spellings in Asfordby, Barrow upon Soar, Humberstone); with an el. signifying the nature of the soil, e.g. *Butterclifes* (f.n. Hoby), *le Cleyclif* (with various spellings in Barkby, Cossington, Rearsby), *radecliue* (Kirby Bellars), *Steinclif* (Cold Newton); with an el. indicating location, e.g. *Middelclyf* (Barkby), *the Nether Cliffe* (Burton on the Wolds), *Southcliff* (Barrow upon Soar), *Thuerclif* (Kirby Bellars); or aspect, e.g. *Blacclif* (Burton on the Wolds), *Greneclyffe* (Barrow upon Soar); occasionally with a pers.n., e.g. *Hosulweclif* (Gaddesby).

clofen OE, pa.part., 'cloven, split'. Clovengore Bault (f.n. Sileby).

***clōh** OE, **clo(u)gh** ME, 'a deep valley or ravine, a dell'. Cluegate (f.n. Queniborough).

clos(e) ME, 'a close, an enclosure'. Very freq. in f.ns.: early examples are *Boreclos* (1477 (e.16), Gaddesby), *Cleyclos* (1349, Cossington), *Duffehous Yerde close* (1486, Kirby Bellars), *le Prestes Clos*, *le Woldclos* (1467 × 84, Barkby), *Thorslos* (1322, Hoby).

closing eModE, 'an enclosure'. *the Closing* (f.n. Seagrave), *Between the Closeing*, Gatsby Closing, Raisby Closing (f.ns. Queniborough), *the towne Closynge* (f.n. Twyford).

clot(t) OE, 'a mass, a lump, a clod'. *Clottiland'* (f.n. Thurmaston).

clump eModE, 'a cluster of trees'. The Clump, Big Clump, Small Clump.

cnæpp OE (Angl), 'a hill-top, a short sharp ascent'. Knapt-thorn (f.n. Ratcliffe on the Wreake).

cnafa OE, 'a boy, a young man, a servant'. *Knaves holme* (f.n. Rearsby).

cnoll OE, 'a knoll, a hillock'. The Knoll. *greenknowles*, *Horsnoll* (f.ns. Cossington), *the knole* (f.n. Rearsby), *knole haydes* (f.n. Rotherby), *the knowle* (f.n. Barsby), *the knowl(e)s* (f.n. Hungarton, Seagrave), Royal Knowl Cl (f.n. Sileby).

***cobb(e)** OE, 'a round lump', **cob** ModEdial., 'a mound, a hillock'. *cobb hadland* (f.n. South Croxton), Cob Headland Furlong, ?the Cob Yard (f.ns. Barsby).

cocc[1] OE, 'a heap, a hillock'; as a first el., difficult to distinguish from **cocc**[2]. ?*Coccroft* (f.n. Barsby).

cocc[2] OE, 'a cock, a woodcock'; difficult to distinguish from **cocc**[1]. ?*Coccroft* (f.n. Barsby), (the) Cock Cl (f.n. Walton on the Wolds), ?*Cockislandis* (f.n. Cossington), *Cokkiscomb* (f.n. Thurmaston), *Cokpoole* (f.n. Barrow upon Soar).

cofa OE, 'a chamber'; poss. later used topographically of 'a recess in the steep side of a hill, a sheltered place among hills or woods'. ?Melcoff Hole (f.n. Tilton).

***cogg** OE, 'a cog wheel', prob. used topographically of 'a small round hill'. ?*Cogling croft* (f.n. Walton on the Wolds).

col[1] OE, 'coal, esp. charcoal'; cf. **col-pytt**. *the Coalcart Road* (Saxelby), Coal-cart Way (Ratcliffe on the Wreake), *the Cole Cart Way* (Rearsby), Coal Place Fd (f.n. Kirby Bellars).

cole ME, 'cabbage'. ?*(the) Cole close* (f.n. Gaddesby).

college ME, 'a college, a community of clerks'. *the Colledge land* (f.n. Wymeswold).

col-pytt OE, 'a place where charcoal is made'. *the coale pitt way* (Belgrave), Coalpit (f.n. Seagrave), Coal Pitt Cl (f.n. Thrussington), *the Cole Pitt close* (f.n. Burton on the Wolds), *Colepitte gate*, *Cole Pit Hill* (f.ns. Hoby), Colepitt Fd (f.n. Quenby).

coltefote eModE, 'coltsfoot (*Tussilago farfara*)', a common weed in waste or clayey ground. Coltsfoot hole (f.n. Halstead).

commun ME, used both as a sb. as 'common land' and as an adj. as 'shared by all, of a non-private nature'. Freq. in f.ns.: Banks Common, Ilemore Common (Sileby), *Bilsdon Common* (Tilton), Broad Plat Common (Hoby), Campion brook Common, Conigreen Brook Common (Barrow upon Soar), *the common* (Hoton, Humberstone, Queniborough), Lings Common (Hoton); *Barkby Common Moore*, *Barkby Common Pasture* (Barkby), *the Common Lyme Pitt(e)s* (Barrow upon Soar), *the Common pasture* (Beeby, South Croxton, Frisby on the Wreake, Humberstone, Saxelby).

conestable OFr, ME, 'a constable'. Constable Hades (f.n. Asfordby, Hoby), *Constable peice* (f.n. Cossington), ?Constables Mdw (f.n. Walton on the Wolds), (the) Constable way (Loddington).

coni ME, 'a rabbit'. Coney Cl (f.n. Belgrave, Walton on the Wolds), *the conie platt furlong* (f.n. Rearsby), ?Conigreen Brook Common (f.n. Barrow upon Soar), *the Connyborrowe* (f.n. Queniborough).

coningre, **coninger** ME, 'a rabbit-warren'. Conery Lane. ?Conigreen Brook Common, *Cuningrie Feilde*, *Walton Cunyngre* (f.ns. Barrow upon Soar), *Conniegrey close* (f.n. Cossington), Conygree Leys (f.n. Prestwold), the Cunnery (f.n. Belgrave, Hoby, Humberstone, Loddington), the Cunnery Cl (f.n. Wymeswold), *the Cunnery End* (f.n. Walton on the Wolds), *Cunny Grey* (f.n. Baggrave), Old Cunnery (f.n. Rearsby), *the twoo Cuneryes* (f.n. Launde).

convent ME, 'a convent; a community of monks or nuns'. Convent or Garlands Fd (f.n. Rearsby), *le Covent Close* (f.n. Kirby Bellars).

copis ME, (OFr *copeiz*), 'a coppice'. The Coppice. Mr Cheslyns Coppice (f.n. Walton on the Wolds), Far ~, Near ~, Copy (f.ns. Welby), Oak Coppice (f.n. Thurmaston).

copp OE, 'a summit, a hill or ridge which has a narrow, crest-like top'. Copley (f.n. Hoby), *Coplow hill close* (f.n. Cold Newton), *Copmore* (f.n. Barsby), ?*Tilton cowpwodis* (f.n. Tilton).

copped[1] ME, adj., 'having a peak'. Copthill Fm. *coptehyll'* (f.n. Hungarton).

copped[2] ME, pa.part., adj., 'having had the head removed, pollarded'. *Copthorn* (f.n. Barrow upon Soar), Copthorn(e) (f.n. Queniborough), *Coppetre* (f.n. Launde).

***corf** OE, 'a cutting, a gap'. *le corf* (f.n. Wymeswold).

corn[1] OE, 'corn, grain'. Corn Cl (f.n. Beeby, Cossington, Cotes, Prestwold, Tilton), the Corn Clay Fds (f.n. Queniborough), *the Corn Mill* (Sileby).

corner ME, 'a corner, a nook'. Common in f.ns., e.g. Barbers Corner, Corner Cl (Frisby on the Wreake), Corner Bit (Cold Newton), (the) Corner Fd (Barkby, Rearsby, Twyford), Corner Mdw (Allexton), Polly Flinders Corner (Walton on the Wolds), Rodhills Corner, Sikes Corner, Slade Field Corner (Halstead) etc. Note the unusual *William corner dame Edeson*(*e*) (of 1319, Kirby Bellars).

cot (**cotu** nom.pl.) OE, **cotes** (nom.pl.) ME, 'a cottage, a hut, a shelter'. Cotes, Goscote Hundred, Storklt Lane. *Coates headland* (f.n. Cossington), Coathills (f.n. Hungarton), *Cotcliffe hill* (f.n. Seagrave), *Cotewong*, *Cotte Croft*, Court Cl (f.ns. South Croxton), *cots lane* (Hoton), *Harcott Hill* (f.n. Belgrave), *Lambcote dale* (f.n. Halstead), *Lambecotehou* (f.n. Thrussington), *Lamcotte hill* (f.n. Burton on the Wolds), *litel cot* (f.n. Hoton), *Shirdiccotes* (f.n. Thurmaston), Shouldercoates (f.n. Twyford).

cotage ME, 'a cottage, a hut, a shelter'. Brancliff Cottage, Dun's Lane ~, Harborough ~, Kirby ~, Queniborough Cottage. Cottage Cl (f.n. Cossington, Frisby on the Wreake, Halstead, Hoby, Cold Newton, Rotherby), the Cottage Croft (f.n. Walton on the Wolds), (the) Cottage Pasture (f.n. Wymeswold), Little Cottage Cl (f.n. Barkby). Note also the range of examples of cottages in Burton on the Wolds (1701).

cotager eModE, 'one who lives in a cottage', used especially of the labouring population in rural districts. Cottagers Cl (f.n. Baggrave, Hoby), the Cottagers Pasture (f.n. Wymeswold), *the Cottagers* (*Old*) *Pasture* (f.ns. Ashby Folville, Rotherby).

cottere OE, 'a cottar, a cottager'. *Ashby Coters Pastuer* (f.n. Ashby Folville), *the Cottiers Close* (f.n. Rotherby, Tilton), Cottyers Cl (f.n. Lowesby).

counsayl ME, 'consultation, deliberation'. Council Cl (f.n. Humberstone).

co(u)nte ME, 'the female private parts, a cunt'. *Grop(e)cuntlane* (Kirby Bellars).

court OFr, ME, 'a large house, a manor house; a space enclosed by walls or houses, a yard'. Keythorpe Court. *the Pump Court* (Cossington).

cover(t) ME, 'a covert, a shelter for game'. Bailiff's Covert, Botany Bay Fox Covert, Foxcovert Ho., Foxholes Covert, John o'Gaunt's Cover, Lord Aylesford's Covert, Lord Merton's Covert, New Covert (South Croxton, Hoton). Carvers Covert, Reed Pool Covert (f.ns. Hungarton), Cover Fd (f.n. Lowesby), Fox Covert (f.n. South Croxton, Syston), Gorse Cover, New Covert (f.ns. Grimston), Gorse Covert (f.n. Syston), Walton New Covert (f.n. Walton on the Wolds).

cowgate ModEdial., 'pasturage for a single cow'. *cowe gates* (f.n. Humberstone).

cowpenn eModE, 'a pen or enclosure for cows'. Cowpen (f.n. Barkby).

crabbe ME, 'a crab-apple, a crab-apple-tree'. Crab Hays (f.n. Belgrave), ?*Crabs Close* (f.n. Allexton).

crabtre ME, 'a crab-apple-tree'. (*the*) *Crabtree* (f.n. Barkby, Belgrave, Queniborough), Crabtree Cl (f.n. Allexton, Loddington, Thorpe Satchville, Thrussington), Crabtree Furlong Cl (f.n. Humberstone).

***craca** OE, **kráka** ON, **crake** ME, 'a crow, a raven'. *Crackhole* (f.n. Burton on the Wolds).

***cramb** OE, 'land in the bend of a river'. *Cramborow syck*, *Crombdale* (f.ns. Wymeswold), (the) Cramp Cl (f.n. Walton on the Wolds), Cramp Fd (f.n. Keyham), ?Cramp Lane (Syston).

cran, cron OE, 'a crane, a heron'. Cranes Nest (f.n. Belgrave, Hungarton), *Crondale hille* (f.n. Twyford).

crāwe OE, 'the crow'. Crow Wood. *Croosick* (f.n. Seagrave), *Crowedale* (f.n. Thorpe Satchville), *Crowe holme garden* (f.n. Cossington), Crow Hill Syke (f.n. Wymeswold), Crow Holm Cl (f.n. Syston), Crow Legs Furlong (f.n. Ratcliffe on the Wreake), *Crow nest furlong* (f.n. Gaddesby), Crow Park (f.n. Kirby Bellars), Crowthorne Furlong (f.n. Barsby).

crew-yard ModE, 'a close or yard with sheds for cattle'. Crew Yard (f.n. Lowesby).

crocc OE, 'a crock, an earthenware pot', in toponyms prob. alluding to places where pots and sherds were discovered or where pots were made. *Crochou* (f.n. Barkby), *Crokehou* (f.n. Hoby).

croft OE, 'a small enclosed field, a small enclosure near a house'. Breadcroft, Fox Croft Spinney, Ryecroft Fm, Tentercroft Ave. Very freq. in f.ns.: especially with pers.ns. and surns., e.g. *Brounyngcroft* (Barsby), *Lentoncrofte* (Barrow upon Soar), *Gagyscroft*, *Pakyscroft*, *Stykeryscroft* (Welby), *Kent croft* (Belgrave), *Lawesoncroft*, *Wasteneyscroft* (Kirby Bellars), *Wilgercroft* (Queniborough); with crops or wild flora, e.g. *Banecroftis* (with various spellings in Barrow upon Soar, Hoby, Kirby Bellars, Queniborough), *Barlicroft* (Seagrave), Pease Croft (Humberstone), Hazel Croft (Barrow upon Soar), *Riscroft* (Kirby Bellars); with structures, e.g. *le Barnecroft* (Humberstone), *Bincroft* (Thorpe Satchville), *Cotte Croft* (South Croxton), *Dufhows croft* (Hungarton), *le Milnecroft* (Asfordby, Barrow upon Soar, Brooksby), *Pencroft* (Cossington); with farm animals, e.g. *Calvercroft* (Kirby Bellars), *Hogcraft* (Seagrave), *horse croft* (Cossington), Lamb Croft (Barrow upon Soar); with an adj. of size or shape, e.g. *le littilcroft* (Kirby Bellars), *Long Croft(s)* (Barkby, Cotes, South Croxton, Welby), *Shortecrofte* (South Croxton); with an indicator of direction, e.g. *East Croft* (Barsby), *le*

Estcroftis (Hoby), *Incrofte* (Asfordby). Occasionally as a simplex, e.g. *le Croft* (Barrow upon Soar, Humberstone). Note *Spitelcroft* (Queniborough).

***crōh**[2] OE, 'a nook, a corner'. ?*Crooesick*, *horsecroe bushe* (f.ns. Seagrave), ?Crow Legs Furlong (f.n. Ratcliffe on the Wreake).

croked ME, adj., 'crooked, twisted'. *Crokedmedowe* (f.n. Hoby), Crooked Cl (f.n. Lowesby).

crop(p) OE, 'a swelling, a mound, a hill'. *Thorscroppis* (f.n. Skeffington).

cros late OE, ME, 'a cross'; difficult to distinguish from **cross** *infra* when acting as a qualifier. Stump Cross. *babgraue crosse* (Hungarton), *Bernardes Crosse*, Parr Cross (Kirby Bellars), ?*Croshou* (f.n. Kirby Bellars), *Croswell* (f.n. Barkby), Great Stump Cross (Ashby Folville), *Headless Cross* (Allexton), *Helot(e)cros* (Loddington), *le Holly Crosse* (Belgrave), *Peres Crosse* (Halstead), *Twyforde Crosse* (South Croxton), *Whadale Crosse* (Wymeswold).

cross ME, adj., 'athwart, lying across, crosswise'. In some modern minor names, used of cross-roads. Cross St. Freq. in f.ns.: e.g. *Crosfurlang* (Cossington, Cold Newton, Seagrave), ?*Croshou* (Kirby Bellars), *Croslands* (Cossington, Seagrave), Cross Hills (Hoby), Cross Leys (with various spellings in Barsby, Cossington, South Croxton, Quenby) etc. As a cross-roads: Ratcliffe Cross (Cossington), *v.* **cros**.

cū OE, 'a cow'. Cowdam Hades (f.n. Frisby on the Wreake), *le Coweclose* (f.n. Old Ingarsby), *the cowe pasture* (f.n. Frisby on the Wreake, Hoby, Humberstone, Rotherby), *Coweswade* (f.n. Belgrave), *Cow(e)gate* (f.n. Belgrave, Hoby, Skeffington), *Cumedwe hauedes* (f.n. Burton on the Wolds).

cubb ME, 'a stall, a pen, a shed for cattle'. Cub Mdw (f.n. Keythorpe).

culfre OE, 'a dove'. *Culurewang'* (f.n. Cold Newton).

cumb OE, 'a valley, a short broad valley with three steeply rising sides'. ?*Cokkiscomb* (f.n. Thurmaston), *(the) Combes* (f.n. Barkby Thorpe), ?Holcombs (f.n. East Norton), Hollow Combs, *the Kombys* (f.ns. Humberstone).

cumber ME, 'an encumbrance'; prob. used of ground encumbered with rocks, stocks, stumps of trees etc. ?Cumberland Cl (f.n. Halstead).

***Cumbre (*Cumbra** gen.pl.) OE, 'the Cymry, the Welsh, the British'. Cumberdale (f.n. Wymeswold), *Cumberlea sicke* (f.n. Seagrave).

cundite eModE, 'a conduit, an aqueduct'. Conduit Spinney. Conduit Cl (f.n. Loddington), Conduits (f.n. Baggrave), the Conduits Fd (f.n. Kirby Bellars).

***cung** OE, 'a mound'. ?Cungen Mdw (f.n. Rearsby).

***cūpe** OE, **cupe** ME, 'a coop, a basket'. ?*Tilton cowpwodis* (f.n. Tilton).

curlewe ME, 'the curlew'. ?*Curley dale* (f.n. Halstead).

cū-sloppe OE, 'the cowslip, the wild flower *Primula veris*'. Cowslip Mdw (f.n. Thorpe Satchville).

cutte ME, 'a cut, a water-channel'. ?*Cutt wonge* (f.n. Rearsby).

cutting ME, 'a piece cut off'. Cuttings (f.n. Grimston).

***cwelle** OE (Angl), 'a spring, a well'. *Qweyldale* (f.n. South Croxton).

cwēn OE, 'a queen'. ?Quenby, Queniborough.

cwene OE, 'a woman'. *Quenemylnleys* (f.n. Kirby Bellars).

cweorn OE, 'a quern, a hand-mill'; some p.ns. refer to a place where mill-stones were obtained. *Qwerinhou* (f.n. South Croxton).

cyln OE (Angl), 'a kiln, a furnace for baking or burning'. *Kilneclose* (f.n. Barrow upon Soar, Burton on the Wolds, Wymeswold), *kilne dike meere* (f.n. Hungarton), *Kylnewong'* (f.n. Kirby Bellars), *le kylne yard* (f.n. with various spellings in Belgrave, Cossington, Halstead).

cyrps OE, adj., 'curly, curling'. ?Cripwell Fm.

cȳta OE (Angl), 'the kite'. *Kitenest* (f.n. Hoby).

dægesēge OE, 'the daisy'. *Daizy Nook* (f.n. Hoby).

dæl[1] OE, 'a pit, a hollow', especially 'a valley'. Ragdale. *Cumberdale* (f.n. Wymeswold), *Cusingedale* (f.n. Thorpe Satchville).

dāl OE, **dole** ME, 'a share, a portion; a share in a common field'. Freq in f.ns.: with a pers.n. or surn., e.g. *Dunnesdole* (Hoby), *Thuruerdesdole* (Cold Newton), *Togdoles* (Cossington); with wild flora, e.g. *le Mapeldole*, *Wyllydowles* (Thorpe Satchville), *Thirndole* (Kirby Bellars), *Whinidoles* (Sileby); with an el. describing the nature of the soil, e.g. *Bony dolys*, *fuldolys*, *flintedole* (Kirby Bellars); with livestock, e.g. *le Oxdoles* (Wymeswold), *sheepe dooles* (Cossington); with minor locational names prefixed, e.g. *Blindewelledole* (Cold Newton), *Stocweldole* (Barkby Thorpe). Recurring are instances of *le Brodedole* (Cossington, Hoby, Kirby Bellars), *le Longedoles* (Barkby Thorpe, Hamilton) and *Newedoles* (Hoby, Kirby Bellars).

dalk ME, 'a hole, a hollow, a depression in the ground'. *the Dalke* (f.n. Humberstone).

dalr ON, 'a valley'; in later spellings, very difficult to distinguish from **deill** 'a share, a portion of land'. Dale Hill. Freq. in f.ns.: common is Debdale/Deepdale (with various spellings in Asfordby, Ashby Folville, South Croxton, Keyham, Kirby Bellars, Lowesby, Queniborough/Burton on the Wolds, Grimston, Saxelby, Skeffington); with an el. indicating size, shape, e.g. *Brodale* (Barkby), *Langedale* (Barkby, Rotherby), *litle dale* (Beeby), *Micheldale* (Saxelby); or with birds and animals, e.g. *doudale* (Cossington), *Hulfstaredale* (Burton on the Wolds), Ozingdale (Barsby), *Calfdale* (Barkby), *Hyndesdale* (Kirby Bellars), Swan Dale (Gaddesby); or with wild flora, e.g. Brackindale (Grimston), *Brimblisdale*, Hawthorn Dale (Shoby). Note the important Dimsdale (with various spellings in Asfordby, Frisby on the Wreake and Sileby).

dame ME, 'the mistress of a household, a housewife'. *William corner dame Edeson(e)* (f.n. Kirby Bellars).

damesyn ME, 'a small plum; the damson-tree (*Prunus communis* or *domestica*, variety *damascena*)'. *damasyn hadlands* (f.n. Wymeswold).

damme ME, 'a dam', usually created either for use at mills or for the watering of farm livestock. Cowdam (f.n. South Croxton), Cowdam Hades, Top ~, Dam (f.ns. Frisby on the Wreake), *the Dames* (f.n. Launde), Dambank (f.n. Tilton), Dams Cl (f.n. Seagrave), Dams-end Lays (f.n. Ratcliffe on the Wreake), Mill Dam (f.n. Belgrave, Old Ingarsby, Loddington), *le milnedame* (f.n. Cossington), *Monkesdam* (f.n. Barrow upon Soar).

dēad OE, adj., 'dead'; often used in p.ns. with reference to a site of violent death or to the discovery of human bones; but also may indicate infertile soil. The Dead Hole (f.n. Belgrave), *the dead sand(e)* (f.n. Rearsby), *Dedewong* (f.n. Barrow upon Soar), Dedford, *Deydmore* (f.ns. Skeffington), *Dedhauedlond* (f.n. Hoby).

dēaw OE, 'dew'. *Dewell* (f.n. Humberstone), *Dewell furlong* (f.n. Barkby Thorpe), *Dewelstreme* (Skeffington), *the Dew wong* (f.n. Belgrave).

dede-man ME, 'a dead man, a corpse'. Deadmans Grave (f.n. South Croxton, Wymeswold), *Dedmanysgraue* (f.n. Skeffington), Deadman's Sty (f.n. Sileby).

deierie ME, 'a dairy'. Dairy Cl (f.n. Lowesby).

deill ON, 'a share, a portion of land'; in later spellings, very difficult to distinguish from **dalr** 'a valley', but pl. forms with *-dales* are sometimes indicators of *deill*. Freq. in f.ns.: compounded with a pers.n. or a surn., e.g. *Fintesdale* (Burton on the Wolds), *Raunsdale* (South Croxton), *Stovesdale* (Kirby Bellars); or with an el. specifying the nature of the soil, e.g. Flindell's Cl (Kirby Bellars), *Flintideles* (Skeffington), Marsh Dale (Cossington), *morlondeale* (Hungarton), *raddells* (Beeby); or size or shape, e.g. *longdele* (Kirby Bellars), *Scoueldale* (Burton on the Wolds); or location, e.g. *Farr dales* (Hungarton), *Fordelis* (Sileby), Holdel (Beeby), *kyrkdales* (Humberstone), *Woolldales* (Saxelby); or the nature of tenancy, e.g. *Mansdale* (Belgrave). Rare as a simplex, e.g. *le Dales* (Barkby), *Dayls* (Thurmaston).

(ge)delf OE, 'a digging, a pit, a quarry'. Delph Cl (f.n. Wymeswold), *delph dales* (f.n. Burton on the Wolds), *v.* **stān-(ge)delf**.

demeyn OFr, ME, 'demesne'. *the Hall demeanes* (f.n. Queniborough).

denu OE, 'a valley'. *the Deynys* (f.n. Skeffington), *Flintedene* (f.n. Kirby Bellars), *sowsmer' syk deyn* (f.n. Hungarton), *Theuisdene* (f.n. South Croxton).

dēop OE, adj., 'deep'. Freq. in the f.n. Debdale/Deepdale (with various spellings in Asfordby, Ashby Folville, South Croxton, Keyham, Kirby Bellars, Lowesby, Queniborough, Walton on the Wolds/Burton on the Wolds, Frisby on the Wreake, Grimston, Halstead, Saxelby, Skeffington, Thorpe Satchville, Wymeswold). Note also *Depforou* (f.n. Barkby).

derne OE, adj., 'hidden, obscure'. Denford (f.n. Queniborough), *le Dernforthe* (f.n. Barrow upon Soar).

dīc OE, 'a ditch'. *Banecroft diche* (f.n. Kirby Bellars), *Beneath the Ditch* (f.n. Humberstone), *Betwixte the ditches*, *Holme dyche* (f.ns. Barrow upon Soar), *denmarke ditch(e)*, *the parsonadge ditch* (f.ns. Asfordby), *the East Medow dich* (f.n. Belgrave), *Henditch*, *the Wash ditch* (f.ns. Rearsby), *Little Inn(e) Ditch*, *Oxback Ditch* (f.ns. Hoby), *Longbenelondichend* (f.n. Wymeswold), Merry Ditch, Water Ditch (f.ns. Sileby), Mill Ditch Furlong (f.n. Skeffington). *Aspedic* (f.n. Welby) and *Doddesdic* (f.n. Hoby) may contain *dīc* or *dík*, *v.* **dík**.

dík ON, 'a ditch'; the el. varies with OE **dīc** in some f.ns. Austen Dyke. *Abdykis* (f.n. Barsby), *Bancroftdike*, *Brantcroftdyke*, *Closdyke*, *Fouchedyke*, *Newdyke* (f.ns. Kirby Bellars), *Betwynedeke*, *le brock dick*, *Dickforlong* (f.ns. Cossington), *denmark dike*, *holmes dike*, *manyedikes*, *oodykes* (f.ns. Asfordby), *Dikefurlongfelde*, *le Dykeshende*, *Newdikes*, *Osmoundesdikys* (f.ns. Barkby), *Haregharedyke* (f.n. Barrow upon Soar), Howbeck Dyke (f.n. Frisby on the Wreake), Match Dike (f.n. South Croxton). *Aspedic* (f.n. Welby) and *Doddesdic* (f.n. Hoby) may contain *dík* or *dīc*, *v.* **dīc**.

docce OE, 'a dock' (the wild plant); poss. also 'a water-lily' when combined with an el. denoting water or a location beside water. Dockey Fm. Dockhams (f.n. Frisby on the Wreake), Dock Hill (f.n. Cold Newton), Docksey (f.n. Twyford), Dock Wong (f.n. Humberstone).

doctour ME, 'one who has attained the highest degree conferred by a university; a learned divine; one who is proficient in knowledge of law; a medical practitioner'. Doctors Cl (f.n. Cossington, Quenby, Wymeswold), *Doctors*

Orch(y)ard, Doctors stints (f.ns. Cossington).

donoke ME, 'the hedge-sparrow, the dunnock'. *Downaclease* (f.n. Queniborough).

dora OE, 'a humble-bee'. *dorendale gate* (Cossington).

douse ME, adj., 'sweet, pleasant', sb., 'a sweetheart'. *Dowsewong* (f.n. Humberstone).

dove-cot(e) ME, 'a dove-cote'. the Dove Coat (Lowesby), Dovecote (Ragdale), Dovecote Cl (f.n. with various spellings in Belgrave, Frisby on the Wreake, Hungarton, Keyham, Cold Newton, Ratcliffe on the Wreake), *the Dovecoats yard* (f.n. Burton on the Wolds), the Dovecote Fd (f.n. Kirby Bellars).

dove-hous ME, 'a dove-cote'. the Dovehouse (Lowesby), *le Dovehouse close* (f.n. Kirby Bellars), *Dufhows croft* (f.n. Hungarton).

dowe ME, 'paste of bread, dough'; later 'a soft, pasty mass'. ?*Douuecrofteshende* (f.n. Barrow upon Soar), ?*Dowwongus* (f.n. Humberstone).

drabbe eModE, '?mire'. *Long Drabs* (f.n. Cossington), Long Drab(b)s (f.n. Sileby).

draca OE, 'a dragon'. *Drakestan* (f.n. Burton on the Wolds).

drain eModE, 'a channel for carrying off water'. *the Drain at the bottom of the Nether Pease Lands* (Hoby), Holow Drain Cl (f.n. Welby), the Marsh Drain (Wymeswold), *the parsonadge dreane* (Asfordby).

drift ModE, 'a track along which cattle are driven'. *the Drift*, Oxey Drift (Loddington), *Drift Nooke* (f.n. Barrow upon Soar).

drinkinge ME, vbl.sb., 'swallowing of liquid'. the Drinking Piece (f.n. Queniborough).

drit OE, 'dirt'. *Catts dirt Hadland* (f.n. Humberstone).

drȳge OE, adj., 'dry'. *drye layes* (f.n. Humberstone), Dry Leighs (f.n. Queniborough).

duble ME, adj., 'double'. *Double Hedges* (f.n. Humberstone, Sileby).

dūc (dūcena gen.pl.) OE, 'a duck'. *dukenpites* (f.n. Asfordby).

dūfe OE, **dúfa** ON, 'a dove'; prob. also 'a pigeon'. ?*Nether douedale* (f.n. Cossington), Dove Bank (f.n. Thorpe Satchville), Dove Hole (f.n. Twyford).

***dumbel** OE, 'a hollow', ModEdial. *dumble*, 'a deep shady dell'. Dumble (f.n. Beeby).

dump[1] ModEdial., 'a deep hole in the bed of a river; a deep depression in the ground'. ?Walton Dump Fd (f.n. Walton on the Wolds).

dump[2] ModE, 'a place where refuse from a mine or quarry is deposited', ?Walton Dump Fd (f.n. Walton on the Wolds).

dūn OE, 'a tract of hill-country, an upland expanse; upland pasture'. ?Cussington Hills (f.n. Thorpe Satchville), ?*Down Hill* (f.n. Hoby), ?Greedon (f.n. Sileby), ?*(on) Longton* (f.n. Humberstone), ?Weldon (f.n. Twyford).

duru OE, 'a door, a gate; a gap'. *the milne doore* (Cossington Old Mill).

dyncge OE, 'dung; manured land, fallow land'. Dungehill Fm. Dungeon Mdw (f.n. Hoby), Dunspool (f.n. Asfordby).

dyrty eModE, adj., 'dirty'. Dirty Balk (f.n. Rotherby), Dirty Lane (Skeffington).

ēa OE, 'a river, a stream'. Eye Brook. *Eyfurlong'* (f.n. Rearsby), *the Eye Meadow* (f.n. Kirby Bellars).

***ēan** OE, 'a lamb'. *Yenbrook field* (f.n. South Croxton).

ears OE, 'an arse, a buttock'; transferred topographically to 'a rounded hill'. *Broadarses* (f.n. Humberstone, Hungarton), Broaders (f.n. Twyford), Gilbrodas (f.n. Tugby), *Pekesers* (f.n. Kirby Bellars), Sanders (f.n. Hoby, Hoton), ?Stanner

Furlong (f.n. Barsby). Note also the attraction to *ears* in Burnt arse Leys (f.n. Hungarton).

ēast OE, adj., 'east, eastern'. East Norton. East Fd, Eastings (f.ns. Asfordby), East Mdw (f.n. Belgrave), *Eastwell, estowlandes* (f.ns. Barrow upon Soar), *Estgate* (South Croxton), *le Estmede* (f.n. Frisby on the Wreake), *Est medue* (f.n. Barkby).

ēasterra OE, comp.adj., 'more eastern'. *Esterpeseland* (f.n. Skeffington).

eating ModE, vbl.sb., 'the action of taking food'; in f.ns. presum. referring to grass used only for grazing and not for a hay crop. ?*the Cottiers Eaton Close* (f.n. Rotherby).

eb ME, adj., 'shallow'. ?Abel Meer Cl (f.n. Hungarton).

ecg OE, 'an edge; the edge of a hill, an escarpment'. *edgecroft* (f.n. Asfordby).

edisc OE, 'an enclosure, an enclosed park'. ?*the Middle Hedge* (f.n. Queniborough), ?*ye Paylehedge furlong* (f.n. Walton on the Wolds), ?Stone Hedge Leys (f.n. Rearsby), ?*Strithill hedge* (f.n. South Croxton), ?Sweet Hedge, ?*West Hedge* (f.ns. Allexton), *Wymundedisch* (f.n. Wymeswold), *v.* **hecg**.

efen OE, adj., 'even, flat, level'. Even Gate Hedge Furlong (f.n. Barsby).

ēg OE (Angl), 'an island, a piece of raised ground in wetlands, land partly surrounded by water'. ?*Cungie* (f.n. Rearsby).

eik ON, 'an oak-tree'. Eagland Wood (f.n. Skeffington).

elbowe ME, 'an elbow'; topographically 'a sharp bend'. *the elboes* (f.n. Cossington), Elbow Pieces (f.n. Ratcliffe on the Wreake).

ellern OE, 'an elder-tree'. *Elderstubbes* (f.n. Ratcliffe on the Wreake), Elder Stump Furlong (f.n. Humberstone), *Ellerenestubbe* (f.n. Skeffington), *Elrenestub* (f.n. Burton on the Wolds, Kirby Bellars, Seagrave), *Elrinstubbes* (f.n. Barkby).

elm OE, 'an elm-tree'. The Elms, Elms Fm. *the Ellmes* (f.n. Asfordby), Elm Cl (f.n. Cold Newton), The Elms, Elms and Wytches (f.ns. Belgrave).

ende OE, **endi** ON, 'the end of something; the end of an estate, district or quarter of a village or town', *v.* **lane-ende**. Cheap End, South End Terrace, Town End Plantation, West End, West End Fm. Freq. in f.ns.: e.g. *atte pol sik ende* (Barkby Thorpe), *Blacclifueshende* (Burton on the Wolds), *Brockhole hades end*, *Chicken wong end* (Asfordby), *le Dykeshende*, *Estmedewende* (Barkby), *Shepdoules ende* (Cossington) etc.; recurring in the compound *town*(*s*)*end* (with various spellings in Asfordby, Barrow upon Soar, Barsby, Belgrave, Brooksby and 20 other townships).

ened OE, 'a duck'. *Enedewell* (f.n. Kirby Bellars).

eng ON, 'a meadow, a pasture'. Austen Dyke, ?Gunsell. Freq. in f.ns.: with an el. indicating size, e.g. Broading (with various spellings in Frisby on the Wreake, Rotherby, Skeffington, Tugby), *lytleinges* (Hoby, Humberstone), Smellings (Thorpe Satchville); with a directional adj., e.g. Eastings (Asfordby, Kirby Bellars), *Northings* (Barkby, Cossington, Sileby, Syston), Southins (Sileby), *the Westinges* (Hoby); with an el. specifying the nature of the soil, e.g. ?*flintinges* (Humberstone), *Steyning* (Cold Newton); with livestock, e.g. *the Bullins* (Kirby Bellars); with a pers.n., e.g. *Wlfinges* (Hoby).

eowestre OE, 'a sheep-fold'. Ostir Ford (f.n. Gaddesby).

eowu OE, 'a ewe'. Ewe Cl (f.n. Prestwold), Little Ewe Cl (f.n. Hoton).

erber OFr, ME, 'a grass-covered piece of ground; a garden'. The Arbour (f.n. Rearsby), *the arbour hades* (f.n. Asfordby), *Perkin Arbor Layes* (f.n. Belgrave).

ermitage OFr, ME, **hermitage** ME, 'a hermitage'. The Hermitage.

erð OE, 'ploughed land'. *Edemerth* (f.n. South Croxton).

eski ON, 'a place growing with ash-trees'; sometimes replacing OE **æsc** 'an ash-tree'. *Eske*, *Eskelund'* (f.ns. Skeffington).

estren ME, adj., 'lying towards the east'; later 'having an eastward direction'. *Estrenegate* (South Croxton).

ēðe OE, 'wasteland'. ?*Edimar'* (f.n. Thurmaston).

***etisc** OE, 'a plot of land' (prob. 'pasture-land'). ?Sweet Hedge (f.n. Allexton).

-ett(e) ME noun suffix, denoting a place characterized by what is named. *Bankett Close* (f.n. Tilton).

fæger OE, adj., 'fair, beautiful, pleasant'. *Faire pasture* (f.n. Loddington), *Fairwellefeld*, *Fayrwellecroft*, *Fayrwellehil* (f.ns. Skeffington).

fætt OE, adj., 'fat, rich'. Fat Cl (f.n. Lowesby), *fatlande sickes* (f.n. Seagrave), Fatlands (Cls) (f.ns. Baggrave, Rotherby), *fattebanlond'* (f.n. Kirby Bellars).

fald OE, 'a fold, a small enclosure for animals'. ?Fold Hill (f.n. Barsby), *Foldhull* (f.n. South Croxton), ?Folds (f.n. Frisby on the Wreake), ?*le Infal'* (f.n. Kirby Bellars).

falg, falh OE (Angl), 'land broken up for cultivation, ploughed land'; later 'ploughed land left uncultivated for a year, fallow land'. Fallow Cl (f.n. Cold Newton).

***(ge)fall** OE (Angl), 'a falling, a place where something falls', whence 'a felling of trees, a clearing'. *Falhul(l)* (f.n. South Croxton), Fall Hill (f.n. Halstead), False Acres (f.n. Hoton), ?*le Infal'* (f.n. Kirby Bellars).

farmyard ModE, 'the yard or enclosure attached to a farmhouse or surrounded by farm buildings'. *Farm(e) Yard* (f.n. Barkby Thorpe, Tilton), the Hall Farm Yard (f.n. Frisby on the Wreake).

farther ModE, adj., 'farther off'. *farther Stoney lands* (f.n. Thurmaston).

fearn OE, 'ferns; a ferny place'. Firn Mdw (f.n. Allexton), Frannum Cl (f.n. Frisby on the Wreake), *the Furne Hades* (f.n. Asfordby).

feeding ModEdial., vbl.sb., 'grazing ground, pasturage'. Feeding Fd (f.n. Lowesby).

fé-hús ON, 'a cattle-shed'. *le Feehous* (Kirby Bellars).

feld OE, 'open country', **feld(e)** ME, 'land for pasture or cultivation; a common or great field of a township', **field** ModE, 'an enclosed or fenced-in plot of land'. Field Fm, Highfield Fm, Highfield Spinneys, Highfields Fm, Netherfield, Northfield, South Fields. Of East Goscote Hundred's 56 townships, 38 have the names of their three great fields surviving in records. In only Ashby Folville, Ragdale and Quenby have the names of what are recognizably great fields failed to survive. In contrast to such names in Framland Hundred (there for 27 townships), in East Goscote Hundred only 4 townships (Hungarton, Keyham, Skeffington, Thorpe Satchville) have fields which are designated by combinations of the simple directional adjectives *north*, *south*, *east*, *west*. Asfordby, Barsby, Frisby on the Wreake, Kirby Bellars, Queniborough and Thrussington each have two great fields with names which are formed by directional adjectives plus a Middle Fd. There are 18 townships which have a Middle Fd (with various spellings). For Allexton, Barsby, South Croxton, Hoton, Ratcliffe on the Wreake and Rotherby are recorded pairs of great field names which indicate height in relation to the township, such as *upper*, *lower*, *over*, *nether*. Mill Fd (with various spellings in Gaddesby, Grimston, Hamilton, Old Ingarsby, Launde, Lowesby, Prestwold, Skeffington, Tugby, Twyford and

Welby) is common, being second only to Middle Fd in recurrence. Otherwise, the great fields are named from topographical features, e.g. *Bowwood feild* (Belgrave), *Brincke Feilde* (Seagrave), *Galloborrowe feild* (Barkby Thorpe), *Strangcliffelde* (Barrow upon Soar); or wild flora, e.g. *the Ash feild* (Gaddesby, Queniborough), *Brymble feild* (Beeby), *Scrib Feild* (Tugby); or principal crops, e.g. *Ote Feild* (Baggrave), *the Pesefeld* (Wymeswold), *Ryefelde* (Queniborough, Rearsby); or soil type, e.g. *the clea fiellde, the sand fielde* (Hoby), *Hardacer feld* (Wymeswold), *Redland field* (Saxelby). Changes in the names of a township's great fields may or may not indicate the reorganization of the township's arable, but such changes of names or alternative names for fields are evidenced in Barrow upon Soar, Barsby, Beeby, Cossington, Hoton, Queniborough, Rearsby, Saxelby, Seagrave, Skeffington, Thrussington, Thurmaston, Walton on the Wolds and Wymeswold. It is uncertain whether the names *Cotesfeld* (Cotes) and *Whatbore Felde* (Whatborough), both in very small upland townships, are indicative of only one great field possible for each of these townships through lack of territory.

felte OE, a plant-name (cf. *felt-wurme* 'wild marjoram', *felt-wyrt* 'mullein', Scots dial. *felt* 'couch grass'), cognate with OE *felt* 'felt, a thick woollen cloth', with reference to something matted. ?Felford Furlong (f.n. Sileby).

fence ME, 'a fence' (a shortened form of OFr *defence* 'a defensive work'). Fence Cl (f.n. Allexton).

fenn OE, 'a fen, a marsh, marshland'; also 'mud, clay, mire', **fen** ON, 'a fen, a marsh'. *le fen* (f.n. Kirby Bellars), *Quakefensike* (f.n. Hoby), *Quake feyne* (f.n. Humberstone), *Saltfengate* (South Croxton), Sauving (f.n. Barsby).

feor OE, **fur(re)** ME, **fur** ModEdial., **far** ModE, adj., 'far, distant'. Common in f.ns.: e.g. *le Farre Close* (Kirby Bellars), *Farr dales* (Hungarton), Far(r) Hill (Cold Newton), *the Farr Sicke* (Burton on the Wolds), *Ferredoles* (Queniborough), Fir Dales (Thorpe Satchville), *Forlawmbull* (Cossington), *Furbywadis* (Rearsby), *furleis* (Ratcliffe on the Wreake), *the furr furlong* (Gaddesby).

fēorðung, fēorðing OE, 'a fourth part, a quarter'; in later f.ns. it may denote either a measure of land or a rental of a farthing. South Farthing. *Bosseferthyng* (f.n. Kirby Bellars), Farthings (f.n. South Croxton, Sileby), *the further furthinge* (f.n. Asfordby).

fēower OE, num., 'four'. *the foure leas* (f.n. Cossington), Fourheadlands (f.n. Asfordby), *fourwell hades*, *fowre landes* (f.ns. Rotherby), *Whistobrooke fowre roades* (f.n. Seagrave).

ferme OFr, ME, 'rent', eModE, 'land held on lease, an agricultural tenement, a farm'. Common in modern minor p.ns. In earlier instances, usually prefixed by a surn., e.g. *Baresbys farm*, *Crosons farm*, *Hodges farm*, *Masons farm* (Gaddesby), *Beebyes farme* (Cossington), *Fowlers Farme* (Asfordby), *Hentons Farme house* (Burton on the Wolds); or with pers.n. plus surn., e.g. *Tho. Hardes Farme* (Queniborough), *Ralph Toones Farme* (Old Ingarsby). Farm Cl (f.n. Loddington), *le Ferme* (f.n. Hoby).

fermier OFr, 'one who cultivates land for the owner; a bailiff, a steward'; later 'a farmer'. ?Farmer Leys (f.n. Grimston).

ferreter ModE, 'one who searches for rabbits etc. with a ferret'. Feriter Leys (f.n. Ratcliffe on the Wreake).

fīf OE, num., 'five'. *Fiuea(c)kres* (f.n. Barkby), Five Acres (f.n. Asfordby).

finc OE, 'a finch'. Finchley Bridge. ?Finch Ades (f.n. Seagrave).
finol OE, **fenel** ME, 'fennel'. *finall' gatte* (Hungarton).
fiscere OE, **fiskari** ON, 'a fisherman'. ?*Phiscur acur* (f.n. Skeffington).
fisc-pōl OE, 'a fish-pond'. Fishpool Brook, Fishpool Spinney. Fish Pool (f.n. Thorpe Satchville), *Fishpoole yard* (f.n. Skeffington).
fithelere ME, 'one who plays on the fiddle, a fiddler', esp. for hire. ?Fiddlers Green.
flagge ME, 'a reed, a rush'. *les Flagges* (f.n. Barrow upon Soar), Flag Pool Furlong (f.n. Barsby).
flanke ME, 'a flank, the side of something'. *Holgate flanke*, *Peyslande flank'* (f.ns. Skeffington).
flasshe ME, 'flooded grassland; a swamp'. *the Flash* (f.n. Walton on the Wolds).
flat ON, 'a piece of flat, level ground'. *Berricliff Flatt*, the Flatt, Toardale Flatt (f.ns. Barsby), Broad Flatt (f.n. Hungarton), The Flat (f.n. Hoby, Tilton), The Flats (f.n. Barkby), *the Flatt* (f.n. Humberstone, Walton on the Wolds), Flatt End (f.n. Syston), *the Flatt nookes* (f.n. Burton on the Wolds), Hall Flatt, the Hall Goss Flatt (f.ns. Queniborough), (*the*) *hie flate* (f.n. Asfordby), the Ten acre flat (f.n. Cossington).
flatr ON, adj., 'flat, level'. Flat Brant (f.n. Hoby), *Flat mydo* (f.n. Skeffington), Flatsick (f.n. Barrow upon Soar).
flaxen eModE, adj., 'consisting of flax, pertaining to flax'. *flaxen furlong* (f.n. Asfordby).
fleax OE, **flax** ME, 'flax'. (*the*) *flax*(*e*) *furlong* (f.n. Asfordby), Flaxland Cl (f.n. Wymeswold), *Flaxlands* (f.n. with various spellings in Asfordby, Barkby, Cossington, South Croxton, Hoby, Humberstone, Ratcliffe on the Wreake, Seagrave, Sileby), *Flaxleys* (f.n. with various spellings in Barkby, Belgrave, Burton on the Wolds, Ratcliffe on the Wreake, Seagrave), *ye flax leasowes* (f.n. Seagrave).
flēot OE, **fljót** ON, 'a small stream, a rivulet'. ?*Alfletford'*, ?*Alfleteþorn* (f.ns. Wymeswold), Fleet Cl, Fleet Leys (f.ns. Ratcliffe on the Wreake).
flint OE, 'flint'. *Flentdole* (f.n. Thorpe Satchville), *Flintedene*, *flinttedele* (f.ns. Kirby Bellars), *flintinges* (f.n. Humberstone), the Flints (f.n. Keyham).
flinti ME, adj., 'flinty, full of flint-stones'. *Flintideles*, *Flyntydole* (f.ns. Skeffington), *Flynty aboue the gate* (f.n. Humberstone).
(ge)flit OE, 'strife, dispute', used in p.ns. of land in dispute. Flithill (f.n. Barsby), *Flithulleswong* (f.n. South Croxton), *Flittelandes* (f.n. Hoby), *Flitwong* (f.n. Barrow upon Soar), *flytbarow* (f.n. Hungarton).
flod-gate ME, 'a flood-gate, a sluice'. Floodgates.
fogge ME, 'aftermath, the long grass left standing during the winter'. Fog Fd (f.n. Quenby).
fola OE, **foli** ON, 'a foal'. ?Fold Hill Furlong (f.n. Barsby).
folie OFr, ME, 'folly; a foolish enterprise; an extravagant or foolish building'; in f.ns., sometimes used of a small plantation (*v.* **folly**, Db 756). the Folley (f.n. Cold Newton), Folley hill (f.n. Belgrave).
foot-road ModE, 'a footpath'. Asfordby ~ ~, Gadsby ~ ~, Kirby ~ ~, Rotherby foot road (Frisby on the Wreake), Foot Road Cl, Foot Road Holdel (f.ns. Beeby), Foot Road Cl (f.n. Humberstone), Footroad Mdw (f.n. Tilton), Old Foot Road Cl (f.n. Halstead).

ford OE, 'a ford'. ?Asfordby, Twyford. Freq. in f.ns.: esp. common are locations, either minor topographical features, e.g. *Holtforth* (Halstead), *Lytulhawforth* (Skeffington), *Stringham foorde* (Hoby), or neighbouring townships, e.g. *Burstalforth* (Thurmaston), *Siwoldeby forthe* (Hoby); the names of the streams forded may occur, e.g. *Brockwell foord* (Hungarton), *the Caudal(l)s forde* (Seagrave), *Hobeck ford* (Asfordby); or human activity, e.g. *Salterforde* (Hoby), *Waschyngforth* (Skeffington), *Wayne ford* (Humberstone); or birds frequenting the fords, e.g. *Fynchefordebrig* (East Norton), *Titfordemere* (Barrow upon Soar); or the appearance of a ford may be specified, e.g. *Atteblakeforth* (Barkby), *Dedford* (Skeffington), *le Dernforthe* (Barrow upon Soar); or its quality, e.g. *Fulforthe* (Thurmaston), *Stonyforth* (Barrow upon Soar). Spellings in *-forth(e)* (arising from late ME *-rd* > *-rth* in unstressed syllables, which occur only in the Danelaw and may be due to Scand influence) represent one third of surviving forms in East Goscote Hundred.

fore OE, prep., 'in front of, before'; elliptically '(land, place, thing) in front of, or lying or standing before something'. *Fordelis* (f.n. Sileby), *Fordolus*, *the Fore meadowe* (f.ns. Queniborough), the Fore Mdw (f.n. Syston), *le Formedowes* (f.n. Hoby), *West Littelhil Fordole* (f.n. Baggrave).

foreward OE, adj., 'the front part of (anything material), forward, inclined to the front'. *Foreworde Wold* (f.n. Thorpe Satchville).

***forst** OE, 'a ridge'. *Forsland Sick* (f.n. South Croxton).

***foss**[1] OE, 'a ditch'. *in to Fosse* (f.n. Thurmaston), *the fosse way* (Ratcliffe on the Wreake), *le Fostretewong'* (f.n. Queniborough).

fōt OE, **fótr** ON, 'a foot; the foot of something; the bottom of a hill'. *le bryggefotte* (f.n. Twyford), *Fotwong* (f.n. Barrow upon Soar), ?Goose Foot Cl (f.n. Wymeswold), *Hartcliffe foote* (f.n. Humberstone), ?Holt Foot Hill (f.n. Halstead), *New Pasture Foot*, *Red Hill Foot* (f.ns. Belgrave), Red Gore Foot (f.n. Ratcliffe on the Wreake), *Twelue foote* (f.n. Asfordby).

fote-waye ModE, 'a footpath'. Footway Cl, Footway Mdw (f.ns. Tilton), *Tilton footway* (Skeffington), Wysall Foot Way (Wymeswold).

fowl-house ModE, 'a shelter for domestic fowl'. Fowl House Fd (f.n. Tilton).

fox OE, 'a fox'. Fox Croft Spinney, Foxhill Fm. Fox Burgh (f.n. Brooksby), Fox Cl, Fox Furlong (f.ns. Hoton), *Fox Close* (f.n. Prestwold), Fox Covert (f.n. Halstead, Syston), *Foxe grauel(l)* (f.n. Beeby), *Foxhou*, Foxley Gate Cl (f.ns. Hoby), *Foxlandes* (f.n. Thurmaston), *Foxwell'* (f.n. South Croxton).

fox-hol OE, 'a fox-hole, a fox's earth'. Fox Holes Spinney. *Foxeholes* (f.n. Shoby), (*the*) *Foxholes* (f.n. Hoby), Foxholes (f.n. Belgrave, Rearsby, Thurmaston), *foxholl'* (f.n. Cossington), *bosci de Foxoles* (Cold Newton), Foxstoles (f.n. Frisby on the Wreake).

frehold ME, 'a tenure in absolute possession'; adjectivally, 'held by freehold'. *the Freehold* (*Land*), *Wesson freehold* (f.ns. Tugby).

frēo OE, adj., 'free; free from service or charge'. Freeborough (f.n. Thurmaston), *the Freeland* (f.n. Tugby), *Lower Freewood* (f.n. East Norton).

Frīsa, Frēsa OE, **Frísi** ON, 'a Frisian, a native of Friesland and the Frisian Isles'. Frisby on the Wreake.

frið OE, 'protection'. ?*frithelund* (Cold Newton).

***friðen** OE, adj., 'protected; fenced in'. ?*frithelund* (Cold Newton).

frogga OE, 'a frog'. Frogg Hole (f.n. Sileby).

front OFr, ME, 'the forehead; the side of something which is seen first'. Frontcliff Furlong (f.n. Barsby), *Front Cliff Sick* (f.n. South Croxton).

frothe ME, 'foam, spume, froth'. *Frot*(*t*)*hewellessyke* (f.n. Barkby).

fūl OE, adj., 'foul, filthy, dirty'. *le fouleforye* (f.n. Seagrave), Foulpoole (f.n. Queniborough), Fowl Sick (f.n. Thrussington), Fulbacks (f.n. Cold Newton), *fuldolys* (f.n. Cossington), *Fulforthe* (f.n. Thurmaston), *Fulwelle* (f.n. with various spellings in Gaddesby, Humberstone, Cold Newton, East Norton), *Ful*(*le*)*wellegate* (Barrow upon Soar, Hoby), *the Fulus* (f.n. Humberstone).

fullere ME, 'a fuller'. ?*Follerscroft* (f.n. Barrow upon Soar).

fulling ModE, vbl.sb., 'the process of cleansing and thickening cloth by washing and beating'. *the Fullinge Mires* (f.n. Hoby).

furh OE, 'a furrow, a trench'; in ME, also used of 'a piece of arable land'. *Depforou* (f.n. Barkby), *le fouleforye* (f.n. Seagrave), Furrow Hill Cls (f.n. Hoton), The Furrows(f.n. Barrow upon Soar), ?*the hall furres* (f.n. Thrussington), *Hollowe furre*, *Schortfurholme* (f.ns. Cossington), *thorow hilles* (f.n. Beeby), *the Waterfurrowes* (f.n. with various spellings in Asfordby, Barkby, Barrow upon Soar, Cossington, Frisby on the Wreake, Hoby, Hoton, Humberstone, Hungarton, Kirby Bellars, Ratcliffe on the Wreake, Rearsby, Rotherby, Seagrave, Skeffington, Tugby), Water Furrow Cls (f.n. Syston), Waterfurrow Furlong (f.n. Barsby, Sileby), *Wetforow'* (f.n. Queniborough), *Wetfurrowes furlong* (f.n. Gaddesby). Later pl. forms are easily confused with **fyrs**.

furlang OE, 'the length of a furrow, a furlong, a piece of land the length of a furrow (esp. in a great field)'; in ME, 'a division of a great field cultivated as a unit'. Furlong's Barn. Very freq. in f.ns., e.g. *le Brokfurlong*, *Dale furlong*(*e*), *le Houeforlong*, *Hunger hill furlong*, *Marlepit furlong*, *Morfurlong*, *Plumtree sick furlonge* (Barkby), *Five Land Furlong*, (*the*) *flax*(*e*) *furlong*, *Riggate furlong*, *Stannion furlong*(*e*), *stooney furlong* (Asfordby). Many of the 'field-names' in ME sources are furlong-names.

furmente ME, (OFr *frumentee*), ModE **furmety**, 'a dish made of hulled wheat boiled in milk and seasoned with cinnamon, sugar etc.'; later 'a kind of wheat or spelt'. Furmety Mdw (f.n. Cotes).

furðra OE, adj., 'more distant'. Farther Sike (f.n. Ratcliffe on the Wreake), *Forther morefeld* (f.n. Welby), *further dewell* (f.n. Humberstone), *the further furthinge* (f.n. Asfordby).

fyrs OE, 'furze'. Freezeland Lodge. *Blakberd fyrrys*, *Frysbek'*, *Tutbury furze* (f.ns. Thurmaston), Buck Furs End, Forceland Sick Furlong (f.ns. Barsby), *Firreswong* (f.n. Kirby Bellars), *Fulwell fyrrys*, *Furry leyes furlonge*, *Quacksick furry*(*e*) *leys*, *quak feild furrs* (f.ns. Humberstone), *the furry close* (f.n. Walton on the Wolds), Furze Lands (f.n. Queniborough), ?*the Hall furres* (f.n. Thrussington), *fussull* (f.n. Beeby). Later spellings are easily confused with pl. forms of **furh**. F.ns. with *furry* may perh. be better attributed to a headword ***fyrsig** OE, adj., 'growing with furze', but surviving forms do not occur before the mid 17th century.

galga OE, **galgi** ON, 'a gallows'. ?*Gallow Hill* (f.n. Barkby).

galg-trēow OE, **gálga-tré** ON, 'a gallows-tree, a gallows'. The Gaultry (f.n. Cossington).

galla OE, 'a sore'; used topographically of 'a wet or barren place in a field'. the Galls (f.n. Kirby Bellars), The Gauls (f.n. Gaddesby), *le Watergall* (f.n. Queniborough), *the Watergalls* (f.n. Thurmaston).

gandra OE, 'a gander'. *Ghonderesyke* (f.n. Wymeswold), Gunder Pits (f.n. Welby).

gang OE, **gangr** ON, 'a way, a path, a track'. *Ouergong* (f.n. Thurmaston).

gap ON, 'a gap, an opening', **gappe** ME, 'an opening in a wall, fence or hillside'. Grimston Gap, Skeffington Gap. Barley Whom Gap (f.n. Queniborough), Barrow Gap Furlong, *Southholme Gap Platt* (f.ns. Sileby), *Congie gap* (f.n. Rearsby), *Croston gapp* (f.n. Barkby), Crotton Gap (f.n. Twyford), *Melton gap*(*p*), *the water gapp* (f.ns. Asfordby), Pitch Gaps (f.n. Humberstone).

gāra OE, 'a gore, a triangular plot of ground, a point of land'. Clovengore Bault (f.n. Sileby), *Gares* (f.n. Prestwold), *le Gore* (f.n. Barrow upon Soar, Cossington, Kirby Bellars), *le Gores* (f.n. with various spellings in Barkby, Hoby, Humberstone, Sileby), *gr' gorr'* (f.n. Hungarton), Langer Leys (f.n. Syston), Red Gore (f.n. Ratcliffe on the Wreake), *Wyngargore* (f.n. Skeffington).

gardin ME, 'an enclosed plot, a garden'. *Crowe holme garden*, Sough Garden (f.ns. Cossington), Field Garden (f.n. Thrussington), Garden Cl (f.n. Belgrave, South Croxton, Thurmaston), Garden End, Garden Spot (f.ns. Halstead), Garden Fd, the Parsonage Gardens (f.ns. Seagrave), Garden Mdw (f.n. Brooksby), *the orchard garden* (f.n. Barkby Thorpe), Ratcliffe Garden (f.n. Ratcliffe on the Wreake), Tookeys Garden (f.n. Syston).

gārlēac OE, 'garlic'. ?*Garleygate* (Rearsby).

garðr ON, 'an enclosure'; later 'a courtyard'. *Barneȝarte* (f.n. Barrow upon Soar).

gata ON, 'a way, a road, a street'. From its later use in the sense 'a right of way for leading cattle to pasture, a right of access to pasture-land', the el. came to mean 'right of pasturage' and 'an allotment of pasture' as in **bullgate** and **cowgate** (*q.v.*). Bradgate Lane, Church Gate, Gate Lane, Kirby Gate, Muckle Gate Lane, Woodgate, Woodgate Ho. In road-names, it is the dominant el.: it may be prefixed by a township name (as destination), e.g. *Baggrave Gate* (South Croxton), *Barnesbygate*, *Bebygate* (Barkby), *hungarton gate* (Beeby), *Sewolbygate* (Asfordby), or compounded with an el. indicating topography, e.g. *Howesgate* (Barkby), *Howgate* (Cossington), *mores gate* (Asfordby), *le Woldgate* (Barkby, Cossington), *Wudegate* (with various spellings in Hoby, Humberstone, Kirby Bellars); or with a minor name defining a more precise location, e.g. *Crokhougate* (Barkby), *dorendale gate*, *Horseydylgate* (Cossington). Local flora may be specified, e.g. *finall' gatte* (Hungarton), *Gossegate* (Saxelby), *Thorn Gate* (Barsby). Grassy tracks are freq. recorded, e.g. *Grenegate* (with various spellings in Allexton, Hungarton, Loddington, Saxelby). Man-made structures are represented, e.g. *Kyrkegate* (Barkby), *le milne gate* (Cossington), *Wynd*(*e*)*mylnegate* (Kirby Bellars); and human occupations are sometimes recorded, e.g. *Saltergate* (Barkby, Thurmaston). Surnames may feature, e.g. *Arpingate* (South Croxton), *Hubbert*(*e*)*s gate* (Frisby on the Wreake). A road's quality or capacity may be indicated, e.g. Even Gate (Barkby), *Ston*(*i*)*gate* (Hoby, Cossington), Bridle Gate (Beeby, Cotes), *Wayngate* (with various spellings in Asfordby, South Croxton, Saxelby). Compounding with a directional adj. is occasionally found, e.g. *Estgate*, *Estrenegate* (South Croxton), *Westgate* (Barkby). Roads for movement of livestock are specified, e.g. *Beaste gate*, *Sheepgate* (Cossington), Neats Gate (East Norton) and presum. the 15th cent. examples of *Cowgate* (Belgrave, Skeffington). *Hol*(*e*)*gate* recurs, as in Cossington, South Croxton and Hungarton. Note the important early *Marthegrevegate* (Wymeswold). Many of these road-names have survived as furlong-names, even when not specifically designated as such.

geard OE, 'an enclosure; a yard, a courtyard'. Freq. in f.ns., esp. with a surn. indicating ownership or tenancy, e.g. *Belmans yard* (Cossington), Burdricks ~, Jacksons Yard (Welby), Kempe's ~, Marks ~, Ortons ~, Welshes Yard (Belgrave); with reference to principal buildings, e.g. *Chapell yard* (Baggrave, Launde), Hall Yards (Beeby), *the parsonadge yard* (Asfordby); or to minor structures, e.g. *the Dovecoats yard* (Burton on the Wolds), *Duffehous Yerde* (Kirby Bellars), (*le*) *kylne yard* (Belgrave, Cossington), *Shepecote yarde* (Launde); or to farm animals, e.g. Bullock Yard (Cotes), the Hogg Yard (Cossington).

geat OE, 'an opening, a passage; a gate'. *the Hall close yate* (f.n. Cossington).

geiri ON, 'a triangular plot of ground'. ?*Gerehow* (f.n. Hoby).

geirr ON, 'a spear', poss. used topographically of shape. ?*Gerehow* (f.n. Hoby).

geoc[1] OE, 'a yoke, a wooden device for coupling together oxen for drawing a plough'; 'a pair of oxen yoked together'; 'a measure of land'; 'something resembling a yoke in appearance'. *Yocacre* (f.n. Hoby), *yokefurlong* (f.n. Cossington).

gerd OE, 'a rod, a spar'. *yerdgatehil* (f.n. Cold Newton).

gild OE, 'tax, payment'. *Gildal Dale* (f.n. Barrow upon Soar).

gipsy ModE, 'a Romany'; a member of a wandering people coming originally from India to Europe in the early 16th cent. and believed at that time to have come from Egypt. Gipsy Lane (Belgrave, Humberstone, Seagrave).

glæppe OE, 'the buck-bean'. (the) Glapings, *Glappi*[ ] (f.ns. Hoby).

glebe ME, 'glebe', i.e. land belonging to an ecclesiastical benefice. Glebe Fm (Cossington, Gaddesby, Hoby, Keyham, Saxelby, Skeffington), Glebe Rd. (the) Glebe (f.n. Barkby, East Norton), *Glebe bastard Ley*, *the Glebe Seaven Landes*, *the Glebe two land*(*e*)*s* (f.ns. South Croxton), Glebe Cl (f.n. Allexton, Beeby, Belgrave, Loddington), Glebe Fd (f.n. Rearsby), Glebe Land(s) (f.ns. Barsby, Hungarton, Lowesby), *the Glebe Meadow* (f.n. Asfordby), Top Glebe (f.n. Frisby on the Wreake).

gleoda OE (Angl), **gleða** ON, 'a kite, a bird of prey'. *Glodurwong* (f.n. Barsby).

gōd[2] OE, adj., 'good'. *Godelis* (f.n. Kirby Bellars), ?*god' pytt* (f.n. Hungarton), *Gudemares* (f.n. Thurmaston).

gold OE, 'gold'; poss. also used in the sense 'gold-hued'. ?Gold Hill (f.n. Rearsby), ?*Goldhou* (f.n. Cossington); but difficult to separate from **golde**.

golde OE, 'a (marsh) marigold'. *Gowborn close* (f.n. Cold Newton), ?Gold Hill (f.n. Rearsby), ?*Goldhou* (f.n. Cossington).

golden ME, adj., 'golden'. *Golden Bank*(*e*) (f.n. Seagrave).

gonele ME, 'a channel, an artificial course for running water'. *Brokesbymilnegonele* (f.n. Brooksby), *Foxhowgonele* (f.n. Hoby).

gorebrode ME, 'a broad strip in a gore of a great field'. (*le*) *Gorebrode* (f.ns. Barkby, Cossington, Queniborough), *Gorebrodewong* (f.n. Cold Newton).

gorst OE, 'gorse, furze'; freq. in modern minor names and f.ns. in the sense 'a piece of ground covered with gorse, a fox-covert of gorse bushes'. Adam's Gorse, Cossington ~, Cream ~, Eller's Gorse, Gorse Fm, Gorse Lane, Gorse Spinney, Grimston Gorse, Lord Wilton's ~, Thrussington Wold ~, Willoughby Gorse. The Gorse (f.n. Ashby Folville), Gorse Cl (f.n. Beeby), Gorse Hill (f.n. Cold Newton), Gorse Sic (f.n. Hoby), ?*Gossick* (f.n. Barsby). *Munday's Gorse* (f.n. Burton on the Wold), *Saxelby Gorse* (f.n. Saxelby). Note the dial. form *goss*(*e*) as in

Copthorne Goss (f.n. Queniborough), *the Goss* (f.n. Hoby), Goss Cl (f.n. Rearsby, Saxelby), *Gossegate Baulk*(*e*) (f.n. Saxelby), (*the*) *Gosse close* (f.ns. Burton on the Wolds, Welby), *Goss ground* (f.n. Frisby on the Wreake), *lamble gos*(*s*)*e* (f.n. Cossington).

***gorstig** OE, adj., 'overgrown with gorse'. Gorsey Cl (f.n. Welby), The Gorsey Mdw (f.n. Belgrave). The spellings *gossy close* (f.n. Asfordby, Thrussington), *the Gossey close* (f.n. Burton on the Wolds) record dial. *gossy* (cf. *goss*(*e*) in **gorst** *supra*).

gōs OE, **gás** ON, 'a goose'. ?Goscote Hundred. Goose Cl (f.n. Barkby), Goose Foot Cl, Goose Nest (f.ns. Wymeswold), Goose Green (f.n. Barkby, Sileby), Gooseholme (f.n. Rearsby), Goose Nook (f.n. Humberstone, Ratcliffe on the Wreake, Syston), *Goseholme* (f.n. Belgrave), *Gosewelsyke* (f.n. South Croxton), *Gosewong* (f.n. Cold Newton), *Gosmastal'* (f.n. Cossington), ?*Gossick* (f.n. Barsby).

goter ME, 'a gutter'. *le Gutterefurlong* (f.n. Queniborough), *Lunsdall Gutter*, *Paddocke Gutter* (f.ns. Tugby), *Northinges Gutter* (f.n. Barkby), *Quake fyld gutter*, *Quakesick Gutter*, Stean Gutter Furlong (f.ns. Humberstone).

goule, gole ME, 'a ditch, a channel'. *le Gowiyl* (f.n. Hoby).

græf OE, 'a digging, a grave, a pit, a trench'. Deadmans Grave (f.n. South Croxton, Wymeswold), *Dedmanysgraue* (f.n. Skeffington).

grǣfe OE, 'a grove, a copse'. *le Greyvedole* (f.n. Thorpe Satchville).

***grǣg**[2] OE, 'a wolf; a badger'. *Grahalega* (f.n. Cossington). (*v.* C. Hough, 'OE **grǣg* in place-names', *Neuphilologische Mitteilungen* 4 xcvi (1995), 361–5).

græs, gærs OE, 'grass, pasture'. *Mr Ashbies grasse grounde*, *Mr Lanes grass ground*, *the Parting*(*e*) *grass*(*e*) (f.ns. Rotherby), *Gilbert Bishops grasse hadland*, *the Grass headland*, *John Morrice his side grasse*, *Morris grasse hadland* (f.ns. Asfordby), *Thomas Dalbeys grasse* (f.n. Skeffington), *James Goodmans* ~ ~, *James Quickes grasse headland* (f.ns. Frisby on the Wreake), *Quacksick partinge grasse* (f.n. Humberstone), *Redegres* (f.n. with various spellings in South Croxton, Cold Newton, Thorpe Satchville, Twyford), Seagrass Mdw (f.n. Kirby Bellars), *the towne gresse hadland*(*e*) (f.n. Ratcliffe on the Wreake).

grāf OE, 'a grove, a copse, a coppiced wood'. Baggrave, Belgrave, Seagrave; Grove Lane. *Haliday grove* (f.n. Old Ingarsby), *Verges grove* (f.n. East Norton).

***grafa**[1] OE, 'a trench, a ditch'. *Newegrove* (f.n. Kirby Bellars).

grāfet OE, 'a grove, a copse'. *le Midlefelde grovett*, *le Wynmyll grovett* (f.ns. Old Ingarsby), *Quenby grovett* (f.n. Quenby).

grange, graunge OFr, ME, 'a grange'; originally 'a granary, a barn', later 'a farm'; also 'an outlying farm belonging to a religious house or to a feudal lord, where crops were stored'; often used in modern p.ns., usually with an older p.n. prefixed, to convey a pretence of antiquity. Ashby Grange, Barkby ~, Beeby Spring ~, Brooksby ~, Cossington ~, South Croxton ~, Frisby ~, Gaddesby Grange, The Grange (South Croxton, Hoby, Hungarton, Saxelby, Thurmaston), Grange Cottage, Halstead Grange, Humberstone ~, Keythorpe ~, Lowesby ~, Cold Newton ~, Rearsby Grange, Seagrave Grange Fm, Spring Grange, Syston ~, Thrussington ~, Tilton ~, Walton ~, Welby Grange; *Burton Grange*, *Colley Grange*. *the Cow Grange Plot*(*t*) (f.n. Burton on the Wolds), *the Grange Close* (f.n. Skeffington).

gravel ME, 'gravel'. Freq. in East Goscote Hundred f.ns.: *Foxe grauel(l)* (Beeby), ye Gravell (Asfordby), Gravel Hill (Lowesby, Thorpe Satchville), Gravel Hole(s) (with various spellings in Baggrave, Frisby on the Wreake, Old Ingarsby, Keyham, Lowesby), Gravel Hole Cl (Gaddesby, East Norton), Gravel Pit(s) (with various spellings in Keyham, Loddington, Lowesby, Cold Newton, Rotherby, Skeffington, Tugby, Walton on the Wolds), Gravel Pit Cl (with various spellings in Beeby, South Croxton, Hoby, Humberstone, Launde, East Norton, Rearsby, Thorpe Satchville, Thrussington, Tilton, Twyford, Welby), Gravel Stones (Rearsby).

grēat OE, adj., 'massive, bulky', ME, 'big in size'. *the Great close* (f.n. Allexton, Gaddesby, Whatborough), *the greate ground* (f.n. Burton on the Wolds), *the grete Ryfelde*, *Mr Whalleyes great peace* (f.ns. Cossington).

greensward ModE, 'grassy turf'. *Sir Alexanderes grene swarde* (f.n. Rotherby).

grein ON, 'a fork (of a stream)'. *in the grayne*, *graynwell* (f.ns. Beeby), *Grenishou* (f.n. Cossington), *Greynedegates* (Thurmaston), ?*Greynel* (Green Hill, f.n. Humberstone).

grēne[1] OE, adj., 'green, grass-grown'. Gambers Hill Lodge, Green Lane. Green Croft, *Greneslade* (f.ns. Hoby), *Greene Stye*, *greenknowles*, *Green shawe*, *grenehou* (f.ns. Cossington), *Green(e) willow sick* (f.n. Asfordby), Green Gate (with various spellings in Allexton, Hungarton, Loddington, Saxelby), *Greneclyffe* (f.n. Barrow upon Soar), *Grenedale*, *Grenestrete* (f.ns. Welby).

grēne[2] OE, 'a grassy spot; a village green'. Fiddlers Green, The Green. Fairly freq. in f.ns.: as a simplex, e.g. (*the*) *Greene* (Asfordby, South Croxton, Hungarton), *la Grene de Segraue* (Seagrave), *atte Grene* (as a pers.n. recorded in various styles for Barkby Thorpe, Barrow upon Soar, Belgrave, Grimston). Recurring are Goose Green (Barkby, Sileby) and Thurn Green (Barsby, South Croxton). Note also *Brechougrene*, *Long(e)grene*, *Scortegrene* (Kirby Bellars), *Lampert greene* (Barkby Thorpe), Maiden Green (Sileby), *Peyseland(ys) grene* (Cossington).

grund OE, 'ground; a stretch of land', **grund** ON, 'earth, a plain'; later also 'an outlying farm, outlying fields' and 'a piece of land enclosed for agricultural purposes'. Hamilton Grounds. Freq. in f.ns., esp. indicating ownership/tenancy, e.g. *Widdow Alleins ground*, *Mr Herricks* ~, *George Taylers* ~, *John Worths ground* (Old Ingarsby), *the Earl of Shaftesbury's ground* (Beeby), *the Parsons Ground* (Hoby). Adjacent townships may be specified, e.g. *Dalby grounds*, *Welby Grounds* (Saxelby); or quality of land, e.g. *Goss ground* (Frisby on the Wreake), *Mr Lanes grass ground*, *the marishe grounde* (Rotherby). Recurring is Middle Ground (Allexton, Thorpe Satchville). Appears only occasionally as a first el., as in *Grundisbutts* (South Croxton), *Grundlees* (Skeffington).

gryfja ON, 'a hole, a pit'. Bottom ~, Top Griff (f.ns. Gaddesby), *Griff hole* (f.n. Tugby), Grift Lane (Keyham), (*le*) *Holegrift* (f.n. Thurmaston).

gryppe ME, 'a ditch, a drain'. *the Grype* (f.n. Thurmaston).

***gylde** OE, 'a golden flower'. *Gildehow* (f.n. Prestwold).

gylden OE, adj., 'golden'; literally as to material or colour, figuratively as to richness or fertility. *Gildenthorn* (f.n. Halstead).

***hæfera** OE, **hafri** ON, 'oats'. *averyll syck* (f.n. Wymeswold), *hauerberghe* (f.n. Kirby Bellars), *Longhauerhul* (f.n. South Croxton).

(ge)hæg OE, **hay** ME, 'a fence, an enclosure'. Hayhill Lane, The Hays. *Calforthehey* (f.n. Humberstone), *Haesike*, *Litelhaye* (f.ns. Skeffington), the Hay Brook

(Sileby), The Hays (f.n. Belgrave), Haysick (f.n. Barrow upon Soar), *longkebithehee* (f.n. Kirby Bellars), *Northaye* (f.n. Thurmaston), *ouirhay* (f.n. Queniborough), Oxey (f.n. Loddington), *Thornheya* (f.n. Seagrave).

hænep OE, ***hemp** ON, **hemp** ME, 'hemp'. *the hempe pyttes* (f.n. Humberstone), Hemp Plick (f.n. Hoby), ?Hemps Cl (f.n. Barkby).

hæpse OE, 'a hinge'; poss. used topographically of a feature which bends. ?*Aspedic* (f.n. Welby).

***hær** OE, 'a heap of stones, stony ground'. ?*Harle* (f.n. South Croxton).

hærg OE, 'a heathen temple'. ?Arrow Fd (f.n. Wymeswold).

***hæs** OE (Angl), 'brushwood'. *Hassowe* (f.n. Ratcliffe on the Wreake), ?*Heyscroft'* (f.n. Cossington).

hæsel OE (Angl), **hesli** ON, 'the hazel'. Hazlewood (f.n. Hoby), Hazelwood Cl (f.n. Rotherby), Hazle Croft (f.n. Barrow upon Soar), *Shorthasylis* (f.n. Hungarton).

hafoc OE, 'a hawk'. Hawkshill Spinney (f.n. Skeffington).

hafocere OE, 'a hawker'. ?*Hauekeremedowe*, ?*Hauekerescroft* (f.ns. Barrow upon Soar).

haga[1] OE, 'an enclosure'. *Hawlandis*, *Littelhagh*, *Wylinghaw* (f.ns. Barrow upon Soar), *Hawsyke*, *Lytulhawe* (f.ns. Skeffington), ?Little Haw Wood (f.n. Tilton), *Martinhaw* (f.n. Wymeswold).

hagu-þorn OE, **hag-þorn** ON, 'the hawthorn, the whitethorn'. ?*Haghorne furlonge* (f.n. Seagrave), Hawthorn Dale (f.n. Shoby), Hawthorn Hill (f.n. Loddington), *Hothornhull* (f.n. Barrow upon Soar).

hald[1] OE (Angl), 'protection', **hald**, **hold** ME, 'shelter, refuge; a stronghold'. Halstead. *le Hold*, *Holdhull* (f.ns. Barrow upon Soar), Horshold seek (f.n. Loddington).

half OE (Angl), adj., sb., 'half; a half part; a half-acre'. Half Roods (f.n. Humberstone), *homhalf' ~*, *huthalf' pipesdale* (f.ns. Kirby Bellars).

half-aker ME, 'a half-acre'; in early f.ns., poss. 'a measure of land which a yoke of oxen could plough in half a day'. the Black half Acres (f.n. Grimston), Dick half-acre Furlong (f.n. Ratcliffe on the Wreake), *haulfe acre*, *Parsey half Acre*, *Wakoe half acre* (f.ns. Asfordby).

halh OE (Angl), 'a nook, a corner of land; a water-meadow; a tongue of land between two streams; a hollow, a secluded valley' etc. ?Padge Hall. ?*yarmshalle* (f.n. Cossington).

hālig OE, adj., 'holy, sacred'. *Haliwell(e)* (f.n. Kirby Bellars, Seagrave), *Halywell herne* (f.n. Thurmaston), *le Holly Crosse* (Belgrave), ?Holy Plat (f.n. Halstead), *le holywell dall'* (f.n. Hungarton).

hall OE (Angl), 'a hall, a manor house'. Allexton Hall, Asfordby ~, Asfordby Old ~, Baggrave ~, Belgrave ~, Burton ~, Gaddesby Hall, The Hall (Barkby, Brooksby, Cossington, Rotherby), Hall Fm, Hall Orchard, Harbrook Fm, Keythorpe Hall, Loddington ~, Lowesby ~, Nether ~, New ~, East Norton ~, Old Hall (Ashby Folville, Keyham, Queniborough, Rearsby, Welby), Prestwold ~, Quenby ~, Ragdale ~, Ragdale Old ~, Ratcliffe ~, Skeffington ~, Thurmaston ~, Wymeswold Hall. Occasionally in f.ns., e.g. All Wong Cl (Saxelby), the Hall Cl (Cotes, Frisby on the Wreake, Hoby), *Hall dales* (Barkby Thorpe), Hall Leys, Hallsick (South Croxton), *Hall Orchard* (Barrow upon Soar).

hals OE (Angl), **hals** ON, 'a neck', **hals** ME, 'a narrow neck of land'. *Peiseland hals* (f.n. Hoby).

hām OE, 'a village, an estate; a homestead'. Keyham. *homhalf' pipesdale* (f.n. Kirby Bellars), ?*Luffnum* (f.n. Humberstone); *v.* **hamer**.

hamer ME, adj., comp., 'nearer home, nearer the village'. *Hameriholm, Hamerneudole, Hamerousterdale, le Hamerrede, Hamerrischebuskes, Hamerroutes, Hamersalterewonges, Hamerskeges, Hamerwonges, Hamircalacre, Hamirwyuelisbuskes* (f.ns. Hoby), *Hamer pippesdale* (f.n. Kirby Bellars); *v.* **hām**.

hamm OE, 'a water-meadow, land hemmed in by water or marsh, wet land hemmed in by higher ground'. Nettleham Fm. Dockhams, Frannum Cl, Tuckham (f.ns. Frisby on the Wreake), ye Ham in Holme, *Sawtrum Stones* (f.ns. Asfordby), ?*Luffnum* (f.n. Humberstone), *the Oakham* (f.n. Loddington), (the) Pineham (f.n. Quenby), *Sinam* (f.n. Saxelby), *Stringham foorde* (f.n. Hoby), *Syrehamdyk'* (f.n. Thurmaston), ?*Thackham* (f.n. Thrussington).

***hamol, *hamel** OE, adj., 'maimed, mutilated'; used topographically in hill-names in the sense 'crooked, scarred'; also used of a flat-topped hill, of one which appears to have been cut off or mutilated. ?Hamilton.

hām-stall OE (Angl), 'a homestead, home buildings; the enclosure of a homestead'; surviving as **homestall** ModEdial., 'a farm-yard'. A common compound el. as a simplex, e.g. *the Homestall* (with reference to the vicarage, parsonage or rectory buildings of Asfordby, Barrow upon Soar, Beeby, Belgrave, Cossington, South Croxton, Frisby on the Wreake, Hoby, Humberstone, Hungarton, Loddington, Lowesby, Saxelby). Note also *Robert Bayleys Homestall* (Hungarton), *the Homestall of Thomas Brewande* (Hoby), ~ ~ ~ *William Gamble* (Asfordby), ~ ~ ~ *John Milner* (Frisby on the Wreake), *the Homestall of Mr Smith* (South Croxton).

hām-stede OE, 'a homestead, the site of a dwelling', **homestead** ModE, 'the home buildings'. The Homestead (Queniborough, Walton on the Wolds), Homestead Fm, Homestead Spinney. Freq. as a simplex, e.g. (The) Homestead (Allexton, Barrow upon Soar, Beeby, Burton on the Wolds, Cossington, Cotes, South Croxton, Frisby on the Wreake, Hoton, Humberstone), Homesteads (Belgrave). Often prefixed by a surn., e.g. Agar's Homestead (Humberstone), *Brewings homestead, Chamberlains ~, John Fishers ~, Wm. Hulses homestead* (Cossington), Sarsons Homestead (South Croxton). Note also First Homestead (Hoby), Hall Homestead, *the parsonage homestead* (Cossington), Lane Homestead (Hoton) and the seven instances dated 1669 of such dependent building complexes listed for Loddington.

hān OE, 'a hone; a stone, a boundary stone'. ?*Hanmul* (Skeffington), Hone Hill (f.n. Barkby).

hangende OE, **hengjandi** ON, pres.part., 'hanging'; used in p.ns. of places on a steep slope or hillside. *the hang(e)inge Brant, the hanging furlong, the hanging lays, le Hengondehul* (f.ns. Hoby), Hanging Mdw (f.n. Brooksby), *le Hengende* (f.n. Cossington), Hingin Brinks (f.n. Sileby), Hingings Furlong (f.n. Humberstone), South Hangings Side (f.n. Halstead).

hangra OE, 'a wood on a steep hillside'. Hinger Spinney (f.n. Skeffington).

hār[2] OE, adj., 'hoar, grey', esp. 'grey through being overgrown with lichen'; prob. came to mean 'boundary' because of its freq. use with features forming boundary marks or lying on boundaries. *Harcott Hill* (f.n. Belgrave), *Haregharedyke* (f.n. Barrow upon Soar), *Harewelmere* (f.n. Barkby), ?*Harle* (f.n. South Croxton), *Harwell* (f.n. Thurmaston), *Herstenhow* (f.n. Cossington), *Horson Hill* (f.n.

Loddington), *Horston'*, *Little Hairston* (f.ns. Humberstone), *Longharepittes* (f.n. Hoby).

hassuc OE, 'a clump of coarse grass'. ?the Haddocks (f.n. Kirby Bellars), *hassokbregge* (f.n. Welby).

haugr ON, 'a hill, a hill-top; a burial mound'; sometimes difficult to distinguish from OE *hō(e)*, dat.sg. of **hōh**. Freq. in f.ns.: *Ayleshou*, *Belloue*, *Brecchou*, *Cattishou*, *Croshou*, *Hayleshou*, *Horshou*, *Stokhowe*, *surhowes*, *Wythowe* (Kirby Bellars), *Brakenowe* (Rearsby), *Bremehou*, *Brounshow*, *Goldhou*, *grenehou*, *Grenishou*, *Herstenhow*, *Howgate*, *Hundehoge*, *Stonehou* (Cossington), *Byhou*, *Crochou*, *Heluhou*, *le Houeforlong*, *Howesgate*, *Mothowes*, *le Thyrnhou*, *Whythows* (Barkby), *Crokehou*, *Foxhou*, *Gerehow*, *Hennow*, *Littelhows* (Hoby), *estowlandes* (Barrow upon Soar), *Frisebyhoue*, *Thingou* (Frisby on the Wreake), *Gildehow* (Prestwold), *Hassowe* (Ratcliffe on the Wreake), *Lambecotehou* (Thrussington), *Qwerinhou* (South Croxton), *Sapehou* (Saxelby), *Segehishou* (Burton on the Wolds), *Sheperdowe* (Barrow upon Soar), *Snelleshou*, *Thirnhou*, *Threhowes* (Queniborough), *Syxhows* (Hungarton), *Thre Howes* (Thrussington), *Trumpeshou* (Cold Newton).

heading ModE, vbl.sb., 'the highest part, that which is at the top; a headland'. The Headings (f.n. Barrow upon Soar).

headley ModEdial., '?a swarded-over or 'grass' headland; ?an end unit of grassland'. *Mr Ashbies head(e)lea*, *Mr Lanes* ~, *Sir Alexander hadlea* (f.ns. Rotherby), *Mr Ashbyes hadley* (f.n. Hungarton), *Church hadley* (f.n. South Croxton), *Matthew Feildings* ~, *John Gambles Hadley* (f.ns Seagrave), the Gleab Headley (f.n. Queniborough), *Gregory's headley* (f.n. Asfordby), *the Hadley Hade*, *Prior* ~, *presgraue hadleye*, *Mr Suttons* ~, *Walkers headley*, *William Wilsons Hadley* (f.ns. Humberstone), *Wid. Kirbyes hadlea* (f.n. Cossington), *Jo. Simpson's Headley* (f.n. Saxelby).

hēafod OE, 'a head; the (top) end of something, a headland, unploughed land at the end of the arable where the plough turns', cf. **hēafod-land**. Wellhead. Freq. in f.ns., and very often in the pl., referring to headlands at the end of the arable, e.g. *the arbur hades*, *arlestub* ~, *bawlands* ~, *Brockhole(s)* ~, *the cunstables* ~, *crokes* ~, *Crosse* ~, *Cust wong* ~, *duckenpittes* ~, *the Furne* ~, *the hie* ~, *hoback* ~, *long land* ~, *(the) ouer flate* ~, *Thurnborow Hades* (all Asfordby). Occasionally in the sg., referring to a more major physical feature, e.g. *Neytysheyde* (Barsby), *Rauenshyd* (Barkby).

hēafod-land OE, 'a strip of land at the head of a furlong, left for turning the plough'. Headland Ho. Freq. in f.ns., usually with a villager's name prefixed, e.g. *Gilbert Bishops hadland*, *William Blunts hadlands* (Asfordby), *Tho. Chamberleins headland*, *Widdowe Kirbyes hadland* (Cossington). The parish church may be specified, e.g. *the Church hadlande* (Barkby, Beeby, South Croxton), or other religious institutions, e.g. *hadland Sancti Johannis* (Humberstone), *Seyntemariesedlond* (Barrow upon Soar), *Seynt Mary hadland'* (Cossington). A locational prefix is sometimes used, e.g. *Crook sick hadland* (Barkby Thorpe), *Five Acres Headland* (Asfordby), *Hewet hadland* (Humberstone), *Thromerson Hadland* (Barkby).

hēafodlēas OE, adj., 'headless; without a top'. *(the) Headless Cross* (Allexton).

hēah[1] (**hēan** wk.obl.) OE, **hēh** (Angl), **high** ModE, adj., 'high, tall; important; lying high up, standing in a high place'. Highfield Fm, Highfield Spinneys, Highfields

Fm, Highthorn Fm. Fairly freq. in f.ns., e.g. (*the*) *hie flate*, *the hie hades* (Asfordby), *Highmeare* (Barkby, Belgrave), *Hyboro*, *Hyclyf* (Cossington). The wk. obl. form is present in *Heynorstorth* (Skeffington). Note also *Hegh Strete* (Barrow upon Soar) and *Hi*(*e*)*gate* (South Croxton).

hēah-weg OE, 'a highway, a main road'. Highway Rd. *the highe waye* (South Croxton, Frisby on the Wreake, Gaddesby), *the Kinges highe way* (Barkby, Saxelby), *the queenes hye way* (Asfordby), *sto hie way* (Asfordby); Highway Cl (f.n. Beeby), *the Highway plott* (f.n. Cossington), Syston Highway Cl (f.n. Thurmaston).

hēap OE, 'a heap'; topographically 'a hill'. ?Heaps Lane (Keyham), Muckheaps Furlong (f.n. Queniborough), Stone Heap (f.n. Rearsby).

hēard OE, adj., 'hard; hard to till; uncomfortable, cheerless', **harðr** ON, adj., 'hard'. Hartfield Lodge. the Hardacre Fd (f.n. Wymeswold), *hardebanland* (f.n. Kirby Bellars), *le Hardemedwe* (f.n. Barkby), *Hardhill* (f.n. Cold Newton), *Hardhurst* (f.n. Humberstone), Hardmeats (f.n. Brooksby), the Hardsick (f.n. Seagrave), ?*Hartclif* (f.n. with various spellings in Asfordby, Barrow upon Soar, Humberstone), *the hart*(*e*) *furres* (f.n. Rearsby), ?*Hartlandis* (f.n. Barrow upon Soar).

hearpe OE, 'a harp'; topographically, used of something resembling a harp in shape. *le Harpe* (f.n. Queniborough), *the Harpe* (f.n. Tugby), *Harp Leys* (f.n. Humberstone), Harp(s) Cl (f.n. Thrussington).

hearty ModE, adj., 'in good heart, well fitted to bear crops'. Hearty Cl (f.n. Thorpe Satchville).

hecg OE, 'a hedge'. Freq. used with reference to the boundary hedges of adjoining townships, e.g. *Asfordbie hedge* (Saxelby), *Beeby Hedge* (Hungarton), *shobie headge*, *Sisonbie headge*, *welbie headge* (Asfordby). Topographical features may be prefixed, e.g. *ho*(*o*)*me headge*, *Marsh heage*, (*the*) *more headge* (Asfordby). A surn. may be prefixed, indicating hedges of private property, e.g. *Roger hedge* (Belgrave); or minor agricultural units may be specified, e.g. *Ballance hedge* (Barsby), *Waterish Wong hedge* (Cossington). Note the unusual *Double Hedges* (Humberstone, Sileby). Some modern forms with *hedge* may conceal an original **edisc** (*q.v.*).

hēg OE (Angl), 'hay, mowing grass'; difficult to distinguish from **(ge)hæg** and **hēah**[1] in initial positions in ME names. (*the*) *Hay Close* (f.n. Allexton), (the) Hayfield, *Hay hill* (f.ns. Queniborough), Hay Furlong Leys (f.n. Rearsby), Hey Hole (f.n. Barrow upon Soar), *Heyrigg* (f.n. Belgrave).

***hegn** ON, 'an enclosure'. Heandale (f.n.Barsby).

hegning ON, 'enclosed land'. Heaning Fd (f.n. Wymeswold).

hēhðu OE (Angl), 'height, a high place'. *Heytlund* (f.n. Skeffington).

hei-ward ME, 'an officer in charge of fences and enclosures'. ?*Heywards acre* (f.n. Rearsby).

helde OE, 'a slope, a declivity'. Heeld Acre Furlong (f.n. South Croxton).

hell OE, 'hell'. ?*Hell* (f.n. Thurmaston), *Hell Hadland* (f.n. Barkby), Hell Hole (f.n. Humberstone).

hemp-yard ME, 'an enclosure in which hemp is grown'. *the Hemp Yard* (f.n. Burton on the Wolds, Gaddesby).

henn OE, 'a hen (esp. of wild birds), a water-hen'. *Hendike* (f.n. Rearsby), Hen-holes (f.n. Twyford), *Hennelandys* (f.n. Cossington), *Hennes neste* (f.n. Halstead), *Hennow* (f.n. Hoby).

heord OE, 'a herd'. ?*Herdewell* (f.n. Kirby Bellars).

heorde OE, 'a herdsman'. ?*Herdewell* (f.n. Kirby Bellars).

heorde-wīc OE, 'a herd farm'. *Herdwych* (f.n. Kirby Bellars).

heort OE, **hjǫrtr** ON, 'a hart, a stag'; difficult to distinguish from **heard, harðr**, to which the recurring *Hartclif* esp. may belong. ?*Hartclif* (f.n. with various spellings in Asfordby, Barrow upon Soar, Humberstone), ?*Hartlandis* (f.n. Barrow upon Soar).

herberȝe, herborouȝ ME, 'a shelter (for travellers), a lodging, an inn', (OE *here-beorg* 'shelter or protection for a number of men', ON *herbergi* 'shelter'). ?*Harborrs Well* (f.n. Tugby).

(ge)hērness OE (Angl), 'a jurisdiction, a district'. *Friseby Hernis* (Frisby on the Wreake).

hēr(r)a OE (Angl), **herre** ME, **her** eModE, adj., comp. of **hēah**[1], 'higher'. *the Heier fielde* (f.n. Ratcliffe on the Wreake).

hestr ON, 'a horse, a stallion'. *Hestecrofte* (f.n. Cossington).

hider ME, adj., 'nearer'. *hither hangings, hyther dewell* (f.ns. Humberstone), *Hydurbywadis* (f.n. Rearsby).

hīewet OE, 'hewing, cutting'; topographically 'a place where trees are cut down'. *Hewet hadland* (f.n. Humberstone).

higre OE, 'a jay, a magpie'. ?*Hyridolis* (f.n. Cossington).

hind OE, ON, 'a hind, the female of the deer'. *Hyndesdale, Indewell* (f.ns. Kirby Bellars).

hind-berige OE, 'a hindberry, a raspberry'. ?*Imber Hill* (f.n. Saxelby).

hinder ME, adj., 'lying behind'. Horse Hinderlands (f.n. Queniborough).

hjallr ON, 'a shed'. ?*Heluhou* (f.n. Barkby).

hjǫrð ON, 'a herd, a flock'. ?*hortebe aker* (f.n. Wymeswold).

hlāw OE, 'a mound, a hill'. ?Big Tiplow Mdw (f.n. Tilton), *Coplowe hill close* (f.n. Cold Newton), *Lowton'* (f.n. Humberstone), Rowlow Fd (f.n. Skeffington), Spellows Mdw (f.n. Asfordby), *Wadlowhadlond'* (f.n. Belgrave), *Whorlo* (f.n. South Croxton).

***hlēp** OE (Angl), 'a leap, a jump, a leaping place; a steep place, a sudden drop in the ground'. *Birdlip* (f.n. Cossington).

hlēt OE (Angl), 'a share, a lot'. Bunlett (f.n. Hoton), ?*Letty-wonge* (f.n. Saxelby).

hnecca OE, 'a neck'; topographically 'a neck of land'. *Neckacres* (f.n. Asfordby).

***hobb(e)** OE, 'a tussock, a hummock'. ?*Hobb Baulk* (f.n. Barkby).

hōc OE, 'a hook, an angle, a bend in a river, a spit of land in a river-bend, a corner or bend in a hill'. *Armeston Hookes, Croson hooks, the hook furlong*, Hooks Furlong, *Langley Hoockes, Stackhill bridge hooke* (f.ns. South Croxton), Baggrave Hooks, Lewin Hooks (f.ns. Baggrave), Beever hooks, Bridge-hook, *Sower Hookes* (f.ns. Queniborough), the Bull Hook (f.n. Skeffington), *le Church Hooke, Sliperhook(e)* (f.ns. Asfordby), *le Hocdole* (f.n. Hoby), (the) Hooks (f.ns. Barsby, Beeby, Gaddesby), Humberston Hook (f.n. Syston), *Neast hooke* (f.n. Thurmaston), *the Nether Hook* (f.n. Hungarton), Peaseland Hook (f.n. Rearsby).

***hōd** OE, 'a shelter'. Hoads Furlong (f.n. Barsby), *Hodes* (f.n. South Croxton).

hogg OE, ME, 'a hog, a pig'; also used in ME and later of a young sheep from the time it ceases to be a lamb till its first shearing. *Hogcraft* (f.n. Seagrave), *the Hogpoole, the Hogg yard* (f.ns. Cossington), Hogmores Cl (f.n. Tugby), Hog Pool (f.n. Halstead), Hogs Fd (f.n. Welby), ?*Hogston side* (f.n. Sileby), *the Stone* *hoggs Close* (f.n. Loddington). Note *John Swan Sherrhoges close* (f.n. Loddington).

hǫgg ON, 'a cutting or felling of trees'. Frisby Hags. Haggs, (*le*) *Hogge* (f.ns. Barrow upon Soar), ?*Haghorne furlonge* (f.n. Seagrave), Hogg Field Mdw (f.n. Old Ingarsby).

hogging ModE, vbl.sb. and ppl.adj., 'the process of keeping a hog (i.e. a lamb) over the winter for sale in the following year'. Hoggin Hole (f.n. Walton on the Wolds), *v.* **hogg**.

hōh (**hōas**, **hōs** nom.pl.) OE, 'a heel; a hill-spur'; in the Danelaw, difficult to distinguish from **haugr**. Hoby, Hoton. Ballow Woulds (f.n. Wymeswold), *Caluero* (f.n. Skeffington), ?*Crackhole*, ?*Segehishou* (f.ns. Burton on the Wolds), *Gosecoteho*, ?*Howesgate*, ?*Mothowes* (f.ns. Barkby), *hoobarrow* (f.n. Beeby), *Steynho* (f.n. Gaddesby), *Wakah Wong* (f.n. Saxelby), Wakoe, Wiggo (f.ns. Asfordby).

hol[1] OE, **hol** ON, 'a hole, a hollow'. Freq. in f.ns.: relating to mineral extraction, e.g. Gravel Hole(s) (Baggrave, Frisby on the Wreake, Gaddesby, Hoby), *Lymepittholes* (Barrow upon Soar), Marl Hole (Barkby); prefixed by a locational name, e.g. *Bandlandhole* (South Croxton, Kirby Bellars), *Herdwykhole*, *scelflondehole* (Kirby Bellars). A range of animals feature, e.g. Badger Hole (Hoby), *Martholes* (Prestwold), ?Oxen holes (Thrussington), Rabbit Hole (Rotherby), Swine Hole (Walton on the Wolds). *The Dead Hole* (Belgrave) and *Hell Hole* (Humberstone) may refer to soils infertile and difficult to till. Note the early *Wlfholes* (Cold Newton), poss. alluding to traps for wolves.

hol[2] OE, **holr** ON, adj., 'lying in a hollow, running in a hollow; deep'; esp. in road-names and stream-names, also 'sunken'. Freq. in road-names, e.g. *Holgate* (with various spellings in Cossington, South Croxton, Hungarton); and in stream-names and those of springs, e.g. *Holbek* (with various spellings in Asfordby, Frisby on the Wreake, Kirby Bellars, Launde), *Holborne* (Barrow upon Soar), *Holewell* (with various spellings in Barkby, Cold Newton, East Norton). Note also *Holands slade* (f.n. Barkby), Holdel (f.n. Beeby), *Hollandys* (f.n. Barrow upon Soar).

holh OE, 'a hole, a hollow'. Ingarsby Hollow. Far ~, Near Hollow (f.ns. Thorpe Satchville), Hardys Hollow, Lound Hollows (f.ns. Halstead), Hollow Cl (f.n. Ashby Folville), Hollow Combs (f.n. Humberstone), *Hollowe furlonge*, *Hollowe furre* (f.ns. Cossington), Hollow Tongue (f.n. Rearsby), Holow Drain Cl (f.n. Welby), *Holubalc* (f.n. Queniborough), (*the*) *Rain hollows* (f.n. Ratcliffe on the Wreake).

holmr ON, 'a small island, an inland promontory, a piece of drier ground amid marshes; a water-meadow'. Holmlea, Walton Holme. Very freq. in f.ns.: as a simplex, e.g. *le Holm* (with various spellings in Asfordby, Frisby on the Wreake, Hoby, Launde), Holme Cl (with various spellings in Barrow upon Soar, Belgrave, Burton on the Wolds, Cossington) and *Holme meddow* (Cossington); with a prefixed early pers.n., e.g. *Gamelisholm*, *Scrapholm* (Hoby), or a surn., e.g. Cox Holme (Ashby Folville), *Johnsons holme* (Barkby). Livestock may be specified, e.g. *Calfholme* (Asfordby, Kirby Bellars), *Gooseholme* (Belgrave, Kirby Bellars), *Oxholm* (Cossington, Queniborough), *Swinholmes* (Hoby); or produce, e.g. *Apple Holme* (Cossington), *Chalhoum* (Kirby Bellars), *Riholm* (Hoby), Wheatholm (Barkby); or wild flora, e.g. *Bromholme* (Gaddesby), *Okeholme* (East Norton),

Seghoome (Asfordby), *Tasilholm* (Hoby). Shape may be indicated, e.g. *Brodhome*, Long Holme (South Croxton); or a topographical feature, e.g. Belholme (Belgrave, Kirby Bellars). Recurring are *the Mill Holm* (with various spellings in Allexton, Asfordby, Barkby, Belgrave, Cossington, Frisby on the Wreake), presum. with reference to watermills, *Padocusholm* (Barsby, Queniborough), alluding to amphibians in wet locations, and *Senholm(e)* (Kirby Bellars, Saxelby), referring to disputed land.

holt OE, ON, 'a small wood, a single-species wood'. Barkby Holt. Holt Cl (f.n. Syston), Holt Foot Hill, *Holtforth*, Willow Holt (f.ns. Halstead), Loddington Holt (Loddington), (the) Osier Holt (Frisby on the Wreake, Welby), Seggs Willow Holt, Willow Holt (Cossington).

home ModE, adj., 'near home'. (The) Home Fm (Asfordby, Beeby, Keythorpe). Very common in f.ns., e.g. Home Cl (Allexton, Ashby Folville, Barsby and 15 other townships; the earliest is *the Home Close* 1674, Rotherby), Home Fd (Barkby, Barrow upon Soar, Frisby on the Wreake), Home Park (Cotes), *the Home plott*, *John Oswins Home Plott*, *Mr Stavelys Home meadow* (Cossington). Note that some 17th and 18th cent. spellings of *holme* appear as *home* and the pair may thus be confused.

hop[1] OE, 'a small hemmed-in valley, esp. one opening into or overhanging the main one; a recess in a hill; a remote enclosed place; a plot of enclosed land, esp. in marsh or wasteland'. *Staffhopps* (f.n. Cold Newton).

hōp[2] OE, 'a hoop'; used topographically in some uncertain sense. ?*Houphing* (f.n. Cold Newton).

***hopping** OE, 'a hop-garden, a place where hops grow'. ?*Houphing* (f.n. Cold Newton).

hop-yard ModE, 'a hop-yard, a hop-garden, an enclosure where hops are grown'. (The) Hop Yard (f.n. Belgrave, South Croxton).

hord OE, 'treasure', sometimes referring to a storage place, but also to hidden treasure. *Hordpit* (f.n. South Croxton).

horn OE, ON, 'a horn, a projection; a projecting feature or piece of land'. ?*Haghorne furlonge* (f.n. Seagrave), *horn* (f.n. Barkby), Horndale, *welbie horne* (f.ns. Asfordby), *hornetoft* (f.n. Rotherby).

***horning** OE, 'a headland; something shaped like a horn, a bend, a spit of land'. Horninghold Furlong (f.n. Skeffington).

hors OE, 'a horse'. Horse Leys Fm, Horsepools Fm. *le Horseclos* (f.n. with various spellings in Allexton, Old Ingarsby, Rearsby, Rotherby), *horse croft*, *Horshades*, *Horsnoll* (f.ns. Cossington), Horse Hinderlands (f.n. Queniborough), *Horse Leyes* (f.n. Barkby Thorpe, Gaddesby), Horse Pool Cl (f.n. Rearsby), Horshold seek (f.n. Loddington), *Horspolgate* (Skeffington), *Horswey*, the Hossups (f.ns. Kirby Bellars), *the two Horse crafts* (f.n. Launde).

hospital ME, 'a hospital, a hospice'. Briggs's Hospital, Old Men's ~, Old Women's Hospital. Hospital (f.n. South Croxton), (The) Hospital Cl (f.n. Belgrave).

hos(s) OE, 'a shoot, a tendril'; also 'brambles, thorns'. ?*Hosewong* (f.n. Wymeswold).

hovel eModE, 'a hovel, a shed; a frame or stand on which a stack of corn is built'. Black Hovel Fd (f.n. Tilton), Goss Hovel, Kilby's Hovel Fd (f.ns. Seagrave), Hovel Cl (f.n. Barkby, Cossington, South Croxton, Hamilton, Lowesby, Thorpe Satchville, Thrussington, Thurmaston, Tilton, Walton on the Wolds), Hovel Fd (f.n. Hoby, Ragdale, Seagrave, Walton on the Wolds), Hovel Mdw (f.n. Belgrave, Gaddesby, Lowesby), Hovel Sick (f.n. Queniborough), Hovel Yard (f.n. Tilton), Steels Hovel Cl (f.n. Barkby), Waggon Hovel Cl (f.n. Halstead), ?Wagon Holes (f.n. Walton on the Wolds).

hræfn OE, **hrafn** ON, 'a raven'. Rancliff Wood. ?Raven Cl (f.n. Walton on the Wolds), ?Ravens Bush (f.n. Humberstone).

hrēac OE, 'a rick'. *Doctor Chippingdales Ricke place*, *Mr Higgs Rickplace*, *the Ricke place*, Rick Leys (f.ns. Humberstone), *the rickes* (f.n. Sileby).

hrēod OE, 'a reed, a rush; a reed-bed'; sometimes difficult to distinguish from **rēad** 'red'. Loddington Reddish, Reedpool Spinney. ?Red Banks (f.n. Asfordby), *le Rede* (f.n. Hoby), *Redeforth* (f.n. Thurmaston), *Redegres* (f.n. with various spellings in South Croxton, Cold Newton, Thorpe Satchville, Twyford), *Redemere* (f.n. Barkby), *Redemoram* (f.n. with various spellings in Barkby, Barsby, Skeffington, Syston), *Redespire* (f.n. Twyford), Reed Bed (f.n. Belgrave), *the Reed(e)s* (f.n. Cossington), Reed Pool Covert (f.n. Hungarton), *the Reyd(e)* (f.n. Humberstone), *Reydwelle* (f.n. Kirby Bellars).

hrēodig OE, adj., 'growing with reeds'. *Reddysyke* (f.n. Launde).

hrīs OE, **hrís** ON, 'shrubs, brushwood'. *Endris* (f.n. Skeffington), the Risborough (f.n. Tilton), *Riscroft* (f.n. Kirby Bellars).

hrúðr ON, 'scurf'; topographically perh. 'rough, shaly ground'. ?*Hamerroutes* (f.n. Hoby), ?Routholme (f.n. Queniborough).

hrycg OE, 'a ridge, a long narrow hill'; also in ME f.ns., 'a cultivated strip of ground, a measure of land'. In the Danelaw, it is often replaced by **hryggr** ON, 'a ridge'. Ridgemere Lane (Barkby, Queniborough). *Between the Ridges*, Ridgeways, *Rigslade* (f.ns. Queniborough), Broadridge Cl (f.n. Wymeswold), *Heyrigg* (f.n. Belgrave), *long rigges furland* (f.n. Rotherby), *Nyne Ridges* (f.n. Barkby Thorpe), Over Ridge Cl (f.n. Syston), the Ridge Cl (f.n. Twyford), *Riggeweyegate* (Skeffington), Riggers (f.n. Tugby), *Rigges* (f.n. Kirby Bellars), Robinrig (f.n. Asfordby).

hulfestre OE, 'a plover'. *Hulfstaredale* (f.n. Burton on the Wolds), *Hulwestergate* (Cold Newton).

hullok ME, 'a hillock', *v.* ***hylloc**.

***humol** OE, **humul** ON, 'a rounded hillock'. *Humblibanland* (f.n. Kirby Bellars).

hund OE, **hundr** ON, 'a hound' ?*Hundehoge* (f.n. Cossington), *Hundou* (f.n. Thurmaston).

hundred OE num., 'one hundred', sb., 'an administrative division of a county, prob. consisting originally of 100 hides'. Goscote Hundred. Short Hundred (f.n. Ratcliffe on the Wreake).

hūne OE, 'hoarhound'. ?*Hunwell'* (f.n. Barrow upon Soar).

hung ModE, ppl.adj., 'steeply sloping'. *Hungdalle* (f.n. Tugby), Hung Leys (f.n. Ratcliffe on the Wreake).

hungor OE, 'hunger, famine', usually an allusion in f.ns. to 'barren ground'. Hungarton. *Hungerfelde* (f.n. with various spellings in Barkby, Barrow upon Soar, Thurmaston), *Hungerhil* (f.n. with various spellings in Barkby, Cossington, Thurmaston, Wymeswold), *Hungerland(e)s* (f.n. Tugby).

hunig OE, 'honey'; in f.ns., usually alluding to places where honey was found or produced, or perh. to 'sweet land'; but sometimes also used of sites with sticky soil. *Honyaker* (f.n. Thurmaston).

hunisuccle OE, 'honeysuckle'. the Honeysuckle (f.n. Wymeswold), *the Honey Suckles close* (f.n. Burton on the Wolds).

huntinge ME, vbl.sb., 'the action or practice of chasing game or other wild animals for profit or sport'. Hunting Brigg Cl (f.n. Halstead).

hūs OE, **hús** ON, 'a house'; usually 'a dwelling house', but sometimes used of buildings for special purposes; **house** ModE, 'a residence, a mansion, a manor-house', also *v.* **maner**, **mansion-house**. Asfordby Ho., Barley Hill ~, Barnstaple ~, Beeby ~, Brook ~ (Rearsby, Sileby), Brookfield ~, Chantry ~, Charnwood ~, Cheney ~, Chippingdale ~, Cliff ~ (Barrow upon Soar, Burton on the Wolds), Cliffe ~, Dale ~, Falcon ~, Granville ~, Halstead ~, Hill ~ (Hoby, Cold Newton), Hoby ~, Hollytree ~, Hoton ~, Ivy ~, Keythorpe ~, Lock ~, Loseby ~, Maida ~, Markham ~, Mill ~ (Barkby, Tilton), Napier ~, Oak ~, Park ~, Pasture ~, Quebec ~, Rearsby Ho., Red House Fm, Shoby House Fm, Stack House Fm, Stoneham Ho., Stonesby House Fm, Strancliffe Ho., Welby ~, Wembley ~, Wetherley Ho., White House Fm (Beeby, Old Ingarsby), Woodgate Ho., Wreake House Fm, Yaxley Ho. Early examples may be prefixed by a surn. indicating the residing family and/or ownership, e.g. *Durrands Howse* (Barrow upon Soar), *Pye howse* (Asfordby); or by an el. indicating ecclesiastical use, e.g. *the Parsonage House* (with various spellings in Allexton, Asfordby, Barkby and 10 other townships), *the Rectory House* (Hoby, Rotherby, Saxelby, Walton on the Wolds), *the Vicarage House* (with various spellings in Ashby Folville, Barkby, Barrow upon Soar and 12 other townships). *The Manor House* (with various spellings) is recorded for Allexton, Ashby Folville, Barkby and 15 other townships. Note *Sekemaneshous* (Kirby Bellars), Woodhouse Leys (f.n. Tugby) and the range of instances of named houses in Burton on the Wolds (of 1701) and in Wymeswold (of the early18th cent.).

huswyf ME, 'a woman who manages or directs the affairs of a household; the mistress of a family'. *Hussiffe Close* (f.n. Launde).

hut eModE, 'a hut, a shed'. Hut Cl (f.n. Ashby Folville, South Croxton, Rearsby), Tin Hut Fd (f.n. Thorpe Satchville).

hveiti ON, 'wheat', *v.* **hwǣte.**

hwǣg OE, 'whey', poss. used topographically in allusion to 'sour land'. Waydall Cl (f.n. Wymeswold).

hwǣte OE (Angl), 'wheat'; occasionally replaced by ON **hveiti**. Whatborough. *Weteberusike* (f.n. Seagrave), *Weteborow* (f.n. Cossington), *Wetelond'*, *Whetedal(l)e*, *Whethill* (f.ns. South Croxton), Wheat Cl (f.n. Baggrave), ?*Wheathead Close* (f.n. Cotes), Wheat Hill (f.n. Barsby, Sileby, Skeffington), Wheatholm(e) (f.n. Barkby, Syston), *Whetdalle* (f.n. Wymeswold), *Whetebergh'* (f.n. Kirby Bellars), *the Whetefelde* (f.n. Humberstone), *wheteland gate* (Beeby), *Wheytlandys* (f.n. Barsby), *Whitland* (f.n. Halstead).

hwearf OE, 'a wharf, an embankment built along navigable waters, and later beside railway lines, for loading and unloading goods'. Barkby Wharf (Syston), Hopkins' Wharf, Rearsby Wharf (Rearsby), *le Milne Wharf* (Queniborough), Station Wharf (Halstead, East Norton), The Wharf in Gaultry Cl (Cossington), Wharf Cl (f.n. Rearsby).

hwerfel OE (Angl), **hvirfill** ON, 'a circle; something circular'. *Weruel* (f.n. Asfordby *s.n.* Warblong f.ns. (a)), *Werueldike* (f.n. Queniborough), *the whorle sicke* (f.n. Hungarton), ?*Whorlo* (f.n. South Croxton).

hwīt OE, **hvítr** ON, adj., 'white'; in eModE, *white* 'infertile' may be contrasted with *black* 'fertile'. White Lees. *Whitacres*, *le Whytemarlepitt* (f.ns. Thurmaston), White Close Stile (f.n. Ratcliffe on the Wreake), *Whythows*, *le Witeston'*, *le Witewong'* (f.ns. Barkby), *witelangeland* (f.n. Cold Newton), *Witelondes* (f.n. with various spellings in Belgrave, Saxelby, Thurmaston), *Wythowe* (f.n. Kirby Bellars).

hyll OE, 'a hill'. Barley Hill Ho., Copthill Fm, Dungehill Fm, Foxhill Fm, Red Hill Lane, Rodhill Fm, Streethill Fm. Very freq. in f.ns.: soil types may feature, e.g. *Calkhill'* (Cossington), Sandhill (Barkby, Loddington), *Steynhull* (Kirby Bellars), or suitability or unsuitability for tillage, e.g. *Hardhill* (Cold Newton), *Hungerhil* (Barkby, Cossington), *Mirehilles* (Cossington), Muckhill (Gaddesby). A hill's size, shape or aspect may be signified, e.g. *blakhyll'*, *coptehyll'* (Hungarton), *Charphyll* (Cossington), *le Hengondehul* (Hoby), *litlehil* (Kirby Bellars), Red Hill (Belgrave). Crops esp. may feature, e.g. *barleyhyll'* (Hungarton), Beanhill (with various spellings in Barrow upon Soar, Belgrave, Skeffington, Twyford), *Colhille* (Kirby Bellars), *Longehauerhul*, *Peysul* (South Croxton), *Ryele* (Cossington), Wheathill (Barsby, South Croxton); or wild flora, e.g. *Burbladehyl* (Cossington), *Hothornhull* (Barrow upon Soar), *Thornhill* (South Croxton). Structures may be indicated, ecclesiastical or lay, e.g. *kirkehil* (Belgrave, Cold Newton), *the Mill hill* (with various spellings in Barrow upon Soar, Cossington, Hungarton, Old Ingarsby), *Wyndmill hill* (South Croxton). Streams related to hills may be prefixed, e.g. *Bydewellhyl*, *Honwellhyll* (Barrow upon Soar), *Tralleswellehul* (Burton on the Wolds). Meeting places are indicated, e.g. Porthill (Lowesby), Ting-hill (Rotherby), as is a hill's location, e.g. *Merehull'* (Burton on the Wolds), *Queniburhull* (Barkby), *Vtterhull* (Barrow upon Soar). A pers.n. or surn. may feature, e.g. *Bernardhull'* (Kirby Bellars). Note also Streethill (South Croxton) and Sunhill (Cossington), Sunnell (Sileby).

hyllig OE, **hilli** ME, adj., 'hilly'. Hillybanks (f.n. Kirby Bellars).

***hylloc** OE, **hillok, hullok** ME, 'a hillock'. Hillockey (f.n. Lowesby), Hullocky (f.n. Ragdale).

hymlic OE, **hemelok** ME, **hemblock** eModE, 'hemlock'. Hemplock Nook (f.n. Grimston).

hyrdel OE, 'a hurdle, a wicker-work frame'. ?*Hurdlegate Bush* (f.n. Seagrave).

hyrid ME, ppl.adj., 'hired out, let out in return for payment'. ?*Hyridolis* (f.n. Cossington).

hyrne OE (Angl), 'an angle, a corner; a recess in a hill, a corner in a valley, a spit of land in a river-bend'. *Bondehirne* (f.n. Asfordby), *Halywell herne* (f.n. Thurmaston), *Iron furlong* (f.n. Frisby on the Wreake).

hyrst OE (Angl), 'a hillock, a wooded hill'. *Blakehyrst* (f.n. Rearsby), *Elthornhurst* (f.n. Barkby), *Hardhurst* (f.n. Humberstone), Hirst Croft (f.n. Beeby), *le Hurst* (f.n. Thurmaston).

-ig[3] OE, suffix, mostly adj., **-ig**, **-i(e)**, **-y(e)** ME, **-y** ModE, adj. suffix. Dockey Fm. Ashey Cl, First Seedy Cl (f.ns. Welby), Banky (f.n. Cold Newton), *Banky(e) Close* (f.n. Allexton, Tilton), Banky Fds, Hullocky (f.ns. Ragdale), *Flaggymere* (f.n. Barrow upon Soar), *Furry leyes furlonge*, *Quacksick furry(e) leys* (f.ns. Humberstone), Hillockey (f.n. Lowesby), ?*Munetilandes* (f.n. Burton on the Wolds).

igil OE, 'a hedgehog; a leech', ***igli** ON, 'a leech'. Ilemoor (f.n. Sileby), I(s)lemoor Cls (f.n. Syston).

in OE, prep., 'in', sometimes with the adj. force 'inner'. Incroft Gate (Asfordby), Incroft Mdw (f.n. Asfordby), *le Infal'* (f.n. Kirby Bellars), *the ingate* (Beeby), *le Inwonges* (f.n. Queniborough).

inclosure eModE, 'an inclosing, an enclosure'; a variant form of *enclosure*, being the statutory form of reference to the inclosing of waste lands, commons etc. *the old Inclosure*, *Sileby Inclosure* (f.ns. Cossington).

-ing[2] OE, toponymic suffix; difficult to distinguish in later spellings from **eng**. ?*flintinges* (f.n. Humberstone), ?(*the*) *Glapings* (f.n. Hoby), *Houphing* (f.n. Cold Newton), *le thickinc* (f.n. Kirby Bellars).

-ingtūn OE, added to a pers.n. to denote an estate associated with that particular person. Cossington, Loddington, Skeffington. ?Cussington Hills (f.n. Thorpe Satchville), *Dodyngton'* (f.n. Rearsby).

***innām** OE, **innám** ON, 'a piece of land taken in or enclosed'. *Hoome Innam*, *Innoms*, *Larpit* ~, *Shobye* ~, *Stoo Innam* (f.ns. Asfordby), *Innhams* (f.n. Thurmaston).

innar ON, adj., 'inner'. Innergate (Wymeswold).

inntak ON, 'a piece of land taken in or enclosed', **intack, intake** ModEdial., 'a piece of land enclosed from a moor or waste'. Intake (f.n. Belgrave, Gaddesby, Tilton), New Intake (f.n. Barkby).

-isc OE, noun suffix, with the sense 'that which pertains to'. Loddington Reddish.

island eModE, 'a piece of land completely surrounded by water, a piece of elevated land surrounded by marsh'; also 'a piece of woodland surrounded by open country'. The Island (f.n. Belgrave), *the Island* (f.n. Cossington).

jack ModEdial., adj., 'unused'. ?Jack Cl, ?Jack Leys (f.ns. South Croxton).

jackanapes eModE, 'a mischievous boy'; but also *Jackanapes on horseback* was a 17th cent. name for a proliferous variety of cowslip (and daisy). *Jackanap(e)s hole* (Jacks Hole, f.n. Walton on the Wolds).

kelda ON, 'a spring, a marshy place'. *Keldalegate* (Twyford).

kenel ME, 'a kennel'; sometimes in later names relating to kennels in which hunting dogs were kept. Kennel Cottage. Dog Kennel Cl (f.n. Welby, Wymeswold), Dogkennel Mdw (f.n. Quenby), Kennel Fd (f.n. Seagrave).

kervinge ME, 'a cutting, a carving out'. *Kiwynge* (f.n. Kirby Bellars).

kirkja ON, 'a church'. *Abouethekirke* (f.n. Thurmaston), *kirkehil* (f.n. Cold Newton), *kyrkdales*, *Kyrkehadlond'* (f.ns. Humberstone), *Kyrkefelde* (f.n. Thurmaston), *Kyrk(e)gate* (Barkby, Thurmaston), *Kyrkehull*, *Kyrkland furlong'* (f.ns. Belgrave), *kyrkewylows* (f.n. Hungarton).

kirkju-bý(r) ON, 'a village with a church'. Kirby Bellars.

kjarr ON, 'brushwood', **ker** ME, 'a bog, a marsh, esp. one overgrown with brushwood'. ?Car Bridge, ~ ~ Spinney. the Car (f.n. Asfordby, Brooksby), Bottom ~, Top Car (f.ns. Frisby on the Wreake), Kirdale Furlong (f.n. Barsby).

kona (**kvenna** gen.pl.) ON, 'a woman'. ?Quenby.

krá ON, 'a nook, a corner of land'. ?Crow Legs Furlong (f.n. Ratcliffe on the Wreake).

kráka ON, **crake** ME, 'a crow, a raven'. *Crokenest* (f.n. Cossington).

krókr ON, 'a crook, a bend; land in the bend of a river; a nook, a secluded corner'. Croaks (f.n. Asfordby), *le Crokedole* (f.n. Kirby Bellars), *le Crokefeld* (f.n.

Barkby), *Crokesgate* (Barkby), Crook Cl (f.n. Lowesby), *Crook*(*e*) *sick*(*e*) *hadland* (f.n. Barkby Thorpe), *the Crooks* (f.n. Humberstone).

la OFr, fem. def.art., 'the'.

lache ME, 'a slowly-moving stream'. *lytyllachemere* (f.n. Welby).

***lǣge** OE, adj., 'fallow, unploughed, lying untilled'. *laylondes* (f.n. Welby), *Leylandys* (f.n. Cossington).

lǣs (**lǣswe** gen.sg., dat.sg.) OE, 'pasture, meadowland'; extremely difficult to distinguish from the pl. of **lēah** (**lǣh** (**lǣs** nom.pl.) (Angl)) to which some of the following may rather belong, *v.* **leys**. *Blackemore Leyes*, *Bradmerholelese*, *Bromholme lees* (f.ns. Gaddesby), *Corbits leasow*, *ye flax leasowes*, *Hoggecroft leasowes* (f.ns. Seagrave), *Corduwanleyes*, The Leasures, ?The Pleasures, *lez Smythleis* (f.ns. Barrow upon Soar), *Croseleys*, Lambleys, *Leypulleyes* (f.ns. Cossington), *Endlieȝ*, *Esthorpleys*, *Godelis*, *Longleys*, *middilthorpleys*, *Quenemylnleys* (f.ns. Kirby Bellars), *Grundlees*, *Orchardleyes* (f.ns. Skeffington), the Leasures (f.n. Syston), *Moreleys* (f.n. Humberstone), *le Oxlesuwe* (f.n. Barrow upon Soar), Scampton leases (f.n. Belgrave), *Westeleys*(*e*) (f.n. Hungarton).

la(g)h ME, **low** ModE, adj., 'low, low-lying'. Low Farm (Manor Lodge Fm). Lafalong Cl (f.n. Humberstone), *le Louuefurlong* (f.n. Cotes), Low Mdw (f.n. Queniborough), Low Street (f.n. Keyham).

laie ME, 'a stream, water, a pool'. *Leapoole* (f.n. Cossington), *le Ley Close* (f.n. Kirby Bellars).

lair ME, 'a place for farm animals to lie down in'. Calf Lairs (f.n. East Norton), (the) Cow Layer (f.ns. Tugby, Wymeswold), Sheep layers (f.n. Tilton).

lām OE, 'loam, clay'. Lambles (f.n. Cossington).

lamb OE, 'a lamb'. *Lambcote dale* (f.n. Halstead), Lamb Croft (f.n. Barrow upon Soar), *Lambecotehou* (f.n. Thrussington), *Lamcotte hill* (f.n. Burton on the Wolds).

lambing eModE, vbl.sb., 'the parturition or yeaning of lambs'. Lambing Paddock (f.n. Tilton).

lammas eModE, 'Loaf Mass'; the 1st of August, in the early English Church observed as a harvest festival at which loaves of bread made from the first ripe corn were consecrated. In f.ns., referring to land which was under cultivation until harvest and reverted to common pasture from Lammas-tide until the following Spring. *le Lammas close* (f.n. with various spellings in Belgrave, Frisby on the Wreake, Hoby, Hoton, Loddington, Sileby, Thrussington, Thurmaston, Wymeswold), Wards Lammas Cl (f.n. Rotherby).

land, **lond** OE, **land** ON, 'land', either in the general sense 'ground, part of the earth's surface' or 'an estate or small tract of land' or 'a selion, a strip of arable in a common field'. Bridgeland Fm. Freezeland Lodge, Longlands Fm, The Peaslands, Sandlen's Lodge. Very freq. in f.ns.: the colour of the soil may be specified, e.g. Black lands (with various spellings in Belgrave, Gaddesby, Keyham, Loddington), *Redlandes* (with various spellings in Barkby, Loddington, Rotherby, Saxelby); or its fertility may be indicated, e.g. *badland* (Barsby), Fatlands (Rotherby); or difficulty of tillage, e.g. *Stanilandes* (with various spellings in Barsby, Beeby, Cossington, South Croxton, Kirby Bellars); or geological type, e.g. *Calkland* (Kirby Bellars, Seagrave), Clay Lands (Belgrave), Sandlands (Gaddesby, Kirby Bellars). Crops may be alluded to, e.g. *Banlandis* (with various spellings in Barkby, Barrow upon Soar, Barsby and 6 other townships), *Cawland* (Kirby Bellars), *Flaxlands* (with various spellings in Asfordby, Barkby, South Croxton, Hoby), *Peselondys* (with various spellings in Cossington, South Croxton, Kirby Bellars, East Norton), *wheteland* (with various spellings in Barsby, Beeby, Belgrave). Wild flora may be indicated, e.g. *Aslande* (Hoby), Eagland (Skeffington), *Shrubland* (South Croxton), the Taslands (Frisby on the Wreake), *thislie landes* (Asfordby). Shape or extent are freq. specified, e.g. Bratlands (Belgrave), *longelandes* (Asfordby, Belgrave, Hungarton), *Narowelandes* (Ratcliffe on the Wreake), Petty Lands (Barrow upon Soar), *Schortlond* (South Croxton, Hungarton), *Wrangelandes* (Asfordby, South Croxton, Kirby Bellars). Ownership or tenure may be specified by a pers.n. or a surn., e.g. *Adeynetlond*, *Rauenoldland'* (Kirby Bellars), *Sproweslond'* (South Croxton), *Thokeslandys* (Cossington), and later, *William Gambles land*, *Richard Hensons lands* (Asfordby), *Jasper's Land* (Saxelby), *Widdow Masons land* (Cossington); or by an el. alluding to larger institutions, e.g. *the Colledge land* (Barkby Thorpe), *Kyrkland* (Belgrave), *the queenes man(n)or land* (Asfordby), *Templeland(s)* (Belgrave, Gaddesby). The type of tenure may be indicated, e.g. *Manlandes* (Hoby), *the severall landes* (Rotherby). Location may be specified, e.g. Eastlands, *Eastwell landes*, *estowlandes*, *Hollandys* (Barrow upon Soar), *Gatelandes* (South Croxton), *le Schelland* (Kirby Bellars). F.ns. such as *the Broken lands* (Thrussington), *Brokenlond* (Barrow upon Soar), *Newlond* (Welby) allude to the development of formerly uncultivated ground. Units made up of specified numbers of selions of common fields appear, e.g. *ye Eight Lands*, *the Glebe Seaven Landes* (South Croxton), *Five Land Furlong* (Asfordby), *fowre landes* (Rotherby), Nineteen Lands (Thrussington). In later f.ns., common is the close formed from an unspecified number of selions of a former great field, e.g. Land Cl (Brooksby, Hoby, Loddington, East Norton).

land-(ge)mǣre OE, 'a boundary'. *Landmeresikfurlonges* (f.n. Hoby).

lane OE, 'a lane, a narrow road'. Abbey Lane, Blackberry Lane, Dun's Lane Fm, Narrow Lane, Perkin's ~, Snows ~, Storkit ~, Water ~, Wide Lane. Freq. in f.ns., esp. with a pers.n. or surn., e.g. *Bardolflane* (Seagrave), Bellars Lane (Grimston), *Bennetts lane* (Cossington), *Bonners Lane* (Hoby), *Digby lane* (Tilton), *Herbert lane* (South Croxton). Occasionally with a stream-name, e.g. *Fulwell Lane* (Barrow upon Soar), *Stocwellelane* (Kirby Bellars); or the name of an adjacent township, e.g. Sholby Lane (Grimston), *Wimeswould Lane* (Burton on the Wolds). Local clergy are sometimes alluded to, e.g. *the Parsons Lane* (Saxelby), *le Vicarslane* (Barkby). Recurring is *Lane Close* (Burton on the Wolds, Cossington, Rearsby, Thorpe Satchville). Note *Grop(e)cuntlane* (Kirby Bellars).

lane-ende ME, 'a lane-end; land at the end of the lane' (*v*. Löfvenberg 117 and Ch **5** (1. ii), 262–3). *Banar lane eynd* (f.n. Barsby), Bellars Lane end (f.n. Grimston), *the Lane end* (f.n. Skeffington), Lane end Cl (f.n. Beeby), *Langworth lane end* (f.n. Thurmaston), Mill Lane End, *ye Stalkott lane End* (f.ns. Wymeswold), Prestwold Lane End Shoot, *Whitoths lane end* (f.ns. Hoton), *Swans lane end* (f.n. Tugby), *Water Lane End* (f.n. Frisby on the Wreake).

lang[1] OE, **langr** ON, adj., 'long'. Longlands Fm. Freq. in f.ns. with a range of aspects of agricultural land, e.g. Langleys (Welby), *lankeley* (Beeby), *Long breche* (Belgrave), *Longcroft* (Barkby), *le Longedoles* (Barkby Thorpe, Hamilton), *Longelandes* (Asfordby, Belgrave). Note also the el. in compound with topographical features, e.g. *Langedale*, *Longclif*, *le Longewold* (Barkby).

lang[2] ME, 'a long strip of land'. *Holebeckhelongke*, *longkebithelee* (f.ns. Kirby Bellars), *the longe* (f.n. Rearsby), *Longs furlong* (f.n. Sileby), *Siwordlong* (f.n. South Croxton), Top Long (f.n. Seagrave).

lanterne ME, 'a lantern; a structure above an opening in a roof which has glazed or open sides for light or ventilation'. *Lantern yerd* (Launde).

launde OFr, ME, 'an open space in woodland; woodland pasture'. Launde. *la Launde* (f.n. Barrow upon Soar), ?Launsdale (f.n. Thrussington), The Lawn (f.n. Prestwold), Lawn Way (Frisby on the Wreake).

lavedi, ladi ME, 'a lady'; often referring to a dowager or to a female proprietor or to the lady of a manor. Our Lady, the Virgin Mary, may be alluded to, esp. with reference to rents for the upkeep of a chapel. Ladies Cl (f.n. Frisby on the Wreake), *ladyacre*, *ladyredyng* (f.ns. Welby), Lady Acre (f.n. Barkby), Lady Fd (f.n. Seagrave), Lady Orchard (f.n. Queniborough), *Ladywell sicke* (f.n. Hungarton), *Lady Wonge* (f.n. Rearsby), *lauedywong* (f.n. Kirby Bellars).

lāwerce, lāferce OE, 'the lark'. ?*lafrickethorn* (f.n. Kirby Bellars).

le OFr, masc. def.art., 'the'.

lēac OE, 'a leek, garlic'. *leke beddes* (f.n. Wymeswold).

lēah OE, **lǣh** (**lǣs** nom.pl.) (Angl), 'woodland, a woodland glade, a clearing in a wood'; later, 'pasture, meadow', *v.* **leys**. Shipley Hill. *Ansley*, *Bryntle*, *Cumberlea sicke* (f.ns. Seagrave), *Brechlahil* (f.n. Skeffington), Brockley Hill (f.n. Ratcliffe on the Wreake), Copley (f.n. Hoby), Foxley Gate (Hoby), *Grahalega* (f.n. Cossington), Harle, *Langley Hoockes* (f.ns. South Croxton), *Langley wonge* (f.n. Barkby), Langleys (f.n. Quenby), *lankeley*, *martley* (f.ns. Beeby).

leggr ON, 'a leg'. ?Crow Legs Furlong (f.n. Ratcliffe on the Wreake).

leirr ON, 'mud, clay'. *Leyrstedes* (f.n. Barkby).

lengthe ME, 'a long stretch of something'; in the case of land, poss. referring to selions which were particularly long. *the lengthes* (f.n. (Hoby).

lēoht OE, **līht** (Angl), adj., 'light, light-coloured'; also used as a sb. 'a light place' (*v.* Löfvenberg 122). *Lighte hill* (f.n. Whatborough).

levenges ME, vbl.sb., 'leavings, residue, remainder; ?aftermath'. *Leyvynges* (f.n. Cossington).

ley ModE, 'a meadow, a pasture', *v.* **leys**. Common in f.ns., e.g. *Mary Chamberlyns Lay*, *the Viccaridge Ley* (Humberstone), *Glebe bastard Ley*, *Margyt(t)s laye* (South Croxton), *John Gregorie lea* (Asfordby), the Lea (Kirby Bellars), Ley Furlong, Whinney Ley (Queniborough), *the midle high lea* (Rotherby), Rough Ley Cl(s) (Syston).

leyne, lain ME, 'a tract of arable land' ?Lane Homestead (f.n. Hoton), ?Manslain (f.n. Thrussington).

leys ModE, 'meadows, pasture; grassed-over selions of a common field (lying fallow)'. F.ns. with *leys* (spellings also in *layes*, *lays*, *leas*, *leaes*, *leaies*, *lease*, *leayes*, *leays*, *leease*, *lees*, *leies*, *leis*, *leyes*) may have developed variously from the pl. of **lēah** (**lǣh** (**lǣs** nom.pl. (Angl)) in its later sense 'pasture, meadow' and from **lǣs** 'pasture, meadow' and it is very difficult to assign with confidence an individual name to either source, except where forms with *leasow* (from **lǣswe**, gen.sg. of the latter) survive. Professor K. Cameron argues that most later f.ns. with *leys* (*ley* sg.) are prob. from **lēah**, *v.* L **2** 66 *s.n.* Carr Leys Wood. However, the modern sg. form *ley* (with spellings too in *lay*, *laye*, *lea*, *lee*) may also be the result of the reduction of *leys* (from **lǣs** 'pasture, meadow') as a perceived plural. Barley Leas, Briery Leys Spinney, Church Leys, Holmlea, Horse Leys Fm, The Leys, Sheep-Le Fm, Summer Lees Plantation, White Lees. Very freq. in f.ns., esp. with a locational prefix, e.g. Clapperdale Leys (South Croxton), Easting Meadow Leys (Asfordby), *Old Pinfold Leyes* (Barkby); or with a surn., e.g. Hoods leas (Asfordby), *Nortons leas* (Allexton), Simison Leys (Barkby), *Stevens leas* (Cossington). Crops may signify, e.g. Barley Leys (South Croxton), *Flaxleys* (Barkby, Belgrave, Burton on the Wolds) (such f.ns. may be the result of the late substitution of *leys* for *lands*); or animal husbandry, e.g. *Bull leyes* (Barkby Thorpe), *the Cunigrie leaies* (Barrow upon Soar, Belgrave), Horse Leys (Barkby Thorpe, Gaddesby), *the Sheep leyes* (Burton on the Wolds). Mineral extraction may feature, e.g. *Quallerie leyes* (Cossington), *Sandpit leas* (Asfordby). Recurring are *the hall layes* (Beeby, South Croxton) and *Longleyes* (Beeby, Burton on the Wolds, Welby). Note the early irrigation system recorded in *the water leas* (Rotherby) and local cloth-making in Tenter Leys Cl (South Croxton). In compound with a numeral, *leys* represents grassland units of tenure corresponding to *lands* (i.e. selions or strips) similarly used of arable, e.g. *Five Leys* (Asfordby), *the foure leas*, *(ye) Six Leas*, *Nyne leyes* (Cossington), Seven Leys (Hoby), *the Twenty Leas* (Burton on theWolds).

les, lez OFr, pl. def.art., 'the'.

līm OE, 'lime'. *les Limstalles* (f.n. Thurmaston), *Lymstall* (f.n. Belgrave).

lim-kilne ME, 'a lime-kiln'. Limekiln Spinney. Lime Kiln (f.n. Skeffington), Lime Kiln Cl (f.n. Barrow upon Soar), Limekilns (f.n. Loddington).

līn OE, **lín** ON, 'flax. *lillandes* (f.n. Asfordby).

linet ME, 'the linnet'. ?Linnet Hill (f.n. Seagrave).

-ling OE, diminutive suffix. ?*Cogling croft* (f.n. Walton on the Wolds).

loc OE, 'a lock, a fold', **loca** OE, 'an enclosure'. *Lokholm(e)* (f.n. Barrow upon Soar).

lock ModE, 'an enclosed section of a canal which has gates at each end and in which water can be raised or lowered to move boats from one level to another'. Barrow Lock, Belgrave Lock, Lock Ho. Locks (f.n. Frisby on the Wreake).

loge OFr, **log(g)e** ME, 'a hut, a small house'; later 'a house in a forest for temporary use (a forester's house or a hunting lodge), a house at the entrance to a park'. Freq. in modern house-names as a pretentious term for a country villa, often prefixed by an older p.n. by analogy with names of genuine hunting-lodges, forest-houses or manorial estate-houses. Alma Lodge, Ashby ~, Austin's ~, Barkby ~, Bell Dip ~, Bigg's ~, Brutnall's ~, Coles ~, Cream ~ (Barrow upon Soar, Kirby Bellars), Freezeland ~, Frisby ~, Gaddesby ~, Gamber's Hill Lodge, Hamner's Lodge Fm, Ingarsby ~, Inkerman ~, Isset's ~, Jenner's ~, Jericho Lodge, Kirby Lodge Fm, Lady ~, Launde ~, Loddington Lodge, The Lodge (Beeby, Seagrave), Messenger's Lodge, Newfoundland ~, Cold Newton ~, North's ~, Paudy ~, Pick's ~, Porter's ~, Queniborough ~, Quenby ~, Rearsby Wharf Lodge, Red Lodge Fm, Rotherby Lodge, Ryefield ~, Sandlen's ~, Scot's ~, Sileby Lodge, Skeffington Lodge Fm, South Lodge, Southfield ~, Spurr's ~, Stone Pit ~, Syston ~, Thrussington Lodge (x2), Thurmaston ~, Underwood's ~, Welby ~, White ~, Wymeswold Lodge. *Angraves Lodge* (Top Fm, Burton on the Wolds), *Brooms* ~ (Broom's Fm, Launde), *Browncliffe* ~ (Brancliffe Fm, South Croxton), *Chandlers* ~ (Ivy Cottage, Kirby Bellars), *Cossington* ~ (1) (College

Fm, Cossington), *Cossington* ~ (2) (White Lodge, Cossington), *Flendell* ~ (Ashby Pasture, Kirby Bellars), *Hanover* ~ (Hanover Fm, Sileby), *Isle* ~ (Belle Isle, Sileby), *Keepers* ~ (Park Wood Fm, Launde), *Launde* ~ (Abbey Fm, Launde), *Launde Wood* ~ (Hill Fm, Launde), *The New Close* ~ (Ash Tree Fm, Kirby Bellars), *Porthills* ~ (Portels Fm, Cold Newton), *Quebec* ~ (Quebec Ho., Sileby), *South Croxton* ~ (South Croxton Grange, South Croxton), *Streethill* ~ (Streethill Fm, Lowesby), *Whatborough* ~ (Whatborough Fm, Whatborough), *Wildbore's Lodge* (Robin-a-Tiptoe Fm, Tilton). Lodge Cl, Lodge Close Mdw (f.ns. Baggrave).

***lort(e)** OE, 'mud, a muddy place, a swamp'. Lorput Gate (Asfordby).

lowsy ME, adj., 'lousy, infested with lice', cf. **lūs-þorn**. *lowsy bushe* (f.n. Rotherby).

lundr ON, 'a small wood, a grove'. *Andreslund*, *Crokislundeswong'*, *Endryslund*, *Eskelund'*, *Heytlund*, *Longedalelund*, *Lundesbroc*, Lunsdale (f.ns. Skeffington), *frithelund*, *Menelund*, *suinelund* (f.ns. Cold Newton), Great ~, Little Lound (f.ns. Halstead), Lounds (f.n. Tilton), Lount (f.n. Loddington), *Lunsdall(e)* (f.n. Tugby), ?*Skelund* (f.n. Kirby Bellars).

lūs OE, 'a louse'. ?Lusty gate (South Croxton).

lūs-þorn OE, 'a spindle-tree'. ?Lusty gate (South Croxton).

lyme-pytt ME, 'a lime-pit'. Lime Hole Plantation. *lympittes* (f.n. Sileby), *Lymputes* (f.n. Barrow upon Soar).

lyng ON, 'ling, heather'. Big Ling Spinney. *Belegraue Ling* (f.n. Belgrave), Bonsers Lings, *Glovers Lings*, Lings (f.ns. Prestwold), ?Buttlings Cl, the Lingens (f.ns. Gaddesby), Hoton Lings (f.n. Hoton), *the Ling Close* (f.n. Burton on the Wolds), *Lyng close* (f.n. Lowesby), *Lynge Landes* (f.n. Wymeswold), Two Lings (f.n. Belgrave), *over Westerling(e)s* (f.n. Barkby Thorpe).

lȳtel, lītel OE, **lítill** ON, adj., 'little, small'. Freq. in f.ns., e.g. *Liteldoles*, *Litileberwe*, *Litleclyff*, *Littelhagh* (Barrow upon Soar), *litle dale*, *the lytle feild* (Beeby), *le littilcroft*, *litlehil* (Kirby Bellars).

mǣd (mǣdwe obl.sg.) OE, **mēd** (Angl), 'a meadow'. Examples in f.ns. from the nom.sg. are comparatively few; earlier instances are *Abbottesmede* (Asfordby), *Brook mead* (Loddington), *le Estmede*, *le Westmede* (Frisby on the Wreake), *Litlemede* (Humberstone), *longemad* (Welby), *Northen-Mead* (Barkby), *Pynemyll mead* (Grimston), *le Watermeade* (Kirby Bellars), while post-1750 examples are Cartwright's Mead (Belgrave), Little Mead (Tilton), Styway Mead (Barkby). Freq. in f.ns. as *meadow* from the oblique case: with a directional indicator, e.g. *le Estmedowe* (Barkby, Belgrave), *le Foremedowes* (Hoby); or with a locational indicator, e.g. *Incroft meadowe* (Asfordby), *Ryecrofte medowe* (Barrow upon Soar), *Westhorpbirimedow(e)* (Barkby). Size may be described, e.g. *Littelmedowe* (Barkby), *Mykul Mydow* (Cossington); or aspect, e.g. *Crokedmedowe* (Hoby), *Flatmedo(w)* (Skeffington), *le Hardemedewe* (Barkby). Livestock may feature, e.g. *Cumedwe* (Burton on the Wolds), *(le) Weddermedow(e)* (Barrow upon Soar). Note *Bondman medow*, *Hauekeremedowe* (Barrow upon Soar), *Saint Nicholas Meadow*, *Saint Pulchres Meadow* (Asfordby).

mægden OE, 'a maiden, a young unmarried woman'; in p.ns., usually in allusion to places owned by them, or to places which they habitually frequented. Maiden Green (f.n. Sileby), *Maydens well* (f.n. Humberstone).

mǣl[2] OE, 'speech'. ?Melborough (f.n. Seagrave).

(ge)mǣne OE, adj., 'common'; in p.ns., denoting property or land held communally. *Manholme* (f.n. Kirby Bellars), *Manlandis* (f.n. Hoby), *Menelund* (f.n. Cold Newton).

(ge)mǣnnes OE, 'a community'; in p.ns., used of 'common land, a common holding'. West Mains. *Mannesmor* (f.n. Hoby), ?*Mannsfyld slade* (f.n. Humberstone), *Mansdale* (f.n. Belgrave), ?Manslain (f.n. Thrussington).

(ge)mǣre OE, 'a boundary, a border; a strip of land forming a boundary'; difficult to distinguish from **mere**[1]. Ridgemere Lane (Barkby, Queniborough). Fairly freq. in f.ns.: most often with the name of an adjoining township, e.g. *grymson meare*, *Saxelbie meare* (Asfordby), *Humberston Meare* (Belgrave), *Ratcliff meere* (Cossington), *Sison Meere* (Barkby); or with an indication of wild flora, e.g. *Arland Bush meare* (Barkby), *Ashmeere* (Cossington), *thornye meare* (Humberstone). Boundary markers are alluded to, e.g. *Harewelmere* (Barkby), *Merehull'* (Burton on the Wolds), Streethill Meer (South Croxton). *Highmeare* recurs (Barkby, Belgrave).

***malm** OE (Angl), 'sand, sandy or chalky soil, soft stone', **malmr** ON, 'sand'. *Malmberthorn* (f.n. Cossington), Mow Macre Hill (f.n. Belgrave).

malte-mylne ME, 'a mill for grinding or crushing malt'. *the Malt mill* (Tilton).

maner ME, 'a manor (house), a mansion'. The Manor, Humberstone Manor, Old Manor, Manor Fm (Beeby, Burton on the Wolds, Cotes, Humberstone, Queniborough, Tugby), Manor Ho. (Ashby Folville, Beeby, Gaddesby, Cold Newton, East Norton, Rearsby, Rotherby, Saxelby, Tilton, Twyford, Wymeswold), North ~ ~, South Manor Ho. (South Croxton); *Chamberleyns maner* (Rearsby), *the Man(n)or House* (Allexton, Barkby, Loddington, Thurmaston). Manor Covert, (the) Manor Piece (f.ns. Thrussington), *the queenes man(n)or land* (f.n. Asfordby).

manig OE, adj., 'many'. *manyedikes* (f.n. Asfordby), *Maynihows* (f.n. Thurmaston).

mansion-house eModE, 'the house of a lord of the manor; an official residence, esp. that belonging to the benefice of an ecclesiastic'. *the Mansion House* (Frisby on the Wreake, Lowesby, Rotherby).

***mapel** OE, 'a maple-tree'. *le Mapeldole* (f.n. Thorpe Satchville).

māra OE, adj. (comp. of **micel**), 'greater, bigger'. *Marwaterlandes* (f.n. Wymeswold).

mare ME, 'a mare; the female of the domestic horse'. *Mare Close Meadow* (f.n. Tugby).

mareis OFr, ME, 'a marsh'. *le Brademares*, ?*Edimar'*, *Gudemares*, *Litelmares*, *Longmaresende* (f.ns. Thurmaston), Marehouse furlong (f.n. Sileby), ?Long Marrows (f.n. Asfordby).

market ME, 'a market, a market-place'. *Marketgate* (Kirby Bellars).

marle ME, 'marl'. Marl furlong, Marl Hole (f.ns. Barkby).

marled(e) ME, adj., 'marled, fertilized with marl'. *the Mauld Close* (f.n. Burton on the Wolds).

marle-pytt ME, 'a marl-pit'. *Marlepitte* (f.n. with various spellings in Barkby, Beeby, Belgrave, Cossington, Hoby, Queniborough, Thorpe Satchville, Thrussington), *Marlepitt hades* (f.n. Frisby on the Wreake), *marlepittgate* (Rotherby), *Marlepytwong* (f.n. Rearsby), *le Whytemarlepitt* (f.n. Thurmaston).

marr[1] ON, 'a fen, a marsh'. ?*Edimar'* (f.n. Thurmaston).

mealt OE, 'malt'. the Malt Sic (f.n. Barkby).

mealt-hūs OE, 'a malt-house'. *Malthous* (Kirby Bellars).

mealwe OE, 'mallow'. Mallows Bush piece (f.n. Halstead).

mearc OE, 'a boundary'. *le Merksfurlonges* (f.n. Hoby).

mearð OE, 'a marten, a weasel'. *Merdegrave* (Belgrave). *Martholes* (f.n. Prestwold), *martley* (f.n. Beeby).

mēl OE (Angl), 'a cross'. ?Melborough (f.n. Seagrave).

meoluc, meolc OE, 'milk'; prob. used topographically of rich pastures etc. yielding good milk. ?Melcoff Hole (f.n. Halstead).

mere[1] OE, 'a pool, a lake', also 'wetland'; difficult to distinguish from **(ge)mǣre**. *Rerisby en le Mere* (Rearsby). Abel Meer Cl, *kilne dike meere*, *sowsmer' syk deyn* (f.ns. Hungarton), *Bradmerholelese* (f.n. Gaddesby), *Flagmere*, ?*Merelond*, *Titfordemere* (f.ns. Barrow upon Soar), ?*Holland meare*, ?*Longmeyrewong'*, *Redemere*, ?*Schortmerewong* (f.ns. Barkby), *lytyllachemere* (f.n. Welby), the Meer (f.n. Lowesby), ?*Meare Willowes* (f.n. Queniborough), *the middle meere*, ?*Rychemere* (f.ns. Cossington), *the mylne meare* (f.n. Humberstone), *Wildgoose meer* (f.n. Saxelby), ?Wisemoor Hill (f.n. Wymeswold).

mere-stall OE, 'a (stagnant) pool, a pond' (*v*. Ch **3** 158–9). *Gosmastal'* (f.n. Cossington), *Merestall'* (f.n. Wymeswold), *Merstalwong'* (f.n. Barkby).

merisc OE, 'a marsh'; an older form of **mersc**. *the marishe grounde* (f.n. Rotherby).

mersc OE, 'a marsh, watery land'. *barle marche*, the Marsh Drain (f.ns. Wymeswold), *the Holt Marsh* (f.n. Loddington), The March (f.n. Ragdale), Marsh dale (f.n. Cossington), *the Marshe* (f.n. Hoby), Marshside (f.n. Asfordby), Marston Mdw (f.n. Humberstone), *Martch Dale* (f.n. Barkby), Match Dike, *Suthenmersche* (f.ns. South Croxton), *le Mersche* (f.n. Queniborough).

mete OFr, ME, 'a boundary'. Hardmeats (f.n. Brooksby).

meðal ON, adv., 'among, between'; in p.ns. with adj. function 'middle', influencing or replacing OE **middel** in the Danelaw. *Medelward*, ?*Melland* (f.ns. Gaddesby).

micel, mycel OE, **mikill** ON, adj., 'big, great'; the OE el. is much influenced by the ON el. in the Danelaw and is difficult to distinguish. *Mikeberkby* (Barkby), Muckle Gate Lane. Freq. in f.ns., e.g. *Micheldale* (Saxelby), *Michelennow*, *Mikilbanland* (Hoby), Mickle Mdw (Cossington), Muckil Hill (South Croxton), Muckle Brinks (Keyham).

mid OE, prep., adv., 'among, amidst'; prob used also in an elliptical fashion, as of land between two ridges or valleys. ?Midland (f.n. Queniborough).

middel OE, adj., 'middle'. Freq. in f.ns., e.g. *Middelclyf* (Barkby), Middle Cl (Allexton), Middle Fd (Asfordby), *le Midulthorp* (Kirby Bellars), *Mydulfelde*, *Mydulfurlong'* (Cossington).

mīl OE, 'a mile'. ?Mile End (f.n. Sileby), *Milethorne* (f.n. Asfordby).

milking eModE, vbl.sb., 'drawing of milk from the udders of cows and other animals'. *the Milking close* (f.n. Old Ingarsby), Milking Cunnery (f.n. Loddington).

milne-stone ME, 'a millstone'. Millstone Lane. Mill Stone Furlong (f.n. Ratcliffe on the Wreake), *Millstone way* (Barkby).

mīl-stān OE, 'a mile-stone'. Milestone Fd (f.n. Rearsby).

minte OE, 'mint'. ?*Munetilandes* (f.n. Burton on the Wolds).

mōdor OE, 'a mother'. *the Modyr and the Chylde* (f.n. Thurmaston).

molde OE, 'earth, soil'. *Blackmole* (f.n. Asfordby).

mōr[1] OE, **mór** ON, 'a moor; marshland, barren wasteland, barren upland'. Black-a-Moors Spinney, Bleak Moor, Welsh Myers. *berkmore*, *Blackemore Leyes* (f.ns. Gaddesby), *Burstall moor*, Moor furlong (f.ns. Belgrave), *Copmore*, *Reedmore* (f.ns. Barsby), *Deydmore* (f.n. Skeffington), *Forthermorefeld*, *le more* (f.ns. Welby), *Hungarton More* (f.n. Hungarton), *Mannesmor*, Moor's Beck, *Osbernmor* (f.ns. Hoby), the Moor, *Redemoram* (f.ns. Barkby), *the Moore balke*, *Mordale* (f.ns. South Croxton), Moor Ley Cl (f.n. Saxelby), More Side (f.n. Asfordby).

morter ME, 'mortar, a mixture of cement, lime etc. with sand and water, that hardens and is used to join bricks and stones in building'. Morder Hill (f.n. Keyham), Morter Pits (f.n. Halstead).

mōt OE, 'a meeting, a moot'. Moat Hill. ?Moat Cl (f.n. Kirby Bellars), Moota Bush, *Mothowes* (f.ns. Barkby).

mote ME, 'a moat, a protective ditch filled with water around a building'. The Moat (f.n. South Croxton, Kirby Bellars), Mott Fd (f.n. Quenby).

mouldy ModEdial., 'the mole'. Mouldy Banks (f.n. Barsby, Queniborough).

mowing ME, vbl.sb., 'the action of mowing'; or ModE, 'the action of putting into a *mow* (a heap, a stack)'. Mowings Cl (f.n. Lowesby).

muk ME, 'dung, muck, dirt'. Muckheaps Furlong, *Mukslade* (f.ns. Queniborough), Muckhill Gate (Gaddesby), Muck Pitt (f.n. Thrussington), *Mukwong* (f.n. Kirby Bellars).

munuc OE, **monke** ME, 'a monk'. *atte Monekes* (Kirby Bellars), ?*Monke his land* (f.n. Gaddesby), *Monkesbroke*, *Monkesdam* (f.ns. Barrow upon Soar), *Monkkewode* (Welby), ?the Munchings (f.n. Rearsby).

mūs OE, **mús** ON, 'a mouse'. Mushill Lane. Mouse Dale Cl (f.n. Twyford), *Mouswell'* (f.n. Kirby Bellars), *Mowsholme* (f.n. Skeffington), Mushills Cls (f.n. Wymeswold), Mussells Furlong (f.n. South Croxton).

mustard OFr, ME, 'mustard'. *Mustardlond'* (f.n. Hoby).

mūða OE, 'a mouth'; later, topographically, 'a valley mouth'. *Deepdale Mouth* (f.n. Halstead).

***mylde** OE (Angl), 'soil, earth'. *Blackmyles* (f.n. South Croxton), *Blakemilde* (f.n. Barkby, Humberstone, Kirby Bellars, Cold Newton).

mylenweard OE, 'a keeper of a mill, a miller'. *Millewarde breche* (f.n. Wymeswold).

mylker ME, 'one who milks (cows etc.)'. Milkers Bridge (f.n. South Croxton), *Milkers Style* (f.n. Hoby).

myln, **mylen** OE, 'a mill', cf. **water-mylne**, **wind-mylne**. Barrow Mill, Belgrave Mill, Cossington Old Mill, Loddington Mill, Mill Fm, Mill Ho., Mill Lane (Asfordby, Thurmaston), Ratcliffe Mill, Rearsby Mill, Sileby Mill, Syston Mills, Thrussington Mill. Mills recorded only in MSS sources are: *Brokesbymilne* (Brooksby), the Mill (Frisby on the Wreake), *Queneby mylnes* (Quenby), *Quenildemilne* (Kirby Bellars). Freq. in f.ns., usually as the first el.: most common are Mill Hill (with various spellings in Barrow upon Soar, Burton on the Wolds, South Croxton, Welby), *Mill Holme* (Allexton, Barkby), *the milne close* (Barrow upon Soar, Cossington), *the Milne field* (Hamilton, Welby etc.).

mylnere ME, 'a miller'. (The) Millers Holme (f.n. Belgrave), *Robert the Millers close* (f.n. Burton on the Wolds), ?Millery Leys (f.n. South Croxton).

mylne-stede ME, 'a place where there is a mill; a place in which a mill stands'. *Alwolmilnestede*, *Bihouerthwertmilnestede* (f.ns. Hoby).

mýrr ON, 'a mire, a bog, swampy ground'. *Blackmires furlong* (f.n. Barkby), ?First Myres, ?Myres Cl (f.ns. Thorpe Satchville), *the Fullinge Mires* (f.n. Hoby), *Mirehilles* (f.n. Cossington), *the Mires* (f.n. Halstead, Humberstone, Tilton).

myry ME, adj., 'miry, muddy'. Merry Ditch, Merry Wong (f.ns. Sileby), ?Merrygate (Old Ingarsby), Miry Wong (f.n. Thrussington).

næss OE (Angl), **nes** ON, 'a projecting piece of land (esp. jutting into water or marsh)'. Burgness (f.n. Whatborough), ?Goose Nest (f.n. Wymeswold), ?*nesborrow* (f.n. Hungarton), the Nest Mdw (f.n. Thurmaston), Widness (f.n. Sileby).

nagge ME, 'a nag'. *nagges peece* (f.n. Seagrave).

nān mann OE, 'no man, nobody'. No Man's Land (f.n. Tilton).

napperone ME, 'an apron'; later used topographically of a small piece of land fronting another. the Apron piece (f.n. Allexton).

nattock ME, of unknown origin and meaning, poss. related to OE *næt* 'wet', with the OE noun suffix *-oc* which usually formed diminutives; perh. referring to a small wet patch of ground or to a small raised dry patch in wet ground. No Clock (f.n. Rearsby).

nearu OE, adj., 'narrow'. Narrow Lane. *Narowelandes* (f.n. Ratcliffe on the Wreake), *Narow Merstallus* (f.n. Cossington), *the Narrow Sick* (f.n. Hoby).

nēat OE, 'cattle'. *the neates pasture* (f.n. Ratcliffe on the Wreake, Rotherby), Neats Gate (East Norton), *the Neets Penn*, *Ould Neetes Penn* (f.ns. Barkby), *Neytysheyde*, *the towne net pasture* (f.ns. Barsby).

neetherd ME, 'a cowherd'. *Netharde yarde* (f.n. Cossington).

neoðera OE, adj., 'lower'. Netherfield. Fairly freq. in f.ns., e.g. *neþerbremhou*, *Nether doudale*, *Netherefouldoles*, *Nethur furlong'* (Cossington), *le Neþerehauedis* (Seagrave), *le Nethirdykefurlong'* (Barkby), *Stondelfnethirende* (Hoby). Nether Fd recurs (e.g. Allexton, Barkby etc.).

nest OE, 'a nest'. Cranes Nest (f.n. Belgrave, Hungarton), *Crokenest* (f.n. Cossington), *Crow nest furlong* (f.n. Gaddesby), *hennes neste* (f.n. Halstead), *the Swannysneste* (f.n. with various spellings in Baggrave, Rearsby, Saxelby).

netel(e) OE, 'a nettle'. Nettleham Fm. Nettlebed Furlong (f.n. Queniborough), Nettle Hill (f.n. Tilton).

nigon OE, num., 'nine'. *Nyne leyes* (f.n. Cossington), *Nyne Ridges* (f.n. Barkby Thorpe), *Nyngates* (Barsby).

nīwe OE, adj., 'new'. Cold Newton, *Newbold Folville*. *Hamerneudole*, New Field Paddock (f.ns. Hoby), *le New(e)close* (f.n. Launde), Newdales Furlong (f.n. Humberstone), *Newdikes* (f.n. Barkby), *Newdyke*, *Newedoles*, *Newegrove* (f.ns. Kirby Bellars), *Newlond* (f.n. Welby), Nuball end (f.n. Sileby).

nōk ME, 'a nook; a nook of land, a triangular plot of ground'. The Nook, Nook Fm, Spinney Nook. Freq. in f.ns.: esp. with a surn., signifying ownership, e.g. *Gilesnoke* (Barrow upon Soar), Huttins Nook (Gaddesby), *Sharpes nooke* (Cossington), Syson's nook (Loddington). A minor p.n. may be prefixed, e.g. Brancliff Nook (South Croxton), *Litel Barrow nooucke* (Seagrave), *Penborrow nook* (Hungarton); or a topographical feature, e.g. (the) Cliffe nooke (Hoby), *March Nook*, Spongs Nook (Asfordby), Wood Nooks (Cossington). Wild flora may be alluded to, e.g. *Daizy Nook* (Hoby), Hemplock Nook (Grimston); or birds, e.g. *Goose Nook* (Humberstone, Ratcliffe on the Wreake, Syston), *Wild(e)goose nooke* (Saxelby).

norð OE, ON, adj., 'northern, north'. East Norton; Northfield. the Northings (f.n. Barkby), *Northwillodole*, *le Norty* (f.ns. Barrow upon Soar).

nursery eModE, 'a piece of ground in which young plants or trees are reared until fit for transplantation; a nursery garden'. Harwood Nurseries, The Nursery. *Nursery* (f.n. Kirby Bellars, Welby), Nursery Cl (f.n. Cossington).

***ofer**[2] OE, 'a slope, a hill, a ridge'. ?*Heynorstorth* (f.n. Skeffington).

ofer[3] OE, prep., 'over, above, across'; difficult to distinguish from **uferra**. *Ouerdorindale* (f.n. Cossington), *Ouerthorpgate* (f.n. Kirby Bellars), *le Overholborne* (f.n. Barrow upon Soar), *over Posterne Hill* (f.n. Barkby Thorpe), *Ovirgreneslade*, *Ovirthewoldgate* (f.ns. Hoby).

ofer-þwart ME, adj., adv., 'across'. *Bihouerthwertmilnestede* (f.n. Hoby), *the ouerthourt furlong*, *the Overthwart Headland* (f.ns. Saxelby), *Overtwart the Way* (f.n. Skeffington).

omere OE, 'the bunting, the yellow hammer'. *Omber layes* (f.n. Humberstone).

open OE, adj., 'open, unenclosed'. Open Wards Cl (f.n. Sileby), *þe opon' woddes* (f.n. Skeffington).

ōra[1] OE, 'a flat-topped ridge with a rounded shoulder at one or both ends'. ?Copnor Hill, ?*Heynorstorth* (f.ns. Skeffington).

orceard, **ort-geard** OE, 'a garden'; later in OE, 'an orchard'. *Doctors Orch(y)ard* (f.n. Cossington), *Hall Orchard*, *le Orchard* (f.ns. Barrow upon Soar), Hall Orchard, *John Miller's Orchard*, *the Orcharde of Mr Bartholomew Brookesbie* (f.ns. Frisby on the Wreake), *Orchard corner*, *the Orchyard end*, *the Parsonage orchard* (f.ns. Queniborough), *Orchardleyes* (f.n. Skeffington), *the Parsonedge Orcharde* (f.n. Rotherby), Swan's Orchard (f.n. Humberstone).

osiery ModE, 'a place where osiers are grown'. the Osiery Beds (f.n. Tilton).

ōsle OE, 'an ouzle, a blackbird'. ?*Osebec* (f.n. Welby), ?*Owsley leyes* (f.n. Gaddesby), Ozingdale Leys (f.n. Barsby).

oter, **otor** OE, 'an otter'. Otterdale (f.n. Thrussington).

oxa (**oxna** gen.pl.) OE, 'an ox'. Ox Brook. Oxback Ditch, *Thoretheoxeneworeslaine* (f.ns. Hoby), *Oxe close* (f.n. Shoby), *Oxdale*, Oxen holes (f.ns. Thrussington), *le Oxdoles* (f.n. Wymeswold), Oxey (f.n. Loddington), *Oxholm* (f.n. Cossington, Queniborough), *le Oxlesuwe* (f.n. Barrow upon Soar).

oyser ME, 'osier, willow'. Welby Osier Beds. ?*Osebec* (f.n. Welby), Osier Beds, the Osier Holt (f.ns. Frisby on the Wreake).

packeman eModE, 'a pedlar'. Packmans Road (Walton on the Wolds).

pad ModEdial., 'a path', *v.* **pæð**.

***padde** OE, **padda** ON, 'a toad'. ?Padge Hall.

paddock eModE, 'a small field or enclosure; a plot of pasture land usually adjoining a house or stable'. Fairly freq. in f.ns.: often as a simplex, e.g. (The) Paddock (Allexton, Barkby, Barrow upon Soar, etc.); with a surn. indicating ownership, e.g. Checkitts Paddock (Belgrave), Pick's Paddock (Hoby), Randalls Paddock (Thrussington), Wildbores Paddock (Keyham); or size may feature, e.g. Great Paddock (Barsby), Little Paddock (Rotherby); or animals, e.g. Pony Paddock (Frisby on the Wreake), Ram Paddock (Rotherby).

***padduc** OE, **paddok** ME, 'a frog'. Paddecombs (f.n. Barsby), ?*Paddoccroft* (f.n. Kirby Bellars), *Padocusholm* (f.n. Queniborough).

pæð OE, **pad** ModEdial., 'a path'. Nosely Path (Tugby), *Oueston path* (Halstead), *Path Lands* (f.n. Hungarton), *over the foot pad* (f.n. Asfordby).

pale ME, 'a fence'. Pale Cl (f.n. Thrussington), *Palecroft* (f.n. Shoby), *ye Paylehedge furlong* (f.n. Walton on the Wolds).

paradis ME, 'a garden, an enclosed pleasure ground'. Paradise (f.n. Halstead, Tilton).

park OFr, ME, 'an enclosed tract of land for beasts of the chase'; later also 'an enclosed plot of ground, a field'. Kirby Park, Launde ~, Lowesby ~, Quenby ~, Saxelbye Park; Park Hill, Park Hill Lane, Park Ho., Parkleigh, Parks Fm. Crow Park (f.n. Kirby Bellars), Great Park (f.n. Brooksby), *Old Park* (f.n. Belgrave), (The) Park (f.ns. Barkby, Gaddesby, Ragdale, Tilton), Park Cl (f.n. Rotherby), The Parks (f.n. Barrow upon Soar, Wymeswold).

parkere ME, 'a park-keeper; an officer in charge of a park'. *Parckeers closs* (f.n. Launde).

parlur ME, 'a parlour, a private room'; in later f.ns. 'a secluded piece of ground'. House and Parlour (f.n. Lowesby), Nan Dennis Parlour (f.n. Seagrave), Kate's Parlour (f.n. Thurmaston), Little Parlour (f.n. South Croxton), The Parlour (f.n. Rearsby), the Parlour End (f.n. East Norton).

part ME, 'a part, a portion'. Barn Close First Part, Coopers Close Third Part (f.ns. Rotherby), Blunts Part, First Part, Horse Part, Mantons over part (f.ns. Tilton), Breaky Part (f.n. Keythorpe), Over Part (f.n. Ashby Folville).

parting ModE, ppl.adj.; in f.ns. prob. meaning 'that which may be divided or shared'. *the Parting(e) grass(e)*, *Parting grasse hades* (f.ns. Rotherby), Parting Peace (f.n. Barrow upon Soar), *Quacksike partinge grasse* (f.n. Humberstone).

pasture OFr, ME, 'a pasture, a piece of pasture-land'. Ashby Pastures, Pasture Fm. Common in f.ns.: esp. with reference to cattle, e.g. *the Cow Pasture* (Barkby, Cossington, Grimston, Frisby on the Wreake, Hoby, Humberstone, Rotherby), *the neates pasture* (Ratcliffe on the Wreake, Rotherby); or specifying a township, e.g. *Barkby Common Pasture* (Barkby), Belgrave Pasture (Belgrave), Burton Pasture (Burton on the Wolds). Location in a parish is sometimes alluded to, e.g. *Bille pasture* (Kirby Bellars), *Coplowe pasture* (Old Ingarsby). Recurring is *the common pasture* (Beeby, South Croxton, Frisby on the Wreake, Humberstone). Note *Rauenold pasture* (Kirby Bellars).

patche eModE, 'a patch; a small piece of ground'. Middle Patch (f.n. Seagrave).

pathwaye ME, 'a path'. *over the path waye* (f.n. Hungarton), *the path waye at Symkyns Townes end* (Humberstone).

paued(e), **paved** ME, ppl.adj., 'paved'. ?Paudy Lane (Barrow upon Soar, Seagrave).

***pearr(e)** OE, 'an enclosure'. Parr-gate Cl (f.n. Twyford).

pece OFr, ME, 'a piece; a piece or plot of land'. Freq. in f.ns.: with a surn. indicating ownership, e.g. *William Adlingtons piece* (Hoby), Hentons piece (Brooksby), *Mr Hills great piece* (Asfordby), *Mr Whalleys great peace* (Cossington); with the title of a township officer, e.g. *Constable peice* (Cossington), *Pindars piece* (Rotherby); with a common structure, e.g. the Bridge Pieces, Church Piece, *the Hall pieces*, *the Mill Piece* (Hoby), the Church peece (Rotherby), Workhouse Piece (Keyham); or with an indication of assignment to parish church requirements, e.g. *Bell peice* (Allexton), the Clock Pieces (Sileby). Size is sometimes alluded to, e.g. *The 40 rood piece* (Belgrave), Four Acre Piece (Hamilton); or agricultural processes, e.g. *the leavings peece* (Cossington),

Parting Peace (Barrow upon Soar), Ploughed piece (Gaddesby); or location, e.g. Fishpond piece (Frisby on the Wreake), Road Piece (Beeby). Recurring is Bull Piece (Belgrave, Cossington, Humberstone, Rotherby).

pegge ME, 'a peg; a post, a stump'. ?*Peghill* (f.n. Hoton).

penn[2] OE, 'a small enclosure, a fold'. Fairly freq. in f.ns.: esp. with a surn., e.g. Bennets Pen, *Johnsons Pen(n)* (Barkby), *Bentlys penn*, *Harris penn*, *Wells penn* (Humberstone), Iliffe's Penn, Warner's Penn (Belgrave); or with reference to cattle, e.g. Cowpens (Walton on the Wolds), *Neets Penn*, *Ould Neetes Penn* (Barkby). Common as a simplex, e.g. *the penns* (Humberstone), Pen Cl (Barkby, South Croxton, Hamilton), Pen Fd (Walton on the Wolds), Pen Mdws (Old Ingarsby).

personage ME, 'a parsonage'. The Old Parsonage; *the Parsonadge* (Asfordby), *The Parsonage Howse* (with various spellings in Allexton, Barkby, Beeby, Belgrave, Cossington, South Croxton, Hoby, Loddington, Rearsby, Saxelby, Seagrave, Walton on the Wolds). In f.ns., Bottom Parsonage Croft (Halstead), *the parsonage backside*, *the Parsonedge Orcharde*, *the personage land* (Rotherby), *the Parsonage Close* (Barsby, Beeby, Saxelby), *the Parsonage Hadland* (Humberstone), *the Parsonage land* (Sileby).

persone OFr, ME, 'a parson, a beneficed cleric'. *parson crafte hades* (f.n. Beeby), *the Parsones bushe*, *the Parsons home Close*, *the Parsons further close* (f.ns. Rotherby), Parsons Cl (f.n. with various spellings in Barrow upon Soar, Barsby, Halstead, Hoby, Prestwold, Rearsby, Shoby), *the Parsons Ground* (f.n. Hoby), *the Parsons Lane* (Saxelby), Parsons nook (f.n. Loddington), Parsons Plat (f.n. Burton on the Wolds), *the Parsons sevynstynt'* (f.n. Cossington), *the parsons ston(e)* (Asfordby).

pertre ME, 'a pear-tree'. *the peartree close* (f.n. Barkby, Rearsby), (*the*) *Pear Tree Furlong* (f.n. Hoby), Pear Tree Lane (Barsby).

peru OE, 'a pear', also poss. used as 'a pear-tree'. *Perecliues* (f.n. Saxelby).

pety ME, (OFr *petit*), adj., 'little'. Petty Lands (f.n. Barrow upon Soar).

pīc OE, 'a point; a pointed hill; a pike (the fish)'. *the Picks furlonge* (f.n. Humberstone), the Pikes (f.n. Gaddesby), *the Pike wonge*, *Pykwelle thorn* (f.ns. Rearsby).

piche ME, 'a pitch, a small plot of land marked out'. Pitch Gaps (f.n. Humberstone).

pie OFr, ME, 'a magpie'. Pye thorns (f.n. Loddington).

piggery ModE, 'a place where pigs are kept'. Piggery Fd (f.n. Rearsby).

pightel ME, 'a small enclosure, a croft'. Pightles (f.n. Hoby).

***pīl-āte (pīl-ātan** nom.pl.) OE, 'pill-oats'. *pilartonwong'* (f.n. Tilton).

***pinc** OE, 'a minnow'. *Pinchepol'* (f.n. Kirby Bellars).

***pinca** OE, 'a finch, a chaffinch'. ?*Pinchewang'* (f.n. Queniborough).

pinder ME, 'a pinder, an officer of a manor or township who impounded stray beasts'. *Pindars piece* (f.n. Rotherby), *Pinder balke* (f.n. Frisby on the Wreake), *Pindermedowedole* (f.n. Hoby).

pine ME, 'labour, toil, exertion, effort'. (the) Pineham (f.n. Quenby).

pingel ME, 'a small plot of ground'. Fairly freq., esp. as a simplex, e.g. (The) Pingle (f.ns. Barkby, Barkby Thorpe, Beeby, Belgrave, Burton on the Wolds, Cossington, Gaddesby, Hoton, Quenby, Welby), The Pingles (f.n. Barrow upon Soar), Pringle (f.n. Kirby Bellars). Otherwise prefixed by a surn. indicating ownership, e.g. *Marshalls pingle* (f.n. Cossington), *Jasper Simpson's Pingle* (f.n. Saxelby), *Worths Pingle* (f.n. Humberstone).

pīpe OE, 'a conduit, a pipe'. *Pipesdale* (f.n. Kirby Bellars).

pirige OE, 'a pear-tree'. *Peryfeld* (f.n. Welby).

pise OE, 'pease'. Pease Hill Fm, The Peaselands. Freq. in f.ns.: esp. in the compound *Peaseland(s)* (with various spellings in Cossington, South Croxton, Hoby, Kirby Bellars, East Norton, Queniborough, Rearsby, Skeffington, Wymeswold). *Pease Field* recurs (with various spellings in Cossington, Welby, Wymeswold), as does *Peasehill* (Cossington, South Croxton). Note also Pease Cl (Humberstone, Keythorpe), Pease Croft (Humberstone), *Peseclif* (Twyford), Peaseborough Sick, *Pesesike* (Wymeswold).

place OFr, ME, 'an area surrounded by buildings'; later 'a plot of ground, a residence'. Derby Gate Place (Keyham), *Doctor Chippingdales Ricke place*, *Mr Higgs Rickplace*, *the Ricke place* (f.ns. Humberstone), *Dokeplace* (Kirby Bellars), *Lombe place* (Barkby), *Power place* (Barkby Thorpe).

***plæsc** OE, 'a pool', **plash** ModEdial., 'a marshy pool'. *Lokholmeplassh* (f.n. Barrow upon Soar), *Plashe* (f.n. Cotes).

plain OFr, ME, 'a great open tract'; also 'a piece of flat meadowland'. The Plain (f.n. Quenby), The Plains (f.n. Seagrave), Plane (f.n. Sileby).

planke ME, 'a plank, a plank bridge'. Plank Furlong (f.n. Queniborough).

plantation ModE, 'a wood of planted trees'. Ash Plantation, Icehouse ~, Park ~, Rookery Plantation. Plantation Cl (f.n. Hoby), Plantation Pond, Plantation Watering (f.ns. Beeby).

planting ModE, vbl.sb., 'a plantation'. New Planting (f.n. Beeby).

plaster ME, 'gypsum, sulphate of lime'. Plaster Pit Barn. Plaster Hill Fd (f.n. Walton on the Wolds).

plat ME, 'a plot, a small piece of ground'; varies with **plot**. Fairly freq. in f.ns.: with a surn. indicating ownership, e.g. Clayton Plat, Leesons Platts (Beeby); as a simplex, e.g. *the Platts* (Burton on the Wolds, Cossington, Kirby Bellars); or locational, e.g. *the Brooke Platt*, *the Watering Platt* (Burton on the Wolds); or Church-related, e.g. *the gleab platt* (Cossington), Parsons Plat (Burton on the Wolds). Note also *the conie platt furlong* (Rearsby) and *the Gardeners Platt* (Burton on the Wolds).

plega OE, **plaga** (Angl), 'play, sport'; in p.ns. 'a place for games'. (the) Play Cl (f.n. Gaddesby).

plek ME, 'a small plot of ground'. Hemp Plick (f.n. Hoby).

plōg OE, **plógr** ON, 'a plough'. the Bottom Plough Cl (f.n. Twyford), *Daddyplowe* (f.n. Barrow upon Soar), Guilford Plough Fd (f.n. Keyham), Plough Cl (f.n. Asfordby, Beeby, Cold Newton, Seagrave, Syston, Tilton, Welby), Plough Piece (f.n. Tilton).

plōg(a)-land late OE, ME, **plógs-land** ON, 'a plough-land', a measure of land; in ON an acre; in the Danelaw, it was about 120 acres and was the equivalent of the carucate of DB or what a team of eight oxen could plough in the year. *the First Plowland* (f.n. Humberstone, Thurmaston), *the Whyne plowlands* (f.n. Barkby Thorpe).

plot late OE, ME, 'a small piece of ground'; varies with **plat**. Fairly freq. in f.ns.: with a surn. indicating ownership, e.g. *Matthew Babingtons plott*, *Caunts plot*, *John Goffs plot*, *John Oswins Home Plott*, *Pears his plott*, *Robt. Spencers plot* (Cossington), *Crosses Plots*, *Foulkes Plots*, *Johnsons Plot*, *Moores Plot* (Belgrave); with a locational prefix, e.g. (*the*) *Ash Plot(t)*, *the Barne Plott*, *the*

Highway plott, *the Home plott*, *the Lawmble plott*, *Round hill plott*, *Seagrave End Plott*, *Sun hill plot* etc. (Cossington), *the Cow Grange Plot*(*t*), *Grange Leyes Plott* (Burton on the Wolds). Note *the Poores Plot* (Belgrave, Cossington).

plūm-trēow OE, 'a plum-tree'. Plumb Tree Syke (f.n. Barkby), Plumtree Mdws (f.n. Kirby Bellars).

poket ME, 'a pocket'; topographically, alluding to a round field with a narrow entrance. the Pockets Mdw (f.n. Hoton).

pōl[1] OE, 'a pool'. Chalk Pool Hill, Reedpool Spinney. Freq. in f.ns.: with farm animals, e.g. Cow Pool (Barkby), *the Hogpoole*, *Swine poole* (Cossington), Horse Pool(s) (?Loddington, Rearsby, Skeffington); with minor wild life, e.g. *Cokpoole* (Barrow upon Soar), *Pinchepol'* (Kirby Bellars); with an el. or pers.n. indicating ownership, e.g. *Abbotispool* (Belgrave), *Swanildepol* (Skeffington); with an el. describing aspect, e.g. Bare Pool (Syston), *Blind Pool*, Foulpoole (Queniborough), *bloepoole*, Dunspool (Asfordby); with wild flora, e.g. Flag Pool (Barsby), Reed Pool (Hungarton), *Ruchepole* (Kirby Bellars), *Thornepoole* (Queniborough); as a simplex, e.g. (*le*) *Pole* (Barrow upon Soar), Pool Cl (Burton on the Wolds, Hoby).

pole ME, 'a long slender piece of wood'; later, 'a pole of definite length used as a measure', hence a lineal measure, esp. for land; as a measure of area, 30¼ square yards. (*the meadow called*) *the Poles* (f.n. Hungarton).

ponde ME, 'a pond, an artificial or natural pool'. the Pond Fd (f.n. Twyford).

pony ModE, 'a horse of any small breed'. Pony Paddock (f.n. Frisby on the Wreake).

port[2] OE, 'a market-town, a market'. *Porteford'*, *Portsike* (f.ns. Cold Newton), *Portegate* (Barrow on Soar), *Portfelde* (f.n. Thurmaston), *le Portstrete* (Thurmaston), *Porthill* (f.n. Lowesby), *port sicke* (f.n. Beeby), *Portisty* (f.n. Kirby Bellars).

port-weg OE, **port-wey** ME, 'a road to a (market) town, a road to a market'. The Portwey. *Port way* (Queniborough), *le Portwey*(*e*) (Barkby).

pot(t) late OE, 'a pot'. ?Butterpot Lane (Skeffington), ?*Potwelle* (f.n. Hoby).

potte ME, 'a deep hole, a pit, a deep hole in a river-bed'. ?Butterpot Lane (Skeffington), ?*Potwelle* (f.n. Hoby).

***pottere** OE, 'a pot-maker'. Potter Hill. ?*Poters meadow* (f.n. Launde), ?Potters Ford (Wymeswold).

potterye ME, 'a pot-factory, a potter's workshop'. Lowesby Pottery. the Pottery (f.n. Lowesby).

pouer(e) ME, adj., 'poor'; in modern f.ns., 'poor' for 'the poor' refers to land dedicated to poor-law relief or charity. Harringworth Poors Cl, Norton Poor's Land, Poors Piece (f.ns. East Norton), Poor Cl (f.n. Tilton), (The) Poor Mdw (f.n. Allexton), (the) Poor's Cl (f.n. Gaddesby), Poors Cls (f.n. Rearsby), *the Poores plot* (f.n. Belgrave, Cossington).

prairie ModE, 'a tract of level or undulating grass-land' (from OFr *praerie* 'a tract of meadow land'). the Prairie (f.n. Tilton).

prēost OE, 'a priest'. Prestwold; Priest Hill. *le Preestes Clos* (f.n. Barkby), *prestwellesike* (f.n. Seagrave), *Westprestgate* (Seagrave), *the priestes baulke*(*s*), Priest's Wong (f.ns. Hoby), *Priests sicke* (f.n. Skeffington).

primerose OFr, ME, 'the primrose' (*Primula veris*). Primrose Hill (f.n. Cold Newton).

prior OFr, ME, 'the prior of a religious house'. ?*Prior hadlaye* (f.n. Humberstone), *Prior(s) slade* (f.n. Skeffington), *Le Pryours Close* (f.n. Launde).

priorie ME, 'a priory'. Kirby Bellars Priory.

pudding ME, 'sticky land, clayey soil'. *Pudyng Row* (f.n. Belgrave).

***pull** OE, 'a pool'. *Leypulleyes* (f.n. Cossington).

pumpe ME, 'a pump'. Pump Lane. Pump Cl (f.n. Frisby on the Wreake), *the Pump Court* (Cossington), Pump Fd (f.n. Barkby).

pund ME, 'a pound, an enclosure into which stray cattle were put'. Pound (f.n. Cossington).

pynd OE, 'an enclosure, a pound'. *Pynslade* (f.n. Thurmaston).

***pynd-fald** OE, 'a pinfold'. Pinfold (f.n. with various spellings in Allexton, Barkby, Gaddesby, Humberstone, Hungarton, Kirby Bellars, Saxelby), Pinfold Cl (f.n. Belgrave), Pinfold Fd (f.n. Tilton), *Pinfold Green(e)* (f.n. Queniborough), Pinfold Mdw (f.n. Thorpe Satchville).

pynne-mylle eModE, 'a revolving drum in which hides were washed'. the Pyne miln Cl (f.n. Grimston).

pytt OE, 'a pit, a natural hollow, an excavated hole', cf. **cley-pytt**, **cole-pytt**, **marle-pytt**, **sand-pytt**, **stān-pytt**. Chalkpit Fm, Plaster Pit Barn. Freq. in f.ns.: common is Gravel Pit (South Croxton, Hoby, Humberstone, Loddington, Rotherby, Welby) and *Wash Pit* (Allexton, Ashby Folville, Hungarton, Lowesby). Location is sometimes signified, e.g. *Banlondpit*, *Longharepittes* (Hoby), *Sandhill pitt(e)s* (Barkby Thorpe); or (wild) fowl, e.g. *dukenpites* (Asfordby), Gunder Pits (Welby); or aspect, e.g. Bellpits (South Croxton), Blew Pits (Sileby), Rough Pit (Barsby). Note *the hempe pyttes* (Humberstone) and *Hordpit* (South Croxton).

quagmire eModE, 'a piece of wet and boggy ground, too soft to sustain the weight of men or larger animals; a quaking bog; a marsh'. *Quagmire* (f.n. Asfordby), *Quagmire Meadow* (f.n. Thorpe Satchville).

quake ME, 'a stretch of quake-fen'. Quakesick Spinney. *Quakefeild*, *Quake feyne*, Quakesyke Mdw (f.ns. Humberstone), *Quakefensike* (f.n. Hoby).

quarrelle ME, 'a quarry', cf. **quarriere**. ?*Quallerie* (f.n. Cossington), *Quarell'* (f.n. Humberstone).

quarrere ME, 'a quarry'. ?*Quallerie* (f.n. Cossington), Old Quarry (f.n. Tilton).

quarter ME, 'a quarter; a fourth part; a division of, or locality in, a larger area'. Quarter Mdw, Quarters (f.ns. Keythorpe), *quartreacres* (f.n. Cold Newton).

quillet(t) eModE, 'a strip of land'. Quillets (f.n. Loddington).

rabet ME, **rabbit** ModE, 'a rabbit'. Rabbit Hole (f.n. Rotherby), Rabbits Hill (f.n. Barkby), Rabbit Warren (f.n. Frisby on the Wreake, Wymeswold).

***rǣc** OE, 'a reach; a strip of land; a stretch of water'. *Long Ratche*, Thackracks (f.ns. Cossington).

***rǣde** OE, adj., 'suitable for riding on'. ?*Redegate* (Launde).

raile OFr, ME, 'a bar of wood'; later 'a fence or railing'. *the Reale Close* (f.n. Burton on the Wolds).

rake ME, 'a narrow path; a drove, a back-lane'. (*the*) *Longrake* (f.n. Thurmaston).

ramm OE, 'a ram'. Ram's Head Spinney. *the Rammes close* (f.n. with various spellings in Beeby, Hamilton, Humberstone, Old Ingarsby), Ram Fd (f.n. Baggrave), Ram Paddock (f.n. Rotherby).

raton OFr, **ratoun** ME, 'a rat'. *le Raton rowe* (Kirby Bellars).

rāw OE, 'a row', esp. of houses. *le Raton rowe* (Kirby Bellars).

rēad OE, adj., 'red'; in f.ns., sometimes difficult to distinguish from **hrēod**. Ratcliffe on the Wreake; Red Hill Barn, Red Hill Lane, Rodhill Fm. *raddells* (f.n. Beeby), *radecliue*, *Redehill* (f.ns. Kirby Bellars), Red Banks (f.n. Asfordby), *Rederodes*, Red Hill (f.ns. Barrow upon Soar), *le Rederodes* (f.n. Thurmaston), Red Hill Cl (f.n. Belgrave), Redlands (f.n. with various spellings in Barkby, Barrow upon Soar, Loddington, Queniborough, Rearsby, Rotherby, Saxelby).

rectory ModE, 'the residence appertaining to a rector'. The Rectory (Allexton, Asfordby, Beeby, Cossington, South Croxton, Hoby, Rearsby, Rotherby, Saxelby, Seagrave, Skeffington, Walton on the Wolds), Rectory Fm (Barrow upon Soar, Rearsby); *the Old Rectory* (The Vicarage, Ratcliffe on the Wreake).

rein ON, 'a boundary strip'. *Eastmore Reine* (f.n. Hoby), *the Raine* (f.n. Rotherby), *the Rane* (f.n. Ratcliffe on the Wreake), Rainy Mdw (f.n. Loddington), *Reygn midow hylle* (f.n. Skeffington).

reke-yard ME, 'an enclosure containing ricks, a stackyard'. *le Rekyart* (f.n. Barkby), *the Rick yard* (f.n. Rearsby), the Rickyard Fd (f.n. Thorpe Satchville).

***ric** OE, 'a narrow strip; a strip of land; a ditch'. *Rychemere* (f.n. Cossington), ?Sostridge Baulk (f.n. Wymeswold).

rickstead ModE, 'an enclosure containing ricks'. *Clement Dormans Rickstead*, *Mr James Wilsons Rickstead* (f.ns. Tugby), *the old rickstead* (f.n. Rearsby), Rickstade (f.n. Queniborough), the Rickstead Cl (f.n. East Norton).

riggett eModE, 'a furrow, a channel', ModEdial., 'a water-channel, a surface-drain'. Rigget (f.n. Twyford).

rinnende OE, pres.part., adj., 'running, flowing'. Running Furrow (f.n. Wymeswold).

risc, ***rysc** OE, 'a rush'. *Broade Rushe*, Rushes Sick (f.ns. Wymeswold), *Rischebusk'* (f.n. with various spellings in Barkby, Grimston, Hoby, Kirby Bellars, Rearsby), *Rishlandes* (f.n. Thurmaston), *Ruchepole* (f.n. Kirby Bellars), *Rush Balk* (f.n. Barkby), *Rushe meadowe* (f.n. Whatborough), The Rushes (f.n. Hoby), *Wadethornrissches*, *Waterresschus* (f.ns. Cossington).

***riscig** OE, **rushy** ModE, adj., 'rushy, growing with rushes'. Rushey Fields. (the) Rushy Cl (f.ns. Cossington, East Norton), Rushey Fd (f.n. Rearsby).

rise ModE, 'a piece of rising ground'. Paudy Rise Fm. Loddington Rise (f.n. Loddington).

rivulet eModE, 'a small stream'. the Ramble rivulet (Wymeswold).

***rod**[1] OE, 'a clearing'; difficult to distinguish from **rōd**[3]. ?*Brakenrodis*, ?*Brakrodis* (f.ns. Thurmaston), ?*Caterrode furlong'* (f.n. Belgrave), ?*Rodeburge* (f.n. Skeffington), ?Rod Hill (f.n. Ratcliffe on the Wreake).

rōd[3] OE, 'a rood of land, a rood measure'. *Achterode*, *Anchrerode* (f.ns. Kirby Bellars), *Banerodys*, ?*Brakenrodis*, ?*Brakrodis*, *le Smalrodes* (f.ns. Thurmaston), Black Roods (f.n. Thrussington), ?*Caterrode furlong'*, Forty Rood (f.ns. Belgrave), *Half rood furlong* (f.n. Tugby), Half Roods (f.n. Humberstone), *the Nether Roode* (f.n. Queniborough), *Rederodes* (f.n. Barrow upon Soar, Thurmaston), ?*Rodeburge* (f.n. Skeffington), ?Rod Hill (f.n. Ratcliffe on the Wreake), *Six Roods* (f.n. Sileby), *þe thre rudes* (f.n. Barkby), (*the*) *Three Roods* (f.n. Asfordby), *Twelfrodisbrod*(*e*) (f.n. South Croxton), *Whistobrooke fowre roades* (f.n. Seagrave).

rokke ME, 'a rock'. Red Rock Cl (f.n. Halstead).

rookery ModE, 'a colony of rooks'. The Rookery (Barrow upon Soar, Walton on the Wolds), Rookery Plantation. Rookery (f.n. Allexton).

round OFr, ME, adj., 'round'; in modern f.ns., sometimes describing fields not necessarily circular, but equilateral rather than oblong or irregular polygons. Round Hill, Round Spinney. Round Cl (f.n. Barrow upon Soar, Skeffington, Thrussington), Round Hill (f.n. Gaddesby, Tilton), *Round hill plott* (f.n. Cossington), *the Round Hole* (f.n. Hoby, Queniborough), Round Mdw (f.n. Old Ingarsby).

roundabout eModE, 'a circle, a circular object'. Roundabout (f.n. Ashby Folville).

ruddle eModE, 'a red dye for marking sheep, reddle'. ?Ruddle Cl (f.n. Barkby).

rūh[1] OE, adj., 'rough'. Common in f.ns., e.g. Roborough Cl (Humberstone), Rough Cl (Baggrave, Barkby, Barrow upon Soar and 6 other townships), Rough Mdw (Hoby, Seagrave), *rowdal* (Beeby), *Roweburrough haydes* (Rotherby), Rowlow Fd, *Rowwardis* (Skeffington).

rūst OE, 'rust'. ?the Rustalls (f.n. Twyford).

***rūt** OE, 'rough ground'. ?*Hamerroutes* (f.n. Hoby), *Routholme* (f.n. Queniborough).

***ryde** OE, 'a clearing'. *le rid* (f.n. Cossington).

***ryding** OE, 'a clearing'. *ladyredyng* (f.n. Welby), *Redyng* (f.n. Kirby Bellars).

ryge OE, 'rye'. Ryecroft Fm. *the Rie field* (f.n. Barkby), *Rie meare*, *Ryefoxoles*, *Ryele*, *the grete ~*, *the Lytul Ryfelde*, *Ryhades* (f.ns. Cossington), *le Riewong*, *Ryefeilde* (f.ns. Queniborough), *Riggate furlong* (f.n. Asfordby), *Riholm* (f.n. Hoby), Royal Knowl Cl (f.n. Sileby), Royborough (f.n. Ratcliffe on the Wreake), Rye Cl (f.n. Keyham, Rearsby), (*le*) *Ryefurlong* (f.n. Thurmaston), *Ryeland* (f.n. Skeffington).

rynel OE, **rundle** ModEdial., 'a runnel, a small stream'. *rundell* (Cossington).

sadol OE, 'a saddle'; topographically 'a saddle-shaped dip in hills'. *Sadelback* (f.n. with various spellings in Asfordby, South Croxton, Shoby, Thurmaston).

sǣd OE, 'seed; sowing'; in modern f.ns. often used of areas of sown grass. Old Seeds (f.n. Rearsby), Seagrass Mdw (f.n. Kirby Bellars), Seed Cl (f.n. Gaddesby, Humberstone, Keyham, Thrussington), Seed Fd (f.n. Barkby, South Croxton, Quenby), Seed Hill (f.n. Keyham), Seed Park (f.n. Cotes), the Seeds (f.n. Lowesby, Tilton), Seeds Fd (f.n. Brooksby), Top Seed (f.n. Welby).

sænna ODan, **senna** ON, 'a dispute, a quarrel'. *Senholm*(*e*) (f.n. Kirby Bellars), *Senlond* (f.n. South Croxton), *Sinam* (f.n. Saxelby).

sǽtr ON, 'a hill pasture, a shieling'. ?*Woolseters* (f.n. Saxelby).

salh OE (Angl), 'a willow, a sallow'. *the Sallowes* (f.n. Humberstone), the Sallow Watering (f.n. Wymeswold), *Salou* (f.n. Cold Newton), ?Thompsons Shallows (f.n. Barrow upon Soar).

salt[1] OE (Angl), 'salt'. *Saltgate* (Kirby Bellars), *Saltestrete* (Wymeswold).

salt[2] OE (Angl), adj., 'salty, brackish'. *Longesaltfen* (f.n. Barsby), *Saltfengate* (South Croxton).

saltere OE (Angl), 'a salt-merchant'. *Hamersalterewonges*, *Salterforde* (f.ns. Hoby), *the Salters Close* (f.n. Keyham, Rearsby), *Saltergate* (Barkby, Thurmaston), Saltersford Bridge (Humberstone), *Sawtrum Stones* (f.n. Asfordby).

sand OE, **sandr** ON, 'sand, sandy soil'. Sandlen's Lodge. Common in f.ns.: e.g. *the dead sand*(*e*) (Rearsby), Sanders (Hoby, Hoton), *Sand feylde* (with various spellings in Barkby, Hoby, Ragdale), Sand Hill(s) (Barkby, Humberstone, Loddington), Sandlands (Barsby, Gaddesby, Kirby Bellars).

***sand-hol** OE, **sand-hole** ME, ModE, 'a sand-pit, a place from which sand is extracted'. Sandhole (f.n. Hoton), Sand Hole Platt (f.n. Cossington), Sandholes (f.n. Barsby).

sandig OE, adj., 'sandy'. (*the*) *Sandie Furlonge* (f.n. Barrow upon Soar), *Sandy lands*, *Sandy lays* (f.ns. Hungarton), Sandy Leys (f.n. Ratcliffe on the Wreake, Thrussington), Sandy Nook (f.n. Thorpe Satchville).

sand-pytt OE, 'a sand-pit', cf. **sand-hol**. Sandpit(s) (f.ns. with various spellings in Barrow upon Soar, Gaddesby, Hungarton, Kirby Bellars, Walton on the Wolds), Sandpit Cl (f.n. Cossington, Thorpe Satchville, Thrussington), *Sandpitt hill* (f.n. Hoby, Skeffington), *Sandpit leas* (f.n. Asfordby, Cold Newton).

***sāpere** OE, **sopere** ME, 'a soap-maker'. ?Sopers Cl (f.n. Belgrave).

scabbed ME, adj., 'having scabs'; topographically perh. describing ground with a scarred appearance. ?Scabdale (f.n. Old Ingarsby).

scacol OE, 'a shackle', in p.ns. used esp. in the sense 'a place where animals are tethered or shackled'; note also **shackle** ModEdial., 'quaking grass', which may have a long history (*v.* Elements **2** 98–9). Shackell Headland, Shackell Mdw (f.ns. Twyford).

sceaga, **scaga** OE, 'a small wood, a copse, a strip of woodland'. *Green shawe* (f.n. Cossington).

sceard, **scard** OE, 'a cleft, a gap'. *Brodescherd* (f.n. Barkby), *Schardewelforlong* (f.n. Cossington).

scearp, **scarp** OE, adj., 'sharp, pointed; steep'. ?Shipley Hill. *Charphyll* (f.n. Cossington), *Sharplegate* (Ratcliffe on the Wreake).

scēat OE, 'a corner of land, an angle, a projecting piece of land'. ?*le Shetewong* (f.n. Skeffington).

sceld OE, 'a shield, a protection', whence 'a shelter'. ?*Sheldisaker* (f.n. Kirby Bellars), *Tipperscheld'* (f.n. Skeffington).

scelf OE, 'a ledge, shelving terrain'. *le Schelland* (f.n. Kirby Bellars).

sc(e)oppa OE, 'a booth, a shed'. Blacksmith's Shop (Cossington, South Croxton, Gaddesby, Keyham, Loddington, Tugby), Carpenter's Shop (Cossington), Wheelwright's Shop (Cossington, Gaddesby). Shop Lane (Halstead).

sc(e)ort OE, adj., 'short'; also used as a sb. Common in f.ns., e.g. *Scortfoshol'*, *Schortfurholm*, *Schortsowtholme* (Cossington), *le Schortewolde*, *Schortmerewong*, Short Mdw (Barkby), *Scortewellebrok* (Barrow upon Soar), *Schort schepis wong'* (Belgrave); *the short*(*e*) (Rearsby).

scēot[3] OE, 'a steep slope'. the Herring Shoot, the Long Hedge Shoot (f.ns. Walton on the Wolds), *Long Shoot* (f.n. Humberstone), Prestwold Lane End Shoot (f.n. Hoton), *the Sonne shoote* (f.n. Cossington).

scēp OE (Angl), 'sheep'. Sheep-Le Fm, ?Shipley Hill. *Sapehou* (f.n. Saxelby), *schepis wong'* (f.n. Belgrave), Sheep Dole (f.n. Cossington), *the Sheep leyes* (f.n. Burton on the Wolds).

scēp-cot OE (Angl), 'a shelter for sheep'. *Schepecotes* (f.n. Cossington), Sheep Cote (f.n. Thrussington), Sheepcote Leys (f.n. Cold Newton), *Shepecote close* (f.n. Cold Newton, Shoby, Walton on the Wolds).

scēp-hirde OE (Angl), 'a shepherd'. *Sheapheards borde* (f.n. South Croxton), *Sheepheard borde* (f.n. Hungarton), *Sheperdowe*, Shepherds Hill Fd (f.ns. Barrow upon Soar), Shepherds House (Tilton), ?Shepherds nook (f.n. Belgrave).

***scēp-hūs** OE (Angl), 'a shelter for sheep', cf. **scēp-cot**. *the sheephosse* (f.n. Beeby).

scēp-wæsce OE (Angl), 'a place for dipping sheep, a sheep-wash'. Sheepwash (Allexton, Sileby, Wymeswold).

scīr[1] OE, 'a shire, a jurisdiction, an administrative district'. ?Circles (f.n. Ratcliffe on the Wreake), ?*Schirdiccotes* (f.n. Thurmaston), ?*Shirremilneholm* (f.n. Skeffington).

scīr[2] OE, adj., 'bright, clear'. ?*Schirdiccotes* (f.n. Thurmaston), ?*Shirremilneholm* (f.n. Skeffington).

scite OE, 'shit, dung'. ?*le Shetewong* (f.n. Skeffington).

scofl OE, 'a shovel'. *Scoueldale* (f.n. Burton on the Wolds), *shouells* (f.n. Humberstone).

***scofl-brǣdu** OE, 'a shovel's breadth', i.e. a very narrow strip of land. *schulbrode* (f.n. Hungarton), *Scouilbrodes* (f.n. Hoby), Shelboard (f.n. Barsby), *Shelboards* (f.n. Saxelby), ?Shobries Cl (f.n. Thrussington), *sholbreade* (f.n. Asfordby), *Shovell broad* (f.n. Rotherby).

***scor(a)** OE, 'a river-bank, a steep slope'. *Schoretoft* (f.n. Skeffington), *Schormere* (f.n. South Croxton).

scoure eModE, 'a channel with fast-flowing water used for cleansing; a drain'. *the parsonadge scoure* (Asfordby), *the Scower* (Frisby on the Wreake).

scræf OE, 'a hole in the ground' and 'a hovel, a hut'. *the screave leys* (f.n. Humberstone), Screaves Furlong (f.n. Barsby).

***scrubb** OE, 'a shrub, brushwood, a place overgrown with brushwood'. *the Ouldes shrubbes* (f.n. Seagrave), (*the*) *Shrubb feild* (f.ns. Cossington, Sileby), *the Shrubbs* (f.n. Hoby), Shrubb Sty (f.n. Sileby), *Shrubland* (f.n. South Croxton), *Shrubs* (f.n. Queniborough), *the Shurbbs alias Srubbs* (f.n. Burton on the Wolds).

scrubby ModE, adj., 'covered with scrub or brushwood'. *the Scrubby close* (f.n. Burton on the Wolds).

scrybb OE, 'a shrub, brushwood, a place overgrown with brushwood'. Scribb (f.n. Tugby), *Scrybestreme* (Skeffington).

sculdor OE, 'a shoulder'; topographically alluding to the brow of a hill. Shouldercoates (f.n. Twyford).

scylfe OE (Angl), 'a ledge, shelving terrain'. Shil(l)gates Furlong (f.n. Queniborough).

scypen, scipen OE, 'a cow-shed'. *Ketilsschepine* (Kirby Bellars), ?Skip-a-dale (f.n. South Croxton).

scyte OE, 'a shooting', prob. used of 'a steep slope'; also used later of 'a steep channel of water, a rush of water, a mill-shoot'. *dale schyte* (f.n. Humberstone).

***scytel**[2] OE, adj., 'unstable'; topographically perh. referring to shaky or unstable ground such as quake-fen. ?*Skittils* (f.n. Tugby).

scyt(t)el, scyt(t)els OE, 'a bolt, a bar'; in p.ns. prob. used of something which could be bolted or barred. *Scuitelsty* (f.n. South Croxton), ?*Skittils* (f.n. Tugby).

sēað OE, 'a pit, a hole'. Seagrave.

secg[1] OE, 'sedge, a reed, a rush'. *Seghoome*, *Segwonge* (f.ns. Asfordby), *þe Seygys* (f.n. Cossington), ?Sledge Cl (f.n. Barrow upon Soar).

***sende** OE, 'a sandy place'. *Sendebusk* (f.n. South Croxton).

seofon OE, num., 'seven'. *the Glebe Seaven Landes* (f.n. South Croxton), *the Parsons Sevynstynt'* (f.n. Cossington).

(ge)set OE, 'a place for animals, a fold'. ?*Anstilsike* (f.n. Seagrave), the Wygmore Sets (f.n. Thurmaston).

***set-copp** OE, 'a hill with a fold', poss. also 'a seat-shaped hill', i.e. a flat-topped hill. *Setcophul* (f.n. Hoby), *Seytcoppis* (f.n. Humberstone).

severall eModE, adj., 'privately owned', referring to land in individual ownership as opposed to common land. *the severall landes* (f.n. Rotherby).

shed ModE, 'a shed, a slight structure built for shelter or storage'. Black Shed Fd (f.n. Tilton), Shed Cl (f.n. Hoby), Shed Fd (f.n. Barkby), Shed Piece (f.n. Brooksby).

shepe-gate ME, 'pasturage for sheep' (*v*. Sheep Gates, L **2** 244). *Sheepgate* (f.n. Cossington), Sheepgate Cl (f.n. Walton on the Wolds).

sīc OE, 'a small stream', **siche** ME, 'a piece of meadow along a stream'. *Northsichehede*, *Northsicheshende* (f.ns. Gaddesby), Willow Sich (f.n. Baggrave).

sīde OE, 'a side; the long side of a slope or hill, a hill-side, the land alongside a stream, village, wood, etc.'. *Arpingate Side*, *Lusty gate side*, Streethill Side Furlong, Thurn Side Furlong (f.ns. South Croxton), *the hie way side*, Marshside, *Melton Gate side*, More side (f.ns. Asfordby), *Northmedowgate syde* (f.n. Humberstone), Side Cl, *Syde furlong*, Townside Cls (f.ns. Belgrave), Thurnside (f.n. Barsby), *ye Towne Side* (f.n. Allexton, Barkby, Cossington), *ye Water syde* (f.n. Cossington).

***sīdling** OE, ME, 'a strip of land lying alongside a stream or some other piece of land'. *ye Hall sideling* (f.n. Seagrave).

sík ON, 'a ditch'; later 'a piece of meadow along a stream'. Catsick Hill, Catsick Lane, Little Gunsel, Quakesick Spinney. Freq. in f.ns.: with a minor p.n., e.g. *Depedalesyke* (Kirby Bellars), *Ladyacar sicke*, *Smereberwesyke* (Barkby); with names for associated watercourses, e.g. *Caldwellesyke* (Barrow upon Soar), *Foxwellesyke*, *Gosewelsyke* (South Croxton), *Frot(t)hewellessyke* (Barkby); or fen, e.g. *Fensyke* (Kirby Bellars), *Quakefensike* (Hoby); with an el. specifying wild flora, e.g. *Burblad(e)syk* (Belgrave), *Green(e) willow Sick* (Asfordby), *Thurne sicke* (South Croxton); or size/shape, e.g. *Broadsick* (South Croxton, Cossington, Saxelby), *the Narrow Sick* (Hoby), *the whorle sicke* (Hungarton). A surn. may be prefixed indicating ownership, e.g. *Armson sicke* (South Croxton), *Rowell Sick(e)* (Barkby), *wattes sicke* (Beeby). Minor local buildings sometimes occur, e.g. *Bossycke*, *Mill Sick* (South Croxton), *Toftessike* (Frisby on the Wreake).

sikeman ME, 'a person who is ill'. *Sekemaneshous* (Kirby Bellars).

six OE., num., 'six'. *ye Six lands* (f.n. Seagrave), (the) Six Rood Furlong (f.n. Wymeswold), *Six Roods* (f.n. Sileby), *Syxhows* (f.n. Hungarton).

skáli OWScand, 'a temporary hut or shed'. Shoby Scholes. *Scole furlong(e)* (f.n. Asfordby).

skant ME, adj., 'stinted in measure, not abundant, existing in barely sufficient amount or quantity'. *Skonte brooke* (Saxelby).

skegg ON, 'a beard'; used topographically of something jutting out (and perh. covered with scrub). Skeg Hill. *Hamerskeges*, *Skeggedale* (f.ns Hoby).

skial ODan, 'a boundary'. ?*Skelund* (f.n. Kirby Bellars).

skil ON, **scyl** late OE, 'a boundary' ?*stylbecke* (Wymeswold).

skinn ME, 'an animal hide'. Dry skins (f.n. Loddington).

skot ON, 'a projecting piece of land, a projecting hill'. *Skotgate* (Skeffington).

slæd OE (Angl), 'a valley'. Common in f.ns., e.g. *Benelondeslade*, *Lytelbaro slade*, *the Slade Baulk* (Barrow upon Soar), *dallyslade*, *fulwell slade*, *greine hyll slade*, *Mannsfyld slade* (Humberstone), *Harewelslade*, *Holands slade*, *Holewell slade* (Barkby).

slag ME, adj., 'slippery with mud'; poss. used of 'a place slippery with mud'. ?The Slag (f.n. Walton on the Wolds).

slagg eModE, 'refuse matter separated from metals in the process of smelting'. ?The Slag (f.n. Walton on the Wolds).

slang eModE, 'a long narrow (sometimes sinuous) piece of land; the ground beside a (winding) stream'. Hoothill Slang. Little Slang (f.n. Seagrave), Slang (f.n. Tilton), the Slang (f.n. Cold Newton, Rearsby, Thorpe Satchville, Twyford), The Slangs (f.n. Barkby).

slash eModE, 'a gash, a deep cut', poss. transferred topographically to 'a cleft in the ground'; note also dial. *slashy* 'miry' and American English *slash* 'a piece of wet or swampy ground overgrown with bushes'. Slash (f.n. Prestwold), *Slash* (f.n. Syston).

slidor OE, adj., 'slippery'. Slither Wong (f.n. Thrussington).

slidyng ME, ppl.adj., 'slippery, steeply sloping'; as a sb. 'a slippery, steeply sloping place'. (the) Slidings (f.n. Gaddesby).

sling ModEdial., 'a long narrow piece of land', *v.* **slang**. Long Slings (f.n. Humberstone), *Sling meadow hill* (f.n. Skeffington).

slipe ME, 'a slip, a long narrow piece of land'. Pinfold Slip (f.n. Thorpe Satchville), the Slip (f.n. Frisby on the Wreake, Gaddesby, Kirby Bellars), Slip (f.n. Seagrave, Tilton), the Slipe (f.n. Rotherby).

slipor OE, adj., 'slippery'. *Sliperhook(e)* (f.n. Asfordby).

slory ME, 'thin, sloppy mud'. Slarry Cl (f.n. Thorpe Satchville).

smæl OE, adj., 'narrow, thin'. *Smalbregge* (Welby), *Smaldolus*, Smallbrook(e) (f.ns. Queniborough), *Smal(e)hilles* (f.n. Twyford), *Smalmedow*, *Smalrodes* (f.ns. Thurmaston), *smale more* (f.n. Asfordby), *Smalethornes* (f.n. Kirby Bellars), *Small Acres* (f.n. Barrow upon Soar), *smallgatte* (Hungarton), Smallings (f.n. Wymeswold), Smallthorns (f.n. Hoton), Smellings (f.n. Thorpe Satchville); used as a sb. in *le Longesmale* (f.n. Queniborough).

smeoru OE, 'fat, grease, lard', **smjǫr** ON, 'grease, butter'; in f.ns. alluding to rich pasturage, productive of milk and butter. Smallborough (f.n. Barkby), *Smereberwe* (f.n. Queniborough).

smið OE, **smiðr** ON, 'a smith, a worker in metal'. ?Smith Cl (f.n. Walton on the Wolds), ?Smithill (f.n. Beeby), ?Smith Mdw (f.n. Barkby), *lez Smithleies*, *Smithisbuttes* (f.ns. Barrow upon Soar), *Smithishakyr* (f.n. Kirby Bellars), *smythesyke* (f.n. Hungarton).

smiððe OE, 'a smithy, a metal worker's shop'. *Smithie meadowe* (f.n. Halstead), Smithy Cl (f.n. Cossington).

snape ME, 'a piece of poor pasture'. *Snapis* (f.n. Skeffington).

snotte ME, 'the mucus of the nose, snot'; topographically 'oozing mud', **snotty** eModE, adj., 'slimy'. *snottybott'* (f.n. Hungarton).

***sōg**, ***sōh** OE, **sogh** ME, 'a bog, a swamp', **sough** ModEdial., 'a bog, a marsh; a drain'. *nedd'soue*, *ouersoue* (f.ns. Hungarton), the Sough (f.n. Keyham), Sough brook (Twyford), Sough Garden (f.n. Cossington), *Souuesdale* (f.n. Kirby Bellars), *Trunsowhyll* (f.n. Rearsby).

soss ModEdial., adj., 'wet, soaking'. ?Sostridge Baulk (f.n. Wymeswold).

sowthward ME, adj., 'lying towards the south'. Southward Dole, the Southward Pasture (f.ns. Thurmaston).

spang OE, 'a clasp, a buckle', topographically as **spong** ModEdial., 'a long narrow strip of land'. *a little spong called the Apron* (f.n. Allexton), *le Sponges* (f.n. Hoby), *Spongs Nook* (f.n. Asfordby).

spearwa OE, 'a sparrow'. *Sparoughhull* (f.n. Wymeswold).

spell OE, 'speech, discourse'; used in p.ns. esp. of places where speeches were made in assemblies and freq. denotes a hundred-site or other meeting-place. Spellows Mdw (f.n. Asfordby).

***spic** OE, 'brushwood'. Spickacre Fd (f.n. Barkby).

spinele OE, 'a spindle'; used in p.ns. of something resembling a spindle in shape. *Spensar Spindle* (f.n. Barkby), Spindle Banks (f.n. South Croxton).

spinney ME, 'a copse, a small plantation'. Barkby Thorpe Spinney, Black-a-Moors ~, Briery Leys ~, Brooksby ~, Conduit ~, Fishponds ~, Fox Croft ~, Fox Holes ~, George's ~, Gorse ~, Hall ~, Moat Hill ~, Quakesick ~, Red pool ~, Rigget's ~, Round Hill ~, Watson's Spinney. *le Espinee*, Hallsick Spinney, Spinney Cl, Thorney Spinney (f.ns. South Croxton), *Loesby Spiney* (f.n. Halstead), Oat Field Spinney, *Old Spiny* (f.ns. Baggrave), *Spenyfeld* (f.n. Welby), (the) Spinnies (f.n. Lowesby), Spinney Cl (f.n. Barkby, Frisby on the Wreake, Gaddesby, Old Ingarsby, Rotherby), Spinney Fd (f.n. Ragdale), Spinney Headland (f.n. Ashby Folville), Spinney Mdw (f.n. Allexton, Hoby), Spinney Merrygate (Old Ingarsby), Spinney Wolds (f.n. Cossington).

spīr OE, 'a spike, the blade of a plant; reeds, rushes'. *Redespire* (f.n. Twyford).

spitel ME, 'a hospital, a religious house, a house of the Knights Hospitallers'. ?*Spigellsti* (f.n. Barsby), *Spitelcroft* (f.n. Queniborough), *Spittle Close*, *Spytell felde* (f.ns. Cold Newton); note also *Newton Grange alias Le Spittell alias Le Spittell Grange alias Le Spittell Hills*).

spotte ME, 'a small plot of ground'. Garden Spot, Mill Spot, ?the Spot (f.ns. Halstead), Mill Spot, Top Spot (f.ns. Tilton).

spoute ME, 'a spout, a gutter'. ?the Spot (f.n. Halstead).

sprigge ME, 'a shoot, a twig or spray of a plant or shrub'. Sprig Thorne (f.n. South Croxton).

spring[1] OE, 'a spring, a well, the source of a stream'. Beeby Spring, Spring Grange, Springfield, Springfield Fm, Springfield Hill. *Cawdewell Springe* (f.n. Seagrave), Dale Spring Cl (f.n. Hoton), Spring Cl (f.n. Beeby, Burton on the Wolds, Cotes, Lowesby, Rotherby), *Springe Poole bauck* (f.n. Halstead), Springfield (f.n. Barkby, South Croxton), Spring Merry Gate (Old Ingarsby), *the Vicars Springes* (f.n. Thrussington), *Wellespringe* (f.n. Barrow upon Soar).

squar(e) ME, adj., 'square'. Square Cl (f.n. Seagrave).

staca OE, 'a stake'. *Stacfurlang'* (f.n. Cossington), *Stackhill bridge hooke* (f.n. South Croxton).

stæf OE, 'a staff, a stave, a rod'. *Staffhopps* (f.n. Cold Newton).

stæpe OE, 'a step'. ?Step Cl (f.n. Ashby Folville).

***stak-ȝeard** ME, 'an enclosure for ricks, a stack-yard'. Stackyard (f.n. Beeby, Cold Newton), Stackyard Cl (f.n. Frisby on the Wreake), Stack Yard Fd (f.n. Barrow upon Soar, Hoby).

stakkr ON, 'a stack, a rick'. Stack House Fm, Stack Cl (f.n. Seagrave), Stackups (f.n. Lowesby), *Stakys* (f.n. Humberstone).

stall OE (Angl), 'a place', esp. 'a standing place, a stall for cattle etc.', 'a site (of a building or other object or feature)' (*v.* Sandred 37–41). Storkit Lane. *les Limstalles* (f.n. Thurmaston).

stallion ME, 'an uncastrated male horse'. Stallions Fd (f.n. Tilton).

stān OE, 'a stone, stone'; when used as a first el., often has the adj. function 'stony', esp. in the names of roads, streams, fords and plots of ground; or may refer to something stone-built. Humberstone; Washstones Bridge. Very freq in f.ns.: referring to standing stones, boundary stones etc., e.g. *above the stone*, *Herstenhow* (Cossington), Cussington Stone (Sileby), *Doleston* (Rearsby), *Drakestan* (Burton on the Wolds), Horson Hill (Loddington), *Horston'*, *Little Hairston* (Humberstone), *the parsons ston(e)* (Asfordby), *le Witeston'* (Barkby); to stone structures, e.g. *Stanbryg* (South Croxton), *the stone bryge* (Asfordby); to roads, e.g. *Stongate* (Cossington); to fords, e.g. *Stanford* (Barrow upon Soar); to stony land, e.g. *Schortstones* (Hoby), *stanlond* (Kirby Bellars), Stonefield Cl (Allexton). Recurring is *Stonhill* (Barkby Thorpe, Cossington), ?*Standilwong'* (Queniborough).

***stand** OE, 'a stand, a standing-place'. ?*Standilwong'* (f.n. Queniborough).

standard ME, 'the standing stump of a tree'. *Standard'* (f.n. Kirby Bellars), *Standart* (f.n. Burton on the Wolds, Hoby), *Standartgate* (Seagrave), *Standart hill*, *Standordfeld* (f.ns. Seagrave).

standing ME, 'a standing place, a place in which cattle and horses may stand under shelter'. Cow Standing (f.n. Gaddesby).

stān-(ge)delf OE, 'a stone-quarry'. *Stondelues* (f.n. Hoby).

stānig OE, 'stony, rocky, made of stone'. *Stanilandes* (f.n. with various spellings in Barrow upon Soar, Barsby, Beeby, Cossington, South Croxton, Kirby Bellars), Stoney Leys (f.n. Rearsby), *Stonie hill* (f.n. Cossington), *Stonigate* (Hoby), *Stonyforth* (f.n. Barrow upon Soar), Stonyfurlong (f.n. Asfordby), *Stonyhyll* (f.n. Kirby Bellars), *Stony More* (f.n. Rearsby), *Stonyslade* (f.n. Barsby).

***stān-pytt** OE, **stone-pit** ModE, 'a stone-pit, a quarry'. Stone Pit Lodge. *Oselweston Stone pittes* (f.n. Halstead), *Stonepit furlong* (f.n. Walton on the Wolds), Stone Pit Mdw (f.n. Loddington), Stone Pits (f.n. Halstead, Tilton), *Stone Pitt Close* (f.n. Burton on the Wolds, East Norton).

stapol OE, 'a post'. *Stapelfurlong'* (f.n. Queniborough).

star ODan, 'sedge'. *Star ende* (f.n. Skeffington).

stede OE, 'a place, a site, a locality'. Halstead. ?*Elsted* (f.n. Skeffington), *Leyrstedes* (f.n. Barkby), *Milnested* (f.n. South Croxton), *Wymanstead* (f.n. Cossington).

steinn ON, 'stone'; used adj. as 'stony'. *Elsteyn* (f.n. Skeffington), Stain Bridge (Twyford), *Staingate* (Skeffington), *Stainsborough* (f.n. Hungarton), *Stayne leas* (f.n. Seagrave), *Stean Hill* (f.n. Asfordby), ?Steans (f.n. Tilton), Steen Mdw (f.n. Humberstone), *Steinclif*, *Steyning* (f.ns. Cold Newton), *Steynho* (f.n. Gaddesby), *Steynhull* (f.n. Kirby Bellars), *Steynrows* (f.n. Barsby).

steort OE, 'a tail'; used topographically of 'a tail or tongue of land, the end of a piece of land, a projecting piece of land'. *Haghtrodesterte* (f.n. Kirby Bellars).

stepping-stone ModE, 'a stone for stepping on, a stone placed in the bed of a stream or on muddy or swampy ground to facilitate crossing on foot'; usually pl., referring to a line of such stones. Stepping Stones Ford. Stepping Stones (f.n. Queniborough).

stīg OE, **stígr** ON, 'a path, a narrow road, an upland path' (*v.* **sty-gate**); almost impossible to distinguish formally from **stig** 'a sty, a pen', and as in some cases the el. develops late as *stile*, it thus may be confused also with names formed with **stigel**. Examples are: *Abovedingesti* (f.n. Hoby), *darbie style*, *bawlandes stye* (Asfordby), *Bene(e)hilstye*, *Understile* (Barrow upon Soar), Breach Sty (Sileby), *Greene Stye* (Cossington), *Grenesti*, *Portisty* (Kirby Bellars), *Milkers Stile* (Hoby), *Pease Hill Stye* (South Croxton), *Spigellsti* (Barsby), Tween Stiles (f.n. Thrussington).

stig OE, 'a pen, a sty'. Almost impossible to distinguish from **stīg**, **stígr**. Such f.ns. as the following may reasonably be attributed to this el.: *Rauenesedesti*, *Rauenesty* (Barkby), *Scuitelsty* (South Croxton), *le Steyes* (Queniborogh), *steyse* (Hungarton), Sties (Wymeswold), *the sty* (Ratcliffe on the Wreake), *le Styes* (Kirby Bellars), Styes Cl (Twyford), *Swynstyse* (Humberstone), the Upper Stigh, Viccars Sty Furlong (Queniborough).

stigel OE, 'a stile'; topographically, prob. 'a steep ascent'. Bennets Stile (f.n. Frisby on the Wreake), *Cobbe stile* (f.n. Barsby), Cow Close Stile (f.n. Shoby), *Henses stile* (f.n. Tugby), Normans Close style (f.n. Rearsby), *Oke stile* (f.n. Whatborough), Stiltons (f.n. Loddington), Swan Style (f.n. Old Ingarsby), White Close Stile (f.n. Ratcliffe on the Wreake).

stille OE, adj., 'peaceful, quiet'. ?*stylbecke* (Wymeswold).

stint ME, 'a portion of common meadow set apart for an individual's use'. *Doctors stints*, *the Parsons sevynstynt'* (f.ns. Cossington), *the Middle Stint* (f.n. Hungarton), *the North ~*, *the South Stints* (f.ns. Barkby), *the Pitt stints*, *the Styntes* (f.ns. Ratcliffe on the Wreake).

stoc OE, 'a place where cattle stand for milking in outlying pastures; a cattle-farm; a dairy farm (esp. an outlying one); a secondary settlement'. *Stoc(h)*, ?*Stokhowe* (f.ns. Kirby Bellars), ?*Stochil* (f.n. Skeffington).

stocc OE, **stokkr** ON, 'a tree-trunk, a stump, a log, a stock'. Stockwell. *Stocforlong'*, ?*Stokhowe*, *Stokkylnewong'* (f.ns. Kirby Bellars), ?*Stochil* (f.n. Skeffington), *Stocwellelane* (Kirby Bellars), Stockwell (f.n. Thorpe Satchville), *Stocweldole* (f.n. Barkby Thorpe), *Stocwellfurlonges* (f.n. Hoby), *stoxclif* (f.n. Seagrave).

***stoccing** OE, **stocking** ME, 'a piece of ground cleared of stumps'. Stocking Dike (f.n. Loddington), Stocking Gorse (f.n. Wymeswold), Stocking(s) (f.n. Allexton), *Stokkyng* (f.n. Thurmaston).

stōd OE, 'a stud, a herd of horses'. *Stodwellewong* (f.n. Barrow upon Soar).

stōd-fald OE, 'a stud-fold, a horse-enclosure'. *Stotfold(e)* (f.n. Gaddesby).

stoned ModE, ppl.adj., 'cleared of stones'. Ston Mdw (f.n. Asfordby).

storð ON, 'a young wood, a plantation; land growing with brushwood'. *Heynorstorth* (f.n. Skeffington), Storthe (f.n. Brooksby).

stōw OE, 'a place (of assembly), a holy place'. Alestow (f.n. Asfordby), *Caytestou'* (f.n. Kirby Bellars), *Luq'stoa* (f.n. Thurmaston), *Stoe hill* (f.n. Seagrave), *stou* (f.n. Hungarton), the Stow (f.n. Grimston), *stowgatte* (Hungarton).

strá ON, 'straw'. *Strowhades* (f.n. Kirby Bellars).

strǣt OE, **strēt** (Angl), 'a Roman road, a paved road, a street'. Streethill Fm. *The Common Street* (Rotherby), *le Fostretewong'* (f.n. Queniborough), *Grenestrete* (Welby), *Hegh Strete* (Barrow upon Soar), High Street, Low Street (f.ns. Keyham), Main St (Tilton), *le Portstrete* (Thurmaston), *the Queens street* (Saxelby), *Saltestrete* (Wymeswold), *the Street(e)* (Frisby on the Wreake, Loddington), *the Street close* (f.n. Burton on the Wolds), Streethill (f.n. South Croxton), (the) Street Hill Fd (f.n. Walton on the Wolds), *le Stret'*, *le Stretes*

(Barkby), *the Strete* (Skeffington), *strete hauedis* (f.n. Wymeswold), *the Town*(*e*) *Street*(*e*) (Cossington, Keyham, Queniborough, Ratcliffe on the Wreake, Rearsby, Thrussington, Twyford, Walton on the Wolds).

strang OE, **strangr** ON, adj., 'strong'; used of 'firm, compact soil'. Strancliffe.

strēam OE, 'a stream'. *le Deuondestrem* (Hoby), *Dewell streame* (Barkby Thorpe), *Dewelstreme*, *Peyslond' streme*, *Redmorestrem*, *Scrybestreme* (Skeffington), *Newton Streame* (Hungarton).

streberie ME, 'a strawberry'. Strawberry Fd (f.n. Thorpe Satchville), *Strawberrys close* (f.n. Burton on the Wolds).

street-waie eModE, 'a paved road or highway'. *the Streetewaie* (Barrow upon Soar), Streetway (Frisby on the Wreake), (*the*) *Streetway* (Rotherby, Saxelby).

streng OE, 'string'; poss. used topographically of something long and thin. ?*Stringham foorde* (f.n. Hoby).

strengr ON, 'a water-course'. ?*Stringham foorde* (f.n. Hoby).

***strīp** OE, 'a narrow tract of land'. Long Stripes (f.n. Thrussington).

strōd OE, 'marshy ground overgrown with brushwood'. *Strode Wong* (f.n. Barsby).

stubb OE, 'a tree-stump, a stub'. *le apiltrestub* (f.n. Cossington), *Appeltrestubbe* (f.n. Thurmaston), *arlestub hades* (f.n. Asfordby), *Elderstubbes* (f.n. Ratcliffe on the Wreake), Elder Stump Furlong (f.n. Humberstone), *Elrenestub* (f.n. Burton on the Wolds, Kirby Bellars, Seagrave), *Elrinstubbes* (f.n. Barkby), *Stubbes* (f.n. South Croxton), Long ~, Short Stubs, Stubs Cl (f.ns. Barsby), Stub Whong (f.n. Wymeswold).

stubbil, stuble ME, 'stubble'. *Schortstobullys* (f.n. South Croxton).

***stump** OE, 'a tree-stump', **stump** ME, 'the broken-off stump of something'. Great Stump Cross, Stump Cross.

stybb OE, 'a stub, a tree-stump'. *Stybbdale Wong* (f.n. South Croxton).

***sty-gate** ME, 'a pathway, a narrow road, a footpath' (*v*. **stīg, stígr, gata**), cf. ***sty-way**. *le Stygate* (Prestwold).

***sty-way** ME, 'a pathway, a narrow road, a footpath', cf. ***sty-gate**. The Styway Fds (f.n. Barkby).

***succa** OE, 'a sparrow'. *Succewels* (f.n. Skeffington).

sumor OE, **sumarr** ON, 'summer'; in p.ns. usually in allusion to sites which were used or could be used only in summer. Summer Leys Plantation. *Somer Leys* (f.n. Syston), the Summer Fd (f.n. Kirby Bellars).

sundor OE, adv., 'asunder, apart'; referring to land or property detached or separated from an estate, or to land or property of a special kind, e.g. private or privileged, cf. **sundor-land**. *sunderhaker* (f.n. Kirby Bellars).

sundor-land OE, 'land set apart for some special purpose, private land, detached land'. *le Halsonderlond* (f.n. Queniborough).

sunne OE, 'sun'; alluding to ground which caught the best of the sun. *the Sonne shoote* (f.n. Cossington), Sun Hill (f.n. Cossington, Ratcliffe on the Wreake, Thrussington), Sunnell (f.n. Sileby).

sūr OE, adj., 'sour, damp, coarse' (of land). Soure Butts (f.n. Barkby Thorpe), *Sower Hookes* (f.n. Queniborough), *surhowes* (f.n. Kirby Bellars).

sūtere OE, **sútari** ON, 'a shoemaker'. ?*Souterdole* (f.n. Barkby).

sūð OE, adj., 'south, southern'. South Croxton; Southfield Lodge, South Fields. South Brook (Beeby), *Southcliff*, *Southolm*, *South Willoes*, *Suthwude* (f.ns. Barrow upon Soar), Sowbrook Cl (f.n. South Croxton), *Sowtholme* (f.n.

Cossington), *Sowthrowes* (f.n. Kirby Bellars), *Suthforth* (f.n. Belgrave).

sūðan OE, adv., 'south, southerly', used in p.ns. elliptically as '(a place) south of'. *Suthenmerche* (f.n. South Croxton).

sūðer OE, adj., 'south, southern'. Southerdole (f.n. Barkby, Thurmaston).

sviða ON, 'burning'; 'woodland cleared by burning'. ?*Swetebuske* (f.n. South Croxton), ?Swithorn Cl (f.n. Syston).

***sviðinn** ON, 'land cleared by burning'. Sweden Furlong (f.n. Ratcliffe on the Wreake), ?Swithorn Cl (f.n. Syston).

***swalg** OE (Angl), 'a pit, a pool'. *Swallow dale* (f.n. Thrussington).

swan[1] OE, 'a swan'. *the Swannysneste* (f.n. Rearsby), *the Swans Nest* (f.n. Baggrave, Saxelby).

swān[2] OE, 'a herdsman, a swine-herd, a peasant'. Swan Style (f.n. Old Ingarsby).

swathe ME, 'a strip of grassland'. *Hydurswath* (f.n. Rearsby), *le Swathis* (f.n. Hoby), *Swathland sickes*, *Thomas Wyldes Swath* (f.ns. Seagrave).

sweart OE, **svartr** ON, adj., 'black, dark'. *Swarth furlong* (f.n. Rearsby).

sweard OE, 'grassland, greensward'. Swarflings (f.n. Grimston).

swēte OE, adj., 'sweet, pure, pleasant'. Sweet Hedge (f.n. Allexton), ?*Swetebuske* (f.n. South Croxton), *Sweytesyke* (f.n. Skeffington).

swift ModE, 'the swift', i.e. the bird of this name. ?the Swifts Pasture (f.n. Thurmaston).

swīn[1] OE, **svín** ON, 'a pig, a swine'. *Suinelund* (f.n. Cold Newton), Swan Dale Hole (f.n. Gaddesby), Swine Hole (f.n. Walton on the Wolds), *Swinholmes* (f.n. Hoby), *Swynstyse* (f.n. Humberstone), ?*Swine poole* (f.n. Cossington), ?*Swines-poole* (f.n. Tilton).

***swin**[2] OE, 'a channel'. ?Swine bridge (f.n. Loddington), ?*Swine poole*, ?Swines Bridge Mdw (f.ns. Cossington), ?*Swines-poole* (f.n. Tilton).

***tacca** OE, 'a teg, a young sheep'. ?*Tacwelle* (f.n. Hoby).

tǣsel OE, 'teasel'. *Tasilholm* (f.n. Hoby), the Taslands (f.n. Frisby on the Wreake), *Tasleclif* (f.n. Kirby Bellars), *Tassells* (f.n. Humberstone).

***tagga** OE, **tag, teg** ModEdial., 'a teg, a young sheep'. Tags Hill (f.n. Beeby).

tare ME, 'vetch', in early times, used esp. of vetch/tares appearing as weeds in corn crops; in later ME, also applied to cultivated vetch (*Vicia sativa*) grown for fodder. Tear-sick (f.n. Twyford).

tēag OE, 'a close, a small enclosure'. ?The Lanty Fd (f.n. Barkby), ?*Lustygate* (South Croxton), *le Norty* (f.n. Barrow upon Soar).

temple ME, 'a temple', used in allusion to former properties of the Knights Templars. *Temple clos*, *Templelands* (f.ns. Belgrave), Temple Cl (f.n. Gaddesby).

tēn OE, num., 'ten'. *Teynebrygis* (f.n. Rearsby).

tenement ME, 'a tenement, a dwelling'. *Summer(e)stenement* (Barrow upon Soar).

tentour ME, 'a tenter, a frame for tenting cloth'. Tentercroft Ave. ?Ten Foot Pool (f.n. Barsby), Tenter Leys (Cl) (f.ns. South Croxton, Thurmaston), *(the) Tenters* (f.ns. Rearsby, Wymeswold).

tēoða OE, 'a tithe, a tenth'. Tithebarn Fm, Tithe Fm. *le tithemedowe* (f.n. Thurmaston), Tithe Pieces (f.n. Syston), *Tith Medow* (f.n. Loddington), *the Tyth Barn* (Rearsby, Saxelby), *Tythemedowe* (f.n. Queniborough), *the tythe pece* (f.n. Seagrave), Tythe Piece (f.n. Ratcliffe on the Wreake), the Tythes (f.n. Keyham).

þæc OE, **þak** ON, 'thatching material'; used in p.ns. of places where thatching materials were got. *Thacholm* (f.n. Hoby), the Thack (f.n. Queniborough),

Thackholms (f.n. Thrussington), Thackracks, *Thakecroft* (f.ns. Cossington), ?Tuckham (f.n. Frisby on the Wreake).

þe ME, def.art., 'the'. *Abouethebrok'*, *þe thre rudes* (f.ns. Barkby), *longkebithehee* (f.n. Kirby Bellars), *þe opon' woddes* (Skeffington).

***þefa** OE, 'brushwood, bramble'. ?Thief Lane Cl (f.n. Syston), Thieves Cl, Thieves Mdw (f.ns. Brooksby), Thieving Furlong (f.n. Barsby).

þēof OE, 'a thief'. *Theuisdene* (f.n. South Croxton), ?Thief Lane Cl (f.n. Syston).

þicce[1] OE, 'a thicket, dense undergrowth'. *le thickinc* (f.n. Kirby Bellars).

þicce[2] OE, adj., 'thick, dense'. *Thickebusk* (f.n. Cossington).

þing OE, ON, 'an assembly, a council, a meeting'. ?Dings (f.n. Hoby), Ting-hill (f.n. Rotherby), Ting Hills (f.n. Frisby on the Wreake).

thing ME, 'property'. *Bayles thing* (f.ns. Humberstone), *Lenton Thing*, *Lokyngton thynge* (f.ns. Barrow upon Soar).

þing-haugr ON, 'an assembly mound or hill'. *Tingoe* (f.n. Saxelby).

þistel OE, 'a thistle'. *the Fisele Close* (f.n. Burton on the Wolds), Thistle Hill (f.n. Barkby).

thist(e)ly ME, adj., 'thistly, abounding with thistles'. *thislie landes* (f.n. Asfordby), Thistley Cl (f.n. East Norton).

þorn OE, 'a thorn, a thorn-tree'; collectively 'a stand or thicket or a wood of thorn-trees'. Highthorn Fm, Walton Thorns. Freq. in f.ns.: with an el. indicating size/shape of the thorn-patch, e.g. Little Thorns (Gaddesby), *Long* ~, *Short thorne* (Cossington), Smallthorns (Hoton, Kirby Bellars); or an el. specifying partic. characteristics of the thorns, e.g. *Banethorn'* (with various spellings in South Croxton, Grimston, Shoby), Sprig Thorne (South Croxton), *Wynterthornis* (Skeffington); or location, e.g. Copthorn (Barrow upon Soar, Queniborough), *Birdlip thornes*, *Croknest thornes*, *Malmberthorn*, *Wadethorn* (Cossington); with a pers.n. or surn. indicating ownership, e.g. *Crokisthorn* (South Croxton), Jordan's Thorns (Thrussington); with an el. referring to birds, e.g. Crowthorne Furlong (Barsby), *lafrickethorn* (Kirby Bellars), Pye thorne (Loddington). Recurring are the simplex *le Thorn* (South Croxton, Hoby), *Thornehill* (South Croxton, Barkby), *Threthornis* (Barsby, South Croxton).

þornig OE, adj., 'thorny, growing with thorns'. Thorney Plantation. *Thorn(e)y Balk(e)* (f.n. Asfordby, Kirby Bellars), Thorney Cl (f.n. Gaddesby, Hamilton), *thornye meare* (f.n. Humberstone), Thorney Spinney (f.n. South Croxton).

þorp OEScand, ON, 'a secondary settlement, a dependent outlying farmstead or hamlet'. Barkby Thorpe, Keythorpe, Thorpe Satchville. Cow Troops (f.n. Shoby), *le Esthorp*, *le Midulthorp*, *le Westhorp* (f.ns. Kirby Bellars), *Northorpe*, *Sewisthorpe*, *Thurmodesthorpe* (f.ns. Thurmaston), *Thorpesgatte* (Kirby Bellars), *Thorp on le Toftis* (f.n. Belgrave), the West Rope end (*Westrope*, f.n. South Croxton).

þrǣll ON, late OE, 'a thrall, a serf, a slave'. ?*Tralleswellehul* (f.n. Burton on the Wolds).

three-corner ModE, adj., 'having three corners, triangular'. Three Corner Cl (f.n. South Croxton), Three Corner Fd (f.n. Twyford).

three-cornered ModE, adj., 'having three corners, triangular'. Three Cornered Cl (f.n. Belgrave, South Croxton, Gaddesby, Grimston, Halstead, Prestwold), Three Cornered Fd (f.n. Kirby Bellars, Cold Newton, Ragdale, Rearsby), Three cornered Piece (f.n. Hungarton).

þrēo neut., fem., **þrī** masc., OE, num., 'three'. *Threhowes* (f.n. Queniborough, Thrussington).

þveit, þveiti ON, 'a clearing, a meadow, a paddock'. *Burgthueit* (f.n. Whatborough), *Peytheweyt syke* (f.n. Skeffington).

þverr (**þvert** neut.) ON, adj., 'athwart, lying across'. *Thuerclif* (f.n. Kirby Bellars), *le Thwerdoles* (f.n. Gaddesby), *le Thwerewong* (f.n. Barkby), Thwart Lands (f.n. Sileby), Whart Ley Cl (f.n. Saxelby).

þwang OE, 'a thong'; in p.ns., prob. 'a narrow strip of land'. *ned'thong, ouerthong* (f.ns. Hungarton).

þyrne OE, **þyrnir** ON, 'a thorn-bush'. Freq. in f.ns.: *Brotherne, le Thyrne, Thyrnwong* (Kirby Bellars), *Clipstherne* (Thurmaston), *Esturn*, Thurns (Barsby), *Longthirndale, Thirnebothim* (Hoby), *le Thirne, Thurnclyf, Thurne fur', Thurnwell furlong, le Thyrnhou* (Barkby), *Thirnhou* (Queniborough), Thuns Cl, Thuns Mdw (Brooksby), *Thurndale* (Saxelby), *Thurne* (Gaddesby), *thurnebarrow hill* (Asfordby), Thurney Cl (Syston), Thurn Side Furlong (South Croxton), *Wolsterne* (Whatborough).

***þyrning** OE, 'a place growing with thorns'. *High Thurning Lodge* (South Croxton Grange).

tillage eModE, 'the act of tilling or cultivating land so as to fit it for raising crops'. Tillage Land (f.n. Belgrave).

tit, tyt ME, 'a tit, a small bird'. *Titfordemere* (f.n. Barrow upon Soar).

tod-hole ME, 'a fox-hole'. Toardale Cl (f.n. Barsby).

toft ODan, late OE, 'a curtilage, a messuage, a plot of land in which a dwelling stands'. *Clipthorntoftes, Scoretoft* (f.ns. Skeffington), *hornetoft, toftsike* (f.ns. Rotherby), *oustontoftis* (f.n. Barkby), Taft Leys (f.n. South Croxton), (*the*) *Tafts* (f.n. Hoton), Tafts Cl (f.n. Barsby), *Thorp on le Toftis* (f.n. Belgrave), *Toftes* (f.n. Humberstone, Kirby Bellars, Twyford), *Toftessike* (f.n. Frisby on the Wreake), *Wistoft* (f.n. Seagrave).

toll OE, ME, 'a tax, a toll'. Tol Grass Lands (f.n. Queniborough).

toll-bar ModE, 'a toll-bar, a toll-gate'. Cotes Toll Bar.

toll-gate ModE, 'a toll-gate, a turnpike'. Toll Gate Ho. Tollgate Cl (f.n. Prestwold).

top ModE, adj., 'topmost, uppermost'. Top Bowling Leys, Top Cl (f.ns. Cossington).

topp OE, 'the top, the top of a bank or hill'. *Debdale Top hade* (f.n. South Croxton), *the Top of Bran Cliffe* (f.n. Queniborough), *the Topp of the hill* (f.n. Rotherby), *the Topp of the Meare* (f.n. Queniborough, Ratcliffe on the Wreake), Top of Township (f.n. Baggrave).

***tōt-hyll** OE, 'a look-out hill'. Hoothill Slang. Tootils (f.n. Quenby).

tounshipe eModE, 'the site of a former village, now deserted'. The Township (f.n. Hamilton, Ragdale), Township Mdw (f.n. Baggrave).

trēow OE, 'a tree'. *Coppetre* (f.n. Launde), Trouleway (Queniborough).

trog OE, 'a valley; a trough, a long narrow vessel'. *Water Mill Trofe* (f.n. Skeffington).

troll ON, 'a troll, a supernatural being'. ?*Tralleswellehul* (f.n. Burton on the Wolds).

***trun, *turn** OE, adj., 'circular, round'; 'something which turns'. *Trunsowhyll* (f.n. Rearsby), (The) Turnwater (f.n. Cossington).

trussell ME, (OFr *troussel*), 'a bundle'; poss. used topographically of 'a small clump of trees'. ?Thorpe Trussels.

tūn OE, 'a farmstead, a village, an estate', **tún** ON, 'a farmstead'. Allexton, South Croxton, Grimston, ?Hamilton, Hoton, Hungarton, Cold Newton, East Norton, Syston, Thrussington, Thurmaston, Tilton, Walton on the Wolds; *Alwolton* (Hoby), *Cussington* (Thorpe Satchville), *Dodyngton'* (Rearsby), *Hogston* (Sileby), *Lowton'*, *Marston* (Humberstone), *Rencheston* (Cossington), *Stilton* (Loddington), *Weston* (Beeby) and note the problematical ?*Batelston'* (Thurmaston) and ?*Longton* (Humberstone); Top Town Plantation, Town End Plantation. Common in later f.ns. denoting land adjacent to a township, e.g. Town Cl (Barrow upon Soar, Belgrave, Rotherby, Welby), Town(s)end (Cl) (with various spellings in Asfordby, Barrow upon Soar, Belgrave, Burton on the Wolds and 12 other townships), *the towne side* (with various spellings in Allexton, Barkby, Belgrave, Cossington, Hoby).

tunge OE, 'a tongue; a tongue of land'. Debdale Tongue (f.n. Queniborough), Hollow Tongue (f.n. Rearsby), *Holowell tong'*, *the tounges* (f.ns. Hungarton), *Mikeltungis* (f.n. Twyford), Tongue Leys (f.n. Tugby), *le Tunge* (f.n. Kirby Bellars), Woodgate Tongue (f.n. Sileby).

tūn-mann OE, 'a villein', **tunman** ME, 'a villager'. *Tunmannemedwe* (f.n. Thorpe Satchville).

tup ME, 'a ram, a tup'. Tup Cl (Welby), ?Tup Cl (Ratcliffe on the Wreake).

turnepe eModE, 'a turnip'. Turnip Cl (f.n. Brooksby), *the Turnopp close* (f.n. Burton on the Wolds).

turnepike ME, 'a turnpike, a revolving pole bearing spikes and serving as a barrier', **turnpike** ModE, 'a road on which a toll is payable and along which movement is controlled by barriers'. Rearsby Turnpike Cl (f.n. Rearsby), Turnpike Cl (f.n. Barkby, Brooksby, Hoton), Turnpike Plantation (f.n. East Norton), Turnpike Potter Hill (f.n. Welby), the Turnpike (Road) (Humberstone, Queniborough, Syston, Walton on the Wolds).

twelf OE, num., 'twelve'. *Twelfeacres* (f.n. Welby), *Twelue foote* (f.n. Asfordby), *Twelfrodisbrod(e)* (f.n. South Croxton); used as a sb., *the Twellues* (f.n. Hoby).

twī- OE, prefix, 'double, two'. Twyford.

twinn OE, adj., 'double, two-fold'. *Thwinford'* (Twyford).

***tyrl** OE, 'that which turns'. *Tyrle meadowe* (f.n. Whatborough).

uferra OE, adj., comp., 'higher, upper'; difficult to distinguish from **ofer**[3] 'over, above, across'. *Houerbremhou*, *Houerfuldolys* (f.ns. Cossington), *Ouerbanlondes*, *Ouirdikefurlong'*, *Overlady acre*, the Over Pasture (f.ns. Barkby), (*the*) *ouer flate*, *ouer Milethorne* (f.ns. Asfordby), *ouersoue* (f.n. Hungarton), *the Over Close* (f.n. Gaddesby), *the Over feelde* (f.n. Allexton, South Croxton), Over Mdw (f.n. Cotes, Hamilton), *Over Plaister Pitts* (f.n. Burton on the Wolds).

under OE, adv., prep., 'under, beneath, below'. *Ounderhoundecrofte*, *Underdingesti* (f.ns. Hoby), *Vnderclyf* (f.n. Cossington), Understile (f.n. Barrow upon Soar), *Vnder the Well* (f.n. Queniborough), *Undur peyslandis* (f.n. Rearsby).

up, **uppe** ME, adv., prep., 'up, higher up'. *uplandes* (f.n. Cold Newton).

uppan OE, prep., 'upon'. Barrow upon Soar, Burton on the Wolds, Ratcliffe on the Wreake.

upper ME, adj., 'higher'. Upper End, *Upper Feild* (f.ns. South Croxton), *Upperlady-Acar-Furlonge* (f.n. Barkby).

uppermoste eModE, adj., 'highest in place, occupying the highest position'. *ye Uppermost side Brackendale* (f.n. Tugby).

ūt OE, adj., 'outer, more distant'. *huthalf' pipesdale* (f.n. Kirby Bellars), *utlant* (f.n. Cold Newton).

ūterra OE, adj., comp., 'outer, lying on the outside, more remote'. *Oterehelland, Vttre pippesdale* (f.ns. Kirby Bellars), *Otterousterdale, le Otterrede, Otterskeges, Otterwiuelisbuskes, Outircalacre, Utteralwolton, Utteriholm, Uttermanlandes, Utterpeiselandes, Utterscheggedale* (f.ns. Hoby), *Vtterhull* (f.n. Barrow upon Soar).

val OFr, **vale** ME, 'a vale, a wide valley'. Skeffington Vale. the Vale Road (Wymeswold).

valeie ME, 'a valley'. The Valley. Valley Fd (f.n. Tilton).

vangr ON, 'an in-field'. Very freq. in f.ns.: esp. with a pers.n. or surn. indicating ownership, e.g. *Arnoldiswong, Bagodeswong, Snypwong* (South Croxton), *Starkeswong'* (Barkby), *Toukwong'* (Kirby Bellars), *Wlfethwong* (Cossington); or with a locational minor name, e.g. *Depedalewong* (Kirby Bellars), *Dumenyngedalewange* (Asfordby), *Kettellbarrow woonge, Langley wonge, Merstalwong'* (Barkby), *Stybbdale Wong* (South Croxton). Stream-names may be prefixed, e.g. *Caldewellewong, Stodwellewong* (Barrow upon Soar), *Caystowellwong* (Kirby Bellars); or road-names, e.g. *Marketgatewong* (Kirby Bellars), *Wayngatewong'* (South Croxton). Disputes over land may feature, e.g. *Flithulleswong, Kalengewong'* (South Croxton), *Flitwong* (Barrow upon Soar). Birds frequenting the field may be specified, e.g. (*the*) *Chickenwong*(*e*) (Asfordby), *Culurewang', Gosewong* (Cold Newton); or soil or fertility, e.g. *the Dew wong* (Belgrave), *Mukwong* (Kirby Bellars), *Waterish Wong* (Cossington); or size/shape, e.g. *Bradewong* (Cossington), *Broadewong* (Barsby), the Little Wong (Belgrave). Major or minor township edifices may also feature, e.g. All Wong Cl (Saxelby), *Cotewong* (South Croxton), *Milwong* (Launde), *Kylnewong'* (Kirby Bellars).

vápnatak ON, **wæpengetæc** late OE, **wapentac** ME, 'a wapentake, a sub-division of a county', corresponding to OE **hundred**. Goscote Wapentake.

varða, varði ON, 'a heap of stones', esp. one on the top of a hill. *Warteborow* (f.n. Cossington).

vað ON, 'a ford'. the Langworth Mdw (f.n. Thurmaston).

verge ModE, 'the bounds or limits of a place; a planted strip at the side of a road'. (*the*) *Varges* (f.n. Tugby), (the) Verges (f.n. East Norton).

vestr ON, adj., 'west', **vestri** ON, comp., 'more westerly'. ?*Westerling*(*e*)*s* (f.n. Barkby Thorpe).

vikerage ME, 'a vicarage'. The Vicarage (Ashby Folville, Barkby, Barrow upon Soar, Belgrave, Frisby on the Wreake, Humberstone, Hungarton, Loddington, Lowesby, Queniborough, Ratcliffe on the Wreake, Sileby, Syston, Thrussington, Thurmaston, Tilton, Tugby, Wymeswold). *the Vicarage Barn, the Vicarage Lane* (Barkby), *the Vicarage Close* (f.n. Hungarton, Lowesby, Ratcliffe on the Wreake), *the Vicarage house* (Twyford), Vicarage Mdw (f.n. Hungarton), *the vicarage yarde* (Ratcliffe on the Wreake), *the Viccaridge Ley, the Vickeridge land* (f.ns. Humberstone).

vikere ME, 'a vicar'. *the Vicars hades* (f.n. Frisby on the Wreake), *the Vicars house* (Ashby Folville), *le Vicarslane* (Barkby), *the Vicars Springes* (f.n. Thrussington), Viccars Sty Furlong (f.n. Queniborough), *the Vickers Lay*(*e*)*s* (f.n. Barsby).

village ME, 'a village; the houses of the settlement nucleus as distinct from the lands of the township'. Village Mdw (f.n. Rotherby).

vǫndr ON, 'a wand; a measure of land' (poss. a virgate, i.e. approximately 30 acres, *v.* OED *s.v.* wand sb. 9b). *the Wand' under the croft'*, *Wands* (f.ns. Humberstone).

vrá ON, **wro** ME, 'a nook, a corner of land', **wro** ModEdial. 'a secluded spot; a cattle shelter'. *Gilby Rowe*, *le Wro* (f.ns. Cossington), *Pudyng Row* (f.n. Belgrave), Row Mdw (f.n. Loddington), *Sowthrowes* (f.n. Kirby Bellars), *Steynrows* (f.n. Barsby), *Williamwro* (f.n. Thurmaston), Worm Row (f.n. South Croxton). Note also *in the Wro* (p) (Belgrave), *in le Wroo* (p) (Gaddesby), *in le Wro* (p) (Ragdale).

***wācor** OE, 'an osier, wicker'. ?*Wakah Wong* (f.n. Saxelby).

***wacu** OE, 'a watch, a wake'; poss. also 'a watching place'. ?*Wakah Wong* (f.n. Saxelby), Wakoe (f.n. Asfordby).

wād OE, 'woad'. Wad Cl (f.n. Halstead), *Wadhomes* (f.n. Seagrave), Wadland (f.n. Tilton), ?*Wadlowhadlond'* (f.n. Belgrave).

(ge)wæd OE, 'a ford'. *Bywades* (f.n. Rotherby), *Coweswade* (f.n. Belgrave), *Holebeckewade*, *le Wade* (f.ns. Kirby Bellars), Wad Acre(s) Furlong (f.n. Queniborough), *Wadefurlong*, *Wadethorn* (f.ns. Cossington).

wægn, wægen, wǣn OE, **wag(g)on** ModE, 'a wagon, a cart'. Waggon Hovel Cl (f.n. Halstead), Wagon Holes (f.n. Walton on the Wolds), *the wayn balk* (f.n. Barkby), *Wayneford* (f.n. Humberstone), *Waynes bridge* (Barkby Thorpe), *Wayngatewong'* (f.n. South Croxton), Wayne way (Queniborough), *weangate* (Saxelby), *Weans Gate* (Asfordby).

wælisc OE (Angl), adj., 'British (not Anglo-Saxon); unfree, servile'. Welsh Myers.

wæsce OE, 'a place for washing'. Washstones Bridge. *the Wash ditch* (f.n. Rearsby), (the) Wash Pit (f.n. Allexton, Lowesby), Washpit Cl (f.n. Ashby Folville), Wash Pit Yard (f.n. Hungarton, Tilton).

wæter OE, 'water, an expanse of water, a lake or pool, a stream or river' or, as first el., 'near to a stream or pool; wet, watery'. Water Lane. Freq. in f.ns.: *Barlie Water*, Water Mdw (Hoby), *brawater*, *the water gapp* (Asfordby), *the Broad water* (Rearsby), Calves Water (Thurmaston), Two Waters (Barrow upon Soar), (The) Turnwater, *Waterresschus*, *ye Water syde* (Cossington), Water Cl (Thrussington), Water Ditch (Sileby), Waterfurrow Furlong (Barsby, Sileby), *the Waterfurrowes* (with various spellings in Asfordby, Barkby, Barrow upon Soar and 14 other townships), *le Watergall* (Queniborough), *the Watergalls* (Thurmaston), Water Hill (Keyham), Water Holm (Syston), Waterland Leys (Wymeswold), *the water leas* (Rotherby), Water Leys (Ratcliffe on the Wreake), *le watermeade* (Kirby Bellars), *Watirland* (Cold Newton). Note also *atte Watere* (p) (Barrow upon Soar).

wæter-(ge)fall OE, 'a rapid; a cascade, a waterfall'. *le Waterfal* (f.n. Barrow upon Soar).

wæterig OE, adj., 'watery'. *þe Watriforoues* (f.n. Cossington).

wald OE (Angl), 'woodland, high forest land', **wald, wold** ME, 'an elevated stretch of open country or moorland'. Burton on the Wolds, Prestwold, Walton on the Wolds, Wymeswold; Burton Wolds, Ragdale Wolds Fm, Seagrave Wolds, Thrussington Wolds Gorse, Wolds Fm. Freq. in f.ns.: with a township name, e.g. *Cosyngton Woldys* (Cossington), *Sison Woult* (Barkby), Thorpe Would (Thorpe

Satchville), Walton Wolds (Walton on the Wolds); with a surn., e.g. Ashby far Wolds, *Babingtons Woulds* (Cossington), Ashby's ~, Blore's ~, Dennis's Wold (Thorpe Satchville); with an el. indicating size/shape, e.g. the Big Wolds (Cold Newton), *le Longewold*, *le Schortewolde* (Barkby); as a simplex, e.g. *le Wolde* (with various spellings in Barkby, Cossington, Kirby Bellars, Syston, Welby). Recurring is *Woldgate(s)ende* (Cossington, Gaddesby, Hoby). Note the important *Seggeswalda* (Six Hills) and the problematical Horningold (f.n. Sileby).

walh OE (Angl), 'a Briton, a serf'. Walton on the Wolds.

walke-milne ME, 'a walk-mill, a fulling-mill'. *Walkemylnenoke* (f.n. Barrow upon Soar), *the Walk mill meadowe* (f.n. Rotherby), *ye Walkmill Nook* (f.n. Walton on the Wolds).

wall OE (Angl), 'a wall, a rampart, a dike'. *atte Wall'* (p) (Welby), Old Wall (f.n. Queniborough), ?*Walbrygge*, ?*le Walwode* (Welby).

walu OE, 'a ridge of earth, an embankment'. ?*Walbrygge*, ?*le Walwode* (Welby).

wamb, womb OE, 'a womb, a belly', used topographically as 'a hollow'. ?Big ~, ?Little Worm (f.ns. Barrow upon Soar), ?Hall Worm (f.n. Wymeswold). These f.ns. may poss. belong with **vangr**. Note *Burne Wong/Burn woome* in South Croxton f.ns. (b).

wareine ME, 'a game preserve, a piece of ground for breeding rabbits, a warren'. Hall Warren (f.n. Barkby), Rabbit Warren(s) (f.ns. Frisby on the Wreake, Rotherby, Wymeswold), The Warren (f.n. Hoby), Warren Cl (f.n. Prestwold, Rearsby), Warren hedge Furlong (f.n. Barrow upon Soar).

warth, ward ME, 'a flat piece of meadow along a stream; marshy ground near a stream'. *Medelward*, *Northsikeward*, *Woldward* (f.ns. Gaddesby), *Rowwardis* (f.n. Skeffington).

wash-dyke ModEdial., 'a sheep-dip'. Wash Dike Cl (f.n. Welby).

washyng ME, vbl.sb., 'the action of cleansing by water, washing'. *le Wassingford* (f.n. Skeffington).

waste ME, 'waste land'. the Waste (f.n. Halstead, Loddington).

water-mylne ME, 'a water-mill'. Sileby Water Mill (Sileby Mill), Syston Water Mill (Syston Mills); *Tylton waturmylne* (Tilton), the Water Mill (Allexton), *the Watermill* (Rearsby Mill). *(the) Watermill lease* (f.n. Twyford), Water Mill Mdw (f.n. Rotherby), *Water Mill Trofe* (f.n. Skeffington).

wateryng eModE, vbl.sb., 'a place where cattle are taken to drink'. Bottom Meadow Watering, Plantation Watering (f.ns. Beeby), Cumberdale Watering, the Sallow Watering (f.ns. Wymeswold), *the Watering* (f.n. Hungarton), *the Watering Platt* (f.n. Burton on the Wolds), *the Watring places* (f.n. Barkby).

weard OE, 'watch, protection'. *Warteborow* (f.n. Cossington).

weg OE, 'a way, a road'. Fairly freq., esp. with the name of a township, e.g. *Barsbye waye*, *gadsbye waye* (South Croxton), *Ingersby way* (Hungarton), *Leycestre way* (Rotherby); or prefixed by the name of a local feature, e.g. *Riecroftwey*, *Stanford waie* (Barrow upon Soar). Note *The Ridgeway* (Barkby), *Riggeweyegate* (Skeffington) and *Saltersway* (Barkby Thorpe Lane).

wella, well(e) OE, 'a well, a spring, a stream'. Stockwell, Wellhead. Very freq. in f.ns.: esp. with a pers.n., e.g. *Grimmeswelle* (Barrow upon Soar), Osgar Well (Asfordby), *Wolfrichwell* (Humberstone), *Wolstonwell'* (Wymeswold), *Wulfitewell* (Thurmaston). Wild fauna may be specified, e.g. *Catwelle* (Hoby), *Foxwell'* (South Croxton), *Mouswell'* (Kirby Bellars); or wild flora, e.g.

Cresswell (Lowesby), *Reydwelle* (Kirby Bellars), *Thurnwell* (Barkby). Water birds occur occasionally, e.g. *Enedewell* (Kirby Bellars), *Gosewelsyke* (South Croxton). The nature of the spring/stream may be indicated, e.g. *Blindewelle* (Cold Newton), *Caldewelle* (with various spellings in Barrow upon Soar, Grimston, Lowesby, Cold Newton, Queniborough, Rotherby, Seagrave, Sileby), *Dewell* (Barkby Thorpe, Humberstone), *Frot(t)hewellessyke* (Barkby), *Fulwell* (with various spellings in Barrow upon Soar, Gaddesby, Hoby, Humberstone, Cold Newton, East Norton). Recurring also are *Haliwell* (with various spellings in Hungarton, Kirby Bellars, Seagrave, Thurmaston), *Harwell* (Barkby, Thurmaston), *Holwell* (Barkby, Cold Newton) and *Stocwelle* (Barkby Thorpe, Hoby, Kirby Bellars). *Croswell* (Barkby) and *Ladywell* (Hungarton) were presum. once sacred springs. Note the intriguing *Tralleswelle* (Burton on the Wolds).

wer, **wær** OE, 'a weir, a river-dam, a fishing-enclosure in a river'. Weir Mdw, *Wyghtwere* (f.ns. Barrow upon Soar), *Weyre welus* (f.n. Rearsby), Wire willows (f.n. Queniborough).

west OE, **vestr** ON, adj., 'western, west'. *West brook*, *Westgate* (Barkby), West Fd (f.n. Asfordby), the Westerns (f.n. Hoby), *le Westfeilde*, *le Westmede* (f.ns. Frisby on the Wreake), *Westthorpbirimedow(e)* (f.n. Barkby), *Weston feild* (f.n. Beeby), *Westrope*, West Wong Cl (f.ns. South Croxton).

***wester** OE, adj., 'west, western'. ?*Westerling(e)s* (f.n. Barkby Thorpe).

westerne OE, adj., 'west, western, westerly'. (the) Western Cl (f.n. Walton on the Wolds).

wēt OE (Angl), adj., 'wet, damp'. *Wetforow'* (f.n. Queniborough), *Wetfurrowes furlong* (f.n. Gaddesby), Wetlands (f.n. Wymeswold), *Wetlond* (f.n. Thurmaston), Wet Mdw (f.n. Frisby on the Wreake).

weðer OE, 'a wether, a castrated ram'. Weather Cl (f.n. Old Ingarsby), ?Weathers Acres (f.n. Kirby Bellars), ?Weatherstone Cl (f.n. Baggrave), *(le) Weddermedow(e)* (f.n. Barrow upon Soar).

whelewryght ME, 'a wheelwright'. Wheelwright's Shop (Cossington, Gaddesby).

whinny ME, adj., 'growing with whins and gorse-bushes'. *Wenie clyffe* (f.n. Ratcliffe on the Wreake), *Weynnylande* (f.n. Seagrave), *Whinidoles* (f.n. Sileby), Whinney Ley, (f.n. Queniborough), *Whinny Leas* (f.n. Walton on the Wolds), *the Whyne plowlands*, *le Wynnidole* (f.ns. Barkby Thorpe), *Wyn(n)ywong'* (f.n. Thurmaston).

wice OE, 'a wych-elm', or other tree with pliant branches. Elms and Wytches (f.n. Belgrave).

wīd OE, adj., 'wide, spacious'. Widness (f.n. Sileby), *Wydeboro* (f.n. Cossington).

widuwe OE, 'a widow'. Widows Cl (f.n. Wymeswold).

wīf OE, 'a woman, a wife, a married woman'. *John Morrice his wiues land* (f.n. Asfordby).

wīfmann OE, 'a woman'. ?*Wymanstead* (f.n. Cossington).

wigga OE, 'a beetle'. ?Wiggo (f.n. Asfordby), ?the Wygmore Sets (f.n. Thurmaston).

***wiht** OE, 'a bend (in a river)'. *Wyghtwere* (f.n. Barrow upon Soar).

wilde-gōs OE, 'a wild goose'. *Wild(e)goose nooke* (f.n. Saxelby).

wildernesse ME, 'a wilderness, a wild place'. (The) Wilderness (f.ns. Barkby, South Croxton).

***wilig** OE (Angl), 'a willow'. *Willoughes*; The Willows. Fairly common in f.ns.: esp. with a prefixed surn. indicating ownership, e.g. Cockram Willow(e)s (Queniborough), *harris wyllowes* (Humberstone), Ortons Willows (Belgrave), Rawlinsons Willows (Barsby); with an el. specifying a township edifice, e.g. *kyrkewylows* (Hungarton), Mill Willows Cl (Rearsby). Appears with an el. signifying a small local feature, e.g. *Meare Willowes*, Wire willows (Queniborough), *Weyre welus* (Rearsby). Appears as a simplex, e.g. First ~, Second Willows (South Croxton), *le Wyllose* (Humberstone), *Wyllows* (Rearsby). May be prefixed to an agricultural unit, e.g. the Willow Beds (Lowesby), Willow Cl (Brooksby, Hoby), Willow Mdw (Belgrave), Willow Sic(h) (Belgrave, Old Ingarsby), *Wiloforlong'* (Cossington).

***wiligen** OE, adj., 'growing with willows'. ?*Wylinghaw* (f.n. Barrow upon Soar).

***wilign** OE, 'a willow' or 'a willow copse'.?*Wylinghaw* (f.n. Barrow upon Soar).

***wilig-trēow** OE, 'a willow-tree'. Willow Tree (f.n. Wymeswold), *Willow Tree Ford* (f.n. Queniborough), *the Willow Trees* (f.n. Humberstone).

wind-mylne ME, 'a windmill'. The Windmill, Old Windmill; *the windemilne* (with various spellings in South Croxton, Humberstone, Rearsby). Windmill Cl (f.n. Seagrave, Thurmaston), Windmill Croft (f.n. Halstead), Windmill Fd (f.n. Barkby, Cotes, Grimston, Kirby Bellars), Windmill Hill (f.n. Barkby, South Croxton, Frisby on the Wreake, Sileby), Windmill Pingle (f.n. Seagrave), Windmills (f.n. Frisby on the Wreake), *Wynd(e)mylnegate* (Kirby Bellars), *le Wynmyll grovett* (f.n. Old Ingarsby), Syston Windmill (Syston), *Tilton windmilne* (Tilton).

winter[1] OE, **vinter** OEScand, 'winter'; in p.ns., referring to streams that ran or to places that were used only in winter. ?*Wynterthornis* (f.n. Skeffington).

***wisse** OE, 'a marshy meadow'. Wisemoor Hill (f.n. Wymeswold), ?*Wistoft* (f.n. Seagrave).

wīðig OE, 'a withy, a willow'. *Wethybuscus* (f.n. Queniborough), *Whity Bush furlong* (f.n. Sileby), *Wyothebroche* (f.n. Skeffington), *Wythibusforlong'* (f.n. Thurmaston).

workhouse ModE, 'a workhouse, a place of public employment for the poor'. The Workhouse (Humberstone), Workhouse Cl (f.n. Cotes), Workhouse Orchard (f.n. Beeby), Workhouse Piece (f.n. Keyham).

wrang OE, **vrangr** ON, adj., 'crooked or twisted in shape'. In f.ns., almost invariably compounded with **land**, as *Ranglandes*, *Wrangelandes*, *Wrongelandes* (with various spellings in Asfordby, Barsby, Cossington and 10 other townships), Rang Back (f.n. Thrussington), *Wrongdoles* (f.n. Humberstone), *Wrong' mer'* (f.n. Hungarton).

wudu OE, 'a wood, a grove, a tract of woodland'. Allexton Wood, Launde Big Wood, Tilton Wood, Woodgate, Woodgate Ho. *Bow(w)ood* (Belgrave), *Cummaneswode* (Launde), *Freewood* (East Norton), *Herewardeswde* (Whatborough), *Lousbywode* (Lowesby), *Monkkewode*, *le Walwode* (Welby), *Philypwode*, *Suthwude* (Barrow upon Soar), *Randulfwde* (Skeffington). *Wodegate* is common (in Barkby, Hoby, Humberstone, Kirby Bellars, Wymeswold). Occasionally in f.ns., e.g. *Woodefeld* (Welby), *Woodford* (Barsby), Wood Furlong (Grimston).

wulf OE, **ulfr** ON, 'a wolf'. *Wlfholes* (f.n. Cold Newton), ?*Wolfhull'* (f.n. Kirby Bellars).

wyrm, wurm OE, 'a reptile, a snake; a dragon; an insect', **worm** ME, 'an earthworm'. Worm Hill (f.n. Ratcliffe on the Wreake), Worm Row (f.n. South Croxton).

yardland eModE, 'a square measure of about 30 acres of land'. Freemans Half Yard Land, Freemans Half Yard Land Mdw, Palmers Yard Land, Taylors Yard Land (f.ns. Tilton), *the hall two yard lands*, *~ ~ three yard lands* (f.ns. Humberstone), *Kimberley's Yard land* (f.n. Barkby), *Sheffeildes yardland* (f.n. Thurmaston).

INDEX OF THE PLACE-NAMES OF EAST GOSCOTE HUNDRED

This index includes all the major names and minor names in the Introduction and in the main body of the work but not in the section The Elements in East Goscote Hundred's Place-Names. Field-names are not indexed. The names of the townships are printed in capitals. Lost names are printed in italic.